READINGS

IN

FEDERAL TAXATION

SECOND EDITION

By

MICHAEL J. McINTYRE

Professor of Law, Wayne State University

FRANK E. A. SANDER

Bussey Professor of Law, Harvard Law School

and

DAVID WESTFALL

John L. Gray Professor of Law, Harvard Law School

Mineola, New York
THE FOUNDATION PRESS, INC.
1983

COPYRIGHT © 1970 THE FOUNDATION PRESS, INC.
COPYRIGHT © 1983 By THE FOUNDATION PRESS, INC.
All rights reserved
Printed in the United States of America

Library of Congress Cataloging in Publication Data

Main entry under title:

Readings in Federal taxation.

    1. Taxation—Law and legislation—United States—Addresses, essays, lectures. 2. Taxation—Law and legislation—Canada—Addresses, essays, lectures.
I. McIntyre, Michael J., 1942-   . II. Sander, Frank E. A. III. Westfall, David, 1927-   . IV. Title.
KF6289.A2R42 1983   336.2'0097   83-16356

ISBN 0-88277-145-0

M., S. & W. Fed. Tax. 2nd Ed. FP

PREFACE

Like the little girl with the curl, an income tax can be very, very good, or it can be horrid. At its best, an income tax distributes its burdens in accord with popular notions of fairness while imposing modest costs in economic efficiency. At its worst, it rewards the politically influential and seriously distorts economic decision-making. An article appearing a decade ago in the first edition of this book declared that "Congress has shown remarkable collective wisdom in shaping our federal tax structure, and its accomplishments in this field may be measured favorably against the tax systems of other countries."[1] Today, the author of that article describes federal tax policy as "troubled" and suggests it may be "in total disarray."[2] This viewpoint is widely shared by tax specialists and the taxpaying public. Although the federal income tax may not be bad enough to curl one's hair, most commentators believe that it is needlessly complex and riddled with special interest provisions. And it seems to be getting worse rather than better.

Reform of the income tax is not easy, partly because of the inherent complexity of income taxes and partly because of the reluctance of Congress to bite the hand that feeds it. Students of the federal income tax can contribute to its reform by offering workable solutions to its problems and supporting the sensible solutions of others. Without the lively support of at least some of those who understand its technical rules, the cause of federal income tax reform will be seriously handicapped.

This book contains a broad sampling of the proposals that commentators have offered for reform of the income tax. In selecting articles for inclusion in this book, we have favored provocative pieces over those that downplay the conflicts in values that underlie all worthwhile tax policy debates. We have also favored recent articles over equally-valuable older ones, due to our limited ability to update articles for changes in the tax code. To compensate for our inability to include all important perspectives in the main selections, we have presented excerpts from a large number of articles at the end of each chapter in what we call our Points and Counterpoints sections.

1. Surrey, "The Congress and the Tax Lobbyist—How Special Tax Provisions Get Enacted," 70 *Harvard Law Review* 1145 (1957).

2. Surrey, "Our Troubled Tax Policy: False Routes and Proper Paths to Change," *Tax Notes*, February 2, 1981, pp. 179-97, 179.

PREFACE

This book has been designed to serve as a principal text for tax policy seminars offered to law and economics students. Sufficient materials are provided for a fourteen week seminar, meeting two hours per week. Chapters II, III, IV, VI, and VIII each might be compressed into a single two-hour session, although a less torrid pace would be advantageous. Chapters I, V, and VII would require at least twice as much time. The introductory materials to each chapter offer some suggestions for additional readings. Many of the entries in the Points and Counterpoints sections could serve as starting points for student research papers.

Like its predecessor, this second edition can be used to supplement the traditional law school course in basic taxation. Instructors using casebooks that do not provide extensive policy analysis might choose to integrate this book into their course. Others might want to recommend the book to students as a convenient reference work.

The first edition of this book was edited by Frank E. A. Sander and David Westfall. Michael J. McIntyre took the laboring oar in editing this edition, in writing the materials that introduce each chapter, and in preparing the Points and Counterpoints sections that close each chapter.

We acknowledge with gratitude the suggestions we have received from a number of colleagues and friends in the course of putting together this book. We welcome additional comments from our readers. We wish to thank Rick Davidson of Wayne State University Law School for research assistance. We also thank May Ping Soo Hoo and Bridget Klink for their help in preparing the manuscript for publication.

MICHAEL J. McINTYRE
FRANK E. A. SANDER
DAVID WESTFALL

Detroit, Michigan
Cambridge, Massachusetts
July, 1983

SELECTIONS AND ACKNOWLEDGMENTS

Chapter 1

Richard Goode, "The Economic Definition of Income," in *Comprehensive Tax Reform*, Brookings Institution (Joseph A. Pechman, Ed. 1977), pp. 1-10. Copyright © 1977 by The Brookings Institution, Washington, D.C. Reproduced with permission.

Institute for Fiscal Studies, *The Structure and Reform of Direct Taxes: Report of a Committee Chaired by Professor J. E. Meade*, George Allen & Unwin (1978), pp. 30-40, 44-45. Copyright © 1978 by George Allen & Unwin Ltd. Reproduced with permission.

Richard A. Musgrave, "Tax Reform or Tax Deform," in *Tax Policy Options in the 1980's*, Canadian Tax Foundation (Wayne R. Thirsk & John Whalley, Eds. 1982), pp. 19-23. Copyright © 1982 by the Canadian Tax Foundation. Reproduced with permission.

Treasury Department, *Blueprints for Basic Tax Reform* (1977), pp. 33-52.

William D. Andrews, "Fairness and the Personal Income Tax A Reply to Professor Warren," 88 *Harvard Law Review* 947 (1975), pp. 953-56. Copyright © 1975 by The Harvard Law Review Association. Reproduced with permission.

Alan Gunn, "The Case for an Income Tax," 46 *University of Chicago Law Review* 370 (1979), pp. 370-78. Copyright © 1979 by the University of Chicago. Reprinted by permission from 46 U.Chi.L.Rev. 370 (1979).

Alvin Warren, "Would a Consumption Tax Be Fairer Than an Income Tax?" 89 *Yale Law Journal* 1081 (1980), pp. 1090-93 Copyright © 1980 by The Yale Law Journal Co., Inc. Reprinted by permission of The Yale Law Journal Company and Fred B Rothman & Company from *The Yale Law Journal*, Vol. 89, pp 1081, 1090-93.

Stanley S. Surrey, "Reflections on the Revenue Act of 1978 and Future Tax Policy," 13 *Georgia Law Review* 687 (1979), pp. 703-6. Copyright © 1979 by Georgia Law Review Association, Inc This Article was originally published in 13 *Georgia Law Review* No. 3 and is reprinted by permission.

SELECTIONS AND ACKNOWLEDGMENTS

Chapter 2

Arthur M. Okun, "Further Thoughts on Equality and Efficiency," in *Income Redistribution*, American Enterprise Institute (Colin D. Campbell, Ed. 1977), pp. 19-22, 25-30. Copyright © 1977 by American Enterprise Institute for Public Policy Research, Washington, D.C. Reproduced with permission.

Walter J. Blum, "Revisiting the Uneasy Case for Progressive Taxation," 60 *Taxes—The Tax Magazine* 16 (1982). Copyright © 1981 by Walter J. Blum and Commerce Clearing House, Inc. This article appeared in the January 1982 issue of *TAXES—The Tax Magazine*, published by Commerce Clearing House, Inc., in Chicago, and appears here with permission.

Robert S. McIntyre, "Flat-Rate Talk," *New Republic*, July 19 & 26, 1982, pp. 20-22. Reprinted by permission of *The New Republic*. Copyright © 1982 by The New Republic, Inc.

Report of the Task Force on Tax Reform (New Zealand, 1982), pp. 128-34. Crown copyright © 1982. Reproduced with permission of the Government of New Zealand.

Congressional Budget Office, *Indexing the Individual Income Tax for Inflation* (1980), pp. 5-25, 29-33.

Chapter 3

Stanley S. Surrey & Paul R. McDaniel, "The Tax Expenditure Concept: Current Developments and Emerging Issues," 20 *Boston College Law Review* 225 (1979), pp. 226-42, 253-63. Copyright © 1979 by Stanley S. Surrey and Paul R. McDaniel. Reproduced with permission.

Office of Management and Budget, *Special Analysis G: Tax Expenditures, Special Analyses, Budget of the United States Government 1984*, pp. G-1 to G-7, G-26 to G-33.

Michael J. McIntyre, "A Solution to the Problem of Defining a Tax Expenditure," 14 *U. C. Davis Law Review* 79-103 (1980). Copyright © 1980 by *U. C. Davis Law Review*. Reproduced with permission.

Robert S. McIntyre, "Lessons for Tax Reformers from the History of the Energy Tax Incentives in the Windfall Profit Tax Act of 1980," 22 *Boston College Law Review* 705 (1981), pp. 732-41. Copyright © 1981 by Boston College Law School. Reproduced with permission.

SELECTIONS AND ACKNOWLEDGMENTS

Chapter 4

William F. Hellmuth, "Homeowner Preferences," in *Comprehensive Income Taxation*, Brookings Institution (Joseph A. Pechman, Ed. 1977), pp. 163-72. Copyright © 1977 by The Brookings Institution, Washington, D.C. Reproduced with permission.

Jerome Kurtz, "Comments by Jerome Kurtz," in *Comprehensive Income Taxation*, Brookings Institution (Joseph A. Pechman, Ed. 1977), pp. 197-201. Copyright © 1977 by The Brookings Institution, Washington, D.C. Reproduced with permission.

Michael J. McIntyre & Oliver Oldman, "Taxation of the Family in a Comprehensive and Simplified Income Tax," 90 *Harvard Law Review* 1573 (1977), pp. 1607-24. Copyright © 1977 by The Harvard Law Review Association. Reproduced with permission.

Section of Taxation, American Bar Association, Committee on Simplification, "Evaluation of the Proposed Model Comprehensive Income Tax," 32 *Tax Lawyer* 563 (1979), pp. 567-84. Copyright © 1979 by the American Bar Association. Reproduced with permission.

Chapter 5

Robert S. McIntyre & Dean C. Tipps, *Inequity & Decline: How the Reagan Tax Policies Are Affecting the American Taxpayer and the Economy*, Center on Budget and Policy Priorities (1983), pp. 32-48. Copyright © 1983 by Center on Budget and Policy Priorities. Reproduced with permission.

Treasury Department, "Entertainment Expenses," in *The President's 1978 Tax Program* (1978), pp. 195-202.

Richard Goode, *The Individual Income Tax*, Brookings Institution (Rev. Ed. 1976), pp. 133-8. Copyright © 1976 by The Brookings Institution, Washington, D.C. Reproduced with permission.

Robert S. McIntyre & Dean C. Tipps, *Inequity & Decline: How the Reagan Tax Policies Are Affecting the American Taxpayer and the Economy*, Center on Budget and Policy Priorities (1983), pp. 75-8, 81-2. Copyright © 1983 by Center on Budget and Policy Priorities. Reproduced with permission.

Michael J. McIntyre, "An Inquiry Into the Special Status of Interest Payments," 1981 *Duke Law Review* 765 (1981), pp. 766-   . Copyright © 1981 by Duke University School of Law. Reproduced with permission.

SELECTIONS AND ACKNOWLEDGMENTS

William D. Andrews, "Personal Deductions in an Ideal Income Tax," 86 *Harvard Law Review* 309 (1972), pp. 344-56. Copyright © 1972 by The Harvard Law Review Association. Reproduced with permission.

Alan L. Feld, "Abortion to Aging: Problems of Definition in the Medical Expense Tax Deduction," 58 *Boston University Law Review* 165 (1978), pp. 166-7, 177-81, 193-6. Copyright © 1978 by Alan L. Feld. Reproduced with permission.

Note, "Costs and Consequences of Tax Incentives: The Individual Retirement Account," 94 *Harvard Law Review* 864-886 (1981). Copyright © 1981 by The Harvard Law Review Association. Reproduced with permission.

Chapter 6

Roger Brinner & Alicia Munnell, "Taxation of Capital Gains: Inflation and Other Problems," *New England Economic Review*, September-October 1974, pp. 3-21. Reproduced with permission.

James W. Wetzler, "Recent Developments in U.S. Capital Gains Taxation," in *1978 Conference Report*, Canadian Tax Foundation (1980), pp. 368-75. Copyright © 1980 by the Canadian Tax Foundation. Reproduced with permission.

Note, "Realizing Appreciation Without Sale: Accrual Taxation of Capital Gains on Marketable Securities," 34 *Stanford Law Review* 857-876 (1982). Copyright © 1982 by the Board of Trustees of the Leland Stanford Junior University. Reproduced with permission.

Chapter 7

Boris I. Bittker, "Federal Income Taxation and the Family," 27 *Stanford Law Review* 1389 (1975), pp. 1391-1414. Copyright © 1975 by the Board of Trustees of the Leland Stanford Junior University. Reproduced with permission.

Michael J. McIntyre, "Individual Filing in the Personal Income Tax: Prolegomena to Future Discussion," 58 *North Carolina Law Review* 469-489 (1980). Copyright © 1980 by the North Carolina Law Review Association. Reproduced with permission.

Note, "The Case for Mandatory Separate Filing by Married Persons," 91 *Yale Law Journal* 363 (1981), pp. 367-78. Copyright © 1981 by the Yale Law Journal Co., Inc. Reprinted by permission of the Yale Law Journal Company and Fred B. Rothman & Company from *The Yale Law Journal*, Vol. 91, pp. 371-8.

SELECTIONS AND ACKNOWLEDGMENTS

Martin J. McMahon, Jr., "Expanding the Taxable Unit: The Aggregation of the Income of Children and Parents," 56 *New York University Law Review* 60 (1981), pp. 64-8, 71, 77-9, 80-93. Copyright © 1981 by the New York University Law Review. Reproduced with permission.

Dan Throop Smith, *Federal Tax Reform*, McGraw-Hill (1961), pp. 291-4. Copyright © 1961 by McGraw-Hill Book Company. Reproduced with permission.

David Westfall, "Trust Grantors and Section 674: Adventures in Income Tax Avoidance," 60 *Columbia Law Review* 326 (1960), pp. 326-42, 345-7. Copyright © 1983 by The Directors of the Columbia Law Review Association, Inc. All rights reserved. This Article originally appeared at 60 *Colum.L.Rev.* 326 (1960). Reprinted by permission.

Chapter 8

Richard M. Bird, "Why Tax Corporations?" in *Taxing Corporations*, Institute for Research on Public Policy (1980), pp. 9-24. Copyright © 1980 by The Institute for Research on Public Policy. Reproduced with permission.

Charles E. McLure, Jr., *Must Corporate Income Be Taxed Twice?* Brookings Institution (1979), pp. 19-38. Copyright © 1979 by The Brookings Institution, Washington, D.C. Reproduced with permission.

Martin Norr, *The Taxation of Corporations and Shareholders*, Kluwer Law & Taxation Publishers (1982), pp. 71-82. Copyright © 1982 by the President and Fellows of Harvard College. Reproduced with permission of International Tax Program, Harvard Law School, and Kluwer Law and Taxation Publishers, Deventer, Netherlands.

American Law Institute, *Federal Income Tax Project—Subchapter C*, "Reporter's Study of the Taxation of Corporate Distributions" (1982), pp. 341-55. Copyright © 1982 by The American Law Institute. Reprinted with the permission of the American Law Institute.

*

TABLE OF CONTENTS

	Page
PREFACE	iii
SELECTIONS AND ACKNOWLEDGMENTS	v

I. THE CHOICE OF THE BASE FOR A PERSONAL TAX SYSTEM: INCOME VERSUS CONSUMPTION ... 1

A. An Overview ... 3
R. Goode, "The Economic Definition of Income" ... 3
Institute for Fiscal Studies, *The Structure and Reform of Direct Taxes* ... 13
R. Musgrave, "Tax Reform or Tax Deform" ... 24

B. A Consumption Base ... 29
Treasury Department, *Blueprints for Basic Tax Reform* ... 29
W. Andrews, "Fairness and the Personal Income Tax: A Reply to Professor Warren" ... 47

C. An Income Base ... 51
A. Gunn, "The Case for an Income Tax" ... 51
A. Warren, "Would a Consumption Tax Be Fairer Than an Income Tax?" ... 60
S. Surrey, "Reflections on the Revenue Act of 1978 and Future Tax Policy" ... 64

POINTS AND COUNTERPOINTS ... 68

II. DESIGN OF THE RATE STRUCTURE ... 74

A. Progressive Rates ... 77
A. Okun, "Further Thoughts on Equality and Efficiency" ... 77
W. Blum, "Revisiting the Uneasy Case for Progressive Taxation" ... 85
R. McIntyre, "Flat-Rate Talk" ... 91
Report of the Task Force on Tax Reform (New Zealand) ... 94

B. Control of "Bracket Creep" Through Indexing ... 101
Congressional Budget Office, *Indexing the Individual Income Tax for Inflation* ... 101

POINTS AND COUNTERPOINTS ... 126

III. TAX EXPENDITURES ... 130

S. Surrey & P. McDaniel, "The Tax Expenditure Concept: Current Developments and Emerging Issues" ... 132

TABLE OF CONTENTS

III. TAX EXPENDITURES—Continued

	Page
Office of Management and Budget, *Special Analysis G: Tax Expenditures*	160
M. McIntyre, "A Solution to the Problem of Defining a Tax Expenditure"	175
R. McIntyre, "Lessons for Tax Reformers From the History of the Energy Tax Incentives in the Windfall Profit Tax Act of 1980"	200

POINTS AND COUNTERPOINTS 210

IV. THE TAXATION OF NONMONETARY BENEFITS 212

A. Home Ownership 214
   W. Hellmuth, "Homeowner Preferences" 214
   J. Kurtz, "Comments by Jerome Kurtz" 224

B. Self-Performed Services 228
   M. McIntyre & O. Oldman, "Taxation of the Family in a Comprehensive and Simplified Income Tax" 228

C. Fringe Benefits 246
   Section of Taxation, American Bar Association, Committee on Simplification, "Evaluation of the Proposed Model Comprehensive Income Tax" 246

POINTS AND COUNTERPOINTS 264

V. DEDUCTIONS AND EXCLUSIONS FROM MONEY INCOME 266

A. Business-Related Costs 269
   1. Depreciation 269
      R. McIntyre & D. Tipps, *Inequity & Decline* 269
   2. Entertainment Expenses 284
      Treasury Department, "Entertainment Expenses" ... 284

B. Tax-Exempt State and Local Bonds 293
   R. Goode, *The Individual Income Tax* 293
   R. McIntyre & D. Tipps, *Inequity & Decline* 298

C. Quasi-Business and Investment Related Adjustments: The Deduction for Interest Payments 302
   M. McIntyre, "An Inquiry Into the Special Status of Interest Payments" 302

D. Personal Expense Deductions 347
   1. Charitable Contributions 347
      W. Andrews, "Personal Deductions in an Ideal Income Tax" 347
   2. Medical Expenses 360

xii

TABLE OF CONTENTS

		Page
D.	Personal Expense Deductions—Continued	
	A. Feld, "Abortion to Aging: Problems of Definition in the Medical Expense Tax Deduction"	360
E.	Deductions for Personal Savings	370
	Note, "Costs and Consequences of Tax Incentives: The Individual Retirement Account"	370
POINTS AND COUNTERPOINTS		393

VI. CAPITAL GAINS 400

R. Brinner & A. Munnell, "Taxation of Capital Gains: Inflation and Other Problems" 402
J. Wetzler, "Recent Developments in U.S. Capital Gains Taxation" 421
Note, "Realizing Appreciation Without Sale: Accrual Taxation of Capital Gains on Marketable Securities" 428

POINTS AND COUNTERPOINTS 448

VII. THE PROPER TAX CONSEQUENCES OF FAMILY SHARING PRACTICES 452

A. Historical Context 454
    B. Bittker, "Federal Income Taxation and the Family" 454

B. Taxation of Marital Partners 478
    M. McIntyre, "Individual Filing in the Personal Income Tax: Prolegomena to Future Discussion" 478
    Note, "The Case for Mandatory Separate Filing by Married Persons" 499

C. Taxation of Dependent Children 511
    M. McMahon, "Expanding the Taxable Unit: The Aggregation of the Income of Children and Parents" 511

D. Taxation of Family Trusts 532
    D. Smith, *Federal Tax Reform* 532
    D. Westfall, "Trust Grantors and Section 674: Adventures in Income Tax Avoidance" 535

POINTS AND COUNTERPOINTS 555

VIII. TAXATION OF CORPORATIONS AND THEIR SHAREHOLDERS 558

R. Bird, "Why Tax Corporations?" 560
C. McLure, *Must Corporate Income Be Taxed Twice?* 576
M. Norr, *The Taxation of Corporations and Shareholders* 596
American Law Institute, *Federal Income Tax Project —Subchapter C*, "Reporter's Study of the Taxation of Corporate Distributions" 608

POINTS AND COUNTERPOINTS 623

READINGS
IN
FEDERAL TAXATION

*

I. THE CHOICE OF THE BASE FOR A PERSONAL TAX SYSTEM: INCOME VERSUS CONSUMPTION

The base of a personal tax system specifies what material benefits are relevant in determining each taxpayer's taxable capacity. A traditional starting point in formulating the base of the personal income tax has been the Haig/Simons income definition, described by Richard Goode in the first selection, below. According to that definition, taxable income would equal the sum of a taxpayer's consumption during the taxable period plus the increase (or minus the decrease) in the taxpayer's net worth during that period. A personal consumption tax, in contrast, would exclude from the tax base any increase in a taxpayer's savings and would include in the base any decrease in savings. Both bases would tax consumption financed out of current income and neither base would tax previously acquired wealth not currently consumed.

A tax system's measure of taxable capacity depends not only upon its base but also upon its taxable period rules and its taxable person rules. The relationships among these complementary rules have only begun to be explored by tax commentators. Consumption tax advocates have brought to the fore some of the relationships between the tax base and the taxable period, since their fairness defense of the consumption tax depends in part on the choice of the "lifetime" as the appropriate period for measuring taxable capacity. Some links between the tax base and the taxable person rules are addressed in Chapter VII.

Every real life tax system, whether informed by an income ideal or a consumption ideal (or some hodgepodge of both) uses a taxpayer's money income as the starting point in assessing and collecting taxes. Chapter IV examines the arguments for going beyond that practical starting point to include in the tax base a variety of economic benefits received in kind. Chapter V examines the possible policy justifications for deductions and similar mechanisms that permit taxpayers to adjust monetary receipts downward in computing their taxable capacity. Chapter VI examines the case for preferential treatment of capital gains. Chapter VIII addresses the problems that arise in taxing the income of corporations.

The two remaining chapters address issues that do not relate to the definition of an individual's taxable income or taxable consumption. Chapter III examines the Congressional attempts to disentangle the tax code provisions intended primarily to reward favored economic activity—tax expenditures in common parlance—from those intended to raise revenue according to whatever fairness standard Congress may have adopted. Chapter II examines the issues that relate to the design of a tax rate structure.

The three selections in Section A, below, present several alternative ways of thinking about an individual's taxable capacity. The selections in Section B were written by persons who generally favor a progressive consumption tax over a progressive income tax. The authors of the selections in Section C are all defenders of an income tax, although not necessarily an income tax based on the Haig/Simons model.

Supplemental Readings. Surrey, "Our Troubled Tax Policy: False Routes and Proper Paths to Change," *Tax Notes*, February 2, 1981, pp. 179-97; *What Should Be Taxed: Income or Expenditure?* (J. Pechman, Ed., 1980) (especially articles by D. Bradford, R. Goode, and M. Graetz); Andrews, "A Consumption-Type or Cash Flow Personal Income Tax," 87 *Harvard Law Review* 1113 (1974); P. Mieszkowski, "The Advisability and Feasibility of an Expenditure Tax System," in *The Economics of Taxation* (H. Aaron & M. Boskin, Eds., 1980); Section of Taxation, American Bar Association, Committee on Simplification, "Complexity and the Personal Consumption Tax," 35 *Tax Lawyer* 415 (1979); Musgrave, "ET, OT and SBT," 6 *Journal of Public Economics* 3 (1976); Bittker, "Equity, Efficiency, and Income Tax Theory: Do Misallocations Drive Out Inequities," 16 *San Diego Law Review* 735 (1979); Hettich, "Henry Simons on Taxation and the Economic System," 32 *National Tax Journal* 1 (1979).

A. AN OVERVIEW

RICHARD GOODE, "THE ECONOMIC DEFINITION OF INCOME"

Comprehensive Tax Reform, Brookings Institution
(Joseph A. Pechman, Ed. 1977), pp. 1–10.*

MUCH OF the discussion of the individual income tax in the United States over the past two decades has stressed inequities and economic defects due to the erosion of the tax base and has led up to recommendations for a broader-based tax. This approach implies that there is an income concept against which practice can be meaningfully appraised. While tax specialists have often stated a formal definition, they have not always paid heed to it in their policy prescriptions. Many other participants in the extensive talk and writing about the tax base appear to assume that everyone knows what income is, or that adjusted gross income as identified in the Internal Revenue Code or personal income as estimated by the Department of Commerce is a suitable measure.

Economic theorists have not agreed on the definition of income. There is an extensive and tedious literature on the subject, enlivened by a few notable contributions. Some of the keenest analysts have

---

* I gratefully acknowledge helpful comments received from Sijbren Cnossen, Federico Herschel, George E. Lent, Leif Mutén, Joseph A. Pechman, Stanley S. Surrey, and Vito Tanzi. They, of course, are not responsible for errors, omissions, or misjudgments, particularly since I did not—and could not—accept all their suggestions, which clashed on some points.

concluded that it may well be impossible to define income rigorously. Thus Henry Simons said: "That it should be possible to delimit the concept precisely in every direction is hardly to be expected"; in another passage he wrote about "insuperable difficulties to achievement of a rigorous conception of personal income."[1] Kaldor asserted that "the problem of *defining* individual Income, quite apart from any problem of practical measurement, appears in principle insoluble."[2]

But fortunately the total absence of ambiguity is not required to make a concept useful. If rigor were the ruling criterion, discourse on public policy would be short. Despite the difficulties, income is in practice measured and taxed, though unsatisfactorily in many respects. A premise of this paper is that individual income can be defined reasonably clearly in a sense that is relevant for taxation. If, as I believe is true, there is more than one definition that meets the requirements, a choice can be made by reference to general usage and, more important, to notions of justice and ability to pay. Measurability is also essential.

A good definition of income is an indispensable intellectual foundation for the evaluation of an income tax statute. It serves as a basis for the orderly consideration of specific questions about inclusions, exclusions, and deductions. Without such a basis, discussion is likely to be unnecessarily discursive and the ad hoc conclusions reached may lack force. But the definition should not be viewed as a Platonic ideal to which unquestioned deference is owed. Income, in the words of an able lawyer, is "a concept calling for creative elaboration to effectuate the practical implementation of the purposes of the [income] tax."[3] Few important issues can be resolved merely by appealing to a definition.

This paper is concerned with the economic definition of personal income for tax purposes. Definitions for use in the theory of capital, social accounting, and other fields may properly differ from that which is preferred for individual taxation. No systematic attention is given in the paper to special problems related to the definition and measurement of business income.

---

1. Henry C. Simons, *Personal Income Taxation: The Definition of Income as a Problem of Fiscal Policy* (University of Chicago Press, 1938), pp. 43, 110.

2. Nicholas Kaldor, *An Expenditure Tax* (London: Allen and Unwin, 1955), p. 70.

3. William D. Andrews, "Personal Deductions in an Ideal Income Tax," *Harvard Law Review*, vol. 86 (December 1972), p. 324.

Proposed Definitions

This section reviews several definitions of income that have been advanced by economists, sometimes explicitly for taxation but more often for other purposes, and briefly indicates some of their implications. One of the definitions has received far more support—from American specialists at least—than the others for use in taxation, and I shall try to explain why this is so. The preferred definition, nevertheless, is subject to a number of conceptual and practical difficulties that will be considered in later sections.

Definitions Stressing Capital Maintenance

Since 1976 was the bicentennial of *The Wealth of Nations* as well as of the Declaration of Independence, the filial piety proper for an economist impels me to begin my survey with Adam Smith. He wrote:

The gross revenue of all the inhabitants of a great country, comprehends the whole annual produce of their land and labour; the neat revenue, what remains free to them after deducting the expence of maintaining; first, their fixed; and, secondly, their circulating capital; or what, without encroaching upon their capital, they can place in their stock reserved for immediate consumption, or spend upon their subsistence, conveniences, and amusements.[4]

Smith's definition in form pertains to what would now be called national income or social income, but in content it resembles other definitions that are clearly intended to apply to individuals. While the two concepts are related and many common problems are involved in their quantification, important differences in purpose justify differences in coverage and in the treatment of particular items. In national income statistics the primary objective is to estimate the aggregate value of goods and services produced, whereas in individual income accounts the objective is to measure an individual's (or a family's) command over economic resources. It should not be expected that the summation of individual incomes, so conceived, will equal national income.[5]

---

4. *An Inquiry into the Nature and Causes of the Wealth of Nations*, Edwin Cannan, ed. (Modern Library, 1937), bk. 2, chap. 2, p. 271.

5. In the U.S. national accounts, personal income comprises factor incomes plus transfer payments from government and institutions but not from individuals, minus personal contributions for social insurance. In estimating factor incomes no deduction is made for depletion. Personal income includes the income of individuals, un-

The concept of income as what a person can consume without impairing his capital is a persistent one. It still appeals to economists. For example, J. R. Hicks in his influential treatise *Value and Capital*, first published in 1939 and revised in 1946, is reminiscent of Smith in the following:

The purpose of income calculations in practical affairs is to give people an indication of the amount which they can consume without impoverishing themselves. Following out this idea, it would seem that we ought to define a man's income as the maximum value which he can consume during a week, and still expect to be as well off at the end of the week as he was at the beginning. . . . I think it is fairly clear that this is what the central meaning must be.[6]

Behind Smith's dignified eighteenth-century prose and Hicks's self-consciously homely phrasing lie many complexities relating to the meaning of "encroaching upon . . . capital" or being "as well off at the end of the week as . . . at the beginning." Even the meaning and measurement of consumption are unclear on close examination, though this difficulty has received much less attention than has the problem of capital maintenance.

Moving out from the "central meaning" of income, Hicks elaborates three definitions, or approximations to the central concept, which differ in the interpretation of keeping capital intact. The third version—and the one he prefers but acknowledges to be imperfect—is "the maximum amount of money which the individual can spend this week, and still expect to be able to spend the same amount *in real terms* in each ensuing week."[7] By thus asserting that recurrence, or permanence, is an essential attribute of income, Hicks links his definition with an idea that has been common in Great Britain but less so in the United States. The idea, however, was endorsed in a presidential address to the American Economic Association entitled "The Concept of Income, as Recurrent, Consumable Receipts."[8]

---

incorporated enterprises, nonprofit institutions, private trust funds, and private pension, health, and welfare funds but does not include retained profits of corporations or capital gains and losses. See U.S. Department of Commerce, *National Income, 1954 Edition* (Government Printing Office, 1954), pp. 49–51. On the relationship between national income and individual income, see Simons, *Personal Income Taxation*, pp. 44–49, 58; and Joseph A. Pechman and Benjamin A. Okner, *Who Bears the Tax Burden?* (Brookings Institution, 1974), pp. 12–15.

6. *Value and Capital: An Inquiry into Some Fundamental Principles of Economic Theory*, 2d ed. (Oxford: Oxford University Press, 1946), p. 172.

7. Ibid., p. 174.

8. Carl C. Plehn, *American Economic Review*, vol. 14 (March 1924), pp. 1–12.

Although the central meaning of income, as seen by Hicks, can be reconciled with what I regard as the best definition of income for tax purposes, his own elaboration is different. Basically, income as defined by Hicks is subjective, dependent on the expectations of the individual, and hence not usable as a tax base.[9] If an effort is made to salvage the idea of recurrence or permanence by relating it to market values rather than to individual expectations, the outcome is not a measurable concept of income suitable for all individuals. What may be evolved is a rationalization for omitting capital gains and losses from income while including interest, dividends, and rent.[10] A distinction between change in capital value and yield may be meaningful in an agricultural society with certain legal institutions,[11] or in the world of abstract economic theory,[12] but it does not fit contemporary reality. There is in fact no clear difference between the function of changes in the market value of assets and the interest, dividend, or rental payments associated with them. Nor is it possible to distinguish for tax purposes between recurrent and nonrecurrent or expected and unexpected changes in market value. Another objection to Hicks's interpretation of income is that it concentrates on the yield of capital and applies awkwardly, if at all, to earnings from personal effort, which make up the greater part of what is commonly regarded as income and are taxed as such.

Source and Periodicity Concepts

Akin to definitions incorporating the criterion of recurrence or permanence are definitions that would restrict income to periodic flows from continuing sources.[13] This approach may have been influ-

---

9. Hicks cautioned against the use of the income concept in economic theory, characterizing income as a "very dangerous term" (*Value and Capital*, p. 180).

10. Strictly, part of the capital gain or loss should be reflected in current income, according to the Hicks definition, because it will affect the interest yield that can be obtained and spent in each future period. If the gain is not expected to recur, the amount that should be included is $rg/(1+r)$, where g is the gain and r is the interest rate. See George F. Break, "Capital Maintenance and the Concept of Income," *Journal of Political Economy*, vol. 62 (February 1954), p. 59.

11. Lawrence H. Seltzer, *The Nature and Tax Treatment of Capital Gains and Losses* (National Bureau of Economic Research, 1951), pp. 25–46.

12. In addition to Hicks, *Value and Capital*, chap. 14, see Erik Lindahl, *Studies in the Theory of Money and Capital* (London: Allen and Unwin, 1939), pp. 96–111; and "The Concept of Gains and Losses," in *Festskrift til Frederik Zeuthen* (Copenhagen: Udgivet af Nationaløkonomisk Forening, 1958), pp. 208–19.

13. For reviews of these and other definitions, see Paul H. Wueller, "Concepts of Taxable Income," *Political Science Quarterly*, vol. 53 (March and December 1938),

enced by the origin of income taxation in several European countries as partial taxes or groups of schedular taxes on income from particular sources, as distinguished from a unitary tax on an individual's total income. The implications of the source and periodicity concepts are similar to those connected with Hicks's version of the capital-maintenance concept: the exclusion of capital gains and losses and "casual" receipts such as gambling or lottery winnings and various lump-sum payments on retirement or loss of employment. The weaknesses are also similar: the artificiality of the distinction between capital gains and other investment yields, the inconsistent treatment of income from personal effort and income from other sources, and—more generally—the omission of items that contribute to the ability to pay taxes.

Fisher's Definition

Another definition that grew out of theorizing about capital and its yield is that of Fisher. According to him, income is fundamentally "yield," consisting of the services rendered by property or persons. Since the only services desired for themselves are those that satisfy consumers' wants, income, as defined by Fisher, is what others call consumption.[14] Savings and increases or decreases in the value of capital assets are explicitly excluded. Apart from the saving decisions of owners, no provision is made for capital maintenance, and no attention is paid to the question of permanence or recurrence. Income is equivalent to consumption, regardless of whether spending is financed out of current earnings or by using up capital.

Fisher developed his definition before the modern income tax was

---

pp. 83–110, 557–83, and vol. 54 (December 1939), pp. 555–76; Edwin R. A. Seligman, "Income Tax," *Encyclopaedia of the Social Sciences* (Macmillan, 1932), vol. 7, pp. 626–39; and Henry Laufenburger, "Die Einkommensbesteuerung," *Handbuch der Finanzwissenschaft*, 2d ed. (Tübingen: J. C. B. Mohr [Paul Siebeck], 1956), vol. 2, pp. 460–69.

14. See the following works by Irving Fisher: *The Nature of Capital and Income* (London: Macmillan, 1906); "Income," *Encyclopaedia of the Social Sciences* (Macmillan, 1932), vol. 7, pp. 622–25; "Income in Theory and Income Taxation in Practice," *Econometrica*, vol. 5 (January 1937), pp. 1–55; and "The Concept of Income: A Rebuttal," *Econometrica*, vol. 7 (October 1939), pp. 357–61. See also Irving Fisher and Herbert W. Fisher, *Constructive Income Taxation: A Proposal for Reform* (Harper, 1942). Fisher objected at times to the assertion that he defined income as merely consumption, calling this a "misrepresentation" of his views (see, for example, "The Concept of Income," pp. 358–59); but this interpretation has been accepted by all critics and, finally, by Fisher himself (*Constructive Income Taxation*, p. 51).

adopted in the United States and, he assures us, independently of any views that he came to hold on social policy and taxation.[15] He later, however, enthusiastically advocated its use for taxation and argued that an "income" tax based on his definition would be fairer and economically superior to the existing tax.

For a long time Fisher insisted that the meaning of income should be restricted to his concept, but finally he gave up this point and conceded that in addition to "services" or "yield" income, as he defined it, there was another useful concept, "enrichment" income or "accretion," consisting of consumption plus capital increase (or minus capital decrease).[16] Indeed he remarked: "While yield is the more fundamental concept, accretion is, for some purposes (other than taxation), the more useful."[17]

Although Fisher's argumentation sometimes appears to be reducible to the proposition that the correct base for the income tax must be "income" as he defined it for another purpose—and in a sense different from common usage—his writings are intellectually far superior to many others on the subject. When he does discuss tax policy Fisher makes a respectable case for preferring an expenditure tax (personal consumption tax) to a conventional income tax. He also deserves credit for addressing many of the practical problems that would have to be solved in order to put into effect an expenditure tax. I am not persuaded that the expenditure tax is better than the income tax, but I shall reserve for my discussion of the accretion concept the few comments on the advantages of the income tax for which there is space in this paper.

The Schanz-Haig-Simons Definition

The income definition that has received most support from American tax specialists is usually called the Haig-Simons concept but more accurately and less parochially could be named the Schanz-Haig-Simons (S-H-S) concept or definition.[18] Developed explicitly for tax

---

15. *Constructive Income Taxation*, p. x; and "The Concept of Income," p. 360.
16. "The Concept of Income," p. 357; and *Constructive Income Taxation*, pp. 48–51.
17. *Constructive Income Taxation*, p. 50. Fisher said that accretion may be more useful in that it conveys information about future yields as well as the yield of the period under consideration.
18. Georg von Schanz (1853–1931) was a German economist and founder and editor of *Finanz-Archiv*. His definition is set forth in his important article, "Der

purposes, this is the accretion concept, which defines personal income as the sum of consumption and accumulation.

Haig stated that income is "the increase or accretion in one's power to satisfy his wants in a given period in so far as that power consists of (*a*) money itself, or, (*b*) anything susceptible of valuation in terms of money. More simply stated, the definition of income which the economist offers is this: Income is the *money value of the net accretion to one's economic power between two points of time*."[19] He emphasized that the definition is in terms of the power to satisfy economic wants rather than the satisfactions themselves and pointed out that this means that income is received when the power is obtained and not when it is exercised. This is to say, income includes savings as well as consumption.

Simons defined personal income for tax purposes as "the algebraic sum of (1) the market value of rights exercised in consumption and (2) the change in the value of the store of property rights between the beginning and end of the period in question." He added, "In other words, it is merely the result obtained by adding consumption during the period to 'wealth' at the end of the period and then subtracting 'wealth' at the beginning."[20]

In an enumeration that may have appeared deliberately provocative in 1896 in the light of much doctrine and tax practice, Schanz made clear that his definition included not only ordinary profits but also the usufruct of property, gifts, inheritances, legacies, lottery winnings, insurance proceeds, annuities, and windfall gains of all kinds and that all interest paid and capital losses should be deducted.[21]

As noted above, the S-H-S definition can be reconciled with a concept going back at least as far as Adam Smith. Income is the amount that one could consume without experiencing any increase or decrease

---

Einkommensbegriff und die Einkommensteuergesetze," *Finanz-Archiv*, vol. 13, no. 1 (1896), pp. 1–87. See the article on Schanz by Hans Teschemacher in *Encyclopaedia of the Social Sciences* (Macmillan, 1934), vol. 13, pp. 563–64. According to Leif Mutén (*On the Development of Income Taxation Since World War I* [Amsterdam: International Bureau of Fiscal Documentation, 1967], p. 25), Schanz was anticipated by David Davidson, writing in Swedish in 1889.

19. Robert Murray Haig, "The Concept of Income—Economic and Legal Aspects," in Haig, ed., *The Federal Income Tax* (Columbia University Press, 1921), p. 7, reprinted in Richard A. Musgrave and Carl S. Shoup, eds., *Readings in the Economics of Taxation* (Irwin for the American Economic Association, 1959), p. 59.

20. *Personal Income Taxation*, p. 50.

21. As quoted in ibid., p. 61.

in his capital. The reconciliation is valid, however, only on the basis of a particular and relatively simple view of the meaning of maintaining capital intact: capital comprises only nonhuman wealth, and it is intact if its money value does not change within the period.[22] In this sense, capital is equivalent to what is commonly called net worth in accounting statements.

Adherents to definitions stressing capital maintenance, however, usually have in mind a quite different interpretation. Only rarely is this clearly stated, and reliance is frequently placed on figures of speech—often a harvest metaphor—rather than on accounting statements. The intention is to exclude from income capital gains and losses and many nonrecurrent accretions to capital. Hicks has provided the sophisticated version of this interpretation of maintaining capital intact. As argued above, Hicks's version is unusable for taxation because it cannot be objectively measured; even if it could be approximated its policy implications would be unacceptable. The emphasis on the permanence of the real level of consumption accords with the rentier's aspiration in a world of uncertainty and inflation. A parallel concept can hardly be applied to entrepreneurs or recipients of income from personal effort. A definition of taxable income that omits capital gains and nonrecurrent or "casual" receipts will favor investors and speculators in securities, real estate, and commodities.

The Fisher definition, in contrast, is objective and measurable in principle (although there would be practical difficulties in applying it). Concern about capital maintenance and permanence or recurrence drop out of the formal requirements, or more accurately, the tax authorities would accept whatever provision the individual thought it appropriate to make for capital maintenance. But I do not believe that legislators or the public thought that a direct tax on consumption was being imposed when the income tax was enacted.

The reasons for preferring the S-H-S concept to Fisher's concept are really the reasons for preferring an income tax to an expenditure tax. This is not the place to elaborate the arguments, but a brief statement is essential, even at the risk of dogmatism. As I see it the income tax is superior in principle to the expenditure tax, first because income is generally a better index of ability to pay than is consumption. Both the amount of income obtained and the amount consumed depend on the decisions and opportunities of the individual, but con-

22. Break, "Capital Maintenance and the Concept of Income."

sumption reflects an additional choice, that is, the disposal of the power to consume that accrues to one within a period of time. It is intuitively appealing to say that an individual's ability to pay is measured by the whole set of his additional consumption opportunities rather than by the subset that he elects to utilize currently.[23] Another reason for preferring the income tax is that accumulation itself is an objective and a source of satisfaction distinguishable from current or future consumption. To the extent that progressive taxation is regarded as a means of preventing excessive inequality, total income or wealth is preferable to consumption as a tax base because accumulation enhances the economic and political power and the social status of the individual. The proposition sometimes advanced that a tax on consumption is superior because it is apportioned according to the use of resources rather than according to one's contribution to production is misleading. Savers and investors direct the use of economic resources no less than do consumers. Whether private consumption or private investment should be displaced to make room for government expenditure is an important question of economic policy that ought to be debated on its merits.[24]

Although the S-H-S definition has been accepted by most American specialists as the best available for tax purposes, a number of conceptual and practical questions are encountered in trying to apply it. I turn now to some of these issues. Before doing so, however, I should like to emphasize that my concentration on issues relating to the S-H-S concept should not be taken to imply that the difficulties could be avoided by adopting one of the other definitions. Many of the problems to be discussed would arise in connection with the other definitions, and there would be some special difficulties as well.

INSTITUTE FOR FISCAL STUDIES, THE STRUCTURE AND REFORM OF DIRECT TAXES: REPORT OF A COMMITTEE CHAIRED BY PROFESSOR J. E. MEADE

George Allen & Unwin (1978), pp. 30–40, 44–45.

INCOME AS THE TAX BASE

A taxpayer's *income* is an obvious candidate to serve as the base for his tax liability; but there are unfortunately difficulties in establishing what in principle is meant by a taxpayer's income, quite irrespective of any practical difficulties of ascertaining and measuring his income when it has been defined. A natural and commonsensical approach is to draw a distinction between a man's capital and his income by regarding his *capital* as the stock of resources from which the flow of income proceeds; in terms of the familiar analogy, the tree is the capital from which the annual income of the fruit crop is derived.

But on examination this distinction is found to involve many difficulties. Should the whole of the fruit crop be counted as taxable income if the fruit trees are ageing and depreciating in value, so that part of the proceeds of the crop must be used to maintain the productive power of the orchard? Or to take an example at the other extreme, if a forester is growing trees from which there is no annual crop but which are ultimately cut down and sold for timber, does he have no income at any time but only a realisation of the gain in the capital value of his trees when he cuts them down and sells them? Or consider two Government bonds both of which are issued at a price of £100, the difference being that on bond A the government undertakes to pay no interest but to redeem the bond at a price of £110 in a year's time, whereas on bond B the government undertakes to redeem the bond at its issue price of £100 in a year's time but meanwhile to pay £10 in interest on its borrowing. Is there no income but only gain in capital value on bond A, while there is income but no capital gain on bond B?

The above are only some extremely simple and obvious examples of the relationships between gains and losses in capital values on the one hand and net income on the other. As rates of income tax have risen to their present high levels, the distinction between income and capital gains has become more and more important; more and more sophisticated ways have been devised by taxpayers to turn highly taxable income into less highly taxable capital gains; and the importance of finding, if it is possible, a definition of income which does not permit these uncertain and often irrelevant distinctions to continue has correspondingly increased. Two such definitions of income are in principle possible, which we shall call definition A and definition B.

DEFINITION A OF TAXABLE INCOME

In the first of these two definitions it is argued that the proper measure of a taxpayer's income in any one year is the value of what he could have consumed during the year without living on and so diminishing his capital wealth in the process. This comprehensive measure would take account of any capital gains or losses which had accrued in the course of the year and would include any other windfall receipts in addition to more narrowly defined income receipts from wages, dividends, rents, profits, etc. This measure, it may be argued, is the fairest one for tax purposes, because whatever the taxpayer may choose to do with these resources they constitute a true measure of the total economic opportunity accruing to him in the year in question.

We call this definition A. To accept definition A of income for the principal or sole measure of an individual's taxable capacity could lead to some very strange results. Consider a millionaire whose £1 million is invested at 10 per cent in a way which ensures an annual flow of £100,000 in interest. If in one year the market rate of interest rises from 10 per cent to $11\frac{1}{9}$ per cent, so that the capital value of his investment falls by £100,000 in the course of the year, his taxable income will be zero. His capital loss will have offset his receipt of interest or dividends, and he must save the whole of his receipt of interest of £100,000 in order to restore the value of his capital investment to £1 million. If income so defined were strictly used as the sole measure of riches or poverty for fiscal purposes, the millionaire, worth £900,000 at the end of the year and with the certain prospect of a future flow of interest of £100,000 a year, would be poverty stricken and would presumably qualify for supplementary benefit.

DEFINITION B OF TAXABLE INCOME

There is, however, an alternative principle upon which income may be defined for fiscal purposes, which does not lead to unacceptable results of the kind described in the previous paragraph. This is to define an individual's income not as the amount which he could consume in any one year without diminishing his capital wealth in the course of that year, but as the amount which he could consume in any one year and yet be left with the resources and expectations at the end of that year which would enable him to maintain that same level of consumption indefinitely in the future. Let us call this definition B of income as a tax base. In this case the millionaire's income is defined as £100,000.

Unfortunately this definition of income would be a quite impracticable criterion for tax purposes, because it depends essentially upon future expectations. The level of consumption expenditure which any individual can enjoy this year and expect to enjoy indefinitely in the future depends upon what his future earnings will in fact turn out to be, upon what will happen to the rate of interest in the future, and upon all such things as may affect what he should save this year in order to maintain his future spending power. It is not easy to envisage the tax inspector agreeing with each taxpayer upon what may reasonably be expected to constitute a maintainable level of consumption.

For this reason when it is suggested that comprehensive income should be chosen for the tax base, this is usually taken to imply the use of definition A, which – difficult as it may be to make the necessary valuations – does in principle rest on hard historic facts about what happened in the year in question, rather than definition B, which involves choosing between different expectations about the future.

In spite of the impracticability of making use of definition B it is helpful to an understanding of the problems involved to consider some of the implications of the choice between definitions A and B.

The difference between the two definitions of income can be illustrated by considering their implications for the treatment of capital gains, which may fall into at least three different categories:

1. A capital gain may be a change of the kind which occurred to the millionaire discussed above as a result simply of a fall in the rate of interest, which altered the present value of his constant assured stream of future purchasing power. On definition A the capital gain must be added to his other income, while on definition B it has no effect upon his taxable income.

2. But a capital gain might indicate that there was a once-for-all unexpected improvement in the efficiency of the company in which the taxpayer had invested his money, so that, for example, with a constant 10 per cent rate of interest the millionaire's property rises in value from £1 million to £1·1 million because the prospect of assured annual future return on the property has risen from £100,000 to £110,000. The capital gain is £100,000; and on definition A his income in the year in question has been increased by £100,000, while on definition B the rise in his income is £10,000.

3. But there is another possibility. Our millionaire may have invested his money in a concern which makes £100,000 profit each year, distributes none of this in dividend, but adds £100,000 to the value of its own assets each year. If the value of the millionaire's investment rises similarly by £100,000 a year, he will make a capital gain equal to this sum, the whole of which on definition B should be included in his taxable income. He can indefinitely realise and spend £100,000 worth of his shares at the

end of every year and maintain his consumption at that level without impairment. In this case the capital gain should be included in taxable income on both definitions.

Or consider the treatment of a windfall or exceptional receipt – e.g. the receipt of £100,000 from the winnings in a football pool, or from an author's sale of the copyright of a best-seller, or from an inventor's sale of a patent right. Suppose further that there is an assured return of 10 per cent on any long term investment. On definition A the lucky gambler, author or inventor has an income this year of £100,000, while on definition B he has an income of £10,000.

CONSUMPTION AS A TAX BASE

An alternative to taking income, whether defined on the A principle or the B principle, is to take expenditure on consumption as the essential base for personal taxation. A strong case can be made for this base in that it levies a tax on the claims which a taxpayer makes at any one time on the community's resources which he uses up for his own consumption purposes. If he saves his income instead of consuming it, he is putting resources back into the productive pool; if he dissaves, he is taking resources out of the productive pool in addition to his other income. His relatively low consumption in the case of savings and his relatively high consumption in the case of dissavings are measures of what he is appropriating at any one time for his own personal use.

This expresses what is normally regarded as the essential case for the choice of expenditure on consumption as the base for progressive personal taxation. A *progressive expenditure tax* (as it is usually called) falls more heavily than progressive income tax on the wealthy who are financing high levels of consumption out of capital resources, but at the same time it gives much greater opportunity than does a progressive income tax for the finance of the development and growth of private enterprises out of private savings.

The implications of this difference are very far reaching. With a progressive income tax a wealthy man with a high marginal rate of income tax of 83 per cent will be able to use only £17 out of £100 of profit for the development of his business, whereas with a progressive tax on expenditure he could use all his profit to develop his business. At the same time with the income tax a wealthy man could live on his capital without paying any tax, whereas with a progressive expenditure tax he could purchase only £17 worth of additional consumption out of each additional £100 of his capital which he realised. A progressive expenditure tax is the one form of tax which could have the political appeal of encouraging enterprise and economic development and at the same time heavily taxing high levels of consumption expenditure which at present, if it is financed out of capital, goes untaxed.

INCOME, CONSUMPTION AND CAPACITY TO PAY

It may, however, be asked whether it is fair and equitable to tax rich Mr Smith who chooses to save a large part of his income very much less heavily than equally rich Mr Brown who chooses to spend his income. Both have the same power of command over resources. Can the fact that Mr Smith chooses to use this power one way and Mr Brown in another way affect their present capacities to pay tax? If attention is confined to the immediate situation, the ability to pay of the two men is apparently the same, although their tax burdens are very different. The picture is, however, changed if the whole lifecycle of the two men is considered. Something will happen in the future to the wealth which Mr Smith is accumulating. If he spends it during his life time, he will pay tax on it and will then be subject to a heavier burden of tax than Mr Brown, who will not possess the same wealth to spend. Mr Smith may hand on his wealth to someone else by gift during his life or by bequest at his death; but according to the regime for the taxation of such capital transfers a tax will then be paid which Mr Brown will avoid, because he has no wealth to transfer. Over their lives Mr Smith's tax burden may well be considerably greater than Mr Brown's. However, it will be true that Mr Smith will have enjoyed the advantages of security, independence and influence which are associated with ownership of property over a period of his life, which Mr Brown will not have experienced. This fact, as we shall consider later, supports the case for some form of annual tax on the amount of a taxpayer's wealth, even if it is considered otherwise equitable to tax Mr Smith and Mr Brown on the basis of their lifecycle of consumption or giving rather than on the year-to-year basis of their capacities to save, to consume or to give.

SIMILARITIES AND DIFFERENCES BETWEEN CONSUMPTION AND INCOME AS A TAX BASE

The measurement of a taxpayer's actual consumption expenditure in any one year is, like income on definition A, a matter of historic fact and does not, like income on definition B, depend upon subjective views about the future. What the taxpayer does in fact decide to spend on consumption in any one year is, of course, likely to be much affected by his expectations about future events. If he expects his future income to fall in his old age, he is likely to reduce his consumption now in order to be able to maintain his future consumption out of his savings. But he makes the decision what to spend, and the tax inspector then inspects what he has in fact spent. This can be a troublesome task (as discussed in Chapters 9 and 22); but at least the tax inspector does not have to reach agreement about the future subjective expectations on which the taxpayer has based his action.

It would be one thing if definition B for income could be used as a tax base; but that is not a practical possibility. If, however, it was wished to use income on definition B as a tax base, it might be better to use consumption expenditure rather than income on definition A as the actual operative base. In the extreme case, if individuals always attempted to plan their affairs so as to maintain indefinitely a constant level of consumption expenditure, then consumption as a tax base would coincide with income on definition B as a tax base, provided that the tax inspector always accepted the taxpayer's views about the future.

In the light of these distinctions of principle it is of interest to compare the choice of income on definition A with the choice of consumption expenditure as the tax base for personal taxation.

There are a number of problems of definition which are common to both tax bases.

It is a well-recognised fact that to obtain a fair comparison of the comprehensive incomes of different taxpayers a decision must be made on how to handle benefits in kind and certain elements of real income which do not involve monetary transactions. A familiar problem of this kind is the need to distinguish between income and business costs. To what extent is the use of a company car provided for an employee of the company an addition to the personal comfort and standard of living of the employee, and to what extent is it merely a business expense like the cost of his office desk? If Mrs Smith goes out to work and uses part of her earnings to hire a babysitter while she is away from home, but Mrs Brown stays at home and looks after the children herself, is the Smith family income for that reason higher than the Brown family income, and, if so, by how much?

Exactly similar problems arise with the definition of consumption. How far does the use of the company's car increase the personal consumption of the user? Is Mrs Smith consuming the services of a babysitter, or is this a business expense which gives the family no net rise in its standard of consumption?

But some problems of definition which arise in the case of an income base are irrelevant in the case of a consumption base, and vice versa. Thus whether an increase in state pension rights should or should not be regarded as adding to the value of an individual's wealth and thus included in income or not is irrelevant for the definition of consumption; in either case it clearly is not an item of current consumption. On the other hand, there may be doubt as to whether an individual's expenditure on education should be included in his consumption or should be regarded as money which he saves and invests to yield a future return in the form of increased earning power. But this distinction is irrelevant for the definition of income: the expenditure comes out of his income whether it is regarded as consumption or savings.

INCOME TAX, EXPENDITURE TAX AND THE RETURN ON SAVINGS

A basic difference between an income base and a consumption expenditure base for personal taxation is to be found in their effects upon the return to the taxpayer's savings. This is illustrated in Table 3.1. We assume that Mr

AN OVERVIEW

Brown has earned £150 and that there is a tax either (i) on his income, or (ii) on his expenditure on consumption. We illustrate this with tax at a (tax-inclusive) rate of $33\frac{1}{3}$ per cent in section 1 of the table and at a (tax-inclusive) rate of 50 per cent in section 2 of the table. We assume that Mr Brown can invest any savings which he makes in machinery or some other form of physical investment which produces a return of 10 per cent on the investment.

Table 3.1 *The difference between an income base and an expenditure base (in £s)*

	Section 1 Tax rate $33\frac{1}{3}$% (tax-inclusive)		Section 2 Tax rate 50% (tax-inclusive)	
	(i)	(ii)	(i)	(ii)
	IT	ET	IT	ET
	A	B	C	D
Earnings spent				
Earnings	150	150	150	150
Less IT	(50)	—	(75)	—
Less ET	—	(50)	—	(75)
Consumption	100	100	75	75
Earnings saved				
Earnings	150	150	150	150
Less IT	(50)	—	(75)	—
Less ET	—	nil	—	nil
Savings invested	100	150	75	150
Annual yield	10	15	7·50	15
Less IT	($3\frac{1}{3}$)	—	(3·75)	—
Less ET	—	(5)	—	(7·50)
Annual consumption	$6\frac{2}{3}$	10	3·75	7·50
Rate of return on postponed consumption (% a year)	$6\frac{2}{3} \div 100$ $= 6\frac{2}{3}$%	$10 \div 100$ $= 10$%	$3·75 \div 75$ $= 5$%	$7·50 \div 75$ $= 10$%

Section 1 of the table makes it clear that, with a $33\frac{1}{3}$ per cent tax rate, under the income tax (IT) regime Mr Brown has the choice of spending on consumption either a single lump sum of £100 or £$6\frac{2}{3}$ a year thereafter, and under the expenditure tax (ET) regime a choice of spending on consumption either a single lump sum of £100 or £10 a year thereafter. Thus if Mr Brown decides to save rather than to spend, he will obtain a return of only 6⅔ per cent on his postponed consumption under the income tax regime but a full 10 per cent on his postponed consumption under an expenditure tax regime.

From section 2 of the table it is clear that, with the higher tax rate of 50 per cent Mr Brown has the choice under the income tax regime between consumption this year of £75 or £3·75 a year hereafter and under the expenditure tax regime between £75 this year or £7·5 a year hereafter. In this case under the income tax regime he can now obtain a rate of return of only 5 per cent on his postponed consumption, whereas under the expenditure tax regime he can still obtain the full 10 per cent return. Of course, the higher the rate of expenditure tax, the lower his consumption. In section 1 he can consume £100 now or £10 a year hereafter, while in section 2 he can consume only £75 now or £7·5 a year hereafter. He can consume less in section 2 than in section 1, but the rate of return on postponed consumption is the full 10 per cent in both cases, whereas with the income tax the higher the rate of tax, the lower the level of consumption *and* the lower the rate of return on any postponed consumption.

It is indeed the characteristic feature of an expenditure tax as contrasted with an income tax that, at any given constant rate of tax, the former will make the rate of return to the saver on his reduced consumption equal to the rate of return which can be earned on the investment which his savings finances, whereas the income tax will reduce the rate of return to the saver below the rate of return which the investment will yield.

In later chapters of this Report we shall frequently use this phenomenon as a basic criterion. We shall treat a tax regime as being equivalent to an expenditure tax if, at a constant rate of tax, it leaves the yield to the saver equal to the yield on the investment. Although we shall use this as our test, there is no implication that this is the sole reason why an expenditure tax regime may be preferred to an income tax regime; there are many other considerations (discussed in this chapter and in Chapter 6 on the effects of inflation on the two bases).

The equality between the rate of yield to saver and the yield on the investment is, however, more than just a test of the existence of an expenditure tax regime, since it does mean that there is no marginal tax incentive inducing taxpayers to substitute at the margin present consumption for future consumption simply because the future yield on savings has been reduced below the true yield.

But the equality between yield to saver and the yield on investment will rule only if the rate of expenditure tax is constant. If the rate of tax is lower at the time of saving than it will be at the future time when the yield on the saving is itself consumed, then the net rate of yield to the saver will be reduced below the rate of yield on the investment.[1]

---

[1] In the example in section 1 of Table 3.1, if the rate of expenditure tax on the yield of £15 had risen to 40 per cent, the saver would have had only £9 instead of £10 to spend – a rate of return of only 9 per cent on his initial abstinence from consumption of £100.

Thus with a progressive expenditure tax there will be a tax incentive to even expenditures out over time, even though, because of concentrated needs or otherwise, lumpy concentrations of expenditure would in the absence of tax considerations have been preferred, just as under a progressive income tax there is a tax incentive to even income receipts out over time.

THE EVEN SPREADING OF INCOME AND OF CONSUMPTION

With a consumption, instead of an income, base for taxation the distinction between once-for-all windfall receipts and regular income receipts becomes less important. If Jones wins a football pool or if author Smith sells his single best-seller in one year for a large lump sum, the individual concerned can, with a consumption tax base, spread the consumption of the windfall over a number of future years; and he will therefore not be liable to tax at the high progressive rate to which he would be liable if the windfall was treated as part of the single year's income. It may be regarded as a desirable feature of an equitable tax system that liability to tax should depend upon a taxpayer's average standard over his lifetime rather than on a current year-by-year standard. With a tax system with progressively higher marginal rates of tax, a fluctuating base will involve a heavier tax burden than a steady base. Thus if the average tax rate on an income of £3,000 were $33\frac{1}{3}$ per cent but on an income of £6,000 were 50 per cent, a taxpayer with a year's income of £6,000 followed by a year's income of zero would pay £3,000 in tax, whereas a taxpayer with two years at a steady £3,000 would pay only £2,000 in tax.

But this consideration tells in favour of a tax on consumption only if a taxpayer's consumption is likely naturally to be spread more evenly over his lifetime than is his income. If his consumption were more variable than his income, this particular argument would tell in favour of an income tax. We can in fact give the same example as in the previous paragraph, simply substituting 'consumption' for 'income'. 'If the average tax rate on a consumption of £3,000 were $33\frac{1}{3}$ per cent but on a consumption of £6,000 were 50 per cent, a taxpayer with a year's consumption of £6,000 followed by a year's consumption of zero would pay £3,000 in tax, whereas a taxpayer with two years at a steady £3,000 would pay only £2,000 in tax.' The balance of advantage will depend very much on what is regarded as consumption. We discuss later how owner-occupied houses should best be treated for such tax purposes. If the purchase of a house were itself treated as an item of consumption expenditure, there clearly could be much greater fluctuations in consumption expenditures than would be the case if the purchase of a house were considered as an act of saving not liable to a tax on consumption, and if instead a regular annual value imputed to the house were regarded as the value of the annual consumption of dwelling space. Equity in progressive taxation as between taxpayers with a steady and taxpayers with a fluctuating tax base requires some arrangements for averaging lumpy tax liabilities over a period of years in both the cases of an income tax and of a consumption tax. The need may be less under a consumption tax depending upon the definitions of consumption used for the purpose of the tax.

THE DIFFERENCE BETWEEN EARNED AND INVESTMENT INCOME

For income tax purposes there is an important difference between earned and investment income. Earned income is neither relieved of tax on its decay nor is it taxed on any capital gain in the human capital which produces the income. Thus no allowance is made for deduction from earnings of a depreciation allowance which will make up for the fact that in old age and by death an earner will lose his power of earnings, although his income will have disappeared in old age and he cannot hand on his earning power to his heirs. On the other hand, if a worker receives an unexpected promotion and increase in his earning power, the present capital value of his future earnings (suitably discounted) will rise; but he will not be taxed on this capital gain.

Investment income may or may not be relieved of tax on its decay and may or may not be taxed on any underlying capital gain. Thus a machine will wear out and lose its productive power, and it is normal to take this into account by refraining from taxing the gross profit on a machine and permitting deduction of some allowance for depreciation from the gross return before assessment of liability to tax. But such allowance for the decay of investment income is not always made. An outstanding example of this occurs in times of rapid inflation (a phenomenon discussed fully in Chapter 6) if in the case of the interest and capital of a money debt no allowance is made for the fact that its real value is being eroded by price rises. Thus a man who owns £100 of government debt with, say, a nominal annual interest of £10 on it will be receiving no allowance for the falling real value of his income if he is taxed on the whole of the £10 of interest. On the other hand, real capital gains on investments sometimes are and sometimes are not liable to income tax or a capital gains tax. The existing differentiation in favour of earned income, previously implemented through the earned income allowance and now through the investment income surcharge, is largely based on the principle that earned income is not lasting, since it will inevitably disappear with old age and death, whereas investment income is normally lasting if proper depreciation allowances are made. But for the reasons discussed above this is an oversimplification of the situation, particularly in times of rapid price inflation, the effect of which (as argued in Chapter 6) greatly complicates this issue.

But this set of problems simply does not arise if consumption rather than income constitutes the tax base. The taxpayer would, of course, prefer an income which was expected to last or better still to rise rather than an income which was expected to be eroded by old age or inflation. He will take his expectations into account when he makes his decisions as to how much he should save and how much he should spend. He can put aside out of earned or investment income in his savings whatever he considers necessary to maintain his position, and with an expenditure tax he will not be taxed on these savings. He can, as it were, decide on his own depreciation allowance and avoid all tax on it. He will be taxed only on what he consumes. Thus if Smith has an income of £5,000 a year which he expects to decline (e.g. because it is an earned income and he is ageing), while Jones has an income of £5,000 a year which he expects to be permanently maintained (e.g. because it is derived from a company whose profits are expected to be maintained in real terms), Smith will not be in a position to maintain as high a standard of consumption as Jones. With a consumption tax their differing abilities will be automatically recognised. In so far as Jones consumes more because he can afford to consume more, he will automatically pay more in tax.

Differences in lasting power are not, however, the only relevant differences between earned and investment incomes. Investment incomes are compatible with a life of leisure or can be supplemented by earnings. Earned incomes are derived from work and do not give the same opportunities for leisure or for a further supplementation of incomes. It is therefore not unreasonable with a consumption tax regime to give some differential treatment to earned income over investment income as alternative sources of purchasing power for the finance of consumption. The case for such differentiation and the degree to which it should be carried is, however, much less with a consumption tax than with an income tax.

* * *

CONCLUSIONS

There are serious difficulties in defining an individual's income satisfactorily for tax purposes and in particular in finding the appropriate treatment for windfall receipts and for different kinds of capital gain. Taking expenditure on consumption in place of income as a tax base raises less acute problems of definition; it taxes what a person takes out of the economic production system rather than what he puts into it; it combines greater opportunities for economic enterprise with heavier taxation of high levels of consumption financed out of the dissipation of wealth; and it avoids problems arising from the distinction between earned income and investment income. On the other hand it may involve somewhat higher rates of tax.

In addition to income or consumption as the main base for direct taxation, there is a case for direct taxes based on the amount of wealth owned by the taxpayer and (if gifts are not treated as taxable income or taxable consumption) on the amounts of wealth transferred by way of gift or inheritance.

While a strong case can be made out in theory for a multiplicity of different rates of tax on a large number of different types of transaction, we see merit in confining direct taxes to one or two well defined bases whose nature can be readily appreciated by the taxpayer.

RICHARD A. MUSGRAVE, "TAX REFORM OR TAX DEFORM"

Tax Policy Options in the 1980's, Canadian Tax Foundation
(Wayne R. Thirsk & John Whalley, Eds. 1982), pp. 19–23.

Legislation to change the tax system—be it in Canada, the United States, or anywhere else—is referred to fondly as tax reform. Reform, so Webster tells us, is "amendment of what is defective, vicious, or depraved." There is first a question, then, of whether today's tax structure, as it exists, exhibits any of these characteristics and thus lends itself to reform. While I do not regard the system as depraved or vicious, I readily grant that it is defective. Legislation may amend its defects, or reform the system, but equally it may serve to *deform*: "misshape, disfigure, render displeasing," as Webster defines the term. Before commenting on tax prospects for the 1980s, I therefore think it prudent to inquire whether legislative changes—and such changes there will be—are going to be of the reforming or deforming variety. To begin with, we need a point of calibration; that is, an agreed-upon concept of a good tax structure. Without such a norm, perceptions of tax reform, like those of beauty, remain in the eyes of the beholder.

Analytical and empirical investigations into taxation effects are important. Taxes are what they turn out to be, and this is not necessarily the same as what they are meant to be. It is all to the good, therefore, that the young generation, armed with indirect utility functions and computer outlets in their kitchens, if as yet limited observations, should set out to measure these effects. But in order to evaluate the outcome for purposes of policy, we have to know first what the good tax structure *should* accomplish, and what it should look like.

Adam Smith was well aware of this when, at the beginning of his chapters on taxation, he presented the four requirements of a good structure: equity, certainty, convenience, and efficiency. Within this framework, he set out his conception of a good tax: "The subjects of every state ought to contribute towards the support of government as nearly as possible in proportion to their respective abilities, that is in proportion to the revenue which they respectively enjoy under the protection of the state."[1] It is not quite clear just what this dictum implies—whether it calls for benefit or ability taxation, and how the two are related to a person's revenue—but Smith's insistence that the tax structure should be equitable was, and surely remains, correct.

Concern with tax equity is still strong in our society. Indeed, a popular sense that the tax structure is reasonably equitable is prerequisite to a sound social

---

[1] Adam Smith, *An Inquiry into the Nature and Causes of the Wealth of Nations* (London: printed for W. Strahan and T. Cadell, 1776), 423.

structure and to the functioning of democracy. Of course, this is not the entire story. "Every tax," Smith continues, "ought to be so contrived as both to take out and keep out of the pockets of the people as little as possible, over and above what it brings into the public treasury of the state."[2] I doubt that this statement should be interpreted as the origin of optimal taxation theory, but it is certainly compatible with the emphasis of recent tax research. The tax system, in short, must be both equitable and efficient. So far so good, but consensus thins out as we move to tighter specifications of the rules.

Horizontal Equity

I begin with the requirements of horizontal equity, not only because it has long been a major interest of mine, but also because it is among the most fundamental concepts in tax structure design, especially in the modern economy with its complex institutional structure and thousands of ways in which income can be received and used. Horizontal equity may be said to precede the issue of vertical equity. Vertical equity deals with distribution; but before we can discuss distribution, we have to decide what is being distributed.

The idea of horizontal equity rests on two propositions. One is that tax burdens are borne by people, not by things or legal entities. All tax burdens must therefore be traced to people, and the system must be judged in terms of its effect upon individuals. From the outset, this premise establishes a strong bias in favour of personal taxes, since only such taxes can be related effectively to the taxpayer's economic position. The personalization of taxes is *reform*; resort to *in rem* taxes, unless acceptable as a proxy for fees, is *deform*. The second proposition is that people in equal positions should be treated alike. There should be no discrimination, be it by accident or, worse, by design. As a general rule of fairness, this is an unobjectionable requirement. Reasonable people may differ on whether taxes should be progressive, or by how much, but they must agree on the principle of equal treatment. It is not, however, obvious how equal treatment should be interpreted—that is, how the index of equality should be defined. To my generation of public finance economists, it was axiomatic that equality be defined in terms of income, which, in the Henry Simons tradition, means accretion. We also accepted as axiomatic that people with equal accretion should pay the same amount of tax. Now the first of these two assumptions has ceased to be self-evident, and the second is in need of amendment.

The concept of income as index of equality was celebrated magnificently, and I hope not for the last time, in the Carter Commission report published 15 years ago. While there have always been rumblings, from John Stuart Mill to Irving Fisher, that the inclusion of interest constitutes "double taxation," it is only recently that the consumption base has emerged as a serious rival. With the consumption base viewed in the context of a personal expenditure rather than a sales or value-added tax, the old objection on vertical equity grounds no longer applies. The consumption as well as the income base may be adjusted to the taxpayer's personal circumstances, and progressive rates may be applied. But this has not been the focal point of recent advocacy of the consumption base. The

[2] Ibid., 425.

argument, rather, has been based on the hypothesis that the expenditure tax is more efficient. This outcome follows if leisure is fixed; but, as pointed out long ago by Little, there is no a priori presumption in favour of the consumption base if leisure is variable. The outcome then depends on the triangular substitutability between leisure and present and future consumption. It also depends on the comparative levels of marginal rates that may be required (a) to obtain the same revenue and (b) to do so with similar distributive outcomes.

I prefer to take a different tack and to compare the merits of the two bases in terms of horizontal equity. I realize that horizontal equity is difficult to define precisely in a world where preferences among individuals differ; some formulation must, however, be attempted. I suggest the proposition that people with equal options should be treated equally. Since the purpose of income is potential consumption, it is reasonable to measure options as present value of potential consumption. Given a long list of idealized conditions, it appears that a good case can be made for the consumption base. These conditions are, however, rather stringent. They include lifetime taxation, perfect foresight, perfect capital markets, disregard of the sizable transition problem, and—very important— inclusion of gifts and bequests in the consumption base. Such conditions, of course, do not prevail; and without them, ranking of the two bases is by no means evident.

Moreover, it is a mistake to compare a perfect expenditure tax with an imperfect income tax. The expenditure base, to be sure, bypasses some of the central difficulties of the income tax, particularly the problems associated with capital gains and depreciation, problems that have become increasingly severe with inflation. But an expenditure tax would also pose new problems as yet unknown, and the difficulties of transition would be substantial. Nevertheless, the issue is sufficiently open that I am prepared to rate experimentation with a personalized expenditure tax as potential reform.

I must, however, draw a sharp distinction between replacing part of the income tax by a bona fide expenditure tax and dismantling the income tax by going easy on income components that are saved. Although there is little prospect that the theorist's vision of a pure expenditure tax will be realized in the foreseeable future, its unguarded advocacy may well generate side effects that will only weaken the income tax. After all, so goes the siren song, if we ought to tax consumption and not income, why not begin with having the income tax go easy on income components that are not consumed? Is this not the more plausible since the income tax already is more effective in reaching wage than capital income? Why should we not move further in that direction? Seekers of improvements in the tax system, like Odysseus when passing the isle of the Seirens, should lash themselves to the mast of reform, lest they yield to temptation and be left with the worst of both worlds: an income tax on wage income only, without there being an alternative personal tax on global consumption.

Maintenance or, better, strengthening of the tax base is an essential condition for reform. This at least follows if one takes the view—and I suppose that most (though a declining fraction of) observers still do—that the major direct tax in the system should be progressive, if only to offset regressivity in the remainder of the system. Thus, as long as major reliance is placed on the income tax, tax reform calls for rendering the base more, not less, comprehensive. Specifically, we should continue our traditional quests for full taxation of capital gains, imputed rent, tax-exempt interest, pension plans, for corporate tax integration, and so forth; in short, implement the spirit of the Carter Commission. Politicians may not like this approach, but true tax reformers should. They may, at the same time, plead for partial replacement of income tax revenue by an expenditure tax, but only in a package that contains a bona fide expenditure tax along with a broad-based income tax, not via *deform* of the income tax. This perhaps is my main message to the tax reformers of the 1980s.

A word might be added on whether the expenditure tax scheme should be supplemented by a wealth tax. I think not. Taxing wealth is more or less equivalent to taxing capital income; and if consumption is chosen as the base, then a supplementary tax on capital income is out of order. Taxation of wealth might remain appropriate, not in the context of tax equity, but in response to concern with the social implications of excessive concentration of wealth and power. But such a tax would be a progressive tax on gross wealth, rather than a tax on net wealth, and might be added to either an income or an expenditure tax approach.

I now turn to the second axiom underlying the traditional view of horizontal equity: the rule that people with equal global income should pay the same amount of tax. Income from all sources should be combined and treated alike. This is the argument for uniformity on which we all used to agree. But we must now recognize that equal treatment and equal amount of tax are not the same. A person's tax burden includes not only the dollars of tax paid, but also the deadweight loss resulting from not paying. As recent taxation theory stresses, the triangle as well as the rectangle should be counted. If equal rate taxation of different sources of earnings generates different efficiency cost, people with equal total incomes but different earnings sources may incur different burdens if they pay the same amounts. To equalize the burden, people with equal incomes should not necessarily pay the same amount of tax; rather, a person's liability should be a function of both the income total and its composition. This, I note, does not call for moving to nonglobal and separate taxation of various income sources—that is, the old schedular approach—nor would it be the same as taxing so as to minimize aggregate deadweight loss. The approach I have in mind would set liabilities in such a way as to equate the economic losses suffered by various taxpayers. Similar considerations would apply to the taxation of various types of outlays under a global expenditure tax. The question is, can these principles be practically applied? Although I want to amend the traditional concept of horizontal equity, in the manner that I have described, I confess that I do not see how a multidimensional rate structure of this sort could be designed and implemented.

I have focussed on these issues of horizontal equity because they have been central to the tax structure thinking of my generation of tax economists, and rightly so. I must, however, take note of the contrary view, that horizontal equity matters little. Horizontal inequities, once embedded in the system, cease to be such, so the argument goes, because differential burdens have become capitalized. This effect has long been noted with regard to the integration of the corporation income tax. Present owners have paid the capitalized price; thus, they no longer benefit and would indeed be penalized by their removal. But the argument has been expanded and given new emphasis in recent discussion.[3] Not only are differential rates on capital income capitalized, but it has been noted that workers who may choose employment in industry x or y, or consumers who may consider consumption of product a or b, may allow for tax differentials in their choice. Since they have equal options to choose, no horizontal inequities can result. Horizontal equity matters in the first round of *de novo* tax design; but, as I put it 25 years ago, tax mistakes are like original sin: nothing can be done after the fall. Tax reform to remove inequalities remains valid on the grounds of efficiency, but not on those of equity. Indeed, new inequities are created by attempting to undo past mistakes.

There is some merit to this argument, but it applies only to old taxes and to the taxation of income from sources that can be capitalized. Also, it assumes that taxpayers have equal options to adjust, and that their tastes and abilities are identical. These assumptions are wrong. Individual positions differ, adjustments are imperfect, not all taxes are on income, and not all income is derived from sources that permit capitalization. I thus conclude that tax reform remains important in terms of horizontal equity as well as efficiency. Of course, if all individuals are alike, a favoured assumption of optimal tax theory, the issue of horizontal equity disappears; but, alas, they are not. Tax theory, I think, should recognize this simple fact.

As to inflation, there can be no doubt about what the principles of equitable taxation demand. The very concept of horizontal equity requires that we define the index of equality in real terms. Capital gains should be taxed fully, but they should be adjusted for inflation. The depreciation base should be adjusted to allow for changes in the price level, meaning (in the context of a tax philosophy that calls for integration) the cost of living rather than replacement cost. The inflation component of interest income should not be taxed, and decline in the real value of net indebtedness should be treated as accretion and taxed accordingly. Rate brackets should be indexed so as to maintain the intended relationship between effective rates and real income; then legislators would be required to enact rate increases, if they so desired, rather than enjoy a free ride via bracket creep. Although there are difficulties in adjusting a nominal tax system for inflation, they can be handled; in the past, failure to address them seriously has done much damage. Tax reform calls for inflation adjustment to the largest possible degree. This requirement should be evident particularly to those who favour strengthening of the income tax, since greater immunity to distortion by inflation is a main advantage of the expenditure tax approach.

---

[3] See Martin Feldstein, "On the Theory of Tax Reform" (July-August 1976), 5 *Journal of Public Economics* 77.

B. A CONSUMPTION BASE

TREASURY DEPARTMENT, BLUEPRINTS FOR BASIC TAX REFORM

(1977), pp. 33–52.

THE PRESENT TAX BASE

Is the Present Base Consumption or Income?

While the present income tax system does not reflect any consistent definition of the tax base, it has surprisingly many features of a "standard-of-living" consumption base.

The idea of consumption as a tax base sounds strange and even radical to many people. Nonetheless there are many similarities between a consumption base tax and the current tax system. Adoption of a broad-based consumption tax might actually result in less of a departure from current tax treatment of savings than adoption of a broad-based income tax.

The current tax system exempts many forms of savings from tax. In particular, the two items that account for the bulk of savings for most Americans, pensions and home ownership, are treated by the present tax code in a way that is more similar to the consumption model than to the comprehensive income model.

Retirement savings financed by employer contributions to pension plans (or made via a "Keogh" or "Individual Retirement Account" (IRA)) are currently treated as they would be under a consumption tax. Under the current system, savings in employer-funded pension plans are not included in the tax base, but retirement benefits from those plans, which are available for consumption in retirement years, are included. Employee contributions to pension plans are treated somewhat less liberally. The original contribution is included in the tax base when made, but the portion of retirement income representing interest earnings on the original contributions is not taxed until these earnings are received as retirement payments. If the tax on those interest earnings were paid as the earnings accrued, treatment of employee contributions to pension plans would be the same as that under a comprehensive income tax. However, the tax on interest earnings in pension funds is lower than under a comprehensive income base because the tax is deferred. If no tax were paid on the interest earnings portion of retirement pay, then the present value of tax liability would be exactly the same as the present value of tax liability under a consumption tax. Thus, the current treatment of employee contributions incorporates elements of both the comprehensive income model and the consumption model, but because of the quantitative importance of tax deferral on pension fund earnings, the treatment is closer to the consumption model.

The current tax treatment of home ownership is very similar to the tax treatment of home ownership under a consumption tax. Under present law, a home is purchased out of tax-paid income (is not deductible), and the value of the use of the home is not taxed as current income. Under a consumption tax, two alternative treatments are possible. Either the initial purchase price of the house would be included in the tax base (i.e., not deductible in calculating the tax base) and the flow of returns in the form of housing services would be ignored for tax purposes, or the initial purchase price would be deductible and an imputation would be made for the value of the flow of returns, which would be included in the tax base.

In equilibrium, the market value of any asset is equal to the net present value of the flow of future returns, either in the form of monetary profits or value of consumption services. For example, the market value of a house should equal the present value of all future rental services (the gross rent that would have to be paid to a landlord for equivalent housing) minus the present value of future operating costs (including depreciation, operating costs, property taxes, repairs, etc.). Thus, in both cases, the present value of the tax base would be the same. For example, if an individual purchases a $40,000 house, the present value of his future tax base for that item of consumption would be $40,000 regardless of how he chose to be taxed. Because the initial purchase price is easier to observe than the imputed service flow, it would be most practical, under a consumption tax, to include the purchase of a house in the tax base and exclude net imputed returns. In that case, capital gains from sale of a house would not be taxable.

In the current tax system, as in the consumption tax system, the down payment and principal payments for an owner-occupied residence are included in the tax base, and the imputed net rental income in the form of housing services is excluded from tax. Capital gains from housing sales are taxable at preferential capital gains rates upon realization (which allows considerable tax deferral if the house is held for a long period), and no capital gains tax is levied if the seller is over 65 or if the gain is used to purchase another house.

In contrast, under a comprehensive income base, the entire return on the investment in housing, received in the form of net value of housing services, would be subject to tax and, in addition, the purchase price would not be deductible from the tax base.

Many special provisions of the tax law approximate a consumption tax in the lifetime tax treatment of savings. For example, allowing immediate deduction for tax purposes of the purchase price of an item that will be used up over a period of years (i.e., immediate expensing of capital investments) is equivalent to consumption tax treatment of investment income because it allows the full deduction of savings; thus, accelerated depreciation approximates the consumption tax approach. While depreciation provisions under the present law are haphazard, a consumption base tax would allow the immediate deduction of saving to all savers.

In conclusion, taxation of a significant portion of savings under the current system more closely resembles the consumption model than the comprehensive income model. For owner-occupied housing, a large fraction of pension plans, and some other investments, the tax base closely approximates either the present value of imputed consumption benefits or the present value of consumption financed by proceeds of the investment.

Is the Tax System Presently on an "Ability-to-Pay" or a "Standard-of-Living" Basis?

Three possibilities may be considered for the income tax treatment of a gift from one taxpaying unit to another: (1) the gift might be deducted from uses in calculating the tax base of the donor and included in sources in calculating the base of the donee; (2) it might be left in the base of the donor and also included in the base of the donee; or (3) it might be left in the base of the donor but excluded from the base of the donee.

The first of these treatments is that implied by a "standard-of-living" basis for determining relative tax burdens. The second treatment expresses an "ability-to-pay" view. The third treatment is that of the present income tax (excluding the estate and gift tax) law, at least with respect to property with no unrealized appreciation at the time the gift is made.

The first and third treatments are similar in that there is no separate tax on the transfer of wealth from one taxpaying unit to another. The tax burdens under those two options may differ with a progressive tax structure, however. Under the third treatment, aggregate tax liability is unaffected by the gift, but under the first, it will rise or fall depending on whether or not the marginal tax bracket of the donee is higher than the marginal tax bracket of the donor. Under the second treatment, with the gift or bequest in the tax base of both the donor and the donee, the consumption or change in net worth financed by the gift is, in effect, taxed twice. It is taxed as consumption by the donor, and then taxed again as consumption or an increase in net worth of the donee.

To illustrate the alternative treatments of wealth transfers, consider the case of taxpayers A and B, who start life with no wealth and who are alike except that A decides to accumulate an estate. Their sons, A' and B', respectively, consume their available resources and die with zero wealth. Thus, A has lower consumption than B; A' (who consumed what his father saved) has higher consumption than B'. Under a "standard-of-living" approach, the pair A-A' should bear roughly the same tax burden as the pair B-B'. This is so because the higher consumption of A' is simply that which his father, A, did not consume. Under an "ability-to-pay" approach, the combination A-A' should bear more tax than B-B'. A and B have the same ability to pay, but because A chooses to exercise his ability to pay by making a gift to his son, A' has a greater ability to pay than B', by virtue of the gift received.

Neglecting the effect of progressivity, present income tax law taxes the combination A-A' the same as it does the combination B-B' (whether or not A and A' are related). In this respect, present income tax law incorporates a "standard-of-living" basis. The way this is accomplished, however, is "backward." That is, instead of taxing A on his "standard-of-living" income and then taxing A' on his "standard-of-living" income, present law taxes A on his consumption plus increase in net worth <u>plus</u> the gift given (i.e., the gift is not deductible in calculating the income tax due from A), while A' is taxed on the value of his consumption plus increase in net worth <u>minus</u> the value of the gift received (i.e., the receipt of the gift is not included in calculating the tax due from A').

This procedure clearly mismeasures the income of A. It mismeasures the income of A', as well, if a "standard-of-living" concept of income is used. The income of A' is understated (gift received is not included) and that of A is overstated (gift given is not excluded). However (continuing to neglect the effect of progressivity), the impact of the tax system on A and A' is the same as if the treatment were the other way around, at least as far as intentional gifts are concerned. Suppose, for example, that A wants to enable A' to have an extra $750 worth of consumption. Under present law, A simply gives A' $750 cash and A' consumes it. Under a "standard-of-living" concept of income (assuming A and A' are both in the 25-percent rate bracket), A would give A' $1,000. After paying taxes of $250, A' would have $750 to consume. At the same time, A would deduct $1,000 from his tax base, saving $250 and making the net cost of his gift $750.

Although the effects of progressivity would alter this somewhat, it is not clear that the differences in rates between giver and receiver would be likely to be large if a lifetime view were taken. Naturally, under present law, an adult donor will tend to have a higher marginal rate of income tax than a child donee. It is for this reason that present income tax law treatment of gift and bequest transactions may come closer than the more intuitively obvious one -- excluding to donor, including to donee -- to measuring "standard-of-living" income correctly. Certain administrative aspects also favor the present treatment of gifts and bequests for income tax purposes.

In summary, whether by accident or design, present income tax law incorporates a rough sort of "standard-of-living" view of the concept of income because it does not include an extra tax on wealth transfers as an integral part of the income tax. Such treatment approximates a provision where a gift given is included in the income of the donee and excluded from the income of the donor, even though the mechanics of calculating the tax are on the opposite basis.

It is, then, mainly the estate and gift tax that introduces the "ability-to-pay" element into the tax system, because it results in a gift or bequest being taxed twice to the donor, once under the income tax and again under the transfer tax. The value implicitly expressed is that taxes should generally be assessed on a "standard-of-living" basis, except in the case of individuals whose ability to pay is very large, _and_ _whose standard of living is low relative to ability to pay_ (i.e., those who refrain from consuming in order to make gifts and bequests).

ALTERNATIVE BASES: EQUITY CONSIDERATIONS

The previous section considered what tax base is implicit in present law. In a sense, the answer itself is an equity judgment, because equity traditionally has played an important role in the tax legislation process. This section considers the relative equity claims of a "consumption" as compared with an "income" basis, _of either_ "ability-to-pay" or "standard-of-living" type, and the "ability-to-pay" or "standard-of-living" version of _either_ consumption or income.

Consumption or Income: Which is the Better Base?

Involved in the choice between consumption and income as the basis for assessing tax burdens is more than a simple subjective judgment as to whether, of two individuals having different incomes in a given period but who are identical in all respects in all other periods, the one with the higher income should pay the higher tax. Examples of tax burdens considered within a life-cycle framework suggest that a consumption base deserves careful attention if the primary consideration is fairness, whether one takes an ability-to-pay or a standard-of-living view.

Many observers consider income and consumption to be simply alternative reasonable ways to measure well-being; often, income is regarded as somewhat superior because it is a better measure of ability to pay. However, in a life-cycle context, income and consumption are not independent of each other. Of two individuals with equal earning abilities at the beginning of their lives, the one with higher consumption early in life is the one who will have a lower lifetime income. This is true because saving is not only a way of using wealth, but also a way of producing income. Thus, the person who saves early in life will have a higher lifetime income in present-value terms. Although his initial endowment of financial wealth and of future earning power is independent of the way he chooses to use it, his lifetime income is not independent of his consumption/savings decisions.

The examples presented below show that a consumption base would be more likely to maintain the same relative rankings of individuals ranked by endowment than an income base, if "endowment" is defined as an individual's wealth, in marketable and nonmarketable forms, at the beginning of his working years. Wealth so defined consists of the total monetary value of financial and physical assets on hand, the present value of future labor earnings and transfers, less the cost of earning income and less the present value of the "certain other outlays" discussed in the accounting framework above. If endowment is regarded as a good measure of ability to pay over a lifetime, this implies that a consumption base is superior to an income base as a measure of lifetime ability to pay.

If individuals consume all of their initial endowment during their lifetime (that is, leave no bequest), a consumption tax is exactly equivalent to an initial endowment tax. However, an income tax treats individuals with the same endowment differently, if they have either a different pattern of consumption over their lifetime or a different pattern of earnings.

A CONSUMPTION BASE

Consider first two individuals with no initial financial or physical wealth, no bequest, the same pattern of labor earnings, and different patterns of consumption. Intuition suggests that, unless these individuals differ in some respect other than how they choose to use their available resources (e.g., with respect to medical expenses or family status), they should bear the same tax burden, measured by the present value of lifetime taxes. The tax system should not bear more heavily on the individual who chooses to purchase better food than on the one who chooses to buy higher quality clothing. Nor should it bear more heavily on the individual who chooses to apply his endowment of labor abilities to purchase of consumption late in life (by saving early in life) than it does on the one who consumes early in life.

While an income tax does not discriminate between the two taxpayers in the case where the two taxpayers consume different commodities, it does in the case where they choose to consume in different time periods in their lives. An income tax imposes a heavier burden on the individual who prefers to save for later consumption than on the one who consumes early, and the amount of difference may be significant. The reason is the double taxation of savings under an income tax. The "use" of funds for savings is taxed, and then the yield from savings is taxed again. The result is that the individual who chooses to save early for later consumption is taxed more heavily than one who consumes early.

The tax burden may be reduced most by <u>borrowing</u> for early consumption, since the interest cost is deducted in calculating income.

Now, suppose that the two individuals have different time paths of labor earnings but that the two paths have the same present discounted value. For example, individual A may earn $10,000 per year in a given 2-year period, while individual B works for twice as many hours and earns $19,524 in the first of the 2 years, but earns nothing in the second. (The figure of $19,524 is the total of $10,000 plus the amount that would have to be invested at a 5-percent rate of return to make $10,000 available one year later.) Each individual prefers to consume the same amount in both periods, and in the absence of tax, each would consume the same amount, $10,000 per year. Intuition suggests these two individuals should bear the same tax burden. However, under an income tax (even at a flat rate, i.e., not progressive), they would pay different taxes, with B paying more than A. The reason, again is the double taxation of B's savings. The differences may be very large if a long time period is involved. An income tax imposes a higher burden on the individual who receives labor income earlier even though both have the same initial endowments in present-value terms and the same consumption paths.

"Standard-of-Living" or "Ability-to-Pay": Which Criterion?

Although for the vast majority of individuals' bequests and gifts of cash and valuable property constitute a negligible portion of sources and an equally negligible portion of uses of funds, the tax treatment of these transactions will have significant consequences for a minority of wealthy individuals and, therefore, for the perceived fairness of the tax system.

The equity judgment embodied in present law is that large transfers should be subject to a substantial progressive tax under the estate and gift tax laws and that relatively small transfers need not be taxed. For income tax purposes, amounts given are taxed to the donor and are not taxed to the donee. This has general appeal. The usual reaction to the idea that gifts given should also be included in the tax base of the donee is that this would be an unfair double taxation.

As has been pointed out, the circumstances under which large transfers occur are relatively large wealth and low consumption of donor. The imposition of a substantial transfer tax (estate and gift tax) is consistent with a common argument for this tax; namely, that it is desirable to prevent extreme accumulations of wealth. If this is, indeed, the equity objective, it suggests that the code's present allowance of relatively large exemptions and imposition of high rates on very large transfers is sensible.

Summing Up: The Equity Comparison of Consumption and Income Bases

As a general matter, the important conclusions to be drawn from the foregoing discussion are:

- Either an income or a consumption tax may be designed to fulfill "ability-to-pay" or "standard-of-living" objectives. The difference is not between these two types of tax, but rather between a tax in which gifts given are considered part of the tax base of either donor or donee or, instead, part of the tax bases of both donor and donee. In the latter case, the tax embodies an "ability-to-pay" approach; in the former, the tax follows from a "standard-of-living" approach. The present income tax system expresses a "standard-of-living" basis of comparison, while the present estate and gift tax system combines with income tax to give an "ability-to-pay" approach in certain cases.

- The difference between a consumption base and an income base of either the "standard-of-living" or the "ability-to-pay" type is between one that depends upon the timing of consumption and earnings (and gifts, in the case of an "ablity-to-pay" tax) during an individual's lifetime and one that does not. The income tax discriminates against people who earn early in life or prefer to consume late in life. That is, if a tax must raise a given amount of revenue, the income tax makes early earners and late consumers worse off than late earners and early consumers. A consumption tax is neutral between these two patterns.

- A consumption tax amounts to a tax on lifetime endowment. It may be viewed as an ideal wealth tax, that is, a tax that makes an assessment on lifetime wealth. An income tax will tend to assess tax burdens in a way presumably correlated with lifetime wealth, but because it depends upon matters of timing, the correspondence is nowhere near as close as would be the case under a consumption base tax.

- As previously noted, present law introduces an "ability-to-pay" element into the tax system through the estate and gift provisions. The same device is equally compatible with either an income base or a consumption base tax. As will be discussed in chapter 4, in some respects an estate and gift tax system fits more logically with a consumption base system, which allows deduction of gifts by the donor and requires inclusion by the donee.

ALTERNATIVE TAX BASES: SIMPLICITY CONSIDERATIONS

Of central importance in determining the complexity of a tax system -- to the taxpayer in complying and to the tax collector in auditing compliance -- is the ease with which the required transaction information can be assembled and the objective nature of the data. Three desirable characteristics are readily identifiable:

- Transactions should be objectively observable -- as in the case of the transaction of a wage payment. Such transactions are called "cash" transactions in this report. "Imputed" transactions, i.e., values arrived at by guesses or rules of thumb -- as in the case of depreciation -- should be kept to a minimum.

- The period over which records need to be kept should be as short as practicable.

- The code should be understandable.

Consumption or Income Preferable on Grounds of Simplicity?

With respect to simplicity criteria, the consumption base has many advantages, as can be seen on examination of the accounting relationships. At this stage, both the concept of consumption and the concept of increase in net worth must be complicated by adding imputed elements to the simple example.

The portion of consumption calculable from cash transactions includes cash outlays for goods and services and transfers to others (optional, depending upon the choice between "standard-of-living" and "ability-to-pay" versions). In addition, an individual usually obtains directly the equivalent of certain consumption services that he could purchase in the marketplace. The most important of these are the services from durable goods, such as owner-occupied houses, and household-produced services, such as child care, recreation, etc.

The change in net worth over a given time period, the other component of income, is calculable in part by cash transactions. These include such items as net deposits in savings accounts. Imputed elements, however, are extensive and lead to some of the most irksome aspects of income tax law. Among these are the change in value of assets held over the period, including the reduction in value due to wear and tear, obsolescence, etc. (depreciation); increases in value of assets due to retained earnings in corporate shares held, changed expectations about the future, or changed valuation of the future (accruing capital gains); and accruing values of claims to the future (such as pension rights, and life insurance).

Thus, both consumption and the change in net worth can be expressed as the sum of items calculable from cash transactions within the accounting period and items that must be imputed. The cash items are easy to measure, but imputed items are a source of difficulty. Because the imputed consumption elements are needed for a comprehensive income or consumption base, consider first some of the more significant imputed elements of the change in net worth, representing necessary additions to complexity if an income base is used.

Four problems commonly encountered in measuring change in net worth are depreciation, inflation adjustment, treatment of corporate retained earnings, and treatment of unrealized capital gains on nonmarketed assets.

Measurement Problems

Depreciation. Depreciation rules are necessary under an income base to account for the change in value of productive assets due to wear and tear, obsolescence, and increases in maintenance and repair costs with age. Because productive assets often are not exchanged for long periods of time, imputations of their annual change in market value must be made.

Inevitably, depreciation rules for tax accounting, as in the present code, can only approximate the actual rate of decline in the value of capital assets. Because changes in depreciation rules can benefit identifiable taxpayers, such rules become the object of political pressure groups and are sometimes used as instruments of economic policy, causing the tax base to depart even further from a true accretion concept. Thus, accelerated depreciation, at rates much faster than economic depreciation, has been allowed in some industries as a deliberate subsidy (e.g., mineral industries, real estate, and some farming). To the extent that the relationship between tax depreciation and economic depreciation varies among industries and types of capital, returns to capital investment in different industries and on different types of equipment are taxed at different effective rates. Differences in the tax treatment of capital income among industries create distortions in the allocation of resources across products and services and in the use of different types of capital in production.

Unrealized depreciation of an asset is neither added to nor subtracted from the consumption base. Thus, the time path of depreciation imputed to assets does not affect the tax base of asset owners. Adoption of a consumption base tax would automatically eliminate current tax shelters that operate by allowing depreciation in excess of economic depreciation in some industries. Alternative tax subsidies to the same industries, if adopted, would have to be much more explicit and would be easier to measure. The accidental taxation of returns to capital in different industries at different rates that arises under the current system because of imperfect knowledge of true economic depreciation rates would not occur.

Inflation Adjustment. During a period of rapid inflation, the current income tax includes inflationary gains along with real gains in the tax base. For example, an individual who buys an asset for $100 at the beginning of a year and sells it for $110 one year later has not had any increase in the purchasing power of his assets if the inflation rate is also 10 percent. Yet, under the current system he would include at least part of any gain on the sale of the asset in the sources side of his tax calculation.

An ideal income base would have to adjust for losses on existing assets, including deposits in savings banks and checking accounts, resulting from inflation. Such adjustments would pose challenging administrative problems for assets held for long periods of time. The current tax system effects a rough compromise in its treatment of "long-term capital gains" by requiring that only half of such gains be included in taxable income and by allowing no inflation deduction. (However, this treatment has been substantially modified by the minimum tax and by denial of maximum tax benefits for "earned income" if the taxpayer also has capital gains.) Dividends and interest income are taxed at the same rate as labor income even though the underlying assets may be losing real value.

A second type of inflationary problem under the current tax system is that rising nominal incomes move taxpayers into higher marginal tax brackets, and thus increase the average tax rate even when real income is not growing. Inflation will automatically raise the average tax rate in any tax system with a graduated rate structure, whether based on income, consumption, or the current partial-income base. A possible solution is some type of indexing plan, such as automatic upward adjustment of exemption levels. Because this problem does not affect the relative distribution of the tax base among individuals, it is not an issue in choosing between a consumption and an income base.

Under a consumption tax, inflation would not lead to difficulties in measuring the relative tax base among individuals because consumption in any year would be measured automatically in current dollars. A decline in the value of assets in any year because of inflation would be neither a positive nor a negative entry in the consumption base.

Treatment of Corporate Income. Given the difficulty of taxing gains in asset values as they accrue, the present corporate income tax serves the practical function of preventing individuals from reducing their taxes by accumulating income within corporations. Naturally, this is but a rough approximation of the appropriate taxation of this income and the difficulty of identifying incidence and allocation effects of this tax is well known. Under a fully consistent income tax concept, as outlined below in chapter 3, "corporation income" would be attributed to individual stockholders. This integration of the corporation and personal income taxes is desirable for a progressive income tax system because the variation among individuals in marginal tax rates makes it impossible for a uniform tax on corporate income, combined with exclusion of dividends and capital gains, to assess all individual owners at the appropriate rate. Although feasible and desirable in an income tax system, full corporate integration is sometimes regarded as posing too many challenging administrative problems. A partial integration plan that allowed corporations to deduct dividend payments and/or allowed shareholders to "gross up" dividends by an amount reflecting the corporation income tax, taking a credit for the same amount in their individual income tax calculations, would eliminate the problem of "double taxation" of corporate dividends. This could be done without introducing significant complexity into the tax code, but the problem of how to treat corporate retained earnings would remain unresolved.

Treatment of corporate income under a consistent consumption tax is simpler than under a comprehensive income tax. The corporation profits tax as such would be eliminated. Individuals would normally include in their tax base all dividends received and the value of all sales of corporate shares, and they would deduct the value of all shares purchased. There would be no need to treat receipts from sales of shares differently than other sources or to attribute undistributed corporate profits to individual shareholders.

Treatment of Unrealized Asset Value Changes. The increase in net worth due to any changes in value of assets, whether realized or not, would be included in the accretion concept of income. An individual who sells a stock at the end of the year for $100 more than the purchase price at the beginning of the year and an individual who holds a parcel of land that increases in value by $100 during the same time interval both experience the same increase in net worth. However, unrealized asset value changes are often difficult to determine, especially if an asset has unique characteristics and has not been exchanged recently on an open market. Further, there is a question as to what is meant by the value of an asset for which the market is very thin and whether changes in the value of such assets should be viewed in the same way as an equal dollar flow of labor, interest, or dividend income. For example, if the value of an individual's house rises, he is unlikely to find it convenient to realize the gain by selling it immediately. Any tax obligation, however, must ordinarily be paid in cash.

Similar questions arise with respect to the treatment of increases in the present value of a person's potential income from selling his human services in the labor market. It is not practical to measure either the increase in an individual's wealth from a rise in the demand for his labor or the depreciation of the present value of future labor earnings with age. Present law makes no attempt to recognize such value changes nor would they be captured in the comprehensive income tax proposal presented in chapter 3.

Under a consumption tax, unrealized changes in asset value would not need to be measured because consumption from such assets does not occur unless either cash flow is generated by the asset or the asset is converted into a monetary value by sale.

Finally, the problem of income averaging can be minimized with techniques of cash flow management. Averaging is desirable under an income tax because, with a progressive rate structure, an individual with an uneven income stream will have a higher tax base than an individual with the same average income in equal annual installments. Equity requires that two individuals pay the same tax when they have the same lifetime endowment, regardless of the regularity of the pattern in which earnings are received (or expended).

The consumption tax may be viewed as a tax in the initial time period on the present value of an individual's lifetime consumption expenditures. Deferral of consumption by saving at positive interest rates raises total lifetime consumption but leaves unchanged the present value of both lifetime consumption and the tax base.

Although the annual cash flow measure of the consumption tax correctly measures the present value of lifetime consumption, averaging problems may arise if annual cash flow varies from year to year. The major averaging problem results from large irregular expenditures, such as the purchase of consumer durables. As described in chapter 4, there are two alternative ways of dealing with loans and investment assets in measuring the tax base. Both methods yield the same expected present value of the tax base over time but enable an individual to alter the timing of his recorded consumption expenditures. The availability of an alternative treatment of loans and assets enables individuals to even out their recorded pattern of consumption for tax purposes and represents a simple and effective averaging device under a consumption tax.

The same type of automatic averaging cannot be introduced under an income tax because an income tax is <u>not</u> a tax on the present value of lifetime consumption. Under an accretion income tax, the present value of the tax base rises when consumption is deferred, if interest earnings are positive, because the income used for saving is taxed <u>in the year it is earned</u> and then the interest is taxed again. Thus, allowing deferral of tax liability under an income tax permits a departure from the accretion concept, lowering the present value of tax liability.

The discussion above suggests that, contrary to popular belief, a consumption-based tax might be easier to implement, using annual accounting data in an appropriate and consistent fashion, than an income-based tax.

"Standard-of-Living" or "Ability-to-Pay" Preferable on Simplicity Grounds?

The choice between an "ability-to-pay" and a "standard-of-living" approach under the consumption or income tax has significant implications for simplicity of administration. It is relatively easy to insure that the amount of a gift is counted in the tax base of either the donor or the donee. Under present law, gifts (other than charitable gifts) are not deductible from the tax base of the donor. If gifts were deductible, the donor could be required to identify the donee. A requirement that both donor and donee be taxed, as would be implied by an "ability-to-pay" approach, would introduce a great temptation to evade. Taxing both sides would require that the gift not be deductible by the donor and that it be included in the tax base of the donee. Particularly for relatively small gifts and gifts in-kind, auditing compliance with this rule, where no evidence is provided in another person's return of having made the gift, could be a formidable problem. For much the same reason, compliance with the existing gift tax law is believed to be somewhat haphazard.

The issue of gifts in-kind is important. It is difficult to establish whether a gift has been given in these cases (e.g., loan of a car or a vacation home). Again, if the gift need only be taxed to one of the parties to the transaction, failing to report a gift simply means it is taxed to the giver and not the recipient.

Gifts in-kind are significant in another sense. Gifts and bequests can be considered a minor matter to most people only if the terms are taken to refer to transfers of cash and valuable property. If account were taken of the transfers within families that take the form of supporting children until their adulthood, often including large educational outlays, inheritance would certainly be seen to constitute a large fraction of the true wealth of many individuals. Any discussion of gifts and bequests should take into account that the parent who pays for his child's college education makes a gift no less than the parent who makes a gift of the family farm or of cash, even though this equivalence is not recognized in present tax law.

Where large gifts of cash and property are involved, it seems likely that enforcement of a double tax on transfers will be less costly than when gifts are small. This has proved to be the case under current law.

EFFICIENCY ISSUES IN A CHOICE BETWEEN AN INCOME AND A CONSUMPTION BASE

In public discussions, the efficiency of a tax system is often viewed as depending on its cost of administration and the degree of taxpayer compliance. While these features are important, one other important characteristic defines the efficiency of a tax system: As a general principle, <u>the tax system should minimize the extent to which individuals alter their economic behavior so as to avoid paying tax</u>. In other words, it is usually undesirable for taxes to influence individuals' economic decisions in the private sector. There may, of course, be exceptions where tax policies are used deliberately to either encourage or discourage certain types of activities (for example, tax incentives for installation of pollution equipment or high excise taxes on consumption of liquor and tobacco).

Both an ideal consumption tax and an ideal income tax, though neutral among commodities purchased and produced, do have important incentive effects that are unintended by-products of the need to raise revenue. Specifically, individuals can reduce their tax liability under either tax to the extent it is possible to conduct economic activities outside of the marketplace. For example, if an individual pays a mechanic to repair his automobile, the labor charge will enter into the measurement of consumption or income and will be taxed under either type of tax. On the other hand, if the individual repairs his own automobile, the labor cost will not be accompanied by a measurable transaction and will not be subject to tax. Phrased more generally, both an income and a consumption tax distort the choice between labor and leisure, where leisure is defined to include all activities, both recreational and productive, that are conducted outside the process of market exchange.

While both consumption and income taxes distort the choice between market and nonmarket activities, only an income tax distorts the choice between present and future consumption.

Under an income tax, the before-tax rate of return on investments exceeds the after-tax interest rate received by those who save to finance them. The existence of a positive market interest rate reflects the fact that society, by sacrificing a dollar's worth of consumption today and allocating the dollar's worth of resources to the production of capital goods, can increase output and consumption by more than one dollar next year. Under an income tax, the potential increase in output tomorrow to be gained by sacrificing a dollar's worth of output today exceeds the percentage return to an individual, in increased future consumption, to be derived from saving. In effect, the resources available to an individual for future consumption are double-taxed; first, when they are earned as current income and second, when interest is earned on savings. The present value of an individual's tax burden may be reduced by shifting consumption from future periods to the present.

A consumption tax, on the other hand, is neutral with respect to the choice to consume in different periods because current saving is exempted from the base. The expected present value of taxes paid is not affected by the time pattern of consumption. A switch from an income tax to an equal-yield consumption tax would thus tend to increase the fraction of national output saved and invested, and thereby raise future output and consumption.

The fact that a tax is neutral with respect to the savings-consumption decision is not, of course, decisive in its favor even on efficiency grounds. No taxes are neutral with respect to all choices. Thus, for example, it has already been pointed out that neither the income nor the consumption tax is neutral in the labor/leisure choice; that is, both reduce the incentive to work in the marketplace. Economic theorists have developed measures of the amount of damage done by nonneutrality in various forms. Although it is not possible on the basis of such research to make a definite case for one tax base over the other based on efficiency, when reasonable guesses are made about the way people react to various taxes it appears that the efficiency loss resulting from a consumption tax would be considerably smaller than that from an equal yield income tax.

The possible efficiency gains that would result from adopting a consumption base tax system relate closely to the frequently expressed concern about a deficient rate of capital formation in the United States. Switching from an income to a consumption base tax would remove a distortion that discourages capital formation by U.S. citizens, leading to a higher U.S. growth rate in the short run, and a permanently higher capital/output ratio in the long run.

SUMMING UP

The previous discussions have attempted to provide a systematic approach to the concept of income as composed of certain <u>uses</u> of resources by individuals. The current income tax law lacks such a unifying concept. Indeed, as has been suggested here, income as implicitly defined in current law deviates from a consistent definition of accretion income especially in that it excludes a major part of income used for savings (often in the form of accruing rights to future benefits). Eliminating savings from the tax base changes an income tax to a tax on consumption.

This chapter has considered whether there is any sound reason for considering substitution of a consumption base for the present makeshift and incomplete income base. It has been suggested that there is much to be said for this on grounds of equity; such a base would not have the drawback, characteristic of an income tax, of favoring those who consume early rather than late in life, and of taxing more heavily those whose earnings occur early rather than late in life. The argument has been made that the choice is <u>not</u> between a tax favoring the rich (who save) and the poor (who do not), as some misconceive the consumption tax, and a tax favoring the poor over the former rich by the use of progressive rates, as some view the income tax. The choice is between an income tax that <u>at each level of endowment</u>, favors early consumers and late earners over late consumers and early earners and a consumption tax that is <u>neutral</u> between these two types of individuals. The relative burdens of rich and poor are determined by the degree of progressivity of the tax. <u>Either tax is amenable to any degree of progressivity of rates</u>.

A distinction has been drawn between a tax based on the uses of resources for the taxpayer's own benefit and one based on these uses plus the resources he gives away to others. The shorthand term adopted for the former is the "standard-of-living" approach to assigning tax burdens; for the latter, it is the "ability-to-pay" approach. It has been suggested that either a consumption or an income tax could be designed to fit either concept. Examination of current practice suggests that the basic tax -- the present income tax -- is, broadly speaking, of the "standard-of-living" type. An "ability-to-pay" element is introduced by special taxes on gifts and estates.

WILLIAM D. ANDREWS, "FAIRNESS AND THE PERSONAL INCOME TAX: A REPLY TO PROFESSOR WARREN"

88 Harvard Law Review 947 (1975), pp. 953-56.

II. Consumption Taxes and Wage Taxes

Professor Warren points out that under certain conditions a tax on consumption alone is the equivalent of an income tax on wages alone, with investment income excluded.[15] He is then curiously careful not to denounce the latter too freely. For my part, I find the notion of taxing wages but not investment income quite objectionable, and I therefore find it necessary to examine the equivalence between consumption and wage taxes more closely.

The equivalence is indeed an exact mathematical one if certain conditions are met. But like some other such paradigms, this is one whose chief interest lies in the way in which the conditions are not met.[16] Among the necessary conditions are (1) all wealth must be traceable to original savings out of wages plus simple investment income and the two must be capable of separation so that the former can be taxed while the latter is exempted; and (2) there must be a single rate of tax applicable to all earnings (or all consumption expenditures) throughout all time.[17] As will be shown, neither of these conditions comes close to being met in fact.

Gain or accretion is not limited to wages and investment income. One example is that of a windfall gain. A tax on wages alone would capture neither the windfall nor the fruits of its investment. Such a tax would be quite obnoxious, for it would allow complete escape to one who can show meticulously that he did not do a useful thing of any kind to earn the wealth he enjoys, while requiring honest workmen to pay in full.[18]

---

[15] The idea of such an equivalence is not entirely new. Musgrave mentions "an income tax under which interest income is not taxable" as one that would, like a consumption tax, "leave the marginal rates of substitution between present and future consumption unaffected." R. Musgrave, The Theory of Public Finance 153, 261 (1959).

[16] *Cf.* Polinsky, *Economic Analysis as a Potentially Defective Product: A Buyer's Guide to Posner's* Economic Analysis of Law, 87 Harv. L. Rev. 1655 (1974).

[17] Another condition for equivalence is that all wealth eventually be spent for consumption. Whether wealth on hand at any particular time will eventually be spent for consumption is more a question for speculation than for investigation, however, and Warren and I both seem ready to rest on the fact that accumulated wealth remains available for future consumption. *Cf.* R. Musgrave, *supra* note 15, at 266–68.

[18] Professor Warren gives an example to show that elements of windfall investment profit in the income from property will not impair the equivalance between a flat-rate wage tax and a flat-rate consumption tax. His example, however, depends on the assumption that the windfall will be proportionate to the amount invested, so that a wage tax will cut the benefit of the windfall by cutting

Moreover, in the real world it is often impossible to isolate wage from investment income, or to sort out the windfall element in either. People with wealth, in particular, may devote substantial amounts of their time and talent to the supervision and management of their investments, and it would be virtually impossible to separate return to services from return to investment in order to tax the former while exempting the latter. Indeed, the most successful accretions to wealth often result from a fusion of personal effort with capital investment in circumstances that make any attribution of income to separate factors largely arbitrary. A wage tax is quite inferior because it requires such an isolation and sorting out, which a consumption tax does not. And this is not just a practical objection, it has to do with notions of fairness; a wage tax would be unfair because it would fail to pick up every original input from which wealth may grow. A consumption tax is not subject to that objection since it applies to funds spent for consumption without regard to source.

Even a fixed, flat-rate consumption tax is not, therefore, the equivalent of a simple wage tax. It is rather the equivalent of a tax on every form of original gain attributable to personal effort or to pure windfall or to anything else except pure investment return. And a consumption tax so limits the exemption automatically, without having to sort out what is and what is not purely fruit from previously taxed investments.

Whatever the case with a flat-rate tax, a consumption tax with graduated rates and personal exemptions cannot be converted into an equivalent wage tax, because when wages are earned and saved there is no way to determine whether they will ultimately be used to support consumption at a high or a low level. Professor Warren recognizes this limitation on the equivalence between consumption and wage taxes, but seeks to dismiss it by indicating that rate graduation in a consumption tax is inconsistent with the maintenance of nondiscrimination between current and deferred consumption in any event. And so it is, if present and future levels of consumption are different. But from an equal-consumer perspective no such inconsistency emerges: a graduated consumption

---

the amount available to invest. The windfall in his example is a doubling in value of an investment asset. Warren at 939-40. The result would be quite different if the windfall took the form of an absolute increase in value. Suppose an investment asset purchased by the retiree for $100 in the initial year increases $100 in value. The resulting $200 invested at 9% would yield $1600 after 24 years, and a consumption tax of 33% applied at that time would leave $1066 after taxes. A wage tax of 33% in the initial year would leave $67 after taxes to invest in that year, which the $100 windfall would boost to $167. That would yield $1333 after 24 years at 9%. Thus, where the windfall gain is not proportional, the equivalence between a flat-rate wage tax and a flat-rate consumption tax does not hold.

tax imposes the intended degree of burden on particular achieved levels of consumption and comfort, without discrimination of any sort between taxpayers whose consumption is financed from current income and those whose consumption is out of prior income saved for the present.

It is a mistake to think much about personal taxes in flat-rate terms as if graduation were only a minor additional complication. Under the existing rate schedule, the difference between a high rate of tax and a low rate of tax is much greater than the difference between a low rate and no tax at all. Moreover, graduation has become quite central in our whole ideology of personal taxation. Any mathematical equivalence that works only for flat-rate taxes is therefore of very limited utility in appraising bases of personal taxation.

Further, rates are not unchanged over relevant periods of time. Whatever might be the utility of a wage tax if it had always existed or if it could be imposed retroactively to the beginning of time, if it were imposed now it would be very unjust because it would do nothing about previously accumulated wealth. It would have the effect of exempting altogether and forever all consumption supported by income from savings out of prior wages. A consumption tax involves no such discrepancy — all consumption is forthwith to be taxed alike, however it may be financed. The only question is whether to give some credit for taxes already paid with respect to accumulation subsequently devoted to consumption.[19]

This problem with a wage tax is more than a mere transition problem, because its effects will be long-lasting. Wealth persists, in some families at least, for many generations. Moreover, it is not just a one-time problem because surely rates will change in the future, and each increase in wage tax rates would produce long-lasting variations in the tax burden associated with any particular level of consumption according to whether the earnings with which the consumption is paid for arose before or after the change.

If one wants to think about a consumption tax as a deferred version of something else, there is another similar equivalence to be considered: a consumption tax with flat, fixed rates would be

---

[19] This question is not really a correlative, as Professor Warren suggests, *id.* at 939, of the discrepancy produced by introducing a wage tax, since it does not arise from the introduction of a consumption tax, as such, but rather from the necessity of making appropriate allowance for the prior existence of the tax we have. Moreover, the difficulties in making an appropriate allowance arise mostly from the inconsistencies and contradictions in the existing tax. Introduction of a consumption tax into a previously taxless world would not produce the same lasting discrepancies in treatment as would introduction of a wage tax.

the mathematical equivalent of a one-time, lump-sum tax on wealth, wealth being defined to include the present discounted value of all future earnings as well as material wealth. Such a tax would be partially equivalent to a wage tax, since a lump-sum tax on the present discounted value of future wages is equal to the present discounted value of a tax on the wages as received. But we would feel quite differently about the equity of such a lump-sum tax, since it would also embrace previously accumulated material wealth.

Of course such a lump-sum tax would be wholly impractical, partly because of the impossibility of evaluating future earnings and of raising money with which to make current payment of the tax. Moreover, we still want rate graduation, and we probably will want rate changes from time to time. A consumption-type personal tax can usefully be regarded as an equivalent of a lump-sum tax on wealth, but with the added virtues of being capable of practical implementation and of having rates that are capable of sensible adjustment and graduation.[20]

[20] The chief virtue of a lump-sum tax in economic speculation is that it is neutral with respect to the choice between work and leisure and with respect to investment choices. *See* R. MUSGRAVE, *supra* note 2, 211, 447. In this respect, of course, the lump-sum tax is supoerior to a consumption tax. But it is equally superior in this respect to a wage tax or an accretion tax or any other kind of income or sales tax. A bias against all economic activity, including work, is a general characteristic of income and sales taxes, which we seem to be willing to accept, partly because there is a contervailing income effect and partly because there is no evidence to show that the distortion actually produced is substantial. *See, e.g.,* R. GOODE, THE INDIVIDUAL INCOME TAX 53-57 (1964).

C. AN INCOME BASE

ALAN GUNN, "THE CASE FOR AN INCOME TAX"
46 University of Chicago Law Review 370 (1979), pp. 370–78.*

Recent studies by the United States Treasury Department[1] and the Meade Committee[2] in England recommend a progressive tax on personal consumption as an alternative to an income tax. Neither adds anything fundamental to the expenditure-tax controversy, but each contains one intriguing feature: a discussion of the practical problems of substituting consumption for income as the tax base.[3] This development may mean that the replacement of the income tax by an expenditure tax should be taken as a serious practical possibility. And even if the possibility of so radical a change in our tax structure is remote, the arguments of the expenditure-tax theorists may encourage changes in the income tax in the form of additional relief for savers or a supplemental tax on expenditure. The time when the expenditure tax could be dismissed as lacking practical significance has long passed.

Arguments based on considerations of equity, administrative convenience, and economic efficiency play an important role in the case for an expenditure tax.[4] I will not address the question of

---

* Professor of Law, Cornell University.

[1] DEPARTMENT OF THE TREASURY, BLUEPRINTS FOR BASIC TAX REFORM (1977) [hereinafter cited as BLUEPRINTS]. This report presents two alternative "model tax systems"—an expenditure tax and a comprehensive income tax with rates much less progressive than the existing rates—without choosing between them.

[2] INSTITUTE FOR FISCAL STUDIES, THE STRUCTURE AND REFORM OF DIRECT TAXATION (1978) [hereinafter cited as MEADE COMMITTEE REPORT].

[3] BLUEPRINTS, supra note 1, at 204-12; MEADE COMMITTEE REPORT, supra note 2, at 187-92.

[4] The most important recent defense of an expenditure tax is Andrews, *A Consumption-Type or Cash Flow Personal Income Tax*, 87 HARV. L. REV. 1113 (1974). Among older proponents of an expenditure tax, Irving Fisher was especially influential. The most concise and forceful expression of his views is I. FISHER, THE INCOME CONCEPT IN THE LIGHT OF EXPERIENCE (n.d.) (pamphlet) [hereinafter cited as THE INCOME CONCEPT], which appears to be Fisher's own translation of a paper originally published in German in 3 DIE WIRTSHAFTTHEORIE [sic] DER GEGENWART (1927). See also I. FISHER, THE NATURE OF CAPITAL AND INCOME (1906); I. FISHER & H. FISHER, CONSTRUCTIVE INCOME TAXATION (1942); N. KALDOR, AN EXPENDITURE TAX (1955); A. PIGOU, A STUDY IN PUBLIC FINANCE 118-26 (3d ed. 1951). For defenses of the income tax, see generally H. SIMONS, PERSONAL INCOME TAXATION (1938), and Warren, *Fairness and a Consumption-Type or Cash Flow Personal Income Tax*, 88 HARV. L. REV. 931 (1975). Professor Andrews responded to Professor Warren's criticism in Andrews, *Fairness and the Personal Income Tax: A Reply to Professor Warren*, 88 HARV. L. REV. 947 (1975).

"efficiency" directly, although some of my "equity" arguments may bear on efficiency as well as equity. I will focus on the most important noneconomic issues in the debate between expenditure and income taxation: whether an income tax imposes "double taxation" on savings, how income compares with other bases for taxation in terms of fairness, whether "ability to pay" is a meaningful test of fairness in a tax base, and whether an expenditure tax will be easier than an income tax for the government to administer and more convenient for most taxpayers to pay.[5] Finally, in the last section, I will touch on some collateral policy issues and suggest that attempts to reform the income tax may be more fruitful than the radical strategy of changing our tax base.

I. The Expenditure Tax, The Income Tax, and The Double Taxation of Savings

A. The Basis of Expenditure-Tax Theory

The earliest proposal for an expenditure tax that is still cited today was made by Thomas Hobbes. Hobbes thought consumption to be the best tax base because it measures the benefits taxpayers receive from society: an expenditure tax would charge individuals equally in proportion to the goods they withdraw from the common stock.[6] Hobbes's ideas are recognizable in the position of some mod-

---

[5] The tax base defended here resembles that of the existing federal income tax, tidied up somewhat, perhaps, but not fundamentally altered. I have no desire to defend an "ideal" tax based on the Haig-Simons definition of income:

Personal income may be defined as the algebraic sum of (1) the market value of rights exercised in consumption and (2) the change in the value of the store of property rights between the beginning and end of the period in question. In other words, it is merely the result obtained by adding consumption during the period to "wealth" at the end of the period and then subtracting "wealth" at the beginning.

H. Simons, *supra* note 4, at 50. Haig's earlier formulation was: "Income is the *money-value of the net accretion to economic power* between two points in time." Haig, *The Concept of Income—Economic and Legal Aspects,* in The Federal Income Tax 7 (R. Haig ed. 1921), reprinted in American Economic Association, Readings in the Economics of Taxation 54, 59 (R. Musgrave & C. Shoup eds. 1959).

Nor do I mean to defend a progressive income tax. Indeed, I shall argue that one advantage of income over expenditure as a base for taxation is that an income tax need not be progressive to be fair. *See* Part IV(C) *infra*.

[6] T. Hobbes, Leviathan 298 (A. Lindsay ed. 1959):

To equal justice, appertaineth also the equal imposition of taxes; the equality whereof dependeth not on the equality of riches, but on the equality of the debt that every man oweth the commonwealth for his defence . . . . [T]he equality of imposition, consisteth rather in the equality of that which is consumed, than of the riches of the persons that consume the same. For what reason is there, that he which laboureth much, and sparing the fruits of his labour, consumeth little, should be more charged, than he that living idly, getteth little, and spendeth all he gets; seeing the one hath no more protection from the commonwealth, than the other? But when the impositions, are laid upon those things

ern expenditure-tax theorists that the income tax is unfair to investors and wage earners because it taxes them while not taxing rich people who choose to be economically idle and live off their principal.[7] Few people today accept Hobbes's principle that taxes should be levied in proportion to benefits received, and the idea that only those who spend receive benefits from society seems bizarre.

Modern expenditure-tax theory is closer to the position of John Stuart Mill.[8] Mill viewed an income tax without an exemption for income saved as discriminating against savers because taxpayers would be "taxed twice on what they save, and only once on what they spend."[9] He argued that an income tax taxes savers both upon principal (the money originally earned) and the earnings from investing that principal. This, Mill argued, is unfair to the saver, because "if he has the interest, it is because he abstains from using the principal; if he spends the principal, he does not receive the interest. Yet because he can do either of the two, he is taxed as if he could do both . . . ."[10] Mill's fundamental idea, that the income tax is unfair to savers, is common today, as is the picturesque language with which he expressed this conclusion: the saver is "taxed twice" under an income tax.[11]

Some influential proponents of the expenditure tax have gone beyond Mill in important respects. Mill thought a consumption tax impractical because measuring annual personal consumption directly was impossible.[12] Modern writers have shown, however, that consumption can be measured, perhaps even more easily than income. Irving Fisher pointed the way by demonstrating that modern accounting techniques make it no harder to compute personal savings or dissavings than business savings.[13] He argued for an "income" tax (really an expenditure tax) under which all receipts—including gifts, inheritances, and withdrawals from savings—would enter into the definition of taxable income, but savings would be deductible, thus adding only two steps to present computations.[14] William Andrews has argued, more recently, that a spend-

---

which men consume, every man payeth equally for what he useth; nor is the commonwealth defrauded by the luxurious waste of private men.

[7] *See, e.g.*, N. KALDOR, *supra* note 4, at 14, 53.

[8] 2 J.S. MILL, PRINCIPLES OF POLITICAL ECONOMY 406-09 (1874).

[9] *Id.* at 407.

[10] *Id.*

[11] *E.g.*, M. CHIRELSTEIN, FEDERAL INCOME TAXATION 260-61 (1977) (presenting the notion that savings are doubly taxed under an income tax as fact, with no suggestion that the conclusion is open to doubt).

[12] 2 J.S. MILL, *supra* note 8, at 428.

[13] THE INCOME CONCEPT, *supra* note 4, at 14-17.

[14] *Id.*

ings tax would actually be easier to administer than an income tax, because the underlying computations would be simpler.[15] His claim is that an expenditure tax would not require the resolution of such troublesome problems of present law as distinguishing capital gains from ordinary income, computing depreciation, and drawing a line between business expenses and capital expenditures.

Mill's "double taxation" argument, in the form in which he made it, is circular. To say, as he does, that one who invests money "abstains from using" it is to say, at least implicitly, that consumption is the only "use" of money that should be considered in devising a tax. But modern writers have rescued the "double taxation of savings" argument from circularity. They argue that an income tax discriminates against savers because it makes saving less attractive relative to spending than would be the case in a world without taxes. I will use Andrews's figures to illustrate the argument.[16]

In a world without taxes or with an expenditure tax, a person who decides to save $1.00 of income and invest it at nine percent will have eight times as much to spend after 24 years as he could have spent initially; but with an equivalent[17] income tax he will have only four times as much to spend under the same conditions.

Tax	(1) Available after Taxes if Spent Immediately	(2) Available after Taxes if Spent In 24 Years	Ratio (2) : (1)
No Tax	$1.00	$8.00	8:1
33⅓% Income Tax	$0.67	$2.67	4:1
Equivalent Expenditure Tax	$0.67	$5.33	8:1

Even in this illustration, the expenditure tax does not reproduce the no-tax world in all respects, because any tax, by reducing the total amount a taxpayer has available for saving and spending, will normally affect the proportion he decides to allocate to each use.[18] But

---

[15] Andrews, *supra* note 4, at 1148-65.

[16] *Id.*, at 1125.

[17] For purposes of this example, an equivalent tax is one that takes the same proportion of nonexempt earnings. To do this, the nominal rate would have to be higher under an expenditure tax than under an income tax, if the income tax base is pretax income, and the expenditure tax base is what a person spends after setting aside what he will need for taxes (assuming no savings). This should not be confused with the problem of whether the aggregate tax base would be greater or smaller under an expenditure tax than it is today. The extent, if any, to which rates might have to be raised overall if the income tax were replaced by an expenditure tax is uncertain and cannot be calculated without knowing how people's savings would respond to changes in the rate of return on investment. For a discussion of the problems in this area, see R. GOODE, THE INDIVIDUAL INCOME TAX 37-57, 312-16 (rev. ed. 1976).

[18] The reason an income tax appears to "discriminate" against savers is that it seems to "take" not only money that would have been saved (but for the tax) but also the money that would have been earned by the money used to pay the tax. But any tax, even an expenditure

to the extent that an individual is influenced by what a dollar saved at the margin can earn, the incentive to save appears the same under an expenditure tax as in a no-tax world and different under an income tax that contains no exemptions for saving.

This argument is convincing only if one accepts a no-tax world as a standard for judging the desirability of a tax. Economists use the model of a no-tax world as a heuristic device to measure the likely effect of different taxes on the economy and as a standard of comparison in measuring "efficiency." As a starting point in making rough guesses about the effects of changes in existing arrangements, the "tax-free society" device may serve a useful purpose. But the model rests on so many assumptions about behavior under hypothetical conditions that any conclusions based on it must be problematic and tentative. As Coase has asked in another context:

> In a state of laissez faire, is there a monetary, a legal, or a political system, and if so, what are they? . . . Whatever we may have in mind as our ideal world, it is clear that we have not yet discovered how we get to it from where we are. A better approach would seem to be to start our analysis with a situation which naturally exists, to examine a proposed policy change, and to attempt to decide whether the new situation would be, in total, better or worse than the original one.[19]

B. Reduction to Present Value and Fairness

Even if we assume, for purposes of argument, that "no-tax society" comparisons are useful in determining economically efficient solutions to complex practical problems, it does not follow that "discrimination" against savings under an income tax (when both income and expenditure taxes are compared to a no-tax society) is unfair. The unfairness argument seems to rest on the notion that people generally prefer to consume as they earn and so must be induced by interest to defer consumption.[20] Interest income is thus merely compensation for delaying consumption. It does not represent a true increase in value to the saver, and a tax on that interest—like a tax on a nominal profit that reflects only monetary inflation—is in reality a levy on capital, a second tax on the earnings whose consumption was delayed. The following example illustrates

---

tax, can "discriminate against savers" in this way. The "double taxation" examples assume that the portion of the taxpayer's income that is saved is unaffected by the kind of tax in force. *See, e.g.,* Macgregor, *Taxation of Savings,* 3 ECONOMICA (New Series) 387 (1936).

[19] Coase, *The Problem of Social Cost,* 3 J.L. & ECON. 1, 43 (1960).
[20] *See* note 28 *infra.*

the thrust of this argument.[21] Two people earn $10,000 in one year. One spends all his after-tax income, while the other saves half his after-tax income the first year and spends it the second. With a flat 30 percent income tax and a 10 percent interest rate, net return after taxes is 7 percent. Ignoring their second-year salaries, we get the following results:

	(1) Spends Year 1	(2) Tax	(3) Saves	(4) Interest pre-tax	(5) Tax on Int.	(6) Spends Year 2	(7) Present Value of (5) at 10%	(8) Present Value of (6) at 7%	(9) of (1)+(6)
Spender	7,000	3,000	—	—	—	—	—	—	7,000
Saver	3,500	3,000	3,500	350	105	3,745	95	3,500	7,000

Although the "present value" of what the saver and the spender eventually spend is the same, the saver must set aside more for taxes—not only does the saver pay more taxes in total dollars ($3,105 vs. $3,000), the present value of his taxes is greater ($3,095 vs $3,000). Under an expenditure tax, the present value of their taxes would be the same, no matter how much or how long one saves. The argument that the net interest rate should be used to reduce future consumption and future taxes to their present value, and that, as a consequence, the saver and the spender in the illustration above "really" consumed the same amount but were taxed unequally, is the essence of the modern justification for the view that the income tax is a "double tax" on savings.[22]

Reduction to present value is often an essential step in comparing people's well-being. If two people receive $10,000 each in a taxable transaction, the one who is allowed to pay the tax later needs to set aside less for that purpose than the one who must pay the tax immediately, because money set aside to pay a fixed sum in the future earns interest until the sum is paid. But this type of analysis, so useful for comparing the burden of taxes, cannot be used in a

---

[21] The example in the text is inspired by Fisher's famous three brothers example. THE INCOME CONCEPT, *supra* note 4, at 12-13. Three brothers inherit $100,000 each. The first chooses to spend only the interest; the second allows his interest to accumulate until his money has doubled, and then spends the interest on this sum; the third buys a $20,000 a year annuity for six years, after which he has nothing left. Fisher assumes a 5 percent rate of return and a 10 percent tax. Under a conventional income tax, the first brother could take care of his future tax burden by setting aside $10,000 in the year of the inheritance, the second would have to set aside $17,140, while the third, "improvident," brother would need only $1,577.30. Under a consumption tax, each brother would have to set aside $10,000.

[22] *Id. See also* N. KALDOR, *supra* note 4, which is more explicit on this point than Fisher. Kaldor's discrimination argument is put in terms of "a comparison between the present capitalized value of a man's future prospect and the present capitalized value of his future tax liabilities." *Id.* at 84-85. Pigou, *Taxation of Savings: A Reply*, 4 ECONOMICA (New Series) 204 (1937) and BLUEPRINTS, *supra* note 1, at 39-40, make similar points.

straightforward way as a technique for determining the present value of future consumption to a saver.[23] If a taxpayer can obtain a secure after-tax return of ten percent, he is indifferent whether he pays $1.00 in tax now or $1.10 a year later, and this is true whether the total tax deferred is $1.00 or $1 million. But this does not mean that if a person lends $10,000 at minimum risk for one year at ten percent, he values $11,000 of consumption a year from now no more than $10,000 now.[24]

The interest rate reflects the "time value of consumption," if at all, only at the margin. The interest rate at which a person lends his money measures the value to him of the last dollar he saves.[25] If the interest rate were lower, he would probably still save, although he would probably save a different amount—less or more.[26] The

---

[23] This criticism seems to be implicit in Simons's response to Fisher, although Simons emphasized Fisher's inconsistent use of the term "income." H. SIMONS, *supra* note 4, at 90:

> It seems not unfair to say that Fisher is guilty of no little verbal legerdemain in his double usage of the income concept. Part of the time he is talking about income in the sense of values realized in consumption; but, whenever he is dealing with the valuation of capital goods, he uses income in exactly what we have defined as the yield, rent, or productivity sense . . . . What is discounted in the valuation of property is future yield (*Ertrag*), which may or may not be consumed. What are discounted are yields, not "consumptions."

See also H. GROVES, TAX PHILOSOPHERS 109 (1974).

[24] The differences between straightforward time-value calculations as applied to the receipt of cash and the same calculations as applied to consumption can be easily shown by a simple if somewhat extreme comparison. Suppose a taxpayer who could expect to receive a secure income of $10,000 a year for the next ten years were offered, as an alternative, a present lump-sum payment of $100,000. Ignoring any possible effects of a progressive income tax, any rational person would accept the offer, since the opportunity for an investment return makes $100,000 now worth more than $10,000 a year for ten years to anyone. But it is surely not the case that any rational person who expected to consume $10,000 a year for the next ten years and who could give up that opportunity in exchange for $100,000 consumption this year, on condition he consume nothing for nine years, would accept the offer.

It is also worth noting that whatever conclusions can be drawn about someone's preference for present over deferred consumption, even at the margin, from that person's decision to save at a given rate of interest are conclusions about *expected* enjoyment of consumption, not about actual enjoyment as determined (if, indeed, it could be determined) after the fact. See A. Warren, Income and Consumption Taxes—The Issue of Fairness (1979) (unpublished manuscript on file with author).

[25] If interest income compensates a person for postponing consumption, and if, as is likely, consumption has a declining marginal utility—that is, as more is consumed, each additional unit of consumption is valued less—a person will save only if the interest rate compensates him for the last unit of consumption he is to forego by saving. If the interest rate does not compensate him for postponing that unit of consumption, he will consume it immediately instead of saving it. If it overcompensates, he will save more until it no longer "pays" him to save. *But see* note 26 *infra*.

[26] If consumption had a declining marginal utility for everyone, people would save more as the interest rate went up, and would save less as it went down. This analysis, however, leaves many factors out of account. For example, someone who is saving for a particular goal, such as a college education for his children or a particular level of retirement income, may

money he would save even with a lower rate of interest produces benefits, if invested at the higher going rate, greater than those of current consumption. Use of the after-tax rate of interest to reduce future spending to present value, when applied to measure the present value of savings, ignores that part of a person's interest income that inures to him when he is able to invest part of his savings at a higher rate than he was in fact ready to accept.

Reduction to present value is essential to the argument that the income tax involves "double taxation of savings" and is therefore unfair to savers. Fisher said that it is "unjust" to impose taxes that are different, when reduced to present value, on people whose consumption, also reduced to present value, is the same.[27] This judgment rests on at least two assumptions: first, that a tax is just only if it taxes equal benefits or enjoyments equally;[28] second, that the interest rate measures the benefits forgone by delaying consumption. If the interest rate measures these benefits only at the margin, this second assumption is undermined and the argument loses much of its force. And a case can be made against reducing postponed consumption to present value, even at the margin, for the purpose of assessing the justice of a tax. As is indicated by the title of the revised (1930) edition of Irving Fisher's famous work on the rate of interest. *The Theory of Interest as Determined by Impatience to*

---

reduce the proportion of his earnings that he saves as the interest rate goes up. Just as the income tax tends to encourage some people to substitute nontaxable leisure for taxable work (the "substitution effect") and encourage others to work harder to replace money taken in taxes (the "income effect"), a tax with an exemption for income saved would encourage some people to save more while encouraging others, such as those trying to accumulate a fixed sum, to save a smaller proportion of their earnings than they would under an income tax. For a discussion of these effects, see R. GOODE, *supra* note 17, at 52-57.

[27] THE INCOME CONCEPT, *supra* note 4, at 12-13.

[28] This is discussed at notes 42-47 *infra*. It should be pointed out here that Fisher's view that it is fair to tax equally—and fair only to tax equally—people whose future consumption reduced to present value is the same assumes, among other things, that the only benefit people get from saving is increased future consumption. But as Guillebaud has pointed out,

the saver has immediately a new asset in the shape of his savings as a capital sum, in terms of its present exchange value, which is valuable to him not merely, and often not principally, as a source of future income, but as a protection and reserve against emergencies which may at any time befall him. There also comes into the question the prestige value of accumulated wealth, the desire to bequeath large sums at death, the knowledge of the power that derives from the possession of wealth . . . .

Guillebaud, *Income Tax and the "Double Taxation" of Saving*, 45 ECON. J. 484, 490-91 (1935). A similar argument is made in H. SIMONS, *supra* note 4, at 95-96 ("Time-preference theories are also interesting for their emphasis upon consumption as the unique end of all economic behavior.").

A person who values accumulation for its own sake will save and, under an expenditure tax, never pay tax on his accumulation, because his enjoyment comes from the possession itself. It is hard to see, on Fisher's own "benefits" approach to taxation, why it is "fair" to tax him less than a person whose benefit comes from consumption, present or future.

Spend Income and Opportunity to Invest It, interest can be viewed as payment for the cost of postponing consumption—resisting impatience to spend—rather than for the supposedly lesser value of future consumption. To an economist, a forgone benefit is a cost, but not all costs are equivalent for judging the fairness of a tax.

If we view the interest rate as paying the saver for the cost to him of resisting the impulse to spend immediately, the "double taxation" argument becomes an argument for allowing taxpayers who incur the "resisting impatience" cost a tax benefit to put them on a par with current spenders, who do not incur such a cost. But to allow this cost to be taken into account in devising a tax is inconsistent with accepted principles not only of income taxation but of expenditure taxation as well. The psychological cost of deferring consumption is like any other cost of giving up lost opportunities; such costs are not, and could not be, taken into account generally under either an income or an expenditure tax. We do not say that a worker's cost in boredom, or in giving up leisure, or in physical effort should be deducted in computing either his taxable income or, under an expenditure tax, his expenditures from current earnings, even though these things are regarded as costs by economists concerned with predicting behavior. In effect, the "double taxation of savings" argument for expenditure taxation is an argument for allowing a very common kind of cost to be deducted when incurred by savers, but not by those who earn and spend, even though we know that they also incur such costs.

The foregoing discussion does not mean that an expenditure tax is necessarily less desirable than an income tax, but the case for an expenditure tax cannot rest upon the argument that the income tax subjects savings to "double taxation." The justification for abandoning income as a tax base—if indeed there be one—must derive from other considerations of tax policy.

ALVIN WARREN, "WOULD A CONSUMPTION TAX BE FAIRER THAN AN INCOME TAX"

89 Yale Law Journal 1081 (1980), pp. 1090–93.

B. *Why Tax Income?*

Using the Haig-Simons concept of income in order to compute each taxpayer's share of the annual social product, an income tax serves to deflect to the government a progressive portion of each citizen's share of the product otherwise allocated to him by transfers and the marketplace. Whether the tax proceeds are used for public goods and services or for redistribution to some persons, either in cash or in kind, those uses are funded by the output of labor and private capital during the current period. Levying the tax on income is on this view simply a logical concomitant of the proposition that society in general has a claim on its annual product that is prior to the claims of its individual citizens.

The existence of a collective claim on privately produced resources is so well-established as part of our polity that justification may seem superfluous. Nevertheless, economic theorists have formally shown that certain goods and services are best produced in the public sector,[31]

---

[31] *See, e.g.*, Samuelson, *The Pure Theory of Public Expenditure*, 36 REV. ECON STATISTICS 387, 387–89 (1954); Samuelson, *Diagrammatic Exposition of a Theory of Public Expenditure*, 37 REV. ECON STATISTICS 350 (1955).

while political theorists have argued for centuries over the nature and extent of the collective claim for redistributive purposes, a subject that has commanded renewed attention in recent years.[32] But neither the theories of public goods nor those of distributive justice have depended on the source of revenues used for the two analytically distinct governmental purposes. Discussions of redistribution generally either have considered the appropriate distribution of economic resources without identifying the best measure of such resources or have assumed that it is income (as product) that is or is not subject to a collective claim. As a result, existing theories of distributive justice and public goods have little to add to the case for the income tax beyond establishing a social claim on private resources.

Specifying that claim as on social product can be justified on the theory that a producer does not have a controlling moral claim over the product of his capital and labor, given the role of fortuity in income distribution and the dependence of producers on consumers and other producers to create value in our society—factors that create a general moral claim on all private product on behalf of the entire society.[33] This rationale would apply *a fortiori* to other increments in Haig-Simons income, such as gifts and windfalls, which come to the recipient without even the claim due to production. Such a proposition is, of course, no more demonstrable than the proposition that society has a prior moral claim on wealth or consumption rather than on product. As Professor William Andrews has stated, the ultimate choice among these alternatives is not a matter of logical proof but of exposing the assumptions and identifying the consequences of each.[34]

Given that limitation, the case for taxing income can be stated by identifying as a plausible assumption the view that, for the reasons suggested above, the distribution of social product is a matter for collective decision. The collective decisionmaking apparatus of the society is conceived of as deciding both the amount and type of public goods to be produced and the distribution of that portion of private social product that remains after diversion of resources into the public sector to produce those public goods that are not financed by service charges. Whatever after-tax distribution is decided upon, that decision

---

32. The seminal work in rekindling interest in distributive justice is J. RAWLS, A THEORY OF JUSTICE (1971).

33. *See id.* at 72-74, 100-08, 310-15. For a recent argument that treatment of an individual's genetic endowment as an accident devoid of moral significance is inconsistent with basic concepts of individuality, see Posner, *Utilitarianism, Economics, and Legal Theory*, 8 J. LEGAL STUD. 103, 128 (1979).

34. *Andrews' Reply, supra* note 1, at 950.

is implemented by the income tax, which is levied on the amount of social product otherwise distributed to each taxable unit.[35]

As anticipated, this argument for the income tax does not appeal to some independently demonstrable principle but is tautological in the sense that it follows simply from the premise of the tax: given a legitimate social concern with the distribution of society's product, the income tax is justified as a means of effecting the desired after-tax distribution. The nature of the desired distribution goes to the content of the tax, rather than to its justification. Extreme egalitarianism would presumably argue for a tax characterized by progressivity, culminating in a confiscatory rate on positive income with corresponding provisions specifying a minimum after-tax income. A social decision to reduce inequality in the distribution of product, but not to the extent of eliminating incentives to work and invest, might lead to less progressivity with rates always under one hundred percent. It is a judgment of this latter type that seems to underlie much current discussion of distributive justice.[36]

Unlike the foregoing argument, the traditional case for the income tax in terms of fairness has appealed to some external standard to establish that income is an appropriate basis for taxation. Generally it has been argued that income is a superior index of an "ability to pay," and that the tax should be structured to result in "equal sacrifice" by taxpayers, the latter being especially relevant to the rate structure. Unfortunately, centuries of elucidation have failed to provide sufficient content to these concepts. For example, ability to pay has been defined as "the capacity of paying without undue hardship on the part of the person paying or an unacceptable degree of interference with objectives that are considered socially important by other members of the community."[37] Such definitions reduce to statements that society should appropriately tax what it should appropriately tax. This approach is no less tautological than the one taken here; it just appears so in that

---

35. This view includes the possibility of negative taxes and assumes that the desired after-tax distribution of income is a function of no personal characteristic other than pretax income. For example, if after-tax income were to be allocated on the basis of weight, intelligence, merit, or whatever, the Haig-Simons definition could be used for collection of revenue, but not for the simultaneous achievement of a given after-tax distribution.

36. *See, e.g.*, A. OKUN, EQUALITY AND EFFICIENCY—THE BIG TRADEOFF (1975); J. RAWLS, *supra* note 32, at 150-61.

37. R. GOODE, THE INDIVIDUAL INCOME TAX 18 (1964); *see* Gunn, *The Case for an Income Tax*, 46 U. CHI. L. REV. 370, 378-88 (1979). The theory of marginal sacrifice is discussed in W. BLUM & H. KALVEN, THE UNEASY CASE FOR PROGRESSIVE TAXATION 39-70 (1953).

apparently, but not really, independently verifiable grounds, such as ability to pay, are said to justify the tax.

To summarize, the personal income tax follows from, and is justified by, a societal judgment as to the appropriate distribution of social product or personal income. Society's interest in the distribution of income, in turn, depends on the view that the importance of fortuity and the interrelationships of contemporary society deprive producers of a controlling moral claim to what would be distributed to them in the absence of a tax system.

STANLEY S. SURREY, "REFLECTIONS ON THE
REVENUE ACT OF 1978 AND FUTURE
TAX POLICY"

13 Georgia Law Review 687 (1979), pp. 703-6.

A. *Consumption Taxes*

A significant segment of the academic community has recently spent much of its intellectual effort in strongly advocating abandonment of the individual income tax (and perhaps the corporate income tax) in favor of a progressive individual tax on consumption expenditures. Those advocating this step stress, with varying emphasis, neutrality as between present and future consumption, an allegedly fairer method of taxing over the lifetime of an individual, and the asserted need for increased savings.[19] The Republican Treasury left as its main legacy a blueprint for such a tax.[20] To those who believe in income taxation, this intellectual effort to promote a tax on consumption rather than income is an unhelpful diversion. A recent Brookings Conference in October 1978[21] left, I believe, most of those present with the distinct view that the burden of proof for such a change had not been met. The econometricians were not satisfied with the claims and analysis that savings would be increased or capital formation aided. The technicians discovered many difficult structural problems that were unsolved. The politi-

---

[19] *See, e.g.*, Boskin, *Taxation and Capital Accumulation*, 8 TAX NOTES 51 (No. 3, Jan. 15, 1979).

[20] U.S. TREASURY DEPT., BLUEPRINTS FOR BASIC TAX REFORM (1977).

[21] The proceedings will be published in J. PECHMAN, THE EXPENDITURE TAX (The Brookings Institution).

cally minded observed that many of the tax expenditures now in the income tax would reappear in a consumption tax along with new forms suited to that measure. The income tax advocates continued to see that tax as a fairer and more appropriate way to reach an individual's share of the country's product.[22] They also thought the lifetime pattern image projected by the consumption tax advocates—that of initial accumulation followed by later decumulation (increased consumption)—hardly fitted most of the wealthy, so that without very strong estate taxes the wealthy would be handed a windfall.[23] In addition, along this same line some thought that leaving savings untaxed indicated a disregard for the power of money in our society, a power that could be exercised in ways that did not involve "consumption" through the spending of that money. Moreover, equitable and workable transition rules from an income tax to a consumption tax remain to be discovered, if indeed they can be formulated. Finally, this emphasis on consumption makes it easier for the Congress to erode the income tax through special preferences for savings, because a group of academics would like that course. At the same time that group stands aloof when the Congress chooses to exclude forms of consumption spending from the tax, as in changes in section 911 allowing a deduction for living costs of Americans abroad.

While Congress has not shown an interest in a progressive tax on consumption, Chairman Long has revived discussion of a flat rate national sales tax in the form of the European value added taxes (VAT), and Chairman Ullman has apparently followed along. VAT for the United States appears to be a very flexible sort of tax. In the late 1960's and early 1970's some business groups and academics promoted a VAT in place of the corporate tax. Now Chairmen Long and Ullman seem to want to use it to replace the social security payroll tax and some of the individual income tax. Those who supported VAT in place of the corporate tax are just as willing now to support it in its new role—some supporters presumably want a regressive tax no matter how it gets into the system.[24] Perhaps the best

---

[22] A draft article by Professor Alvin Warren makes this point: *Income and Consumption Taxes—The Issue of Fairness.*

[23] *See, e.g.,* J. BRITTAIN, INHERITANCE AND THE INEQUALITY OF MATERIAL WEALTH 11, 22, 51, 61, 63-64 (1978).

[24] Even a good liberal economist, Gerard Brannon, has bought the "savings argument" and supports VAT. He would reduce the "regressiveness" by providing rebates to low-income taxpayers. Brannon, *The Value Added Tax Again—and Again,* 8 TAX NOTES 691 (1978). But

argument they have for VAT is that they can use those initials or the full expression—value added tax—without having to explain to the general public that it is really a retail sales tax. Furthermore, the European VAT, unlike our state retail sales tax, is often hidden in the price. The VAT also has achieved an aura of legendary effects that, while wholly false, continues to surround it. Thus Chairman Long and many in the business community[25] believe that VAT will aid exports because exports are not subject to the tax. Just how exports will increase although their present prices remain unchanged under the tax is not explained (while perhaps it may be that the employer's share of the payroll tax is passed on in prices, it is doubtful that there would be significant price reductions if that tax were reduced) and most economists have not supported this myth. Also VAT is usually described as a simple measure—the manufacturer charges the wholesaler at the full rate, the wholesaler charges the retailer at that rate and deducts from his payments to the Treasury what the wholesaler was charged, and the retailer, deducting from his payments what he was charged, charges the final consumer the full amount of the tax. Even this brief explanation raises the question of why go through all the preliminary charging and deducting rather than just having the retailer charge the consumer. The answer so far seems to be that the Europeans who started VAT do it that way and so should we—an answer that neglects the history of VAT as replacing European turnover taxes levied at all levels in some countries and the fact that the French, who really introduced the VAT, went to the stages of multiple collection because in the year of its adoption they needed an earlier boost in budget receipts. The European VAT system is on close examination a very complex tax, with many issues as difficult as—and in some respects similar

---

it is not an easy administrative task, as experience has shown, to see that the rebates all get to those entitled to them; *see* Murray, *Value Added Credits—Will They Work,* 8 TAX NOTES 139 (1979). And such rebates do not reduce the regressiveness aspect at higher levels. *See* Pechman, *Value Added Taxes: The Case Against,* 8 TAX NOTES 83 (1979).

[25] *See, e.g.,* Nevin (Chairman of Zenith Radio Corporation), *How Taxes Make for a Trade Deficit,* N.Y. Times, Jan. 28, 1979, § 3, at 14F.
See the statement of Charls E. Walker (note 7 *supra*) in favor of VAT:
> VAT is such a good idea, both politically and economically, that the real question is not whether we should move toward it, but why we've waited so long. It would foster capital formation, reduce our trade and payments deficit, promote greater efficiency in business, raise large amounts of revenue, produce stability in revenue, be simple to administer, and avoid taxpayer revolts.

8 TAX NOTES 406 (1979). VAT sounds more like a patent medicine than a tax!

to—the issues that complicate an income tax. It would be sheer administrative folly to foist such a tax on the Internal Revenue Service to replace the much simpler payroll tax, even apart from the economic arguments against such a step. Also, the Europeans have never developed a theoretical concept of just what should be considered "consumption" and hence what should be the base of a VAT. Consequently the coverage and structure of the VAT differs among the European countries. A similar problem exists with our state retail sales taxes and a solution would be needed if the United States decided to have a national retail sales tax. It is hard to believe that the governors, or even mayors, bemused by the name VAT would stand idly by and allow the Federal Government to adopt a tax that up to now has been considered a revenue source belonging exclusively to state and local governments. It is also difficult to believe that a Democratic President would embrace a sales tax. We must therefore hope that Representative Conable, the ranking Republican member of the Ways and Means Committee, was correct when he said early in 1979 that the current advocacy of VAT was "a red herring. That's a diversion. They want to take pressure off the discontent from social security."

Let us hope that the academics who favor a progressive tax on consumption will not in the end find that their efforts and arguments have been turned into a regressive sales tax. But they should be more aware than they are that they are playing a dangerous political game.

POINTS AND COUNTERPOINTS

1. According to Richard Goode, an income definition is "an indispensable intellectual foundation for the evaluation of an income tax statute" without which "conclusions reached may lack force." How does an income definition add force to the conclusions reached by tax specialists? Is not the definition itself one of their principal conclusions? As Goode notes, income can be defined in more than one way. Should tax specialists first form their definitions and then pick among these definitions on grounds of fairness, as Goode suggests, or should fairness concepts instead be built into the definition? Is Goode suggesting that no one can formulate a fairness standard without first formulating some tentative income definitions? Why does Goode feel the need to instruct economists that the income definition itself cannot settle fairness issues? Do some tax specialists believe that it does? Is Goode likely to interpret the "Schanz-Haig-Simons" income concept as requiring the taxation of small children on their leisure activities? Why not?

2. Is the principle of horizontal equity discussed by Richard Musgrave merely a variation of the rule that equals should be treated equally? Does this principle have any content? What is the source of the horizontal equity principle? Why does Musgrave conclude that it requires taxation of individuals? Does he mean to exclude marital couples, for example, as a proper object of taxation?

What are the practical differences between "equal treatment" and "equal amount of tax" under the horizontal equity principle? What are the policy implications of Musgrave's suggestion that "people with equal options should be treated equally?" What taxable period and taxable person rules, if any, has Musgrave implicitly adopted to give content to that principle? Does that principle reflect utilitarian ethics? Would Musgrave tax lottery winners and lottery losers the same under that principle, or would he impose a "double tax" on those whose options produced a profit?

3. In the *Meade Report*, what taxable period rules are implicit in its use of "Definition A of Taxable Income"? Does it assume the same period for Definition A and Definition B? Are the authors aware that "taxable income" is meaningless without reference to taxable person rules and taxable period rules? When the *Meade Report* argues that an exemption for yield or a deduction for savings are equivalent in a consumption tax, what assumptions, if any, are being made about the taxable period?

The *Meade Report* suggests that a strong case can be made for a consumption base from the fact that "it levies a tax on the claims which a taxpayer makes at any one time on the community's resources which he uses up for his own consumption purposes." What is that strong case? Does the "strong case" require that self-performed services not be taxed, since cleaning one's house, for example, does not use up a community's resources? (Or does it?) If using up resources is the test of taxation, how should those who first create resources and then consume them be taxed?

4. To many economists, the charm of a consumption tax is its similarity to an "endowment tax"—a lump sum tax levied with respect to each person's income producing potential. *Blueprints*, for example, repeatedly appeals to the endowment tax model in making its case for a consumption tax. But no one with a modicum of good sense would want to run for office on an endowment tax platform, for that ideal has some unattractive features. First, an endowment tax would be assessed not only on wealth but on the discounted value of each taxpayer's potential income stream. Volunteer doctors ministering to the poor for free, for example, would pay the same endowment tax as prosperous plastic surgeons, since taxpayers would be assumed to have pursued the most lucrative career available to them. Similarly, the tax would ignore such things as good and bad fortune since the tax would be assessed with respect to expectancies, not outcomes. Second, the tax would be imposed despotically without advance notice, since any debate over its adoption or its design features would introduce inefficiencies. Finally, to forestall tax avoidance, the tax would have to be collected at birth—an inconvenient time for most taxpayers to be worried about tax matters.

5. Should gifts be taxed both to the donor and the donee? Does the answer depend on the choice between a consumption tax and an income tax, or between an ability-to-pay and a standard-of-living tax, as *Blueprints* suggests? Does it depend, instead, on whether "consumption" should be defined to include "the joy of gift-giving," as many economists have insisted? If joy is taxable, should pain be deductible? Is the tax treatment of gifts better understood as a taxable person issue rather than as a tax base issue? *See* Chapter VII.

6. Joe and Maura are good friends. One year, Joe picks out a blue clock radio for Maura. Maura picks out a pink clock radio for Joe which is identical to the one Joe purchased except for the color. On Christmas, they exchange gifts and have a bitter-

sweet chuckle over the similarity of their tastes. How would an ideal personal tax treat this exchange? Are there persuasive policy reasons for taxing Joe and Maura on the market value of both the gift they gave and the gift they received? Should they be taxed one more time if Joe decides he likes the blue clock better and talks Maura into another gift exchange? Should a government that taxes the joy of gift giving be willing to accept payment in kind? How?

7. How does the following quotation bear on the case for the consumption tax outlined in *Blueprints*?

> "Since the amount of lifetime earnings that are not spent, but rather bequeathed, is substantial, and the taste for bequests varies significantly within lifetime earnings class, the consumption tax will exact very different burdens among those with similar lifetime budget constraints. This "horizontal inequity" effect, by our calculation, is at least as great as the horizontal inequity engendered by our annual tax system with all its preferences and exclusions. Finally we calculated the incidence of a proportional lifetime consumption tax by earnings class. Its incidence appears to be inverse U-shaped with the middle class treated more harshly then [sic] the rich *and* the poor. Some qualifications on this last point are presented however.
>
> "One final point should be made. The theoretical support for a consumption tax comes from the life cycle theory of saving. If people save to consume later in their lifetime, an income tax distorts this process. We have found (see the regression model in the appendix) along with others that the evidence supporting the notion that people dissave in old age is weak. Consequently, much of what is earned and saved is not consumed by the earner. To the extent that people save either to bequeath or for other reasons not related to planned future consumption, the consumption tax distorts the saving decision and loses much of its theoretical support."

Menchik and Martin, "The Incidence of a Lifetime Consumption Tax," 35 *National Tax Journal* 189 (1982), p. 200.

8. How appealing is "the lifetime" as the period for measuring a taxpayer's material well-being? Consider, for example, two taxpayers who both have lifetime consumption (or, alternatively, lifetime income) of $100,000. The first taxpayer lives for 80 years and the second dies at the age of twenty. Do they both have the same taxable capacity under any reasonable fairness standard? Would a study showing substantial variations in

lifetimes among the taxpaying population tend to discredit the lifetime as the appropriate measurement period?

9. The appeal to consumption tax advocates of a lifetime measurement period is due at least in part to the equity problems of an annual consumption tax. Consider, for example, a taxpayer who earns $15,000 in year one and then is laid off from his job in year two. During the year of unemployment, he supports himself by drawing down his $5,000 savings from year one and by borrowing $5,000 from his brother-in-law. Under an annual income tax, he would have no taxable capacity during year two and would pay no tax—an intuitively appealing result. Under a consumption tax, however, he would include the $5,000 of consumption from savings and the $5,000 of consumption financed by his loan in the measure of his taxable capacity for year two. What, if anything, can be said for this result?

10. The trend in federal tax policy of exempting many forms of savings has continued since the publication of *Blueprints*. *See* Steuerle, "Is Income From Capital Subject to Individual Income Taxation?" 10 *Public Finance Quarterly* 283 (1982). Is this trend evidence of popular support for the consumption model, as *Blueprints* intimates? Is it relevant that many of the exemptions for savings were adopted by Congress as incentives for arguably desirable economic and social conduct? Is it useful to distinguish popular support for some kind of realization requirement (e.g., no tax on capital gains until disposition; no tax on accrued pension rights until pension payments are received) from popular support for a general savings exemption?

11. Is there any practical way for a consumption tax to reach consumption financed by previously acquired wealth? Would enforcement of a consumption tax require that taxpayers be compelled to submit detailed statements of their wealth at the time the tax went into effect? How could the tax authorities determine when a taxpayer has consumed out of borrowed funds? Would it be fair, under a new consumption tax, to tax *all* consumption financed by previously acquired wealth? Would it be fair to *exempt* all such consumption? How could inflation affect the taxation of gains on assets that were acquired before enactment of the consumption tax and converted to consumption after enactment of that tax? In sum, do transition problems significantly reduce the purported advantages of the consumption tax? For a cavalier dismissal of transition problems in moving to a consumption tax, *see* R. Hall & A. Rabushka, *Low Tax, Simple Tax, Flat Tax* (1983). For a detailed and serious discussion, *see* Graetz, "Implementing a Progressive Consumption Tax," 92 *Harvard Law Review* 1575 (1979), pp. 1649–61.

12. The question of how to tax gifts in the federal estate and gift tax is largely independent of their treatment in an income or consumption tax. A major purpose of wealth transfer taxes is to redress inequalities existing prior to enactment of the income tax or persisting after its enactment due to advantages of birth.

13. How does the following quotation bear on the case for the Haig/Simons income definition? What assumption is the author making about the source of government revenue in his imagined "world without taxes"?

> "Even with identical utility functions, the Haig-Simons tax will violate the principle of horizontal equity when individuals differ in ability *if there is more than one type of ability*. Consider an economy in which individuals are endowed with varying amounts of two abilities, 'wit' and 'strength.' In such an economy, two individuals with different endowments and the same tastes may earn equal money incomes but, because of differences in the work that they do have different utility levels. More formally, each individual's abilities may be measured by the earnings per unit of physical effort ('strength endowment') and earnings per unit of mental effort ('wit endowment'). Each individual's utility is then a function of his money income, his level of physical effort and his level of mental effort. With different endowments of strength and wit, two individuals may select supplies of effort that yield the same income but different utility. Taxing them equally would thus violate horizontal equity.
>
> "The multiple ability model suggests another way in which a comprehensive income tax may not satisfy horizontal equity. Consider now an economy in which each individual has an endowment of only one of the two types of ability. Utility depends on income and the level of effort, with no distinction between physical and mental effort. The distributions of these abilities are such that, with the wages prevailing in the absence of taxation, the corresponding income distributions overlap. The introduction of an income tax will in general change the relative aggregate supplies of the two types of labor and therefore the relative wage rates. Two individuals with equal income and utility in the absence of taxes would have different pre-tax income after the tax system was introduced, and would therefore pay different taxes. The general equilibrium response of

factor prices thus introduces a further source of horizontal inequity." (Footnotes omitted, emphasis in original.)

Feldstein, "On the Theory of Tax Reform," 6 *Journal of Public Economics* 77 (1976), pp. 87–88.

14. In recent years, much of the creative energies of young economists has been directed at developing the design features of an "optimal tax." Optimal tax theorists and endowment tax theorists are often kissing cousins, for both take an "ex ante" perspective in deciding upon the merits of a tax and both define income broadly enough to include as many forms of imputed benefits as they can imagine. In contrast to endowment tax advocates, optimal tax theorists concern themselves entirely with the efficiency implications of alternative tax models. Members of the optimal tax school embrace tax principles that lead them to favor heavy taxes on essential commodities and other price-inelastic goods—a policy prescription that lost much of its political constituency with the fall of the *ancien regime* in 1789. What explains the popularity of this politically unpalatable tax reform agenda with many economists? Richard Musgrave suggests that "the younger generation is now stressing efficiency" because "efficiency considerations are more amenable to the exercise of technical tools, a practice that brings rewards to the young professional but may not be most helpful to a balanced view of reform." R. Musgrave, "Tax Reform or Tax Deform," in *Tax Policy Options in the 1980s* (1982), pp. 19–27, 25. Is this a plausible explanation? Is part of the explanation the utilitarian values which underlie most economic analyses of human behavior?

II. DESIGN OF THE RATE STRUCTURE

The rate structure of an income tax imposes tax burdens on taxpayers (however specified) in accordance with their taxable income (however computed). To the extent that taxable income is an acceptable measure of the material well-being of individual taxpayers, the rate structure can impose its burdens so as to vindicate society's preferences for economic equality. Weaknesses in the definition of taxable income almost always complicate and usually undercut whatever redistributive policies a society may be pursuing. For example, a special surcharge on high income taxpayers could offset, on the average, the disproportionate benefits that high income taxpayers typically obtain from tax preferences. But the surcharge would be more favorable than a tax base correction to high income taxpayers with above average tax preference income and would unfairly penalize members of that class with below average tax preference income—while exacerbating whatever undesirable economic side effects are produced by high marginal tax rates. Exemptions granted to all taxpayers, such as the personal exemption, or exemptions granted to a clearly defined income class, such as the low income allowance, need not undercut redistributive policies, since such measures are functionally equivalent to rate adjustments.

A progressive income tax is one that redistributes taxable income in favor of low- and/or middle-income taxpayers by imposing proportionally higher taxes on upper-income taxpayers. This contrasts sharply with a regressive income tax, which imposes proportionally higher taxes on low- and/or middle-income groups. A proportional income tax, the third possibility, seeks to preserve intact whatever inequalities in income distribution existed prior to its imposition.

Because taxpayers are permitted by the Internal Revenue Code to exclude many kinds of economic benefits from their taxable income, economists usually estimate the progressivity of the federal income tax by reference to some measure of economic well-being that is broader than taxable income, such as, for example, adjusted gross income plus certain tax preferences. They also adjust the burdens imposed by the rate structure by some or all of the tax credits that taxpayers may be entitled to take against taxes otherwise due. In deciding what concept of income to use in estimating progressivity, policy makers must confront almost the same set of issues they face in framing their definition of taxable income.

Most commentators believe that a personal income tax worthy of respect would exempt the poor from taxation. Low-income relief can take the form of a deduction, a credit, a zero tax rate, or some combination of the above, but whatever its form, it is best understood as a tax rate adjustment, since the purpose and effect of low-income relief is to redistribute tax relevant economic goods in favor of the poor. Thus the proper debate over progressive rates is over the degree of progressivity, not over progressivity itself. Some commentators would impose steeply graduated rates on upper-middle-class and high-income taxpayers in order to reduce the great disparities in economic well-being almost inevitably produced by an economy that rewards individuals for the relative scarcity of the goods and services they are able to offer for sale in the market place. Other commentators suggest that redistribution (except in favor of the poor) is an improper governmental function. The middle position would be to tax the great mass of middle-income taxpayers at a flat rate and to reserve graduated rates for those at the extremes of the income spectrum.

Section A, below, examines the pros and cons of imposing graduated rates on middle- and upper-income taxpayers. In the first selection, Arthur Okun argues that a democratic society which aspires to equality of opportunities should use progressive taxes to second-guess the distribution of income produced by market forces. In the second selection, Walter Blum explains why he would give decisive weight to the possible efficiency costs of substantial redistributive policies in setting the rate structure. In the third selection, Robert McIntyre appeals to popular notions of fairness in weighing the significant advantages of a broad-based progressive income tax over the various flat-tax proposals that have surfaced in recent years. The final selection, from a recent study of tax reform options in New Zealand, offers a concrete example of the delicate trade-offs that policy makers face in redesigning a tax rate structure.

In Section B, below, Hyman Sanders and Joshua Green of the Congressional Budget Office summarize the arguments for indexing the federal rate structure. Congress acted in 1981 to index the rates, effective for taxable years beginning after December 31, 1984. Under that legislation, changes in the Labor Department's Consumer Price Index over the prior year would trigger an automatic increase in the size of the personal exemptions and zero-bracket amounts and in the width of the various tax brackets.

Supplemental Readings. J. Pechman & G. Break, *Federal Tax Reform: The Impossible Dream*? (1976); Minarik, "The Future of the Individual Income Tax," 35 *National Tax Journal* 231 (1982); Treasury Department, Statement of John E. Chapoton, Assistant Treasury Secretary for Tax Policy, "Flat-Rate, Broad-Based Income Taxation, Hearings Before the Senate Finance Committee," Sept. 28, 1982, 97th Congress 2d Session; 3 *Report of the Royal Commission on Taxation* (Canada 1966), pp. 3–12, 20–2, reproduced in F. Sander & D. Westfall, *Readings in Federal Taxation* (1970), pp. 219–27; H. Vartiainen, "Progressive Income Taxation, Disincentives and Barter," in *Reform of Tax Systems* 103 (1981); Graetz, "The 1982 Minimum Tax Amendments as a First Step in the Transition to a 'Flat-Rate' Tax," 56 *Southern California Law Review* 527 (1983); *Inflation and the Income Tax* (H. Aaron, Ed., 1976); Allan, Dodge, & Poddard, "Indexing the Personal Income Tax: A Federal Perspective," 22 *Canadian Tax Journal* 355 (1974); *Note*, "Inflation and the Federal Income Tax," 82 *Yale Law Review* 716 (1973); Yoran & Shimer, "Adjusting Taxes for Inflation: The Impact of the Economic Recovery Act," 22 *Boston College Law Review* 1257 (1982).

A. PROGRESSIVE RATES

ARTHUR M. OKUN, "FURTHER THOUGHTS ON EQUALITY AND EFFICIENCY"

Income Redistribution, American Enterprise Institute
(Colin D. Campbell, Ed. 1977), pp. 19-22, 25-30.

The Cost of Equalization

In our capitalistic economy, the marketplace determines the prices of factors of production—labor and various types of physical property. Given the ownership of the productive factors (which is itself strongly influenced by the market over the longer run), the factor prices in turn determine the incomes of the citizenry. That market-determined incomes provide incentives and signals that contribute to efficiency has been the main story told by the economics profession for two centuries. But market-determined incomes also generate the economic inequality we dislike. Equalizing income thus implies modifying, vetoing, or supplanting the market determination, and therein lies its cost.

Doubters raise many searching questions about the efficiency of the real-world (as distinct from the competitive-model) marketplace. Does more real gross national product really mean more welfare? How seriously are consumer choices distorted by misinformers and "hidden persuaders"? How important is monopoly, which confers income as a reward for promoting scarcity rather than productivity? How serious are uncorrected externalities, excess supplies and demands? These issues are crucial, but I will ignore them in this paper—because they are so broad and complex.

All in all, I find the efficiency arguments in favor of the marketplace persuasive. These arguments have both a static and a dynamic component—getting the right things produced today and achieving progress tomorrow. The dynamic component can be further split into two parts: the importance of market incentives to accumulate physical capital (save and invest) and to innovate. I see the dynamic considerations as more important than the static considerations, and innovation as far more significant than accumulation.

Indeed, I believe that concern about accumulation incentives is grossly overemphasized in debates on redistribution.[13] The national saving-and-investment rate is, in fact, a result of political decisions—and should be explicitly faced as such. Society can have the saving-and-investment rate it wants with more or less inequality of income, so long as it is willing to twist some other dials, involving the capital-building component of public budgets, the mix of fiscal-monetary policy, and the taxation of middle-income savers and investors. In the area of innovation, collective action (such as publicly financed basic research) is essential to rescue the market from the appalling inefficiency of private property in knowledge.[14] Yet the market does provide vital incentives for experimentation and innovation that cannot be replaced on a collectivized basis. That is where the really large dynamic costs of any drastic income redistribution are likely to be found.

---

[13] Okun, *Equality and Efficiency*, pp. 98-100.
[14] Ibid., pp. 57-60.

The basic technique of redistribution actually employed in our society lies in the tax-transfer reshuffle. It appeals to me in principle and in practice. It allows a first-round distribution of income that is dictated by market verdicts and then modifies the results by imposing progressive taxation and by supplying resource-using rights (public goods) to all and transfer benefits (the equivalent of negative taxes) to the poor. With very few exceptions, this second-round redistribution cannot be carried out costlessly: as I like to put it, we can transport money from rich to poor only in a leaky bucket.[15] Some obvious leakages include administrative and compliance costs of implementing both tax and transfer programs, altered and misplaced work efforts resulting from them, and distortion of innovative behavior as well as saving and investment behavior. The most insidious attacks on an equalization program are those that view the discovery of any leakage as prima facie evidence against the desirability of the program. Holding it up to a standard of perfection, or zero leakage, guarantees a negative verdict. A social preference for equality implies a willingness to pay some costs for equalization.

Given (1) a social preference for equality (or at least for more equality than market-determined incomes provide), and (2) a cost of altering the market-determined distribution, society faces a trade-off between equality and efficiency. The resulting optimum will normally be a compromise.[16] Some efficiency will be sacrificed by altering the market's verdict through a second-round redistribution in the direction of greater equality. But some economic inequality will be left because it preserves economic efficiency (or some other social value, a point discussed below). Thus, society will carry the leaky bucket to pursue equality up to the point where the added benefits of more equality are just matched by the added costs of lesser efficiency.

These formal principles have significant implications. For one thing, they put into perspective the often-asked question, "How much equalization of income is enough?" That issue is no different from how large a capital stock or how large a police force or how large a computer is "enough." For all, the optimal "enough" is reached when the next unit costs more than it is worth. So long as benefits and costs are continuous, both fanaticism and complacency about equalization are ruled out of bounds. Second, the principles supply sufficient grounds for society's acting to alter the results of the income distribution. In particular, the preference for equality implies that the overall tax structure must be progressive and not proportional.[17] As Henry Simons suggested long ago, the case for progressive taxes rests on the proposition that inequality is "unlovely."[18] In principle, the necessary and sufficient case for the tax-transfer reshuffle is that simple.

---

[15] Ibid., pp. 91-95.

[16] In principle, the possibility of a "corner optimum" cannot be ruled out. If the cost of even the first dollar's worth of redistribution exceeded the benefits of its added equalization, zero redistribution would be optimal. At the other extreme, if the benefits of eliminating the last dollar's worth of inequality exceeded the costs of doing so, zero inequality would be optimal. Neither of these extremes appears to have any empirical relevance, unless one invokes a "principle" against any redistribution or any inequality.

[17] Again, this assumes that there will be no corner optimum.

[18] Simons, *Personal Income Taxation*, pp. 18-19.

The formal rules do not prescribe what public policy ought to do, but they strongly suggest what public policy questions the country ought to discuss. First, the political dialogue should focus explicitly on the intensities of social preference in favor of equality: I wish that the opinion researchers would give us the public's answers to my leaky-bucket experiment. Second, economists and other social scientists should be striving to measure the leakages and the effective equalization accomplished by various programs of taxation, transfer benefits, and public goods. The effort to quantify the trade-off ought to cover not only existing programs but also such proposals as guarantees of job opportunity, subsidization of low wages, and new forms of subsidy to higher education.

* * *

The Relativism of the Market's Verdict

Throughout the analysis this far, I have assumed that citizens have preferences about the *results* of the economic process—the distribution of command over goods and services—that are distinguishable from their feelings about the method by which those results were obtained. This is a crucial assumption. Indeed, every serious analysis that urges society to cease modifying the income distribution is based on the contention that the market method is so good, or any method of modification so bad, that the market's verdict should be left intact.

In some important noneconomic areas, we do regard whatever results emerge as untouchable, because they are generated by an explicitly accepted ideal process. I do not believe that the winner of an election is always the best candidate, but I believe that it would be wrong to overturn the results. Similarly, I do not care whether a jury finds a particular defendant guilty or not; I care only that justice be done. And I am prepared to respect the jury's verdict, unless I learn that the intended process was violated by tampering or the like.

Unlike the jury's verdict, the market's verdict is not accepted as necessarily ultimate. The second-round "reshuffle" is established precisely to allow political decision making to second-guess the market. As revealed by our laws, the first-round process is not regarded as sacred, nor the second-round process as sinful.

The Market as Ideal. To be sure, generations ago the marginal productivity theory of factor pricing was invoked by some economists to demonstrate the justice of the income distribution generated by a competitive market economy. I know of no proponent of that view within the economics profession today (though Milton Friedman is ambivalent).[25]

That normative view dissolved in recognition of the enormous distinction between effort and output, of the accidental ("unmerited") variations in the value of marginal product stemming from shifts in demand, and of the dependence of each unit's marginal product on the inputs of other units, which implies the omnipresence of joint inputs (and really makes the social environment a basic joint input in everybody's production process). These considerations effectively rule out the attribution of merit or desert to the market outcome. The results of the first-round income distribution cannot be defended as fair rewards for personal contribution.

The concept of reward for contribution has an even more fundamental defect. It is the logic—perhaps the magic—of capitalism to make distribution a by-product of production; the value of products determines factor prices which in turn determine incomes. Thus, the value of extra marketable output created by the labor and property inputs of any producer is supposed to be returned to that producer in the form of command over marketable output. In that sense, each contributor takes out what he puts in; and it all appears very natural, very fair, and almost inevitable. But that appearance is convincing only in the narrow cultural context of a market economy.

Until the seventeenth century, productive contribution was not viewed as the key to income distribution. For militaristic, marauding, and slave-owning societies, the name of the game was obtaining command over goods and services *without* engaging in the labors of production. In both feudal and monastic societies, the carving up of the pie was governed by rules and customs that did not have much to do with contributions to the baking of that pie. Across the range of human societies, the penalty for slackers was often ostracism, physical punishment, or the threat of divine retribution, rather than deprivation from consumption. The notion that income rewards geared to productive contribution is a natural or self-evident principle is a symptom of market myopia; an excellent treatment for that disease is a careful reading of the works of Karl Polanyi.[26]

---

[25] See Milton Friedman, *Capitalism and Freedom* (Chicago: University of Chicago Press, 1962), pp. 161-65. For a sampling of libertarian authors who explicitly reject the ethical rationale for income distribution based on marginal productivity, see Frank H. Knight, *The Ethics of Competition and Other Essays* (New York: Harper, 1935), pp. 54-58; and F. A. Hayek, *The Constitution of Liberty* (Chicago: University of Chicago Press, 1960), pp. 93-100.

[26] See Karl Polanyi, "Our Obsolete Market Mentality," in George Dalton, ed., *Primitive, Archaic, and Modern Economies* (Boston: Beacon, 1971), esp. pp. 65-67; and *The Great Transformation* (New York: Farrar, 1944; Boston: Beacon, 1957). Another type of historical perspective on the evolution of market ideology in the nineteenth and twentieth centuries is provided by R. A. Gordon, "Adam Smith in the Twentieth Century," in Leonard S. Silk, ed., *Readings in Contemporary Economics* (New York: McGraw-Hill, 1970), pp. 37-44.

An appreciation of the relativism of market rewards can also be gleaned from contemporary noneconomic institutions. Students, soldiers, amateur athletes, club members, friends, and family members are not rewarded with a command over resources geared to their contribution to the "output" of the relevant community. The laissez-faire market economy is unique in presuming that people *should* take out the value of what they contributed.

The Specter of the State. Most contemporary arguments that oppose altering the market's verdict do not rely on enthusiasm for the market, but instead stress the negative aspects of the political second-guessing process. Rather than deifying the market, these theories vilify political decision making. Such arguments are deeply rooted in basic philosophical conceptions of the desirable role of the state. Two modern laissez-faire theories, developed by Friedrich Hayek and by Robert Nozick, can serve to illustrate the nature of the critical issues in this huge area.

According to Hayek, the function of government is to root out the evil of coercion, but the only way it can carry out that mission is "by the threat of coercion. Free society has met this problem by conferring the monopoly of coercion on the state and by attempting to limit this power of the state to instances where it is required to prevent coercion by private persons."[27] Moreover, except in the case of the monopoly of an essential service, market arrangements do not involve coercion, according to Hayek; they may impose hardship on individuals but not "true coercion."[28] Hence, any policies requiring coercion by the state to mitigate such noncoercive hardships would be improper, since they would serve purposes other than preventing coercion by private persons.[29] In Hayek's view, it is clearly appropriate for the citizens to authorize coercion by the state to keep them from killing one another; but it is wrong to empower the state to exercise coercion in order to prevent death by starvation that is imposed impersonally by the market. Our society is not impressed by that distinction, and neither am I.

In his presentation of the case against redistribution, Nozick offers an even more restricted concept of the desirable role of the state. He develops an invisible-hand explanation of the state: it arises from individuals hiring protective agencies to help enforce their rights; as a result of economies of scale, a single protective agency becomes dominant in the territory and thus achieves a monopoly position. Such a state could emerge "without violating anyone's rights," and only such a state can be justified.[30] The resulting "entitlement theory" of distributive justice

---

[27] Hayek, *Constitution of Liberty*, p. 21.

[28] Ibid., pp. 136-38.

[29] Hayek even manages to justify public services (and the coercive taxation to finance them) as coercion to prevent greater coercion: "We need only remember the role that the assured 'access to the King's highway' has played in history to see how important such rights may be for individual liberty." Ibid., pp. 141-42.

[30] See Robert Nozick, *Anarchy, State, and Utopia* (New York: Basic Books, 1974); a brief summary is presented on pp. 118-19.

makes the appropriateness of any distribution of assets depend entirely on the justice of their acquisition and transfer, and not at all on the dispersion of material welfare among individuals.[31]

Like John Locke, Nozick depends heavily on a concept of natural rights. Indeed, he concedes candidly that, to him, it is an assumption rather than a conclusion that "there is some set of principles obvious enough to be accepted by all men of good will, precise enough to give unambiguous guidance in particular situations, clear enough so that all will realize its dictates, and complete enough to cover all problems that actually will arise." [32]

That assumption about natural principles or laws is indispensable to Nozick's theory. The state obviously punishes people for breaking rules. Such law enforcement can be noncoercive (not violating anyone's rights) only if the rules are "natural"—prior to and independent of the state. Thus, it can be argued that, because of natural rights, no one has the right to steal property from his neighbor: hence, when the government enforces laws against theft, it is not infringing on any right.

Frankly, I find the natural-law approach mind-boggling. One of the many questions that mystify me is how John Locke and his disciples acquired the franchise for stipulating the set of natural laws. (Was that "just acquisition"?) Suppose, for a moment, that some intruder into this game advances, as a principle "obvious enough to be accepted by all men of good will," that no citizen of an affluent society should ever be seriously deprived of material sustenance. Thus he can claim that the state is merely enforcing natural law when it carries the leaky bucket. On what basis can he be told that he is wrong? More generally, why should natural laws restrict the state's function to that of a protective association, rather than including a role as an insurance association or a mutual benevolent association?

Varying Normative Attitudes toward the Market. Empowering the political process to second-guess the market does not imply complete neutrality—a purely instrumental attitude—toward the market. People can have preferences about the dispersion of incomes and still have preferences about the process by which income is obtained. Clearly, many Americans are market fans, who like a recognition of success that takes the form of additional command over material output; others are offended by the reliance on greed and competition, rather than fraternity and cooperation, as the key motivating forces in economic life.

The market fans would pay something (but not an unlimited amount) in terms of both efficiency and equality to extend the scope of market determination, while the others would make some sacrifice to narrow it. My own value judgments come out essentially neutral: I like the impersonality of the market process, and I become

---

[31] Ibid., pp. 150-53.
[32] Ibid., p. 141.

attached to instrumentalities that work well, but I have some negative feelings about greed and competition.

I prefer exceptionally good plumbers to average plumbers—no matter whether they are better because they are more energetic, or better trained, or better endowed genetically. But I personally want average plumbers to get less steak and smaller homes only insofar as such a structure of rewards and penalties elicits better productive performance. I believe, nonetheless, that the majority of my fellow citizens are market fans. Popular expressions of concern about work incentives, handouts, and welfare ripoffs go beyond regrets about waste in the tax-transfer reshuffle, implying some attachment to the market's principles of distribution. Suppose, for example, that the voters were offered two alternative programs that would achieve exactly the same total GNP with the same income distribution. Program *A* would increase transfer benefits, while program *B* would establish an inefficiently large subsidy for the training of unskilled workers, thus permitting some of them to earn higher pay in the marketplace. Even if it could be demonstrated that the two involved the same government expenditures, the same tax burdens, and the same leakages, I would predict that program *B* would be preferred by an overwhelming majority—both of those who would be taxed to finance the programs and of those who would be recipients of the benefits. Equalization that raises the wage income of the poor is more popular than transfers unconnected to work effort, and it would remain so even if it were demonstrably no more efficient.

The development of such attitudes is easy to understand. Once our laws permit affluence and poverty to coexist, our attitudes must allow the wealthy to enjoy their rewards without personal guilt and must countenance the poverty without social guilt. We become committed to make a judgment that the rich and the poor deserve what they get, or else we would feel morally obliged to narrow the disparities. In effect, the rules of the game legitimatize inequality and, at the same time, reinforce pecuniary incentives with invidious socioeconomic distinctions between productive and unproductive citizens. When it rewards success in the marketplace with social approval as well as with affluence and penalizes failure with social disapproval as well as with deprivation, society marshals a broad set of incentives for market-oriented behavior.

The market ethic has been sold to a mass market. Getting paid is "belonging" in the minds of most citizens. Sociological studies reveal that the poor really do want to work and would strongly prefer higher incomes that come from better-paying jobs rather than from more generous transfer benefits.[33] The surprisingly small disincentive effects of some income-maintenance programs may reflect the motivational force of the market ethic. That, in turn, cuts two ways. On the one hand, fairly generous transfers can be provided without encountering major leakages. On the other hand, the more general and generous the transfer programs

---

[33] Leonard Goodwin, *Do the Poor Want to Work?* (Washington, D.C.: The Brookings Institution, 1972), p. 112.

become, the more nonmarket income is legitimized, thereby ultimately weakening the market ethic and increasing the size of the leakages. By that reasoning, welfare checks delivered with a smile may be a dangerous product. Indeed, many affluent voters want to keep the frown in transfers that go to people who, in principle, could work. On the other hand, the careful design of a contributory theology—even mythology—in old-age insurance keeps the frown out of that program, as seems appropriate for recipients for whom work disincentives are not a serious problem. Whether or not he shares them, no egalitarian can afford to ignore these market-oriented ethical attitudes when designing and promulgating proposals for carrying the leaky bucket.

WALTER J. BLUM, "REVISITING THE UNEASY CASE FOR PROGRESSIVE TAXATION"

60 Taxes—The Tax Magazine 16 (1982).

The writer (a co-author of "The Uneasy Case for Progressive Taxation") believes that recent trends in U. S. society, including a decline in economic progress, a high rate of inflation, an increase in welfare payments, and the expansion of the government's role in our society, make the case for highly progressive taxation less easy to support. Walter J. Blum is the Wilson-Dickinson Professor of Law at the University of Chicago.

Has the strength of the case for the progressive taxation of income changed since the early 1950s when "The Uneasy Case for Progressive Taxation"[1] was written? One way of addressing this question is to note four developments that have occurred in our society since then and comment on the bearing they possibly might have on the central progression issue.

Preliminary Considerations

Several preliminary observations are in order. The enquiry will focus on the personal income tax, although the much more significant relationship is that between the distribution of income among persons (or perhaps families) and our whole basket of taxes. The more narrow perspective seems appropriate for this review. Historically, the arguments over progressive taxation have generally revolved about the income tax; and it has been a tax on income that has supplied the main element of progression for our overall system. We will find it easier, moreover, to think about the consequences of a progressive tax levied on income than to talk about the effects of a bundle of taxes whose aggregate burden can be plotted alongside the distribution of personal income.

[1] Walter J. Blum and Harry Kalven, "The Uneasy Case for Progressive Taxation," 19 *University of Chicago Law Review* 417 (1952).

The progessivity of a tax could be measured not only against income but against wealth or consumption. Perhaps the relationship between tax burden and personal consumption, now that there is an increased interest in replacing the tax on income with a tax on expenditures, should be considered. But at the moment there is no widespread enthusiasm for an expenditure tax outside some academic circles; and the difficulty encountered in understanding this generally unfamiliar levy would tend to complicate further the discussion of the progression issue. Very likely there will be more heard on the topic of progressive expenditure taxation a decade from now.

It is also helpful to simplify the discussion by finessing all problems of describing what is meant by greater and lesser degrees of progression. This can be done by comparing two alternative types of rate patterns. One consists of any set of marginal rates graduated so that a higher rate applies to additional increments of income. *Steep* progression can be achieved by this pattern. The other consists of a flat marginal rate applied against all taxable income in excess of a specified excluded amount. The excluded amount is, in effect, subject to a zero rate of tax while the balance of taxable income is taxed at the flat rate. Under this pattern—technically called "degression"—the degree of progressivity in effective rate can be altered mainly by changing the size of the zero rate bracket. This pattern results in *mild* progression. For convenience in making the comparison, it will be assumed that the set of graduated marginal rates which one has in mind includes a zero rate bracket equal in width to that found in the alternative degressive tax. To sharpen the comparison between mild and steep progression, these alternative rate structures will be assumed to produce equal amounts of revenue for the government.

We will be dealing with the progression issue in the context of our own society. The matter likely would appear quite different in a totalitarian society highly controlled from the center. The issue for us is tightly connected with the features of our society, including the fact that most economic enterprise is conducted outside of government, people are generally free to spend or save their after-tax dollars, and individuals usually have considerable latitude in choosing their work patterns.

Finally, for most of the hundred-plus years of controversy over progressive taxation, the debate dealt with tax policy as something apart from policy concerning redistribution of income through the tax system. Among scholars, the prevailing view for a long time was that the progression question could be examined on various tax criteria, such as "fairness" or "ability-to-pay," while assuming that the redistributive impact of alternative tax schemes was a neutral factor— one not to be advanced as a reason for or against adopting a particular tax policy. There are still traces of this separation between taxation and redistribution; but, for the most part, those who speak about "fairness" or "ability-to-pay" are simply using the language of public political controversy. Most serious commentators now recognize that such a separation is artificial and obscures analysis of the progression issue.

Let us turn now to changes that have taken place in our society that may bear upon the question at hand.

Slower Pace of Economic Progress

First, our economy is not as lively as it was a quarter of a century ago. The gross national product, the output per hour of labor and the rate of capital formation are improving at a very slow pace, if at all. The record in the past decade has been poor compared to our own earlier performance and to that of most other developed countries.

While the causes of this decline are uncertain and no doubt diverse, several parts of the puzzle seem to be related to our question. All other things being equal, the economic situation would improve if saving increased relative to consumption, if more ventures were undertaken, if greater investments were made in capital goods, and if people on the whole gave up some leisure and worked more. Let us consider how progressive taxation bears on these matters.

As to saving in the private sector of the economy, steep progression is a depressant. The well-to-do on average save a greater fraction of their income than the less affluent. By imposing relatively higher taxes on the affluent and relatively lower taxes on the others, steep progression will result in a lesser aggregate of private savings. It is, in theory, possible to compensate for this difference by having the government do the saving through running a budgetary surplus year by year. Experience should tell us that this corrective is not likely to be adopted even when there are strong declarations of good intentions.

As to enterpreneurship (which can be thought of as taking business risks), the recent stagnation of the economy again points away from steep progression. An enterpriser is more likely to get a venture off the ground if there is no need to count on others for 100 percent of the capital required. In theory, a good proposition will attract sufficient funds from others; but practical experience suggests that the financiers will be more ready to do business if the enterpriser shares in making the investment. A steep progressive tax that dampens personal savings by those in the potential pool of enterprisers might reduce the total of new ventures.

---

a steep progressive tax that dampens personal savings by those in the potential pool of enterprisers might reduce the total of new ventures

---

More important is the bearing of marginal rates on risk-taking itself. Steep progression, as compared to a mild degressive form, results in imposing sharply higher marginal rates on relatively few taxpayers and slightly lower marginal rates on a relatively large number of taxpayers. Under a structure of sharply graduated rates, gains generally will count more heavily than losses in the computation of taxes. Big net gains will push the taxpayer into higher rate brackets, while big net losses will be deductible against income taxed in lower rate brackets inasmuch as the taxpayer's total taxable income will be smaller. This effect, which is likely to dampen enthusiasm for taking risks, becomes more pronounced when the marginal rates are more steeply graduated.

As to capital formation, the basic relationship between progression and total investment in plant and equipment can be captured in crude terms. A combination of greater savings and more risk-taking by enterprisers will bring about a higher level of capital formation. Businessmen who are seeking profits will find numerous opportunities to improve the "bottom line" by buying or modifying capital goods capable of making their operations more efficient. By retarding savings and risk-taking, steep progression acts to slow down capital formation.

As to inducing people to trade their leisure for working more, a tax on income penalizes work but not the enjoyment of leisure. Steep progression, as we noted, puts relatively heavy penalties on a small number of taxpayers and relatively light penalties on a larger number of taxpayers. Standing alone, such a distribution of penalties plausibly might encourage a broader shift away from work to indulgence in leisure. But we cannot ignore an offsetting consideration: some taxpayers who are highly penalized under steep progression might elect not to give up work for leisure but rather to swap leisure for more work in order to reach a level of after-tax income they regard as desirable. We therefore cannot be confident that steep graduation of rates leads to less total work (and more total leisure) than does mild progression. Likewise, there is no reason to believe that the opposite result will ensue.

On this quick analysis of incentives and penalties, the low economic performance of our society would appear to strengthen the case against a steeply progressive income tax. Yet the contrary has been vigorously urged on political or social grounds.

The core contention is that economic stagnation is now a permanent condition and, as a consequence, our society can be analogized to a zero-sum game. In such a society, new or additional demands on government can only be met by taking resources away from others; no longer can they be satisfied out of the increase in resources that is made available through economic growth. This zero-sum limitation produces greater tensions in society, making it more difficult to achieve the political compromises needed for adjusting to changed conditions or threats to the social fabric. Stalemate, the argument goes, might be avoided if the distribution of income is so altered that it is widely perceived as "fair." A steeply progressive tax has a special role to play: it is an important, if not indispensable, factor in generating a strong consensus that the after-tax distribution is "fair" under the prevailing circumstances.

---

some argue that a steeply progressive tax has a special role to play: it is an important, if not indispensable, factor in generating a strong consensus that the after-tax distribution is "fair" under the prevailing circumstances

---

There may well be a kind of self-fulfilling prophecy in this reasoning. The highly redistributive taxes might themselves contribute significantly to bringing about the economic conditions associated with the zero-sum society idea. Even apart from that prospect, however, the argument runs into a major dilemma.

The dilemma lies in translating the prescription into a schedule of tax rates. As between steep and mild progression, there is no obvious way of deciding which is fairer in the abstract. Surely people will differ on this issue in the future as they have in the past. Some will accent economic considerations, while others will more or less ignore them. Some will take a short-run view, while others will think about a longer term. Some will feel deeply about a particular position they take, while others will not be so certain of theirs. The question itself is intrinsically political in nature. In a representative democracy such an issue is best resolved by the legislature, the only institution that is in a position to read and weigh the views of the populace on fairness and then reach a decision that takes account of the spectrum. If tax policy is to be predicated on public perceptions of fairness, the tax voted by the legislature, I suggest, must qualify as being the fairest of the fair.

But let us suppose for the moment that in a zero-sum society a steeply progressive tax is more widely perceived as fairer than a mildly progressive levy. Would adopting the more redistributive tax achieve the stated goal of reducing political tensions and easing stalemates? On my reading of human nature, the underlying confluence of forces is not likely to move the political process in that direction. Persons subject to sharply higher marginal rates hardly would become more agreeable to government spending programs that resulted in allocating more resources to others in society; and in turn the others, whose taxes have been slightly reduced by adopting steep progression, cannot reasonably be expected to moderate their demands for government funding of their preferred programs. It is even conceivable that high progression could serve to exacerbate political tensions and prolong political stalemates. In short, we need to be reminded that all such projections concerning political responses are merely conjectures.

Stagnation in the economy, I submit, weakens the case for steeply progressive taxes.

Increase in Inflation Rate

Second, our society has experienced a significant degree of inflation during the past decade. We have been unable to stabilize the price level or confine inflation to the much lower rate enjoyed during the prior two decades.

In examining how this change bears upon the progression question, an adjustment in perspective is in order. No knowledgeable person has argued that steeply progressive taxes are at the root of our inflation. Nor has it been argued that inflation can be effectively curbed by doing away with graduated rates. The enquiry at hand is more modest: is a steeply progressive or a mildly progressive tax more compatable with a soundly conceived program to reduce the rate of inflation?

In an analysis of inflation, concededly a complex subject, the most durable and instructive relationship is that between the amount of money and the supply of goods. Roughly put, the general level of prices will increase if the amount of money increases faster than the supply of goods. Conversely, the general level of prices will fall if the amount of money decreases faster than the supply of goods. This unrefined formulation is adequate to approach our question, bearing in mind that we are comparing alternative tax patterns set to yield the same total revenues. Because of this equal-yield assumption, the choice between high and low progression ought not to influence the amount of money in the economy. That amount ultimately rests on the monetary policy pursued by the Federal Reserve—our central bank. There is no reason to believe that the Reserve's decision regarding the "proper" amount of money should be affected by the legislative decision to rely on a highly or a mildly progressive tax for obtaining a given amount of government revenue. This tax choice, however, might impact on inflation through its effect on the supply of goods.

Recall the point that, as compared to mild progression, steep progression would tend to be more of a depressant on the economy because it leads to relatively lower levels of savings, risk-taking and capital formation. Higher levels would result, over time, in a greater total supply of goods. And if the improved levels of savings, risk-taking and capital formation do not cause the Federal Reserve to deviate from its policy for determining the amount of money it otherwise would allow in the economy, the larger supply of goods should tend to hold down prices.

There might be another connection between progression policy and inflation. It is apparent to all that inflation brings about innumerable unintended changes in the relative burdens imposed on individuals or the benefits enjoyed by them. One significant set of such changes concerns the distribution of burdens under an income tax. Inflation creates nominal but not real gains for owners of assets other than money; it creates real losses for moneyowners and creditors and it creates real gains for debtors. Only through the use of fantastically complicated tax rules could the tax base deal generally with gains and losses that are real rather than nominal. As a practical matter, we must live with rules under which the effect of inflation on taxes will impact unevenly on different individuals. These unintended and often undesirable consequences are magnified when the tax is steeply progressive.

Thus, in a society that seeks to reduce a persistently high level of inflation, the case for a steeply progressive tax is weaker than in a society not faced with that challenge.

Increase in Government Welfare Payments

Third, government welfare payments have increased dramatically since the early fifties, both in absolute terms and in relation to total government expenditures. The welfare system has been expanded to provide virtually all our needy people with the necessities of life, although there continues to be much disagreement as to what constitutes an adequate minimum standard of living.

This welfare system does redistribute income from the nonpoor to the poor. There is, moreover, fairly wide agreement in our society that under existing conditions such a reallocation is sound policy. Controversy regarding the welfare system is mainly over its structure and magnitude but not over the principle that the needy are to be protected through welfare measures.

At first impression this development might seem to bolster the case for steep progression in an income tax. The welfare system does reallocate income in favor of the poor. Some commentators contend that it is only logical to finance such a reallocation through redistributive taxes. On closer inspection this notion turns out to be groundless.

Under a soundly constructed income tax, the zero-rate bracket (in conjunction with the definition of taxable income) would be set to shield the poor altogether from payment of tax. To collect a tax on those below the poverty level, as defined for purposes of welfare benefits, would be to incur costly administrative burdens that are a dead loss. If the prescribed support level is to be preserved, then the dollars taken from the poor by the tax would have to be replaced through increasing net welfare benefits by like amounts. So it is reasonable to assume that the poor will not be called upon to pay an income tax whatever degree of progressivity is built into the levy.

The relevant inquiry for us concerns not the poor minority but those above the welfare poverty level who do pay an income tax. Does the case for imposing a relatively greater share of the total income tax burden on the affluent among this majority grow weaker or stronger as the total size of welfare payments to the poor are increased?

If one views the welfare system as designed primarily to provide fall-back support for the needy, welfare expenditures are like all other government expenditures. The case for steep progression is no better or worse merely because the government is spending funds for welfare instead of, say, defense. Increased welfare payments from this perspective are a neutral development in thinking about progression policy.

The matter is not much different if one views the welfare system as designed primarily to be a mechanism for redistributing income to those at the bottom of the range. The fact that society generally agrees on redistributing income to the bottom tier does not carry any necessary implication about how the concomitant burden is to be shared by taxpayers. There are two distinct redistribution issues involved. So long as they are kept separate, the case for steep progression among those who do pay taxes is not advanced.

Cynics or perhaps political realists have contended that the larger the transfer payments, the weaker the case for steep progression. Welfare programs not infrequently come to be treated in some quarters as creating welfare rights which give rise to entitlements. The expansion of entitlements, it has been asserted, might lead to perpetuation of an underclass in our society. The thesis is that the development of an entitlements psychology will undercut efforts to inculcate stronger work motivations and build higher skills among the welfare beneficiaries. The crux of the cynic's concern is that steep progression might facilitate an expansion of entitlements; fewer voters will strongly resist the enlargement if they think the well-to-do alone are bearing the cost.

I leave this argument without comment.

Expansion of the Government's Role in Our Economy

Fourth, the role of government in our society has grown markedly since the early fifties. The public sector of the economy has expanded more rapidly than the private; the welfare program has spread out; government controls, especially over business affairs, have proliferated; and the size of the bureaucracy has increased. On a variety of measurements, the relative power of the government over the lives of individuals has mushroomed. Recent events, moreover, remind us again how difficult it is to cut back on government programs once they are entrenched. Government personnel and their constituents often can be politically potent.

How might these observations enter into consideration of the progression question? It seems futile to speculate whether government on the whole would tend to be less prone to growth under a milder version of progression. Perhaps the public willingness to endorse larger government appropriations might be diminished if more persons felt the heavier weight of a tax burden which they associated with the programs being funded. This is a more general version of the point that the acceptable level of welfare spending might turn out to be loosely linked to the distribution of the tax burden. Put as a general proposition, however, it does not seem persuasive.

Another line of thought seeks to relate government power with progression policy. Many of the values that have been important in our society will be impaired, it is said, if the balance of power shifts too much in favor of the public domain at the expense of the private or quasi-private area. At some point on the scale, dominance by the government saps the vitality of other organizations and inhibits the formation of new institutions that can check its exercise of power.

This concern often is offered in support of plans to confine government power by putting a limit on expenditures or curtailing the amount of revenue to be raised through taxes. It might possibly have special relevance to progression policy. The existence of large pools of private wealth seems to be important in restraining the continual encroachment of government. Steeply progressive taxation inhibits the growth of these pools.

All this is part of an old controversy over the place of sizeable private wealth in a societal system that embraces representative democracy and enterprises whose owners and managers are outside of government. I am not about to rehash that fundamental argument, but wish only to make a limited comment based on the increase in government power that has already occurred. As that power has grown in the past quarter of a century, the case for steeply progressive taxation might seem less attractive to those who place a high value on privately controlled universities, hospitals, research centers and the like; on privately controlled newspapers, periodicals, broadcasting stations and the like; and on new high-risk enterprises, new modes of art, new styles and the like. The necessary financial support for these things conceivably might be obtained by assembling small sums from many interested parties. In the actual event, however, the existence of large pools of private wealth often turns out to be the crucial source of support or the catalyst.

Progressive Taxation in the Present

"The Uneasy Case for Progressive Taxation" was concluded with an observation: "But in the end it is the implications about economic inequality which impart significance and permanence to the issue and institution of progression. Ultimately a serious interest in progression stems from the fact that a progessive tax is perhaps the cardinal instance of the democratic community struggling with its hardest problem." In the early 1950s the case for progressive taxation was not easy. Subsequent developments in our society have made it no less, and perhaps even more, uneasy. ●

ROBERT S. McINTYRE, "FLAT-RATE TALK"

New Republic, July 19 & 26, 1982, pp. 20–22.

CRITICS WHO have called President Reagan ideologically inflexible on economic matters got their comeuppance the other day when David Stockman, director of the Office of Management and Budget, announced that he "would not be surprised" to see repeal of most tax loopholes—apparently including the gaping new ones included in last year's tax act—proposed as part of Reagan's next budget. Of course, there's a catch: the Administration would preserve its commitment to "trickle-down" principles by requesting elimination of progressive tax rates as well. Stockman's remarks suggest that the Administration may be caught up in what a front-page story in *The Wall Street Journal* called an "intellectual groundswell . . . for the notion of a greatly simplified tax system with a single rate and few deductions—if any."

The Washington Post calls a flat-rate, no-deductions income tax the "obvious" answer to the internal revenue mess. Democrats like Senator Dennis DeConcini of Arizona and Representative Leon Panetta of California have introduced specific flat-rate legislation. So have Republicans like Senators Mark Hatfield of Oregon and Jesse Helms of North Carolina. And Presidential adviser Edwin Meese says anything but a flat tax is "immoral." Does all this mean that a flat-rate income tax with few deductions and credits is the wave of the future? Probably not, but the growing fascination with it deserves some serious attention.

Flat-raters are divided into two camps, and each camp makes two basic points. On the first point, they agree, along with almost everyone else: the current system of high tax rates, imposed on a taxable income base that has been heavily eroded by special tax breaks, has given us outrageous complexity, gross inequities, and terrible economic distortions. And it's getting worse. By 1987 the federal government will forgo 86 cents in "tax expenditures" for every dollar it collects in income taxes—up from 53 cents per dollar in 1977. The corporate tax data are even more extreme, with $1.88 in loopholes for every dollar that will be collected in 1987, up from 50 cents on the dollar in 1977.

Robert S. McIntyre is director of federal tax policy for Citizens for Tax Justice, a coalition of public interest, labor, and citizens groups which represents middle- and lower-income taxpayers.

The second point made by traditional flat-rate advocates, like the National Taxpayers Union, former Republican Treasury Secretary William Simon, and others on the political right, is that taxes on the well-off are too high and taxes on moderate-income people are too low—a problem, they say, a flat-rate would solve. The traditional flat-raters forthrightly admit that what they are promoting is more "trickle-down" tax policies. "I don't care what you call it," said Jim Davidson of the National Taxpayers Union in a recent interview. "Trickle-down economics makes reasonable sense."

A rather different second argument is made by some of the newcomers to flat-ratism, such as *The Washington Post*. They claim that the current loophole-ridden system is no longer progressive, and that a flat-rate tax would in fact be at least as tough on the rich, if not more so, than the existing code—and would do away with all the flotsam and jetsam.

Both sides have a point. Until the 1981 tax act, it would have been hard to argue that a flat-rate could possibly be as progressive as the existing tax code. In spite of the loopholes, the pre-1981 law did retain a modest progressivity. Corporations and the top 5 percent of individual taxpayers paid average effective rates of 25 to 30 percent, compared to 15 to 20 percent for the middle class and about 10 percent for taxpayers at the bottom. Thanks to last year's bill, however, there would now be little difference in progressivity between the current individual tax structure and a flat rate of 20 to 25 percent—assuming that there would be generous personal exemptions and standard deductions and that Social Security taxes would be part of the package. From the perspective of corporations, a flat 25 percent rate on real income would be a great improvement in progressivity.

On the other hand, in practice if not in theory, a flat rate would almost certainly mean far less progressivity than even the current approach. First, most of the traditional flat-raters would keep the separate Social Security payroll tax—which would ensure that people earning under $30,000 would pay taxes at a *higher* rate than their richer neighbors. Second, the old-line flat-raters understand that the pressures for tax loopholes would not vanish with a change in the tax rates.

Does any serious person believe, for example, that business taxpayers would cheerfully agree to the loss of their investment "incentives"? Or that charities will be content to lose the benefits of tax-deductible contributions? On the contrary, they would probably ask for more: a *double* deduction, say, or a large tax credit for charitable gifts—proposals seriously put forward by a national commission on philanthropy just a few years ago. What about Social Security recipients? Will they be willing to pay taxes—even a mere 20 percent or so—on half their stipends? Will homeowners gratefully give up their mortgage interest deductions if a single tax rate prevails? Are the oil companies and the banks standing ready with their checkbooks? This is not to say that elimination of many or most or all loopholes would not be a good thing. But, and this is basic point number one, a flat-rate does not necessarily reduce the pressures for tax breaks. The fight against loopholes is separate from the fight over rates.

Which leads us directly to basic point number two: just as one can imagine a flat-rate tax with no deductions and credits, so one can imagine a progressive tax system with none. The latter has long been the goal of traditional liberal tax reformers, whose ideal is a simple tax code with much lower but still progressive tax rates, ranging from, say, 10 percent to 35 percent.

WHY SHOULD an executive earning $500,000 a year contribute a higher share of his income toward supporting the government than a working mother earning $10,000? We can start with the basic themes usually summarized in the "ability-to-pay" principle. Assuming we want to spend a certain amount of money on collective projects such as defense, roads, and aid to the elderly, it's fairer to ask the well-off to contribute more than to burden those with lower incomes. And the redistributive effect adds more to total social welfare. Most economists would agree that a dollar's "marginal utility" is higher in the hands of a poor person than in the hands of a rich person. The extra food that the lower-income worker can buy for his or her children is worth more than the rich person's extra drink at the country club.

Another rationale for progressive rates is basically a benefits argument. Capitalism is a great way to generate innovation, efficiency, and growth, but it is premised on the idea that there should be winners and losers. Given such a system, it's important to smooth out some of the rough edges—and we can do part of that with a tax approach that tells the winners they have to pay more to support the system under which they have done so well.

Finally, real free-market liberals, in the tradition of Supreme Court Justice Louis Brandeis, would argue that progressive rates can help mitigate the concentration of wealth and power which, unless kept in check, undercuts the basic rationale for the capitalist system.

In terms of the tax base—that is, what income is taxed—liberal reformers make the same kinds of points now being made by the flat-raters. A "comprehensive income tax," with few of the government subsidies now included in the tax code, would be simpler, fairer in treating equally situated taxpayers alike, and much sounder economically. Liberal reformers argue persuasively that most tax loopholes, when seen as the government subsidies they are, are foolish, mistargeted, or even perverse, and that almost all the tax preferences either would function better as direct spending programs or would never be enacted at all if they could no longer be hidden in the tax system.

SOMEHOW, IN SPITE of these cogent arguments, loopholes remain—and they're rapidly expanding. Corporate tax breaks are the fastest-growing item in the Reagan budget, outdistancing even defense, and will double between 1981 and 1985. In constant dollars, the only broad functions showing increases between 1981 and 1985 under the Administration's 1983 budget are corporate tax subsidies (up 57 percent), defense (up 45 percent), interest (up 15 percent), health (up 13 percent), individual tax subsidies (up 11 percent), and income security (up 3 percent). (The increases in health and income security, by the way, are misleading. The former is due to growth in the age group eligible for Medicare and to projected inflation in the health sector. The latter is also due to an increasing number of elderly, and masks substantial real cuts in other programs that help poor people.)

The 1981 additions to the tax expenditure list include some of the most foolish ever adopted. The new corporate depreciation breaks will be death to productivity growth unless amended. They lead to effective tax rates on profits from new investments ranging from a 37 percent tax on income from industrial buildings to a subsidy—or "negative tax rate"—of 194 percent on profits from short-lived machinery. The result may be consistent with the President's vision of America as one giant tax shelter, but it will also mean a dramatic shift in investment toward tax-favored areas, even when investment in longer-lived assets makes far more economic sense.

Besides the depreciation changes—which will virtually wipe out the corporate tax—the 1981 act was festooned with Christmas tree baubles ranging from breaks for oil companies and utilities, to the misnamed "All Savers Certificates," to preferential treatment for trucking companies, multinational firms, and people who adopt children. As Stockman has ruefully admitted, the process "just got out of control."

Last year's tax bill was so outrageous, however, that the pendulum appears to be swinging back the other way. The Harris poll shows that 78 percent of the voters want last year's decision to abolish the corporate tax reversed. Fifty-eight percent now want the President to try something other than his current Robin Hood-in-reverse economic policies. At the same time, many in Congress who had talked themselves into believing the economic promises of the special interests are now furious at the lobbyists, as the economy fails to respond to the snake oil. Some Democrats are particularly angry that even though they went out of their way to prostitute themselves on last year's tax bill, their opponents are still garnering the lion's share of the business PAC money.

PART OF THE renewed interest in a no-deductions flat-rate tax comes from the anger over last year's excesses. As another dose of "trickle down," the flat rate is exactly the wrong prescription. But the general attack on tax breaks is a healthy development. Liberals and conservatives alike need to consider what a simplified, less loophole-ridden tax code would mean to them.

In the 1950s, before loophole mania took hold, Democrats and Republicans in Congress were generally united in their opposition to tax breaks, other than long-standing ones with entrenched constituencies, like the oil depletion allowance, and very narrow special-interest measures which had little impact on the overall system. For the Republicans, the main reason was ideological: they believed in the free market, and were opposed to government-created economic distortions. For the Democrats, the major rationale was political: tax breaks generally benefited Republican constituencies, not the poor and working people who voted Democratic.

The anti-loophole coalition began to break up during the Kennedy Administration. Despite Republican opposition on economic grounds and labor antagonism for distributional reasons, the best and the brightest successfully promoted the single biggest (until last year) loophole in the tax code—the investment tax credit, a tax subsidy which was supposed to encourage business purchases of equipment. After briefly reuniting during the first year of the Nixon Administration to enact numerous reforms (including repeal of the investment credit), the anti-loophole coalition completely fell apart in the 1970s.

Beginning with the 1971 Revenue Act, both parties reversed their philosophies toward the tax system. Republicans began playing constituency politics—which meant more loopholes for corporations and the wealthy—and Democrats began indulging their urge to get the government tinkering with the economy. There were plenty of opportunities for both, as inflation-driven "bracket creep" necessitated frequent amendments to the tax laws. As a result, scores of new tax breaks, including reinstitution of the investment tax credit, were enacted in the 1970s, interrupted only briefly by a few reforms in 1975 and 1976. By the end of the decade, effective corporate tax rates had been slashed by at least one-third, capital gains preferences had been increased enormously, and "incentives" for everything from energy conservation to exports had been added to the tax code.

Small wonder that middle-income taxpayers were getting frustrated with the tax system. Although government revenues as a share of the gross national product increased not at all from 1969 to 1980, the tax burden on middle-class wage earners went up substantially, due to the sharp decline in taxes on the well-off, particularly corporations, in combination with "bracket creep" and much higher Social Security taxes. The corporate share of the federal tax burden fell by one-third from 1969 to 1980. In constant dollars, corporate tax payments were 13 percent less in 1980 than in 1969—while constant-dollar after-tax profits were up 70 percent. The 1981 tax act capped the process, as Democrats and Republicans stumbled over each other to provide new tax breaks for every interest group and pet economic project that beckoned.

Yet few members of Congress are happy with their handiwork. Liberal Democrats are discovering that they can't fund social programs without revenues, and that middle-class support for the government has plummeted as the tax burden has shifted increasingly onto wage earners. Conservative Republicans look at the wreckage of the free market which tax preferences have given us—and many are aghast.

SOME STIRRINGS on both sides of the Congressional aisle are already evident. As a counter to the large crop of flat-rate plans which have sprung up, Democratic Senator Bill Bradley of New Jersey and Representative Dick Gephardt of Missouri have introduced a comprehensive reform package with graduated rates and few loopholes, to which they have attached the oxymoronic label, "progressive flat-rate tax." Republican Senators Robert Dole of Kansas and Pete Domenici of New Mexico, chairmen of the Finance and Budget Committees respectively, have tried to make loophole-closing the centerpiece of their budget strategies, both because they think it's right and because they have nowhere else to go after last year.

If Democrats will start representing middle-income wage earners as taxpayers again, the old 1950s coalition may be ready to regroup. If liberals will forswear economic tinkering through the tax code—no "Tax-based Incomes Policies" (TIPs), no energy tax credits, no "targeted" investment tax incentives—and if conservatives will forgo hidden subsidies for corporate and high-income constituents, there may be a way out of our income tax mess.

The idea of throwing out the whole tax code and starting over with a simple system may be impractical. And for many politicians it may even turn out to be an excuse to do nothing. "I'll believe these guys are serious about eliminating all loopholes when I see them vote to close one," says a long-time Hill tax expert. But if the flat-raters succeed in promoting a public debate about the benefits of a loophole-less tax code, they will—in spite of their "trickle-down" bias—have performed a useful service for the economy and for tax fairness.

REPORT OF THE TASK FORCE ON TAX REFORM
(New Zealand, 1982), pp. 128–34.

Avenues for Reforming the Rate Structure

6.141 A recurring theme which has emerged from the Task Force's examination of the present type of personal income tax rate structure, is the desirability (on many grounds) of flattening this rate structure. At the extreme, a uniform proportional rate scale would be consistent with this view. Although it would fully overcome a number of major problems inherent in the present rate structure, it would also entail some serious disadvantages. An acceptable solution, therefore, is more likely to be a scale which is significantly less progressive than the present one but not proportional.

6.142 Nevertheless, it is instructive to consider the pros and cons of a proportional scale as it highlights the issues involved in flattening the present rate structure and so provides a useful reference point. Accordingly, the following paragraphs consider the general characteristics of first a uniform proportional rate scale and, second, several less extreme types of flatter scales.

Proportional Tax Rate Scale

6.143 The impact of a proportional scale depends largely on the level of rate set. For example, the following table shows the variations in the break-even level of taxable income for a shift from the present personal income tax rate scale to several flat rates of tax.

Proportional Tax Rate	Break-even Taxable Income Level[1]
(%)	($ p.a.)
20	7,650
25	11,500
30	15,500
35	20,150

(1) Below the break-even taxable income levels tax liability is increased, and above them it is reduced.

6.144 The choice of break-even level is constrained by the amount of tax revenue that can be forgone altogether or otherwise be obtained—e.g. from the introduction of a broad-based tax on consumption expenditure and/or adoption of a more comprehensive definition of taxable income.

6.145 Irrespective of the rate, any proportional scale has certain general features. These are categorised below into advantages and disadvantages.

Advantages

6.146 Adoption of a proportional scale for assessing personal income tax would:
(a) reduce the fiscal drag effect of the scale to zero;
(b) remove the argument for income splitting—i.e. to overcome inequities due to the individual tax unit in the context of a progressive tax rate scale—and with it the risk of inequities and social problems associated with any version of income splitting which does not embrace all types of households (e.g. is limited to married couples);
(c) make tax liability much simpler to calculate and its collection via PAYE much easier;
(d) facilitate the integration of company and personal income taxation, by permitting the deduction of tax *at source* for dividends paid; and
(e) eliminate "period inequities" of the kind described in paragraph 6.125 above, and the associated need for income averaging to overcome such inequities experienced by people with markedly fluctuating incomes.

6.147 In the Task Force's view the most important advantage of a proportional scale—provided the rate is not set too high (e.g. say does not exceed 25 percent)—is that it would:

> minimise the *perceived* disincentive impact of high marginal tax rates on tax evasion and avoidance, and on work, saving and investment decisions—for any given personal income tax revenue goal—because the level of marginal tax rates for all but relatively low income recipients would likewise be minimised, other things being equal.

Disadvantages

6.148 The main features of adopting a proportional scale which are likely to be perceived by many as disadvantageous are that it would:
(a) clearly not distribute tax liability progressively amongst taxpayers, which may be considered unfair in terms of ability to pay criteria;
(b) increase the tax liability of those persons with relatively low taxable incomes—i.e. those with incomes below the break-even level—which may be considered unfair;
(c) benefit higher income earners proportionately more than low income earners, which may be regarded as unacceptable—particularly because of:
  (i) the limited scope for personal income tax reductions, given the Government's budget constraint; and

(ii) the more so, if personal income tax scale changes were financed by a switch to greater reliance on a broader-based consumption tax (e.g. VAT or an extented wholesale sales tax) the immediate burden of which may be regressive.

6.149 The first disadvantage, however, may be much less of a real problem than it appears at first sight insofar as:
(a) the distribution of taxable income is very compressed in New Zealand and the bulk of taxpayers therefore have average tax rates (under the present progressive scale) which lie in a fairly narrow range. As a result the redistributive impact of shifting to a proportional scale would be less than generally appreciated; and
(b) the narrowness of the present income tax base—despite the present progressive scale—means that the income tax burden is distributed much less progressively than it would be in terms of a more comprehensive definition of income (i.e. one that more accurately reflects ability to pay tax). Indeed, in these terms it may be regressive for the upper taxable income range.

6.150 The second disadvantage—i.e. a higher tax liability for persons with low taxable incomes—also may be a less extensive problem in economic reality insofar as the taxable income of certain types of *individuals* tends to understate their ability to pay tax:
(a) spouses' (e.g. in households with middle to high aggregate incomes) and other dependants' (e.g. a child, young adult apprentice or student) ability to pay tax arguably is a function of both their own income and that of others in their resource-sharing household—notably the principal income earner whose income they supplement.

Given this view it is arguable that such individuals with low *taxable* incomes for years may have paid less income tax than was appropriate in terms of ability to pay, so that an increase in their tax liability is justified. An increase may be further justified to the extent that each such individual's household benefits overall from the scale reducing (often substantially) the tax liability of the household's principal income earner;
(b) social welfare beneficiaries (other than national superannuitants) whose benefits generally are not taxed, but who may earn additional taxable income of up to a maximum of $40 per week ($2,080 p.a.) before ceasing to be eligible for the benefit; and
(c) some principal income earners—e.g. some self-employed individuals— who currently:
(i) can effectively split their income amongst family members; and/or

(ii) have substantial non-taxable benefits (tantamount to income) such as the use of their own production and the provision of a phone, car and other items as deductible business expenses.

6.151 Inevitably, however, there would be some low-taxable-income individuals whose economic circumstances would justify provision of at least partial compensation for the increased tax liability resulting from adoption of a proportional scale. The number of such persons would depend largely on:
(a) the level of proportional rate adopted; and
(b) the level of disposable income (and corresponding taxable market income) deemed to be a generally acceptable and adequate minimum for a single adult supporting himself/herself—on the assumption that different family circumstances (e.g. the presence of dependants) or other special circumstances (e.g. disability) are, or should be, otherwise taken into account (e.g. via tax rebates or social welfare payments).

Summary

6.152 The case for a proportional scale rests essentially on the expectation that it would improve economic efficiency—by generally reducing both the incentive to avoid or evade tax and any disincentive to work—and so lead to a general improvement in economic welfare. The associated demise of fiscal drag due to the underlying scale itself, easier administration, and defusing of tax unit problems may be regarded as secondary benefits.

6.153 The main argument against a proportional scale is likely to be that it would clearly not distribute the burden of personal income tax progressively, whereas many people may wish to see at least some degree of progressivity— even if it effectively is less than the scale suggests. The fact that individuals with low taxable incomes would pay more if a proportional scale were introduced may be of lesser concern, insofar as it arguably is justifiable in some cases and in others can justifiably be compensated for.

Largely Proportional Scale

6.154 If a proportional scale is not acceptable, then it could be modified in one of the following three ways, while still retaining a sizeable degree of proportionality:
(a) by introducing progressivity at the upper end of the scale;
(b) by introducing progressivity at the lower end of the scale; or
(c) by a combination of both—i.e. a so-called "double-ended progressive" scale.

6.155 The impact on the average tax payable by the majority of taxpayers, of choosing one of the foregoing approaches instead of a given proportional tax rate, is shown graphically below in Figure 6.5(i)-(iv).

Largely Proportional Scale with Progressivity in Higher Income Range

6.156 A scale which is proportional for low—to middle-income level taxpayers and thereafter progressive, would have the following advantages:
(a) it would enable a slightly lower rate to apply to all individuals with taxable incomes on the flat step, than under an equi-yield proportional scale (see Figure 6.5 (i) and (ii);
(b) it would reduce the need for changing from the present individual tax unit;
(c) for the majority of taxpayers it would have the other benefits of a proportional scale (see paragraphs 6.146—6.147).

6.157 Its main disadvantages would be:
(a) an increase in the tax liability of people on lower taxable incomes; and
(b) people with higher taxable incomes would be taxed at higher average and marginal tax rates than otherwise necessary.

Largely Proportional Scale with Progressivity over Lower Income Ranges

6.158 A scale which is markedly progressive over the lower range of taxable income and thereafter essentially proportional would have:
(a) the advantages of proportionality for taxpayers with higher incomes while permitting low average rates of tax for those on lower taxable incomes; and
(b) the disadvantage that low marginal rates on the initial income bracket(s) would benefit all taxpayers, not just those in the lower taxable income range; and
(c) the further disadvantage that the flat rate component of the scale would need to be higher than necessary under an equi-yield, proportional scale (see Figure 6.5 (iii)).

Double-Ended Progressive Scale

6.159 This type of scale is a combination of a scale with progressivity at the top end of the income spectrum only and one with substantial progressivity at the bottom due to either a zero or

PROGRESSIVE RATES

Figure 6.5
VARIATIONS ON A PROPORTIONAL SCALE

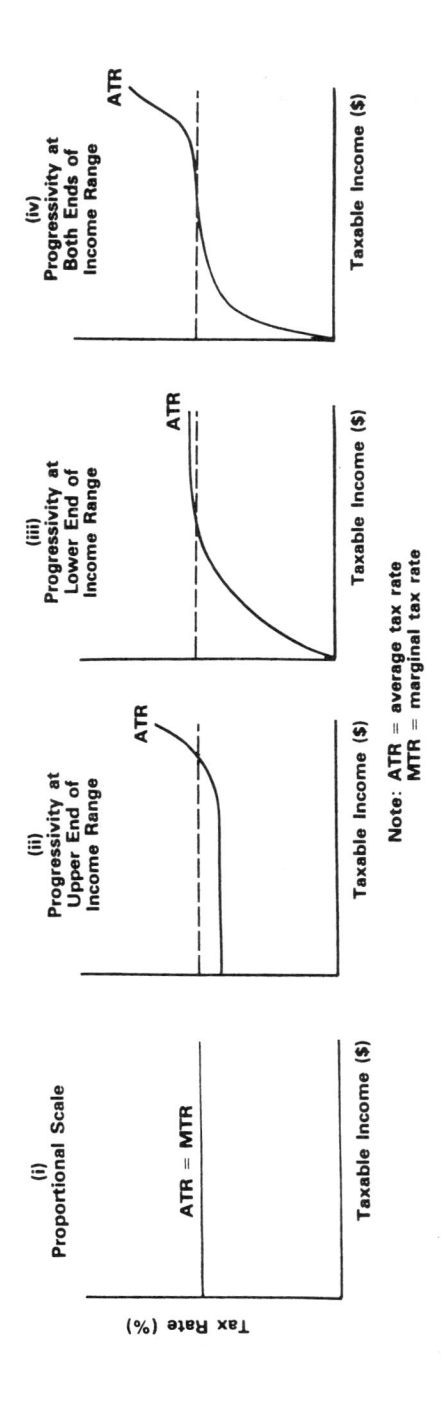

Note: ATR = average tax rate
MTR = marginal tax rate

very low marginal rate on the initial bracket of taxable income. It represents a compromise between a desire to reduce the tax burden of low-income taxpayers and a desire to tax those on high incomes at higher average rates. As a result, introducing such a scale would have:

(a) the effect of distributing the tax burden more progressively than under the present type of scale, the extent depending how low is the initial marginal rate; and
(b) the disadvantage of highly progressive marginal rates for taxpayers with low and high taxable incomes, and therefore
(c) the bulk of taxpayers would face a higher than otherwise degree of fiscal drag; and
(d) higher marginal rates for most taxpayers.

6.160 The marginal rate for the middle-income bracket of this type of scale would be lower:

(a) the higher is the initial marginal tax rate;
(b) the smaller is the income range to which the lower marginal rates apply; and
(c) the lower is the income level at which higher-income progressivity begins.

Summary

6.161 If a proportional scale is unacceptable, then a scale with a modest degree of progressivity over either the lower—or higher-income range, or both, and with a long flat bracket for the majority of individuals, may offer a reasonable compromise between economic efficiency and equity goals. *This is the Task Force's preferred approach.*

B. CONTROL OF "BRACKET CREEP" THROUGH INDEXING

CONGRESSIONAL BUDGET OFFICE, INDEXING THE INDIVIDUAL INCOME TAX FOR INFLATION

(1980), pp. 5-25, 29-33.

CHAPTER II. THE EFFECTS OF INFLATION ON THE INDIVIDUAL INCOME TAX

Inflation has three principal effects on the rate structure of the income tax.

One effect is that taxpayers may pay a larger share of their incomes to the federal government unless tax rates are cut periodically through formal legislation.[1] This occurs because, as money incomes rise, a larger portion of taxpayers' incomes is subject to higher tax rates. A taxpayer with two dependents, for example, earning $15,000 and filing a joint return, would pay $294 more in federal income taxes--a 23.8 percent rise in tax liabilities--if the family's adjusted gross income and itemized deductions both rose by 13.3 percent (see Table 1). Moreover, this taxpayer's overall tax rate--the percentage of income paid in federal income taxes--would rise from 8.2 to 9.0 percent. The share of total personal incomes absorbed by federal taxes thus increases, causing federal revenues to grow automatically as a percentage of national income.

A second effect of inflation on the income tax is that it changes the distribution of the tax burden among taxpayers in different income groups. Larger fractions of cost-of-living increases, for example, will generally be taxed away from middle- and higher-income persons than from others. In addition, the tax law treats differently incomes earned from different sources. Only 40 percent of capital gains income is taxed, for example, while income from state and local bond interest and Social Security is not taxed at all. These sources of income are not evenly distributed among all taxpayers, and inflation may affect

---

1. This problem arises only to the extent that taxpayers' incomes are adjusted upward to keep pace with price increases. Taxpayers whose incomes do not rise will experience a reduction in their real purchasing power, but will not face any tax increase. A recent review of median earnings levels for U.S. workers between 1967 and 1978 found that median earnings kept pace with inflation during this period. See Janice N. Hedges and Earl F. Mellor, "Weekly and Hourly Earnings of U.S. Workers, 1967-1978," Monthly Labor Review, August 1979, pp. 31-41.

TABLE 1. THE EFFECTS OF INFLATION ON THE TAX LIABILITY OF PERSONS IN DIFFERENT ECONOMIC CIRCUMSTANCES, 1980 (Income and tax liabilities in dollars)

Adjusted Gross Income	Current Tax (1)	Tax After 13.3% Inflation[c] (2)	Amount of Tax Increase (3)	Increase As a Percent of Original Tax Liability (4)	Percent Decrease in Real After-Tax Income[d] (5)
Single Person Without Dependents					
$ 5,000	250	362	112	44.8	1.5
10,000	1,177	1,392	215	18.3	0.6
15,000	2,047	2,445	398	19.4	0.9
25,000	4,364	5,234	870	19.9	1.2
50,000	12,559	15,273	2,714	21.6	2.5
100,000[a]	31,424	36,442	5,018	16.0	1.1
Joint Return Without Dependents					
$ 5,000	0	37	37	*	0.7
10,000	702	941	239	34.0	1.4
15,000	1,624	1,947	323	19.9	0.7
25,000	3,399	4,116	717	21.1	1.1
50,000	10,183	12,385	2,202	21.6	1.9
100,000[a]	28,694	33,712	5,018	17.5	1.5
Joint Return With 2 Dependents					
$ 5,000[b]	-500	-500	0	0.0	1.1
10,000	374	587	213	57.0	1.5
15,000	1,233	1,527	294	23.8	0.8
25,000	2,901	3,556	655	22.6	1.1
50,000	9,323	11,525	2,202	23.6	2.1
100,000[a]	27,714	32,732	5,018	18.1	1.6

NOTE: For taxpayers who itemize, deductions are assumed equal to 23 percent of their income.

* Greater than 100 percent

a. All income is assumed to be earned income, subject to a maximum marginal tax rate of 50 percent.

b. Qualifies for the maximum amount of the earned income credit.

c. Assumes incomes increase as much as the rate of inflation.

d. Decrease in real after-tax income after prices and incomes increase by 13.3 percent.

some of these sources more than others--further altering the distribution of the tax burden.

The third major effect of inflation on the income tax is that it makes the tax code less able to distinguish, for tax purposes, among persons with similar incomes but different economic or personal circumstances. For example, inflation causes the personnal exemption to shield a smaller percentage of income from tax. Thus tax liabilities grow relatively faster for taxpayers with more dependents (see column 4). This consequence of inflation also affects the distribution of tax liabilities among taxpayers at different income levels, since a change in the personal exemption has a relatively larger proportional effect on tax liabilities for low-income taxpayers than for taxpayers with higher incomes.[2]

The various effects of inflation on the individual income tax occur for two basic reasons. First, different types and levels of income are not all taxed at the same rate; and second, the tax code relies heavily on fixed-dollar tax provisions. If the income tax were proportional rather than progressive, if all types of income were treated alike and if the percentage of income subject to tax were the same for all taxpayers, inflation would have no effect in real terms on individual tax liabilities.

SIZE OF THE EFFECTS

Estimates of the Effects of Inflation on the Tax Liabilities of Persons at Different Income Levels

Table 1 shows how taxpayers in different types of households and at different income levels would fare under the current tax system if prices and incomes were to increase by 13.3 percent during 1980. In general, although most taxpayers would not actually be pushed into higher marginal brackets by rising incomes, the share of their income collected in taxes would increase. This occurs primarily because a greater fraction of

---

2. In this sense, the interaction of inflation and the tax structure also affects individuals whose money incomes have not risen during inflation, since the tax system neither recognizes nor makes adjustments for the fact that the after-tax purchasing power of these taxpayers has declined.

their income would be taxed at the highest marginal rate to which they are subject.

All but one of the cases depicted in Table 1 would experience tax increases that exceed the rate of inflation (column 4), and all would have lower real after-tax incomes (column 5). The actual tax increase in dollars attributable to inflation grows rapidly in absolute dollar terms as income increases (column 3) but is fairly constant as a percent of current tax liability for taxpayers with adjusted gross incomes of $15,000 to $50,000. Single taxpayers with adjusted gross incomes of $5,000 and joint return filers with adjusted gross incomes of $10,000 experience the largest relative increases in tax liability—increases of 34 to 57 percent (column 4). Taxpayers with adjusted gross incomes of $50,000, by contrast, appear to experience the greatest loss in real, after-tax income: a decline of 1.9 to 2.5 percent (column 5).

Table 1 also highlights another important effect of inflation on tax liabilities: inflation makes the personal exemption less effective at shielding income from tax. This aspect of inflation can be seen by examining column (4) or column (5). Taxpayers claiming a greater number of exemptions experience larger percentage increases in tax liability during inflationary periods and have somewhat larger reductions in their after-tax incomes. For example, a household with two dependents and an income of $15,000 pays 23.8 percent more in federal income taxes during inflation, while for a two-person household at that income level the increase is 19.9 percent—nearly 4 percentage points less. When measured in terms of after-tax income, the taxpayer with dependents suffers a loss of 0.8 percent; the taxpayer without dependents, a loss in real after-tax income of 0.7 percent.

The Effects of Inflation on the Distribution of Total Income Tax Liabilities

Inflation can also change the distribution of total tax liabilities across income groups, again because of the structure of the tax code. This is illustrated in Table 2. If prices and incomes rose on average by 13.3 percent during 1980, without any change in the tax law taxpayers at the bottom of the income scale would face the largest relative tax increase from inflation, with the percentage of the increase generally falling as expanded income[3] increased (column 3).[4] On average, taxpayers with expanded incomes below $5,000 would face the largest relative tax increase, although the actual amounts involved would also average only a few dollars (see columns 2 and 3). Taxpayers in the $5,000 to $10,000 category would receive the next largest relative increase, about 17 percent. Among taxpayers for whom the change in after-tax incomes can be calculated, the greatest reduction in after-tax income, about 2.5 percent, would be incurred by those with incomes of $50,000 to $100,000.[5] Their average tax increase would be only 7.5 percent, however, while persons with expanded incomes of $100,000 or more would have tax liability increases, on average, of 4 percent or less.

---

3. Expanded income is a broader definition of taxpayer income than adjusted gross income. In addition to adjusted gross income, it includes the excluded part of capital gains, percentage depletion in excess of cost depletion, and other tax preferences subject to the minimum tax. At the same time, it excludes the deduction of investment interest to the extent it exceeds investment income.

4. An agreed-upon method for measuring the impact of increasing prices on incomes and in turn on income tax liabilities does not exist. As a rough way of approximating these effects, four of the major income tax provisions--the zero bracket amount, the bracket widths, the personal exemptions, and the earned income credit--were each lowered by 13.3 percent, the projected rate of increase in the CPI for calendar year 1980 as embodied in the first concurrent resolution on the budget for fiscal year 1981. The difference between tax liabilities under these conditions and under current law was then used as the measure of how inflation affects individuals' tax liabilities. This method, however, excludes the effects that inflation-induced distortions in the measurement of capital gains income may have on tax liabilities. In addition, many analysts believe that using the CPI may overstate the size of the income tax revenue change due to inflation. For a further discussion of this issue, see Chapter 4.

5. The change in average after-tax incomes for taxpayers with expanded incomes below $10,000 cannot be accurately estimated, because there is no readily available information on the before-tax incomes of persons and families who would have to file returns when their money incomes increase.

TABLE 2. EFFECT OF A 13.3 PERCENT INFLATION RATE ON INDIVIDUAL INCOME TAX LIABILITY BY EXPANDED INCOME CLASS, 1980[a]

Expanded Income Class (in dollars)	Average Tax Liability Before Inflation (in dollars) (1)	Average Increase in Tax Liability Due to Inflation[b] (in dollars) (2)	Percent Increase in Average Tax Liability Due to Inflation (3)	Percent Change in After-Tax Income Due to Inflation (4)
Below 5,000	-54	69	c	d
5,000- 10,000	475	82	17.2	d
10,000- 15,000	1,226	130	10.6	-1.9
15,000- 20,000	2,054	194	9.4	-1.4
20,000- 30,000	3,350	291	8.7	-1.6
30,000- 50,000	6,365	573	9.0	-2.0
50,000-100,000	15,509	1,164	7.5	-2.5
100,000-200,000	41,122	1,753	4.3	-2.2
200,000 and over	171,849	2,006	1.2	-1.1
All Incomes	2,995	135	4.5	d

SOURCE: Treasury tax model, 1979 law at 1979 income levels.

a. For an explanation of procedures, see description in text footnote 4. Figures may not add to indicated totals because of rounding.
b. Assumes incomes increase by the rate of inflation.
c. Over 100 percent, because average tax liability becomes positive.
d. Cannot be accurately estimated, because data are not available on the before-tax incomes of previous nonfilers who would now have to file returns.

Estimates of the Effect of Inflation on Aggregate Income Tax Revenues

CBO estimates that the rise in tax revenues caused by inflation will generate additional individual income tax receipts of about $22 billion in fiscal year 1981, if the inflation rate is

13.3 percent. This $22 billion estimate hinges on assumptions about the rate of inflation during 1980 and about the "elasticity" of income tax revenue with respect to money incomes--the ratio of the percentage change in income tax revenue to a percentage change in income. The elasticity of income tax revenue with respect to money incomes depends on how much of the increase in money incomes results from inflation and how much from real economic growth; the elasticity with respect to inflation is thought to be higher than that for real growth. Tax revenues should thus increase more if inflation accounts for most of the higher income than if most of it results from real growth.

Studies have shown that aggregate income tax revenues will grow by about one and a half percentage points for every one percent increase in annual incomes,[8] given recent combinations of inflation and real growth. An increase in the inflation rate would cause a rise in the overall elasticity figure, since inflation would be responsible for more of the increase in money incomes. This, in turn, would mean an even greater rise in tax revenues.

CHAPTER III. MAJOR ARGUMENTS FOR AND AGAINST INDEXING

Indexing is only one way to handle the effects of inflation on tax liabilities. Another is to continue making occasional discretionary tax cuts, as the Congress has done in past years. Many arguments have been offered in favor of each approach.

MAJOR ARGUMENTS IN FAVOR OF INDEXING

Proponents of indexing maintain that it would offset the effects of inflation in several ways. First, it would hold constant the share of personal incomes collected in income taxes by the federal government. At the same time, it would assure that the distribution of the federal tax burden did not change because of inflation--that some taxpayers did not, as they have in recent years, incur relatively higher tax burdens than others because of inflation. Furthermore, federal spending as a fraction of total GNP would rise less rapidly than now during periods of inflation, provided the Congress did not permit the federal deficit to grow.

Indexing Would Eliminate Unlegislated Increases in Overall Tax Rates

Many believe that overall tax rates should not be allowed to rise without explicit Congressional action. Unlegislated increases in effective tax rates now occur during inflationary periods, however, because the tax code has progressive marginal tax rates, and most of its provisions--such as the zero bracket amount (the standard deduction) and personal exemptions--are specified in fixed-dollar terms. Advocates of indexing point out that it would adjust these fixed-dollar amounts automatically to keep pace with inflation.[1] Discretionary tax cuts could also

---

1. Advocates do not claim that it would preserve the average taxpayer's real after-tax income, because the incomes of some taxpayers may rise more slowly than the measure of inflation used to index the income tax. Indexing can, however, largely prevent taxpayers whose real incomes did not rise during periods of inflation from paying a higher proportion of their incomes in federal income taxes.

bring about these changes, but they would not be guaranteed. In addition, the time needed to make the adjustments would probably be greater under current law than under indexing.

In practice, indexing could come close to eliminating the inflation-caused rise in tax rates. It would not fully do so, however. To accomplish this objective would require both an accurate measure of the effect of inflation on tax liabilities and a procedure for adjusting all fixed-dollar provisions of the tax code almost instantaneously to offset the increase in liabilities--neither of which is available. First, there is no precise index of the impact of inflation on tax liabilities, and it would be difficult, perhaps impossible, to develop one. Such an index would have to be approximated with some general measure of increases in prices or in incomes. Nor could the tax code be adjusted whenever there was an increase in liabilities. Administrative considerations would probably hold the frequency of adjustment to once each year. These limitations could cause indexing to fall short of offsetting all of the inflation-generated rise in tax liabilities. The net shortfall would normally be small, however.

Indexing could fall still further short of providing full inflation adjustment if it was restricted to only some of the basic fixed-dollar tax provisions, or if only partial automatic adjustments were made. If only some of the basic fixed-dollar tax items were indexed, many taxpayers could still incur higher real tax liabilities, because the real value of non-indexed tax provisions would decline. CBO's estimates indicate that failing to index the personal exemption, for example, would preserve about $6.7 billion, or almost 25 percent, of the disproportionate rise in total liabilities in fiscal year 1981. Taxpayers would also face higher tax rates if indexing was restricted to years in which the inflation rate exceeded some minimum amount, or if the rate of automatic adjustment was set at less than the full increase in the official inflation index. Both of these limitations have been adopted in some other national indexing systems.[2]

The record of tax changes enacted since the beginning of more rapid inflation in the United States during 1967 indicates that, at least in aggregate terms, the Congress has come close to offsetting the effect of inflation on overall tax rates over a period

---

2. For a further discussion, see Chapter IV and Appendix C of this report.

of several years. Table 3 shows that, between 1967 and 1979, the overall tax rate remained on average within 0.4 percentage points of what it would have been under a prototype indexing scheme, although during particular years the difference in overall tax rates was considerably larger.[3] As compared to an indexed law, however, many individual taxpayers experienced a rise in overall tax rates (see Table 4), because the tax cuts enacted during this period were targeted primarily on lower-income groups.[4]

Indexing Would Eliminate an Upward Influence on Government Spending

A second argument often raised in favor of indexing is that the present tax structure tends to cause federal government spending to increase in real terms with inflation, because the more-than-proportionate growth in tax revenues allows the Congress to increase spending without either explicitly raising tax rates or increasing the federal budget deficit. Indexing could eliminate most of the automatic, disproportionate growth in revenues. This effect, in turn, could help to restrain federal spending.

While indexing would reduce federal revenues below what they would otherwise be, this effect need not bring about either a balanced budget or even a decrease in total expenditures. It would depend on many factors, such as general economic conditions and the willingness of the Congress and the public to tolerate deficit spending. If unemployment were to increase sharply, for example, the Congress might decide to increase spending and endure

---

3. The increased liabilities caused by inflation in 1978 were offset by the Revenue Act of 1978, which became effective in the 1979 taxation year.

4. Most of the tax changes enacted between 1967 and 1977 involved increasing personal exemptions and the standard deduction or zero bracket amount. These changes had the greatest relative effect on the tax burdens of low- and moderate-income taxpayers. These kinds of changes were excluded from the indexing simulation used here, although the Congress could also have enacted similar distributional changes under indexing. For a further discussion of tax changes during this period, see Benjamin A. Okner, "Distributional Aspects of Tax Reform During the Past Fifteen Years," National Tax Journal, vol. 32 (March 1979), pp. 11-27.

TABLE 3. INDIVIDUAL INCOME TAX LIABILITIES AND OVERALL TAX RATES UNDER ACTUAL LAW AND UNDER SIMULATED AUTOMATIC ANNUAL INDEXING, 1967-1979

	Actual Law		Prototype Indexed Law[b]	
Year	Income Tax Liabilities ($ billions)	Overall Tax Rate[a] (%)	Income Tax Liabilities[c] ($ billions)	Overall Tax Rate[a] (%)
1967	62.9	11.0	62.9	11.0
1968	76.6	12.3	69.8	11.2
1969	86.6	12.8	77.0	11.4
1970	83.9	11.7	81.6	11.4
1971	85.4	11.2	86.9	11.4
1972	93.6	11.3	97.4	11.7
1973	108.1	11.7	110.8	12.0
1974	123.6	12.3	119.3	11.9
1975	124.5	11.7	124.3	11.7
1976	141.8	12.2	138.4	11.9
1977[d]	159.8	12.4	155.8	12.1
1978[d]	188.6	12.9	178.4	12.2
1979[e]	217.8	13.4	200.1	12.3
Average Overall Tax Rate		12.1		11.7

SOURCE: Emil M. Sunley and Joseph A. Pechman, "Inflation Adjustment for the Individual Income Tax," in Henry F. Aaron, ed., Inflation and the Income Tax (Brookings Institution, 1976); Internal Revenue Service, Statistics of Income: Individual Income Tax Returns; and U.S. Department of Commerce, Survey of Current Business, selected issues.

a. Calculated as a percentage of adjusted personal income (personal income less transfer payments and other untaxed labor income, plus employee contributions for social insurance).
b. Indexed law assumes annual indexing of aggregate revenues by the annual change in the Consumer Price Index, rather than specific changes in individual tax law provisions. It thus differs from the indexed 1967 law used in Table 4, which assumes specific tax changes.
c. A tax elasticity with respect to income of 1.5 is assumed.
d. Preliminary
e. Extrapolated from 1979 returns processed through July 1980.

TABLE 4. COMPARISON OF INCOME TAX LIABILITIES AT 1978 INCOME LEVELS UNDER CURRENT LAW AND UNDER AN AUTOMATICALLY INDEXED VERSION OF THE 1967 TAX CODE PROVISIONS, BY EXPANDED INCOME CLASS

Expanded Income Class[a] (dollars)	Percent of All Returns by Income Class[b]	Liability Under Current Law (dollars)	Average Tax Liability Under Indexed 1967 Law[c] (dollars)	Average Tax Increase (+) or Savings (−) if Current Law were Replaced by Indexed 1967 Law[d] (dollars)	Average Tax Increase (+) or Tax Savings (−) Under Indexing as a Percentage of Current Tax Liability
Below $5,000	26.2	−59	122	+181	[f]
5,000– 10,000	21.7	458	606	+148	+32.2
10,000– 15,000	16.0	1,171	1,202	+31	+2.7
15,000– 20,000	13.1	1,972	1,824	−147	−7.5
20,000– 30,000	14.6	3,262	2,812	−450	−13.8
30,000– 50,000	6.5	6,437	5,021	−1,417	−22.0
50,000– 100,000	1.5	16,778	12,013	−4,765	−28.4
100,000– 200,000	0.3	45,892	36,357	−9,536	−20.8
Above 200,000	[e]	184,965	169,826	−15,138	−8.2

SOURCE: Department of Treasury tax model, 1979 law at 1978 income levels.

a. For a definition of expanded income, see Chapter II, p. 9, footnote 3.
b. Totals may not sum to 100 percent because of rounding.
c. Indexed law is defined as the 1967 tax code with bracket widths, the standard deduction (now the "zero bracket amount") and personal exemptions indexed by the cumulative rise in the Consumer Price Index between 1967 and 1978.
d. The data base utilized to generate these figures is based solely upon the current population of taxpayers. Since 1964, large increases in the standard deduction and personal exemption have reduced the number of low-income persons who must file an income tax return. Thus, average tax savings for persons with expanded incomes below $15,000 may be significantly higher than the figure reported here, even after taking into account effects of the earned income credit on the number of low-income households filing tax returns.
e. Less than 0.1 percent.
f. Greater than 100 percent.

a temporarily large deficit. Thus, indexing would not guarantee lower expenditures.

The Canadian experience with indexing suggests that indexing could reduce spending, but not under all circumstances. Between 1974, when indexing was enacted in Canada, and 1977, Canadian federal expenditures actually increased sharply, in large part because of government policies designed to combat a dramatic rise in unemployment beginning in 1974 (see Appendix B). With the recovery of the Canadian economy in 1977-1978, however, the growth in Canadian federal expenditures began to decrease significantly. Some Canadian observers believe that this decrease can be attributed, at least in part, to the restraining effect of indexing on federal revenues and its implications for the size of the federal deficit.[5] Recent pronouncements by Canadian officials, however, suggest that legislators may be unwilling to curb the growth in Canadian spending still further--in which case the deficit could continue to rise unless steps are taken to increase revenues.[6]

MAJOR ARGUMENTS AGAINST INDEXING

Opponents of indexing, for their part, have made several arguments. First, they contend, any kind of automatic adjustment, whether in outlays or in revenues, would impair the Congress's flexibility in determining the federal budget. Second, indexing would tend to magnify the effects of business cycle changes on the economy by weakening the stabilizing function of the income tax structure--perhaps even to the point of being itself inflationary. Finally, the tighter control of aggregate federal revenues under indexing would limit opportunities to review and revise the tax code.

---

5. See, e.g., statements by Canadian leaders cited in Jerry Edgerton, "The Tax Reform You May Need Most," Money, vol. 7 (June 1978), pp. 48-51. Between 1974 and 1978, the Canadian federal budget moved from a surplus of $1.1 billion to a deficit of $11.4 billion.

6. See testimony of Deputy Minister of Finance Dr. Ian Stewart before the Standing Canadian Senate Committee on National Finance (May 27, 1980), p. 26.

Indexing Would Reduce the Federal Government's Flexibility in Setting Budgetary Policy During Periods of Inflation

Opponents of indexing contend that the more-than-proportionate rise in tax revenues that now occurs during inflationary periods eases the task of setting budgetary policy. If restraint is needed, it can be supplied simply by not enacting a tax cut, since without a tax cut revenues tend to rise more quickly than expenditures for current programs.[7] If, on the other hand, more stimulus is thought necessary, taxes can be cut or spending increased.

The ability to set policy simply through tax cuts, spending increases, and deferrals of tax cuts would be significantly reduced under indexing. Thus, indexing would complicate the development of a budget much as the indexing of certain outlays, such as Social Security, already has. Under indexing, if fiscal restraint were needed, the Congress would have to reduce spending or increase tax rates explicitly. Spending, though, is difficult to reduce.[8] Moreover, legislated tax rate increases have occurred recently only during periods of national emergency (for example, the 1968-69 Vietnam War tax surcharge).

Indexing advocates might agree with this conclusion but would contend that the present system's flexibility also has drawbacks. For example, the automatic rise in federal revenues that now

---

7. CBO has estimated that in the absence of changes in current policies, federal revenues will grow about 15 percent annually between 1980 and 1985, about 6 percent faster than federal outlays. See Five-Year Budget Projections, Fiscal Years 1981-1985: A Report to the Senate and House Committees on the Budget--Part II (February 1980), Summary Tables 1 and 2.

8. Spending cuts are difficult for two reasons. One is that most spending programs affect well-defined groups that will resist any decrease in their benefits. In addition, however, there are few discretionary spending programs. According to Administration estimates, over 75 percent of all federal outlays in fiscal years 1980 and 1981 are relatively "uncontrollable" in the short term, in the sense that these expenditures result from programs such as Social Security or from contracts mandated by existing law. Without changing current legislation, these expenditures would continue. See Budget of the United States Government, Fiscal Year 1981 (January 1980), Table 17.

occurs during inflationary periods may allow more federal spending at a given federal budget deficit. Under an indexed system, either a higher budget deficit or an outright increase in tax rates would be needed to accommodate the same level of expenditures. Since both these steps appear difficult to undertake, the present tax system—which requires neither—may promote higher federal spending during periods of inflation.

Experience from 1967, when the rate of inflation first began to accelerate, until 1977, indicates that overall tax rates during this period were roughly equal, in the aggregate, to what they would have been under indexing (see Table 3). In particular years, however, overall tax rates differed from what they probably would have been under indexing. This record suggests that the Congress may have periodically used the flexibility created by the tax code and inflation to fashion its budgetary policies. Thus, at times taxes were reduced more than enough to offset the effects of inflation on tax revenues; at other times the automatic rise in revenues served to fund new spending programs or to expand existing ones without increasing the federal deficit.

Indexing May Weaken the Ability of the Tax System to Stabilize the Economy During Periods of Inflation and May Itself Be Inflationary

It is often said that the current federal tax system tends to stabilize the economy during periods of inflation, because the rise in demand generated by higher money incomes is checked by the higher tax rates that apply to these incomes. Indexing could be seen as weakening or eliminating this tendency of the tax system. By helping to maintain the demand for goods and services, indexing could weaken some downward influences on prices that might otherwise occur.

While there is much theoretical appeal to the argument that the current tax system stabilizes the economy during inflationary periods, recent studies suggest that this property is slight at best. One macroeconomic simulation of the Canadian income tax system, which resembles that of the United States, has shown it to have had relatively little ability to stabilize the Canadian economy before indexing was adopted, because inflation-caused tax increases tended to lag behind the beginning of a demand-induced surge in inflation. In addition, Canada's unindexed system was found to have a destabilizing influence once the initial surge in demand tapered off, because money incomes—and, thus, overall tax rates--continued to rise even after real incomes leveled off.[9] Another study, which simulated the macroeconomic effects of indexing the income tax in the United States, found that the resulting changes in tax liabilities had almost no effect on the economy's response to large inflationary shocks. The reason was that the magnitudes of the tax changes were very small relative to the overall demand consequences of these shocks.[10] Thus, this study suggests that whether or not the tax code is indexed may not have much overall macroeconomic significance. Both studies tend to weaken the argument that indexing would destabilize the economy by reducing the automatic rise in tax rates caused by inflation.

Proponents of indexing also contend that some of the arguments against indexing may be relevant only during a traditional inflation characterized by excess demand. They point out that when unexpected cost increases, such as a rise in oil prices, are responsible for inflation, an unindexed tax system tends to destabilize economic activity. When inflation of this sort occurs, economic activity tends to diminish because price increases outpace the rise in consumer money incomes. If the cost increases are reflected in higher incomes, the resulting increase in tax rates prevents after-tax income from "catching up" with higher prices. Indexing, by largely eliminating the increase in overall tax rates during periods of inflation, could neutralize this negative impact of the tax structure on economic activity.

Opponents of indexing also say it could generate inflation. Indexing could cause higher prices, for example, by allowing higher levels of consumer demand during periods of inflation. Indexing could also generate inflation if it were interpreted as a sign of government acquiescence to inflation, or as an admission of inability to cure it. Moreover, indexing might weaken popular support for price-restraint measures by insulating households from some of inflation's adverse consequences.

---

9. See John Bossons and Thomas A. Wilson, "Adjusting Tax Rates for Inflation," Canadian Tax Journal, vol. 21 (May-June 1973), pp. 185-199.

10. See James A. Pierce and Jared J. Enzler, "The Implications for Economic Stability of Indexing the Individual Income Tax," in Henry J. Aaron, ed., Inflation and the Income Tax (Brookings, 1976), pp. 173-194.

Advocates argue, however, that indexing could also have some anti-inflationary consequences. For one thing, it might help to restrain government spending by restricting the amount of available revenues in a given year, if the Congress wishes to limit the federal budget deficit. Moreover, if the income tax were indexed, workers might be willing to accept smaller money wage increases because they would know that the tax system would absorb much less of these increases. This reduction in wage demands appears to occur in Europe,[11] although the major studies of wage changes in the United States have not shown this to be true here.[12] With the persistence of inflation, however, workers in the United States may also come to require wage adjustments specifically to offset the tax effects of inflation. If this occurs, indexing could serve as a moderating influence. In that case, indexing could actually be, on balance, noninflationary or even anti-inflationary.

Econometric studies suggest that any inflationary consequences of indexing would be fairly small. Simulations performed for CBO on the Data Resources, Inc. (DRI) quarterly model and on the Wharton Econometric Forecasting Associates (Wharton) annual model found that over a period of three years, from 1979 to 1981, between 0.2 and 0.4 percentage points of the projected increase in

---

11. See D.A.L. Auld, "Taxation and Inflation: A Survey of Recent Theory and Empirical Evidence," Public Finance Quarterly, vol. 5 (October 1977), pp. 403-418.

12. See, for example, Robert J. Gordon, "Can the Inflation of the 1970s Be Explained?" Brookings Papers on Economic Activity, 1977:1, pp. 253-277, in which tax rates were found to have no statistically significant effect on the rate of wage inflation.

the Consumer Price Index could be traced to indexing.[13] These and other results can be criticized, however, because the available models do not incorporate any of the possible psychological effects of indexing on price or wage levels cited earlier. Thus, without more evidence, the net effect of indexing on inflation cannot be predicted.

Indexing Will Tend to "Lock In" the Existing Distribution of Tax Liabilities and Impede Other Tax Changes

A third argument often made against indexing is that the current tax system, with its automatic, disproportionate rise in tax revenues during inflationary periods, tends to promote Congressional review of the tax code by forcing tax cuts onto the Congressional agenda every two or three years, and by allowing adjustments to be made without the need for offsetting tax rate increases, spending cuts, or increases in the budget deficit. With tax revenues rising automatically, the Congress can alter tax expenditures and shift the distribution of tax burdens across income groups simply by enacting tax cuts in which some taxpayers receive larger reductions than others. Moreover, by failing to adjust a particular fixed-dollar tax provision during an inflationary period, the Congress implicitly allows the amount of taxable income shielded by the provision to decline. Thus, the present unindexed tax code tends to facilitate regular reviews of the various tax provisions.

---

13. To simulate indexing, overall income tax rates were decreased during the first quarter of the year, beginning in 1979, by the average annual change in the Consumer Price Index for the previous calendar year. DRI control simulations then assumed a $15 billion tax cut during the first quarter of 1981, including a personal tax cut of $7 billion, a $3 billion corporate tax cut, and a $5 billion decrease in Social Security taxes. The indexing simulation omitted the $7 billion cut in individual income taxes. The Wharton annual control solution included a $12.6 billion cut in personal and corporate taxes effective January 1980, of which $7.7 billion represented a reduction in personal income taxes. In addition, Wharton assumed the Social Security tax rate to remain at its 1979 value and the earnings base to rise by 7 percent per annum. The indexing simulation removed the $7.7 billion cut in personal taxes.

Indexing, by reducing the automatic rise in tax liabilities during inflationary periods, would limit the opportunities for this kind of informal review. Changes in the tax code might be less likely if tax reductions for some groups had to be offset by outright tax increases, rather than smaller money tax cuts, for others--again because of Congressional desires to limit the budget deficit. In addition, with no major tax cut legislation on the agenda, proponents of tax changes would lack a good vehicle for their proposals.

At the same time, these opportunities to review the tax system are, in a sense, a mixed blessing. With less need for ad hoc adjustments to keep up with inflation, legislators might have more time for other issues. Indexing might also reduce the instability and unpredictability involved in subjecting the tax code to broad-scale review every two or three years. Moreover, some would argue that many of the changes resulting from ad hoc reviews of the tax system may be undesirable. Ad hoc tax cuts, for example, can be used as vehicles for special interest tax changes that lack sufficient support to be enacted on their own.

The experience of several other countries with indexing systems shows that discretionary tax changes can still occur under indexing. Canada, Denmark, and the Netherlands have continued to make ad hoc changes after indexing.[14] It is noteworthy that the Congress has undertaken major structural reviews of the tax code during comparatively noninflationary periods (1954 and 1964, for example) when the automatic rise in overall tax rates from inflation was much smaller. In both 1954 and 1964, however, enactment of major tax changes was facilitated by economic growth, which allowed the Congress to reduce nearly everyone's tax liability.

It is not clear what impact indexing might have on tax expenditures by reducing the frequency of ad hoc tax cuts. Between 1967 and 1977, ad hoc tax changes tended to benefit low-income taxpayers relatively more, resulting in higher marginal tax rates for middle- and upper-income persons. For example, in 1967

---

14. For details, see the discussion on "Adjusting Personal Income Taxes: The Foreign Experience," in Henry J. Aaron, ed., Inflation and the Income Tax, p. 227. Critics of this view might argue, though, that Denmark and the Netherlands only partially index their tax systems and thus have more need to review their tax codes periodically.

less than one percent of all taxable returns had income taxed at the 40 percent marginal rate or above (see column 1 of Table 5). CBO estimates that in 1979 this figure climbed to nearly 6 percent (see column 3).[15] Taxpayers facing marginal rates such as these have made increasing use of specialized tax provisions originally expected to be used only by a few taxpayers in unusual circumstances.[16] Although adjustments were made in the rate structure in 1978, indexing the present system would still leave marginal rates at fairly high levels, thus preserving significant incentives to use tax expenditures. The revenue constraints imposed by indexing, however, might limit the creation of further tax expenditures, since under a constant budget deficit the money needed to fund these items would have to come from offsetting tax increases or reductions in existing spending programs.

* * *

15. These figures are similar to those presented in Donald W. Kiefer, "Inflation and the Federal Individual Income Tax," Inflation in 1980: A Survey of Selected Economic Issues, Congressional Research Service, Rept. No. 80-59E (April 9, 1980), p. 122.

16. The increased use of these provisions may also have had some adverse effect on savings and work incentives. For a further discussion of these issues, see Congressional Budget Office, An Analysis of the Roth-Kemp Tax Cut Proposal (October 1978), pp. 11-21.

CHAPTER IV. DESIGNING AN AUTOMATIC RATE STRUCTURE INDEXING SYSTEM: ISSUES AND OPTIONS

If the Congress decides to index the rate structure of the individual income tax, many ways for doing so are available. Countries that have adopted indexing have made different decisions about which tax code provisions to index, how much of the inflationary tax increases to offset automatically, and so on.[1] This chapter sets out some of the issues that would have to be decided and describes several of the options that are available. Among the issues covered are: which index to use in measuring inflation; which tax provisions to adjust; when to apply the indexing mechanism; and how much of the effects of inflation to offset.

INCOME- VERSUS COST-OF-LIVING-BASED INDEXES

Perhaps the first issue that must be resolved is what kind of index to use for measuring inflation. If the goal is to prevent the share of total personal income absorbed by taxes from rising solely as the result of inflation, some measure of the effects of inflation on incomes would seem most appropriate. If, on the other hand, the goal is to offset the effects of higher prices on taxpayers' real incomes, some measure of price increases or increases in the cost of living would be more effective.

An indexing plan may have both of these goals, of course, so the distinction is not as clear-cut as this analysis implies. In addition, the choice of an index is likely to turn to a large extent on such practical questions as the public's familiarity with a given index, the time required to compile it, and whether the index is revised retroactively. It may be helpful in making the choice, nonetheless, to consider briefly the differences between income- and cost-of-living-based indexes, and why one might be preferred to the other.

---

1. For a brief account of indexing systems in other countries, see Appendix C. These systems all provide tax adjustments only when prices increase--not in the event of a deflation.

Inflation is generally accompanied by higher money incomes. As prices rise, wages and salaries tend to be adjusted to keep up; but the process is not automatic, and not all incomes rise at exactly the rate of inflation. Looking only at the domestic economy, however, all increases in price show up in the form of higher incomes for someone, so the total of all incomes tends to rise at about the same rate as the total of all prices.[2] Thus, if the goal is to prevent the share of total incomes paid to the government in taxes from rising solely as the result of inflation, an index measuring the inflation-induced increase in total incomes would be appropriate.

The effect of inflation on the cost of living is more direct. Thus, if the goal is to maintain taxpayers' real, after-tax incomes, some measure of the effects of inflation on the prices most taxpayers pay would be the best index. This kind of cost-of-living "market basket" index could cover a narrower range of prices, however, than an income-based index.

Most countries that have indexed their tax systems have adopted a cost-of-living measure such as the Consumer Price Index (CPI) as their index of inflation.[3] This may have been dictated in part by convenience, because cost-of-living indexes typically are available and well known to most taxpayers. In addition, they have the advantage of already being in place and of being often used to make adjustments in income transfer programs.

If indexing is intended to prevent the ratio of income taxes to the nation's total income from rising, however, the use of

---

2. All income is not taxable, however, so broadly-based income indexes may overstate the effects of inflation on taxable income. In addition, not all taxable income is earned by U.S. taxpayers. A large portion of income from energy resources, for example, is received by foreign governments and individuals.

3. Detailed discussions of the foreign experience appear in Amalio H. Petrei, "Inflation Adjustment Schemes under the Personal Income Tax," *International Monetary Fund Staff Papers*, vol. 22 (July 1975), pp. 539-64; Vito Tanzi, *Inflation and the Personal Income Tax: An International Perspective* (Cambridge University Press, 1980), pp. 23-40; and *Studies on International Fiscal Law: Inflation and Taxation*, International Fiscal Association (Vienna, 1977).

cost-of-living measures may not be desirable for a number of reasons. First, this sort of index measures changes in the prices of goods and services consumed by households. While this covers about two-thirds of GNP, it does not directly reflect inflationary increases in wages, salaries, or other sources of income. In addition, some indexes like the CPI may not measure increases in the cost of living correctly, thus making it even more inaccurate as a measure of income increases. The CPI, for example, is adjusted only infrequently for changes in consumption patterns. It therefore probably overestimates the effects of energy price increases, since consumers are now reducing their consumption of energy in response to higher prices. The housing price component of the CPI is also distorted for a number of technical reasons during periods when prices escalate rapidly.[4] Finally, and perhaps most important over the long run, the CPI takes account of import price increases, which may be reflected only to a limited extent in domestic incomes. If indexing is intended only to keep overall tax rates from rising, including these price rises in the inflation index may cause an overadjustment of tax rates.

Several alternative measures have been proposed for indexing the income tax: the implicit price deflators[5] for gross national product (GNP), personal consumption expenditures (PCE), and national income (NI).[6] Like the CPI, these are available every quarter. Unlike the CPI, however, none of these takes account of the effects of imports on the U.S. economy. The GNP deflator registers the changes in the market value of all goods and services produced domestically or, equivalently, changes in the

---

4. For example, when housing prices escalate, current owners can use the increase to finance additional consumption by selling their homes and moving to less expensive units. Higher prices can thus reduce living expenses for some households. The CPI, however, counts all price increases as an increase in the cost of living.

5. Implicit price deflators are a family of price indexes for GNP and a number of its components. This kind of index is computed by taking the ratio of GNP (or a specific component) in current prices to GNP (or the specific component) valued in prices of a base year, currently 1972.

6. For an extensive discussion, see Edward F. Denison, "Price Series for Indexing the Income Tax System" in Henry J. Aaron, ed., Inflation and the Income Tax, pp. 232-269.

income derived from their production. The PCE deflator is similar to the CPI in that it is intended to measure changes in purchasing power of consumers. However, it avoids measuring imports and uses a current market basket to define consumption. The NI deflator, which measures inflationary (and deflationary) movements in total national income, is adjusted in a number of ways--for example, a deduction is made for indirect business taxes such as sales and property taxes--that allow it to approximate the income tax base more closely.[7]

Table 6 shows the annual rates of increase of the CPI since 1968 and compares these increases with those in the GNP, PCE, and NI deflators. In general, the average percentage rise in the CPI has exceeded that for the deflators by 0.3 to 0.7 percentage points each year, although for the more recent period since 1975 when housing and energy prices have risen rapidly the differences have been greater. Because the CPI has generally exceeded the rise in incomes during the present period of large increases in oil prices, using the CPI to index individual income taxes could actually reduce the percentage of total personal income paid in taxes, because tax provisions would be adjusted downward by more than the rise in taxable incomes. Thus, the PCE or the NI deflator might be a better indexing measure for keeping overall tax rates constant. The same general effect could be achieved by using the more widely-known GNP deflator, however, because the average increase in the GNP deflator has in the past several years been very similar to that for the other two deflators.

---

7. Many analysts prefer using a national income deflator to the GNP deflator for indexing an income tax because they contend that indexing should not be expected to offset legislated increases in indirect business (sales, property, and gross receipts) taxes. Under a system that adopted either the CPI or GNP deflator as an index, taxpayers would be compensated for such increases. It is largely for this reason that the government of the Netherlands chose an index equivalent to a national income deflator as part of its indexing procedure. The Dutch may also have chosen this index, however, to avoid incorporating the effects of higher import prices into their tax adjustment mechanism.

TABLE 6. ANNUAL PERCENTAGE CHANGES IN VARIOUS PRICE INDEXES, 1968-1979

Year	Consumer Price Index	Gross National Product Deflator	Personal Consumption Expenditure Deflator	National Income Deflator
1968	4.2	4.5	4.1	4.0
1969	5.4	5.0	4.6	4.6
1970	5.9	5.4	4.5	5.5
1971	4.3	5.1	4.4	5.0
1972	3.3	4.1	3.5	4.9
1973	6.2	5.8	5.5	6.5
1974	11.0	9.7	10.8	9.1
1975	9.1	9.6	8.1	9.3
1976	5.8	5.2	5.1	5.5
1977	6.5	6.0	5.7	6.3
1978	7.7	7.3	6.8	7.6
1979	11.3	8.8	8.9	9.1
Average				
1968-1979	6.7	6.4	6.0	6.4
1974-1979	8.6	7.8	7.6	7.8

One problem with using either the GNP deflator or one of its related indexes is that these measures are retroactively revised over a period of up to three years by the Commerce Department.[8] The size of any revision is usually small--under one percent--but with higher rates of inflation, the revisions could become larger. If this proved to be a problem, one solution might be to use the most current figure available at the time withholding tables had to be prepared, and then reflect any subsequent revision in the next year's adjustment. Alternatively, subsequent revisions could simply be ignored for purposes of the indexing system.

---

8. These revisions appear annually in the July issue of the Survey of Current Business published by the Commerce Department.

POINTS AND COUNTERPOINTS

1. In judging the very different trade-offs between efficiency and equity recommended by Arthur Okun and Walter Blum, consider the following quotation:

"[I]t is reasonable to expect that every gain, through taxation, in better distribution will be accompanied by some loss in production. The real problem of policy, thus, is that of weighing the one set of effects against the other.

"Two simple points should be noted at the outset. First, the effect of a higher degree of progression in taxation upon the distribution of income is certain; the effect upon production, problematical. One is a matter of arithmetic; the other, largely, of social psychology. Second, if reduction in the degree of inequality is a good, then the optimum degree of progression must involve a distinctly adverse effect upon the size of the national income. Prevailing opinion to the contrary notwithstanding, it is only an inadequate degree of progression which has no effect upon production and economic progress."

H. Simons, *Personal Income Taxation* (1938), p. 19.

2. Assuming that the tax system should redistribute income in favor of the poor, who should bear the burden of that policy? All taxpayers in proportion to their income, as Walter Blum implicitly suggests, or those with above average incomes, as implicitly suggested by Arthur Okun and Robert McIntyre and recommended by The New Zealand Task Force on Tax Reform?

3. Economists have sometimes argued that steeply progressive rates tend to reduce risk taking. But recent studies challenge this view. *See* Schneider, "The Effects of Progressive and Proportional Income Taxation on Risk Taking," 33 *National Tax Journal* 67 (1980).

4. American citizens, through their government, control a valuable asset—the distribution and production network that makes it possible for capitalists to reap large rewards in the marketplace. Should those who defend the distribution of goods and services produced by market forces also defend the right of the citizenry to "rent" its production and distribution asset to capitalists at whatever rate (in progressive taxes) the market will bear? What kind of tax system would result from a policy of taxing according to market principles?

5. In evaluating the relative merits of regressive and progressive rates, consider the following statement of the so-called "trickle down theory":

> "For liberals concerned with the distribution of income, moreover, the Laffer curve offers a promise as seductive as any of the Keynesian strictures against austerity and thrift. Regressive taxes help the poor! It has become increasingly obvious that a less progressive tax structure is necessary to reduce the tax burden on the lower and middle classes. When rates are lowered in the top brackets, the rich consume less and invest more. Their earnings rise and they pay more taxes in absolute amounts. Thus the lower and middle classes need pay less to sustain a given level of government services."

G. Gilder, *Wealth and Poverty* (1981), p. 188.

6. The jury is still out on the impact of progressive rates on the level of savings. But there is little doubt that high rates imposed on a narrow base will cause taxpayers to choose lightly taxed investment areas over highly taxed areas, thereby reducing the redistributive effect of the tax and the size of national income available for redistribution. Thus all advocates of progressive rates should also favor a tax base that includes all (or none) of the yield from investment activities in income. Preferences for certain uses of income, such as charitable gifts and medical expenditures, arguably have less impact on redistributive policies, since taxpayers who want to avoid high tax rates will invest in tax-free securities to the extent of their assets but probably will not run up medical bills or give all their money away just for tax purposes. Of course this is not true for the many tax shelter abuses of the charitable deduction and is not true for phony medical costs.

7. Most flat-tax advocates assert that without progression, the thorny family taxation issues addressed in Chapter VII would disappear. In support of their position, they note that because a flat tax imposes the same tax on all income, it matters not (at least to the fisc) who the taxpayer is on an item of income. They would be largely correct if their flat tax were intended to be a flat-rate excise tax on all income sources (and all family members pooled all their income). But all flat-rate advocates recommend that the income tax remain a personal tax that adjusts for individual circumstances. In fact, they do not actually recommend a single-bracket tax, but instead favor a two-bracket tax, the first bracket being the zero bracket. Once the rate structure includes a zero bracket, the theoretical problem of

whom to tax on income earned by one family member and spent for the benefit of another remains undiminished. Nor is this problem solved by structuring low-income relief in the form of deductions and/or credits; on the contrary, such disguises for zero-bracket relief merely complicate the analysis of family taxation issues.

8. Redistributive policies ultimately rest on a belief in the unfairness of the distribution of marketplace rewards. When is the distribution produced by the market least defensible? Consider the following pairs of taxpayers and decide whether society should attempt to preserve or mitigate the differences in their material well-being:

—A–1 and A–2 both earn $8 per hour but A–1 works 60 hours a week and A–2 works only 40 hours per week;

—B–1 and B–2 both dig for gold, but B–1 is lucky and hits a $1 million vein while B–2 finds nothing;

—C–1 and C–2 both work equally hard and invest equal time and money in training, but C–1 is much smarter and makes a lot more money than C–2;

—D–1 works diligently and makes a good salary, but D–2 is the son of a multi-millionaire, who uses her connections to push D–2 into the big time;

—E–1 makes huge profits clubbing baby seals to death and selling their pelts, while E–2 earns a modest wage as a forest ranger in a state park.

9. How do the economic consequences of progression compare to those of a flat-rate tax that raises an equal amount of revenue? Is a rich man likely to spend more and work less in the face of high marginal progressive rates? Or is he likely to spend less and work more in order to recoup the loss in after-tax income resulting from higher average rates? How is a low-income taxpayer likely to respond to the lower marginal and average rates of tax he would pay in a progressive tax system? Assuming some net loss in savings from progression, how could the government recoup that loss without offending the fairness standards that motivated the imposition of progressive rates? Why have economists expended considerable energy attempting to estimate the response of taxpayers to changes in marginal tax rates and almost none to estimate the impact on taxpayer behavior of changes in average tax rates?

10. Is the reason for indexing the rate structure largely procedural—to force an explicit vote on tax increases? Which groups would have done better with indexing over the past dec-

ade and which did better from the periodic adjustments in rates enacted by Congress? Given the distribution of discretionary tax cuts in recent years, should the business community favor indexing? What should labor's position be? What other organized groups have an important interest in the indexing issue?

11. Do labor and business have conflicting interests in the choice of the price index used in making automatic adjustments in the rate structure?

III. TAX EXPENDITURES

The core function of the federal income tax is to raise revenue for government spending programs in accord with popular notions of distributive justice. Many provisions of the Internal Revenue Code, however, have little to do with justice or revenue raising; indeed, their purpose is to reduce revenue otherwise collected in order to promote some exogenous social or economic goal. Such provisions have acquired a variety of labels—tax incentives, tax loopholes, tax preferences, tax subsidies, "special" tax provisions, tax aids, and tax expenditures. In the late 1960's Treasury officials compiled a list of the tax provisions which they believed were unrelated to the core function of the income tax and estimated the "cost" of these provisions in forgone revenue. They called the resulting document a "Tax Expenditure Budget." They hoped that their work would encourage Congress to subject these "tax expenditures" to the budget review procedures it traditionally applied to the review of functionally related direct expenditure programs.

The first selection below explains the intended functions of a tax expenditure budget and elaborates the criteria for identifying tax expenditures that the Treasury Department employed during the Johnson, Nixon, Ford and Carter Administrations and which Congress and most academics still employ. The authors of that selection have played a central role in the development and institutionalization of the tax expenditure concept. As Assistant Secretary of the Treasury for Tax Policy during the Kennedy and Johnson Administrations, Stanley Surrey directed the research which led to the publication of the Treasury Department's first tax expenditure budget in 1968.

The second selection, from the 1984 Federal Budget, sets forth an alternative to the definitional methodology advocated by Stanley Surrey and Paul McDaniel. The most striking feature of this alternative methodology is that it excludes from the list of tax expenditures the "excess" depreciation permitted under the accelerated cost recovery system (ACRS) adopted in 1981 by Congress as the centerpiece of the Reagan Administration's economic recovery program. The third selection, written by Michael McIntyre, suggests a methodology for identifying tax expenditures that avoids the theoretical difficulties that otherwise confront commentators in unambiguously separating revenue raising provisions from disguised spending programs. The final selection, by Robert McIntyre, discusses some of the political problems that an unsophisticated use of the tax expenditure concept can create for tax reform advocates.

Supplemental Readings. Congressional Budget Office, *Tax Expenditures: Current Issues and Five-Year Budget Projections for Fiscal Years 1982–1986* (1981); "Part Two: The Concept of Tax Expenditures," *The Economics of Taxation* (H. Aaron and M. Boskin, eds., 1980) (Articles by J. Brannon, M. Feldstein, and S. Surrey & P. McDaniel); Surrey and McDaniel, "The Tax Expenditure Concept and the Budget Reform Act of 1974," 17 *Boston College Industrial and Commercial Law Reviews* 679 (1976); R. Smith, *Tax Expenditures: An Examination of Tax Incentives and Tax Preferences in the Canadian Federal Income Tax System* (1979); Bittker, "Accounting for Federal Tax Subsidies in the National Budget," 22 *National Tax Journal* 244 (1971).

STANLEY S. SURREY & PAUL R. McDANIEL, "THE TAX EXPENDITURE CONCEPT: CURRENT DEVELOPMENTS AND EMERGING ISSUES"

20 Boston College Law Review 225 (1979), pp. 226–42, 253–63.

INTRODUCTION

In 1968, the Treasury Department published its first "tax expenditure" budget.[1] Only six years later, the Congressional Budget Act of 1974 made the concept of tax expenditures an integral part of a new congressional budget process. Pursuant to that Act, the 1975 Budget contained a "Special Analysis" entitled "Tax Expenditures,"[2] and all subsequent Budgets have included a similar tabulation. In 1976, both the House and the Senate Budget Committees established a targeted amount of reduction in tax expenditures as a goal of tax reform legislation and this step was a material factor in the

---

[1] ANNUAL REPORT OF THE SECRETARY OF THE TREASURY ON THE STATE OF THE FINANCES FOR FISCAL YEAR 1968, 326-40 (1969) [hereinafter cited as 1968 ANNUAL TREASURY REPORT].

[2] BUDGET OF THE UNITED STATES GOVERNMENT, 1976, Special Analysis F at 101 (1975). See also Special Analysis F in subsequent annual Budget Documents. For the Fiscal Year 1979 Budget this material is in Special Analysis G [the Special Analyses

passage of the Tax Reform Act of 1976.[3] In 1977, the President, in assembling material for his consideration of changes in the tax system, asked the Treasury for a detailed report on the desirability of each item listed in the tabulation of tax expenditures. In 1977 and 1978, the Congress, in its continuing search for ways to make the ever-growing federal budget manageable, again recognized, as it had in 1974, that it must grapple with the role played by tax expenditures. The principal occasions for congressional analysis of tax expenditures were the consideration of "sunset" review for federal programs[4] and the question of the jurisdiction of the Senate Appropriations Committee over "refundable" tax expenditure credits.[5]

These events, along with developments at the state and international levels,[6] evidence a rapid and expanding recognition of the role that the tax expenditure concept plays both in tax policy issues and in budget policy issues. Indeed, once the presence of tax expenditures in a tax system is focused upon, there is a general awareness that unless attention is paid to those tax expenditures, a country has neither its tax policy nor its budget policy under full control. This awareness in turn opens up new facets of the concept of tax expenditures, and leads to new insights in the ways the concept affects the substance of fiscal policy and the political processes by which such policy is formulated. The purpose of this article is to describe current developments and emerging issues concerning the tax expenditure concept.[7]

I. CONCEPTUAL ISSUES

A. *Definition of Tax Expenditure*

1. Background

Essentially, the tax expenditure concept, as applied to an income tax, regards such a tax as composed of two distinct elements. The first element con-

---

are hereinafter cited as 1976, 1977, or 1978 Special Analysis F, respectively, and 1979 Special Analysis G].

[3] *See* Surrey, *Reflections on the Tax Reform Act of 1976*, 25 CLEV. ST. L. REV. 303 (1976), *reprinted in* 6 TAX NOTES No. 12 at 291 (March 12, 1978).

[4] See Part V.D *infra*.

[5] See Part V.B.1 *infra*.

[6] In 1976, California by statute directed that a report on tax expenditures be included in the Governor's Budget. 1976 Cal. Stats. ch. 575. In 1971, the state by statute had directed the Department of Finance to prepare a biennial tax expenditure report. 1971 Cal. Stats. ch. 1762.

In 1976 and 1977, the two major international tax organizations chose the concept of tax expenditures as a principal subject for their annual meetings—the International Fiscal Association at its 1976 Jerusalem Congress, INTERNATIONAL FISCAL ASSOCIATION, GENERAL REPORT, TAX INCENTIVES AS AN INSTRUMENT FOR ACHIEVEMENT OF GOVERNMENT GOALS, LXIa CAHIERS DE DROIT FISCAL (Jerusalem Congress, 1976) [hereinafter cited as IFA 1976 Congress], and the International Institute of Public Finance at its 1977 Varna Congress, INTERNATIONAL INSTITUTE OF PUBLIC FINANCE, SUBSIDIES, TAX RELIEFS AND PRICES (Varna Congress, 1977) (to be published) [hereinafter cited as IIPF 1977 Congress].

[7] This article covers primarily developments in the period 1976 to 1978 and is a companion piece to a previous article which had the same purpose for the period from 1974 to early 1976. *See* Surrey & McDaniel, *The Tax Expenditure Concept and the Budget Reform Act of 1974*, 17 B.C. IND. & COM. L. REV. 679 (1976).

tains the structural provisions necessary for implementation of a normal income tax. These structural provisions include the definition of net income; the specification of accounting periods; the determination of the entities subject to tax; and the specification of the rate schedule and exemption levels. These provisions compose the revenue raising aspects of the tax. The second element consists of the special preferences found in every income tax system. These special preferences, often called tax incentives or tax subsidies, are departures from the normal tax structure, designed to favor a particular industry, activity, or class of persons. Tax subsidies partake of many forms, such as permanent exclusions from income, deductions, deferrals of tax liabilities, credits against tax, or special rates. Whatever their form, these departures from the "normative" income tax structure essentially represent government spending for the favored activities or groups through the tax system rather than through direct grants, loans, or other forms of government assistance.

Put differently, whenever government decides to favor an activity or group through monetary assistance, it may elect from a wide range of methods in delivering that assistance. Direct assistance may take the form of a government grant or subsidy, a government loan, perhaps at a special interest rate, or a private loan guaranteed by the government. Instead of direct assistance, the government may work within the income tax system to reduce the tax otherwise owed by a favored activity or group. Examples of this indirect government assistance are investment credits, special depreciation deductions, deductions for special forms of consumption, or low rates of tax for certain activities. These tax reductions, in effect monetary assistance provided by the government, represent tax expenditures.[8]

Most tax expenditures are readily recognizable since they are usually treated by their supporters as tax incentives or as hardship relief, and they are not urged as necessary to correct defects in the income tax structure itself. The Treasury Department, in establishing the first tax expenditure tabulation in 1968, basically utilized the general economic definition of income—the increase in net economic wealth between two points in time plus consumption during that period. The Treasury modified this general definition by adding a reference to the "generally accepted structure of an income tax." The modification had the narrow, explicitly described function of excluding from the category of tax expenditures certain nontaxable items which economists would cover under the general economic definition of income but which historically have not been regarded as essential aspects of the structure of the Sixteenth Amendment income tax. These nontaxable items include such things as unrealized appreciation in the value of an asset and income imputed from an asset (for example, rental income imputed from ownership of a house). With the exception of its reference to the "generally accepted structure of an income tax," the Treasury closely followed the general economic definition of income. Thus, it included as tax expenditures those provisions allowing deductions for personal consumption items or other items not incurred in the

---

[8] *See generally* Surrey & McDaniel, *supra* note 7, at 679-80.

earning or production of income. As to the "timing" criteria for defining income for the taxable period, the Treasury referred to widely accepted "standards of business accounting" used to determine income for financial reports.[9]

---

[9] *See* Surrey & McDaniel, *supra* note 7, at 683. The definitional process was described for an international audience in Address by Stanley Surrey, The Concept of Tax Reliefs—Its Relation to Tax Policy and Budget Policy, IIPF 1977 Congress, *supra* note 6 (the 1977 Varna Congress used the term "tax relief" interchangeably with "tax expenditure" and in the excerpt below "tax expenditure" has been substituted for "tax relief" in several places).

Tax expenditure analysis is based on the concept of a normal or normative tax of the type under consideration. This paper focuses on the income tax and hence discusses the normal structure of such a tax. But the analysis is appropriate to any broad based tax intended to have a general application, as a consumption tax (such as a retail sales tax or a value added tax, or a progressive expenditure tax), a death tax, a general property tax, or a wealth tax. In terms of the income tax, the normative structure involves the determination of the base of the tax (net income); the accounting period; the taxable unit; and the rate schedule, including personal exemption levels. In the United States' analysis of tax expenditures, the normative concept of net income is the general economic definition of income under the "Haig-Simons" approach, i.e. increase in net economic wealth between two points of time plus consumption during that period. "Consumption" is broadly applied, and in essence covers all expenditures except those incurred as a cost in the earning or production of income and hence are proper offsets to gross income to arrive at taxable net income. Since the Haig-Simons approach does not identify appropriate accounting techniques, resort in establishing a normal structure is made to widely-accepted "standards of business accounting" used to determine income for financial reports. The application of these economic and accounting norms is then tempered by also referring to the "generally accepted structure of an income tax." This reference, it was pointed out, excluded as normative the inclusion of unrealized appreciation in asset values and of imputed income from homes or other assets, since in the United States, and largely elsewhere, these items are not commonly regarded as income for tax purposes though they fall within the economic definition of income.

The taxable unit is not defined by the Haig-Simons defintion nor is there a normative concept of that unit. Rather, the choice of taxable unit—e.g., how to tax single persons versus married persons, working spouses as against non-working spouses, and the family in general—is regarded as a policy issue wider than tax policy per se and embracing a country's attitudes toward marriage, women in general, women in the work force, etc. Also the rate schedule itself is not a normative concept. Instead such matters as how progressive the rates should be or at what starting point in the income scale the rates should generally apply are matters for fiscal policy to determine. While factors such as the taxable unit or a rate schedule are necessary to the structure of an income tax, their particular determination—unlike the determination of the tax base and the accounting techniques to identify the net income of a given period—are not part of a normative concept of the income tax. However, once a general rate schedule is decided upon as a matter of fiscal policy, a special variation in that rate intended to confer a special tax benefit becomes a departure from a normal structure. But a general reduction of tax rates would not be a tax expenditure—though it would be relief from taxes.

The basic Treasury formulation of the tax expenditure concept and of the criteria utilized in classifying tax expenditures has stood up quite well as both the concept and the classification criteria have obtained wider application and consequently wider scrutiny. Using this formulation, technicians in the executive branch and in Congress charged with preparing the annual tabulation of tax expenditures have been able to maintain a high degree of consistency and uniformity in approach, even when faced with the need to classify a constant stream of legislative changes in the income tax. Although the Budget Act of 1974 required a legislative definition of the term "tax expenditure," since a number of operative provisions of that Act utilize the term,[10] this def-

> Essentially, then, the concept of a normal (or normative) income tax to be used in identifying tax expenditures is one of applying a general rate schedule (determined under fiscal policy) against a taxable unit's (determined under fiscal and social policy) net income base—with that base ascertained by including all items of gross income and deducting all expenditures associated with the earning or production of that income, with capital expenditures allocated over time in accordance with generally accepted accounting practices. This analysis extends to both the corporation income tax and the individual income tax. The norm, however, does not specify any particular general relationship between these two taxes, and thus does not specify a classical corporate tax structure, a completely integrated corporate tax, or a partially integrated corporate tax. However, once given a country's general choice of a corporate tax-individual income tax relationship, then special departures from that choice can be tax expenditures. (The United States tax expenditure analysis is made against the background of the present classical separation of the two taxes.) The analysis also does not specify whether the determination of the tax base is in terms of nominal accounts or in terms of inflation-adjusted accounts. However, here also, once a clear choice is made, any special departure can be a tax expenditure. Thus an approach that would adjust the cost of an asset for inflation in computing gain or depreciation but fail to make an adjustment in the real cost of funds borrowed to acquire the asset would be effecting only a partial or preferential change to reflect inflation and would thus involve a tax expenditure. (In the United States, tax expenditure analysis is made against the background of the present general nominal dollar determination of the base.) The "indexing" of the rate schedule for inflation is not a tax expenditure, since the shape of the rate schedule itself is not involved in the normative structure and hence a decision to change rate brackets because of inflation is equally outside the analysis.
>
> It will be seen that the essential aspect of the definition of a normal income tax is the determination of the net income base allocated to the particular yearly accounting period utilized to compute tax liabilities. Generally speaking, in countries using a broadly-applied modern income tax, the determination of that base is not a matter on which informed fiscal experts would exhibit much disagreement if their function were solely to establish a normative structure.

[10] For a description of the operative tax expenditure provisions in the Budget Act of 1974, Pub. L. No. 93-344, 88 Stat. 297 [hereinafter cited as Budget Act], see Surrey & McDaniel, *supra* note 7, at 683-84. Examples of these operative provisions include the requirement in section 601 that the President include tax expenditures in his annual Budget, and the requirement in section 708(a) that committees reporting bills which provide for new or increased tax expenditures include statements concerning the effect of the bill on current levels of tax expenditures and a five-year projection of the revenue effect of the change.

inition has not proved helpful. The language used by the drafters to define tax expenditure indicates their problem in capturing the concept in statutory words: "[tax expenditures are those] revenue losses attributable to provisions of the Federal tax laws which allow a special exclusion, exemption, or deduction from gross income or which provide a special credit, a preferential rate of tax, or a deferral of tax liability . . . ."[11] The word "special" is not explicit enough to carry the definition, and the legislative history essentially resorted to references to existing tax expenditure tabulations to convey the congressional intent. The government technicians therefore have generally followed the original Treasury formulation, and, as stated above, have found that formulation sufficient to handle legislative tax changes and other matters.[12] The fiscal 1977-1979 tax expenditure lists are set forth in Appendix A.

There remains in some discussions of tax expenditures the feeling that the concept somehow implies that the government is entitled to a taxpayer's entire income and that the enumerated tax expenditures, instead of being regarded as subsidies, should be seen as examples of governmental restraint in not taxing all of that income.[13] But clearly, the tax expenditure concept

---

[11] Budget Act, *supra* note 10, § 3(a)(3).

[12] Tabulations of tax expenditures are to be found in the following documents, so far published annually: BUDGET OF THE UNITED STATES GOVERNMENT, Special Analyses (see *supra* note 2); CONGRESSIONAL BUDGET OFFICE, FIVE-YEAR BUDGET PROJECTIONS, SUPPLEMENT ON TAX EXPENDITURES [hereinafter cited as CBO TAX EXPENDITURE TABULATION]; STAFF OF JOINT COMM. ON TAXATION, ESTIMATES OF FEDERAL TAX EXPENDITURES (annual) [hereinafter cited as JOINT COMM. ESTIMATES]. *See also* SENATE BUDGET COMM., 94TH CONG., 2D SESS., TAX EXPENDITURES: A COMPENDIUM OF BACKGROUND MATERIAL ON INDIVIDUAL PROVISIONS (Comm. Print March 17, 1976) [hereinafter cited as S. BUDGET COMM. COMPENDIUM], and 95TH CONG., 2D SESS., TAX EXPENDITURES: RELATIONSHIPS TO SPENDING PROGRAMS AND BACKGROUND MATERIAL ON INDIVIDUAL PROVISIONS (Comm. Print September 1978). The 1977 CBO TAX EXPENDITURE TABULATION, *supra*, contains in Appendix a brief description of each item listed; the 1979 Special Analysis G also contains such descriptions.

While earlier Budget Special Analyses differed from congressional tax expenditure lists in not including deferral of tax on the income of controlled foreign corporations, the asset depreciation range, and capital gains at death, 1979 Special Analysis G includes these items. The functional categories are now identical with those used in the congressional lists.

[13] The homey example used by Chairman Long in his testimony on S. 2, *The Sunset Act of 1977, Hearings on S. 2 Before the Subcomm. on Intergovernmental Relations of the Senate Comm. on Governmental Affairs*, 95th Cong., 1st Sess. 468-69 (1977) [hereinafter cited as *Hearings on the Sunset Act of 1977*], illustrates this point. Chairman Long states:

> Some people would like to say, since we put a top tax bracket at 70 percent on individual income, that theoretically, the Government owns 70 percent of everything you make. That being the case, they would like to assume that an individual is getting some sort of tax advantage or escaping something if he fails to pay that 70 percent of his income. You could just as well take the same attitude about the personal exemptions, although they don't necessarily do that. So you can define "tax expenditure" however you want to do it. You may include one thing and I include another—it makes me think of this situation:
>
> > You could say that I saved 40 cents, because, instead of taking a bus downtown, I decided that I would walk. But you could just as

merely states that if *only* an "income tax" is desired and no other social or economic objectives are sought, such a tax should reach fully the normative scope of "net income." Whether that net income base is taxed at rates that are high or low is a decision apart from tax expenditure analysis. A deliberate decision to exclude certain items from that base because of particular social or economic goals becomes a tax subsidy since the conceded base of the tax has not been followed. As the Congressional Budget Office appropriately describes:

> [A] tax expenditure is analogous to an entitlement program on the spending side of the budget; the amount expended is not subject to any legislated limit but is dependent solely upon taxpayer response to the particular provision. In this respect, tax expenditures closely resemble spending programs that have no ceiling.[14]

This view of tax expenditures is becoming clearer as discussion in the area proceeds, although some still attempt to make debating points based on the "all income belongs to the government" syndrome.[15]

2. Classification of Legislative Changes

As to fiscal 1979, all three tax expenditures lists—Special Analysis G in the President's Budget, the Congressional Budget Office Tax Expenditure

---

easily say that I saved $1.50, because I could have hired a taxicab to go down there. Or you could say I saved $50 because I seriously considered taking a limousine, and that would have cost me 50 bucks.

Now that type of logic is implicit all through this argument about tax expenditures.

Clearly the Chairman understands the concept and his example is but a debating point. Compare Chairman Long's statements, for example, in *Tax Reform Act of 1975: Hearings on H.R. 10612 Before the Senate Comm. on Finance*, 94th Cong., 2d Sess. 191, 503, 1637, 1664-65, 2404 (1976), that some provisions clearly are tax expenditures. In his above example, one could of course find a norm for a given individual and the "saving" would be readily measurable, though different if individuals had differing norms as presumably they would. But the income tax has but one normative base. The tax expenditure saving does vary with an individual's rate bracket, but that is simply an aspect that demonstrates a problem—and generally a defect—in utilizing a tax expenditure device to provide government assistance.

For examples of the mistaken view that the tax expenditure concept implies that all income belongs to the Government, see Friedman, *What Belongs to Whom?*, Newsweek, March 13, 1978, at 71; Stutsman, Brookes, Jewett and McCaskey, *Tax Reform, reprinted in* 123 CONG. REC. E3538-39 (daily ed. June 6, 1977) (statement of Rep. Goldwater); Smith, *Taxation of Capital in a Political Economy*, 38 TAX FOUNDATION'S TAX REV. No. 7, 25 (July 1977); I. KRISTOL, TWO CHEERS FOR CAPITALISM 208 (1978).

[14] 1977 CBO TAX EXPENDITURE TABULATION, *supra* note 12, at 1.

[15] As discussed *infra* in text at notes 310-28, an amendment to the Revenue Act of 1978 was offered by Senator Glenn to subject tax expenditures to a "sunset process." During the course of the debate on that amendment, several members of the Senate Finance Committee opposed the amendment in part on the rhetorical assertion that the tax expenditure concept implies that all income belongs to the government. *See, e.g.,* the remarks of Senators Bentsen and Hansen, at 124 CONG. REC. S17494, 17760 (daily eds. Oct. 7 and 9, 1978). Senator Long, ever resourceful in debate, produced a new image:

Tabulation in its Five-Year Budget Projections, and the Estimates of Tax Expenditures prepared by the Staff of the Joint Committee on Taxation—agree on which provisions of the tax code constitute tax expenditures.[16] With each new piece of tax legislation, however, new classification issues emerge. For example, the Tax Reduction and Simplification Act of 1977 combined the minimum standard deduction (the low income allowance) and the regular standard deduction into a zero bracket amount in the rate scale, and defined itemized deductions in terms of the excess over the zero bracket amount. These changes eliminated the standard deduction from the list of tax expenditures. The zero bracket amount is now regarded as a part of the rate schedule; it is essentially a transformation of the minimum standard deduction into the rate schedule. The various itemized deductions remain, and their amounts are to be estimated by reference to the "floor" of the zero bracket amount.[17]

Looking ahead, welfare reform legislation may affect the list of tax expenditures. For example, the present tax expenditure lists include the exclu-

---

    In my left hand I hold a big cigar, which I borrowed from a friend. It is an object of value.

    I hold in my other hand a pencil. The Congress thought about the matter and decided to put a tax on the cigar, so we pay a tax on the cigar, and that results in some revenue for the Government. We once had a tax on pencils, but we took the tax off pencils, so the pencil bears no tax and the cigar does.

    To apply [Senator Glenn's] argument to the cigar and the pencil, pencil users are being provided an unjust advantage because they are not paying the same tax we pay on cigars. Congress thought about what it wanted to tax and it said, "We want to tax the cigar." But to use the Senator's argument, the Government is losing a fantastic amount of money because the tax we have on the cigar does not apply to a pencil.

124 CONG. REC. S17491-92 (daily ed. Oct. 7, 1978).

    Chairman Long confuses the issue by selecting metaphorically different tax bases. If the tax base is cigars (*i.e.*, income), no tax expenditures result *within that tax* from the failure to tax pencils (*i.e.*, net wealth). In contrast, if the tax is on cigars (income), but one-half the tax is deferred on cigars manufactured by small business to encourage their growth (small corporation income tax rates), a tax expenditure is present within the tax. *See* S. SURREY, PATHWAYS TO TAX REFORM 27 (1973), discussing the application of tax expenditure analysis to excise taxes.

    [16] The Congressional Budget Office stated that the 1976 Tax Reform Act involved forty-one tax expenditure changes. While most of the changes resulted in increases or decreases in existing tax expenditures, some tax expenditures were dropped and others were added. The items *dropped or phased out* were: exclusion of gross-up on dividends of LDC corporations; special rate for Western Hemisphere trade corporations; credit for purchases of new homes; five-year amortization of railroad rolling stock; five-year amortization for employer child care facilities.

    The items *added* were: tax incentives for preservation of historic structures; contributions in aid of construction for certain utilities; credit (instead of deduction) for child and dependent care expenses; deduction for eliminating in buildings, etc., barriers for the handicapped; exclusion of contributions to prepaid legal services plans; employee stock ownership plans (ESOPs) funded through investment tax credits. *See* 1977 CBO TAX EXPENDITURE TABULATION, *supra* note 12, at Table 2 and the descriptive material in 1979 Special Analysis G.

    [17] See the discussion of estimates in the text at notes 28-29 *infra*.

sions from taxable income of government direct cash payments, such as social security payments and unemployment insurance payments. Yet, the tax expenditure lists do not include the government benefits in kind, such as food stamps, which are also excluded from taxable income. This difference in approach has been previously mentioned in the Special Analyses in the President's Budget as an aspect that may require reexamination. Where the benefits in kind closely resemble cash payments, as in the case of food stamps, so that problems of measurement are not really involved, it appears that their exclusion from taxable income should be considered a tax expenditure. The 1968 Treasury decision to exclude as a tax expenditure the non-inclusion in taxable income of the imputed income from homes and personal property did not really explore how that decision affected government services generally, or more particularly, government in-kind transfer programs.[18] Furthermore, it is not clear that the "equivalent of cash" characterization which may fit food stamps would apply to any other in-kind program. Perhaps the discussion of welfare reform will clarify the area. Presumably in that discussion it will be necessary to determine whether conversion to monetary terms of existing government in-kind programs must itself be included in taxable income. The decision on that issue and the grounds advanced to support the decision may also clarify views regarding the treatment in the tax expenditure budget of remaining in-kind programs.

The 1978 changes in the corporate tax rate structure present an emerging classification issue. To date, all tax expenditure budgets have treated the corporate surtax exemption as a tax expenditure, while regarding the corporate tax as a flat rate tax. The lower rates, provided within the corporate surtax exemption range, traditionally were justified as aids to small business and, accordingly, were included in tax expenditure lists. In the Revenue Act of 1978, the existing "normal tax" and "surtax" structure was repealed and replaced by a five-step rate structure on corporate taxable income, with rates ranging from 17 to 46 percent. Concerning this change, the Ways and Means Committee Report stated: "With respect to business taxpayers, the basic corporate tax structure is changed and taxes are reduced, but the Committee does not consider a new tax structure to be a tax expenditure, even though the change reduces tax liabilities. The Congressional Budget Office does not agree."[19] In some respects, the Ways and Means Committee justification of the changed rate structure is consistent with its view that the change simply implemented a new rate system for corporations. The Committee was concerned that the former "abrupt jump in tax rates" from 22 to 48 percent was undesirable. Moreover, it argued that the new system of graduated rates would reduce the impact of the tax provisions on a small business' selection of operating form.

These arguments appear to be structural rather than tax expenditure justifications. Nevertheless, the Committee also stated that it was making the

---

[18] 1968 ANNUAL TREASURY REPORT, *supra* note 1.
[19] H.R. REP. No. 1445, 95th Cong., 2d Sess. 143 (1978). The Senate Finance Committee took the same position. S. REP. No. 1263, 95th Cong., 2d Sess. 253 (1978).

change because tax relief was "especially needed for small companies."[20] The "small business" aspect was highlighted by the Committee decision to halt the progression of the rates at $100,000 of taxable income, since 78 percent of corporate net income and 93 percent of corporate taxes are attributable to corporate income above $100,000. And, despite the Committee's statement, the tables on changes in tax expenditures provided in the Committee Reports treat the revenue loss from the lower corporate rates on the first $100,000 of taxable income as a tax expenditure.[21]

The 1978 changes in corporate rate structure do present an interesting conceptual issue. Certainly, tax expenditure analysis does not imply that a country can only adopt a flat rate corporate tax. Progressive rates traditionally have not been applied to corporations since a progressive rate schedule has largely been justified on "ability to pay" concepts, a concept that has little relevance to corporations. A country could choose, however, to have a truly graduated and progressive rate scale for corporations. But the 1978 legislation does not represent such a scheme. As noted above, the benefits of the new rate schedule are largely confined to "small business" because of the failure to extend the five-step rate schedule farther up the income scale. Moreover, the changes amount to only a $7,750 reduction in tax impact on the first $100,000 of income. This seems a relatively minor revenue change and not significant enough to take the five-step corporate tax rates out of the tax expenditure category in which the present two-step system is classified. On balance, we are therefore of the view that classification of the graduated rate system for corporations as a tax expenditure program for small business would be correct.

A renewed interest in the "integration" of the corporate and individual income taxes could present a classification problem if legislation integrating the two taxes were to develop. Budget Special Analysis G stated in 1978:

> *Treatment of individuals and corporations as separate tax-paying entities.*—A theoretically pure income tax would integrate the taxation of individual and corporate income to avoid multiple taxation of any particular type of income. Only individuals would be taxed; corporate income would be taxed to shareholders, whether or not it was distributed in the form of dividends. However, *for practical reasons*, separate taxation is accepted as part of the normal tax structure for purposes of this analysis.[22]

In contrast, the Treasury analysis in 1968 simply stated that "[t]he assumption inherent in current law, that corporations are separate entities and subject to income taxation independently from their shareholders, is adhered to in this analysis."[23] The Treasury analysis thus did not determine whether a "theoretically pure income tax" would integrate the two taxes. If the "practical

---

[20] H.R. REP. No. 1445, *supra* note 19, at 79. The Senate Finance Committee Report emphasized the "small business" thrust of the new rate schedule even more heavily. S. REP. No. 1263, *supra* note 19, at 110.

[21] S. REP. No. 1263, *supra* note 19, at 144.

[22] 1979 Special Analysis G at 152 (emphasis added).

[23] 1968 ANNUAL TREASURY REPORT, *supra* note 1.

reasons" mentioned in Special Analysis G extend to the fact that economists and others are not agreed on the "pure" treatment of corporate and individual income taxes, and that a country therefore may choose among various relationships between these taxes—just as it may choose among various family unit decisions in constructing its "normative income tax"—then the expression "for practical reasons" may be acceptable.

The recent discussion of "integration" does exhibit a large degree of difference in viewpoint as to the appropriate relationship between corporate and individual income taxes, in terms of economic theory, financial attitudes, and structural aspects. Indeed, much of the discussion is in terms of incentives to capital formation and investment rather than in terms of theoretical concepts. Moreover, the more serious legislative approaches to integration that surfaced in 1977 and 1978 appeared to extend only to limited tax relief for dividends, though it was difficult to decide whether a reduction in tax at the shareholder level or a reduction in tax at the corporate level was being discussed.[24] If only a limited tax relief for dividends were to be enacted, then presumably the relief would be classified as a tax expenditure, especially if enactment rests on incentive grounds.[25] It may be that continued theoretical analysis of "integration" approaches will lead to more insight on appropriate classification, as well as to more guidance on the appropriate legislative response to the substantive questions. The experience in the United States certainly supports the view that the discussions thus far as to the economic, financial, accounting, and legal ramifications of the various suggested approaches to integration have not come close to the extensive exploration of these factors that sensibly should precede such a basic change in the income tax system.

In summary, the definition of tax expenditures has not as yet presented any basic problems.[26] There may be borderline situations in determining

---

[24] *See generally* C. McLure, Jr., Must Corporate Income Be Taxed Twice? (1979). *See also* McLure, Jr. & Surrey, *Integration of Income Taxes: Issues for Debate*, 55 Harv. Bus. Rev. 169 (1977); *The President's 1978 Tax Program: Hearings on the President's Tax Proposals Before the House Comm. on Ways and Means*, 95th Cong., 2d Sess. (1978); M. Blume, J. Crockett & I. Friend, Financial Effects of Capital Tax Reforms (1978).

[25] In this connection, theoretical analysis in Europe has not yet resolved the question whether the various European shareholder credits (and the German corporate rate reduction for dividends) should be considered as permissible responses within a set of possible normative relationships between the corporate and individual income taxes which a country can adopt or whether they constitute tax expenditures (in a system that views the classical system as normative) or tax penalties (in a system that views a *fully* integrated corporate tax as normative).

[26] Surrey & McDaniel, *supra* note 7, at 685-88, pointed out some definitional misconceptions. A few additions may be described here. Richard Goode states, "In my opinion . . . the present tax expenditure budget rests on a shaky conceptual foundation and for this reason is less convincing to skeptics than it would be if more rigorously derived." Goode, *The Economic Definition of Income*, in Comprehensive Income Taxation 1, 27 (J. Pechman ed. 1977). He then suggests two alternatives, one being a broader tabulation using the Schanz-Haig-Simons definition, described *id*. at 7, and the other being a narrower tabulation including only those provisions where the legislative history indicates a dominant tax incentive or hardship relief motivation. *Id*. at 28. But as Charles Davenport in his Comments points out, Goode's second alternative using legislative history would result in the present tax expenditure list and not a narrower

whether a particular provision of the Code constitutes a tax expenditure, but

---

tabulation. *Comments by Charles Davenport*, in COMPREHENSIVE INCOME TAXATION 33, 34-35 (J. Pechman ed. 1977). Moreover, Goode's first alternative would not greatly differ from the present tabulation but would include net imputed rental income from owner-occupied homes, death benefits from life insurance policies, and accrued gains on capital assets. *Id.* at 34. These omissions have been explicitly discussed, however, in tax expenditure analysis. The Treasury 1968 guidance, which excluded these items—Goode calls that guidance "pragmatic," Goode, *supra*, at 26—simply saw no point in pressing inclusion of these items especially when Congress and the public certainly do not come close to conceiving of their exclusion from the tax base as tax incentives. Indeed, much of the confusion over capital gains results from the inability of legislators to conceive of the use of the "realization concept" as a benefit to recipients of capital gains. Goode's criticism thus either disappears or is very narrowly confined and by no means supports his term "shaky conceptual foundation."

A curious aberrational concern over the definitional aspect appeared in Treasury Secretary Blumenthal's testimony on the proposed Sunset Act of 1977:

> I think it is important from the beginning to recognize that tax expenditures is not a clearly defined concept. . . .
> . . . .
> It is not clear under this definition that the personal exemption or the standard deduction might not be categorized as a tax expenditure. [The definition referred to is the definition of tax expenditures in the bill, which was almost identical to that adopted in the Budget Act, quoted in text at note 11, *supra*].

Hearings on the Sunset Act of 1977, *supra* note 13, at 109.

> Senator Kennedy in his testimony readily pointed out the Treasury's errors:
>
> In his testimony last week, Secretary Blumenthal indicated that there might be problems in identifying tax expenditures. But the examples given do not suggest that the problems are significant. . . .
>
> With respect to the specific examples cited by the Secretary, no tax expenditure budget for the past 10 years has included personal exemptions as a tax expenditure; every budget has included the standard deduction as a tax expenditure. To my knowledge, there is no disagreement as to either treatment.
>
> Moreover, the Treasury seems to be concerned in its other examples by items that are not included in the tax expenditure budget. But the suggested definitional difficulties seem to be resolved in light of the thorough analysis that has characterized the efforts of the Congressional Budget Office and the Joint Committee on Taxation on this issue in recent years.
>
> The Budget Reform Act of 1974 contains a workable definition of tax expenditures. So, too, do S. 2 and the legislation developed by Senator Glenn. Moreover, under the Budget Reform Act, the committee reports of the House Ways and Means Committee and the Senate Finance Committee must identify new or increased tax expenditures.
>
> Therefore, the Joint Tax Committee and the Congressional Budget Office—as well as the Treasury—are given guidance by Congress as to the items that should be included in the tax expenditure budget.

Id. at 329-30.

> Later, the Treasury, on further reflection, recognized that the definitional problem did not really exist and submitted a letter from Secretary Blumenthal which came back to the basic Treasury position:
>
> In my testimony, I discussed the definitional difficulties in the tax expenditure concept. Section 401(a)(1) of Title IV contains a broad definition of tax expenditures which is subject to the difficulties cited by me in my testimony. On the other hand, tax expenditures are listed and *ipso facto*

any useful classification has borderline problems.[27] The important point, and one overlooked by some economists and others, is that the assertion of definitional impossibility is an assertion that a country has lost control of its tax and budget policies. The Congress at least understands that it must separate tax expenditures from the regular tax system if it is to have rational budget controls. Once those who seem to despair or agonize over definitional problems realize that an operative tax expenditure analysis is a legislative necessity—as well as an executive branch tool—then perhaps there will be more helpful discussion of the definitional boundary.

B. *Estimates of Tax Expenditures*

The technicians working on the tax expenditure tabulations have been able to handle the problems presented in estimating the various items.[28] This is not surprising since the analytical problems which arise in estimating tax expenditures are precisely the same as those presented in estimating revenues for any proposed legislative tax changes. These problems include: the handling of an estimate for one item when the item is affected by changes in other items—the so-called "stacking" of changes in interrelated items; the

---

defined in three places: the special analysis of the budget prepared by the Executive; the annual reports of the Congressional Budget Committees; and, the annual estimates of tax expenditures prepared for the Committee on Ways and Means and the Senate Finance Committee by the staff of the Joint Committee on Taxation. The definitional difficulties can be avoided if an abstract definition is replaced by reference to any of the currently used lists of specific tax expenditures. Furthermore, budget procedures already enacted require the specific identification of new tax expenditures as they are legislated.

Id. at 120.

Apparently the initial Treasury statement was prompted by its dislike at being caught between a directive by OMB at the last moment to support in principle the entire proposed Sunset legislation even as to termination of tax expenditures on lines parallel to termination of direct Budget programs—a Carter campaign position—and the Treasury's awareness that Chairman Long disagreed with the tax expenditure termination provisions (though not with the basic concept of reviewing tax expenditures, *see id.* at 470). The later Treasury letter reflected a more reasoned approach. *See also* text at notes 310-28.

Another definitional misconception surfaced in the 1977 Sunset Act Hearings. Senator Glenn indicated a preference for the term "tax incentive" instead of tax expenditure, *id.* at 87, not realizing that his terminology would leave out tax subsidies for the relief of hardships, *e.g.*, many of the income security items, which his basic position on Sunset legislation would want covered by the review and termination provisions.

[27] Professor Carl Shoup has pointed out:
The listing of tax expenditures will no doubt be "incomplete" (or overcomplete), but if publication were to be denied to any listing that was sure to be incomplete, on the grounds that incompleteness is "potentially misleading" . . . as indeed it is, national income accounts would never have appeared and no censuses would have been taken.
Shoup, *Surrey's Pathways to Tax Reform—A Review Article*, 30 J. FINANCE 1329, 1334 (1975).

[28] Much that has already been said about defining tax expenditures equally applies to estimating them. Surrey & McDaniel, *supra* note 7, at 688-90 discusses tax expenditure estimating techniques and some misconceptions about them.

assumption that economic behavior remains unchanged if an item is eliminated—the so-called "first-order" estimates; and the assumption that economic conditions remain unchanged by microeconomic measures. The technicians who supply these revenue estimates for tax reform proposals are the same individuals who furnish the tax expenditure estimates. Hence, any critical observations made of the tax expenditure estimates are essentially criticisms and observations concerning the basic revenue estimating procedures used by the Treasury and Congress. The criticisms may or may not be proper, but they must be seen as relating to basic revenue estimating procedures and not as criticisms of the tax expenditure concept itself.[29]

---

[29] Hence the remark of Richard Goode in his paper at the Brookings Institution Conference on Comprehensive Income Taxation that "the tax expenditure estimates are less firmly based than would be desirable for official statistics," Goode, *supra* note 26, at 28, seems strange indeed. Likewise strange, for a different reason, are Henry Aaron's remarks in the same conference:

> But it is futile to dream of a "grand budget" that sums direct expenditures—a set of affirmative actions actually taken—and tax expenditures—a set of actions *not* taken or revenues *not* collected. The list of things we have chosen not to do is infinite and unspecifiable. The futility of such an endeavor is revealed by the fact that if we try correctly to estimate the aggregate level of tax expenditures, the level of each particular tax expenditure depends on the number of tax provisions that are *defined* as tax expenditures. The level of social security outlays does not depend on whether we define, say, Federal Home Loan Bank Board advances to be in or out of the budget; but the revenue implications of, say, permitting the deduction of property taxes does depend on the fact that unemployment insurance is excluded. The impossibility of constructing an unambiguous grand tax expenditure budget should not divert attention from the immense value of program analysis that includes both direct and tax expenditures.

Comments by Henry Aaron, in COMPREHENSIVE INCOME TAXATION 30, 31 (J. Pechman ed. 1977) (emphasis in original). However, as Charles Davenport points out in his *Comments*, the same problem is presented in direct program estimates:

> For example, if food stamps were eliminated, the outlays for aid to families with dependent children might increase, but no one suggests that estimates for the food stamp program are in error for this reason.

Comments by Charles Davenport, *supra* note 26, at 35.

The International Fiscal Association 1976 Congress, on the subject of incentives, said as to estimates:

> Another difficulty was seen in determining the initial cost to be attributed to a tax incentive in cases where e.g. foreign capital or foreign technicians would not be attracted in the absence of such incentive.

Summary of Proceedings, [1976] I.F.A.Y.B. 46 (1976) [hereinafter cited as *IFA Summary*]. However, this comment indicates the problems that persist because of a failure to recognize that tax incentives are really spending programs. Thus, suppose a country, to attract foreign capital or foreign technicians, adopted a direct grant program of roughly the same cost magnitude as a tax incentive program for the same purpose. Surely the "cost" of the direct program would appear in the budget, even though without that program there might have been no foreign capital or foreign technicians. The revenue obtained from such attraction becomes an offsetting item. But the choice of a tax incentive spending program should show a similar "cost," offset by the revenue brought in by the foreign capital and foreign technicians (including the "cost" itself). The two programs are thus comparable and the "cost" of each is in effect obtained in the same fashion, each cost being open-ended.

The President's 1978 tax reform proposals presented a descriptive prob-

---

Stiglitz and Boskin, in *Impact of Recent Developments in Public Finance Theory on Public Policy Decisions*, 67 AM. ECON. REV. 295 (1977), also misconceive the estimating process and fail to state that, to a great extent, their observations equally apply to all revenue estimates (the observations may be accepted as statements, but estimators and others familiar with the process have long been fully aware of the situation):

> The other concept, the use of which is now written into law, is that of tax expenditures: the loss of revenue due to a particular provision. We have three major objections to this concept. First, as presently formulated, the measurement of foregone revenue implicitly assumes zero elasticities; the estimates of aggregate tax expenditures are correct only when one contemplates eliminating *all* deviations from taxing real economic income *simultaneously and* if the factors of production are in *perfectly inelastic supply* [which Boskin in 1977 and Heckman in 1974, among others, demonstrated is not the case]. Further, the estimates for particular so-called tax preferences are often extremely inaccurate. For example, if the tax law allows a deduction for charitable contributions, it is not correct to argue that abolishing the deduction will increase tax revenue by (the summing over all contributors who itemize deductions) the product of the marginal tax rate and the amount currently given to charity. The amount of resources flowing into each such "tax expenditure" category reflects the tax treatment of that category as well as others. Since the charitable deduction reduces the price for a dollar of charitable contributions from $1 to $(1-t), where t is the marginal tax rate, any price elasticity at all in charitable giving would imply that abolishing the deduction would also reduce charitable contributions. Take the case of a family with a marginal tax rate of 20% which currently gives $300 a year to charity. The tax expenditure budget counts .2 times $300, or $60, as a tax expenditure. Yet abolition of the deduction implies a 25 percent price increase; with the elasticity of -1.2 estimated by Feldstein (1976), contributions fall to $210, and at the other extreme the "revenue foregone" is only $42 if the extra $90 does not flow into taxable income. The tax expenditure budget thus overestimates the revenue loss by more than 40 percent!

Id. at 296-97 (emphasis in original).

But the phrase "if the extra $90 does not flow into taxable income" misses the issue. The $90 is *already* in taxable income since the $300 was a deduction from taxable income. The taxpayer would have to use the $90 for some expense that would still qualify as deductible and would not be within the tax expenditure list. This is unlikely and hence the criticism of the estimate is unsound.

Another criticism in the same article is as follows:

> [T]he tax expenditure concept suffers from a further defect: the legislation implicitly assumed that the "natural" tax base is income, broadly defined; as we shall argue below, there is little justification for this. That is, to know what is being "exempted" from taxation one needs to know what "ought" to be taxed.

Id. at 297.

The article then discusses, for example, whether "consumption" is a more appropriate tax base than "income." It may or may not be, but the present federal income tax is accepted as a tax that uses "income" as its base. It is therefore appropriate to structure a tax expenditure list for *that* tax accordingly. A different tax expenditure list would be—and could be—structured for a tax using "consumption" as the base, since the legislature, contrary to the assumptions of many economists who prefer the consumption base, would undoubtedly also work into such a tax a large number of "incentive" and "relief" exceptions.

Another aspect of the estimation process is the "feedback," or second order

lem for the technicians handling tax expenditures.[30] Those 1978 proposals involved major tax rate reductions which in turn reduced the value of all tax expenditures other than those utilizing a credit against tax technique. The proposals also recommended the elimination or direct scaling down of specific tax expenditures. To separate these varying effects, Budget Special Analysis G in 1978 first showed the existing tax expenditures under existing tax rates, and then showed the combined results of the recommended rate reductions and the revisions in particular tax expenditure items.[31]

---

effects, of proposed tax changes. Renewed interest has been expressed in efforts to estimate these effects. Attention has focused especially on proposals to reduce the tax on capital gains. *See, e.g.*, M. Evans, An Alternative to the Fiscal Stimulus Act of 1978: A Reduction in Capital Gains Tax Rates (Chase Econometrics Assoc., Inc., May 1978). The hazards of such endeavors and the sometimes truly heroic assumptions required to be made are discussed and debated in Bristol, *Pitfalls in Using Econometric Models: The Chase and DRI Capital Gains Estimates*, 6 TAX NOTES No. 20 at 531 (May 15, 1978); Evans, *Capital Gains Taxes and Econometric Models*, 6 TAX NOTES No. 22 at 593 (May 29, 1978); Eckstein, *The Use of Econometric Models to Evaluate Capital Gains Changes*, 6 TAX NOTES No. 23 at 611 (June 5, 1978); Bristol, *Pitfalls in Equation Construction*, 6 TAX NOTES No. 23 at 635 (June 5, 1978). *See also* Gravelle, Study by Chase Econometrics on Effects of Reducing the Capital Gains Tax Rate, Library of Congress, Congressional Research Service (1978), *reprinted in* 124 CONG. REC. E2616 (daily ed. May 16, 1978). At this writing it appears that economists generally agree on the desirability of developing techniques that would provide accurate data on feedback effects in appropriate situations. However, there is no agreement that reliable techniques have yet been developed. Moreover, considerable care must be employed where tax expenditures are involved. Usually tax expenditures affect only the allocation of available resources and do not involve the creation of new resources. Hence, models showing net increases in jobs or capital from changes in tax expenditures are highly suspect. See the discussion of this subject in 124 CONG. REC. 14610-18 (daily ed. Sept. 6, 1978), which includes a Treasury Department technical analysis of the appropriate use of feedback estimates.

In proposing an increase in the capital gains deduction for individuals from 50 percent to 70 percent of the realized gain, the Senate Finance Committee reduced its estimated revenue loss of $3.394 billion by an assumed $1.092 billion "feedback," resulting from estimated increased realizations of gains. *See* S. REP. No. 1263, 95th Cong., 2d Sess. 193 (1978). While there seemed to be general agreement among economists that the reduction might produce a short-term increase in realizations, Treasury economists concluded that there would be no long-term increase in the level of realizations by investors. *See Hearings Before the Senate Finance Committee on the Revenue Act of 1978*, 95th Cong., 2d Sess. 197-201 (1978) (statement of Secretary of the Treasury Blumenthal).

[30] Some estimating situations presented by the 1976 Tax Reform Act change—e.g., minimum tax changes, at-risk provisions, and the termination of some tax expenditures which had involved deferrals of tax liabilities—are discussed in the text at notes 156-62 *infra*.

[31] *See also* CONGRESSIONAL BUDGET OFFICE, THE PRESIDENT'S FISCAL YEAR TAX EXPENDITURE PROPOSALS (April 1978).

The estimates for the tax expenditures involving itemized deductions—e.g., mortgage interest, charitable contributions—are made as follows: Since, in general, only the total of itemized deductions in excess of the zero bracket amount ($2300 single, $3400 married) is allowed, where there is an allowable excess considering itemized deductions as a group, then as to any particular itemized deduction the tax expenditure value of that item is computed by applying the marginal rate used by the estimators to the lesser of the amount of the excess or the amount of the specific item. As a consequence, the total of the separate estimates for the various itemized deductions *overstates* the revenues that would be collected in the event that several of the *deductible* items were eliminated. In contrast, the total of the tax expenditure estimates of *exclusions* from gross income *understates* the revenue gain that the elimination of several of the exclusions would provide.

Thus, as to the conceptual problems involved in estimating tax expenditures, we may conclude that a consensus among fiscal experts as to the estimates to be attached to those expenditures should be readily obtainable. The problems of estimating tax expenditures are similar, in this respect, to those involved in the identification of tax expenditures. Indeed, a moment's thought should indicate how serious are the consequences of asserting that tax expenditures cannot be identified or, if identified, that their costs cannot be ascertained. At bottom, this would be an assertion that the fiscal experts of a country do not know what is contained in their income tax or how much particular programs cost the government. In short, as stated earlier, the assertion would be an admission that the country has lost control of both its tax policy and its budget policy. Ten years ago the United States did not know what its tax spending programs were or how much they cost. The United States now realizes that in January, 1978 it had around 85 such programs involving over $135 billion, a total equal to 27 percent of the estimated $500 billion of direct budget outlays. Unquestionably, this figure represents too large an amount of revenue to allow its distribution to evade scrutiny or analysis. Yet, without the tax expenditure analysis commenced in 1968, that would be the situation today in the United States. The obvious point is that once experts are given the assignment of identifying and quantifying tax expenditures, the task can be accomplished, and a new dimension opened for fiscal policy.

* * *

II. Tax Policy Issues

The tax expenditure concept, as it is gradually internalized by those responsible for and involved in the formulation of tax policy, has produced some discernible shifts in several areas normally denominated as "tax policy" issues. It has become increasingly clear that a number of matters traditionally treated as concerns of "tax policy" would more accurately be classified as "spending policy" issues. It remains true, however, that decisions to utilize the tax system to expend federal funds do have important implications for normative tax policy issues. In this part, we consider the impact of the tax expenditure concept on both tax and spending policy issues.

A. *Tax Reform Aspects*

Recent legislative efforts for tax reform centered almost exclusively on items in the tax expenditure list. Data showing that very high income individuals pay little or no income tax [69] have continued to fuel the quest for tax

---

[69] See U.S. TREAS. DEPT., HIGH INCOME TAX RETURNS: 1974 AND 1975 (Mar. 3, 1977); U.S. TREAS. DEPT., HIGH INCOME TAX RETURNS: 1975 AND 1976 (Aug. 1978), for reports on high income taxpayers emphasizing those tax returns that incurred little or no tax liability. The 1977 Report revealed that in 1975, 215 returns with adjusted gross income (AGI) of $200,000 or more paid no federal income tax; 2,858 returns with AGI of $50,000 or more paid no tax. The Treasury report complacently reassured us, however, that "most" high income taxpayers pay "very substantial amounts of tax," although the data supplied by the Treasury indicated that these "substantial" amounts were in fact considerably below the taxes that would have been paid had these same taxpayers not been the beneficiaries of tax preferences. The 1978 Report disclosed that, as a result of the Tax Reform Act of 1976, the number of no-tax individuals with adjusted gross incomes in excess of $200,000 had declined to 22 in 1976. The 1978 Report emphasized that the problem of low effective rate-high income individuals was even a greater problem than the no-tax individuals. Finally, the report noted, the average effective tax rate for the over-$200,000 income group was only 35%, which the Treasury described as "substantial." 1978 Report at 5-7.

reform.[70] The reasons why wealthy individuals do not pay the effective rates of tax at the levels indicated by the tax rate schedules are almost without exception to be found in the tax expenditure budget.[71]

Appendix B sets forth the distribution by income class of tax expenditures provided through the individual income tax for fiscal 1977. These statistics clearly reveal both the reasons why the progressivity of the federal income tax system is so much less than a 14-70 percent rate schedule would imply, and why taxpayers with the same economic incomes can pay substantially different amounts of federal income taxes. Specifically, Appendix B indicates the quantitative extent of the upside-down character of the tax expenditures employed in the United States. In fiscal 1977, the top 1.4 percent of taxpayers, with "expanded gross income"[72] of $50,000 or more, received 31.3

Some have seized on the Treasury studies to conclude that the income tax bears disproportionately on the upper income groups in the country. They reach this rather startling conclusion by referring to such facts as the upper one-half income group pays 94% of all personal income taxes, the top 25% pay over 70% of personal income taxes, and the top 1.4% (over $50,000 adjusted gross income) pay 23% of the taxes. See 124 CONG. REC. H1975-76 (daily ed. Mar. 13, 1978) (statement of Rep. Kemp). The conclusion that upper income groups pay a disproportionate amount of tax, on the basis of these facts, is a non sequitur. The data merely reflect the use of a progressive income tax in the United States. Similar results would be expected if the marginal rates ranged from 2% to 20%. The only relevant data to determine the appropriateness of the tax burden on upper income individuals are data pertaining to effective rates of tax. Here, studies have repeatedly shown that, on the average, the effective rate never exceeds about 32% to 36%, even for taxpayers with incomes in excess of $1 million annually. Such data hardly seems to justify a picture of an "overburdened" upper income class. For recognition of this point, see 124 CONG. REC. H7924 (daily ed. Aug. 4, 1978) (statement of Rep. Wright); 124 CONG. REC. E1819 (daily ed. Apr. 12, 1978) (statement of Rep. Vento).

[70] Nevertheless, the reduction in the tax rate on capital gains, in the Revenue Act of 1978, demonstrated little concern for this situation.

[71] The period from 1976 to 1978 did not produce significant developments in, or require modification of, our earlier analysis of the use of effective rates in formulating tax policy. Surrey & McDaniel, *supra* note 7, at 698-706. Those studies on effective rates that have appeared confirm our prior conclusion that traditional effective rate analysis—comparing actual taxes paid to actual economic income—remains a valid and useful tool in determining the effects of tax expenditures. See, e.g., the following studies by the Library of Congress, Congressional Research Service: Gravelle, Tax Provisions and Effective Tax Rates in the Oil and Gas Industry (Oct. 6, 1977), *reprinted in* 123 CONG. REC. S16946 (daily ed. Oct. 11, 1977) (statement of Sen. Kennedy); Gravelle, Provisions Reducing the Effective Tax Rate of Commercial Banking Organizations (Jan. 19, 1977). *See also* U.S. TREAS. DEPT., EFFECTIVE INCOME TAX RATES PAID BY UNITED STATES CORPORATIONS IN 1972 (May, 1978). See note 69 *supra*.

[72] "Expanded gross income" is adjusted gross income plus tax preferences subject to the minimum tax. The term does not include items of income that do not appear on tax returns, notably interest from tax-exempt bonds.

A curious aspect of the "expanded gross income" definition is that it treats the deduction for investment interest up to the amount of investment income as not a tax preference. Apparently, in the view of the Treasury economists, high income taxpayers routinely borrow funds and make investments with no objective of making a profit. But the Treasury assumption seems clearly wrong and results in an overstatement of the effective rates of tax paid by high income taxpayers. More analysis is required to allocate properly investment interest. One suspects, for example, that a percent of the Treasury "tax checks" delivered through the tax expenditure mechanism—over $26 billion out of a total of almost $84 billion spent. On the average, taxpaying units in this select group received, in effect, federal subsidies of $71,429. The 49,000 taxpayers with incomes above $200,000, representing 5/100 of 1 percent of total returns, on the average received federal tax subsidies of $535,653. Tax sheltered individuals live in stately mansions!

The upside-down character of tax expenditures is also strikingly apparent when individual items in the tax expenditure budget are considered. The top 1.4 percent of taxpayers, with expanded gross incomes of $50,000 or more, received from 66.7 percent to 80 percent of tax expenditures for natural resources; 85.4 percent of the tax expenditures resulting from exemption of the interest on state and local bonds; 87 percent of the revenues from tax-exempt industrial development bonds issued for pollution control purposes; 86.3 percent of the tax expenditures involved in industrial development bonds generally; 75.6 percent of the tax expenditures for rental housing; 60 percent of the benefits from the Asset Depreciation Range (ADR) system; 73.3 percent of the revenues involved in the charitable contributions deduction for education; 58.8 percent of the revenues from the charitable contributions deduction for health; 43.2 percent of the revenues for all other charitable contributions deductions; 67.7 percent of the tax expenditures resulting from preferential treatment of capital gains; and 100 percent of the benefits of the maximum tax on earned income.

While some tax expenditures provide relatively greater benefits to those with incomes below $50,000, only 14 of the 69 tax expenditures set forth in Appendix B reflect a progressive distribution pattern, that is, the greatest percentage of benefits going to the low income groups, with the percentage declining as income increases. Moreover, these 14 tax expenditures involve only $10.9 billion. In short, less than 13 percent of the total tax expenditures are distributed on a progressive basis.[73]

It thus remains true, after a decade of tax reform efforts sharpened by tax expenditure analysis, that the overwhelming majority of tax expenditure programs, and of the funds distributed thereunder, benefit the upper income groups. Not only are the tax expenditure provisions the primary cause of tax inequity, but it seems safe to say that the provisions do not even achieve what most Americans would perceive to be a fair distribution of funds, measured by criteria applied to direct spending programs. Major strides toward tax equity—horizontal and vertical—could be achieved by eliminating all the tax expenditures from the Internal Revenue Code. But, short of total repeal, ac-

---

large part of the investment interest should be allocated to untaxed, unrealized appreciation. The 1978 Treasury Report, *supra* note 69, at 12-14, reflects a greater sensitivity to the problem, recognizing that the decision to treat only investment expenses in excess of investment income as the tax preference element is an "arbitrary" one. Existing data do not, however, permit a more precise method of matching interest deductions and income.

[73] *See* Manvel, *Tax Expenditures by Income Classes*, 7 TAX NOTES No. 3 at 55 (July 17, 1978) (describing the allocation of tax expenditures to income classes in terms of transfer payments, capital gain items, and all other tax expenditures).

tion can be taken to improve the fairness of both the tax system and of the tax expenditure programs. The 1976-1978 legislative experience revealed some significant trends in this "second best" approach to tax reform.[74]

B. *The Trend to Tax Credits*

1. Tax Credits Versus Special Tax Deductions: Efficiency, Equity, and Program Funding Issues

A trend continued during the period from 1976 to 1978 was the increased reliance on tax credits, instead of special deductions or exemptions, as the mechanism for providing federal financial aid or incentives through the tax system. The reasons for the shift to tax credits vary depending on the type of preferential provision which they replace. In determining whether tax credits should be utilized in lieu of special business deductions, for example, the tax expenditure concept indicates that the same cost-benefit analysis must be made of tax spending programs as is made of direct spending programs. The results of such analysis tend to favor using tax credits rather than special deductions, assuming, of course, that the studies demonstrate a need for some federal financial assistance.

Cost-benefit studies have been particularly effective in exposing the inefficiencies in the program areas supported by the "tax shelter" deductions. For example, studies have demonstrated an unacceptably high level of inefficiency in the tax expenditures used to construct oil and gas, and real estate tax shelters.[75] This inefficiency results from passive tax shelter investors retaining a substantial portion of tax expenditure funds which should be expended in actual drilling or construction operations. The waste, in large part, results from the interaction of progressive rates with the special deduction technique. In effect, the tax shelter syndicator is selling the tax benefits that the driller or developer is unable to use. While the special deductions for oil or real estate are valuable for the 70 percent tax bracket investors, there are not enough 70 percent investors to provide the driller or developer with needed funds. Accordingly, the tax shelter deal is modified to make it attractive to the 50 percent investor, with a resulting windfall to the investors in brackets above 50 percent, and a waste of federal funds. A tax credit to the driller or developer, even if available to passive investors, would largely eliminate this type of inefficiency.[76]

---

[74] For a general discussion of tax reform issues, vintage early 1978, see Surrey, *Current Tax Developments in Perspective*, 11 CREIGHTON L. REV. 807 (1978).

[75] Regarding real estate tax shelters, *see* H. AARON, SHELTER AND SUBSIDIES: WHO BENEFITS FROM FEDERAL HOUSING POLICIES? (1972); Kurtz, *Tax Incentives for Real Estate Have Failed*, 3 REAL ESTATE REV. No. 2 (Summer 1973); McDaniel, *Tax Reform and the Revenue Act of 1971: Lesions, Lagniappes and Lessons*, 14 B.C. IND. & COM. L. REV. 813 (1973). Regarding oil and gas tax shelters, *see* G. BRANNON, ENERGY TAXES AND SUBSIDIES (1974); McDaniel, *Tax Shelters and Tax Policy*, 26 NAT'L TAX J. 353 (1973).

[76] Additionally, the studies have shown that even where the funds are employed by drillers and developers, investments with low national priorities result, *e.g.*, development wells instead of exploratory drilling, or shopping centers instead of low-income housing. This aspect of the efficiency problem, however, is one of proper program design, rather than one of credits versus deductions.

A 1977 Congressional Budget Office study of real estate tax shelter subsidies reached a similar conclusion, and recommended that consideration be given to replacing the accelerated depreciation deduction for real estate with a tax credit for builders of low income housing. Similarly, it has been proposed that the deduction for intangible drilling and development costs be replaced with a tax credit.[77] In recent years, the enactment of new tax subsidies to business via the tax credit technique, such as the WIN tax credit[78] and the target jobs tax credit,[79] further illustrate this response to the inefficiency of certain special deductions.

More recently, the 1977 National Energy Plan, as proposed by the President, contained new or expanded tax expenditure programs, almost all of which were structured as tax credits. The President recommended that taxpayers' costs of undertaking certain energy conservation and conversion actions be reduced. The cost reduction was provided in some instances by tax credits and in others by direct spending programs. The President's National Energy Plan unfortunately did not articulate why tax spending was to be preferred over direct spending in any given program area. Where the tax route was proposed, however, the tax credit mechanism was almost exclusively employed. Thus, in the business area, the President's plan included a 10 percent tax credit for investment in approved conservation measures and a 10 percent tax credit for investment in energy saving equipment. The lone exception to the credit approach was a proposal to extend the special deduction for intangible drilling costs to geothermal drilling.[80]

In Congress, the House generally followed the President's approach to national energy policy, although it did add a percentage depletion allowance for geothermal resources.[81] The Senate nevertheless rejected the Presidential and House bill reliance on taxes as regulatory or penalty measures. The Senate Finance Committee version shifted entirely to the tax incentive route, providing for some $40 billion in new and expanded tax expenditures between 1978 and 1985.[82] Additional tax expenditures were added on the Senate floor. With only a few exceptions, both the Finance Committee and the floor amendments relied on tax expenditures in the form of tax credits, rather than special deductions or exemptions.[83] The Energy Tax Act of 1978, as it fi-

---

[77] As to housing, *see* CONGRESSIONAL BUDGET OFFICE, REAL ESTATE TAX SHELTER SUBSIDIES AND DIRECT SUBSIDY ALTERNATIVES (May 1977) [hereinafter cited as CBO HOUSING STUDY]. As to oil, *see* McDaniel, *Tax Shelters and Tax Policy*, 26 NAT'L TAX J. 353, 375 (1973); *Tax Reform Act of 1975: Hearings on H.R. 10612 Before the Senate Comm. on Finance*, 94th Cong., 2d Sess. 193 (1976) [hereinafter cited as *SFC 1976 Hearings*].

[78] I.R.C. §§ 40, 50A-50B.

[79] I.R.C. §§ 44B, 51-53. The targeted jobs tax credit was adopted in the Revenue Act of 1978 to replace the expiring new jobs tax credit.

[80] EXECUTIVE OFFICE OF THE PRESIDENT, ENERGY POLICY AND PLANNING, NATIONAL ENERGY PLAN 78 (1977) [hereinafter cited as NATIONAL ENERGY PLAN].

[81] H.R. 8444, 95th Cong., 1st Sess. (1977). *See also* H.R. REP. No. 543, 95th Cong., 1st Sess. 129-30 (1976).

[82] S. REP. No. 529, 95th Cong., 1st Sess. 19-26 (1977).

[83] *See e.g.*, the Senate version of the energy tax bill, H.R. 5263, 95th Cong., 1st Sess. (1977) § 1012 (energy cost credit for the elderly); § 1013 (credit for increased

nally emerged from Congress, more closely followed the Senate than the House approach, although a modified regulatory "gas guzzler" tax was included.[84]

The tax expenditure concept inevitably does drive advocates of tax preferences toward the use of credits as opposed to special deductions or exemptions. As the 1977-1978 energy tax legislation demonstrated, tax credits and direct grants result, or can result, in identical economic consequences to the government and to beneficiaries of the programs.[85] This result does not mean, however, that tax policy makers therefore should be indifferent to the use of tax credits as opposed to direct grants. There are important differences in, and consequences of employing, the two approaches which to date have not been sufficiently appreciated or analyzed by proponents of tax expenditures. Some of the more crucial of these differences and consequences will be identified below.

The trend to tax credits in lieu of special deductions in the business area continues to demonstrate that neither Congress nor a number of departments in the executive branch have yet mastered the technique of evaluating tax credits as alternatives to direct grants. The Senate Finance Committee Report and the Senate floor debates on the proposed energy tax credits demonstrated that the Senate had very little concrete evidence before it (1) as to the need for a given credit; (2) if there was a need, why the level of funding provided by the credit was appropriate; or, (3) whether the program design implicit in the credit reflected the program design which would have been adopted had a direct spending program been under consideration.

This last point requires a caveat. The tax expenditure analysis should not lead policy makers unthinkingly into substituting tax credits for special business deductions. Assuming that a need for federal financial aid for a particular activity has been established, the next question is the most effective form

---

cost due to imported oil); § 1028 (credit for electric motor vehicles); § 1044 (tax credit for production of oil and gas from nonconventional sources); § 1055(e) (credit for home heating oil). Exceptions to the tax credit approach included § 1027(b) (exclusion from employer income of value of employer-furnished van pooling services); § 1042 (percentage depletion for peat and geopressured methane gas); § 1043 (intangibles deduction for geopressurized methane gas).

[84] The final bill included tax credits for residential insulation and other energy conserving components; for residential solar, wind, and geothermal equipment; for vehicles used in van pooling; for personal use electric or hydrogen motor vehicles; for business investment in "alternative energy property" and "specially defined" energy property; for business insulation costs; and, for business investment in congeneration and recycling equipment. Tax expenditures that did not employ the credit technique included the exclusion from income of employer-provided van pooling service; percentage depletion for geothermal deposits and geopressured natural gas; and, immediate deduction of intangible drilling costs for geothermal wells. S. REP. No. 1324, 95th Cong., 2d Sess. (1978).

[85] For example, the President proposed a tax credit for certain business energy conservation costs. He proposed, however, direct grants to tax-exempt organizations that incurred the same costs. No explanation was offered why the direct grant approach was adopted for tax-exempt entities rather than refundable tax credits, and tax credits for business rather than direct grants. See NATIONAL ENERGY PLAN, *supra* note 80, at 42.

of providing that aid. Generally, the alternatives to tax credits are outright grants and loans. Assume that the loan approach is adopted. If it is then decided to provide the loan through the tax system, three techniques are available: (1) accelerated deductions in which the amount of the loan is the tax saving in the early years of the life of the asset; (2) an income exclusion with a corresponding basis adjustment, in which the amount of the loan is the amount of tax that would have been due had the excluded amount constituted currently taxable income; or, (3) a tax credit repayable in full over time with no basis reduction, in which the amount of the loan is the creditable amount itself. The amount of the "tax loan" under the first two techniques is a function of the tax rates—the higher the tax bracket the larger the amount of the federal loan.

The repayable tax credit approach in (3) makes the same federal loan available regardless of the bracket of the taxpayer. In this sense, therefore, the results in approach (3) seem fairer than those in approaches (1) and (2). But, if one compares the results to commercial lending practices, that conclusion is less certain. Private lending institutions do, after all, lend larger amounts to those with higher incomes than to those with lower incomes. The rationale for this practice is obvious and it would seem not patently unreasonable for the government to adopt the same view in the loan programs that it administers. Thus, the shift from an accelerated deduction to a tax credit is not necessarily called for if (a) a loan rather than a direct grant is the desired form of federal assistance, and (b) the variation in the size of loans under the accelerated deduction is roughly equivalent to that observed in commercial lending practices. On the other hand, because it is the government making the loan, attention must be focused on the question whether individuals and corporations with large net incomes merit larger loans than do their lower income counterparts.

There is, moreover, one marked difference between private and most direct government loans and the loans made available through techniques (1) and (2) above. This difference lies in the failure to charge interest on the "tax loan" programs.[86] Possibly, an interest charge would be imposed if Congress adopted technique (3). This situation could be remedied by imposing a direct annual interest charge on taxes deferred as the result of accelerated deductions, or deferred income inclusion. The interest incurred could be paid to the Treasury each year with the taxpayer's tax return. Such a procedure would complicate tax administration. Moreover, Congress to date has not displayed much concern over the interest free use of government funds through accelerated deductions. If that concern develops, then it is possible that a shift to repayable tax credits in technique (3) would take place since the amount of the loan in the case of tax credits would appear simpler to determine than would the amount of the loan generated by the tax savings from accelerated deductions. Again, to emphasize a familiar point, the foregoing analysis does

---

[86] The minimum tax may be viewed as an annual interest charge on the tax loans effected through the accelerated deductions to which it applies. The interest charge is quite erratic, however, varying (1) from taxpayer to taxpayer as a result of the basic exemption and offset for one-half of the regular taxes paid, and (2) from asset to asset depending on its useful life.

not suggest that the government should use the tax system to provide loans. It simply points out that *if* the tax system is to be used (a very big if!), proper construction of the loan program does not necessarily involve the use of tax credits rather than accelerated deductions.

In the area of business tax subsidies, therefore, the waste resulting from the interaction of deductions and progressive rates that has been identified and quantified by the tax expenditure concept appears to have been an important factor in the congressional and executive branch decisions to employ tax credits rather than special deductions as the mechanism for providing the subsidies. But, in terms of clearly demonstrating the need for federal financial support, identifying effective program design, establishing proper levels of federal funding, and articulating the criteria for choosing the tax as opposed to the direct spending route to aid business, Congress and the executive branch still fall considerably short of full implementation of the tax expenditure analysis.[87]

In the area of federal tax subsidies for personal expenditures, a similar trend to tax credits is emerging. New tax expenditure proposals more frequently take the form of tax credits rather than itemized personal deductions, and a number of proposals have been advanced to convert existing deductions to tax credits. Three major aspects of tax expenditure analysis appear to have contributed to this trend.

First, tax expenditure analysis has been particularly effective in exposing the upside-down results produced by special deductions for personal costs.[88] The tax credit technique is perceived to avoid an increase in benefits as a

---

[87] For example, the targeted jobs tax credit enacted as part of the Revenue Act of 1978 provides tax credits to employers who hire qualified employees from seven specific "target groups." I.R.C. § 51(d). Qualified employees are those certified as such by the Secretary of Labor and the Secretary of the Treasury. Since the Labor Department appears to be the appropriate agency to handle employment programs, its presence in the certification procedure is logical. What was never made clear, however, was why the Department of Labor was not also authorized to issue the subsidy checks directly, since its certification constituted the critical program eligibility requirement. In short, the program was structured to require both Labor and Treasury involvement, when it appeared Labor alone would have been sufficient. Perhaps the real answer lies not in program design issues, but in the issue of which congressional committees would exercise control over the program. See *infra*, Part V.

Two 1978 changes in tax expenditures did not employ the tax credit approach. One was the increase in the exclusion for long-term capital gains from 50% to 60% of the gain. This change was viewed as an expansion of an existing tax expenditure in a form that it had traditionally taken. No thought was given to converting the exclusion to a tax credit. The other change was the introduction of a series of special deductions for United States citizens living overseas. Here again, tax credits could have been employed. However, the use of deductions in I.R.C. § 913 appears to have been grounded in part on the mistaken view that the excess expenditures incurred by a United States citizen living abroad for higher costs of living, education, housing, home travel and living in "hardship" areas represent extraordinary costs of producing income. Although the items appear to be personal under normal United States tax principles, use of the deduction technique would be appropriate if one were persuaded that in fact they represented costs of producing income.

[88] Some commentators have asserted that the "upside-down" argument is not applicable to the deduction for charitable contributions. This conclusion is reached,

function of higher tax brackets, a result that is produced automatically when the deduction technique is employed. It is not clear whether tax credit proponents philosophically believe that benefits should not rise with income or whether they simply wish to eliminate an argument against their proposed tax expenditure. In any event, it is evident that an expenditure program effected through a tax credit usually more closely resembles a corresponding direct program than does one implemented through a special deduction or exemption (we, at least, are unaware of any direct spending programs that are structured to provide progressively increased financial benefits as income or wealth rises). The impact of the equity issues so dramatically posed by tax expenditure analysis of personal deductions is reflected in the evolution in the proposed tax expenditure for the costs of higher education. Initially, such proposals were almost always advanced in the form of special deductions for such costs or for contributions to a "qualified higher education fund."[89] Subsequently, however, proponents of tax expenditures for higher education costs converted their proposals to the tax credit approach approved by the Senate in 1976 and 1977,[90] and by both the House and Senate in 1978.[91]

---

however, by using an "after tax and after charitable deductions disposable income" test and then observing that, under this test, changing the deduction for charitable contributions to a credit would be more beneficial to the rich, since the consequent decline in their charitable contributions caused by the decline in tax benefit would give the rich more disposable income. Since the price elasticity effect of the tax deduction is greater than one, the rich would save more in lower charitable contributions than their increased tax, and the poor would give up in higher contributions more than their lowered tax. But one can ask whence comes the "disposable income" test. The fact that the rich are moved to change the consumption patterns previously induced by the tax system to patterns that involve less in charitable contributions and more in, say, travel or entertainment is not an argument against the upside-down characterization. The increase in disposable income produced by the tax change, as compared to the prior pattern, is just the reflection of the earlier shift in how disposable income was utilized. An increase in disposable income could equally result if a previously allowed deduction for, say, travel expenses, were eliminated, but that is hardly an argument that the elimination would favor the rich or that the initial allowance of the deduction hurt the rich.

Essentially the above argument must rest on the view that contributions to charity are not "consumption" under the Haig-Simons definition. This view hardly seems supportable when, for example, one reads literature urging the wealthy and corporations to contribute only to those colleges that would employ more conservatively-inclined professors. The view that the charitable contribution is not "consumption" really comes from changing "consumption" in the Haig-Simons definition to refer to a "standard of living" and then concluding that since charitable contributions do not increase a "[material] standard of living" they are not "consumption." There is some of this same shift in definition in U.S. TREASURY DEPT., BLUEPRINTS FOR BASIC TAX REFORM (Jan. 17, 1977), 31 *et seq.* But the shift in definition does not seem an acceptable modification of the Haig-Simons definition. One doubts that Simons would approve this reworking of his definition.

[89] *See, e.g.,* H.R. 9678, 92d Cong., 1st Sess. (1971).
[90] *See* The Tax Reform Bill of 1976, H.R. 10612, § 2601, 94th Cong., 2d Sess. (as passed by the Senate); The Social Security Financing Amendments of 1977, Senate Amendment No. 1057 to H.R. 9346, 95th Cong., 1st Sess. (as passed by the Senate), 123 CONG. REC. S18792-93 (daily ed. Nov. 4, 1977).
[91] *See* H.R. REP. NO. 1790, 95th Cong., 2d Sess. (1978) (the Conference Committee report on the Tuition Tax Credit Act of 1978).

A second aspect of special itemized personal deductions thrown into sharp relief by tax expenditure analysis is the exclusion of standard deduction (zero bracket amount) taxpayers from the tax expenditure program. With the higher standard deduction figures approved in 1975, 1977, and 1978,[92] every tax expenditure program implemented as an itemized personal deduction automatically excludes some 77 percent of all taxpayers—almost all of whom are low and middle income individuals—from the program. Although the result could be avoided by allowing the itemized deduction outside the standard deduction, that is, removing the implicit floor imposed on all itemized deductions by the zero bracket amount, such an action would not eliminate the upside-down effect of the subsidy. The tax credit approach may therefore be the more acceptable way to include in the tax spending program those whose itemized deductions are below the zero bracket amount. Such considerations appear to account in part for the decisions in the 1978 Energy Tax Act to provide individual tax credits instead of itemized personal deductions for solar energy equipment, energy saving devices such as windmills, energy saving efforts such as installing storm windows or more energy-efficient heating equipment, and for the purchase of electric powered automobiles.[93] Similarly, suggestions to convert the present itemized deductions for charitable contributions and home mortgage interest and property taxes to credits appear motivated in part by the equity issues raised by the tax expenditure analysis.[94]

Third, tax expenditure analysis has accelerated the trend towards tax credits by demonstrating that when an itemized personal deduction is viewed as a spending program, the level of funding for the program fluctuates up and down as the result of decisions totally unrelated to the program itself. An increase in tax rates automatically increases the federal spending inherent in a special deduction or exemption. Conversely, a tax reduction automatically reduces the size of the tax expenditure program. Once this fluctuation is perceived, it becomes evident that beneficiaries of a special deduction have a direct financial stake in every tax change considered by the Treasury or Congress.[95] Some specific examples of this phenomenon are discussed in Part IV.

Recognition that general tax trends are in the direction of reducing the value of the itemized personal deductions, and that support of the deduction

---

[92] The Tax Reduction Act of 1975, Pub. L. No. 94-12, 89 Stat. 26, increased the standard deduction to 16% of adjusted gross income with an overall maximum of $2,600 for joint returns and $2,300 for single individuals. The Tax Reduction and Simplification Act of 1977, Pub. L. No. 95-30, 91 Stat. 126, converted the standard deduction (and the prior low-income allowances) to a $3,200 "zero bracket amount" for joint returns ($2,200 for single individuals). The Revenue Act of 1978 increased the zero bracket amounts to $3,400 and $2,300 respectively.

[93] See note 84 *supra*.

[94] 123 CONG. REC. S11408 (daily ed. July 1, 1977) (statement of Sen. Kennedy).

[95] See 124 CONG. REC. H2395 (daily ed. Apr. 3, 1978) (statement of Rep. Conable), for a discussion of the estimated decline in charitable receipts resulting from increases in the standard deduction since 1969.

mechanism involves beneficiaries of special deductions in tax issues in which they should have little interest, may lead to the conclusion that each itemized deduction should be replaced with a tax credit. For example, some charitable organizations [96] and some congressional supporters [97] of incentives for private philanthropic giving have recommended that a tax credit be substituted for the charitable contribution deduction. A tax credit equal to, for example, 30 percent of the donor's contribution would insure that aggregate amounts received by charity would be increased somewhat over present levels. Moreover, the credit would be much more insulated from extraneous shifts in tax policy than is a deduction. Consequently, it seems likely that we shall see a greater interest in the use of tax credits instead of itemized personal deductions as the beneficiaries and supporters of programs financed via the itemized personal deduction mechanism become more cognizant of the arbitrary variations in federal funding levels for their programs, produced by actions completely unrelated to the tax expenditure program itself.

---

[96] The National Committee for Responsive Philanthropy, a group of social action exempt organizations, is conducting a study of the desirability and effects of such a change.

[97] See note 94 *supra*.

OFFICE OF MANAGEMENT AND BUDGET, SPECIAL ANALYSIS G: TAX EXPENDITURES, SPECIAL ANALYSES, BUDGET OF THE UNITED STATES GOVERNMENT 1984

Pp. G–1 to G–7, G–26 to G–33.

The Congressional Budget Act of 1974 (Public Law 93–344) requires a listing of a "tax expenditures" in the Budget. The act defines "tax expenditures" as "revenue losses attributable to provisions of the Federal tax laws which allow a special exclusion, exemption, or deduction from gross income or which provide a special credit, a preferential rate of tax or a deferral of liability."

The definition of tax expenditures used in this analysis is based on the distinction between the "normal" or "reference" provisions of the tax structure needed to make the tax operational, and the "special" provisions that are exceptions to the reference tax provisions. Such exceptions are designed to further other objectives, such as health care, export promotion, or employment of the handicapped. Their operation is, therefore, comparable to outlay programs, such as milk price supports and rent subsidies that also provide a subsidy to particular activities. For this reason, the expressions "tax subsidies" and "tax expenditures" are often used synonymously. Because the term "tax subsidies" is somewhat more descriptive than "tax expenditures," the former will be used in the remainder of this analysis.

The reference tax provisions are those which deal with the basic structural features of the Federal income tax. These features include such concepts as the definition of income subject to tax; taxable units and their threshold levels of taxability; the relationship between the taxation of corporations and their shareholders; the tax rate schedules; the basic tax accounting rules; the treatment of international transactions; and the system of tax administration. All of these structural features must be dealt with in some manner in order to have an operational income tax. In contrast to such reference provisions, it would be possible to have a fully operational income tax that did not contain any of the special provisions that give rise to tax subsidies.

While the distinction between the reference and special provisions of the Code may be clear as general concepts, there are numerous difficulties encountered when applying these concepts to obtain an actual list of tax subsidies. The inclusion of wages in the tax base is a clear example of a reference tax provision; the exclusion of fringe benefits is due to special provisions, and therefore clearly constitutes a tax subsidy. On the other hand, a less clear

TAX EXPENDITURES

example is provided by the capital gains provisions, which apply to a broad class of transactions and taxpayers, but are exceptions to the general rules governing taxation of income from all other sources. As explained more fully below, the capital gains provisions are considered a tax subsidy.

ALTERNATIVE DEFINITIONS OF TAX EXPENDITURES

While the current income tax is a useful reference standard, it is not the only one that might be used. Some analysts would prefer using a "pure income tax" under which the tax base is equal to an individual's consumption plus the change in his net worth during a year. Other analysts would prefer to use income used for consumption as the reference tax base for measuring tax subsidies. In this latter view, income that is saved would not be taxed.

If the current tax system is compared with a pure income tax for purposes of identifying tax expenditures, the list of tax expenditures would be quite different from the list presented in table G-1. For example, the following would be considered tax expenditures if the reference system were a pure income tax:

(1) the accelerated cost recovery system (ACRS);
(2) the exemption of tax on the imputed income from housing;
(3) the lack of inflation indexation of capital gains, taxation of capital gains only upon realization and the 60-percent exclusion of long-term capital gains; and
(4) the double taxation of corporate dividends.

The first of these would be a tax expenditure because a pure income tax would allow as a deduction only the economic depreciation on an asset—i.e., the true reduction in the value of the asset. ACRS is a system designed to provide more rapid depreciation than true economic depreciation.

The second of these, the exemption of the imputed income from housing, arises from the fact that owner-occupied housing provides income in kind to the owner. A house is a capital asset. The difference between a house and a corporate bond is that the return on the house is in the form of free rent whereas the return on the corporate bond is in the form of cash. Nonetheless, both assets return income and under a pure income tax, that income would be taxed in the same manner. Thus, the value of the free rental services provided by an owner-occupied home would be included in a pure income tax base. However, a deduction for mortgage interest payments (indexed for inflation) would be allowed just as there is a deduction for investment interest when one borrows money to invest in a corporate bond. If the reference tax is a pure income tax, the mortgage interest deduction would not be treated as a tax expenditure. Instead, there would be a tax expenditure based on the exemption of the imputed rent from the owner-occupied home, adjusted for depreciation.

The case of capital gains is quite complicated. Under a pure income tax, real accrued capital gains, i.e., accrued capital gains adjusted for a purely inflationary rise in the value of an asset, would be taxed just as any other income. Thus current law, when compared to a pure income tax, has three tax expenditures with regard to long-term capital gains. The first is that these gains are not indexed. This is a negative tax expenditure, i.e., it may cause a higher tax liability that would occur under a pure income tax. Offsetting this, however, is the 60-percent exclusion of long-term capital gains from adjusted gross income. This is the usual positive tax expenditure resulting in lower tax liability. Finally, capital gains are taxed only when realized, not as they accrue.

Under a pure income tax, all income would be taxed only once to the recipient. Consequently, the double taxation of the corporation income, when compared to a pure income tax, is a negative tax expenditure. It may raise the tax liability above that which would apply under a pure income tax.

If a tax on income used for consumption were used as the reference point, the list of tax expenditures is different from that which would result from a pure income tax and from that which would result from use of the normal provisions of the tax code as the reference structure. The following provisions of current law would be treated as tax expenditures if a pure consumed income tax were used as the reference point:

(1) the nondeductibility of saving other than saving contributed to individual retirement accounts and Keogh plans;
(2) the nontaxability of borrowing used for consumption; and
(3) the nontaxability of bequests consumed by recipients.

Under a consumed income tax, income that is saved would be deducted from the tax base. Consequently, except for contributions to IRA plans and pension plans, the nondeductibility of saving under current law would constitute a negative tax expenditure.

Just as saving would be deducted from the tax base, borrowing would be included in the tax base to the extent it is used for consumption. If an individual borrows $1,000 in a year and uses that $1,000 to increase consumption, a tax that is based on consumption would include that $1,000 in the tax base. Current law has no such provision and thus the absence of a tax on borrowing, if a consumed income tax were used as a reference point, would constitute a positive tax expenditure.

Since a consumed income tax would allow accumulations of wealth to be deductible because they are not consumption, the corresponding treatment of consumption out of wealth requires that such consumption be included in the tax base. Thus, an individual who inherits wealth and consumes it over his lifetime would have to include the bequest in his tax base. For example, if a person inherited $1 million and proceeded to spend $150,000 a year and, in doing so, reduced the principal amount, all of the $150,000 a year of consumption would be taxable. Under current law, consumption of wealth does not enter the tax base. Therefore, when current law is compared with a consumed income tax, a positive tax expenditure results from exclusion of spending out of inherited wealth.

While there are valid arguments in favor of identifying and measuring tax expenditures relative to a pure income tax or a consumed income tax, the existing Federal income tax is the best practical alternative available now for listing and computing the amounts of existing tax subsidies. Consequently, the remainder of this analysis is based on existing law.

The Relationship Between Tax Subsidies and Outlays

Tax subsidies often have objectives similar to government programs funded through direct appropriations. There are numerous examples of this. Direct expenditures and tax subsidies both reduce the cost of ships; direct interest subsidies and the issuance of tax-exempt bonds both result in lower financing costs for eligible issuers of mortgage bonds and businesses. Similarly, State and local governments benefit both from direct grant programs and from the ability to borrow funds at tax-exempt rates. Individuals benefit both from direct medicare payments and from the deductibility of medical expenses for income tax purposes. And individuals also benefit from social security payments as well as the exemption of these payments from income tax.

This special analysis contains quantitative estimates of tax subsidies that can be used in conjunction with the consideration of direct budget outlays. Like the listing of comparable direct oulays, the listing of specific tax items implies neither approval nor disapproval of the special provisions of the tax system that authorize them. Neither does it imply that only the special provisions are worthy of analysis. Many features of the normal tax structure such as the rates, exemption levels, and basic accounting rules, have major effects upon the level and composition of economic activity and the distribution of income. Thus, it is important that both the reference tax structure and exceptions that provide tax subsidies be subject to periodic analysis and review.

The Internal Revenue Code contains provisions relating to individual income, corporate income, estate and gift, excise, and employment taxes—all of which include special provisions that provide subsidies. Nevertheless, this analysis deals only with deviations from the reference structure in the taxation of individual and corporate income.

Defining Tax Subsidies

For a provision to involve a tax subsidy, two conditions are necessary:
—The provision must be "special" in that it applies to a narrow class of transactions or taxpayers; and
—There must be a "general" provision to which the "special" provision is a clear exception.

If these two conditions are satisfied, the special tax provision clearly has the characteristics of a direct outlay program—a program objective and a method of reimbursing program costs. Some examples will illustrate the application of these conditions to specific provisions of the Federal income tax.

Under the general provisions of the income tax, interest received from any source is includable in income subject to tax. However, a special provision allows interest on obligations of State and local governments to be excluded from taxable income. The exclusion is therefore considered a tax subsidy. A second example is the allowance of deductions for homeowners' mortgage interest and property tax payments. Under the general provisions of the Code, deductions are not allowed for any expenses allocable to income that is exempt from tax. However, the income from homeownership, that is, the (imputed) gross rental value of owner-occupied housing, is exempt from tax under the reference income tax rule requiring "realization." The special provisions that allow homeowners to reduce their housing costs by deducting mortgage interest and property taxes are, therefore, considered tax subsidies.

More difficult definitional issues are raised by the capital gains provisions. These provisions apply to a very broad class of transactions and taxpayers, and they constitute the basic provisions governing the taxation of gains from the sale of capital assets held more than one year. On these grounds it could be argued that the capital gains provisions do not involve a tax subsidy. However, under the capital gains provisions of the Code, income from the sale of capital assets held more than one year is taxed in a different manner than income from any other source. Because the reference provisions for taxing income without regard to source are more general than the capital gains provisions, capital gains are retained on the list of tax subsidies.

A further illustration of the definition of tax subsidies is provided by the Accelerated Cost Recovery System (ACRS) provisions enacted in the Economic Recovery Tax Act of 1981. Any income tax requires a set of rules for determining how the cost of depreciable assets is recovered. The ACRS provisions now constitute the general income tax rules for that purpose. To see this, one need only ask: "If ACRS is 'special,' what is the 'general' tax accounting rule to which ACRS is an exception?" The ACRS provisions are clearly a divergence from any measure of economic income, but this is not a criterion for designating a tax subsidy.

Because they set forth general rules, the ACRS provisions do not appear in table G-1. They are, nevertheless, very important provisions of the reference tax structure, both because of their sizable revenue cost as compared with prior law ($10.6 billion in 1982, $16.7 billion in 1983, and $25.6 billion in 1984) and because of their importance as investment incentives.

The treatment of ACRS may be contrasted with that of the investment tax credit, which has very similar economic effects. The investment credit is considered a tax subsidy because, unlike ACRS, it does not deal with one of the basic structural elements of the income tax.

Several other issues relating to the distinction between the reference structure of the income tax and tax subsidy provisions are discussed below.

- *Threshold income levels for tax liability.*—The reference structure includes those Code provisions that determine threshold levels of income below which no tax liability is imposed upon different types and sizes of taxpaying units. These levels have been affected by legislated changes in the dollar amounts allowed for personal exemptions and the standard deduction in recent years. However, the additional personal exemptions for taxpayers age 65 and over and for the blind result in tax subsidies because they are special provisions directed at demographic groups in special circumstances.
- *The progressive rate schedules.*—The progressive rate schedules for the individual and corporate income taxes are a part of the reference tax structure, as would be proportional or even regressive rate schedules. Tax subsidies do not result because some income is taxed at lower rates than other income. The income averaging provision of the Code for individuals is also part of the reference structure.
- *Separate rate schedules for single and married taxpayers, married taxpayers filing separately, and heads of households.*— Existing provisions regarding the definition of taxpaying units and the separate rate schedules for different kinds of taxpayers are considered part of the reference tax structure. The tax subsidy concept is not characterized by any specific set of rate schedules applicable to particular kinds of tax filing units. Similarly, the deduction for second earners, en-

acted in the Economic Recovery Tax Act of 1981, is part of the reference tax structure.
- *Forms of business organization.*—The tax law recognizes different forms of business organizations, including corporations, partnerships and Subchapter S Corporations, and individual proprietorships. Generally, provisions of the tax law that accommodate different forms of business organization do not result in tax subsidies so long as income is subject to tax at either the corporate or the individual level.
- *Treatment of individuals and corporations as separate taxpaying entities.*—The separate taxation of individuals and corporate entities is considered part of the reference tax structure.
- *Deduction of business expenses.*—The deduction of business expenses is necessary to determine taxable income under the reference rules of the tax code. Tax subsidies, therefore, do not result from deductions for "ordinary and necessary" business expenses. No attempt is made in this analysis to determine whether certain expenses such as those for entertainment and meals not only should reduce the taxable income of employers, but should also be included in the taxable income of the employees receiving such in-kind benefits.
- *Foreign tax credits.*—The reference structure of the income tax includes tax credits for foreign income taxes paid; this prevents the double taxation of income earned abroad.

No estimates are made in this analysis for "negative tax subsidies" or tax penalties—that is, exceptions to the reference tax structure that result in increased tax liabilities for certain groups of taxpayers to discourage specified kinds of activities. At present, there are only a few such provisions. One example is the deductibility of gambling losses in excess of gambling gains only when gambling is engaged in for profit. Also, under the Tax Reform Act of 1976, deductions for the costs associated with the demolition of certain historic buildings were disallowed, and the credit for foreign taxes paid was denied taxpayers who cooperate with, or participate in, an international boycott.

* * *

Table G-1. OUTLAY EQUIVALENT ESTIMATES FOR TAX SUBSIDIES BY FUNCTION

(In millions of dollars)

Description	Fiscal years 1982	1983	1984
National defense:			
Exclusion of benefits and allowances to Armed Forces personnel	2,890	2,780	2,820
Exclusion of military disability pensions	165	165	160
Total (after interactions)	3,055	2,945	2,980
International affairs:			
Exclusion of income earned abroad by United States citizens	1,850	2,155	2,165
Deferral of income of domestic international sales corporations (DISC)	2,870	2,565	2,000
Total (after interactions)	4,720	4,720	4,165
General science, space, and technology:			
Expensing of research and development expenditures	115	−1,160	−1,070
Credit for increasing research activities	640	1,060	1,180
Total (after interactions)	830	−115	120
Energy:			
Expensing of exploration and development costs:			
Oil and gas	3,285	1,830	1,710
Other fuels	45	45	50
Excess of percentage over cost depletion:			
Oil and gas	3,065	2,545	2,295
Other fuels	600	730	790
Capital gains treatment of royalties on coal	310	275	295
Exclusion of interest on State and local government industrial development bonds for certain energy facilities	5	15	20
Residential energy credits:			
Supply incentives	390	515	690
Conservation incentives	435	400	390
Alternative, conservation and new technology credits:			
Supply incentives	250	240	255
Conservation incentives	290	155	100
Alternative fuel production credit	20	45	70
Alcohol fuel credit [1]	5	5	5
Energy credit for intercity buses	10	15	15
Total (after interactions)	6,170	4,485	4,245
Natural resources and environment:			
Expensing of exploration and development costs, nonfuel minerals	85	90	100
Excess of percentage over cost depletion, nonfuel minerals	595	640	690
Exclusion of interest on State and local government pollution control bonds	870	1,020	1,150
Tax incentives for preservation of historic structures	245	320	385
Capital gains treatment of iron ore	40	40	40
Capital gains treatment of certain timber income	565	730	910
Investment credit and seven-year amortization for reforestation expenditures	20	30	40
Total (after interactions)	2,380	2,825	3,265
Agriculture:			
Expensing of certain capital outlays	550	570	590
Capital gains treatment of certain income	775	725	745
Total (after interactions)	1,410	1,375	1,415
Commerce and housing credit:			
Dividend and interest exclusion	1,530	615	605
Exclusion of interest on State and local industrial development bonds	1,795	2,250	2,625
Exemption of credit union income	225	245	270
Excess bad debt reserves of financial institutions	660	680	1,090
Exclusion of interest on life insurance savings	6,625	6,780	7,310
Deductibility of interest on consumer credit	10,900	10,710	10,530
Deductibility of mortgage interest on owner-occupied homes	23,495	25,255	28,335

Table G–1. OUTLAY EQUIVALENT ESTIMATES FOR TAX SUBSIDIES BY FUNCTION—Continued

(In millions of dollars)

Description	Fiscal years		
	1982	1983	1984
Deductibility of property tax on owner-occupied homes	8,405	8,810	9,645
Exclusion of interest on State and local housing bonds for owner-occupied housing	955	1,185	1,315
Capital gains (other than agriculture, timber, iron ore and coal)	26,590	22,865	23,465
Deferral of capital gains on home sales	2,090	2,225	2,515
Exclusion of capital gains on home sales for persons age 55 and over	710	765	865
Carryover basis of capital gains at death	3,120	3,330	3,685
Investment credit, other than ESOP's, rehabilitation of structures, energy property, and reforestation expenditures	19,255	17,170	18,325
Safe harbor leasing rules	2,880	3,270	3,035
Amortization of start-up costs	125	195	290
Exclusion of interest on certain savings certificates	1,970	840	105
Reinvestment of dividends in public utility stock	400	590	670
Total (after interactions)	111,905	108,300	115,635
Transportation:			
Deferral of tax on shipping companies	25	35	40
Exclusion of interest on State and local government bonds for mass transit	*	5	15
Total (after interactions)	25	40	55
Community and regional development:			
Five-year amortization for housing rehabilitation	45	60	70
Investment credit for rehabilitation of structures (other than historic)	295	360	460
Total (after interactions)	335	425	535
Education, training, employment, and social services:			
Exclusion of interest on State and local student loan bonds	115	175	240
Parental personal exemption for students age 19 or over	1,065	985	945
Exclusion of employee meals and lodging (other than military)	730	755	805
Employer educational assistance	55	55	15
Exclusion of contributions to prepaid legal services plans	20	25	25
Investment credit for ESOPs	2,455	2,220	2,405
Deductibility of charitable contributions (education)	830	770	805
Deductibility of charitable contributions, other than education and health	7,550	7,085	7,170
Credit for child and dependent care expenses	1,830	2,110	2,430
Credit for employment of AFDC recipients and public assistance recipients under work incentive programs	30		
General jobs credit	115	35	5
Targeted jobs credit	360	495	705
Total (after interactions)	15,500	15,050	15,895
Health:			
Exclusion of employer contributions for medical insurance premiums and medical care	22,555	25,412	28,980
Deductibility of medical expenses	3,970	2,950	2,635
Exclusion of interest on State and local hospital bonds	730	925	1,115
Deductibility of charitable contributions (health)	1,240	1,155	1,185
Tax credit for orphan drug research		15	25
Total (after interactions)	28,775	30,755	34,270
Income security:			
Exclusion of social security benefits:			
Disability insurance benefits	1,770	1,675	1,660
OASI benefits for retired workers	14,940	15,765	16,800
Benefits for dependents and survivors	3,735	3,765	3,890
Exclusion of railroad retirement system benefits	790	780	725
Exclusion of workmen's compensation benefits	1,735	1,875	2,105
Exclusion of special benefits for disabled coal miners	185	170	165
Exclusion of untaxed unemployment insurance benefits	2,615	3,330	2,940

TAX EXPENDITURES

Table G-1. OUTLAY EQUIVALENT ESTIMATES FOR TAX SUBSIDIES BY FUNCTION—Continued

(In millions of dollars)

Description	1982	1983	1984
Exclusion of disability pay	190	170	150
Net exclusion of pension contributions and earnings:			
Employer plans	65,805	70,005	78,780
Plans for self-employed and others	5,150	5,875	6,480
Exclusion of other employee benefits:			
Premiums on group term life insurance	2,890	2,910	3,095
Premiums on accident and disability insurance	165	160	160
Income of trusts to finance supplementary unemployment benefits	10	5	5
Additional exemption for the blind	35	35	35
Additional exemption for elderly	2,385	2,360	2,420
Tax credit for the elderly	135	135	135
Deductibility of casualty losses	1,295	705	520
Earned income credit [2]	460	390	340
Exclusion of interest on State and local housing bonds for rental housing	425	580	770
Deduction for motor carrier operating rights	115	115	115
Deduction for certain adoption expenses	15	15	15
Total (after interactions)	107,090	113,165	123,260
Veterans benefits and services:			
Exclusion of veterans disability compensation	1,860	1,815	1,835
Exclusion of veterans pensions	330	305	295
Exclusion of GI bill benefits	175	150	125
Total (after interactions)	2,390	2,290	2,280
General government:			
Credits and deductions for political contributions	185	195	295
General purpose fiscal assistance:			
Exclusion of interest on general purpose State and local debt	7,215	8,335	9,430
Deductibility of nonbusiness State and local taxes other than on owner-occupied homes	19,085	20,000	21,755
Tax credit for corporations receiving income from doing business in United States possessions	2,365	2,150	1,830
Total (after interactions)	28,885	30,720	33,275
Interest:			
Deferral of interest on savings bonds	315	450	500

* $5 million or less. All estimates have been rounded to the nearest $5 million.

[1] In addition, the exemption from the excise tax for alcohol fuels results in a reduction in excise tax receipts of $55 million in 1982, $80 million in 1983, and $90 million in 1984.

[2] The figures in the table indicate the tax subsidies provided by the earned income tax credit. The effect on outlays is: 1982, $1,280 million; 1983, $1,205 million; 1984, $1,125 million.

Proposed Changes in Tax Subsidies

The administration has proposed a number of tax revisions that would introduce new tax subsidies or change the costs of existing ones.

Tuition Tax Credit.—The administration proposes a nonrefundable credit for 50 percent of the tuition paid to private elementary and secondary schools for taxpayers' qualified dependents. This credit, which is subject to certain limitations, will be effective for expenses incurred after July 31, 1983.

Enactment of the tuition tax credit will increase the 1984 revenue loss by $245 million. The corresponding outlay equivalent estimates are $100 million in 1983 and $630 million in 1984.

Enterprise Zone Program.—The enterprise zone proposal provides tax incentives for the redevelopment of economically distressed areas. Beginning in 1983, up to 25 small areas per year will be designated "enterprise zones." Starting in 1984, businesses in the zones will be entitled to exemption from tax for certain capital gains, and to tax credits for capital investment, for increases in employment, and for hiring disadvantaged employees. A tax credit is also provided to employees in the zones.

These incentives will increase the 1984 revenue loss by $85 million. The corresponding outlay equivalent is $265 million in 1984.

Tax Treatment of Health Insurance Premiums.—Under current law, cash compensation paid to employees is fully taxable for income tax purposes, while compensation paid in the form of health insurance benefits is nontaxable. The administration proposes that, effective January 1, 1984, employees be taxed on employer-paid health insurance premiums in excess of $175 per month for family plans and $70 per month for individual plans.

This proposal is estimated to reduce revenue losses by $1,670 million in 1984. The corresponding outlay equivalent is $2,420 million in 1984.

Jobs Tax Credit for the Long-Term Unemployed.—The administration proposes a new tax credit for employers that hire individuals who have exhausted their regular and extended Unemployment Insurance (UI) benefits and who would have met the criteria for Federal Supplemental Compensation (FSC) benefits.

This proposal is estimated to increase revenue losses by $27 million in 1983 and by $174 million in 1984. The corresponding outlay equivalent estimates are $184 million in 1983 and $642 million in 1984.

Social Security Changes.—At present, social security benefits are exempt from the Federal income tax. Under the proposed bipartisan plan, single taxpayers with more than $20,000 ($25,000 for married couples filing a joint return) of adjusted gross income from non-social security sources will be required to include in adjusted gross income one-half of their social security benefits.

In addition, the combined employer-employee Old Age and Survivors and Disability Insurance (OASDI) payroll tax rate is currently scheduled to increase from 10.8% to 11.4% on January 1, 1985 and to 12.4% on January 1, 1990. Under the proposed plan the rate will increase to 11.4% on January 1, 1984, 12.12% on January 1, 1988 and to 12.4%, as currently scheduled, on January 1, 1990. Employees would be allowed a refundable credit on their income tax equal to their portion, .3%, of the rate increase accelerated to 1984.

The taxation of benefits will reduce revenue losses by $1,100 million in 1984. The corresponding outlay equivalent is $2,730 million in 1984.

The refundable tax credit will increase revenue losses by $145 million in 1984. The corresponding outlay equivalent is $3,225 million in 1984.

Tax incentives for higher education.—The Administration proposes that there be an exclusion from tax for earnings on savings deposited in special accounts to pay future higher education expenses of dependent children. This exclusion, which will be subject to certain limitations, will be effective January 1, 1984.

This proposal is estimated to reduce revenue losses by $13 million in 1984. The corresponding outlay equivalent is $35 million in 1984.

REVENUE LOSS ESTIMATES FOR "TAX EXPENDITURES"

Table G-2, which follows, shows the estimated "revenue loss" associated with each tax subsidy item for which an "outlay equivalent" estimate was provided in table G-1. As explained in the text under the heading "Measuring Tax Subsidies," revenue loss estimates do not take into account the additional resources (if any) that would be required to provide the same after-tax incentive if the expenditure program were administered as a direct outlay rather than through the tax system. As was also explained earlier, these revenue loss estimates are *not* equivalent to estimates of the increase in Federal receipts that would accompany the repeal of tax subsidy provisions.

Table G-2. REVENUE LOSS ESTIMATES FOR "TAX EXPENDITURES" BY FUNCTION

(In millions of dollars)

Description	1982	1983	1984
National defense:			
Exclusion of benefits and allowances to Armed Forces personnel	2,250	2,200	2,250
Exclusion of military disability pensions	165	165	160
International affairs:			
Exclusion of income earned abroad by United States citizens	985	1,285	1,300
Deferral of income of domestic international sales corporations (DISC)	1,550	1,385	1,080
General science, space, and technology:			
Expensing of research and development expenditures	450	−870	−1,235
Credit for increasing research activities	415	645	685
Energy:			
Expensing of exploration and development costs:			
Oil and gas	3,430	1,520	1,215
Other fuels	25	30	30
Excess of percentage over cost depletion:			
Oil and gas	2,100	1,850	1,665
Other fuels	410	505	530
Capital gains treatment of royalties on coal	205	180	180
Exclusion of interest on State and local government industrial development bonds for certain energy facilities	5	15	20
Residential energy credits:			
Supply incentives	250	430	575
Conservation incentives	360	330	305
Alternative, conservation and new technology credits:			
Supply incentives	205	195	200
Conservation incentives	220	125	25
Alternative fuel production credit	15	40	70
Alcohol fuel credit [1]	5	5	5
Energy credit for intercity buses	10	10	10
Natural resources and environment:			
Expensing of exploration and development costs, nonfuel minerals	50	55	60
Excess of percentage over cost depletion, nonfuel minerals	405	440	470
Exclusion of interest on State and local government pollution control bonds	825	975	1,105
Tax incentives for preservation of historic structures	185	270	310
Capital gains treatment of iron ore	20	20	20
Capital gains treatment of certain timber income	335	370	515
Investment credit and seven-year amortization for reforestation expenditures	10	15	20
Agriculture:			
Expensing of certain capital outlays	545	560	585
Capital gains treatment of certain income	610	615	585
Commerce and housing credit:			
Dividend and interest exclusion	2,160	445	435
Exclusion of interest on State and local industrial development bonds	1,640	2,120	2,520
Exemption of credit union income	150	170	185
Excess bad debt reserves of financial institutions	405	405	635
Exclusion of interest on life insurance savings	4,535	4,805	4,170
Deductibility of interest on consumer credit	10,825	10,765	10,540
Deductibility of mortgage interest on owner-occupied homes	23,305	25,065	27,945
Deductibility of property tax on owner-occupied homes	8,360	8,765	9,535
Exclusion of interest on State and local housing bonds for owner-occupied housing	905	1,110	1,290
Capital gains (other than agriculture, timber, iron ore and coal)	18,020	15,890	16,615
Deferral of capital gains on home sales	1,625	1,480	1,740
Exclusion of capital gains on home sales for persons age 55 and over	585	535	630

Table G–2. REVENUE LOSS ESTIMATES FOR "TAX EXPENDITURES" BY FUNCTION—Continued

(In millions of dollars)

Description	1982	1983	1984
Carryover basis of capital gains at death	1,995	2,180	2,370
Investment credit, other than ESOP's, rehabilitation of structures, energy property, and reforestation expenditures	16,455	12,985	14,585
Safe harbor leasing rules	3,333	2,990	2,795
Amortization of start-up costs	75	120	180
Exclusion of interest on certain savings certificates	935	1,665	320
Reinvestment of dividends in public utility stock	130	365	415
Transportation:			
Deferral of tax on shipping companies	25	30	40
Exclusion of interest on State and local government industrial development bonds for mass transit	*	5	15
Community and regional development:			
Five-year amortization for housing rehabilitation	45	55	65
Investment credit for rehabilitation of structures (other than historic)	250	335	365
Education, training, employment, and social services:			
Exclusion of interest on State and local student loan bonds	100	155	220
Parental personal exemption for students age 19 or over	1,070	995	950
Exclusion of employee meals and lodging (other than military)	655	680	725
Employer educational assistance	40	40	20
Exclusion of contributions to prepaid legal services plans	20	25	25
Investment credit for ESOPs	1,390	1,250	1,375
Deductibility of charitable contributions (education)	835	775	840
Deductibility of charitable contributions, other than education and health	7,595	7,145	7,190
Credit for child and dependent care expenses	1,175	1,520	1,765
Credit for employment of AFDC recipients and public assistance recipients under work incentive programs	40	*	
General jobs credit	80	25	*
Targeted jobs credit	235	290	465
Health:			
Exclusion of employer contributions for medical insurance premiums and medical care	16,365	18,645	21,300
Deductibility of medical expenses	3,945	3,105	2,630
Exclusion of interest on State and local hospital bonds	680	865	1,055
Deductibility of charitable contributions (health)	1,245	1,170	1,205
Tax credit for orphan drug research		10	15
Income security:			
Exclusion of social security benefits:			
Disability insurance benefits	1,780	1,690	1,660
OASI benefits for retired workers	14,825	15,685	16,680
Benefits for dependents and survivors	3,725	3,765	3,870
Exclusion of railroad retirement system benefits	790	780	735
Exclusion of workmen's compensation benefits	1,730	1,870	2,090
Exclusion of special benefits for disabled coal miners	185	170	165
Exclusion of untaxed unemployment insurance benefits	2,500	3,260	3,020
Exclusion of disability pay	155	145	135
Net exclusion of pension contributions and earnings:			
Employer plans	45,280	49,700	56,560
Plans for self-employed and others	2,835	3,755	4,230
Exclusion of other employee benefits:			
Premiums on group term life insurance	2,035	2,100	2,250
Premiums on accident and disability insurance	120	115	120
Income of trusts to finance supplementary unemployment benefits	10	5	5
Additional exemption for the blind	35	35	35
Additional exemption for elderly	2,385	2,365	2,410
Tax credit for the elderly	135	135	135

Table G-2. REVENUE LOSS ESTIMATES FOR "TAX EXPENDITURES" BY FUNCTION—Continued

(In millions of dollars)

Description	1982	1983	1984
Deductibility of casualty losses	920	575	380
Earned income credit [2]	455	385	330
Exclusion of interest on State and local housing bonds for rental housing	395	530	710
Deduction for motor carrier operating rights	140	75	75
Deduction for certain adoption expenses	10	10	10
Veterans benefits and services:			
Exclusion of veterans disability compensation	1,855	1,825	1,830
Exclusion of veterans pensions	330	310	295
Exclusion of GI bill benefits	180	150	130
General government:			
Credits and deductions for political contributions	180	190	200
General purpose fiscal assistance:			
Exclusion of interest on general purpose State and local debt	6,885	8,000	9,105
Deductibility of nonbusiness State and local taxes other than on owner-occupied homes	19,160	20,060	21,770
Tax credit for corporations receiving income from doing business in United States possessions	1,375	1,245	1,075
Interest:			
Deferral of interest on savings bonds	135	435	475

* $5 million or less. All estimates have been rounded to the nearest $5 million.

[1] In addition, the exemption from the excise tax for alcohol fuels results in a reduction in excise tax receipts of $55 million in 1982, $80 million in 1983, and $90 million in 1984.

[2] The figures in the table indicate the effect of the earned income tax credit on receipts. The effect on outlays is: 1982, $1,280 million; 1983, $1,205 million; 1984, $1,125 million.

MICHAEL J. McINTYRE, "A SOLUTION TO THE PROBLEM OF DEFINING A TAX EXPENDITURE"

14 U. C. Davis Law Review 79–103 (1980).*

INTRODUCTION

In 1968 the Treasury Department published a remarkable document containing a long list of purported tax subsidies and estimates of their costs in forgone federal revenues.[1] This "tax expenditure budget" has enjoyed enormous political success. It has induced Congress to alter its procedures for scrutinizing tax subsidies, now called tax expenditures,[2] and it has focused public attention on the indefensible consequences that often result when Congress uses special deductions, exemptions and other

---

* Professor of Law, Wayne State University Law School, A.B., Providence, 1964; J.D., Harvard, 1969. The author thanks Richard D. Pomp, Professor of Law, University of Connecticut School of Law, for his helpful comments on a draft of this article.

[1] SEC'Y OF THE TREAS. ANN. REP. ON THE STATE OF THE FINANCES, FISCAL YEAR 1968, 326-40.

[2] For an excellent discussion of the current and projected uses of the tax expenditure budget, see Surrey & McDaniel, *The Tax Expenditure Concept: Current Developments and Emerging Issues*, 20 B.C. L. REV. 235 (1979) [hereinafter cited as *Current Developments*]. *See also* Surrey & McDaniel, *The Tax Expenditure Concept and the Legislative Process,* in THE ECONOMICS OF TAXATION (Aaron & Boskin, eds., 1980).

tax mechanisms to achieve its spending goals.[3] At the same time, it has generated a voluminous, often contentious literature, most of which addresses the subject matter of this article—the problem of defining a tax expenditure.[4]

The progenitors of the tax expenditure budget identify as a tax expenditure any provision of the Internal Revenue Code that departs from what they call the "normal" structure of the income tax.[5] They have developed a series of ad hoc tests for dis-

---

[3] *See Lopsided Loopholes*, People & Taxes, No. 4, April 1980, at 2-5 for illustrations of the apparent unfairness of "spending programs" constructed from existing provisions of the Internal Revenue Code. The article states, for example, that the deduction for charitable gifts, often defended as a subsidy for private philanthropy, dispenses 47% of its benefits to the 3% of the taxpayers with incomes over $50,000. Whether or not the deduction for charitable gifts is "properly" classified as a tax expenditure is a subject of some debate among tax specialists. For the argument that the deduction is a tax expenditure, see McDaniel, *Study of Federal Matching Grants for Charitable Contributions*, in U.S. COMMISSION ON PRIVATE PHILANTHROPY AND PUBLIC NEEDS, DEP'T OF TREAS. 4 RESEARCH PAPERS TAXES 2417-532 (1977). For a contrary view, see Andrews, *Personal Deductions in an Ideal Income Tax*, 86 HARV. L. REV. 309 (1972). For a novel defense of the charitable deduction that apparently accepts the tax expenditure classification, see Brannon, *Tax Expenditures and Income Distribution: A Theoretical Analysis of the Upside-Down Subsidy Argument*, in THE ECONOMICS OF TAXATION, (Aaron & Boskin, eds., 1980).

[4] For the best of the early exchanges on the definition of a tax expenditure see Bittker, *Accounting for Federal Tax Subsidies in the National Budget*, 22 NAT'L TAX J. 244 (1971) [hereinafter cited as *Accounting for Federal Tax Subsidies*]; Surrey & Hellmuth, *The Tax Expenditure Budget—Response to Professor Bittker*, 22 NAT'L TAX J. 528 (1971); Bittker, *The Tax Expenditure Budget—Response to Professors Surrey and Hellmuth*, 22 NAT'L TAX J. 538 (1971). For an annotated bibliography, see U.S. ACCOUNTING OFFICE, TAX EXPENDITURES: A PRIMER 64-76 (1979).

A similar definitional controversy arose when the Canadian government announced its interest in developing a tax expenditure budget. *See* R. SMITH, TAX EXPENDITURES: AN EXAMINATION OF TAX INCENTIVES AND TAX PREFERENCES IN THE CANADIAN FEDERAL INCOME TAX SYSTEM (1979). For a lively debate on the utility of a tax expenditure budget in Canada, see *Tax Expenditure Analysis*, 1 CANADIAN TAXATION, No. 2 (Summer 1979); Surrey, *The Concept and Its Uses*, 3-14; Le Pan, *Some Conceptual Problems*, 15-18; Smith, *Definitional Problems*, 19-22; McGillivray, *The Canadian Context*, 23-25; *A Reply by Professor Surrey and Discussion*, 26-28.

[5] Commentators use "normal," "normative," "prescriptive" and "ideal" to describe that part of the tax system designed to raise revenue in a fair and efficient manner. The word "normal" is favored by protagonists of the tax expenditure concept, perhaps in the belief that it carries less of a requirement of theoretical purity. *See* OFFICE OF MANAGEMENT AND BUDGET, SPECIAL ANALYSIS

tinguishing normal rules from special rules.[6] Critics forcefully argue that the list of tax expenditures yielded by this methodology has no serious claim of legitimacy. They insist that the proponents of any list of tax expenditures must set forth and defend the principles of taxation which define the norm.[7] Because of a well-founded fear of being drawn into an inconclusive debate over the proper organizing principles of an income tax, the tax expenditure champions have steadfastly refused to elaborate

---

G: TAX EXPENDITURES, SPECIAL ANALYSES, BUDGET OF THE UNITED STATES GOVERNMENT 1980, at 184 (1979) [hereinafter cited as BUDGET OF THE UNITED STATES GOVERNMENT.] "Normative" is a favorite term of the economists, though Professors Surrey and McDaniel use normal and normative interchangeably. *See, e.g.,* Surrey & McDaniel, *The Tax Expenditure Concept and the Budget Reform Act of 1974,* 17 B. C. INDUS. & COMM. L. REV. 679, 683 (1976). The nuances in meaning of these words is unimportant in the context of this article.

[6] *See, Current Developments, supra* note 2, at 227-28. *See also* BUDGET OF THE UNITED STATES GOVERNMENT, *supra* note 5 317-19; S. SURREY, PATHWAYS TO TAX REFORM 15-24 (1973). These ad hoc tests generally include in the normal tax structure the rules that establish the tax rates, specify who is taxable on particular income items and define the persons and entities subject to tax. They also include the traditional exclusions for most nonmarket or imputed income, unrealized capital gains and some other "esoteric" economic benefits. These ad hoc tests treat as special rules most exclusions from income that depart from the Haig-Simons definition of income. They treat almost all deductions that are not justifiable on business grounds as special rules, even if the deduction arguably conforms to Haig-Simons. Problems in classifying particular code provisions have generally been resolved by reference to the real or assumed intent of Congress in adopting or continuing those provisions. *See* Surrey, *The Concept and Its Uses, supra* note 4, at 4.

[7] Professor Bittker asserts that "[w]hat is needed is not an ad hoc list of tax provisions, but a generally accepted model, or set of principles, enabling us to decide with reasonable assurance which income tax provisions are departures from the model. . .," *Accounting for Federal Tax Subsidies, supra* note 4, at 247. Professors Surrey and McDaniel accept the need for prescriptive rules but contend that these were provided by the drafters of the tax expenditure budget. Surrey & McDaniel, *supra* note 5, at 685 n.23. Professor Andrews, disagreeing with what he perceives to be the normative model of the proponents of the tax expenditure concept, states:

> I agree in the end it is useful to speak in terms of an ideal income tax and to evaluate departures from the ideal as tax expenditures whose purposes, not being reflected in the ideal, must be extraneous to the tax. But the ideal for this purpose must be carefully shaped and refined to reflect the intrinsic objectives of the tax.

Andrews, *supra* note 3, at 312.

their vision of the ideal tax structure.[8] Instead, they have defended their methodology on the practical ground that it has produced a list of tax expenditures acceptable to a majority of tax policy makers in Congress and the Treasury and to many other tax specialists.[9] Needless to say, tax specialists who object to that list have found this defense unpersuasive.

This article proposes a methodology for identifying tax expenditures which bypasses entirely the problem of obtaining consensus on the features of the normal tax structure. This methodology requires the identification of tax expenditures only for limited purposes and thus avoids the complex theoretical problem of developing a general, all-purpose definition of a tax expenditure. After introducing the methodology through a "horticultural metaphor," the article applies it to show how Congress could generate lists of tax rules that it should treat as the functional equivalent of spending programs for purposes of its legislative procedures. Finally, this article demonstrates the practical

---

[8] Professors Surrey and Hellmuth stated:
> [The Treasury] was fully aware of the blood, sweat and tears developed in the debate over a comprehensive income tax base and did not see that as the appropriate approach. Thus, Professor Bittker puts up a straw man which he proceeds to beat without mercy—and a Bittker beating is indeed an awesome sight. This part of [Bittker's] article is in one sense a welcome vindication of the wisdom of not desiring to be pulled into the debate over a comprehensive tax base.

Surrey & Hellmuth, *supra* note 4, at 531 (footnotes omitted).

[9] Professor Surrey makes this point forcefully:
> The application of tax expenditure analysis to separate an income tax into its two elements clearly requires a definitional approach which determines the contours of the normative tax. *But the task of finding that definitional standard is not really a difficult one.* . . . [T]he tax expenditure budget developed by tax technicians in the United States, though representing various agencies—Treasury, the President's Budget Office (OMB), the Congressional Budget Office, the Congressional Budget Committees, and the Staff for the Congressional Joint Committee on Taxation—have been remarkably consistent in their enumeration of the items to be placed in that budget. This consistency has been maintained despite the many legislative changes occurring since 1968. *The technicians . . . have been able to agree on the appropriate classifications of items as either tax expenditures or alterations in the normative structure.*

Surrey, *The Concept and Its Uses, supra* note 4, at 4 (footnotes omitted and emphasis added).

and theoretical advantages of utilizing the methodology in what has come to be called a "tax expenditure analysis."

I. THE NEW METHODOLOGY[10]

Tax specialists believe that a good definition of the term "tax expenditure" must capture the essential meaning of the term. Thus they agree that the definition should unambiguously divide the class of all past, present and potential provisions of the Internal Revenue Code into two mutually exclusive subclasses—tax expenditures and normal tax rules. While defenders of the Treasury Department's definition claim that it accomplishes this task, critics attack the definition by accumulating examples of hard-to-classify tax code provisions.

The following section employs a beguilingly simple horticultural metaphor to introduce an alternative to the generally accepted methodology for identifying tax expenditures. The lesson of this metaphor is used to expose a potential solution to the problem of defining a tax expenditure. The utility of this new methodology is then tested in several exemplary situations.

A. The Fable of the Garden

There was a rich man who bought an old estate that contained a once fine flower garden now engulfed in weeds. He hired a talented gardener to cultivate the garden and remove the weeds. Before undertaking his charge the gardener asked the owner to please define for him what constituted a weed, so that he would be sure to do what the owner wanted. "A weed," said the owner, "is a plant that has no proper place in a flower garden."

The gardener did not feel fully enlightened with this definition, but he nevertheless went to work and removed many, many plants without any problems of classification. After some days the owner visited the garden and saw that great improvements had been made. The gardener then asked what he should do about several types of plants that had foliage he found pleasing but which he suspected might be weeds. The owner suggested that the gardener take samples to experts at a nearby botanical

---

[10] For an introduction to and bibliography of the philosophical literature on definition, see ENCYCLOPEDIA OF PHILOSOPHY 314. *See also* Dewey & Bentley, *Definition*, 44 J. PHILOSOPHY 281 (1947). For a law-related discussion, see Hart, *Definition and Theory in Jurisprudence*, 70 L. Q. REV. 37-60 (1954).

garden for an opinion. The opinion was duly sought, and the gardener learned that the experts classified all of the flora in question as weeds. He began removing them at once.

Some days later, the owner again visited the garden. He saw the gardener about to dig out a row of dandelions that showed signs of having once been cultivated with care. "Stop!" the owner ordered. "Why would you destroy the dandelions when the blooms last so long and the greens are so delicious?" The gardener explained that all of the experts he had consulted had been in agreement that the dandelions had no proper place in a flower garden. "They have a place in my flower garden," the owner announced, and so they did.

B. *The Lesson of the Fable*

The problem of giving content to the definition of a weed—"a plant that has no proper place in a flower garden"—has some similarities to the problem of defining a tax expenditure. One obstacle to defining a weed is that part of what makes a weed a weed is its relationship to things external to it. Almost any plant may be considered a weed under particular circumstances. The water hyacinth, honored in Japan, is the curse of the Congo. Violets, mint, bonesets and morning glories are a pleasure to some and a pain to others. Even the rhododendron, whose blooms and foliage are universally acclaimed, is sometimes considered a weed in the Irish countryside. Similarly, whether a tax rule is "normal" or "special" often depends on its relationship to other rules. For example, a deduction for local property tax on a personal residence may be viewed as a tax expenditure or as part of the normal tax structure, depending on the treatment of imputed income from home ownership.[11] A definition that focused exclusively on the intrinsic qualities of tax code provisions would thus be incomplete. The definition either would miss many tax rules which are arguably within the tax expenditure subclass or would trivialize the classification process by including almost all code provisions within that subclass.

Another shared definitional obstacle is that rules which unambiguously separate weeds from flowers or tax expenditures from

---

[11] *See* Pomp, *Mortgage Interest and Property Tax Deductions: A Tax Expenditure Analysis,* 1 CANADIAN TAXATION, No. 3, 23 (Fall 1979); Hellmuth, *Homeowner Preferences,* in COMPREHENSIVE INCOME TAXATION, 169, 179 (J. Pechman, ed., 1977).

normal tax rules unavoidably incorporate some subjective value judgments. To minimize the subjective element in the definition of a tax expenditure, the framers of the definition could obtain a consensus on the values they implicitly endorse. All of us are entitled, however, to our idiosyncratic preferences when we are the ones for whom the definition is being framed. In the fable, the owner of the garden was the ultimate arbiter of what constituted a weed. In the same way, the person or institution using the term "tax expenditure" has the final say on the contours of its definition. Consequently, the definitional problem would remain even if we could browbeat the world into agreeing on a standardized list of tax expenditures.

Finally, weeds and tax expenditures cannot be identified precisely without changing the core meaning of the terms. Some words have an intrinsic element of vagueness. The term "adult," for example, suggests a person who has fully developed physically and has acquired a measure of maturity. But distilling the vagueness from this term by specifying the age at which a person passes from childhood to adulthood would change the complex concept of "adult" into something simple and different.[12] Similarly, part of what makes a weed a weed is an aesthetic judgment that it is out of place where it is. The same is true of a tax expenditure. Since their meanings depend in part on value judgments, their definitions necessarily have soft, fuzzy edges—not the crisp lines of an itemized list.

In the face of real problems of definition, how was the gardener able to weed the garden to the satisfaction of the owner? More fundamentally, why would we anticipate that any competent gardener would be able to separate weeds from flowers without even addressing the definitional problems discussed above? The answer is that the gardener understood that his purpose for uprooting plants was to enhance the beauty of his employer's garden. This purpose became the touchstone for resolving all sorting issues. By sorting weed from flower by reference to the purpose of the sorting, an enormous theoretical problem was converted into a series of small, practical decisions. The gardener could make these decisions in most instances through the exercise of his aesthetic judgment.

Since the gardener's employer remained the ultimate arbiter

---

[12] For discussion of this famous example, see ENCYCLOPEDIA OF PHILOSOPHY, *supra* note 10, at 315.

of what constituted a weed, he was not limited to the conventional purposes for distinguishing flowers from weeds, as illustrated by his unorthodox treatment of dandelions. But while the power of the owner to specify additional purposes for distinguishing weeds from other plants complicated the gardener's job, it did not create fundamental sorting problems. Once the employer informed the gardener of the special purpose for keeping dandelions, the gardener was able to continue the sorting of plants without further discussions with the owner.

Although the gardener and the owner did not crystallize their definition in a verbal formula, they implicitly defined the term "weed" by their actions. Describing those actions made the definition explicit. Thus a weed, for purposes of weeding the owner's garden, was "either a plant that does not enhance the beauty of the garden in the opinion of the gardener or one that the owner does not specifically identify as desirable in the garden." This definition was in no sense an all-purpose definition of a weed; by its own terms, it was useful only when the purpose of weeding was to enhance the beauty of the owner's garden. Nor was the rule it provided for sorting weeds from flowers self-executing; weeding remained a task that required a knowledge of plants and an artistic touch. For a skilled gardener, however, the definition gave instructions for sorting weeds from flowers that were fully adequate for the owner's purposes. Since the definition accomplished its sorting function, the problem of defining a weed for the limited purposes of the owner was solved.

For an analogous solution to the problem of defining a tax expenditure, we need to examine individually the myriad purposes for distinguishing tax expenditures from normal tax rules. For each such purpose, we must fashion a rule that will permit the persons responsible for identifying tax expenditures to accomplish that task. This methodology yields a definition of a tax expenditure that is not applicable at large, since a definition tied to use obviously must change if the use changes.

II. The Lesson Goes to Congress

Over the past half century, Congress has frequently used the tax system to reward favored economic activity and to relieve the personal hardships of individual taxpayers. These tax subsidies are similar in economic effect to the imposition of a tax otherwise due, followed by a corresponding government subsidy in the amount of the tax collected. Until recently, however, Congress applied entirely different legislative procedures to its consideration of direct expenditures and tax expenditures—excluding tax expenditures, for example, from the budget-setting process. The proponents of the tax expenditure budget have apparently convinced a majority of Congress that radically dissimilar treatment of functionally equivalent policy measures is undesirable. In the Budget Reform Act of 1974,[13] Congress took the first steps toward a uniform system for considering direct and indirect spending programs.[14]

To treat tax expenditures like direct expenditures, Congress must decide which tax rules should be treated as the functional equivalents of spending programs. The tax expenditure budgets prepared by the Treasury Department and by several other government agencies provide a standardized list of purported tax expenditures. But critics contend that Congress should not use this list, since it contains many code provisions that arguably constitute part of the normal structure of the income tax. Both defenders and critics apparently agree that the legitimacy of the list depends on the success of the tax technicians in unambiguously bifurcating the tax code on some principled basis into "normal" and "special" parts.[15] Thus the problem of defining a tax expenditure is central to the movement to apply uniform procedures to the consideration of tax expenditures and direct expenditures.

The new methodology developed above would allow Congress to accomplish its legislative reform objectives without having to distinguish tax expenditures from normal tax rules. Three concrete examples illustrate the potential of that alternative methodology. While the examples do not attempt to take into account every political factor that might influence the definitional process, they are sufficiently realistic to provide a fair test of the methodology.

A. *Example One: The Tax Expenditure Budget*

For Congress to move toward unifying its procedures for eval-

---

[13] 31 U.S.C. §§ 11(e), 1301-1353 (1976).

[14] For a detailed discussion of the Budget Reform Act of 1974 and an analysis of issues that have arisen in implementing it, see Surrey & McDaniel, *supra* note 5, at 709-20.

[15] *See* notes 5-7 and accompanying text *supra*.

uating tax expenditures and direct expenditures, it must have the kinds of cost data on tax subsidies that are regularly available on direct spending programs. The vehicle for providing Congress with such data is the tax expenditure budget. To construct that budget, tax analysts must develop a list of the tax expenditures contained in the Internal Revenue Code. The task of listing tax expenditures differs markedly from the task of listing direct spending programs. For direct expenditures, federal money raised through taxes or loans is physically spent; someone "taking inventory" of direct spending programs would observe the programs in action. But for tax expenditures, "spending" is a logical construct. No money physically enters the federal till and no money goes out, even though the economic impact of a tax subsidy may be equivalent to the impact of a direct spending program. A physical inventory of tax expenditure programs is therefore impossible.

To overcome this special difficulty of identifying tax expenditures, the framers of the tax expenditure budget have attempted to unambiguously bifurcate the Code into normal and special parts.[16] They are needlessly ambitious. The clear purpose of the tax expenditure budget is to give Congress reliable estimates of the costs in forgone revenue of tax provisions that are functionally equivalent to spending programs.[17] Since its purpose is strictly informational, differences of opinion among tax specialists over the proper treatment of particular tax rules become footnotes, figuratively and literally, to the tax expenditure budget.[18] For example, those persons assigned the job of producing a tax expenditure budget could achieve its purpose by including in the budget every tax rule that is arguably a tax expenditure, with an annotation for the controversial items. Since those persons would have conveyed all the information they possessed, their budget surely fulfills its informational function.

An all inclusive list, however, is but one of many solutions to the problem of producing a useful tax expenditure budget. As a

---

[16] See note 6 and accompanying text *supra*.

[17] According to Professors Surrey and McDaniel, "Certainly a government should know how much it is spending and for what purposes. A tax expenditure budget provides this essential and elementary knowledge with respect to the spending channelled through the tax system." Surrey & McDaniel, *supra* note 4, at 692.

[18] This suggestion is made in Shoup, *Surrey's Pathways to Tax Reform—A Review Article*, 20 J. FIN. 1329, 1334 (1975).

perfectly acceptable alternative, those drawing up the list could develop ad hoc rules for limiting the list to items that have been supported in Congress for tax expenditure reasons—that is, because of some nontax goal that the tax rule allegedly advances—since these are the items for which the cost data are most likely to be relevant to congressional budget decisions. Other approaches are also possible—a minimum list with annotations or a consensus list with annotations might be better choices. In choosing among alternative approaches, those drawing up the list of tax expeditures only have to decide which approach best conveys the information at their disposal, taking into account, for example, the costs of acquiring data and the time, convenience and intelligence of those who requested the tax expenditure budget. This decision is a practical one and is obviously independent of the theoretical issue of which tax rules are normal and which ones are special.

B. Example Two: Assigning Tax Expenditures to the Appropriate Congressional Committee

Both the House of Representatives and the Senate manage their legislative business through a complex network of committees. In the House, all tax bills, including bills containing tax expenditure proposals, are routed to the Ways and Means Committee; in the Senate, the Finance Committee has this jurisdiction.[19] Direct spending bills, in contrast, are controlled by the standing committee with jurisdiction over their subject matter. Until recently, no mechanism operated to coordinate congressional consideration of tax expenditure proposals with direct expenditure proposals encompassing the same subject matter.[20]

Logic suggests that tax expenditures should be subjected to the same kinds of cost/benefit scrutiny and political tradeoffs applicable to functionally equivalent direct spending programs. To implement a coordinated approach, Congress must decide which tax rules to treat as tax expenditures. Using the new methodology, Congress could achieve its goal of coordinating re-

---

[19] The tax legislative process is fully described in Surrey, *The Federal Tax Legislative Process*, 31 RECORD OF THE ASSOCIATION OF THE BAR OF THE CITY OF NEW YORK 515 (1976).

[20] For a discussion of the tentative steps Congress has taken to subject tax expenditures to the discipline of the budget process, see *Current Developments, supra* note 2, at 328-30.

view of tax expenditures and direct expenditure proposals without bifurcating the tax code into normal and special parts. Any tax bill containing a provision whose classification was the subject of legitimate dispute could be referred to both the tax and the relevant nontax congressional committee. Congress could instruct the nontax committee to assume that the disputed provision was in fact a tax expenditure and to scrutinize it accordingly. The tax committee would be given the opposite instruction. The result would be that all tax expenditures, plus some tax rules that may or may not be tax expenditures, would be evaluated by the appropriate nontax legislative committee according to traditional budget criteria. At the same time, the tax committee would examine all tax rules which are part of, or are arguably part of, the normal tax structure according to traditional tax policy criteria.

The possibility of concurrent jurisdiction by both the tax and nontax congressional committees eliminates the need for deciding unambiguously which committee has the predominant jurisdictional claim. Concurrent jurisdiction may be desirable even for tax rules that clearly fall into the special classification, since the tax committees have the expertise to disguise the spending program in the appropriate tax language. Congress has already experimented with this technique in considering the energy tax credits contained in the 1978 Tax Act.[21] Concurrent jurisdiction, of course, is the common solution for spending programs that arguably fall within the subject matter of more than one committee.

C. Example Three: Sunset Legislation

Over the past several years, Congress has held hearings on legislation that would subject all federal spending programs, including tax expenditures, to periodic review and the threat of automatic termination.[22] This review procedure, popularly called "sunset," would terminate tax expenditure programs after five

---

[21] I.R.C. §§ 44C, 44D & 44E. For a fascinating account of the politics that led to concurrent jurisdiction over the refundable portion of the energy tax credits and some sophisticated suggestions for extending the technique of concurrent jurisdiction, see Surrey & McDaniel, *supra* note 2, at 130-44.

[22] For discussion of the 1976 sunset proposal, see McIntyre, *The Sunset Bill: A Periodic Review for Tax Expenditures*, Tax Notes, Aug. 9, 1976, at 3. *See also Current Developments, supra* note 2, at 330-35.

years unless they were reenacted following an analysis of their effectiveness by the executive branch and the appropriate congressional committees. The mechanics of sunset obviously require a crisp dividing line between tax expenditures and other tax rules, since only tax expenditure programs would be assigned a cut-off date.

Specifying the purpose of subjecting certain tax rules to sunset poses some difficulties. The basic motive for sunset legislation is clear enough—some federal programs, once enacted, are said to take root and survive as organisms independent of Congress and the voters. By imposing an automatic termination date, sunset would force supporters of these "hidden" federal programs to make a public defense. This motive justifies subjecting obscure federal programs—tax expenditures or direct expenditures—to sunset, but it arguably does not justify imposing the risks of sunset on *all* spending programs. Under sunset, legislation that has already been debated publicly and has majority support in both houses of Congress can be repealed automatically if a reenactment bill is bottled up in committee, filibustered to death on the floor of the Senate or vetoed by the President. Applying sunset to the Medicare program, revenue sharing or the Federal Trade Commission budget, for example, would be unnecessary, even mischievous, like a bank calling the mortgage loans of its reliable and solvent customers just to put them to the test.

Applying sunset to some but not all spending programs would present enormous political problems, however, since the political support for sunset rests on the perception that it is merely a procedural reform, not an attack on specific programs. Selective sunset would require Congress to decide what programs to subject to the threat of termination. An immediate debate on the merits of specific programs would then be unavoidable, contrary to the plan of sunset for orderly review over a period of years.

To apply sunset to tax expenditures, therefore, Congress ideally would want a list of tax expenditures with some claim to legitimacy that could be adopted without precipitating a debate on the classification of particular tax rules. The source of that legitimacy is unimportant. Congress could employ a variety of techniques to produce a consensus list of tax expenditures. One technique would be to adopt without change a list developed for some other purpose, such as for the tax expenditure budget.[23] An alternative would be to modify an existing list by eliminating tax rules that were difficult to classify or that otherwise provoked controversy.[24] A third approach might be for those seeking passage of sunset legislation to negotiate the list, item by item, with those members of Congress whose support was considered necessary. What goes on the list, then, is a question of practical politics—not tax theory. A list that unambiguously bifurcated the tax code into normal and special parts would have no special appeal.[25]

D. The Examples in Perspective

By following the procedures outlined in the above examples, Congress would produce for itself three definitions of the term "tax expenditure."[26] Each of the definitions would be exactly tailored to achieve a narrowly specified congressional purpose. None of the definitions requires an ability to unambiguously divide the tax code into normal and special parts.

Despite the economic equivalence of tax expenditures and direct expenditures, the two forms of "spending" have some inher-

---

[23] *See* text accompanying notes 16-18 *supra*.

[24] Supporters of sunset now realize that many purported tax expenditures can be subjected to automatic termination only by substantially redrafting sections of the tax code. Tax shelter abuses, for example, are the product of the perverse interaction of several "normal" tax rules; to repeal tax shelters, the offending tax rules must be rewritten, not simply repealed. See McIntyre, *supra* note 22, at 6.

[25] The House Rules Committee's Task Force on Federal Spending Limitations has held hearings on a variety of proposals for controlling the growth of federal spending. See McDaniel, *Tax Expenditures and Federal Spending Limitations,* Tax Notes, April 7, 1980, at 475. To be effective, spending limitations should impose controls on disguised spending through the tax system. Implementing a limitation on tax expenditures poses definitonal problems similar to those encountered in identifying tax expenditures for sunset legislation. In both cases an unambiguous list of tax rules is required. Spending limitations enforced through a balanced budget requirement arguably could ignore tax expenditures, since a failure to include a tax expenditure on the spending side of the budget would offset the failure to include a deemed tax receipt on the revenue side of the budget. For a collection of articles on tax and spending limitations, see *Proceedings of a Conference on Tax and Expenditure Limitations,* 32 NAT'L TAX J., No. 2, (Supp. 1979).

[26] As illustrated above in Example 3, see notes 22-25 and accompanying text *supra,* Congress might find reason to use the same list of tax expenditures for more than one purpose.

ent differences, the most obvious being that the budget cost of a tax expenditure cannot be measured by recording outlays from the federal fisc. No one can seriously argue that the identical procedures applicable to direct spending programs should apply to purported tax expenditures. The goal of Congress should be to fashion institutional arrangements for managing tax expenditures that would be comparable in their effects to the necessarily different arrangements applicable to direct spending programs. But the examples above illustrate that a debate over the features of the normal tax structure has little or no relevancy to the achievement of that goal.

III. A Further Application of the Lesson: The Use of a Tax Expenditure Analysis

Only an Alice in Wonderland character would judge the merits of a direct spending program by applying traditional tax policy criteria. Everyone understands, for example, that the case for funding the Navy has nothing to do with its ability to fairly and efficiently raise revenue for the government. Tax expenditure champions have vigorously asserted that tax policy criteria are equally inappropriate in judging the merits of indirect spending through the tax code. They insist that tax expenditures should be recast as functionally equivalent spending programs and then evaluated according to traditional budget criteria. They call this two-step procedure a "tax expenditure analysis."[27] The logic of their position is unassailable.

Tax expenditure critics accept the logic of applying a tax expenditure analysis to tax rules which unquestionably constitute indirect spending programs. They see that procedure as a valuable analytical tool, for example, in judging the merits of the exclusion for interest on state and local bonds—a tax code rule which they concede acts solely as a federal interest subsidy.[28] They balk, however, in applying it to tax rules which are at least arguably defensible on tax policy grounds. Tax expenditure champions accept in principle this limitation on the tax expenditure analysis. But in practice they would apply a tax expenditure analysis to any tax rule that appears in the Treasury De-

---

[27] See, e.g., S. SURREY, supra note 6, at 36.
[28] See, e.g., Andrews, supra note 3, at 311.

partment's tax expenditure budget.[29]

The tax expenditure analysis should be liberated from its historical ties to the consensus list of tax expenditures prepared by the Treasury Department. As long as the tax expenditure analysis is linked to such a list, the results of its application are discredited in the eyes of anyone who is not part of the consensus.[30] Even more significantly, that linkage places unnecessary restraints on the use of a tax expenditure analysis. Tax specialists have mistakenly assumed that a tax expenditure analysis ought to measure the intrinsic worth of a tax code provision.[31] This error has made the definition of the term "tax expenditure" central to the invocation of that procedure. This section argues that tax specialists should use a tax expenditure analysis to evaluate *arguments* made on behalf of a tax rule—not to directly judge the worth of the rule itself. After illustrating the operation and advantages of the proposed new methodology for invoking a tax expenditure analysis, this section provides the theoretical underpinning for that approach.

A. An Example: The Dependency Exemption[32]

Some commentators argue that in a tax structure which ideally defines income in terms of personal consumption plus the net change in savings, the proper taxpayer on an income item is

---

[29] Professor Surrey states:
 We thus can put the basic question of whether we desire to provide that financial assistance at all, and if so in what amount—a stock question any budget expert would normally ask of any item in the regular budget. We can inquire whether the program is working well, how its benefits compare with its costs; whether it is accomplishing its objectives—indeed, what are its objectives? Who is actually being assisted by the program, and is that assistance too much or too little? Again, these are stock questions directed by any budget expert at existing programs. *They all equally must be asked of the items and programs in the Tax Expenditure Budget.*
S. SURREY, *supra* note 6, at 35-36 (emphasis added).

[30] *See* text accompanying notes 8-9 *supra*.

[31] The case for or against a tax rule obviously depends on the strength of all arguments that might support it. Since a tax expenditure analysis is useless in evaluating tax policy arguments, it alone cannot determine the worth of any tax rule that conceivably forms part of the normal structure of the tax.

[32] This subsection uses as an example I.R.C. § 151, which provides a personal exemption of $1,000 for each of the taxpayer's dependent children.

the person who saves or consumes that income.[33] Applying that principle in the family context, the proper taxpayer on income earned by a parent and spent on a child would be the child. Since the tax authorities cannot measure the actual consumption and savings of children in a family, they need some indirect method of calculating the correct theoretical result. The $1,000 dependency exemption crudely approximates the distribution of burdens that would prevail if dependent children were taxed on that share of the family income which they presumptively enjoy.

In evaluating this argument, the tax expenditure analysis should remain on the shelf. The argument asserts that the goal of the dependency exemption is the fair distribution of tax burdens—obviously a traditional tax policy goal. A proper inquiry, therefore, would pose some or all of the following questions: Is the theoretical norm of taxing income to the beneficiary a sound one in terms of notions of fairness in the distribution of tax burdens? Is the ad hoc technique for implementing that norm too crude? Is a better technique available? Does the rule produce undesirable nonneutralities in economic choices? Are these possible nonneutralities significant in light of the alleged fairness gains?[34]

Other commentators argue for the exemption on the ground that support of children is in part a community responsibility and should be subsidized by the government through the tax system.[35] Since the asserted goal of the exemption under this argument is a spending goal—the wise expenditure of public funds—the argument should be evaluated according to budget criteria using a tax expenditure analysis. Analysts should convert the tax rule into a functionally equivalent spending program and subject it to the scrutiny appropriate for related spending programs. They should determine, for example, whether the assumed spending goal of the tax rule is important

---

[33] For a presentation and defense of the proposition that the beneficiary of an income item is the person properly taxable on that income, see McIntyre & Oldman, *Taxation of the Family in a Comprehensive and Simplified Income Tax*, 90 HARV. L. REV. 1573 (1977).

[34] Tax specialists generally agree that a tax rule should not cause an inefficient allocation of resources if that result can be avoided without sacrificing administrative resources or fairness. A tax rule justified for efficiency reasons, however, may be difficult in theory to distinguish from a tax rule adopted to advance an economic goal not germane to a revenue-raising goal.

[35] *See, e.g.*, McIntyre & Oldman, *supra* note 31, at 1602.

or trivial, whether or not the costs of achieving the goal are commensurate with the benefits and whether the benefits are properly targeted or produce windfalls. In all probability, most analysts would judge the $1,000 deduction deficient according to budget criteria.

What could we fairly conclude about the desirability of the dependency exemption if this project were carried out? First of all, if we found, as expected, that the $1,000 allowance could not be justified according to budget criteria, we would know that the spending argument was a false one. If we also found that the tax policy argument was defective, we would know that the allowance was indefensible, unless, of course, commentators could develop additional arguments not previously considered. We might also learn which of its features made it a bad spending rule or a bad revenue-raising rule and whether or not those features were correctable. Alternatively, we might discover that the tax policy argument for the allowance was fundamentally sound. In any event, we would know as much about the merits of the dependency exemption provision as our analytical tools are capable of uncovering.

In contrast, what would we learn about the dependency exemption from the traditional tax expenditure analysis? In my view, virtually nothing. The traditional approach requires us to determine initially whether the dependency exemption is "normal" or "special." Even those tax specialists who are most optimistic about our ability to bifurcate the tax code into normal and special parts concede that the classification of the dependency exemption is problematic.[36] This analysis is thus stuck at square one. An analyst who simply ignored the classification problem and treated the exemption as a tax expenditure would probably conclude that it is unjustified, but only persons oblivious to the constraints of sound reasoning would give any weight to that finding. Similarly, if an analyst arbitrarily treated the exemption as a normal part of the tax code, his defense of the exemption would be tainted beyond redemption. In summary, arbitrary premises about the nature of a tax rule yield arbitrary conclusions about its merits.[37]

---

[36] *See Current Developments, supra* note 2, at 263-65.

[37] This problem arises in many other situations. The deductions for medical expenses and for charitable contributions should be analyzed as tax expenditures when they are defended on the ground that they advance desirable social

B. Another Example: The Business Lunch Deduction[38]

Commentators almost uniformly consider the business meal deduction to be a feature of the normal structure of the income tax, though many oppose it as unsound tax policy.[39] As a normal provision, it would traditionally enjoy immunity from a tax expenditure analysis. But the methodology advocated in this article would employ a tax expenditure analysis to evaluate nontax arguments made in defense of the business expense deduction.

The business lunch deduction is permitted by judicial interpretation of the "ordinary and necessary" language of Internal Revenue Code Section 162.[40] Congress has reinforced this interpretation by specifically excluding "quiet business lunches" from the statutory restrictions on entertainment expenses, which it enacted in 1962.[41] No one, least of all the Congress, has viewed this deduction as the product of an explicit or implicit congressional spending decision, though commentators occasionally speak of the deduction as a subsidy for the well-heeled businessman.[42] This subsidy language probably reflects well-founded

---

goals. They should be analyzed according to traditional tax criteria, however, in other circumstances. See Andrews, *supra* note 3, at 331-43. The deduction for interest payments on personal debts is often treated as a tax expenditure but has been defended on tax policy grounds. See Gunn, *Is the Interest Deduction for Personal Debts a Tax Expenditure?* 1 CANADIAN TAXATION, No. 4, at 46 (1979). The child-care credit can be treated as either a tax expenditure or a part of the normal tax structure, depending on the rationale offered in its defense. See McIntyre, *Evaluating the New Credit for Child Care and Maid Service,* Tax Notes, May 23, 1977, at 7. The same has been said of the casualty loss deduction. See Blum, Book Review (SURREY, PATHWAYS TO TAX REFORM), 1 J. CORP. TAX, 486, 489 (1975). Other ambiguous areas include the exclusion of imputed income from home ownership, the deferral of tax on contributions to pension funds, the gift and scholarship exclusions, the concession rate on earned income and the exemption (or deferral) for controlled foreign corporations.

[38] This subsection analyzes the arguments for and against the Carter Administration's 1978 proposal to deny a business expense deduction for one-half of the cost of a business lunch. U.S. DEP'T OF TREAS., THE PRESIDENT'S 1978 TAX PROGRAM 195-204 (1978) [hereinafter cited as TAX PROGRAM].

[39] See Halperin, *That's Entertainment,* Tax Notes, September 11, 1978.

[40] I.R.C. § 162 states, in pertinent part:
There shall be allowed as a deduction all the ordinary and necessary expenses paid or incurred during the taxable year in carrying on any trade or business. . . .

[41] *See* I.R.C. § 274(e)(1).

[42] *See* Bittker, *Income Tax Deductions, Credits, and Subsidies for Personal*

cynicism about the business necessity of some claimed deductions, rather than an implied assertion that the judicial gloss on section 162 has produced a disguised spending program.

Commentators have defended the proposal to deny a portion of the business meal deduction on two independent grounds. According to one line of reasoning, an expenditure genuinely motivated by business considerations should be deductible, but the tax authorities cannot distinguish genuine and bogus business meals without provoking protracted litigation. A 50% deductibility rule would limit the well-documented abuses that full deductibility has spawned without adding to the complexity of the tax code.[43]

Under the other line of reasoning, business meals should be deductible in computing the net income of the payor but should be taxable income to the beneficiary of the business meal, in much the same way that in-kind wages are deductible to the payor and taxable to the recipient. This argument applies the principle advanced in the preceding example that the beneficiary of consumption goods is the proper taxpayer under a tax system such as ours.[44] Under this argument, the denial of the deduction to the payor is proper as an administratively feasible method of making the payor a "withholding agent" on amounts paid to the beneficiary. Analysts would justify allowing a deduction for 50% of the cost of a meal as a transitional device, a concession to political exigencies or a rough attempt to minimize possible hardships.[45]

Analysts should evaluate both of the above arguments according to tax policy criteria—not budget criteria—under the methodology recommended in this article. Both arguments claim that the 50% deductibility rule raises tax revenue according to consistently applied fairness principles. Both marshall evidence tending to demonstrate that the recommended tax rule is a proper means of achieving an asserted tax policy goal. Since the asserted goal has nothing to do with the expenditure of public funds, a tax expenditure analysis of these arguments would be a useless frivolity.

Expenditures, 16 J. OF L. & ECON. 193 (1973).

[43] *See* Tax Program, *supra* note 38, at 200.

[44] *See* note 34 and accompanying text *supra.*

[45] *See Business and Pleasure,* People & Taxes (December 1977), at 3; Halperin, *supra* note 39.

The main argument advanced by opponents of the Carter Administration's proposal was the possible reduction in jobs within the restaurant industry that enactment of the proposal would produce.[46] Since the maintenance of jobs in a particular industry is typically a spending goal and not a revenue-raising goal, analysts should subject this argument to a tax expenditure analysis. To carry out this analysis, they should recast the business lunch deduction as a spending program and evaluate it according to budget criteria. They should try to determine, for example, the number of jobs, if any, that the constructed spending program is responsible for, its costs per job, the job impact of alternative uses of the forgone tax revenue and the appropriateness of spending government money to achieve the asserted goal. By carrying out the above analysis, they would probably conclude that the business lunch deduction, viewed as a jobs program, is ludicrously wasteful.[47] Whatever they concluded, however, they would have given this argument full consideration without having to determine whether the business lunch deduction was a normal or special part of the tax code.[48]

C. The Theoretical Underpinning of the New Approach

As tax specialists long ago discovered, a tax expenditure analysis can be performed on virtually any tax rule, even on rules which unquestionably are integral to the operation of the income tax.[49] But conducting a tax expenditure analysis indiscrimi-

---

[46] *See, e.g.,* STATEMENT OF V. ROSELLINI, ET AL., BEFORE HOUSE WAYS AND MEANS COMMITTEE, March 20, 1978, in BNA, Daily Report for Executives, Special Supplement, DEP No. 54, 03-5 (estimating 63,000 jobs lost from reform of business lunch deduction).

[47] *See* LIBRARY OF CONGRESS STUDY, cited in Halperin, *supra* note 39, at 301.

[48] The problem in the text could arise in many other contexts. The special treatment of the oil industry is generally defended on tax expenditure grounds, though it was originally adopted for tax policy reasons. The same may be said of accelerated depreciation, cash accounting for farmers, the deduction for interest on personal loans, the exclusion of part of the income of overseas employees and even the capital gains exclusion.

[49] For example, the deduction for amounts paid as rent of a business premises—everyone's idea of a normal tax rule—can be cast as a spending program, with the amount "spent" measured by the amount of tax forgone by allowing the deduction. This constructed spending program then could be evaluated according to budget criteria. The goal of the constructed spending program would not be easy to detect—perhaps it would be an "incentive" to businessmen to engage in profit-seeking activity. *See* text accompanying note 52 *infra*

nately yields no usable information. Proper interpretation of the conclusions of a tax expenditure analysis requires a principled basis for invoking it. Recognizing this, the early proponents of a tax expenditure analysis applied it only to those tax rules which they had first identified as tax expenditures. Their definition of a tax expenditure was the familiar one, requiring tax rules to be characterized unambiguously as normal or special.[50] The overwhelming drawback of this system is that it substantially limits the potential benefits of a tax expenditure analysis. Rigorously applied, it restricts the tax expenditure analysis to an examination of tax provisions that demonstrably are not part of the normal structure of the income tax, thereby barring it from a constructive role in the analysis of many controversial tax issues.

The two preceding examples illustrate a more expansive approach to invoking a tax expenditure analysis. Under this approach, the bare assertion that the tax rule under examination promotes a spending goal triggers a tax expenditure analysis.[51] Once invoked, analysts would conduct the tax expenditure analysis in the same way as is contemplated under the traditional system. The interpretation of the conclusions of the tax expenditure analysis must change, however, to reflect the change in the triggering mechanism. The traditional system employs a tax expenditure analysis after proof that the tax rule is in fact a spending program embedded in the tax code. Evaluation of the constructed spending program, therefore, fairly tests the tax rule itself. Under the new system, we have only an assertion that the tax rule promotes a spending goal. Consequently, the tax expenditure analysis simply determines the merits of the tax rule as a spending program. As illustrated in the two examples above, it says nothing at all about the suitability of the tax rule for promoting tax policy goals.

This approach may appear to differ significantly from the way

---

for a discussion of the problem of evaluating a spending program with unspecified goals.

[50] *See* S. Surrey, *supra* note 6, at 35-39.

[51] Tax analysts cannot always distinguish goals associated with raising revenue from goals associated with spending, since tax policy is a tool of fundamental social and economic policy. Exempting the poor from tax, for example, is typically both a tax policy and a spending policy goal. But this problem poses no difficulty here, since the approach recommended in this article can accommodate an analysis of an argument according to both tax policy and spending policy criteria.

direct expenditure programs are typically evaluated. In fact, however, this approach parallels the mode of analysis that budget specialists employ (or ought to employ) when they attempt to determine the merits of spending programs enacted for mixed or unclear motives.[52] Assume, for example, that Congress has voted to build a dam in the state of an influential senator. Assume further that Congress has completed inconclusive studies of the possible benefits of the dam, and the dam's proponents have alleged multiple and inconsistent goals for it. How should a budget analyst go about evaluating that spending program? I venture that he would postulate possible goals for the dam—flood control, hydroelectric power, flat-water recreation—and test to see if the expenditures for the dam were an appropriate means of achieving those goals, individually and in combination. He would eliminate from his analysis the possible political benefits of the dam, since an evaluation of those benefits would go beyond his professional competence. He would do what I recommend the tax specialists do when faced with legislation with unclear goals: he would evaluate the possible arguments for the legislation—not the legislation itself.

D. Notes from the Flower Garden

In the modified tax expenditure analysis illustrated above, the problem of identifying tax expenditures vanished like dew in the noon sun. The vanishing act was not a linguistic trick, a definitional sleight of hand. The problem was solved by applying the methodology developed in Part I, A above. Once the purpose of the modified tax expenditure analysis—testing nontax arguments—was clearly specified, the solution became obvious. Tax specialists should apply the tax expenditure analysis to any tax provision defended on nontax grounds.[53]

---

[52] Professor Bittker notes the irony of tax specialists' wanting to duplicate for tax rules the review procedures applied to spending programs without understanding how defective those procedures typically are. Bittker, *supra* note 4, at 244 n.1. Also ironic is the complaint that analyzing tax rules as spending rules is inappropriate because of the difficulty of knowing the true purpose of the tax rule, when a similar situation for spending programs commonly arises and presents no great difficulties.

[53] Professors Surrey and McDaniel suggest that "[m]ost tax expenditures are readily recognizable since they are usually treated by their supporters as tax incentives or as hardship relief, and they are not urged as necessary to correct defects in the income tax structure itself." *Current Developments,*

Epilogue

Our tax code has been forged in the cauldron of politics. The goals it has pursued, or allegedly pursued, are multiple and inconsistent. Many code provisions unquestionably function as spending programs, while others arguably serve both spending and revenue-raising goals. This state of affairs poses problems for Congress in managing the tax system and for tax specialists in analyzing it. The progenitors of the tax expenditure budget have articulated a promising system for coping with these problems—a system that has enjoyed remarkable success in Congress. The controversial part of that system is its recommended methodology for identifying disguised spending programs. The alternative methodology presented in this article extends their system and eliminates the feature that has subjected it to attack.[54]

---

supra note 2, at 228. In recognizing tax expenditures by the arguments used to support them, Surrey and McDaniel are following the approach recommended in the text. They depart from this approach, however, when they fail to interpret the conclusion of their tax expenditure analysis in light of the method used for invoking it.

[54] This point is illustrated by examining Professor Kahn's recent attack on the tax expenditure concept. *See* Kahn, *Accelerated Depreciation—Tax Expenditure or Proper Allowance for Measuring Net Income?*, 78 MICH L. REV. 1 (1979). Kahn argues that the debate over the merits of tax policy arguments in favor of accelerated depreciation should not be "stifled" by the Treasury Department's designation of accelerated depreciation as a tax expenditure. Under the methodology of this article, the fact that the tax expenditure budget includes revenue forgone as a result of certain accelerated depreciation deductions merely signifies that Congress views those deductions as an alternative to a direct investment subsidy. Analysts may try to persuade Congress to view them differently, but they can hardly complain that Congress has stifled debate by measuring the revenue forgone through accelerated depreciation.

Kahn offers a novel argument in favor of some form of accelerated depreciation. Under conventional accounting theory, depreciation should allocate the tax cost of an asset to the income earned by that asset. Straight-line depreciation rests on the simplifying assumption that an asset generates income in equal annual amounts over its useful life. Kahn accepts this simplifying assumption but argues that depreciation should allocate the tax cost of an asset to the present worth of the income earned by the asset. Assuming a positive real interest rate, Kahn's allocation method would result in accelerated depreciation for at least some assets.

Under the methodology of this article, tax analysts would evaluate Professor Kahn's argument without first attempting to determine whether accelerated depreciation is a normal or special rule. Since Kahn's argument is obviously a tax policy argument, analysts should test it according to tax policy criteria.

No one should propose a solution to the problem of defining a tax expenditure and expect to bypass completely the heated debate that the tax expenditure idea has engendered. This debate pulls into its vortex all who venture near. Mentioning the "problem" of identifying tax expenditures, for example, implicitly attacks those who proclaim that no problem exists. Similarly, speaking of a "solution" affronts those who contend that no solution is possible. The positions taken in this article are nevertheless genuinely compatible with the core position of both the progenitors of the tax expenditure budget and their critics and furnish no fuel to either side for continuing their apparently unendable debate.

They would learn nothing about the merit of Kahn's argument by casting accelerated depreciation as a spending program and testing it according to budget criteria.

ROBERT S. McINTYRE, "LESSONS FOR TAX REFORMERS FROM THE HISTORY OF THE ENERGY TAX INCENTIVES IN THE WINDFALL PROFIT TAX ACT OF 1980"

22 Boston College Law Review 705 (1981), pp. 732-41.

III. BEYOND TAX EXPENDITURE ANALYSIS

The preceding discussion includes a fair summary of most of the arguments presented to Congress in favor of or in opposition to the various energy tax preferences under consideration for inclusion within the windfall profit tax legislation. Implicitly or explicitly, virtually all of these contentions fit snugly within the framework of what is known as tax expenditure analysis. That is, it was generally conceded by both proponents and opponents that the tax credit proposals were substitutes for direct spending programs, and that they should be analyzed as such.

It is somewhat difficult to imagine the supporters of the energy tax preferences defending their proposals as anything but tax-based spending programs. Certainly it would have have been ludicrous to have tried to justify them as an appropriate means of measuring the decline in real incomes suffered by those who enlisted as soldiers in the moral equivalent of war against excessive use of foreign oil. Such a justification would have been even stranger in light of the fact that most of the tax provisions under consideration were in the form of credits against tax liability rather than deductions from taxable income. It is basic that a credit cannot be the correct tool for accurately measuring income.[107]

The general concession that the proposed energy preferences should be analyzed as tax expenditures may seem trivial, but it actually represents an unusual phenomenon. In the more typical case, there is a great deal of categorical confusion between assertions about the proper way to measure real incomes and arguments about the best way, if any, to encourage socially useful

---

[107] To illustrate: Legitimate business expenses ought to be deductible in computing net income. A credit system could not yield such a fair result, given progressive tax rates. For example, if the business expense deduction were replaced with a 40% credit for such expenses, a taxpayer with $50,000 in gross earnings and $20,000 in expenses would have only about one-third the tax liability of a taxpayer with $100,000 in gross income and $70,000 in expenses. This point is explored at greater length in M.J. McIntyre, *Evaluating the New Tax Credit for Child Care and Maid Service*, TAX NOTES, May 23, 1977, at 7.

behavior.[108] Sometimes the disagreement about the proper characterization of a particular tax provision — as either a tax expenditure or a tool to help measure income properly — represents a genuine, good faith dispute. For example, the charitable deduction is defended by Professor Andrews as a proper adjustment in determining taxable income.[109] His view is based on the plausible conclusion that funds given away constitute neither consumption nor savings on the part of the donor.[110] In contrast, Professor McDaniel criticizes the

---

[108] For a thorough demystification of the confusion often encountered between tax expenditure and income measurement analysis *see* M.J. McIntyre, *A Solution to the Problem of Defining a Tax Expenditure*, 14 U.C. DAVIS L. REV. 79 (1980) [hereinafter *M.J. McIntyre*]. My brother notes that disputes over whether a particular tax provision is a tax expenditure or is rather a "normal" tax rule incorrectly assume that the intrinsic nature of the provision in question should determine the analytical framework in which to evaluate it. He argues that a more fruitful approach would be to eschew *a priori* decisions as the proper mode of analysis, and instead in each case to use the analytical method which responds to how a provision is defended. *Id.* at 94. In other words, "the bare assertion that the tax rule under examination promotes a spending goal [should] trigger a tax expenditure analysis," but only for the purpose of evaluating whether the provision in fact promotes that spending goal in an efficient and acceptable manner. *Id.* at 100. "[A] tax expenditure analysis of . . . arguments [that a rule is appropriate in defining 'income,' on the other hand,] would be a useless frivolity." *Id.* at 98. If a tax provision is convincingly defended on income measurement grounds, he suggests, tax expenditure analysis is both unnecessary and inappropriate. *Id.* at 94-95.

The application of tax expenditure analysis only to tax expenditure *arguments* completely avoids the up-until-now controversial problem of defining what is a tax expenditure and what is a "normal" tax rule. The insight which this approach offers also helps cut through the intentional smokescreens, frequently created by proponents of tax provisions, which cannot adequately be justified on either tax policy *or* spending grounds. *See, e.g.*, the discussion in note 115 *infra*.

[109] See note 110 *infra*.

[110] *See* Andrews, *Personal Deductions in an Ideal Income Tax*, 86 HARV. L. REV. 309 (1972). Under this analysis, the only rationale for not allowing deductions for *all* gifts and taxing them to the donees is administrative convenience.

While Andrews' approach provides a defensible explanation of the proper treatment of charitable donors, the issue remains as to the proper treatment of the charitable organizations themselves — namely, whether charities should be allowed to pay no taxes on gifts received (assuming those gifts are deductible by the donors).

An income measurement analysis would start with the threshhold question of whether charities should be taxed under a comprehensive income tax. Would such a tax on charities be a proxy for taxing the recipients of the charities' largesse, much as the corporate income tax acts as a rough proxy for taxing shareholders on retained earnings (i.e., savings)? In other words, from an analytical perspective, are *recipients* of gifts from charities the proper taxpayers, since they are the ones who actually consume the funds? But if so, given the presumably low tax brackets of many of said recipients, would a "proxy" tax on charities properly be at a very low rate? Moving further, should administrative expenses be deductible? If a charity uses all its gross "income" to provide information to the general public, are the newly-informed the proper taxpayers, or has the charity spent its entire "income" on administrative costs and is its "net income" therefore zero? Would this mean that only organizations which provide grants to individuals should be treated as having taxable income (based upon the proxy theory)? Should charities with a poor clientele (orphanages) be taxed at a lower rate than those who cater to the more affluent (museums)? The proper answers to these and certainly other questions might cause one to conclude that the tax exemption for charity is sensible under an income measurement analysis.

Alternatively, the tax-exempt status of charities might be defended on spending grounds. Is tax exemption the most appropriate way for government to subsidize such organiza-

write-off for donations to charity on the ground that it is an upside-down subsidy which favors wealthy taxpayers and their chosen causes.[111] What is sometimes not understood is that, if Professor Andrews is right, Professor McDaniel's argument is irrelevant.[112] If Professor Andrews is wrong, then the focus should be concentrated on Professor McDaniel's tax expenditure analysis, which some maintain still results in a favorable report on the charitable deduction.

At the legislative level, proponents of a particular tax measure frequently resist the "tax expenditure" label in an attempt to gain a tactical advantage or to defuse criticism. The former chairman of the Senate Finance Committee, Russell Long (D-La.), for example, used to rail against acceptance of the tax expenditure concept,[113] due in part to his fear that the jurisdiction of his committee might suffer were its legislative proposals generally seen in this light.[114] In addition, lobbyists for new tax benefits usually make great efforts to characterize their proposals as necessary to reflect income properly or to deal with some defect in the normative incom tax rules, while simultaneously explaining their desperate need for new "incentives." The proposed increases in business depreciation allowances, for example, are alternatively defended by corporate lobbyists as appropriate to obtain an accurate measure of capital income in an inflationary economy and as a needed subsidy to encourage capital investment. This dual characterization allows them to mitigate the perceived pejorative nature of the "tax expenditure" label and to confuse the argument when necessary to respond to difficult-to-refute attacks on their positions.[115]

---

tions? Given the pluralistic desire to avoid government interference with charitable activity, one could well answer this question in the affirmative. Certainly, such a tax expenditure is far easier to defend as a subsidy to the charities than it is as a benefit to donors.

[111] *See, e.g.*, McDaniel, *Study of Federal Matching Grants for Charitable Contributions*, in U.S. COMMISSION ON PRIVATE PHILANTHROPY AND PUBLIC NEEDS, DEPT. OF TREASURY, 4 RESEARCH PAPERS TAXES 2417-532 (1977).

[112] Professor McDaniel's argument is relevant only to contentions that the charitable deduction is a proper way to subsidize charities and their donors. It does not even attempt to address the income measurement argument put forward by Professor Andrews. See note 66 *supra*.

[113] *See, e.g., Hearings on H.R. 10612 Before the Senate Finance Comm.*, 94th Cong., 2d Sess. 241 (March 1976). More recently, Senator Long has admitted that there is at least "some analogy between a tax program designed to encourage a particular activity and a direct spending program to encourage that activity." R.B. Long, Luncheon Speech, NAT'L TAX JOURNAL, Sept. 1979, at 279.

[114] Several of the leading proponents of the tax expenditure concept have suggested that the tax-writing committees should share jurisdiction with other committees where tax "spending" is involved. *See, e.g., Investment Credit Hearings, supra* note 2a, at 28 (Statement of Paul McDaniel); *id.* at 125 (statement of Fred Werthheimer for Common Cause); CONG. REC. S5703-09 (daily ed. Apr. 17, 1978) (remarks of Sen. Edward M. Kennedy (D-Mass.)).

[115] If an attack is made on the income measurement argument by pointing out, for example, that corporate taxable income is already far less than inflation-adjusted book income, due to the $49 billion in corporate loopholes, the business lobbyists typically counter by raising the incentive argument. *See, e.g.*, the statement of Charles E. Walker (who represents a large number of Business Roundtable clients) and succeeding colloquy during the Senate Finance Committee hearings on tax cut proposals in July of 1980:

No such confusion occurred in the case of the energy tax incentives proposed for inclusion in the windfall profit bill. Moreover, not only were the proposals defended solely as tax expenditures, but they were also generally styled as tax credits, rather than deductions. At first glance, these two occurrences might seem to represent unmitigated achievements for tax reformers. The "tax expenditure" label apparently puts reformers on their home ground; the use of credits is an approach long advocated by some reformers, since it avoids the "upside-down" effect by which the extent of federal subsidy is dependent upon an individual's tax bracket.[116] Unfortunately, these "victories" were not without cost, nor were they clear-cut. As has been illustrated, the level of the congressional debate was not always the highest, and one major negative effect of the credit proponents' concession on the "tax expenditure" label and their general advocacy of credits was to remove some of the arguments which might otherwise have been made against the provisions. Many of the reform-oriented members of Congress and their staffs, schooled only in a rather primitive tax expenditure analysis approach to all tax policy issues, were unprepared to make or to understand further arguments not encompassed within the limited framework with which they are familiar. This problem is illustrated by the large number of normally reform-oriented members who voted in favor of the House motion to instruct the windfall conferees to accept all the Senate's energy credits. Reformers should, therefore, be forced to face up to some of the

---

> Mr. WALKER: [One reason we need faster writeoffs is that] with the underdepreciation that we have seen because of the rapid rates of inflation, the actual corporate tax is much higher than the 46-percent rate.

But when questioned about another proposal (by Professor Dale Jorgensen), which would completely solve the inflation problem but was much less generous than the plan favored by the big business community, Mr. Walker shifted gears:

> Mr. WALKER: I don't think we should argue this in terms of theoretical economics, or how many angels can dance on the head of a pin. . . . I say, let's look around the world and see what is happening . . . . Other countries have very fast depreciation . . . . The people that worked on 10-5-3 [the depreciation scheme favored by Mr. Walker] . . . have as their basic goal to liberalize the depreciation system. Not to offset what inflation has done . . . .

Hearings Before the Senate Comm. on Finance on Tax Cut Proposals, 96th Cong., 2d Sess. 855-65 (June 24, 25, 28, 1980). Conversely, if the business lobbyists' tax expenditure analysis is questioned in light of, say, the dismal economic record of the seventies in spite of the $26 billion in added annual investment tax subsidies, the lobbyists frequently retreat to the inflation/income measurement argument. *See, e.g.*, the comments of Richard W. Rahn, chief economist of the Chamber of Commerce, in response to my article, *Business Tax Cuts In Perspective*, TAX NOTES, Sept. 1, 1980, at 395. Replying to the point made in this article that the 10-5-3 depreciation plan would be more generous than immediate expensing and would therefore cause serious distortions in investment decision-making and generate a huge new tax shelter market, Mr. Rahn states, *inter alia*, that "[e]ven taxpayers who take advantage of maximum acceleration allowed under present law may not be sufficiently compensated for inflation at today's double-digit rates." R. Rahn, *A Critique of the McIntyre Article*, TAX NOTES, Sept. 1, 1980, at 401. (Needless to say, my article had also dealt at length with the inflation argument.)

[116] Even tax *credits* cannot reach those with no tax liability, unless the credits are refundable. It was suggested that some of the energy credits proposed for inclusion in the windfall bill include a refundability feature to remedy this defect.

limits to the scope of tax expenditure analysis, particularly as it is understood in Congress.

The tax expenditure concept is tremendously useful in comparing proposed tax subsidies to direct spending alternatives, and in many cases in illuminating equity problems, particularly when an "upside-down" effect would result from enactment of a proposed tax provision. As a result, tax expenditure analysis has often been an effective lobbying tool in fighting new loopholes. Nevertheless, in recent years, the basic premise of tax expenditure analysis — that loopholes can, and in fact *should*, be analyzed exactly like direct spending programs — has in many instances had the perverse and unintended effect of legitimizing the proliferation of new tax subsidy provisions. This result has occurred due to a number of interrelated factors.

First, it is repeatedly stressed by advocates of the tax expenditure approach that the term is not a pejorative one.[117] This position has been taken largely for tactical reasons, for example, to gain support for inclusion of tax expenditures within the budget process and, more recently, as part of the debate over sunset legislation.[118] The proposition implicitly suggests, however, at least to most members of Congress, that some proposed loopholes must be acceptable.[119]

---

[117] The now official view that the "tax expenditure" label is neutral is emphatically stated in Office of Management and Budget, Special Analyses, Budget of the U.S. Government, Fiscal Year 1982, Special Analysis G, at 203 (1981): "It should be emphasized that the listing of specific tax expenditure items does not imply either approval or disapproval of specific provisions of the tax system." *See also Investment Credit Hearings, supra* note 3, at 35 (statement of Paul R. McDaniel). In fact, the term "tax expenditure" was intentionally chosen for its non-emotional character. *See* Davenport, *Tax Expenditure Analysis as a Tool for Policymakers*, TAX NOTES, Dec. 1, 1980, at 1051, 1052.

[118] *See generally* Surrey & McDaniel, *The Tax Expenditure Concept and The Legislative Process*, in THE ECONOMICS OF TAXATION 123 *et seq.* (Aaron & Boskin, eds. 1980).

Advocates of the sunset concept for tax expenditures have sometimes had to tie themselves in knots to maintain their position that they are not biased against tax expenditures *per se. See, e.g., Investment Credit Hearings, supra* note 3, at 153 (colloquy between Fred Wertheimer of Common Cause and Rep. John Duncan (R-Tenn.)):

 Mr. DUNCAN: . . . Mr. Wertheimer, you have referred to "tax incentives [that] have long outlived their usefulness." Would you identify some that you consider obsolete?
 Mr. WERTHEIMER: I think our basic concern is there is no way to figure out which incentives have long outlived their usefulness under the present process. As I said earlier, we are not here to support or oppose any particular programs. We do believe that the present process does not leave room for evaluation.
 Mr. DUNCAN: You do make a statement, though, that they are obsolete but then can't identify any. Is that your answer?
 Mr. WERTHEIMER: I would prefer not to specifically testify on behalf or against any tax incentives right now.
 Mr. DUNCAN: I take it you don't know any? Are you saying your statement is incorrect?
 Mr. WERTHEIMER: No.
 Mr. DUNCAN: But you don't know of any that is obsolete? I am a little amazed
 . . . .

[119] If not all tax expenditures are necessarily bad, then, *a fortiori*, some must be good. Of course, the advocates of the tax expenditure concept do not always believe their own rhetoric

Second, tax expenditure analysis has tended to focus the political debate over new loopholes on efficiency issues. Admittedly, most proposed tax preferences fail a dispassionate efficiency evaluation — in fact, it is difficult to recall a single loophole proposal which has passed such a test.[120] Careful efficiency analysis, however, is not always an important influence on legislative decisionmaking. By agreeing to fight on an efficiency battleground, reformers have increasingly found themselves overwhelmed by the masses of allegedly scientific research and computer printouts which powerful interests now routinely muster on behalf of their favored new loopholes.[121]

---

about the neutrality of the term. At a 1979 conference on tax expenditures, the following exchange occurred between Professor Stanley Surrey and a member of the audience:

Question. Professor Surrey, . . . you mentioned earlier in your presentation that there were good tax expenditures and bad tax expenditures. Could you give us an example of what you regard as a good tax expenditure . . . ?

[Prof. Surrey:] . . . When you press hard as to whether I can see any useful tax expenditures, I am pushed very hard. . . . I do have some difficulties in finding programs I would run, if I were running the government, through the tax system rather than as direct programs.

Tax Expenditure Analysis: A Reply by Professor Surrey and Discussion, CANADIAN TAXATION 26, 28 (Summer 1979).

Before it became fashionable to maintain the neutrality of the tax expenditure concept, Professor Surrey did not need to be prodded to assert his antagonism to virtually all special tax breaks. *See, e.g.*, Surrey, *The Federal Tax System — Current Activities and Future Possibilities* (speech before Boston Economic Club, May 15, 1968), at 26 ("I doubt that any of these special tax treatments could stand the scrutiny of careful program analysis, and I doubt that if these were direct expenditure programs we would tolerate for very long the inefficiencies that such program analysis would reveal."), *quoted in* Bittker, *Accounting for Federal "Tax Subsidies" in the National Budget*, NAT'L TAX J., June 1969, at 241 n.11.

[120] *Cf.* Professor Surrey's conclusion in note 119 *supra*.

[121] Legislators usually ignore the fact that "one can get almost any answer one wants as to the effects of tax incentives by making sure that the chosen model has specifications appropriate to one's purpose," R. Chirinko & R. Eisner, THE EFFECTS OF TAX POLICIES ON INVESTMENT IN MACROECONOMETRIC MODELS: FULL MODEL SIMULATIONS, OTA PAPER 46, U.S. Dept. of the Treasury 26 (Jan. 1981).

[122] Proposals for major changes in the tax depreciation rules, such as "10-5-3" and the Senate Finance Committee's '2-4-7-10," would so disassociate tax depreciation from financial accounting standards that the concept of a corporate *income* tax would be rendered meaningless, at least for large, capital-intensive companies. Although the Carter Treasury did complain about the loss of linkage between actual and taxable income which these plans would create, *see Miscellaneous Tax Bills III: Hearings Before the Senate Comm. on Finance*, 96th Cong., 1st Sess. 164, 171 (1979) (statement of G. William Miller, Secretary of the Treasury), the significance of this result seems to be lost on most members of Congress. *See Legislating Without a Blackboard*, PEOPLE & TAXES, Aug./Sept. 1980, at 13. It is not lost on some of the proponents of the measures, who hope that, by breaking the link between tax depreciation and service lives, the way will be opened for even further corporate tax reductions in the future. *See* R.S. McIntyre, *The Beginning of the End of the Corporate Income Tax?*, PEOPLE & TAXES, Oct. 1979, at 3.

The focus in the "three martini lunch" debate ought to have been on the valuable form of income that free meals provide to their recipients. Once this is recognized, it is difficult to justify a 100% exclusion on either tax policy or tax expenditure grounds. Congress, however, never seemed to appreciate this point. Instead, it concentrated on whether a meals exclusion is an appropriate way to subsidize the restaurant industry. Although it is demonstrably not, restaurant employees defended themselves with the usual charts and tables showing such enormous job losses from reform of the meals rules that Congress was almost unanimously opposed to change.

Third, by promoting tax expenditure analysis as the key to evaluating most tax proposals, reformers have created a whole generation of members of Congress and their staffers who are wholly innocent of an understanding of traditional tax policy analysis. Issues like proper income measurement techniques are rarely discussed intelligently in the political arena, and the repercussions have been and are being felt in areas ranging from depreciation "reform" to the "three martini lunch" to the so-called "marriage penalty."[122]

Fourth, the focus on direct spending comparisons which tax expenditure analysis encourages has tended in practice to result in substantial disregard of the very special need of the Internal Revenue Service for ease of administration and the importance for taxpayers of simplicity. Certainly these factors can be included within a broad-reaching tax expenditure analysis approach,[123] but such inclusion tends to contradict the assertion that the "tax expenditure" label is not a pejorative one, especially when proposed loopholes are opposed on complexity grounds alone.[124]

Finally, and most important, the premise of tax expenditure analysis that tax incentive proposals should be treated merely as direct spending substitutes has tended to drastically oversimplify issues of tax equity. Assuming a tax benefit is crafted to avoid "upside-down" effects and made refundable to [treat fairly]those with no liability, tax expenditure analysis tends to give it a favorable report as far as equity is concerned.[125] Not everyone is willing, however, to accept the idea that this is all equity entails. Paying to the government one's allotted share of taxes based on an honest report of one's income is never a cheery task, but it becomes positively onerous when one is aware that others have had large chunks of their taxes forgiven — for whatever "incentive" reason. It is all well and good to maintain that a proper appreciation of tax subsidies as merely direct grants routed through the tax system ought to make ordinary taxpayers less critical of the loopholes enjoyed by their betters. The common perception of tax equity in the real world, however, is not so sophisticated. Maintaining a general belief in the fairness of the system is of high importance in ensuring a reasonable level of taxpayer compliance with the

---

For an outline of how the various arguments should have been presented, *see* M.J. McIntyre, *supra* n.108, at 98-99.

The "marriage tax" issue ought to revolve around questions about who should be taxed on pooled income. Instead, it has largely centered on claims that the tax system encourages divorce, or that it discourages women from entering the job market. For a discussion of the problems in the current debate, *see* M.J. McIntyre, *Individual Filing in the Personal Income Tax: Prolegamena to Future Discussion*, 58 N.C.L.REV. 469 (1980).

[123] *See, e.g.*, Surrey, *Tax Expenditure Analysis: The Concept and Its Uses*, CANADIAN TAXATION 3, 8-9 (Summer 1979).

[124] See note [118] *supra*. See text accompanying note [138] *infra*.

[125] *See, e.g., Investment Credit Hearings, supra* note 3, at 35-36 (statement of Paul R. McDaniel) (suggesting that refundable credits solve equity problems, but that administrative considerations may remain).

law[126] — a factor which reformers who advocate refundable investment credits for giant corporations[127] tend to discount.

Somewhat ironically, the widely-held belief that the tax laws should be fair has contributed to the pronounced tendency for tax expenditures to expand once they are established. This phenomenon seems to be most evident in the energy area. The historically classic example is percentage depletion,[128] which was originally enacted only for oil and gas, but eventually grew to cover almost a hundred different "depletable" resources, including gravel, asbestos, peat moss, and clam shells.[129] The pressures to expand the recently enacted energy credits indicate that they have an expansionary potential which may be of even a higher order than that of percentage depletion.

The potential for energy tax credits to grow can be appreciated by perusing almost any issue of *Tax Notes*, the weekly tax journal. The lead item in the summary of incoming Treasury mail will almost invariably describe a letter or series of letters asking that a mechanized awning, or woodburning stove, or special reflective roof paint, or carburetor jet adjusting device, or almost any conceivable device which happens to save energy be made eligible for an energy tax credit.[130] The requests are so voluminous that the Treasury Depart-

---

[126] See Kurtz, *Notes to a New Commissioner of Internal Revenue*, TAX NOTES, June 1, 1981, at 1195, 1202. Congress has understood the political significance of avoiding gross perceived inequities in the tax system, but at the same time has generally been unwilling to attack loopholes directly. Therefore, it compromised by establishing the minimum tax, I.R.C. §§ 55 *et seq.* — a band-aid measure which pure tax expenditure analysis must necessarily condemn as schizophrenic.

[127] See, e.g., *Investment Credit Hearings, supra* note 3, at 202, 205 (statement of Gerard M. Brannon); *cf. id.* at 162-63 (statement of Emil M. Sunley, Jr.) (suggesting that the nonrefundability of the investment credit is largely for "cosmetic" reasons. *But cf. id.* at 180 (statement of Jerome Kurtz, Commissioner of Internal Revenue) (noting that leasing transactions result in a kind of *ad hoc* refundability even under current law).

[128] I.R.C. §§ 613, 613A.

[129] Percentage depletion has been allowed for oil and gas since 1926. Beginning in 1932, it was gradually extended, at lower rates, to most other minerals. TAX REFORM ACT OF 1969, REPORT OF THE SENATE COMM. ON FINANCE ON H.R. 13270, S. REP. NO. 91-552, 91st Cong., 1st Sess. 178 (1969). The 1954 Code made percentage depletion generally available, excluding only "soil, sod, turf, water, or mosses" and "minerals from sea water, the air, or similar inexhaustible resources." B.I. BITTKER AND L.M. STONE, FEDERAL INCOME, ESTATE, AND GIFT TAXATION 332 (4th ed. 1972).

[130] See, e.g., TAX NOTES, Jan. 14, 1980, at 31 (*Residential Energy Credit Requested for Coal Burning Stove; Credit Requested for Heat Exchanges and Wind Turbines; Still Another Residential Energy Credit Request [— for] 'Plasticool'; Sailing, Sailing . . . [A letter asks] whether an ocean-going commercial sailing vessel . . . will be eligible for a tax credit*); *id.*, Jan. 21, 1980, at 77 (*Residential Energy Credit Suggested for Hot Water Heaters; Credits Asked for Zone Control System for Heating and Air Conditioning*); *id.* Feb. 4, 1980, at 156, (*Credits for Wood Burning Stoves Supported*); *id.*, Feb. 11, 1980, at 196 (*Tax Benefits to Encourage Recycling are Urged*); *id.*, Feb. 25, 1980, at 265 (*Credits Sought for Wood Stoves and Solar Heating Systems*); *id.*, Mar. 3, 1980, at 301 (*New England Senators Urge Woodstove Credit*); *id.*, Mar. 10, 1980, at 349 (*Push Continues for Wood Burning Stove Credits*); *id.*, Mar. 17, 1980, at 375 (*Wood Stove Credits Continue To Be a 'Burning' Issue; Why Don't Awnings Qualify for a Credit?*); *id.*, Mar. 31, 1980, at 455 (*Credits Sought for Wood Stoves, Aluminum Siding, Awnings, and Insulation; Credits*

ment pleaded with Congress to remove its never-exercised discretionary authority to expand the list of items qualifying for tax credits. Congress responded, however, only by establishing hard-to-meet standards for the exercise of that discretion.[131]

Sought for Low Temperature Commercial Dishwasher); id., Apr. 7, 1980, at 489 (*Taxpayer Wants to Know Why House Had To Be Completed Before April 20, 1977 To Get Credit for Insulation; Treasury Gets Proposals on Community Recycling Centers*); id., Apr. 14, 1980, at 531 (*Insulation Credit for Landlords Urged; Another Request for Wood Stove Credits*); id., Apr. 21, 1980, at 585 (*Tax Credits for Wood Stoves, Heat Pumps, and Thermocyclers*); id., Apr. 28, 1980, at 623 (*Credits Sought for Temperature Control System*); id., May 5, 1980, at 655 (*Energy Credits Sought for Ground Water Pumps and Other Items*); id., May 12, 1980, at 719 (*Energy Credits Sought for Woodburning Stoves; Qualification for The Business Energy Investment Tax Credit Sought for Solar Cooling System*); id., May 19, 1980, at 751 (*Tax Credit for Wood Stove Sought by Taxpayer; Tax Credit Urged for Wood-Burning Equipment; Company Seeks Insulation Credit for Slag-Type Roofing Material*); id., May 26, 1980, at 793 (*Nine Senators Ask for Wood Stove Credit Meeting; Tax Credit Sought for Small-Scale Hydroelectric Equipment*); id., June 2, 1980, at 831 (*More Letters Are Received Supporting a Credit for Woodburning Stoves*); id., June 9, 1980, at 855 (*Energy Credit Sought for Vapor Compression Hot Water Heaters; Qualification for Tax Credit Sought for Energy Conversion System and for Windmills*); id., June 16, 1980, at 925 (*Viscosity Stabilizer Said To Reduce Fuel Use*); id., June 30, 1980, at 1005 (*Wood Energy Institute Supports Credit for Wood Stoves; Reports on Wood Stove Credit Said To Mislead Homeowners; Fedders Continues to Urge Tax Credits for Vapor Compression Water Heaters*); id., July 7, 1980, at 15 (*Fedders Continues to Urge Tax Credits for Vapor Compression Water Heaters*); id., July 14, 1980, at 75 (*Aluminum Can Eater Said To Qualify for Energy Credit; Energy Credit is Urged for Coal-Fired Furnaces; Treasury Receives More Letters Supporting Wood Energy Credit*); id., July 21, 1980, at 119 (*Treasury Receives Another Inquiry About Energy Credits for Woodburning Stoves; Should Energy-Producing Greenhouses Qualify for Energy Credits?*); id., July 28, 1980, at 161 (*Energy Credit for Coal Burning Furnaces and Boilers Recommended; Woodburning Stove Energy Credit Receives Another Recommendation*); id., Aug. 4, 1980, at 215 (*Taxpayer Seeks Insulation Credit for Second Home; Taxpayer Seeks Amount of Tax Credit for an Unspecified Type of Solar Product*); id., Aug. 11, 1980, at 267 (*Tax Credit Sought for Awnings; Taxpayer Berates Denial of Energy Credit for Gas Furnaces*); id., Aug. 18, 1980, at 323 (*Expansion of Residential Energy Credits Recommended, Specifically for Wood-Burning Stoves and Vapor Compression Water Heaters; Credit Recommended for Energy Saving Window Coatings*); id., Aug. 25, 1980, at 369 (*Heat-Pump Water Heaters, Wood-Burning Stoves, Electric Radiator Heaters, and Evaporative Coolers Recommended for Energy Credits*); id., Sept. 1, 1980, at 407 (*Limits on Energy Credits Opposed; Credit for Hydronic Central Heating Systems Sought; Credit Sought for Geothermal Well With Underground Heat Pump*); id., Sept. 8, 1980, at 465 (*3M Urges Change in Regulations to Permit Credit for Window Coatings; Credits Recommended for Wood-Burning Stoves, Vapor Compression Water Heaters, and Coal Furnaces; More Liberal Energy Credits Recommended As Cure To Energy Problems Of U.S.*); id., Sept. 22, 1980, at 579 (*Energy Credit Recommended for 'Passive Solar Houses'*); id., Sept. 29, 1980, at 631 (*Fedders Applies for Energy Credit for Heat Pump Water Heater*); id., Oct. 6, 1980, at 683 (*Gradison Asks if Saturated Felt Qualifies as 'Roof Insulation'*); id., Oct. 13, 1980, at 739 (*Denials of Energy Credits for Solar Collector and New Furnaces Criticized; Treasury Queried on Eligibility of Thermal Conduction Plates for Energy Credits*). But cf. id., Jan. 7, 1980, at 11; id., Jan. 28, 1980; and id., Sept. 15, 1980, at 531. Through Oct. 13, 1980, these were the only 1980 issues in which there were no energy credit references. These items tend to be at the beginning because the summary is in Internal Revenue Code section order, and credits occur early in the code.

[131] The windfall profit tax bill sets the following criteria for adding energy items to the list of those eligible for a tax credit: Treasury must determine, first, that making the item eligible will result in a reduction in total U.S. consumption of oil and natural gas and that the reduction is sufficient to justify the revenue cost; second, that adding the item cannot result in increased use of anything which is known to be, or reasonably suspected to be, hazardous to the environment or to public health or safety; and, third, that existing federal subsidies are insufficient. Pub. L. No. 96-223, § 201(b) (1980); I.R.C. § 44C(c)(9).

The most obvious reason for the expansionary nature of energy tax expenditures is that there simply is no purely logical stopping place once the principle is established that tax incentives for alternative energy development and conservation are a good idea. If a credit for solar hot water heaters is on the books, what is the argument against extending the credits to greenhouses used in passive solar heating — especially since the greenhouses probably save more energy? Similarly, if a credit for replacing inefficient boiler parts is allowed, why not a credit for replacing the whole furnace? And so on. While some discrimination is expected in direct spending programs, the deeply felt — albeit often violated — principle that the tax laws should be *fair* makes such distinctions seem less justifiable with regard to tax expenditures.[132]

This special fairness requirement which we impose on tax incentives means that no one should think that we can treat tax preference legislation as fully equivalent to direct spending. Tax expenditure analysis in skilled hands can be a very useful tool, but it does not offer a complete means for evaluating new tax loopholes. The need to maintain public confidence in the tax system and to preserve the tax base from even further erosion cautions against enactment of tax expenditures even when an analysis based purely on efficiency may indicate, at least to Congress, that a tax subsidy is appropriate. This point has not been sufficiently stressed in recent years.

---

[132] This feeling may explain why Jim Jeffords (R-Vt.) wanted to make the wood-burning stove credit retroactive to April, 1977. See text at note 42 *supra*.

There are other reasons why energy tax credits are so prone to expansion. One, which may be applicable to subsidies generally, is that once some energy items are eligible, manufacturers or installers of others find it necessary to gain eligibility in order to remain competitive. If insulation is paid for in part by the Treasury, for example, a product which combines insulation with exterior siding needs a similar subsidy if it is to be saleable. Another reason why energy credits are susceptible to expansion is that the normal opposition to tax expenditures on the part of liberals, who are usually concerned about retaining tax revenues for government social programs, has been particularly weak in the case of energy credits. This is due to several factors. One is that such tax expenditures are advocated by many of the do-good groups which are traditionally linked with liberals. Another is pure politics — many of the liberals are from New England, where the wood-burning stove credit is very popular, since everybody seems to be buying such a device. Still another has to do with the liberal opposition to decontrol of domestic oil prices. Having rejected the most effective means of stimulating solar energy and conservation, many liberals have desperately grasped for any substitute in order to present a pro-conservation, pro-solar image.

Until very recently, a notable exception to the tax reform apostasy of many liberals when it came to energy tax credits was the firm antagonism to the tax expenditure approach maintained by Senator Edward Kennedy (D-Mass.). Senator Kennedy coupled his opposition to oil decontrol with a detailed program of *direct* subsidies for conservation and alternative energy use. See 125 CONG. REC. S11507-13 (daily ed., Aug. 2, 1979). With the election of Ronald Reagan, however, even Senator Kennedy appears ready to abandon this effort. Following reports that the Reagan administration would recommend elimination of the Solar and Conservation Bank, see note 74 *supra*, Senator Kennedy proposed to double the business energy conservation tax incentives. See THE JOURNAL OF COMMERCE (Feb. 12, 1981).

POINTS AND COUNTERPOINTS

1. Is the Accelerated Cost Recovery System (ACRS) a tax subsidy? Do you think the business groups that lobbied so hard for its enactment were seeking a subsidy? In classifying ACRS, what is the relevance of the fact that Congress unquestionably was told in 1981 that its enactment would stimulate the economy? Does it matter whether the advice was good, or only that Congress chose to follow it? For discussion of the merits of ACRS, see Chapter V.

2. Given the position taken by Treasury in the 1984 Budget that ACRS is the "general" income tax rule for "determining how the cost of depreciable assets is recovered," should it classify the depreciation rules presently governing assets put in service before 1981 as tax penalties?

3. Is Congress helped or hurt in setting budget priorities by the omission of the revenue loss from ACRS (estimated at $25.6 billion for 1984) from the Treasury's Tax Expenditure Budget? Given the fact that Treasury has computed the revenue cost of ACRS and has, in effect, footnoted its omission, is the omission largely symbolic? Or does it threaten the integrity of the tax expenditure budget? For a pointed criticism of Treasury's action, see McDaniel and Surrey, "Tax Expenditures: How to Identify Them; How to Control Them," 15 *Tax Notes*, May 24, 1982, pp. 595–625.

4. Commentators have frequently warned that an arithmetic total of all tax expenditures in the tax expenditure budget is not an exact measure of the total revenue loss from tax expenditures. Repeal of the medical expense deduction and the interest deduction, for example, might not produce the revenue gain suggested in the tax expenditure budget because of the probable increase in the number of taxpayers electing the standard deduction (zero-bracket amount). Repeal of exclusions, in contrast, might produce more revenue than the Tax Expenditure budget totals. For discussion, see Congressional Budget Office, *Tax Expenditures: Current Issues and Five-Year Budget Projections for Fiscal Years 1982–1986* (1981), pp. 7–8.

5. What do the revenue loss figures in the tax expenditure budget indicate about the government's spending priorities? Must the figures in the tax expenditure budget be linked to real spending decisions in order to reflect spending priorities? Without some link between the definition of a tax expenditure and real budget decisions, do the cost figures in the tax expenditure budget merely show the revenue gains that could be expected from certain reforms of the tax code? For a debate over the

meaning of those cost figures, *see* Dyer, "Measuring the 'Cost' of Tax Expenditures," and M. McIntyre, "The 'Cost' of Tax Expenditures: McIntyre Responds," *Tax Notes*, Feb. 15, 1982, pp. 423–25; Dyer, "The 'Cost' of Tax Expenditures: A Rejoinder," *Tax Notes*, March 15, 1982, p. 653; McIntyre, "Tax Expenditure Costs: A Reprise," *Tax Notes*, March 29, 1982, pp. 801–802.

6. How important has the tax expenditure budget been in improving the tax legislative process? Is Treasury's attempt to keep ACRS out of the Tax Expenditure Budget some indication of its success, a symbol of its limitations, or both? Would some type of Tax Expenditure Budget be necessary in order to impose a meaningful "balanced budget" requirement on Congress?

7. How useful is the tax expenditure concept in analyzing specific reform proposals? Consider, for example, the proposal of those who would discourage what they consider excessive litigation in the United States by disallowing a business expense deduction for attorney's fees. In judging the merits of that proposal, does it matter whether tax specialists would classify the deduction for legal fees as a tax expenditure or as part of the normal structure of the income tax? Assuming the experts all agree that the deduction is not a tax subsidy, how should the proposal be evaluated? Does the definitional approach suggested by Michael McIntyre offer a useful analytical framework for evaluating proposals of this type?

IV. THE TAXATION OF NON-MONETARY BENEFITS

Unless a society wishes to return its economy to the barter system, it is obliged to extend the base of its income tax beyond money income. But how much beyond? Should all marketplace rewards be taxed in principle, including all employee fringe benefits? Is full taxation of marketplace gains enough, or should the tax system attempt to reach gains obtained outside the exchange economy, such as the imputed income from consumer durables and self-performed services? Given the obvious administrative and political obstacles to a tax base that strays too far from monetary income, how can policy makers limit the tax base to something less than "total economic income" without merely drawing arbitrary lines?

This chapter addresses many of these challenging questions. Chapter V addresses the issue of the deduction for interest payments, which most commentators believe relates closely to the proper treatment of imputed income from home ownership. That chapter also examines the proper tax treatment of entertainment expenses—an issue that is problematic because of the general exclusion of entertainment benefits from the income of the recipient.

Since most nonmonetary income is consumed currently, its treatment under an income tax and a consumption tax would generally be the same. But pension contributions and similar in-kind savings would not be taxed currently under a consumption tax yet would be good candidates for current taxation under an income tax.

The first two selections, which were prepared for a Brookings Institution conference on comprehensive income taxation, discuss the proper treatment of imputed income from home ownership in an income tax based at least in part on the Haig/Simons ideal. The next selection challenges the traditional position of economists that an ideal income tax ought to include the economic value of all services that taxpayers provide for themselves outside the marketplace. The final selection reviews some proposals for bringing a little order and fairness to the current federal income tax treatment of in-kind compensation and related fringe benefits.

Supplemental Readings. R. Goode, *The Individual Income Tax* (1976), pp. 114–25; Pomp, "Mortgage Interest and Property Tax Deduction: A Tax Expenditure Analysis," 1 *Canadian*

Taxation 23 (1979); Popkin, "The Taxation of Employee Fringe Benefits," 22 *Boston College Law Review* 439 (1981); Note, "Federal Income Taxation of Employee Fringe Benefits," 89 *Harvard Law Review* 1141 (1976); Tax Section, New York State Bar Association, Committee on Employee Benefits, "Report and Recommendations on the Tax Treatment of Fringe Benefits, *Tax Notes,* January 3, 1983.

A. HOME OWNERSHIP

WILLIAM F. HELLMUTH, "HOMEOWNER PREFERENCES"

Comprehensive Income Taxation, Brookings Institution
(Joseph A. Pechman, Ed. 1977), pp. 163–72.

UNDER A comprehensive individual income tax based on the Haig-Simons definition of income, the income tax base would include imputed net rent for owner-occupied homes. Both Robert Murray Haig and Henry Simons were very explicit that imputed income would be included and that imputed rent on owner-occupied homes is an important imputed income item.[1]

Housing and other durable consumer goods provide services over a period of years. Consumers have a choice of purchasing financial assets that provide taxable monetary income or of purchasing homes that provide untaxed services over time. Simons pointed out that consumers' capital is not a uniform percentage of income for persons in the same income class, nor is it constant between different income classes; thus the omission of such income causes both horizontal and vertical inequities.[2]

---

1. See Robert Murray Haig, "The Concept of Income—Economic and Legal Aspects," in Haig, ed., *The Federal Income Tax* (Columbia University Press, 1921), pp. 7–8, 14–15, reprinted in Richard A. Musgrave and Carl S. Shoup, *Readings in the Economics of Taxation* (Irwin for the American Economic Association, 1959), pp. 59, 65; and Henry C. Simons, *Personal Income Taxation: The Definition of Income as a Problem of Fiscal Policy* (University of Chicago Press, 1938), p. 50 and chap. 4. Also see Chapter 1 in this volume.

2. Simons, *Personal Income Taxation*, pp. 114–15.

If homeowners' imputed net rent were taxable, it would obviously be necessary to calculate the amount of net rent. Generally this would be obtained by estimating a gross rent equal to the rent the housing unit would bring on the market and deducting the actual expenses, including mortgage interest, property taxes, maintenance expense, insurance, and depreciation. This net rent amount would be included in the homeowner's adjusted gross income.

Under current tax treatment all homeowners, whether they take the standard deduction for tax purposes or itemize deductions, benefit from the exclusion of imputed net rent in calculating their income. Further, homeowners who itemize deductions may deduct mortgage interest and real estate taxes to reduce their taxable income, even though the rental income against which these constitute expenses has not been included. Taxpayers who are tenants are permitted no comparable deductions.

Another tax preference for homeowners is the right, when an owner-occupied home is sold at a gain, to defer a tax on the gain if the seller purchases and occupies a new home that costs more than the one sold. This deferral of tax on rollover of a home generally does not apply to other assets sold at a gain. In addition, under certain conditions elderly taxpayers are permitted to exclude part or all of the tax on the gain from the sale of their homes.

The homeowner preferences have several important effects on the tax system and on the economy:

—They create horizontal inequities in the income tax system in that they provide tax savings for homeowners over tenants with comparable incomes, and differential savings between different homeowners with comparable incomes.

—They cause vertical inequities in the tax system. Since homeownership rises with income, the values of homes purchased increase as a proportion of income as incomes rise (that is, are income elastic), and the value of homeowner preferences is directly related to the marginal tax rate of the homeowner, high-income recipients benefit more from these preferences than do low-income recipients.

—They interfere with the allocation of resources between residential construction and other uses of resources. The tax expenditures favoring homeowners lower the cost of housing services and increase the after-tax rate of return on investment in homes, relative to other choices that consumers and individual investors have for the use of their funds. Tax incentives thus draw more resources into housing than would occur in the absence of such preferences.

—They also distort the housing market choices in favor of residential construction suitable for homeowners, creating a demand for more single-family homes and apartments for purchase than for rental units.

But these preferences, which provide higher effective rates of return for homeownership, need to be considered in the broader context of other preferences for other types of investment. Homeowner preferences do not exist alone in a tax system that is otherwise comprehensive and neutral between different forms of investment. Individuals and corporations that invest in rental housing are eligible for accelerated depreciation on the cost of the rental property. And businesses receive tax subsidies for investments in machinery and equipment, for export sales, for research and development expenditures, and for other selected activities.

Further, these homeowner tax preferences are relatively inefficient and expensive if they are considered as incentives to promote homeownership and the construction of more homes. The incentives are most valuable to those with higher marginal tax rates, the income class that would find it easiest to buy homes in the absence of tax incentives. And the incentives for homeownership are much weaker for families in the lower tax brackets whose income levels also make homeownership more difficult. Tax incentives are, of course, of no value to those whose income is so low that they pay no federal income tax. And to the extent that the tax preferences increase the demand for owner-occupied homes, the price of such dwelling units rises and puts them further beyond the reach of low- and modest-income persons. The greater value of these preferences for persons with high incomes and high marginal tax rates is likely to draw more resources into the construction of large and expensive homes; on the other hand, income-neutral incentives would be likely to result in more dwelling units to meet the housing needs of more people.

Income Excluded from Tax Base by Homeowner Preferences

Substantial amounts of income are now excluded from the individual income tax base by the three major homeowner preferences,

Table 5-1. Increase in Taxable Income and Income Tax Revenue Resulting from Changes in Certain Homeowner Tax Preferences, 1977 Levels

Change	Increase (billions of dollars) In taxable income	Increase (billions of dollars) In tax revenue	Percent increase in revenue
Include imputed net rent (all homeowners)	13.0	3.0	2.5
Eliminate deduction for real estate taxes (itemizers only)	26.0	5.8	5.7[a]
Eliminate deduction for mortgage interest (itemizers only)	28.4	5.7	5.6[a]
Eliminate deductions for both real estate taxes and mortgage interest (itemizers only)	54.3	10.7	10.6[a]
Include imputed net rent and eliminate deduction for both taxes and interest (all homeowners)	67.3	13.8	11.4[b]

Source: Brookings MERGE File.

a. The percentage increase shown is for all homeowners who itemize, although some do not deduct all of the items; for all homeowners, including nonitemizers who would have no increase, the increase would be 4.8 percent for elimination of the deduction for real estate taxes, 4.7 percent for elimination of the deduction for mortgage interest, and 8.8 percent for elimination of the deduction for taxes and interest combined. This last total is less than the sum of gain from the elimination of the two deductions separately, since some homeowners shift to the standard deduction.

b. This percentage increase combines a 4.2 percent increase for nonitemizers and a 12.8 percent increase for itemizers.

with consequent large effects on revenues. Estimates from the Brookings MERGE File shown in table 5-1 indicate that homeowners in 1977 will have imputed net rent of about $13 billion. Further, homeowners who itemize are expected to claim deductions of $26 billion for real estate taxes and $28.4 billion for interest on their mortgages. The possible revenue gains would range from $3 billion to $13.8 billion, depending on which preferences were eliminated.[3] These amounts for homeowner preferences do not include mortgage interest and real estate taxes paid by homeowners who do not itemize deductions. Moreover, part of the imputed rent is received by, and some of the interest and tax deductions are taken by, persons whose incomes are too small to be taxable. The loss of deductions for some taxpayers would be partially offset by shifting to the standard deduction, but this is allowed for in the revenue estimates in table 5-1.

A number of different studies have been made of the relation between housing values and gross and net imputed rent. These studies

3. Corresponding estimates in a 1976 study of tax expenditures by the Senate Budget Committee are given by income classes in table 5-9 in the appendix to this chapter.

Table 5-2. Income Tax Subsidy to Homeowners, Selected Studies

Calculation of imputed gross rental income and of subsidy	Shelton[a]	Laidler[b]	Sunley[c]	Aaron[d]	James[e]
	Percent of house value				
Imputed net rental income	4.0	6.0	8.0	4.0–6.0[f]	4.0–9.0
Property taxes	1.5	1.5	1.3	n.a.	2.0
Mortgage interest	3.0	...	...	n.a.	...
Maintenance	0.75–1.0	1.25	1.25	n.a.	...
Depreciation	1.0–1.5	2.25	...	n.a.	1.0–1.2
Imputed gross rental income	10.25–11.0	11.0	10.55	10.0–12.0	6.5–10.0
	Percent of imputed gross rental income				
Subsidy	77.3–82.9	68.2	88.2	n.a.	n.a.
	Percent of reduction in imputed gross rental income[g]				
Subsidy	19.3–20.7	17.0	22.0	n.a.	26.8

Sources: First four columns from Frank A. Clayton, "Income Taxes and Subsidies to Homeowners and Renters: A Comparison of the U.S. and Canadian Experience," *Canadian Tax Journal*, vol. 22 (May–June 1974), p. 299; and last column adapted from Franklin J. James (see note e).
a. John P. Shelton, "The Cost of Renting versus Owning a Home," *Land Economics*, vol. 44 (February 1968), pp. 63–68. Assumes ratio of imputed net rental income to equity of 8 percent and a mortgage interest rate of 6 percent; the homeowner is assumed to have 50 percent equity in the market value.
b. David Laidler, "Income Tax Incentives for Owner-Occupied Housing," in Arnold C. Harberger and Martin J. Bailey, eds., *The Taxation of Income from Capital* (Brookings Institution, 1969), p. 57. Assumes the ratio of imputed net rental income to house value and the mortgage interest rate are both 6 percent.
c. Emil M. Sunley, Jr., "Tax Advantages of Homeownership versus Renting: A Cause of Suburban Migration?" in National Tax Association, *Proceedings of the Sixty-Third Annual Conference on Taxation* (Columbus: NTA, 1971), pp. 377–92. Assumes the rate of imputed net rental income and the mortgage interest rate are the same.
d. Henry Aaron, "Income Taxes and Housing," *American Economic Review*, vol. 60 (December 1970), pp. 789–806.
e. Franklin J. James, "Income Taxes, Homeownership and Urban Land Use" (Urban Institute, 1976; processed), pp. 13–24.
f. Percent of equity.
g. Assuming average marginal tax rates of 25 percent for homeowners.
n.a. Not applicable.

are useful in showing what percentage of the gross rent is excluded from tax for the average homeowner. As shown in table 5-2, the portion of imputed gross rent that is excluded from income by homeowner tax preferences is variously estimated as between 68 and 88 percent. The smaller the amount of maintenance and depreciation relative to the gross rental, the larger the fraction of the gross rental that is excluded from income subject to tax. Applying a taxpayer's marginal tax rate to these percentages determines each unit's tax subsidy. Obviously the higher the marginal tax rate, the greater the tax subsidy portion of the gross rental. Homeowner tax preferences, as shown in table 5-2, have reduced the effective cost of housing, as measured by gross rents, by approximately 20 percent, assuming average marginal tax rates of 25 percent for homeowners.

Renters obtain some reduction in average rentals, resulting from the accelerated depreciation allowed to investors in rental housing. Franklin James estimated this reduction in rents at 11 percent, based on the assumption of a 25 percent tax bracket for the typical investor in rental housing.[4] Emil Sunley suggested the reduction in rents to tenants was somewhat higher, perhaps 17 percent, assuming the marginal investor in rental housing was in the 40 percent tax bracket.[5]

The demand for housing is influenced by the price of housing. The lower the price, the greater the quantity of housing demanded. Numerous studies have led to the conclusion that the price elasticity of demand for housing falls in the range of -1.0 to -1.5.[6] This means that a 1 percent decline in the price of housing will cause the quantity demanded to increase by 1 to 1.5 percent.

These estimates indicate the value of the tax preferences for housing in reducing the rentals, whether paid by tenants or imputed to owner-occupiers. The net subsidy for homeowners over tenants would generally fall in the 10 to 15 percent range for homeowners in the heavily populated $10,000 to $25,000 income brackets. With a price elasticity of -1.0 to -1.5, this indicates an increase of 10 to 20 percent in the demand for homeownership.[7] Obviously the value of the net subsidy from the tax preferences and the increase in demand for homeownership generally varies directly with a person's income level and marginal tax rate.

Thus removal of the tax subsidies would have the effect of raising the net cost of housing and of reducing the demand for owner-occupied homes. The demand for owner-occupied housing usually varies

---

4. Franklin J. James, "Income Taxes, Homeownership and Urban Land Use" (Urban Institute, 1976; processed), pp. 19–21, 24.

5. Emil M. Sunley, Jr., "Tax Advantages of Homeownership versus Renting: A Cause of Suburban Migration?" in National Tax Association, *Proceedings of the Sixty-Third Annual Conference on Taxation* (Columbus: NTA, 1971), pp. 377–92.

6. See Richard F. Muth, "The Demand for Non-Farm Housing," in Arnold C. Harberger, ed., *The Demand for Durable Goods* (University of Chicago Press, 1960), pp. 72–74; Margaret G. Reid, *Housing and Income* (University of Chicago Press, 1962), p. 381; Frank de Leeuw, "The Demand for Housing: A Review of Cross-Section Evidence," *Review of Economics and Statistics*, vol. 53 (February 1971), pp. 8–9; and Sherman J. Maisel, James B. Burnham, and John S. Austin, "The Demand for Housing: A Comment," ibid. (November 1971), pp. 410–13.

7. James, "Income Taxes, Home Ownership and Urban Land Use," pp. 19–25.

directly with income level, with an income elasticity of demand of about 1.5 (that is, for every 1 percent increase in personal income, the quantity of housing demanded rises about 1.5 percent). With the value of the subsidy provided by tax preferences rising with increases in taxable income from 14 percent up to 70 percent at the top marginal rate, the tax preferences add to the stronger demand for homeownership the higher a person's income.[8]

The Commission to Revise the Tax Structure estimated that the sweeping changes it recommended for a very comprehensive income tax base with much lower rates would have caused a small reduction in residential construction estimated at $2.5 billion for 1975, after the new tax structure was fully effective, with a consequently larger flow of capital to corporate investment.[9]

A Fully Comprehensive Income Tax Base

A comprehensive income tax base would include imputed net rent of homeowners in adjusted gross income. Generally the first step would require an estimate of the gross rent the dwelling unit would bring in an arm's-length-market rental. From the gross rent, the normal expenses of property taxes, interest on the mortgage (if any), maintenance, depreciation, and insurance would be deducted to obtain a net rental. In effect homeowners would treat their houses as investment property that they rent to themselves.

The inclusion of imputed net rent in arriving at adjusted gross income would apply to all homeowners. Further, those homeowners who now itemize their deductions would no longer be permitted the separate deductions now taken for mortgage interest and for property taxes, since these deductions would already have been used in calculating net rent.

The increase in individual income tax revenues would be large, estimated at $13.8 billion for projected 1977 incomes, assuming imputed net rent is included and no separate deductions are taken for mortgage interest and for property taxes (see table 5-1). All homeowners with taxable income would probably have some increase, with an average increase of 11.4 percent. (The distribution of this tax in-

---

8. Commission to Revise the Tax Structure, *Reforming the Federal Tax Structure* (Washington, D.C.: Fund for Public Policy Research, 1973), pp. 141–42.
9. Ibid., pp. 35, 140.

crease by income bracket and age group is discussed later and shown in tables 5-7 and 5-8.)

Including imputed net rent in the income of homeowners would present a number of major difficulties. One is the problem of obtaining accurate and consistent estimates of imputed net rent for millions of homeowning taxpayers. Imputed net rent is estimated now on an aggregate basis for various national income purposes. But the calculation of imputed net rent for approximately 45 million different individual and family units would be a complicated task for each taxpayer and for Internal Revenue Service review. There is no background or history in the United States for making estimates of imputed rent or home values on a nationwide basis, unlike the United Kingdom or Germany.

The United Kingdom included imputed rent in taxable income for over a century, from the beginning of its income tax until 1963. Imputed rent was discarded then instead of attempting to correct and update the assessments, which had become obsolete in the period of inflation and other major economic changes following World War II. Imputed rent was abandoned despite a recommendation in 1955 by the Royal Commission on the Taxation of Profits and Income that the taxation of imputed rent be continued.[10]

The Canadian Royal Commission on Taxation (popularly known as the Carter Commission after its chairman, Kenneth L. Carter) stated that the comprehensive tax base

would include imputed income, that is, the gains realized when a person uses or consumes his own personal services or his own property. In most circumstances, however, . . . the valuation and administrative problems involved in including such amounts in income are insuperable.[11]

The Carter Commission stated further specifically in relation to imputed rent:

The most prevalent example of an imputed property gain is imputed rent. . . . To ensure that all taxpayers bore their fair proportion of the total tax burden, it would be necessary to impute rental income to this [homeowner] taxpayer. . . .

10. Richard Goode, *The Individual Income Tax*, rev. ed. (Brookings Institution, 1976), p. 118. Goode cited the Royal Commission's *Final Report*, Cmd. 9474 (London: Her Majesty's Stationery Office, 1955), pp. 249–51. See also Simons, *Personal Income Taxation*, note on p. 112, for reference to both Britain and Germany.

11. *Report of the Royal Commission on Taxation;* vol. 3, *Taxation of Income* (Ottawa: Queen's Printer, 1966), p. 41.

... The exclusion from income of imputed rent is therefore a substantial tax preference for home ownership.

An incentive of this magnitude leads to inequities between owners and renters. If it were administratively feasible, we would recommend that imputed net rental income be included in the tax base or, to compensate for not doing so, that the deduction of some portion of the rent paid by individuals who do not own their own homes be permitted. ...

Because of the administrative difficulty of properly and equitably determining the amount of the net gain, we suggest that imputed rent continue to be omitted from the tax base.[12]

Other approaches provide rough but reasonable approximations of imputed rent without the necessity of estimating or calculating gross rent, mortgage interest, property taxes, depreciation, maintenance, and insurance. A net worth approach would use the market value of the home less any outstanding mortgage. An annual net rent would be obtained by multiplying this net worth by a conservative rate of return. Alternatively, the *net* return on the market value of the home could be calculated by applying a reasonable interest rate to the market value of the home, less the actual interest on the mortgage, if any. The calculated net rent would vary inversely with the relative size of the mortgage and the mortgage interest rate.[13]

This approach still requires a periodic estimate or appraisal of the market value of each owner-occupied unit, the major administrative problem with any tax on imputed rent. And this problem is so likely to result in errors, inconsistencies, and litigation that this approach still creates really major problems from the viewpoint of administration and compliance. The problem of valuation is made more difficult by the rapid changes in real estate values in recent years, and the uneven rates of change between different areas and different types of housing.

An impressive case can be made for including imputed rent in a comprehensive income tax base. William Vickrey made the case very

12. Ibid., pp. 47–49.
13. The Commission to Revise the Tax Structure recommended the determination of imputed rent as follows: (1) the owner-occupant would determine the capital value of the home and would declare this value on his tax return, permitting review by the Internal Revenue Service; (2) Internal Revenue would establish guideline rates for communities by region, these rates to be either gross or net or both; (3) the taxpayer would apply the appropriate return to his declared capital value to get the annual rent; if the taxpayer chose the gross return, deductions for interest and taxes would be permitted. (*Reforming the Federal Tax Structure*, p. 39.)

persuasively in 1947 that although the valuation problems would be rough, no possible inequity due to inconsistent valuations "can be as great as the disparity between tenants and home-owners with equities [in value of their homes] that would remain, even with the deductions for taxes and mortgage interest eliminated."[14] He considered the likely increase in controversy small relative to the greater equity that would result from inclusion of imputed rent.

Comprehensive Income Plus Net Gains Approach

If Henry Simons's broad definition of personal income, including consumption plus accumulation during a period, is accepted as the basis for a comprehensive income tax, the concept and the measurement of the value of homeowner preferences become more complicated. This approach would call for the net change in the value of assets less liabilities to be included in the taxpayer's income subject to tax each year. For owner-occupied homes, a valuation would be required at the beginning of each tax year for the current market value less any outstanding mortgage debt. The net gain (or loss) would be included in taxable income each year. Accrued and unrealized gains based on changes in estimated or appraised values would be taxed just as would realized gains based on market sales. Difficulties would arise from both the problem of annual valuations and the liquidity problem of paying taxes on unrealized gains.

Given the difficulties of obtaining comparable and accurate property tax valuations on residences within local assessing districts and under statewide equalization programs, the administration of an income tax including both imputed rent and annual changes in the net value of owner-occupied homes on a national basis seems impractical. Although the Carter Commission did not consider the problems insoluble, it did recommend that Canada initially should include only realized gains in the tax base.[15]

---

[14] *Agenda for Progressive Taxation* (Ronald Press, 1947). p. 24.

[15] *Report of the Royal Commission*, vol 3, p. 50.

JEROME KURTZ, "COMMENTS BY JEROME KURTZ"

Comprehensive Income Taxation, Brookings Institution
(Joseph A. Pechman, Ed. 1977), pp. 197–201.

I will address some of the practical problems of implementing the taxation of imputed rent on owner-occupied homes. It seems to me that in building the stairway to the paradise of a comprehensive tax base, imputed rent should be one of the last steps.

William Hellmuth suggests two methods of computing net imputed rental income. One is to estimate gross rental value and subtract expenses; the other is to assume an arbitrary interest return on the net investment in the property. I will discuss some of the problems in doing one or the other, but before that let me mention some general problems of implementing either system. These may appear to be fringe matters, but in this area the fringes are important.

The first problem is that of defining a home, and that will involve difficult problems of drawing a line. For example, how should farmers (who seem to have a great deal of legislative influence) be treated? They live on farms or ranches that produce very small incomes, considering the value of the property. Presumably they tolerate low rates of return on their assets because they like to live on a farm or a ranch. It seems to me that additional income should be imputed to them for living on the farm rather than elsewhere.

Other difficult line-drawing problems occur to me. Mobile homes should clearly be included; if so, campers, houseboats, and recreational land cannot be excluded. If a summer home is included, why not a hunting preserve?

While owner-occupied homes are singled out for taxation because they are the largest single class of consumer assets, not enough is known about the ownership of other consumption capital goods to conclude that inclusion only of homes will improve vertical equity. Horizontal equity might be improved, but the question of vertical equity should not be ignored. For example, people invest large sums in antiques, art, and collections of various kinds. To exclude the imputed income from such consumption assets—while including the imputed income of consumption assets owned throughout the scale of incomes—may not improve equity.

It goes without saying that simplification will not be served by taxing imputed rent, no matter what method is used. Inevitably the tax return will be made more complicated and the valuation problems will complicate compliance and tax administration. The question is whether the result is worth the effort.

Another factor that cannot be completely ignored—one mentioned by Richard Goode—is the importance of the taxpayer's perception of equity. Taxpayers generally think in terms of money income, or things that are essentially equivalent to money income; they would have great difficulty in understanding why imputed rent should be taxed.

If imputed rent were taxed on the basis of current values, the tax burden would increase as the value of the taxpayer's home increased. Many people would not view themselves as significantly better off—and therefore having greater taxpaying capacities—because their homes have increased in value. They probably do not view their homes as investment assets; they are not in the business of selling their homes. Homes are the places in which they live, the same places they have always lived. Their money incomes may remain essentially the same, yet their taxes would increase for reasons that would be relatively incomprehensible to most of them. The question is one of ability to pay. I am not sure that a person who lives in a house that appreciates at a faster rate than money income has an increase in his ability to pay taxes.

As to the mechanics of introducing imputed rent into the tax base, the more accurate method is to estimate gross rents and subtract the deductions. But I am not sure how to estimate gross rental values. I have the impression that homes do not command rents that represent a fair return on their value. One reason is that renters are unwilling to make the kind of financial commitment that a homeowner is willing to undertake. The homeowner may be making more of a commitment for his housing because he is hedging against future rent increases.

If that is so, consideration must be given to whether rental value means the amount that would be paid under a long-term lease or a short-term lease; if the former, then when should the lease be considered to have begun? It would not seem entirely inappropriate to regard the homeowner as having entered into a long-term lease at the time of acquisition of the property. According to this analysis, current values may be the wrong measure of imputed income.

Alternatively, suppose a taxpayer leases a house for ten years at a flat rental. Does he have imputed income if, toward the end of the lease term, the current rental value is higher than that which he committed himself to pay in the beginning? How should people living in rent-controlled housing be treated? They may be the beneficiaries of as much imputed income by reason of governmental controls as those who own their own homes.

Once having determined gross rental value, an estimate of expenses must be made. How should depreciation be figured? If the precedent of rental housing is followed, losses rather than gains will be generated on imputed income. Much of the rental housing built today shows no taxable income for eight or ten years. The accounting losses are rather substantial. Since houses turn over about every eight years on the average, this may be a roundabout way of giving tax shelters to middle-income people.

The problems of estimating the cost of repairs and maintenance boggle the mind. It is an extraordinarily difficult problem in business just to distinguish between repairs and capital additions. In addition, in an owner-occupied home, it would be necessary to distinguish between normal repairs and repairs that are incurred solely because the property is a home. One may paint every two years rather than every four. One may keep the property in a condition that would be uneconomical if one were renting the property. Such excess maintenance is really current consumption rather than repairs that are related to the imputed rent. Separating these items seems impossible.

These problems would lead, I think, to taxation based on a net rate of return on either the entire property, or only on the value of the equity. The simpler method is to impute a net rate of return only on the equity. The simpler approach would be inaccurate, however, because it fails to take account of the interest paid on mortgages. Obviously a homeowner paying a lower rate of interest on his mortgage has greater net imputed income than another who is paying a higher interest rate. If only net equities are considered, such differences are ignored.

It must be recognized that the price of achieving this degree of simplicity creates inequities because repairs, maintenance, and other expenditures affecting net income from the property are ignored. The taxpayer may not have realized any real net-imputed income in a particular year, yet he would be taxed in an arbitrary way to achieve greater simplicity.

The question of horizontal equity is frequently illustrated by comparing the owner-occupant of a home with one who rents and has a savings account. The interest on the savings account is taxed and no deduction is allowed for the rent. If the renter cashes in his savings account and buys a house, he avoids adding to his taxable income and improves his tax position while not affecting his ability to pay. While this comparison is valid, the owner-occupant could also be compared with a renter having investments in assets that are appreciating and on which there is no realization.

The appreciation in the value of a home is realized by the occupant by the consumption of the home at the appreciated value. But the owner-occupant may have two motives in owning—investment and consumption. For many people their home is their biggest investment. Taxation based on full fair market value would be equivalent to taxing unrealized appreciation due to the investment rather than the consumption element of the home.

In addition, housing may go up in value because of changes in interest rates. Since interest rates are a cost of construction, rents on newly constructed rental housing will rise as interest rates rise. To some extent, therefore, the tax on imputed income may reflect changes in market interest rates.

I would conclude that net-imputed rent might be included under an *ideal* income tax. Many other reforms are more urgent, however, and I would give the taxation of imputed rent a low priority on the tax reform agenda.

B. SELF–PERFORMED SERVICES

MICHAEL J. McINTYRE & OLIVER OLDMAN, "TAXATION OF THE FAMILY IN A COMPREHENSIVE AND SIMPLIFIED INCOME TAX"

90 Harvard Law Review 1573 (1977), pp. 1607–24.

IV. APPLICATION OF THE CTB IDEAL IN DETERMINING THE RELATIVE BURDENS OF ONE- AND TWO-INCOME MARRIED COUPLES

A direct corollary of our conclusion in Part II that one-half of the consolidated marital income of a couple should be attributed to each of the spouses is that equal-income couples should pay equal taxes. Our discussion there focused exclusively on the rules for attributing the pool of income available to the family without consideration of what should go into that pool. We made the simplifying assumption that only monetary income — income arising through market exchanges — would go into the pool, without direct or indirect adjustment for the imputed income arising from services performed by family members for the benefit of themselves or other family members.[116]

In this Part, we reexamine the proposition that couples with equal monetary income should pay equal taxes in light of the arguments made for adjusting the burdens on one- and two-job couples on account of perceived differences in the imputed income typically available to each. If imputed income should be taxed under the CTB ideal, and if two-job couples have less imputed income than one-job couples, then our decision to tax equally couples with equal monetary income discriminates against two-job couples.[117] Hence, consideration of the issue of imputed income, although principally a problem of defining the appropriate tax base, has implications for the attribution of income within the family.

The case for including at least some self-performed services in income is illustrated by the following example: A_1 and B_1 are married and each has a forty-hour-a-week job with an annual salary of $10,000. At the end of a work day, A_1 and B_1 are seldom in the mood to cook; instead they either eat out at a restaurant or heat up in the oven a frozen convenience dinner purchased at the supermarket. They also hire a maid to clean the house and handle other domestic chores and they send their dirty clothes to the laundry. A_2 and B_2 are married. A_2 has a full-time job paying $20,000 a year and B_2 has no employment outside the home. B_2 spends a good bit of time, however, baking bread, cooking fancy meals, canning fruits and vegetables, cleaning the house, sewing, and doing laundry.

If the services performed by B_2 in the above example produce taxable income as a matter of definition under the CTB ideal, then the value of the services should in principle be included in the pool of income attributed to A_2 and B_2 under the scheme of taxation proposed in Part II. The fact that A_2 and B_2 enjoy a real economic benefit from these services, however, does not necessarily mean that the value of the services should be taxable. Although the view is widely held by supporters of the CTB ideal

---

[116] See p. 1593 *supra*.

[117] Although the discussion is framed in terms of the possible disparity in treatment of one-job and two-job couples in the failure to tax imputed income, similar considerations have been raised as to the comparative treatment of single individuals and one-job couples. It is argued that a couple with only one working spouse obtains the benefits of self-performed household services which the working single person does not enjoy. See Bittker, *supra* note 1, at 1425-26. The issue of imputed income in fact raises a host of issues applicable generally in the income tax. We have attempted, however, to restrict our discussion as much as possible to the problems of one-job and two-job couples. Much of the analysis in Section A, pp. 1609-13 *infra*, however, raises fundamental questions about the tax base that have not yet been adequately explored by tax theorists.

that imputed income from self-performed services is taxable income as a matter of definition, we present several arguments in Section A which challenge that proposition. We conclude, first of all, that the CTB definition of income by itself gives no clear answer as to the proper treatment of self-performed services. Secondly, we suggest that some of the considerations that led to the formulation of the CTB ideal also justify the exclusion of the value of self-performed services from taxable income. Finally, we argue that even if our theoretical objections to taxing imputed income from services are overcome, the case against equal treatment of couples with equal monetary income depends on the existence of a definite pattern to the distribution of imputed income from services that disadvantages two-job couples. In Section B, we attempt to determine how imputed income is distributed between one-job and two-job couples. We conclude that the pattern of distribution of imputed income from self-performed services is so complex that the failure to take imputed income into account in determining relative tax burdens leads to no particular disadvantage for two-job couples.

Although we do not feel that the generalization that one-job couples have more imputed income from services than two-job couples holds sufficiently true to justify special tax measures, we recognize that the opposing viewpoint is tenaciously held and cannot be entirely refuted. In Section C we look at specific proposals for indirectly taxing self-performed services. In our view, all of these proposals have major defects which are traceable to our theoretical objections to taking imputed income into account in devising an ideal tax system. Our major complaint is that no assumptions can be made about the distribution and comparative economic effects of self-performed services that are of sufficient generality to justify the sweeping proposals which have been made. We therefore believe that our tentative conclusion to tax couples with equal monetary income equally need not be altered because of concerns for imputed income from self-performed services.[118]

A. *The Proper Treatment of the Benefits from Self-Performed Services Under the CTB Ideal*

The benefits obtainable from self-performed services pose a dilemma for the designers of a tax system based on the CTB

---

[118] We acknowledge that cases for narrowly tailored allowances for two-job couples have been advanced on grounds of efficiency or inequity because of the "tax on marriage" under the current system of multiple rate schedules. Our approach to efficiency, which we believe is outweighed by fairness in the family context, is set forth in note 127 *infra*. Our proposal for dealing with the "tax on marriage," *see* p. 1596 *supra*, eliminates that problem for all couples.

ideal. On the one hand, there are practical and theoretical advantages in formulating the income concept in terms of the exercise or the accumulation of market rights, thereby omitting the benefits of self-performed services which are obtained outside the market. On the other hand, these benefits can be so similar to benefits purchased out of income earned in the market that they raise the issue of fairness between otherwise similarly situated taxpayers. An analysis of these benefits in terms of the definition of income does not resolve the dilemma. Simons' definition, for example, refers to the exercise or the accumulation of a market right, which would seem to exclude the benefits of self-performed services from taxable income.[119] Simons himself, however, suggested that income includes rights to which a market price could be imputed.[120] Beyond this, however, since income for tax purposes can be defined in whatever manner we wish, it follows that even if we could resolve the ambiguities in the traditional formulation of the income concept, we would be still left with the more basic question of whether or not that formulation is consistent with widely held views as to what is requisite to a satisfactory definition of income. According to Simons, the definition of income (1) should be objective rather than subjective; (2) should be quantitative and measurable; and (3) should have a minimum number of implicit arbitrary distinctions.[121] These three minimum tests for an acceptable definition of income provide a

---

[119] H. SIMONS, *supra* note 5, at 50.

[120] "Personal income . . . has to do . . . with rights which command prices (or to which prices may be imputed)." *Id.* at 49. Simons did not propose the taxation of imputed income from self-performed services but did recommend the taxation of imputed income from home ownership. *Id.* at 111-12. In our view, imputed income from real property raises many fewer problems, practical and theoretical, than imputed income from self-performed services. Imputed income from home ownership is more akin to income in kind received by an employee in exchange for services than it is to imputed income from self-performed services. The most compelling reason for ignoring imputed income from self-performed services in an income tax is the inappropriateness of the market model for most kinds of self-performed services. The concept of imputed income presupposes the appropriateness of imputing first an exchange and then a price. Since a home is purchased in the market for a price which reflects the value of living in it, it is not unrealistic to view home ownership in market terms. Similarly, when an individual exchanges services which he normally sells in the market for tangible goods or for the services of someone else, a market analysis of the exchange is almost unavoidable. When a person makes himself a sandwich, however, it is an artifical construct to say that an exchange has taken place and any value imputed to the gain from the exchange is an artificiality once removed.

[121] "Income must be conceived as something quantitative and objective. It must be measurable; indeed, definition must indicate or clearly imply an actual procedure of measuring. Moreover, the arbitrary distinctions implicit in one's definition must be reduced to a minimum." *Id.* at 42-43 (footnote omitted).

convenient framework for an analysis of the case for taxing the imputed income from self-performed services.

The variety of self-performed services which in some sense constitute income range from the sublime to the ridiculous, from the priceless private poetry of an Emily Dickinson to the thumb-sucking of a small child. Putting a handle on the self-performed service concept is something like defining a capital gain: we think we know what we mean, but if we articulate a definition, we end up with either nothing fitting the description or everything fitting it. For example, which if any of the following services should be taxable: Getting up in the morning? Doing exercises? Singing in the shower? Grooming oneself? Fixing breakfast? Chewing food? Processing it within the stomach? Walking to work? Baking bread? Growing roses? Fixing the car? Driving in the country? Watching T.V.? Reading a novel? Reading bedtime stories to one's children? Playing backgammon?

As these examples illustrate, almost every activity we undertake is in some sense a self-performed service, since the possibility of imposing a market model on nonmarket activity has no logical limits.[122] A general inclusion of all imputed income from personal services in the definition of taxable income would cause the definition to fail all three of Simons' tests, since it would present hopeless problems of subjectivity and measurement and would require entirely ad hoc decisionmaking.[123] At a minimum, therefore, some categories of imputed income ought to be excluded from the tax base.

The examples also show that a definition of income that excluded some but not all items of imputed income from self-performed services would have difficulty satisfying Simons' tests. A logical step in limiting the imputed income concept might be to exclude from consideration all items which cannot be bought

---

[122] The procedure for imposing a market model on a self-performed service is to view the individual as bifurcated into a person who benefits and a person who performs the service. An exchange between these two parts of the individual is then postulated. The logic of an imputed exchange is often not carried to the end. Both sides of a market exchange should have income to the extent that what they receive exceeds the tax cost of what they gave up. The person who benefits has a gain, but the person who performed the services must also have a gain, since he is postulated to have received something equal in value to the services he surrendered. The amount of the gains is also imputed. For services performed for the benefit of family members, the metaphysical problems of bifurcation of an individual are not present, but the double-or-nothing problem remains. This double-or-nothing aspect of an imputed exchange was noted at p. 1603 *supra* in relation to the argument for children-as-consumption.

[123] Simons considered the problems of benefits received in kind by an employee as "clearly hopeless," once the facts did not warrant an inference of a real exchange. H. SIMONS, *supra* note 5, at 53. Outside the context of employment, the question of whether or not to impose a market analysis is even more open-ended.

and sold on the market.[124] That distinction is far from clear-cut, however, since almost all items of imputed income have a market analog. Chewing and digesting food might appear to be bizarre examples of imputed income that are obviously outside the boundary of serious concern. Yet when bodily functions fail to operate, replacement machinery is increasingly available even if the market price is high. The argument behind taxing imputed income — the comparatively greater economic well-being of those who do not have to pay for the services — is clearly applicable to these and countless other items of imputed income not normally viewed in market terms. Thus, even if the line could be drawn clearly enough to overcome problems of specificity and even if a rule of measurement could be devised, the problem of arbitrary distinctions and exclusions could not be avoided.

The examples also show the potential for catastrophic consequences for some taxpayers and intolerable windfalls for others from what appears to be an issue of little or no concern. Take an apparently minor item such as shaving. At the minimum market price of $2 per shave, imputed income from shaving would exceed $700 per year for a person who shaves daily. Similarly the imputed income from dressing oneself each day, measured by the market price for a valet, would be in the thousands of dollars. In fact, potential income from even a narrow definition of self-performed services would be likely to exceed salary income for a majority of taxpayers. Thus a series of de minimis rules would not be very helpful in meeting the requirements of Simons' tests.

Although drawing a line which excluded nonmarket services from the definition of taxable income may well be the fairest practical and theoretical result,[125] the case for defining taxable income in terms of market income cannot be conclusive, since market income is not the most fundamental test of an individual's material well-being which is at base the measure of tax equality.[126] If the supporters of some form of taxation of nonmarket income can identify clearly the items they would tax, the possibility remains that an argument could be constructed that would justify the taxation of those items. To have appeal on fairness grounds,

---

[124] The rationale would be that a problem of fairness arises only when one individual purchases a service in the market and another performs the service himself.

[125] To the extent that our analysis focuses on who benefits, rather than who consumes in the market sense, it might be thought more theoretically compatible with the notion of taxing consumption of personal rather then market goods, but since our rule looks to who benefits from available *income*, it presents the same problem of defining when benefits are to be recognized for tax purposes.

[126] *See* p. 1577 & note 9 *supra*.

however, that argument must rest on the perception that a pattern of distribution of the benefits of certain items of imputed income discriminates against an identifiable group of taxpayers. The existence of a pattern is necessary for two reasons. First, problems of identifying the tax base and attaching values to particular services would make direct taxation of imputed income from self-performed services administratively impossible. The practical policy choice is between ignoring imputed income from self-performed services entirely or employing some indirect method of taxation. All indirect methods require a discernible pattern, since they cannot operate unless there is some factor other than the imputed income item itself for identifying who is being disadvantaged. That factor would be used as a proxy for the presence or absence of the benefits of a particular type of self-performed service.

Second, the theoretical justification for taking particular items of imputed income into account must be related to some systemic defect in market income as an index of an individual's material well-being. A defect of that nature cannot be identified unless patterns of discrimination show up.

A challenge to our tentative conclusion in Part II that couples with equal monetary income should pay equal tax is dependent, therefore, on a showing that the exclusion of certain items of imputed income from the tax base results in a definite pattern of discrimination against two-job couples. The problems in finding a pattern of discrimination are taken up in Section B.[127]

---

[127] Whether or not a pattern of discrimination exists must be judged according to fairness criteria, not efficiency criteria. Much of the support for tax measures in favor of two-job couples nevertheless rests on considerations of efficiency. In analyzing the economic component of the choice between working in and working outside the market, economists find it useful to include income from self-performed services within the concept of income, since the optimum choice for efficiency purposes is the one which maximizes the total of market and nonmarket income. The failure to tax certain types of self-performed services probably creates a distortion in the labor market in favor, for example, of a woman working in the home rather than working at a job which pays a taxable salary. The utility of including self-performed services in the income concept for purposes of eliminating this distortion, however, has no bearing on the merits of including it in income for purposes of determining fairness. Arguments addressed to the social and economic consequences of a particular mode of taxing self-performed services have usually sidestepped the issue of fairness and instead have focused on considerations of efficiency or social engineering. Proposals for accomplishing these nontax goals should be subjected to a tax expenditure analysis and must be justified, if at all, under budget criteria, not tax criteria. A discussion of the merits of proposals for adjusting the burden of one-job and two-job couples on efficiency grounds is beyond the scope of this Article.

If we did reach the merits, we would begin by examining the implicit assumption of all efficiency arguments — that the maximization of economic goods is a desirable social goal. We would want to see what the arguments are for en-

B. Estimating the Patterns of Imputed Income from Self-Performed Services of One-Job and Two-Job Married Couples

Our analysis of imputed income was prompted by the concern that equal tax treatment of couples with equal monetary income might discriminate against two-job couples. As discussed above, a claim of discrimination depends on the existence of identifiable patterns in the distribution of imputed income which disadvantage two-job couples. A stereotyped view of the activities of working and nonworking wives might suggest that a clear pattern exists. In this Section, we attempt to go behind the stereotype and undertake to determine whether patterns actually exist which can be related to the one-job/two-job classification.

To avoid some of the definitional ambiguities discussed above, we will be concerned exclusively with a limited group of self-performed services which many taxpayers commonly purchase in the market — "household services," such as cooking, cleaning, sewing, and caring for children; and "handy-person services," such as shoveling snow, fixing the television, and repairing the roof. In examining the widely held perception that one-job couples have more imputed income from these services than two-job couples have, we are unable to refer to existing empirical studies. In any case, empirical verification of this perception may be impossible. Since we have no organized data, we must rely on intuition, experience, and observation in estimating the distributions of self-performed services among one-job and two-job married couples. We suggest that the pattern of the distribution of self-performed services is more complex than is generally supposed. Although one-job couples do have the advantage of extra hours available for nonemployment activity, there is no necessary relationship between the amount of leisure time and the performance of these services.

First, we can find no predictable difference between one- and two-job couples in the consumption of self-performed child-care

---

couraging market activity at the expense of leisure and self-performed services. Our suspicion is that giving money rewards for some kinds of activities but not for others already distorts the choice among activities in favor of paying jobs. There are a number of possible gains in a tax system which counteract this distortion. We think, for example, that citizen participation in the political processes of the country is desirable and is inhibited by the economic incentives which pull people away from volunteer political work. On the other hand, we can appreciate arguments for encouraging market behavior in other situations. None of the efficiency literature we have seen addresses itself, however, to this fundamental point. For a discussion of efficiency arguments, see H. Rosen, Application of Optimal Tax Theory to Problems in Taxing Families and Individuals (U.S. Dep't of Treasury, OTA Paper 21, November 1976) (also referring to much of the literature on the subject).

services. Obviously, and most importantly, such services are rarely performed by couples without children, in which case disparity between one- and two-job couples is nonexistent. In addition, when there are children a substantial amount of child-care services are performed by both two-job couples and one-job couples.[128] It is true that some one-job couples and even more two-job couples purchase child-care services in the market. Those who purchase probably have less self-performed child-care services than those couples with children who do not purchase. But the ratio of purchased as opposed to self-performed child-care services may be more closely related to inclination than to whether both spouses work, especially if child-care services are defined more meaningfully than as one parent's mere physical presence for long stretches of time.

Second, certain self-performed services, such as carpentry and electrical work, sewing and gourmet cooking, require a definite inclination or skill. These services are distributed in indeterminate patterns among couples: persons who possess the skills perform the services and those without the skills do not. One-job couples may have more time for performing these services, but if the inclination or skill is there, the two-job couple will often arrange their affairs to provide the time. If the skill is possessed by a working spouse, it makes little difference whether or not the other spouse is employed. Most importantly, large numbers of both one-job and two-job couples will have very modest amounts of imputed income from these services.

Third, many self-performed services, such as entertaining and managing one's business affairs, relate much more to lifestyle and type of occupation than to the one-job and two-job categories. Although one-job couples may perform more of these services than two-job couples, it is extremely doubtful whether there is any reasonably close correlation at any given income level.

Of course, many day-to-day services, such as cleaning, maintenance, gardening, and basic cooking, are more likely to be self-performed by one-job than two-job couples. Many two-job couples, however, arrange their lives so as to perform as much

---

[128] Some studies have been made on the patterns of child-care arrangements of working mothers with small children. The most common arrangement is for the child-care to be provided by either the father or another relative. According to a 1973 survey, 49% of working mothers paid nothing for child-care, and in a large number of other cases, the out-of-pocket expenses were "very small," because the services were provided by relatives. In 26% of white two-job families and 14% of black two-job families surveyed, the mother and father arranged working hours to that they could handle their child-care requirements themselves. Child-care in the home is also apparently preferred by the majority of two-job and one-parent families. *See* Woolsey, *Pied Piper Politics and the Child-Care Debate*, DAEDALUS, Spring 1977, at 127, 130-32.

or more of these services than typical one-job couples. Other two-job couples simply allow certain tasks to remain undone, or adopt a living arrangement in which the tasks which must be done are modest — for example, by purchasing or renting space in an apartment building. Still other two-job couples directly purchase the services in the market. On the other hand, significant numbers of one-job couples purchase greater than average quantities of services in the market, and others arrange their lives so that the need for self-performed services is low. Hence, it is difficult to generalize as to the distribution of self-performed services between one-job and two-job couples even with regard to these basic needs.

We recognize that other persons might make estimates quite different from ours and that we would have no reason, beyond our intuition, to claim they were wrong. If, however, our guesses are correct at least within some generous margin of error, the generalization that one-job couples have more imputed income than most two-job couples at the same income level is problematic. Although in a large number of cases it may indeed be accurate, the correlation is too tenuous to justify differential tax treatment of one-job couples to account for the possibility of these additional benefits.

An alternative argument for the differential tax treatment of one- and two-job couples is based not on the nonmonetary income arising from specific self-performed services, but on the theory that in a stable marriage the benefits derived from the marriage contract are the same for each spouse. That theory postulates that in a one-job marriage, the spouse without a job contributes services or other benefits at least equal in value to the market income contributed by the working spouse. If this theory of equivalence of benefits is applied to the tax law, then the more unequal the spouses' contributions of monetary benefits are at any given income level, the more nonmonetary benefits that couple must have in order to match the money contribution. To base tax consequences on this theory, however, seems singularly inappropriate: it presumes a definition of nonmarket gain that goes far beyond that commonly contemplated for tax purposes. For example, the theory implies that the benefits given by a nonworking wife to a husband who earns $50,000 are five times more valuable than those contributed by a nonworking wife to a husband with a $10,000 salary. Such a relative notion of gain, although perhaps theoretically appropriate to a contractual model of marriage, has nothing to do with the economic well-being with which the tax system is concerned.[129]

---

[129] The theory of equivalence of benefits in marriage requires a very broad

The one advantage which a one-job couple consistently has over a two-job couple is the extra time available for nonemployment activity. Although it cannot be assumed that this time is in fact used to perform services the couple would otherwise have to purchase in the market, some advocates of a tax allowance for two-job couples assert that leisure itself constitutes "consumption," and thus should be taxable.[130] Treating leisure as consumption for tax purposes raises most of the problems of treating self-performed services as income. First of all, what is the policy reason for wanting small children, retired persons, students, and the unemployed — those most likely to have substantial amounts of leisure "income" — to pay an increased share of the tax burden?[131] The leisure-as-consumption argument makes sense only if there is some perception that leisure is itself a gain in material well-being that is relevant for income tax purposes.[132] If a link between leisure and gain is made, however, by reference to the benefits obtained through the use of leisure, the leisure-as-consumption argument is a back-door assertion that leisure is a useful surrogate for imputed income from services, a proposition which we have already criticized.

---

definition of benefits and assumes that the benefits are being valued idiosyncratically by the marital partners rather than by the market. Spouses would take into account, for example, beauty, wit, and compatibility, as well as a host of other equally unmeasurable benefits. For a discussion of the theory and for references to the growing literature, see Sawhill, *Economic Perspectives on the Family*, DAEDALUS, Spring 1977, at 115.

[130] Since self-performed services may be thought to involve a sacrifice of leisure, arguably they should be treated equally — or alternatively the leisure itself should be taxed, regardless of the use to which it is put. *Cf.* H. SIMONS, *supra* note 5, at 52 (leisure is a major item of consumption; however, leisure income may be neglected for tax purposes in order to offset the neglect of imputed income).

[131] To tax the housewife for doing her own housework yet not tax the housewife who hires a maid on her increased "consumption" of leisure would arguably penalize industry and subsidize leisure, which may be an undesirable outcome. *See id.* at 111. Although we may wish to encourage certain types of leisure activity such as education, it seems clear that taxing the leisure of the retired and unemployed is both inequitable and self-defeating. At any rate, these considerations are related more to efficiency than fairness.

[132] According to Henry Simons, "[t]he *sine qua non* of income is *gain* . . . ." *Id.* at 50. He states further, "[t]he essential connotation of income, to repeat, is *gain* — gain to someone during a specific period and measured according to objective market standards." *Id.* at 51. Even if leisure is viewed as consumption, it is difficult to see the failure to make productive use of one's time as gain. If leisure is to be treated seriously as consumption, then all available minutes of a tax period should perhaps be seen as a part of an individual's accumulation. Consumption of time in leisure thereby produces no gain, since the loss of time is reflected by a depletion of the accumulation account. The parallel to more serious items of consumption and accumulation is completed by noting that time has no tax cost, so its expenditure in earning income should give no deduction.

Second, the administrative problems in taxing leisure are even greater than those which would arise in attempting to tax self-performed services. It is neither possible to determine directly a market value for leisure, nor proper to assume that the value of leisure is equal to the opportunity cost of an extra hour of work, even if such cost information were available.[133]

Finally, although the two-job couple spends more hours in employment activity than the one-job couple, it is not clear that this actually decreases the opportunities of the two-job couple for obtaining imputed income. The analog of imputed income from services as consumption is imputed income from increases in human capital as accumulation. The distribution, between one- and two-job couples, of imputed accumulation arising from increases in an individual's earning capacity is as problematic as the distribution of imputed income from services. But just as the one-job couple typically has an extra forty hours a week of leisure, so also does the two-job couple have an extra forty hours a week for building up seniority rights and job experience, two of the most important components of human capital.[134]

C. Indirect Methods for Taxing Imputed Income from Self-Performed Services

Despite the preceding analysis, some may still feel that an ideal income tax somehow must take self-performed services into account. In this Section, we assume the validity of that perception and consider practical proposals for taking it into account. Since direct taxation of imputed income is universally acknowledged to be unfeasible, the objective is to find some indirect method of approximating the distribution of tax burdens which would result from direct taxation. We will discuss the merits of three possible indirect methods of taxing imputed income: a deduction for cash outlays for the purchase of personal services, an earned income allowance, and adjustments in the rate schedule. Given the conceptual problems with any definition of imputed income and the complex patterns of distribution of self-performed services among the groups of taxpayers, any indirect method of adjusting burdens will be crude indeed. The most that can be hoped for is a system which reduces the perceived disproportion-

---

[133] A person's pay per hour is a form of return on his skills, and as such may be only incidentally related to the value of leisure if the latter is to be measured by the individual's inclination or disinclination to work. In any case we have data only on marginal cost, not on the average cost figures which would be required were leisure to be included even indirectly in the tax base.

[134] For a critical discussion of increases in human capital as income, see Andrews, *A Consumption-Type or Cash Flow Personal Income Tax*, 87 HARV. L. REV. 1113, 1145-46 (1974).

ate burden arguably imposed currently on two-job couples without creating greater unfairness for other taxpayers. We conclude that none of these proposals achieves even that limited goal.

1. Deductions for Purchases of Personal Services. — Amounts spent on personal services — to hire a maid or gardener, for example — normally constitute consumption, and the income which finances the consumption is taxable. If many taxpayers receive these same benefits tax-free by performing the services themselves, a deduction for cash outlays for services may be in some circumstances a satisfactory indirect method of taxing self-performed services. The function of the deduction would be to equalize the tax treatment of purchased services and self-performed services by in effect making both kinds of services exempt from tax.[135]

A deduction for cash outlays for personal services is defensible in an ideal income tax only if the amount spent to purchase services is a good proxy for differences in the distribution of self-performed services. For example, if all taxpayers either mow their own lawn or hire someone to do it, and if the amount of mowing which must be done is about the same for all taxpayers, then a deduction for the costs of hiring someone else to mow has about the same effect on relative tax burdens as including imputed income from mowing in taxable income. On the other hand, if a significant number of taxpayers do not have a lawn to mow, or mow it very infrequently, then a deduction for the purchase of mowing services is not an acceptable indirect method for taxing self-performed mowing services. The higher tax rates necessitated by the deduction unfairly increase the tax burden on persons who do not mow.[136]

---

[135] As a "second best" adjustment for the failure to tax self-performed services, the child-care deduction originally provided in the Internal Revenue Code of 1954 was defective in that it offered no benefit to the bulk of taxpayers taking the standard deduction and limited the deduction to two-job couples and heads of one-parent families. *See* I.R.C. § 214(e) (repealed 1976). The Tax Reform Act of 1976, Pub. L. No. 94-455, 90 Stat. 1520, which changed the deduction to a nonrefundable credit, I.R.C. § 44A, extended the benefits to families in which one spouse works part-time or is a student. Theoretically the benefits should be available to all purchasers of child-care services and to all taxpayers without children. *See* p. 1620 *infra*. In this case eligibility rules for the benefits were due in part to the view of some supporters that child-care expenses are akin to ordinary business deductions. Most tax specialists would agree, however, that child-care expenses are essentially personal, not business expenses. For a statement of this viewpoint and an analysis of the current credit, see McIntyre, *Evaluating the New Tax Credit for Child Care and Maid Service*, Tax Notes, May 23, 1977, at 7. *See also* Popkin, *Household Services and Child Care in the Income Tax and Social Security Laws*, 50 IND. L.J. 238, 245 (1975).

[136] Assume a universe with only three taxpayers, M, H, and N, each with pecuniary income of 100. The required revenue yield of the tax system is 30. As-

This example illustrates that while a deduction for purchases of any type of services is fair as between persons who typically perform the services themselves and those who purchase, a deduction is unfair as between those who purchase and those who neither purchase nor perform the services themselves. A deduction for mowing is unfair to most renters; a deduction for shoveling snow is unfair to taxpayers in the South.

Of greater practical significance, a deduction for child-care expenditures is unfair to those without children, assuming that the purpose of the deduction is to make allowance for the failure of the tax system to tax imputed income from child-care services. If self-performed child-care services are to be treated as income, the proper adjustment is a large deduction for taxpayers without children, with a more modest deduction for those with children who purchase child-care services.

This analysis suggests that a minimum requirement for permitting a deduction for cash outlays for services must be that the service in question is one which virtually all taxpayers either perform themselves or purchase in the market. This requirement, although a necessary one, is not, however, a sufficient one to identify the purchases for which a deduction is an acceptable "second best" adjustment for the failure to tax self-performed services directly. Cooking may be the most pervasive example of a service which is either performed or purchased. A deduction for amounts spent at restaurants is, however, a poor index of the value of the self-performed services of those who eat at home. Amounts spent at restaurants vary considerably even among persons who frequently eat out; those who eat at expensive restaurants should not be allowed a tax benefit which is only vaguely related to the value of the self-performed cooking services of persons who eat at home. Cleaning house is another chore which is widely purchased or performed for oneself. The allowable deduction would have to be small, however, to avoid unfairness to people with small houses, people without children, and people with a high tolerance for untidiness.[137]

---

sume M mows his lawn, H hires someone to mow, and N has no lawn and never purchases lawn mowing services or performs them himself. If mowing for oneself should be taxable in an ideal income tax system, then M should pay more tax than H or N, and H and N should pay the same tax. If only H is allowed a deduction for mowing, then the tax on M and N will be increased to make up for the revenue loss. This is fair to M, who has more "income" than H, but unfair to N, who has the same income as H. The only fair solution is to give the deduction to both H and N. Assume further that H purchases some mowing services and also performs some for himself. The only way to approximate the "ideal" solution of taxing mowing services would be to give a big deduction to N (perhaps 30), a smaller deduction to H (say 10) and no deduction to M.

[137] A maid service deduction, if regarded as an indirect method of taxing self-

2. Earned Income Allowance. — Unlike those whose income is derived from property, a person whose income is derived from personal services must sacrifice a certain amount of time otherwise available for leisure activities in order to obtain income. A two-job couple will typically sacrifice more leisure time, or time for self-performed services or volunteer work, than a one-job couple in obtaining the same consolidated income. This difference in available time is said to justify some form of earned income allowance — either a deduction or a credit. The most frequently proposed allowance would grant a tax deduction of twenty-five percent of the earnings of the lower income spouse, or a tax credit of ten percent of those earnings, subject to a ceiling of $1,000 in tax benefits.[138] Alternative mechanisms for granting an allowance have been suggested from time to time, but these alternatives are not different in principle from the percentage allowance and will not be analyzed here.

The notion that loss of leisure justifies a tax reduction is based on two distinct theories about what types of benefits should be taxable. The first theory is that "leisure" itself is a form of consumption. As such, it should be taxed, but since it cannot be taxed directly, a deduction for loss of leisure is an acceptable "second best" solution. The second theory is based on the premise that differences in the amounts of self-performed services can be assumed to relate to differences in the amounts of leisure time available. Under this approach, leisure itself is not considered to be income, but its loss is a reasonable proxy for imputed income from self-performed services. The conceptual difficulties inherent in these two rationales were discussed above, where we concluded that taxation of leisure directly or as proxy involved the same problems involved in taxing any other form of imputed income.[139] Leaving aside the conceptual difficulties, an earned income allowance for two-job couples suffers from its own collection of infirmities.

---

performed housecleaning services, should of course be available to all taxpayers, not simply those with a qualifying dependent for whom the expense is somehow job-related. See I.R.C. § 44A. We suspect, however, that a deduction for maid services, if divorced from the business expense rationale which in part explained the political acceptability of the present household services credit, would be perceived by the public as a subsidy to the rich, who are more likely to pay for the performance of housework than are poorer people regardless of whether both spouses work. The problem of an apparent lack of equivalence between self-performed and purchased services may be particularly blatant here even though theoretically the two groups are being treated alike. It is unclear how a system of deductions could deal with this problem.

[138] For a clear presentation of alternative earned income allowances and estimates of their distributional impact, see J. PECHMAN, *supra* note 82, at 98–103.

[139] *See* pp. 1617–18 & note 132 *supra*.

We see two major difficulties in instituting an earned income allowance for two-job couples. First, there is no acceptable justification for limiting the allowance to two-job couples. If the allowance is an adjustment for leisure, it should also be available to single persons on the assumption that single persons have the same leisure available to them, on a per capita basis, as have two-job couples. Moreover, a case can even be made for giving some minimal allowance to one-job couples to make up for the greater amount of leisure enjoyed by couples and singles supported entirely by property income. In addition, persons who habitually work long overtime hours theoretically should receive a larger allowance than persons working a forty-hour week. Extending the earned income allowance to all deserving cases, however, would mean that the size of the allowance would have to be much smaller than is generally proposed. Since from eighty to ninety percent of total adjusted gross income reported for tax purposes is earned income, an allowance available to a substantial part of the population would either have to be very small or would cause a massive shift of tax burdens to property income.

The other difficulty with the earned income allowance arises from the practical problems of distinguishing part-time from full-time workers. In our discussion heretofore, we have assumed that each two-job couple was comprised of two full-time workers. In fact, however, it is common for one spouse in a two-job couple to work on a part-time basis. Since the rationale of the earned income allowance is based on loss of leisure, the allowance should be a function of hours worked and, hence, of leisure forgone. The standard proposal for an earned income allowance nevertheless makes the allowance a percentage of the earnings of the lower income spouse and does not look at all to actual hours worked. This approach is based on two simplifying assumptions. First, it is assumed that the dollar ceiling on the benefits can be pegged high enough so that most persons eligible for the maximum allowance will be full-time workers, and most persons denied the maximum will be part-time workers. The second assumption is that for persons not eligible for the maximum benefits, the amount of income earned is a good proxy for the number of hours worked.

Neither of these assumptions has much intuitive appeal. Our guess is that there are, first of all, a significant number of part-time workers who are highly compensated on a per hour basis. We think it also common for lower income spouses to take jobs which are essentially full-time but which pay close to the minimum wage. Since the tax consequences of being denied or granted a deduction of twenty-five percent of earnings are substantial, we think the simplifying assumptions implicit in the proposal for a percentage allowance mask from view an unacceptable degree of unfairness, even assuming the merits of some form of earned income allowance.[140]

The alternative to a percentage allowance is to require IRS to collect data on the number of hours actually worked by taxpayers. Such data are not now available and would require a major change in current reporting requirements. The collection of the data, however, is certainly feasible, at least for hourly workers. Even crude data — enough to group taxpayers into fulltime and part-time classifications — would be sufficient to devise an earned income allowance which was fairer than the percentage allowance proposal.

3. Rate Adjustments. — Two conceptually distinct proposals have been advanced for taking account of self-performed services through the rate schedules. The first proposal would allow the lower income spouse in a two-job couple to file a separate return, although the property income of the couple would be consolidated with the income of the higher income spouse.[141] The benefits to the two-job couple under this proposal are a function of their income, and bear no particular relationship to loss of leisure or loss of self-performed services. The proposal, in our view, is based almost exclusively on an attempt to avoid the inefficiency consequences of progressive rates.[142]

The second proposal calls for separate rate schedules for

---

[140] An allowance based on percentage of income, rather than hours worked, is appealing to those who support an earned income allowance on grounds of efficiency rather than of fairness. To the extent that the nontaxation of self-performed services induces potential secondary earners to stay at home, any form of earned income allowance improves the efficiency of the labor market. Relating the benefits to income earned, rather than hours worked, also reduces the inefficiency caused by progressive rates. That inefficiency exists for all taxpayers, but is apparently greater for secondary earners. A consistent application of the efficiency criterion would result in a complex pattern of family taxation which we suspect would have little or no political support. It would give the least benefits, for example, to two-job couples at the low end of the income spectrum who are forced to work by economic necessity.

[141] In countries such as the United Kingdom and Switzerland which typically consolidate marital income and assess tax under the same rate schedule used for singles, separate taxation of the earned income of the second working spouse undoubtedly increases the fairness of the tax systems. The tax on marriage under United States law is minor in comparison with that in a number of European countries, even when special allowances for working wives granted in these countries are taken into account. *See generally How Direct Taxes Affect Individuals and Couples: Old Values and New,* OECD OBSERVER, March 1977, at 28.

[142] Our objections to separate taxation of spouses on fairness grounds are presented in Part II, pp. 1589–92 *supra*.

different types of households, expanding the multiple rate system of current law to include rates for two-job couples and families. The relationships among the rate schedules would be a function, in part, of intuitions about differences in the amount of self-performed services enjoyed by different types of household units.

None of the problems of deciding what tax consequences should flow from self-performed services is removed by the multiple rate approach. All that happens is that the critical choices are buried from public view. For example, should the rates for single persons be higher or lower than those for two-job married couples? If imputed income is a factor in that choice, we face the same issue which was raised by the earned income credit: are we willing to raise the rates on property income to cover the loss of revenue which would result if a rate reduction were given to single persons? Similarly, in asking whether or not the rates on two-job couples should be lower than the rates on one-job couples, we have to confront the problem that generalizations about the distribution of self-performed services between one-job and two-job couples are of little help in deciding what burdens individual taxpayers should bear.

A rate schedule for two-job couples would require us to decide whether a full-time working spouse and a part-time working spouse qualify as a two-job couple. That definitional problem was discussed in our analysis of the proposal for an earned income credit.[143] Rate schedules, however, are less flexible in this context than deductions or credits. Part-time workers must be treated as a part of either a one-job or a two-job couple. An intermediate position is possible only if we are prepared to proliferate the number of rate schedules — adding one, for example, for one-and-one-half-job couples.

As has been noted before,[144] many of the effects of special rate schedules can be duplicated through the use of deductions. Any proposal for the use of multiple rate schedules for handling the problem of self-performed services can be reduced, with some effort, to a question of whether or not a series of special deductions should be allowed. We have already discussed the problems in using deductions to take account of imputed income from self-performed services. We fail to see how these issues become less intractable when buried in a rate schedule.

---

[143] See pp. 1622–23 *supra*.
[144] See pp. 1584–85 *supra*.

C. FRINGE BENEFITS

SECTION OF TAXATION, AMERICAN BAR ASSOCIATION, COMMITTEE ON SIMPLIFICATION, "EVALUATION OF THE PROPOSED MODEL COMPREHENSIVE INCOME TAX"

32 Tax Lawyer 563 (1979), pp. 567–84.

II. COMPENSATION

If all compensation for services rendered were paid in cash shortly following the performance of such services, the taxation of such compensation would be simple indeed. The real world, however, presents a vastly different picture: for both tax and non-tax reasons, compensation is frequently paid in kind and/or is deferred. The non-tax reasons for this include both governmental and private paternalism; the tax reasons include the benefits of deferral, special treatment and outright exemption.

In terms of dollars, the biggest issue in this area is, of course, the tax treatment of deferred compensation distributed through *qualified* pension, profit sharing, and stock-bonus plans. In 1976, employer contributions to private plans of this type were estimated at $29.1 billion, the earnings on such plans at $10.4 billion, and the benefits paid out at $19.4 billion. Although involuntary, Social Security retirement benefits complement and supplement the private pension system and raise similar tax questions. Other significant benefits to be discussed herein include employer-provided health and disability insurance; Medicare and Social Security Disability insurance; employer-provided life insurance coverage; unemployment compensation; and the entire panoply of so-called "fringe benefits" paid in kind.

In terms of simplification, the ideal solution would be to tax all of the above items in the same manner—at least to the extent that they are similar to one another. All benefits would be valued at the time they are provided, as if cash had passed instead and the employee had purchased the item provided, be it an annuity policy, term-life insurance, health insurance, or an airplane ticket. If the employee had no immediate right to the benefit, taxation would be deferred until such right vested.

Alternatively, a relatively simple system would be to defer both employer deductions and employee income until the employee receives cash or its equivalent, whether pension distributions, life insurance proceeds, health insurance payments, or airplane tickets. Payments in kind, of course, would still pose serious valuation problems.

The difficulty with the foregoing "simple" solutions is that they run directly counter to other major factors used in determining tax policy such as congressionally mandated "social goals," perceptions of "equity," and administrative feasibility. In considering the various types of compensation, this paper briefly reviews the current tax treatment of compensation, the relevant proposals in *Blueprints*, the "simple" solutions suggested above, some solutions suggested by others, and the impact of the cross-currents of public policy, equity and practicality. As explained in the introduction to this report, the analysis and proposals made herein are based on the belief that major and substantial simplification of income tax laws can best be accomplished by a broad-based, low-rate tax system.

A. *Private Retirement Benefits.*

Under present law, if a retirement plan is "qualified," the employer's contributions to the plan are deductible when made,[4] no one is taxable on plan income, and an employee is taxable only when he receives distributions attributable to such contributions and income.[5] In addition, if the employee contributes to the plan, his contributions are not deductible but the earnings thereon are not taxed and he may include his contributions when distributions are taxed. Finally, certain lump sum distributions are taxed as capital gains.[6]

There is no doubt that the foregoing tax treatment is extremely favorable and has contributed to the dramatic growth of private pension plans. Congress reviewed the entire area of private pension plans when adopting the comprehensive Employees Retirement Income Security Act (ERISA) in 1974. Despite criticism of the cost and complexity of this act, there seems to be uniform political support for the basic tax treatment of pensions under ERISA. It should also be noted that the tax-induced savings under the private system are a major element in capital formation in the private sector. While the Committee accepts these facts, it does not find ERISA acceptable from the standpoint of simplification.

If all compensation were taxed to employees when rights to that compensation vested, an employee would pay tax on the present value of anticipated future benefits when they accrued. This process would be quite complex in the case of defined-benefit plans. Rather than pay tax on dollars they do not receive, employees would presumably forego pension benefits for higher current compensation. If this were the result, the tax law would certainly be simpler, but would such simplification be worth the cost in terms of capital formation and expanded public pension programs?

Blueprints suggests that many of the complexities of taxing pension benefits as they accrue can be avoided by taxing the plan's earnings (to the employee, if vested, and to the employer if not) and fully taxing distributions.[7] *Blueprints* demonstrates that this scheme, despite the ap-

---

[4] I.R.C. § 404.
[5] I.R.C. §§ 402(a)(1), 403(a)(1).
[6] I.R.C. §§ 402(a)(2), 403(a)(2).
[7] BLUEPRINTS, *supra* note 1, at 56-57.

parent double taxation of plan income, has the same net effect as taxing accrued benefits plus plan income. In any event, this would raise havoc with the private retirement plan as it currently exists.

The other "simple" solution suggested is to deny deductions to the employer until benefits are paid and taxed. Plan income would be taxed to the employer. This scheme would be even more destructive to qualified plans than the two preceding suggestions because the revenue gain from denying the employer's deduction would exceed that from taxing accrued benefits.

In terms of broad principles, "simplification" would mandate either taxing accrued benefits or denying employer deductions. Pension benefits could thereby be most easily treated uniformly with all other employee benefits. The details of taxing accrued pension benefits would not be at all simple, however, and denying employer deductions would sound the death knell for funded plans. The *Blueprints* solution is more complex than present law in adding the taxation of plan earnings. While it is less complex than direct taxation of accrued benefits, it is almost as destructive of the incentive to create private pension plans as any of the other proposals.

One commentator recently discussed the apparent conflict between general principles of simplification and the specific congressional mandate to encourage private pension plans:

> ... [S]ubstantial simplification would be achieved, in general, by enlarging the tax base to include in income all economic benefits arising out of the employment relationship. A comprehensive tax base permits a substantially reduced and simplified structure of exemptions and rates, which would be the greatest possible contribution to simplification. *Blueprints*, for example, demonstrates that with a comprehensive tax base, roughly the same degree of progressivity in the income tax system, or vertical equity, may be achieved with a greatly simplified [and reduced] structure of exemptions and rates. ...
>
> On the other hand, the major identifiable and integrated set of benefits reflected in the treatment of qualified employee benefit plans could be excluded from the all-inclusive concept of income without major loss of these simplification achievements. The policy considerations favoring encouragement of retirement savings through the private sector, with the benefits of flexibility, thereby obtained, may be of greater importance.[8]

Despite the anomaly of commencing a paper on simplification with a proposed exception to the search for general rules, there is much to be said for this approach. As a matter of practical politics, of course, there is really no other approach. In any event, much can be done to simplify and streamline ERISA and such work is proceeding. An ALI-ABA conference on the simplification of ERISA was held this spring; the Tax Section's Committee on Employee Benefits is also working on the prob-

---

[8] Nolan, *Taxation of Fringe Benefits*, 30 NAT'L TAX J., 359, 360 (1977).

lem, and various legislative proposals have been introduced in Congress. Further discussion in this area is beyond the scope of this paper.

B. *Social Security Retirement Benefits.*

Under present law, employers may deduct the Social Security taxes they pay.[9] Employees may not deduct Social Security taxes which are withheld and paid to the government by their employers.[10] Retirement benefits are not taxable[11] and there is no attempt to tax earnings on the Social Security "trust fund." Indeed, such earnings are not even computed in the ordinary sense.

Blueprints would allow a deduction, presumably "above-the-line," for all contributions from employees as well as employers, and tax all benefits. *Blueprints* does not, however, seek the equivalent of accrual by taxing fund earnings. The distinction is based on the mandatory nature of Social Security taxes which do not, according to *Blueprints,* create an incentive to convert savings to tax-deferred forms.[12]

As in the case of private pension plans, taxing benefits as they accrue would be extremely complicated. Moreover, the employee tax would have to be allowed as a deduction. The simplification technique of delaying all deductions and taxing all benefit payments is further complicated in the context of Social Security in that all employers who ever contributed on behalf of a certain employee would have to be allowed a prorated deduction when benefits are paid.

On balance, the *Blueprints* solution seems most acceptable. It is simple to apply, and it is consistent with the present treatment of private retirement plans. The *Blueprints* proposal also represents an improvement over the present system in which the deductibility of contributions by the employer leads to pressure to increase only the employer's tax. Finally, it comes much closer than the present system to achieving the base-broadening which is essential to simplicity and equity. Presumably, the Code's pattern of rates and exemptions would be so structured as to exempt persons whose income includes *only* Social Security retirement benefits.

C. *Employer-Provided Health Insurance.*

Under present law, employers can deduct health insurance premiums,[13] employees do not have corresponding income,[14] and benefit payments are nontaxable.[15] This highly favorable treatment is presum-

---

[9] I.R.C. § 162.
[10] I.R.C. § 3502(a) (disallows deduction of taxes imposed pursuant to section 3101, the Federal Insurance Contributions Act, and sections 3201 and 3211, the Railroad Retirement Tax Act).
[11] Rev. Rul. 70-217, 1970-1 C.B. 12.
[12] BLUEPRINTS, *supra* note 1, at 58.
[13] I.R.C. § 162.
[14] I.R.C. § 106.
[15] I.R.C. § 104(a)(3) (an exception to this exclusion of payments from income exists when the payments are attributable to contributions by the employer that were not includible in the gross income of the employee or when such payments are made by the employer).

ably to encourage the purchase of health insurance, which is regarded as socially desirable. This scheme is simple enough taken in isolation, but is it consistent with a broad-based, low-rate taxation program such as the one proposed by *Blueprints?*

The *Blueprints* program would include in taxable income health insurance premiums paid by an employer.[16] This provision appears inconsistent with the notion of delaying the tax on retirement benefits until received, but the inconsistency can be explained if premium taxation is seen as the general rule and pensions as an exception justified by the complexities inherent in allocating the cost of private and Social Security retirement benefits. On the other hand, it is arguably less fair to accelerate the taxation of health insurance since the employee may never receive the proceeds.[17] Finally, one reason why there is little enthusiasm for taxing health insurance benefits is that a serious illness could produce an unreasonable increase in income in the year in question. This problem might, however, be handled by allowing a deduction for catastrophic medical expenses.

In the context of a broad-based, low-rate income tax scheme, it should pose no undue difficulty to require employees to pay tax on health insurance premiums paid by their employers. Since similar coverage is offered on an individual basis, the value of the coverage received could be measured and easily taxed. Under this approach, benefit payments would be tax-free and the employee would be able to deduct such amounts of his imputed income just as if he had purchased an individual policy.[18]

Taxing health insurance premiums, however, presents for the first time in this paper the *wholesale-retail* dilemma in the fringe benefits area. If the cost to the employer of a group health insurance program is less than the sum of the individual policies, should this cost-saving be allocated and passed on to the employees? Since the employees, in most instances, could form their own "group" and achieve approximately the same savings, fairness requires an affirmative answer. This is the result reached in the case of group term life insurance in excess of $50,000, which is taxed to the employee pursuant to Service tables.[19]

The problems of preparing tables to provide the taxable values of health insurance is far more complex than in the case of life insurance, however. This is because of the wider variety of benefits to consider, such as the inclusion or exclusion of maternity and mental health benefits, deductibles, percentages, and the duration of benefits. It is suggested that tables be used whenever possible for the most typical plans

---

[16] BLUEPRINTS, *supra* note 1, at 59.

[17] To the extent that the 1978 administration proposals to limit the benefits of sections 79, 105, 106, and 127 have been enacted, their new nondiscrimination requirements could form the basis of an argument that these statutory fringes should all be treated as favorably as "qualified" pension plans. *See* H.R. 12078, 95th Cong., 2d Sess. § 252 (1978).

[18] I.R.C. § 213(a)(2).

[19] *See* I.R.C. § 79 and the Regulations thereunder.

and that the cost to the employer be allocated among the employees in all other cases.

In summary, since a broad-based, low-rate tax system requires taxing all income whenever practical, it seems that health insurance premiums should be taxable when paid. Finally, note that this discussion has focused only on the most common type of general health insurance available to all employees. Extra insurance provided in recognition of hazardous occupations might well be regarded as a nontaxable condition of employment.

D. *Medicare.*

A portion of the Social Security taxes provide funding for health benefits which closely resemble those paid under private health insurance programs. The only significant difference is that the recipient must be over 65. Since employer-paid taxes provide one-half the cost of this system, the resemblance to private health plans is obvious. A parallel solution is to tax the employees on that portion of the employer's Social Security taxes which is used to fund Medicare. *Blueprints* apparently recommends this procedure.[20] The Committee, somewhat reluctantly, disagrees on the grounds that taxation of a portion of the employer-paid Social Security is both complex and impractical. The Committee suggests that the voluntary nature of the program be seen as a basis of distinction. We would instead favor taxing Medicare *benefits,* like Social Security retirement benefits, but with offsetting deductions for medical expenses to the extent provided in the Code.

E. *Employer-Provided Disability Insurance.*

Under present law, employers may deduct premium payments, but employees do not realize income at the time of such payments. Disability benefits are not taxable except in excess of specific limits.[21]

Blueprints suggests treating disability and health insurance provided by employers in different ways. It concludes that taxing disability premiums to the employees would pose insurmountable administrative difficulties, and therefore recommends full taxation of benefits.[22] It is difficult to appreciate the distinction made by *Blueprints* between disability insurance and health insurance in general. Individual disability policies, like individual health policies, are sold every day, and the same type of extrapolated value should be possible. On balance, it seems most consistent with the concept of taxing all compensation for services to tax the beneficiaries of disability insurance on their ratable share of premium

---

[20] BLUEPRINTS, *supra* note 1, at 59.
[21] I.R.C. § 105(d).
[22] BLUEPRINTS, *supra* note 1, at 59. It also proposes that employees be allowed to deduct their own contributions to such disability plans.

payments. Benefit payments would then be nontaxable, as in the case of individually purchased policies.

If this solution were adopted, the wholesale-retail problem encountered in the case of health insurance would again have to be faced, as would the fact that benefits vary widely. The solution should also be the same: use of tables where possible and wholesale cost allocation otherwise.

F. *Social Security Disability Insurance.*

Once again, under present law, the employer's tax is deductible but no income is allocated to potential beneficiaries at that time. Benefit payments are tax-free. *Blueprints* would allow both employers and employees a deduction for their tax payments but would tax disability benefits when received.[23] The Committee agrees with this proposal for the reasons set forth above with regard to all other Social Security benefits. Thus, all Social Security taxes and benefit payments would be treated alike.

G. *Life Insurance.*

Under present law, life insurance premiums are generally nondeductible[24] and proceeds are nontaxable.[25] If an employer pays life insurance premiums and the employee designates the beneficiary of the policy, then the employer may deduct such payments. The employee is taxed on the premium payments, with the important exception that an employer's premium payments for up to $50,000 of group term life insurance are tax-free to the employee.[26]

Under the *Blueprints* program, term insurance would be taxed the same as under present law, except that the $50,000 exclusion would be removed.[27] In the case of whole life or permanent insurance, however, the owner of the policy would be taxed each year on an amount equal to the increase in its cash surrender value, plus the value of the term insurance protection, minus the net premium. *Blueprints* does not make clear whether the mere right to designate the beneficiary shifts this tax to the employee, or if there should be some concept of "vesting." As with term insurance, employer contributions to the annual premium would be includible in gross income.[28]

Blueprints explains that the increasing cash surrender value represents the increasing value of the insured's right to purchase the same amount of insurance each year at a fixed premium. It might be argued that the

---

[23] *Id.* at 59.
[24] I.R.C. § 101.
[25] I.R.C. § 264.
[26] I.R.C. § 79.
[27] BLUEPRINTS, *supra* note 1, at 60.
[28] *Id.*

insured is being taxed on the earnings of the "investment element" of his policy. In either event, a new item is added to the tax base which resembles the income which the policyholder would have realized had he instead bought decreasing term insurance and invested the premium savings in a mutual fund.

It is beyond the scope of this paper to attempt to resolve, even on simplification grounds, the competing theories pertaining to the measurement of income derived from the investment element of life insurance. The Committee agrees with *Blueprints* that the value of employer-provided term insurance should be taxed to the employees. In addition, if the employer pays the cost of ordinary or whole-life policies, the employee should be deemed to have received cash equal to the allocated premium, and the general rules pertaining to the taxation of life insurance should be thereafter applied. In this situation, the employee should be taxed on each year's cash-value earnings so long as he benefits from them in terms of less expensive coverage or vested rights upon cancellation. The balance of such income, if any, should be taxed to the employer. It may be argued that requiring insurance companies to identify this element of investment income and requiring the employer or the beneficiaries to report it is contrary to the goal of simplification. The Committee believes, however, that the burden on this fully computerized industry would be minimal, and the benefit to the general concept of simplification, through the aegis of a broad-based, low-rate tax system, would be quite substantial.

H. *Unemployment Compensation.*

Although the system is mandatory, unemployment compensation under government programs seems properly includible in this discussion of employer-provided benefits. While the employee is working, the employer must provide for future benefits if such work should cease under certain circumstances. Under present law, unemployment taxes are deductible by the employer but not income to the employee. Until recently, unemployment benefits were not taxable to the recipient.[29] Beginning in 1979, however, they will be taxed in whole or in part to taxpayers earning over $20,000 per year (or $25,000 in the case of a joint return).[30]

Blueprints favors taxing unemployment benefits in their entirety rather than allocating premium payments.[31] The Committee supports this proposal. This is another example of an involuntary plan in which allocation would be quite difficult since unemployment insurance is not customarily sold on an individual basis. Moreover, an individual receiv-

---

[29] Rev. Rul. 70-280, 1970-1 C.B. 13; Rev. Rul. 73-154, 1973-1 C.B. 40.
[30] I.R.C. § 85.
[31] BLUEPRINTS, *supra* note 1, at 61.

ing $5,000 of unemployment compensation as part of his income would be treated the same as one receiving an equal amount of Social Security retirement or disability income. It appears that some consistent patterns are emerging here. This is certainly a step toward simplification.

I. *Withholding.*

In the preceding paragraphs, the Committee recommends taxing employees on the value of employer-provided health, life and disability insurance as well as on retirement benefits. All such "income" could be subjected to withholding taxes. Withholding is the simplest and most effective way for the government to ensure collection of taxes. Indeed even Social Security and unemployment benefits *could* be subject to income tax withholding.

On the other hand, the Supreme Court has recently held that all compensation income is not necessarily subject to withholding.[32] Similarly, there has never been withholding tax on pensions. As will be discussed below, the problems of allocating and valuing benefits may be so severe in certain cases that the imposition of withholding taxes on such compensation would be an unfair burden. Finally, in certain cases it may be more sensible to deny the employer's deduction in lieu of taxation or withholding at the employee level.

In all events, the Committee recommends that employers be required each year to provide their employees with a full statement of taxable fringe benefits whether or not tax has been withheld. The employee may then use this statement in preparing his tax return. This is the simplification issue; withholding *vel non* is primarily a revenue issue.

J. *Statutory "Fringes".*

The most important types of deferred or non-cash compensation for which the Code provides specific treatment have been discussed above. In addition, there are other fringe benefits whose excludability from income is provided by statute. Examples of such compensation include nondiscriminatory medical expense reimbursement plans,[33] qualified group legal service plans,[34] combat pay,[35] mustering-out pay,[36] certain retirement pay of members of the armed services,[37] fellowship grants,[38] veterans disability, survivors, and pension benefits,[39] rental value of

---

[32] Central Illinois Public Service Co. v. United States, 435 U.S. 21 (1978) (lunch reimbursements not wages).
[33] I.R.C. § 105(b), *as amended by* the Revenue Act of 1978, Pub. L. No. 95-600, 92 Stat. 2763.
[34] I.R.C. § 120.
[35] I.R.C. § 112.
[36] I.R.C. § 113.
[37] I.R.C. § 122.
[38] I.R.C. § 117.
[39] I.R.C. § 104.

parsonages,[40] and, commencing in 1979, nondiscriminatory educational assistance plans.[41] An even better known and more frequently used example is the exclusion for meals and lodging furnished for the convenience of the employer.[42]

In terms of simplification, through a broad-based, low-rate tax system, it is desirable to repeal all of these provisions and to deal with the presently excluded income under the rules suggested below for nonstatutory fringe benefits. The policy reasons which have led to these additional statutory exclusions are insubstantial in the face of any real effort to broaden the tax base and to tax compensation in a consistent manner.

K. *"Fringes" Under The Regulations.*

The income tax Regulations exclude certain employee benefits from income for reasons which are not entirely clear under the statute. For example, tuition remission programs for children of faculty members of educational institutions are treated as "scholarships" and excluded from income by section 117.[43] On November 1, 1976, the Treasury Department proposed changes in the Regulations to include such tuition remission benefits in income.[44] These Regulations were subsequently withdrawn in response to a storm of protest.[45] The Regulations also exempt from taxation military subsistence and uniform allowances. Except for their origin, the problems posed by these exclusions are no different from those involving "fringe benefits" in general, and hence are considered below.

L. *All Other "Fringes".*

The final group of benefits to be considered includes all those which have been excluded from income by published rulings or administrative practice, sometimes for reasons of administrative convenience, or whose tax treatment is uncertain and frequently varies according to the audit practices of the Service. These benefits include such items as airline and railroad passes given to employees,[46] discounts allowed employees of retail stores, personal use of company cars, free parking, and many others. In September, 1975, the Treasury Department released a Discussion Draft of proposed Regulations which, in general, attempted to rationalize and continue the longstanding administrative practice of

---

[40] I.R.C. § 107. Consider also the tax-free, nonaccountable expense allowances of the President and Congressmen.
[41] I.R.C. § 127, enacted as part of the Revenue Act of 1978, see note 24 *supra*.
[42] I.R.C. § 119.
[43] Reg. § 1.117-3.
[44] Notice of Proposed Rule Making, Tuition Remission Programs, 41 Fed. Reg. 48132 (Nov. 2, 1976).
[45] I.R.S. News Release 1735, Jan. 13, 1977, 77-9 CCH ¶ 6375, 77-6 P-H ¶ 55,172.
[46] O.D. 946, 4 C.B. 110 (1921).

excluding many of these employee benefits from income.[47] The Draft was the subject of spirited protest, both by opponents and proponents of various exclusions, and was subsequently withdrawn.[48] Finally, on June 28, 1978, the House of Representatives overwhelmingly approved H.R. 12841 which prohibits the Service from issuing new rules on the taxation of fringe benefits until December 31, 1979.[49] The rationale behind the resolution is that Congress needs more time to study this subject. The Ways and Means Committee has appointed a task force which is drafting legislation on fringe benefit taxation.

In considering the proper treatment of the foregoing items from a simplification viewpoint, the overriding consideration is administrative feasibility. Because these benefits are so pervasive and varied, a complex system, frought with problems of valuation, identification, and consistency, would be intolerable both to taxpayers and to the Service. On the other hand, as has often been stressed in the preceding discussion of better-known statutory fringe benefits, the general principle of a broad-based, low-rate tax system should be to tax substantially all income. This is required by simplicity in its broadest sense, and by considerations of equity and consistency. It is also required by sections 61 and 83 of the Code. Exceptions to this general rule should be rare and clearly defined, and the solutions to valuation problems should be clear and simple.

It has been generally suggested that taxing fringe benefits complicates the law by raising many new tax issues and major problems of administration. The Committee rejects this argument. The multiplication of fringes in high-rate countries like Britain has proved very inefficient; employers simply do not get their money's worth. In the United States the present annual value of fringe benefits is estimated at $100,000,000,000. Furthermore, the present uncertainty in such areas as commuting expense allowances and employer provided meals is producing hundreds of cases for audit. This is the essence of complexity. Finally, the confusion surrounding the definition of wages places a terrible burden upon employers deciding whether or not to withhold tax on various benefits.

The Committee believes that now is the time to confront the problem of taxing fringe benefits. Clear rules, emphasizing both taxability and administratibility, will (i) cut down on fringe benefits by making them less attractive; (ii) broaden the tax base, a step which is necessary in order

---

[47] Notice of Publication of Discussion Draft of Regulations, Fringe Benefits, 40 Fed. Reg. 41118 (Sept. 5, 1975), Announcement 75-101, 1975-40 I.R.B. 22.
[48] Treasury Department News Release, Dec. 17, 1976.
[49] In the same bill, the House would provide that the Supreme Court's decision in Commissioner v. Kowalski, 434 U.S. 77 (1977), holding state troopers' meal allowances taxable, would apply only in years after 1977.

to cut rates; and (iii) promote equity in the tax system by recognizing the unequal opportunities among taxpayers seeking this type of tax benefit.

M. *Compensation* Vel Non.

The first step in devising a workable system to tax fringe benefits is to recognize that certain "benefits," generally in the nature of conditions of employment, are simply not compensation. Other items, such as an employer-provided automobile used for both business and pleasure, clearly have elements of both compensation and nontaxable conditions of employment. Finally, some benefits are clearly compensation in their entirety.

The Committee believes that each purported benefit must be analyzed to see if an allocation is possible between business and personal benefit. If so, the latter is income. If allocation is not possible, the *primary* purpose of the benefit must be determined. If personal benefit is primary, the recipient should be taxed. Only at this point must the personal benefits be valued and such questions as *de minimis* exceptions, denial of employer deductions, and withholding be considered.

1. *Examples of Allocation.*

Frequently, it is possible to draw a line between the taxable benefit to the employee and the "excess" which is either provided for the employer's benefit or necessary to make the employment acceptable. Consider, for example, housing provided to overseas employees in certain areas where American-style housing is not otherwise available. A simple apartment that might rent for $400 per month in the United States could command a rental of $2,000 per month in such an area. The provisions of such accommodations to employees and their families who are United States citizens may properly be viewed as providing acceptable conditions of employment according to generally prevailing community standards. On the other hand, there is a clear benefit to the employee and unless some provision such as section 119 is expanded and made applicable to this situation,[50] the employee should be taxed on some amount.

Prior to the Foreign Earned Income Act of 1977, a reasonable solution would have been to include in the employee's income the highest fair rental value of comparable facilities in the United States, less any amount paid by the employee. Effective January 1, 1978, the Foreign Earned Income Act of 1978 provides a different solution to the cost of housing differential problem in the case of an employee who receives cash compensation and pays for his own foreign housing. Under new section 913(b)(2), a qualifying foreign employee is allowed to deduct his "qualified housing expenses." In most cases, such expenses will equal the

---

[50] *See generally,* Reg. § 1.119-1(b).

excess of the employee's actual foreign housing expenses (other than lavish or extravagant expenses) over his "base housing amount." The base housing amount is defined as the excess of twenty percent of earned income less allocable deductions, housing expenses, and all the other foreign living expense deductions allowed under sections 913(b)(1), (3), (4) and (5).

An employee who has his foreign housing provided by his employer, assuming that section 119 does not apply, should fare no differently from the employee who receives a higher salary and pays his own housing costs. Therefore, the employee described above should be taxed on $24,000 of imputed income (twelve months × $2,000 per month rent) and allowed the section 913(b)(2) deduction based on grossed-up "earned income" and a constructive $24,000 rental payment. Without even delving into the subtleties of the new section 913, it seems fair to say that the solution suggested by the Committee above is far simpler. Indeed, if Congress is determined to provide some relief in this area, it may be that the pre-1976 exclusion is the simplest solution available.

Another good example of allocation is the situation when company cars are available for personal use. The use of such cars is an identifiable, measurable benefit to the employee which is sufficiently substantial to be taxed. The Regulations might address the case of an automobile used five days a week in the course of business and for commuting,[51] and used by the employee for his personal use on weekends. It may be reasonable and administratively feasible to prescribe a standard, if general statistics so indicate, whereby an appropriate fraction of the annual rental charge for a comparable car by a commercial lessor of cars would be treated as income to such employees.

2. *Examples of Primarily Nonpersonal, Nontaxable Benefits.*

Those items which are primarily provided to aid the business of the employer and constitute acceptable conditions of employment are not easy to describe in general terms but are easily recognizable. They usually have one or more of the following characteristics: (i) they are "required" by the employer rather than "optional;" (ii) they are provided regularly or continuously rather than sporadically; (iii) they are provided on a nondiscriminatory basis; and (iv) sanctions may be imposed for failure to "accept" the benefit.

Examples in this category of nontaxable items include (i) an executive's large, attractive office, (ii) first class air travel on business trips, (iii) a limousine used as a portable office, but not for commuting, (iv) bus

---

[51] It is well-settled that commuting expenses of employees are not deductible. Accordingly, it follows that in-kind benefits to employees which reimburse commuting expenses should be taxed. *See* Rev. Rul. 76-453, 1976-2 C.B. 86, and cases cited therein. This Revenue Ruling was suspended. I.R.S. News Release 1884, Sept. 23, 1977, 77-9 CCH ¶ 6256R, 77-6 P-H ¶ 55,898.

service for night shift employees where the area is unsafe and public transportation unavailable, (v) meals in the company cafeteria if substantially all employees are expected to and do eat there, (vi) box lunches provided to county patrolmen, (vii) uniforms not usable off the job, (viii) supper money if nondiscriminatory and helpful in increasing productivity, and (ix) a health care unit in a plant.

Certain other items may fall into this category, depending upon the circumstances. For example, employer-provided physical examinations appear to qualify if required for all employees, if required by regulatory agencies (such as FAA), and/or if required by the nature of the work (asbestos factory). On the other hand, if the examination is optional and /or available on a discriminatory basis, the value of such an examination might be income. Finally, if the exam is given in connection with a three-day vacation at a health spa, an allocation would be required.

The bodyguard is another example. If an executive needs protection due to his public identification with the company, he should not be taxed on the value of the bodyguard just as he would not be taxed because there is a security man at the plant gate. On the other hand, if the bodyguard doubles as a chauffeur and gardener, an allocation of his salary seems appropriate.

3. *Examples of Primarily Personal, Taxable Benefits.*

Although there are obviously elements of benefit to the employer present, items taxable under the "primary purpose" test include (i) employer-provided commuting transportation, (ii) the value of a week's accommodations at a resort location at a "meeting" of company employees, if social and recreational elements clearly outweigh the business elements of the meeting, (iii) a limousine used primarily for commuting and pleasure, even though the occupant occasionally does some work, (iv) payment of the expenses of an executive's spouse at a convention where his or her presence is helpful but not vital, (v) meal money which is optional, discriminatory and/or extravagant, and (vi) free parking.

N. *Valuation.*

Once it is determined under the foregoing rules that an employee has received a taxable benefit, either by allocation or under the "primary purpose" test, the Regulations should provide the method for valuing such benefit for tax purposes. The methods of valuation most frequently suggested are (i) objective fair market value, (ii) subjective fair market value, (iii) incremental cost to the employer, and (iv) fair market value less arbitrary discounts. The Committee believes that although objective fair market value raises some problems and calls for some exceptions, it is the only acceptable standard for this broad range of problems. In addition, as noted above, it seems mandated by section 83.

Subjective fair market value, defined as what the employee would give up in cash compensation to obtain the benefit, is an interesting concept but totally impractical as a valuation method. Incremental cost would lead to total or near-total exemption for such items as airline passes and department store discounts. This principle could lead to grave inequities in our system, if it has not done so already. In any event, it runs counter to the statute. The same may be said of arbitrary discounts which would, in addition, involve constant controversy over the proper level of discounts for various situations.

Applying the standard of objective fair market value calls for incisive analysis. For example, the value of a parking space in a downtown office building can be determined by looking at monthly (or yearly) rates in the same or neighboring garages. In a rural or suburban industrial park, the value may be zero if the public generally enjoys free parking.

In the case of airline and railroad passes, if the pass is issued only on a "seat available" basis, it should not be valued at commercial rates. On the other hand, a taxable ride in the company jet could ordinarily be taxed at first class rates.[52] Every effort should be made to find true fair market value through comparability. In the case of department store discounts, sale and discount prices available to non-employees should be considered in valuing the employee's discount. Tuition remission is a very difficult area. Here, the answer may lie in the use of actual scholarship programs based on need, rather than remission benefits available to all faculty. Finally, there is the wholesale-retail problem, referred to above in the context of group insurance purchases. The Committee believes that this is a different problem from that of incremental cost, and that employees should receive the benefit of volume purchase discounts from third parties. In most cases, the employees could form a group or cooperative and obtain similar volume discounts.

O. *Exceptions.*

The Committee has identified two areas where these general rules should be abandoned in the interests of administrability.

1. *Denial of Deductions.*

When it is extremely difficult either to ascertain which employees actually received the benefits or to allocate the value of such benefits among employees, the Committee suggests denying the employer's deduction rather than taxing the employees. Examples include the cost of providing otherwise taxable meals at a company cafeteria in which employee use is optional, and the cost of maintaining a company hunting lodge or yacht which is available to all employees.

---

[52] *Cf.* S. REP. No. 768, 93d Cong., 2d Sess. 167 (1974).

2. A Role for De Minimis Rules.

In the preceding pages, the Committee has suggested a greatly expanded concept of compensation income compared to that currently required by the Code, Regulations, and administrative practice. If simplification is the objective, however, this quest for includibility and consistency can prove self-defeating if carried too far. The year-end search for covert compensation could prove exhausting, and the review on audit could be even more troublesome. At some point, despite sections 61 and 83, enough should be enough.

In the past, the Service has ruled that the value of hams, turkey and other nominal Christmas gifts to employees need not be included in income.[53] The Committee similarly recommends that certain de minimis rules be established to minimize record-keeping for a variety of minor fringes which do not aggregate to a significant amount of increased income. Purists will not tolerate such rules if they come via administrative fiat, but the Code could be amended to authorize these exceptions through Regulations and Rulings with such limits as Congress deems appropriate. This might be a very useful step in obtaining support for the broadest concept of taxable income from those employees who derive very little benefit from the present system.

In promulgating de minimis rules, following congressional authorization, the Treasury Department might consider implementing rules applicable to specific benefits as well as to an aggregation of benefits. In some cases, these rules might be quite specific; in others, general principles might be enunciated; in still others, the role of de minimis might expressly be left to the ad hoc determinations of agents in the field.

As examples, without advocating any particular rule, in the case of discount purchases of an employer's goods, as distinguished from other property such as employer's stock, discounts of less than a specified percentage of the retail price or a specified dollar amount per year might be disregarded. Discounts of less than a small sum per purchase also might be disregarded. On an aggregate basis, all fringe benefits might be disregarded if they total less than the *lower* of a specified percentage of annual compensation exclusive of such benefits, or of a fixed dollar amount. Finally, there might be some specific exclusions along the lines of the Christmas turkey rule to cover benefits such as free coffee and donuts.

The Committee recognizes that the employment of de minimis rules injects elements of complexity in drafting and administration. For example, if both individual and aggregated benefits are to have de minimis exceptions, such provisions must be carefully coordinated and record-keeping minimized. In the examples given above, the creation of

---

[53] Rev. Rul. 59-58, 1959-1 C.B. 17.

annual and/or aggregated exceptions could impose severe burdens on the Service, employers and, perhaps, employees. It is hoped that the rules actually adopted would contain sufficient administrative relief to clearly outweigh any legal complexities and new administrative burdens.

P. *Income and Deductions.*

In terms of simplification in the area of compensation, it is clear that the tax result should be the same regardless of whether the employer provides the benefit or reimburses the employee who has purchased it. If the employee received cash and could not fully deduct the cost of the benefit, he should not be able to exclude the income when the benefit is paid by the employer. The Committee supported this result in the case of health insurance and would reach the same conclusion in the case of employer-provided child care and commuting transportation. The employee should report the value of the benefit as income and then take whatever deductions are allowed. Other examples include interest-free loans, matching charitable contributions, medical expense reimbursement plans, and group legal services.

Although the situation arises much less frequently, it is clear that an employee should not be able to deduct the cost of an item he purchases if the provision of the same item by his employer would have resulted in taxable income with no offsetting deduction. To obviate this possibility, the relatively few rules allowing employee deductions must be modified. For example, an employee would not be allowed to deduct the cost of a uniform which could be used off the job.

Q. *A Taxable Fringe Is Better Than No Fringe At All.*

A taxable benefit is, nevertheless, a benefit. It would be very rare indeed for an employee to prefer no benefit at all to a taxable one. In terms of vertical equity, it is particularly significant that the lower paid employees will derive the greatest after-tax benefit from the fringe benefits in question. A fifteen percent discount to a department store employee is still a twelve percent net discount, even if taxed at a marginal rate of twenty percent, and $4,000 worth of "free" air travel is still quite a deal, even if the flight attendant must pay a tax of $1,000. If, on the other hand, a top executive does not think it is worth fifty percent of the imputed cost of a private jet flight, under the rules suggested above, to bring his wife to a convention, he need not choose this mode of travel. Full recognition of the thrust of this paragraph should make the preceding proposals less objectionable, particularly if, as *Blueprints* and others[54] have urged, the goal of substantially lower tax rates can be achieved by broadening the base of taxable income.

---

[54] Goldstein, *The Case for a Tax on Gross Income,* 30 NAT'L TAX J. 225 (1977); Goldstein, *An Overview of Basic Tax Reform Possibilities,* 14 HOUS. L. REV. 1059 (1977).

R. *Conclusion.*

In developing a comprehensive approach to the taxation of compensation other than current wages and salaries, there is no reason to distinguish among items presently exempted by statute, Regulations, Rulings or administrative practice except, perhaps, in formulating transition rules. All benefits should be considered, with current taxability the strong presumption. Feasibility of administration is an important consideration, however, as is fairness in valuation. The former consideration dictates taxing Social Security and unemployment benefits rather than allocating employer tax payments. The latter suggests a zero valuation for parking space at a plant in a rural location.

Exceptions should be few and far between. The only major statutory exception recommended herein is the continuation of the present favorable treatment of employer-provided retirement benefits. The Regulations should also exempt items for which compensation is not the primary motive or effect. Finally, with congressional authorizations, denial of deduction and de minimis rules should be used to mitigate the record-keeping and audit burdens when allocation problems are severe or relatively small cumulative benefits are involved.

Implementing these recommendations would simplify the Code by eliminating many present provisions which exclude, in whole or in part, certain types of compensation from income. On the other hand, new rules must be prescribed, for example, for taxing the annual interest accrual on employer-provided cash-value life insurance, and new tables designed to set forth the value of employer-provided health and disability insurance. Most important, comprehensive Regulations are necessary to deal with the broad range of present nonstatutory benefits. These must set forth a framework of principle, provide clear guidelines, and be liberally illustrated with specific examples.

The Committee aims at simplification in this area by emphasizing includibility, objective fair market value, and administrative feasibility. It recognizes, however, that simplification will not come easily since the issues presented affect almost every taxpayer and involve hundreds of different fact patterns. Considerations of equity and practicability will frequently dictate that the long range simplest solution is not always the best solution. On the other hand, objections to taxability based solely upon the belief of the affected group that its tax burden will be increased must not be determinative if real progress towards simplification through a broad-based, low-rate tax system is to be achieved.

POINTS AND COUNTERPOINTS

1. In trying to predict whether an individual will choose to work for an additional hour or to spend that time in play, economists must know the market wage for the individual's services and the value he places on his leisure time. What reasons, if any, are there for carrying over this concept of leisure as income to a personal income tax? Should persons who value their leisure highly pay more tax than workaholics who fear leisure? How should people who need a full nine hours of sleep a night be treated in a tax system that distributes burdens according to the value of an individual's leisure?

2. Is "equity" between renters and homeowners a good reason for taxing the imputed income from home ownership? Is the concern for renters due to a belief that renters are often financially unable to purchase a home? Or is the concern largely about efficiency?

3. Consider a taxpayer with two vacation cottages. Assume she never makes them available to friends and spends one week a year in the first cottage and two weeks in the other. How much imputed income does she have from these cottages? Is her actual use relevant, or only her potential use? Since she presumably can only use one at a time, what is the proper measure of her potential use? Does the answer depend upon whether personal taxes should be imposed with respect to outcomes or with respect to opportunities?

4. What distinctions are there between imputed income from home ownership and imputed income from self-performed services? Do persons who buy a house for their own use participate in the market economy in a way that is significantly different than the actions of those who benefit from self-performed services? Do renters living in rent controlled dwellings enjoy imputed income? How much, if any?

5. Some commentators have suggested that an ideal income tax would reach gains from increases in an individual's human capital—the accumulation component of imputed income. They suggest, for example, that a student who is awarded a degree in law should pay taxes under Haig/Simons principles on the increase in his earning capacity which the degree symbolizes. Few, if any, commentators, however, advocate taxation of such imputed income. *See*, e.g., Kelman, "Personal Deductions Revisited: Why They Fit Poorly in an 'Ideal' Income Tax and Why They Fit Worse in a Far from Ideal World," 31 *Stanford Law Review* 831, 842 (1979) ("To force the beachcomber to work as

a doctor . . . would violate the simple libertarian principle that the state should not require people, directly or indirectly, to engage in particular activities.") How, if at all, does the case for the taxation of self-performed services differ from the case for taxing human capital? Is human capital minus market income a reasonable proxy for the value of self-performed services? As a matter of practical administration, what differences would there be in the mechanisms used to tax imputed income from human capital and imputed income from self-performed services?

6. Is it a "logical implication of the concept of income," as some commentators argue, "that human capital should be treated like other capital, so that in theory invested imputed income should be taken into the tax base, just as in theory imputed income that is consumed should arguably be taken into account"? Warren, "Would a Consumption Tax be Fairer than an Income Tax?" 89 *Yale Law Journal* 1081, 1114 (1980). Obviously the taxation of imputed income would not logically follow if income were defined in terms of marketplace rewards. Why do economists and many other analysts typically reject a market oriented definition of income? What are the grounds for the theory that imputed income should be a component of taxable income? To refute those who would tax all imputed income in theory, is it enough to say that any theory which requires young but employable children to pay tax on their enjoyment of leisure is unworthy of serious attention? Is there any way to defend an income tax ideal apart from the fairness of the distribution of burdens it produces?

7. One approach that Congress occasionally has taken in dealing with tax-free fringe benefits is to limit the ability of companies to restrict these benefits to highly compensated individuals. Is this a sensible approach?

8. One commentator has argued that employers should be required to offer money wages as an alternative to tax-free fringes. See Popkin, "The Taxation of Employee Fringe Benefits," 22 *Boston College Law Review* 439 (1981). Would this recommendation, if adopted, tend to limit fringe benefit abuses?

9. What would be the likely long-term consequences of including in income all fringe benefits but then allowing taxpayers to deduct the amounts so included? Consider, for example, the political consequences of a deduction for life insurance, personal travel on an employer's airline, etc. versus the present exclusion. Consider also the differences in information flows to the Internal Revenue Service.

V. DEDUCTIONS AND EXCLUSIONS FROM MONEY INCOME

In an income tax built upon the Haig/Simons ideal, all income from whatever source derived should be included, at least tentatively, in the tax base. Thus exclusions of income from particular sources, such as the exclusion for interest on state and local bonds, always violate Haig/Simons principles. But taxpayers should be allowed to exclude from the base those expenditures that do not finance either consumption or a net increase in savings. In a well ordered income tax, this result is achieved through the deduction provisions.

Section A, below, examines two controversial features of current law—the liberal depreciation deductions enacted as part of the Economic Recovery Tax Act of 1981, and the deductibility, with exceptions, of business related entertainment costs. Haig/Simons principles require that the cost of assets with a useful life that extends beyond the end of the taxable year not be deductible in the year of purchase, since assets acquired during the taxable year out of income and left on hand at the close of the year constitute savings. For wasting assets, the proper amount of depreciation under Haig/Simons would be the amount of their decline in market value during the taxable year, since the decline in value represents a reduction in the taxpayer's net worth. The tax code usually has been more generous than that— in recent years, much more generous. Congress has occasionally relied on accounting practices as authority for its departures from Haig/Simons. Its radical departures from Haig/Simons, however, have usually been explained on tax incentive grounds. The selection in Section A(1) criticizes the 1981 Tax Act on both fairness and economic efficiency grounds. It was written by Robert McIntyre and Dean Tipps of Citizens for Tax Justice, a public interest lobby with ties to organized labor.

The proper treatment of entertainment expenses in a Haig/Simons income tax depends upon the meaning of "consumption." Everyone understands that eating, drinking, going to sporting events, and traveling on exotic cruises normally would constitute consumption under Haig/Simons principles. It is hard to imagine what "consumption" would mean if such items were excluded from its purview. But many commentators have asserted that these expenditures generally should be deductible from income whenever taxpayers engaged in business intend that such expenditures serve a significant business purpose.

The selection in Section A(2), written by Treasury officials in the Carter Administration, challenges this position.

The two selections in Section B address the problems created by the long-standing exclusion of interest on state and local bonds from the tax base. The selection by Richard Goode explains how the exclusion not only violates traditional fairness standards but also provides an inefficient subsidy to state and local governments. The other selection, by Robert McIntyre and Dean Tipps of Citizens for Tax Justice, examines the tax and fiscal problems that have arisen because of the tax-free status of industrial development bonds. In many respects, the tax solution to those problems is obvious—the exclusion should be repealed for *all* state and local bond interest. But in the short term, most pundits think that this solution is politically unacceptable. Deprived of the ideal solution, tax specialists must devise a system that preserves a tax subsidy for obligations that fund traditional governmental functions and ends it for obligations that fund business activities.

The selection in Section C, written by Michael McIntyre, examines the proper role of the deduction for interest payments in an ideal and in a less than ideal income tax. The author challenges the popular belief that interest payments on a loan cannot be linked in a meaningful way with the use made of the loan proceeds.

Section D examines the deduction for charitable contributions and the deduction for medical care—two of the most popular personal expense deductions in the tax code. In the first selection, William Andrews argues that a charitable contribution under some plausible conditions would not constitute consumption in a Haig/Simons tax system. In a part of his article not reproduced here, he makes a similar defense of the medical expense deduction. Whatever the merits of the case for those deductions in theory, the case breaks down in practice unless tax specialists can define the deductions to exclude normal living expenses. The second selection, written by Alan Feld, examines the issues that have arisen in trying to specify what expenses related to medical care qualify for the deduction.

Because of its desire to limit the medical expense deduction to out-of-the-ordinary expenditures, Congress amended the tax code in 1982 to restrict the deduction to qualified medical expenses in excess of five percent of adjusted gross income. In the 1981 Tax Act, Congress authorized those taxpayers who elect to take a standard deduction (zero-bracket amount) in lieu of itemized deductions to deduct nevertheless their charitable contributions.

This new rule is being phased in and will not be fully effective until 1986.

Section E addresses the issues raised by the deduction permitted under the tax code for contributions to an Individual Retirement Account. In the 1981 Tax Act, Congress liberalized the IRA deduction by increasing the limitation on contributions from $1,500 per year to $2,000 ($2,250 for certain married couples). More importantly, it made the IRA deduction available to persons already covered by an employee pension plan.

Supplemental Readings. J. Pechman, *Federal Tax Policy* (3d ed. 1977), pp. 145–53, 83–92; Gravelle, "Effects of the 1981 Depreciation Revisions on the Taxation of Income from Business Capital," 35 *National Tax Journal* 1 (1982); "Investment Neutrality," in *The Economics of Taxation* (H. Aaron & M. Boskin, Eds. 1980) (articles by D. Bradford and A. Harberger); Auerbach, "The New Economics of Accelerated Depreciation," 22 *Boston College Law Review* 1327 (1982); *Growth with Fairness: Progressive Economic Policies for the Eighties* (R.McIntyre, Ed. 1983); Berger, "Simple Interest and Complex Taxes," 81 *Columbia Law Review* 217 (1981); Turnier, "Evaluating Personal Deductions in an Income Tax—The Ideal," 66 *Cornell Law Review* 262 (1981); C. Clotfelter & E. Steuerle, "Charitable Contributions," in *How Taxes Affect Economic Behavior* (H. Aaron & J. Pechman, Eds. 1981), pp. 403–37; Epstein, "The Consumption and Loss of Personal Property Under the Internal Revenue Code," 23 *Stanford Law Review* 454 (1971); Halperin, "Retirement Security and Tax Equity: An Evaluation of ERISA," 17 *Boston College Industrial and Commercial Law Review* 739 (1976).

A. BUSINESS-RELATED COSTS

1. DEPRECIATION

ROBERT S. McINTYRE & DEAN C. TIPPS, INEQUITY & DECLINE: HOW THE REAGAN TAX POLICIES ARE AFFECTING THE AMERICAN TAXPAYER AND THE ECONOMY

Center on Budget and Policy Priorities (1983), pp. 32–48.

CHAPTER 2: WRITING OFF CORPORATE TAXES— AND PRODUCTIVITY

"We are talking about wasting a large portion of our capital formation, our precious investment dollars. . . . These precious dollars are going to be diverted into tax shelters. We are going to create, to use David Stockman's famous simile, a 'coast-to-coast corporate soup line.'"

Harvard economist Dale Jorgenson
Testimony before the House Ways
and Means Committee, May 1981

Although the individual rate cuts received most of the media attention, the most significant aspect of the 1981 tax act was its dramatic reduction in corporate income taxes. Under the guise of "depreciation reform," the 1981 act instituted a system of super-accelerated write-offs and tax credits as a backdoor way of repealing most of the federal corporate income tax. The new approach to depreciation, known as the "Accelerated Cost Recovery System" (ACRS for short), was designed to reduce business taxes (and federal revenues) by more than one-half *trillion* dollars over the 1980s. Together with the tens of billions of dollars in special-interest provisions also included in the act to benefit particular industries or companies, the result was nothing short of extraordinary. As Roger Altman, a former assistant Treasury secretary now with the Wall Street firm of Lehman Brothers, told the *Washington Post*, "the tax bill has virtually phased out the corporate tax in America."[1]

1. *The Washington Post*, November 12, 1981.

The benefits of 1981's corporate tax bonanza were not spread evenly across the business community. Instead:

• About 80 percent of the ACRS cut in corporate taxes was targeted to the country's largest 2,000 firms—the top 0.1 percent of America's businesses. Testifying on an early version of ACRS, a representative of the Small Business Legislative Council told a Senate Finance Subcommittee: "It would be difficult to write a tax bill better designed to speed the extinction of small business."[2]

• Oil and gas interests were granted at least $60 billion in ACRS tax breaks over the course of the 1980s as well as another $20 billion to $30 billion worth of reductions in the oil windfall profits tax. This $60 billion from ACRS does *not* include additional billions of dollars in tax cuts going to the oil companies for their non-oil-and-gas holdings in areas such as mining, chemicals, plastics, retailing, and office equipment.[3]

• Mining companies stood to gain at least $10 billion in federal tax breaks by 1990 under ACRS.

• For chemical companies, the ACRS benefits over the decade came to some $15 billion.

• Electric and gas utilities were granted at least $30 billion under ACRS by 1990. And the law specifically prohibited them from passing their tax credits on to consumers by lowering utility rates.[4] In addition, utilities and their shareholders also benefited from another provision of the tax act that allows up to $1,500 in utility dividends to be reinvested tax-free, at a cost to the Treasury of more than $1.6 billion by 1986.

• Telephone companies such as AT&T and GTE were granted more than $40 billion in federal tax breaks from ACRS by 1990, including a last-

---

2. Statement of William E. Hardman on behalf of the Small Business Legislative Council, Hearings on S. 1435, etc., before the Subcommittee on Taxation and Debt Management of the Senate Committee on Finance, 96th Congress, 1st Session (1979), p. 330. Speaking of attempts by the U.S. Chamber of Commerce and other big-business groups to enlist small business support for ACRS, Mr. Hardman also noted: "To put it bluntly, the small business community was being taken for a ride on a piece of legislation authored by representatives of the major corporate powers in this country. . . . [R]ealistically, the nation's four million small businesses, 99 percent of all U.S. enterprises, would probably end up with less than 20 percent of the benefits [from ACRS]. Maybe much less." *Id.* at 329-330.

3. The official estimates were broken down by line of business rather than by the main business of corporations operating in several fields. The estimates also did not attempt to allocate the benefits of "tax leasing," so that the industry figures presented here are substantially too low, in some cases by as much as 50 percent.

4. Utility rates are set by public utility commissions to provide companies with a "fair" rate of return on their invested capital after all costs, including taxes, have been offset against gross income. The 1981 act *required* that federal "taxes" and other items for which customers are billed be computed as if the tax credits allowed under ACRS did not exist. In other words, customers must pay for what often are referred to as "phantom taxes."

minute special provision that retroactively changed prior depreciation law to add more than $14 billion to the telephone companies' ACRS winnings.

• Railroads, in addition to benefiting from the general provisions of ACRS, were allowed to write off some $8 billion in railroad track, some of it carried on their books since 1887. Seven railroads told *The Wall Street Journal* (October 27, 1981) they would save more than $700 million in 1981 as a result of this provision, and more in subsequent years. In 1980, all U.S. railroads paid a total of only $600 million in federal taxes. Facing such a cornucopia of write-offs, one railroad holding company, IC Industries, told the *Journal* it would use its excess deductions as a tax shelter for the profits of newly acquired businesses.

Tax Leasing

The railroads were not alone in receiving more write-offs and credits than they had income to shelter. In fact, so many companies saw that they would have an overflow of tax breaks under ACRS that the corporate community demanded some way to utilize all these tax breaks more fully. In response, the Reagan administration created the most notorious of the 1981 loopholes: "tax leasing," the procedure allowing corporations already off the tax rolls because of too many shelters or genuinely low profits to sell excess tax credits and deductions to other firms by entering into phantom "safe-harbor leases." The "leases" exist only on paper; the law specifically provided they need have no legal or economic consequences other than for tax purposes.[5] Writing in the June 1982 issue of *Harper's*, Michael Kinsley aptly described "leasing" as "a complicated and fictional transaction somewhat like a welfare mother's selling her children to an affluent childless couple, so the tax deduction doesn't go to waste, then leasing them back for her own use and enjoyment."

"Tax leasing" was preferred by the Reagan administration as less embarrassing than simply writing checks to companies whose tax breaks exceeded their ability to use them. In addition, some corporate lobbyists who initially had pressed for having the government send tax refunds to such companies soon realized that leasing, with its complicated legal and accounting manipulations, would be personally more lucrative. By November 1981, two leading promoters of the leasing provisions each had reported setting up leases covering a billion dollars worth of corporate equipment. Based on a June 1982 report by the staff of the Joint Committee on Taxation, this would translate into more than $5 million in fees for each promoter.

The data in the Joint Committee Report, covering leasing through February 19, 1982, also indicated that:

• Only 14 percent of the leases were sold by the "distressed" money-losing auto and airline industries, the companies whose troubles were

---

5. Tax lawyers soon learned to avoid using the confusing term "leasing" to describe the system, coining instead the phrase "tax-benefit transfers," or "TBTs."

constantly invoked by corporate lobbyists as the justification for creating leasing in the first place. By comparison, oil and gas, chemical, and utility companies sold 25 percent of the tax breaks, and most of the other large sellers also were in profitable industries.

• Less than 77 percent of the tax benefits transferred in leases accrued to sellers of tax breaks. Two percent went in fees to middlemen, and the balance ended up as windfall gains to purchasers, many of whom were earning after-tax returns of 20 percent to 30 percent on leasing "investments" involving virtually no risk at all.

According to a February 1982 Treasury report covering leasing transactions through December 31, 1981, the major buyers of tax breaks were oil companies, with 22 percent of total purchases, and machinery manufacturers, with 18 percent.[6] Specific leasing deals that have become public include:

• Occidental Petroleum added $25 million to its 1981 earnings through tax leasing, Despite its high earnings ($711 million in 1980 and $722 million in 1981, making it the nation's 26th most profitable company), Occidental has so many tax write-offs from its foreign and domestic operations that it has not paid any federal taxes in at least four years.

• General Electric made tax leasing its "most important product." It bought so many tax breaks that it not only avoided paying any U.S. taxes on its $1.6 billion profit for 1981, but actually received a $100 million refund on previous years' taxes.

• In its 1981 annual report, Standard Oil of Indiana (Amoco) revealed it had "invested" more than $400 million to purchase tax benefits through tax leasing. As a result, Amoco said, it was refraining from drilling a number of promising oil and gas properties because of a "tax-induced shortage of capital."

• LTV Corporation, with 1981 pretax profits of $504 million, sold $100 million worth of tax breaks.

• Burlington Northern sold $36 million in excess tax benefits—left over after its $272 million in 1981 profits had been completely sheltered from tax.

• The Treasury's leasing report shows that in 1981, while some auto companies (presumably Ford, Chrysler, and American Motors) sold tax breaks for $201 million, the rest of the auto industry (apparently General Motors) spent $78 million to *buy* tax benefits. In the first quarter of 1982, GM apparently cashed in on its tax-break purchases: its first quarter report shows it turned what would have been a $120 million loss into a $130

---

6. As the figures suggest, oil companies were involved in both buying *and* selling tax breaks, with some firms having an overabundance of write-offs and credits and others able to use more.

million profit with $250 million in tax credits (which it used to get refunds against previous years' taxes).

As was the case with the individual tax cuts, the Reagan administration defended its sharp corporate tax reductions, including the "tax leasing" provisions, as essential to economic recovery. Many who rejected the administration's "Laffer-curve" arguments for the individual tax changes found the added business incentives more plausible. Yet the truth of the matter is that the corporate cuts were not simply inequitable; they also worked counter to the goals of improving productivity and economic growth.

How ACRS Works

The Accelerated Cost Recovery System represents a radical change in the way businesses write off, or "depreciate," their investments in plant and equipment in computing their taxable income.

Although the details of "depreciation" can be arcane, the concept is fairly straightforward. In measuring business income, whether for tax purposes or for reports to shareholders, allowances must be made for the gradual wearing out of plant and equipment. The timing of these allowances is quite critical. At one extreme, for example, writing off the costs of capital investments *immediately*—before the assets have worn out at all— turns out to be the same as exempting from tax entirely the profits generated by the investments.[7] Writing off assets much too slowly, on the other hand, would mean a large overstatement of profits.

Before 1981, the tax laws generally followed rules for depreciation similar in concept to those used by companies when reporting income to shareholders. Tax depreciation allowances were supposed to be "reasonable," and to reflect actual "wear and tear, exhaustion, and obsolescence" of the plant and equipment involved. There were significant exceptions. Many of the costs involved in drilling oil wells, for example, could be written off immediately, and this tax break for "intangible drilling costs" contributed heavily to the low tax rates on the oil industry overall and to the virtual exemption from taxes enjoyed by "independent" oil producers engaged only in drilling and extraction. In addition, companies were generally allowed to write off their equipment about 20 percent faster than the actual "useful lives" of the equipment as calculated by the Treasury

---

7. How can writing off the cost of capital investments immediately—or "expensing"—be the same as tax exemption? Suppose someone wants to invest $100. Under expensing, the cost of the investment will be reduced by $100 times the person's tax bracket. A corporation in the 46 percent bracket, for example, would have to put up only $54. If the investment yields, say, $10 a year, the government will take $4.60 in taxes, but this leaves the $5.40 a year earned on the $54 actually invested by the corporation subject to no tax at all. In effect, expensing makes the government a silent partner in private investments, and any "taxes" it collects are simply a return on its investment. In practice, the government actually will collect very little at all: assuming the private businesses reinvest a reasonable portion of their profits, their ability to shelter income will tend to stay ahead of their duty to pay the government a return on its share of their investments.

Department. And another, much larger "incentive" for investment was provided by allowing a 10 percent "investment tax credit" for most equipment purchases.

Because they are not required by law to report the same depreciation deductions for tax purposes as are reported to shareholders, most companies have one story to tell the IRS—the maximum depreciation allowed by the tax code and therefore lower taxable income—and another to tell Wall Street—not so much depreciation and therefore higher "book" profits. Nevertheless, despite the special tax provisions and the two sets of books, there usually was a significant correlation prior to 1981 between corporate taxable income and the actual earnings reported to shareholders.

ACRS wiped out any such relationship. It established arbitrary "cost-recovery periods" for the depreciation of capital investments. These write-off periods, as the Senate Finance Committee report on the 1981 tax bill noted, are "generally unrelated to . . . useful lives." Under the new system, most equipment is written off over five years; most structures, over 15 years; cars, light trucks, and equipment used in connection with research and development, over three years; and certain public-utility property, over 10 to 15 years. In all cases, the write-offs can be concentrated in the early part of the "cost-recovery periods." ACRS also carried over from prior law the 10 percent tax credit for equipment purchases and upped to 6 percent the credit for cars, light trucks, and equipment used for research and development.

ACRS was defended by some as necessary to offset the impact of inflation on the value of depreciation deductions. Rising prices can diminish the real worth of depreciation write-offs, which are based on the original purchase price of assets. But studies have indicated that the investment tax breaks already on the books before enactment of ACRS had more than compensated for inflation, even at the high inflation levels of the late 1970s.[8]

In fact, the new ACRS write-offs and credits, when fully phased in (and after adjusting for inflation), amounted to the mathematical and practical equivalent of *tax exemption* for profits generated by new equipment, *plus* an outright government subsidy of about a nickel for every dollar invested.[9] As these nickels accumulate, the system was designed to produce subsidies—or "negative tax rates"—of outlandish proportions. In other words, under the 1981 act, *profits from new investments in equipment were made more profitable after tax than before tax.*

---

8. *See, e.g.,* Jorgenson and Sullivan, "Inflation and Corporate Capital Recovery" (1981).

9. As mentioned above, taking an immediate write-off for the full cost of equipment before it has even begun to wear out turns out to be the equivalent of exempting from tax the profits generated by the equipment. The ACRS write-offs plus the investment tax credit were the equivalent of taking an immediate write-off for *110 percent of the cost of new equipment* (when fully phased in).

Investment Tax "Incentives": A History of Failures

The idea of providing investment "incentives" through the tax code did not originate with Ronald Reagan. Over the decade preceding passage of the 1981 tax act, the United States adopted investment tax breaks that by 1980 cost $36 billion a year. This was in addition to the billions of dollars worth of such tax preferences enacted in previous years. These "incentives" were notably successful in shifting more of the federal tax burden onto wage-earners, but they apparently did not succeed in improving the performance of the economy. Instead, the 1970s saw a decline in the growth rate, stagnant productivity, and spiraling inflation. And despite the massive corporate tax breaks, the share of the gross national product going into business fixed investment was exactly the same—10.5 percent—over the 1974-79 period as it had been from 1966 through 1973.

Moreover, the added tax breaks had adverse economic consequences. While the rate of investment held remarkably constant over the 1970s as a share of the GNP, *the tax "incentives" reduced productivity and economic growth by dramatically distorting the allocation of new capital investment.* The problem stemmed from the fact that business tax breaks added during the 1970s were anything but even-handed. Unintentionally, Congress created a pronounced bias in favor of investments in shorter-lived equipment and against investments in long-lived machines and structures—even when the latter were more productive.

As these tax distortions became increasingly pronounced, there emerged what a 1981 Federal Reserve Board study, *Public Policy and Capital Formation,* called a "disturbing pattern in investment." Particularly noticeable was the drop-off in the share of business fixed investment going into structures, which fell from 42 percent in the 1950s and early 1960s to only 30 percent by the mid- and late 1970s.[10]

There is nothing intrinsically "better," of course, about long-lived equipment and structures as compared to short-lived machines. A tax bias in favor of long-lived assets could be just as damaging to the economy. The point is that *distortions* in investment patterns caused by tax preferences are intrinsically bad because they substitute tax factors for economic forces when investment decisions are made.

Tax-based distortions in investment decisions inevitably occur when profits from investments in different assets are taxed at different effective tax rates.[11] The width of the gap between the highest and lowest effective

---

10. The fall-off in investment in structures was not limited to the business side. Contrary to popular misconception, investment in new housing also suffered. Not only did it decline as a share of total private fixed investment—from 34 percent in the 1949-65 period to 28 percent from 1974 to 1979 and to only 22 percent in 1980 and 1981—but it even fell in real dollar value—declining at an annual rate of 1 percent in real terms from 1973 to 1979. By 1981, real investment in new housing was 27 percent below its 1973 level—one factor contributing to the skyrocketing prices of existing homes in the 1970s. (Data are from the 1983 *Economic Report of the President,* Table B-2.)

11. Essentially, the term "effective tax rate" means what it sounds like: the share of the profits from an investment that must be paid to the government in income taxes. As used

tax rate is one good measure of the scope of such distortions. The wider the gap in effective rates, the more likely that investments will be made on the basis of their tax advantages instead of on their economic merits. When this occurs, capital is diverted from its most productive uses into less productive, tax-favored areas and into wasteful and counterproductive tax shelters.[12]

The investment tax distortions in the 1970s were sufficiently severe and the gaps in effective tax rates so wide that by 1979 (as Harvard economists Alan Auerbach and Dale Jorgenson have shown) these distortions had reduced the marginal output of new corporate capital investment by at least 45 percent.[13] During this same period, productivity growth declined even within sectors of the economy where capital investment rapidly increased. In manufacturing, for example, the rate of increase in real capital investment almost tripled in the 1970s and inflation-adjusted capital per worker in manufacturing was 30 percent higher in 1980 than in 1972. Nevertheless, output per hour in manufacturing (manufacturing productivity) grew by only 1.7 percent a year from 1972 to 1980, compared to 2.9 percent annually during the previous 25 years.

Problems created by distortions in the tax code are well-known and have been criticized not only by economists such as Auerbach and Jorgenson but by the Federal Reserve as well. The U.S. capital investment situation, as it existed prior to the 1981 tax act, was well summarized in the Federal Reserve's 1981 study, *Public Policy and Capital Formation:*

> While finding that the overall rate of capital formation is probably adequate, this study concludes that the existing capital stock is misallocated, probably seriously, among sectors of the economy and types of capital, primarily because of distortions caused by inflation and U.S. tax laws. . . . The biases are substantial. . . . As a result, capital is not applied to its most efficient uses. . . . The cost to the nation has been lessened productivity growth and reduced business output.

Two decades of ever-expanding tax incentives for business investment have failed to result in higher productivity or economic growth. To the contrary, as tax incentives intensified distortions in investment

---

here, the term refers to the inflation-adjusted tax rate *expected* to be paid when the investment is made, because it is expectations about profitability that affect investment decision-making, particularly with regard to choices among different investments.

12. For example, suppose an investment in an electronics factory will produce $10 per year, and the same investment in ice-cream-making machines will produce only $8 a year. From society's point of view, the factory is a better investment. But suppose the government taxes profits from electronics factories at 50 percent, but taxes ice-cream-making profits at only 25 percent. The after-tax profit from ice-cream making will now be $6 a year, while the electronics factory will yield only $5 after tax. And, as a result, the nation will get too much investment in ice-cream makers and not enough in electronics factories.

13. In other words, a dollar of investment shifted from the most lightly taxed asset to the most heavily taxed asset would produce a 45 percent higher pretax return (but the same after-tax return). See Auerbach and Jorgenson, "The First Year Capital Recovery System" (1979), p. 13.

patterns, the economy suffered. From the early 1960s to the late 1970s, the average effective corporate tax rate on profits from new investments was cut almost in half. At the same time, the maximum gap between effective corporate tax rates on earnings from different types of new investments nearly tripled. And over the same period, the rate of productivity growth fell by 58 percent.[14]

Of course, many factors contributed to the economic problems of the 1970s. The evidence shows, however, that the $36 billion a year in added investment tax "incentives" which constituted American industrial policy in the 1970s not only failed to achieve their stated goals, but actually were seriously counterproductive to the promotion of the nation's economic health.

ACRS: Compounding the Investment Distortion Problem by Sharply Increasing the Bias Against Long-Term Investments

President Reagan's free-market rhetoric might have suggested that a key goal of the President's tax program would be to reduce government interference in the market-place by curbing tax-based investment distortions. As it turned out, however, this was far from the case. Rather than remedying the harmful distortions caused by prior tax laws, the ACRS provisions proposed by the administration and enacted in 1981 greatly aggravated these problems, at a heavy cost to the well-being of the economy.

In June 1981, when ACRS was being considered by the Congress, a group of more than 200 prominent economists issued a "Public Statement on Depreciation Reform."[15] They warned that ACRS

> would lead to enormous distortion in investment decisions, shifting funds away from their most productive uses and into less productive, tax-favored areas. The distortions . . . could severely impair our economy's productivity growth by diverting capital away from its most productive uses. And it could lead to a new proliferation of wasteful tax shelters.

---

14. The failure of corporate tax-cutting as a growth strategy also is illustrated by comparisons with other countries. A study for the International Monetary Fund, for example, found that even before the 1981 tax act, the United States provided significantly larger business tax breaks than Japan or any of our European allies—with one exception. The exception was Great Britain, the only country studied with lower manufacturing productivity growth in the 1970s than the United States. Kopits, "Tax Provisions to Boost Capital Formation Vary Widely in Industrial Nations," *Tax Notes*, November 17, 1980, p. 955.

15. Among those signing the statements were: former members of the President's Council on Economic Advisers Gardner Ackley of the University of Michigan, Walter Heller of the University of Minnesota, and Charles Schultze of Brookings; Nobel Prize winners Kenneth Arrow of Stanford and James Tobin of Yale; Former Treasury Deputy Assistant Secretary (under President Ford) David Bradford of Princeton; Alan Auerbach, Henrik Houthakker, Dale Jorgenson and Richard A. Musgrave of Harvard; Charles McLure of the National Bureau of Economic Research; Henry Aaron, Barry Bosworth, Joseph Pechman and George Perry of Brookings; Robert Solow and Lester Thurow of MIT; and numerous others whose political views span the right-to-left spectrum.

In 1981, the Reagan Administration and Congress ignored these admonitions about the crucial flaws in ACRS. But the 1982 *Economic Report of the President,* in a surprising display of honesty, acknowledged that these critics were correct. "ACRS does not treat all types of business investment equally," the *Report* observed. It "is relatively more favorable to investment in . . . short-lived equipment. Tax rates vary across industries. . . . Effective tax rates on new equipment are negative for some industries."

Particularly striking was the role of ACRS in promoting "*negative* tax rates." When tax rates on new investment are negative, this means that the government not only exempts from tax the profits generated by the new investments, but actually supplements those profits. In the case of ACRS, the write-offs and credits provided were so excessive that they fully sheltered from taxation the income produced by most types of new investments, and produced an overflow of write-offs that could be used to shelter other income from taxation as well. If a firm had no other taxable income, the excess tax breaks could be sold in tax leasing transactions. Many observers had thought the trend in the 1970s of falling tax rates on profits from new investments would stop when the rate reached zero—and they doubted any administration or Congress would dare go that far. But ACRS was designed to produce, by 1986, an average effective corporate tax rate on profits from new investments of *negative* 63 percent.

The negative tax rates generated by ACRS were greatest for short-lived equipment assets that required frequent replacement. (In effect, every time a dollar would be invested in replacing equipment, ACRS would provide an outright tax subsidy of a nickel—on top of exempting from taxes the profits generated by the new investment.) The 1982 *Economic Report of the President* showed that by 1986, the effective tax rate on the shortest-lived class of equipment would be *negative* 194 percent.[16] In other

---

16. How can a tax rate of negative 194 percent happen? The exact arithmetic is complicated, but a somewhat simplified example can help illustrate this:

  Start with a system under which there are no taxes at all and suppose an investor has $45,000 to invest. If he or she puts the $45,000 into assets with an inflation-adjusted yield of 4 percent a year, after one year the investor will have earned $1,800. (Or, put another way, the $45,000 investment will have grown to $46,800.)

  Now, imagine a tax system in which the investor's tax rate is 50 percent and the government allows an immediate tax write-off for 110 percent of the cost of new investments. Then, to start with the investor's $45,000 can be used to purchase $100,000 worth of assets, since the $100,000 write-off the government allows will save the investor $55,000 in taxes. Suppose the assets wear out at 33 percent a year. To produce a net pretax profit of 4 percent, or $4,000, the assets will have to generate $37,000 in gross income. If the investor decides to cash in after one year and sells the assets for their remaining value of $67,000 he or she will end up with $52,000 in cash after paying 50 percent of the $104,000 in gross receipts in taxes.

  Now look at what has happened. With no taxes at all, the investor earns a net profit of $1,800. With taxes and extra write-offs, the investor ends up making $7,000 in net profits. This would be a "negative tax rate" of minus 289 percent.

  In real life, the tax system generally doesn't let people cash in their investments quite this fast without losing some of their tax breaks, so assume in our "taxable" example that the first year's after-tax gross earnings are reinvested. Now, after one more year has gone

words, such investments would earn almost three times as much after taxes as before taxes. On the other hand, long-lived equipment was only slightly subsidized under ACRS, and profits from corporate investments in structures remained taxable.

The result was to intensify sharply the prior law's bias against long-term investments. The *Economic Report* showed that the maximum gap between effective tax rates on different types of investment (already far too high) was widened by a factor of *ten* under ACRS, to an astonishing 231 percent. This meant, for example, that an investment in an industrial plant would need to be more than four times as profitable before tax as an

FIGURE 8
Average Effective Corporate Tax Rates On Profits From New Investments 1960-1979, and 1981-1986 Under 1981 Tax Act

1960-1964	32%
1965-1969	28%
1970-1974	29%
1975-1979	17%
1981	−8%
1983	−23%
1986	−63%

Source: Based on data and methodology from the 1982 *Economic Report of the President* and Jorgenson and Sullivan, *Inflation and Corporate Capital Recovery* (1981).

investment in office equipment or trucks in order to compete on the after-tax bottom line.

This bias against long-term investments was enacted despite the growing consensus among management experts that the U.S. corporate emphasis on short-term investments has contributed significantly to our

by, cashing in would produce a net profit of $11,220 after tax—compared to $3,670 under a system with no taxes at all. This implies a negative tax rate of minus 195 percent.

Carrying out this pattern for a number of years would give similar answers. Using a little more sophisticated arithmetic, it's possible to calculate average returns on assets of different types, such as the negative 194 percent rate referred to in the text.

economic difficulties. In a penetrating analysis in the *Harvard Business Review*, "Managing Our Way to Economic Decline," Robert H. Hayes and William J. Abernathy wrote in 1980: "By their preference for serving existing markets rather than creating new ones and by their devotion to short-term returns and 'management by the numbers,'" many American managers "have effectively foresworn long-term technological superiority as a competitive weapon." The corporate lobbying for ACRS, with its dramatic favoritism for short-term investment and its reliance on tax incentives rather than market incentives, was one more symptom of these problems.

The *Economic Report of the President* was candid about how ACRS's distortions would adversely affect the economy: "Federal subsidies to

---

FIGURE 9
Gap Between Highest and Lowest Effective Corporate Tax Rates on Different Types of New Investments

	Highest Rate	Lowest Rate	Maximum Gap
1960-1964	34%	26%	8%
1965-1969	33%	24%	9%
1970-1974	38%	24%	14%
1975-1979	34%	12%	22%
1981	39%	−30%	69%
1983	37%	−67%	114%
1986	37%	−194%	231%

Source: Based on data and methodology from the 1982 *Economic Report of the President* and Jorgenson and Sullivan, *Inflation and Corporate Capital Recovery* (1981).

---

particular industries permit them to gain more access to productive inputs than is economically efficient, and different tax treatment of productive inputs can also result in economic inefficiency." When such distortions are introduced, the *Report* added, "the composition of the capital stock will be altered and national output would be produced less efficiently from what would occur with neutral treatment." In short, said the *Report*, "the 1981 act will alter the allocation of existing capital and labor among industries. It will also affect the allocation of new business investment." Since these shifts are based on tax considerations rather than on real economic returns, the inevitable result of such a policy is a lower-quality, less productive capital stock.

ACRS thus effectively transformed bad investments into good ones and good investments into bad. By so doing, it represented not a reduction in government interference in the marketplace, but rather one of the largest intrusions by government into private investment decision-making in the nation's history. In short, ACRS only compounded the tax-policy mistakes of the past.

A Bias Against Labor

ACRS also caused other distortions by providing incentives for employers to replace employees with labor-saving machinery in situations where machines actually are less efficient. The ACRS tax write-offs for machinery are so large that in circumstances where use of labor is more profitable on a pre-tax basis, switching to labor-saving machinery can become more profitable after ACRS is taken into account. This type of distortion helps neither the economy nor the employees involved. As Nicholas von Hoffman observed in the May 1982 *Harper's:*

> Labor-saving machinery really and truly does save labor, which means it puts people out of work. If these changes occur through the play of those vaunted market forces, they may lead to an expanding economy and the new employment possibilities. When they occur because of a distortion of market forces, as in th[e] case [of ACRS], they just mean fewer jobs.

The 1982 *Economic Report of the President* makes the same point in more formal language. Taking note that employers must pay taxes on labor-generated profits but pay little or no taxes on profits generated by capital investments, the *Economic Report* warns that "switching from wage and capital taxation to wage taxation alone can reduce economic welfare and efficiency even though this structural change could lead to more capital formation." The problem is the bias such a shift creates in favor of machines and away from labor.[17]

17. ACRS hurt wage-earners in other ways as well. Even before ACRS, there had been a growing shift from taxation of wages and capital to taxation just of wages. A 1980 study by a member of the Treasury Department's tax policy staff, entitled *Is Income from Capital Subject to Individual Income Taxation?*, answered this question with a straightforward "no." The Treasury study found that the various loopholes and tax preferences for investment income have effectively wiped out most personal taxes on non-wage income. Thus, by 1981, the only real tax on capital income left, the only tax helping retain balance in the system, was the corporate income tax.

Instead of remedying the shift toward labor taxation, however, ACRS made things much worse. While the median-income family will find its wage income taxed at record rates through income and Social Security taxes, ACRS put the federal government in the position of subsidizing rather than taxing corporate profits from new investments. The result was to shift virtually the entire tax burden onto wages.

This built-in bias against labor hits workers with a double whammy. Not only will wage-earners pay more in taxes, but they also must suffer the effects of reduced economic efficiency and lower economic growth, which means fewer jobs and depressed wages.

No Boon Even for the Amount of Investment

Even the Reagan administration eventually acknowledged that ACRS would compound the investment distortions of previous tax policy. It held out the hope, however, that ACRS would generate such a dramatic surge in total capital spending that those capital misallocations would be more than offset.

Exactly why a higher level of private capital spending would be desirable is not readily apparent. The Federal Reserve's 1981 study, *Public Policy and Capital Formation,* which found misallocation to be a very serious problem, concluded that "over the last three decades the average U.S. savings [and investment] rate has probably not been greatly different from a rate that is optimal" from the point of view of a productive and efficient economy. But even if a case could be made for a higher level of investment, the question remains if ACRS would help or hinder that goal.

The nation's experience in the 1970s illustrates that corporate tax "incentives" have little, if any, positive impact on overall business investment levels. From 1974 to 1979, business capital spending as a share of the gross national product averaged 10.5 percent—the same share as from 1966 to 1973—despite the creation of more lucrative tax write-offs during the latter period. Only the composition of business investment showed significant change, with equipment outlays accounting for a 12 percent higher share and investment in structures for a 20 percent lower share of total business capital investment in the latter period.

It is unclear why anyone thought in 1981 that throwing more money at the corporate sector would be more effective in the 1980s than in the past. Companies were not required to increase capital spending to gain the benefits of ACRS's tax subsidies. Nor were they required to plow back the additional cash flow from ACRS into new productive investment. Of course, the tax savings *could* be used to purchase added plant and equipment. The savings also could be used, however, to finance dividend payments, advertising campaigns, higher executive salaries, foreign investments, or corporate takeovers.

Arguments that ACRS would significantly increase the level of private investment also ignored one other problem. Combined with other elements of Reaganomics, ACRS helped fuel enormous government deficits in future years. These in turn—under the tight money policies the administration encouraged the Federal Reserve to pursue—led to high real interest rates, stifling plant and equipment outlays, residential investments, and economic activity generally.

The huge size of the business tax reductions also provided the administration with more leverage in its efforts to secure sharp cutbacks in domestic spending. Hard hit was public investment in physical capital such as roads, bridges, and sewers and in human capital such as education, job training, and research and development. Public capital spending was already in trouble prior to 1981. Real nonmilitary government investment had fallen from 3.6 percent of the gross national product in the late 1960s and early 1970s to only 2.7 percent by the second half of the 1970s. In a cover story on "State and Local Government in Trouble," *Business Week* (October 26, 1981) headlined "The Decay That Threatens Economic Growth," and stated:

> So serious is the decay of the nation's infrastructure and so poor the prospects for refurbishment that many sophisticated businessmen and economists believe the U.S. is entering a period of severe crisis. . . . Compounding the crisis are cuts in federal funding in the no less important area of human capital—job training, vocational education and health care. Letting such public services decline could have high costs not only in social and political terms but also in terms of the operating environment for business.

Concern over the increasing decline in public capital has grown so strong that the Committee for Economic Development (made up primarily of corporate executives) issued a report on February 11, 1982, cautioning localities to avoid new business tax breaks which "decrease tax revenues needed to provide the public services and infrastructure for urban development." Unfortunately, in campaigning for the 1981 Reagan tax act, the corporate community was as blind to these vital public spending needs as it was to other key factors affecting productivity and economic growth.

ACRS: A Disaster for the Economy

ACRS clearly was a major mistake from an economic standpoint. Rather than correcting investment distortions produced by prior tax law, ACRS seriously compounded them. It further reduced the *quality* of business capital investments by encouraging an even greater shift toward investments based on tax considerations instead of economic merit.

In addition, ACRS's sharp bias in favor of short-term investments and against longer-lived plant and equipment dramatically reinforced the disturbing tendency on the part of America's corporate managers to focus only on short-run profits.

ACRS also created a bias for using machines rather than labor even where labor would be more efficient.

And ACRS was not even likely to increase the quantity of productive investment. Its generous tax benefits were not tied to any requirements that companies increase their levels of capital spending.

Finally, ACRS was funded by increasing an already large federal deficit (thereby driving up interest rates), and by cutbacks in federal investment in the physical and human capital needed for future economic growth.

2. ENTERTAINMENT EXPENSES

TREASURY DEPARTMENT, "ENTERTAINMENT EXPENSES"

The President's 1978 Tax Program (1978), pp. 195–202.

Present Law

Present law imposes relatively few restrictions on the deductibility of "business" entertainment. To be deductible, entertainment expenses must be "ordinary and necessary" in the taxpayer's business. Voluminous litigation attests to the difficulty of defining the "ordinary and necessary" standard. However, it is clear that "necessary" does not mean "essential." Rather, courts generally have construed the term "necessary" as imposing only the minimal requirement that an expense be appropriate and helpful for the development of the taxpayer's business.

The regulations require that entertainment expenses be reasonable in amount. Theoretically, an entertainment expense is not deductible to the extent that it is lavish or extravagant. However, since one man's "lavish" is another man's "moderate," this requirement is difficult to apply evenhandedly -- and hence difficult to apply at all.

Theoretically, entertainment is deductible only to the extent that it is allocable to the taxpayer's business. However, it is seldom possible to distinguish between personal and business motives in entertainment, let alone to prove that distinction. Further, even entertainment provided for business reasons must produce personal enjoyment in order to have its intended effect. Thus, the personal element in business related entertainment generally is not disallowed.

In short, some taxpayers are in a position to deduct many of the luxuries of life as business entertainment. Costs of country club memberships, cocktail parties, cruises, hunting lodges, lunches, dinners, nightclub shows, yachts, hotel suites, swimming pools, tennis courts, and vacation trips -- all can be deductible under present law.

In response to President Kennedy's tax reform proposals, in 1962 Congress enacted several provisions intended to prevent abuse of entertainment deductions. However, most entertainment expenses deductible before 1962 still can be deducted today.

One provision enacted in 1962 requires substantiation of entertainment expenses that are deducted. The taxpayer must substantiate, "by adequate records or by sufficient evidence corroborating his own statement," the amount of expense, time and place of entertainment, business purpose of expense, and business relationship to the taxpayer of any persons entertained. To the limited extent the IRS can enforce this requirement, it impedes those who previously created entertainment expenses out of whole cloth or simply guessed at what they had spent. However, the substantiation requirement is not a serious obstacle to those who actually incur expenses and keep careful records.

Another provision enacted in 1962 requires that expenses of entertainment activities be "directly related to" or "associated with" the taxpayer's business in order to be deductible. These tests are easy to meet.

While the "directly related" rules purport to require some expectation that business will be conducted at the entertainment event, entertainment is considered "directly related" without a showing that business benefit resulted from the entertainment, or that more time was devoted to business than entertainment, or even that business was discussed. Even the loose "directly related" standard does not apply if meals are furnished under circumstances "conducive to a business discussion." As described in a prominent publication which advises taxpayers how to obtain "trouble-free" deductions, this exception operates as follows:

> Say you take a customer or a client to dinner at . . .[a] restaurant. Or, perhaps you prefer to take him to a hotel bar or cocktail lounge for a few drinks. As long as he's a business associate, you can deduct the tab whether or not you discuss business, make a sales pitch, or even if it's only for goodwill. The only limitation is that the atmosphere must be conducive to a business discussion.

In short, the "directly related" requirement may have little more practical effect than to disallow deductions for entertainment which offers little or no opportunity for business discussion -- such as entertainment at night clubs, entertainment at cocktail parties where non-business associates are present, or entertainment which the taxpayer does not attend.

Moreover, even entertainment which offers no opportunity for business discussion is deductible if it meets the "associated with" test. Thus, expenses of an entertainment activity which does not qualify as "directly related" still may be deducted if the activity has some proximity to a business discussion. Under the "associated with" rule, expenses for dinner and a night on the town for the taxpayer, a business contact, and their spouses are deductible merely because that afternoon or the following morning some of the participants talked or will talk business.

Like expenses of entertainment activities, expenses of entertainment facilities such as yachts and swimming pools may be deductible. (Dues or fees paid to a social, athletic, or sporting club are also considered entertainment facility expenses.) To be deductible, such expenses must meet the "directly related" test, and more than half of the use of the facility must be for business entertainment.

Reasons for Change

Present law on deductibility of entertainment expenses is an open invitation to charge personal expenses to the Treasury, and many taxpayers accept the invitation. Some who have done so in recent years are described below. The expenses described in these examples are deductible under present law.

> A New York City taxpayer claimed deductible expenses of $9,665 for business lunches throughout the year. According to the taxpayer's records, he entertained a business client or associate each day for 338 days of the year. The taxpayer skipped his business lunch on Thanksgiving Day, but not on the Friday, Saturday, or Sunday of Thanksgiving weekend. He entertained at top restaurants on an average of 6-1/2 days a week all year, at a cost of well over $20 each lunch time.

> In a recent year, an electrical fixture salesman structured his business calls so that he ate breakfast, lunch, and dinner, five days a week, with a customer or purchasing agent either before or after a business discussion. The deductible amount for the year was $8,000, of which $3,000 was spent on the salesman's meals.

> A university professor received $30,000 in annual salary and, in addition, many of his expenses were reimbursed. His department did not reimburse him for $1,300 spent to entertain visiting professors, but these expenses were deductible on the basis of his department chairman's statement that entertaining visiting professors was required as part of the professor's job.

> A surgeon deducted $14,000 a year for expenses of entertaining doctors who referred patients to him. He entertained the doctors on a yacht, where they discussed

patients recently referred. The surgeon claimed that he took care to begin each medical discussion early in the cruise in case a doctor later became seasick.

The corporation of an incorporated dental surgeon had gross income of $500,000, a deduction of $160,000 for the surgeon's salary, and taxable income of only $26,000. An amount close to $17,00 was deducted for the surgeon's expenses of entertaining dentists who referred patients to him during the year. The surgeon entertained the dentists (and sometimes their wives) at home, at a country club, at sporting events, at restaurants, and at a rental cottage. He entertained the same few dentists the preceding year, and they are his personal friends.

A small corporate manufacturer with few competitors owned a yacht. Before and after business discussions, the corporation entertained customers and potential customers on cruises and fishing trips. Yacht expenses of $67,000 were deductible for the year.

A corporation which operated an iron foundry and machine shop in Virginia owned several hunting and fishing lodges on an island off the coast of North Carolina. The corporation used these lodges to entertain employees of its major customers. Deductible costs of lodge operation and depreciation, plus airplane expenses, were over $100,000 a year.

These taxpayers are not isolated examples. As President Kennedy said 16 years ago:

" ... Too many firms and individuals have devised means of deducting too many personal living expenses as business expenses, thereby charging a large part of their cost to the Federal Government. Indeed, expense account living has become a byword in the American scene. This is a matter of national concern, affecting not only our public revenues, our sense of fairness, and our respect for the tax system, but our moral and business practices as well."

Even when entertainment promotes business and hence can be argued to have a business purpose, the entertainment provides substantial personal benefits to the recipient. It is this personal consumption which distinguishes entertainment from other business purchases, such as advertising.

Reading an advertisement is not comparable to dining at an elegant restaurant, sailing on a yacht, or attending a Sunday football game. Entertainment is more closely analogous to wages; they both provide personal benefits. However, the tax collector withholds a portion of wages before they can be spent for personal consumption while entertainment benefits are now received tax-free.

The benefits associated with business related entertainment tend to be disproportionately distributed to upper-income taxpayers. For example, lunches are deductible by a lawyer who eats with clients at a club, but not by a carpenter who eats with other workers at a construction site. Costs of giving a party for friends are deductible by a businessman whose friends are his business associates, but not by a secretary or nurse, for whom entertaining cannot be said to have a business purpose. In light of the personal benefits associated with entertainment, the disproportionate availability of entertainment deductions to upper-income taxpayers makes the allowance of such deductions particularly unfair.

And entertainment expenses intended primarily to promote business are not the whole problem. Frequently "business related" entertainment is personal entertainment in disguise. A taxpayer in the 50 percent tax bracket can purchase two tickets to a football game for the price of one if he deducts their cost. Therefore, he has nothing to lose by inviting a friend who is also a business associate to join him for the game. If the expense account fan happens to pick up a little business as a result of this entertainment or to receive a return invitation from the friend, this is all gravy paid for by Uncle Sam. Since it is extremely difficult to distinguish between personal and business intent in entertainment, entertainment which is intended to provide tax-free personal benefits often cannot be disallowed.

In addition to entertainment expenses which are deductible under present law, some nondeductible expenses are in fact deducted. The subjectivity of present law encourages taxpayers to deduct entertainment expenses which, though not clearly deductible, are "arguably" so.

For example:

A life insurance salesman recently deducted his tennis club dues on the theory that tennis games enabled him to judge the physical fitness of prospective customers.

A large casino operation in Nevada deducted as promotion expenses the costs of using and maintaining a lake property and a hunting lodge. The annual deduction was $110,000 for the lake property and $350,000 for the hunting lodge.

A practicing attorney with gross income of $150,000 entertained clients throughout the year on his yacht. He claimed deductions of $22,000 for operating the yacht, $19,000 for depreciation of the yacht, and $6,000 for operating an airplane to fly clients to the yacht.

A physician deducted $13,000 a year for expenses of entertaining other physicians at parties, dinners, and a hunting cabin -- all on the theory that any physician is a potential source of referrals.

The sole shareholder-officer of a small corporation deducted the costs of entertaining employees of another corporation from which he bought scrap on a "highest bidder" basis.

The owner of an insurance agency deducted $31,000 one year and $32,000 the next on a claim that every single meal during the two years (except for the meals on one day) was motivated by business.

A medium-size corporation which supplies parts to auto manufacturers deducted $35,000 in each of two consecutive years for lunch expenses of the corporation's three owners and three salesmen. According to their oral testimony, supported only by invoices, the owners and salesmen entertained purchasing agents and other representatives of customers under circumstances conducive to business discussion.

The controlling shareholder of a small retail sales corporation received a salary of $19,000. From this, he deducted $26,000 for the expenses of entertaining at a cottage on a Caribbean island.

Taxpayers may claim "arguably deductible" entertainment expenses in the belief that they are properly deductible, or in the hope or expectation that they will not be audited, or in an attempt to obtain bargaining power for use if they are audited. Whatever the reason, many nondeductible entertainment expenses are in fact deducted. IRS data suggest that about 20 percent of all entertainment expenses deducted on individual returns should not be deducted. Overreporting of this magnitude breeds disrespect for the law and impairs the integrity of the tax system.

Stricter enforcement of present law cannot solve the overreporting problem. Present law on the deductibility of entertainment expenses is so generous, and its application so subjective, that it invites taxpayers to test the boundaries. Determinations of "necessary," "reasonable," "directly related," and "associated with," as well as the allowance of substantiation by means other than adequate records, necessarily leave much to the judgment of the individual IRS agent. They make administration extremely difficult, and uniform administration unattainable.

General Explanation

To reduce the unfairness and abuse associated with present law, the Administration proposes to disallow deductions for expenses of entertainment which is not taxed to the recipient as compensation. In general, deductions for expenses of all entertainment activities and facilities will be disallowed. However, 50 percent of currently deductible entertainment expenses for food and beverages will remain deductible.

Regardless of the existence of a business purpose, the high level of personal value associated with entertainment justifies the proposed disallowance of deductions. Disallowance is required to achieve the equivalent of including in the tax base the personal value of the benefit to the recipient. Since entertainment meals often involve business conversations, they may be less likely than other forms of entertainment to have personal value to the recipient equal to cost. Fifty percent disallowance is roughly equivalent to allowing a full deduction to the payor and including half of the cost of the meal in the income of the recipients.

This proposal will affect entertainment expenses only. Costs of business travel away from home will continue to be deductible, subject to the limitations proposed with respect to foreign conventions and first class air fare. Travel is less likely to have personal value to the businessman than entertainment, and travel deductions are less subject to abuse. Therefore, it is appropriate to continue to allow them to be deducted.

However, since entertainment is entertainment, no matter where it takes place, entertainment expenses incurred in connection with business travel will be subject to the Administration proposal. For example, if an employee traveling away from home on business entertains associates by taking them to the theater, the cost of the theater tickets will not be deductible. Also, if the only purpose of a trip is to entertain the traveler, no deduction will be allowed. For example, no deductions will be allowed for costs of a cross country trip by business associates to attend the Masters Golf Tournament or the Superbowl.

Certain employer-provided meals will be excepted from the proposal. Present law excludes from an employee's income the value of meals which are furnished to him by his employer on the employer's business premises and for the employer's convenience. In applying this exclusion, meals are considered to be furnished for the employer's convenience only upon a clear and strong showing of business necessity. The proposals do not modify the statutory exclusion, and costs of providing such meals will continue to be fully deductible under the proposals.

Analysis of Impact

The Administration proposal will not hurt American business. If the increased revenue from the proposal is used to lower tax rates, as recommended, the proposal will simply make it relatively more expensive for businesses to provide entertainment to employees and business associates, and relatively less expensive to lower prices or to increase salaries. [1]

In terms of economic efficiency, the proposed changes will be beneficial. The government will no longer be subsidizing consumption in such forms as yachts, theater tickets, and country club memberships connected with an ostensible business purpose. The government subsidy for entertainment meals will also be reduced. Persons will continue to engage in such entertainment, either on their own or in the company of business associates, if they feel that the benefit derived from the entertainment is worth its cost. Because entertainment expenses will have to be purchased with after-tax dollars, there will no longer be a bias in favor of entertainment over other forms of consumption.

It is true that many forms of business entertainment have become accepted as social custom and are viewed by some businessmen as necessary to attract and keep customers. However, one reason that business entertainment has become accepted as social custom is because the tax system lowers its price. In the long run, social customs related to business entertainment might change if the tax subsidies that encourage it change. Even in the very short run, changes in deductibility of entertainment expenses will affect all business firms engaging in entertainment alike.

The Administration proposal will not have a substantial effect on those industries benefiting from tax incentives for entertainment. Expensive restaurants catering to individuals eating tax deductible meals might

----

1. [Ed.] The estimated revenue gain would have been $1.2 billion for 1979, rising to $1.7 billion by 1983.

suffer some decline in the demand for their services. However, the Administration proposal will cause relatively little, if any, loss of jobs. It is estimated that the total employment reduction in the restaurant industry will be no more than 2 percent, at most, of all such jobs. The rapid employment turnover in that industry will absorb much of any such employment reduction. Hotels and other travel related industries generally will not lose business as a result of the proposal since most costs of business travel and domestic convention attendance will continue to be fully deductible.

It should be emphasized that output and employment in the economy as a whole will NOT decline as a result of the Administration proposal. Any reduced spending on entertainment will be balanced by increased spending on other goods and services by individuals benefiting from the reduced tax rates. [2]

----

2. [Ed.] Congress amended IRC Section 274 in 1978 to curtail the deduction for social, athletic, and sporting clubs. The Senate passed a broad reform of the entertainment expense deduction in 1982 but the measure died in the Conference Committee.

B. TAX–EXEMPT STATE AND LOCAL BONDS

RICHARD GOODE, THE INDIVIDUAL INCOME TAX

Brookings Institution (Rev. Ed. 1976), pp. 133–8.

Interest on State and Local Securities

Of all the omissions from taxable income, the exclusion of interest on state and local government securities has attracted the most attention.[47] It has been attacked by many writers on taxation and by several secretaries of the treasury but vigorously defended by state and local officials and by securities dealers. The question whether the Constitution allows the federal government to tax this interest has been extensively debated but never resolved because the statutes have provided for the exclusion since 1913. Although the constitutional question will not be considered here, authoritative opinion has tended toward the position that Congress could end the exclusion if it wished.

Statistics on interest payments by state and local governments and estimates of the amount received by individuals appear in table 6-7. The estimated amount of tax-exempt interest received by individuals grew at the rapid rate of 13.9 percent a year between 1950 and 1960, but the annual rate of growth declined to 7.0 percent between 1960 and 1970 owing to a slower rate of increase in state and local borrowing and interest payments and to a fall in the proportion of tax-exempt securities held by individuals.

The tax immunity of interest on state and local securities brings out in acute form the issues posed by other exclusions. Because state and local securities can be freely bought and sold with little expense and little risk and without the necessity of buying consumer services

Table 6-7. Interest Paid by State and Local Governments and Estimated Amount Received by Individuals, 1950, 1960, 1970, and 1971
Millions of dollars

Description	1950	1960	1970	1971
Total interest paid	613	2,028	5,123	5,904
Estimated amount received by individuals	235	864	1,693	1,745

Sources: First row, *Statistical Abstract, 1973*, p. 419; second row, total amount of interest paid by state and local governments allocated between individuals and others in proportion to holdings of state and local obligations by households, personal trusts, and nonprofit organizations and by all others (average of beginning and end of year) as estimated in Federal Reserve System, "Flow of Funds Accounts, 1945–1972," pp. 83–84, 88–90.

47. For a convenient review of the facts and issues, see David J. Ott and Allan H. Meltzer, *Federal Tax Treatment of State and Local Securities* (Brookings Institution, 1963).

at the same time, they are ideal for persons who wish to avoid high rates of income tax. A tax-free return is available without the inconvenience and expense associated with homeownership or life insurance. It is true that the market for state and local securities is less fluid than that for many other securities, but state-local bonds are more liquid than houses.

Reliable current information is not available on the distribution of holdings of state and local government securities and of interest received from them by individuals classified by size of income. Statistics from federal estate tax returns and deductive reasoning indicate, however, that, among individuals, ownership is heavily concentrated in the hands of the wealthy. Treasury Department estimates, which are subject to a considerable margin of error, place the federal income tax value of the exclusion of interest on individual holdings at $800 million in 1971, of which virtually all is allocated to holders with incomes above $15,000 and four-fifths to holders above the $50,000 income level.[48]

Many comments exaggerate the effect of the exclusion on the equity and progressivity of the income tax because they take no account of the compensating reduction in market yields of tax-exempt securities. If, for example, all holders of the securities were subject to a marginal tax rate of 50 percent and if yields on state-local securities were only half those on comparable taxable securities, the tax advantage would be fully discounted in the market. Although state and local governments would still gain from the tax immunity, the choice between state-local securities and other securities would be a matter of indifference to high-income investors. In these circumstances, the effective rate of income tax would seem less progressive than it would without the exclusion; however, the distribution of income would not be affected, and investors in state-local securities would receive no unfair advantage.

Questions of income distribution and equity arise because investors are subject to various tax rates and because the market does not fully discount the tax advantages of state and local securities for holders as a group. Even if yields on tax-exempt securities were half those on other securities, the holders of tax-exempts who were subject to marginal rates above 50 percent would gain an advantage. For example, a person subject to a marginal tax rate of 70 percent would have no preference between a taxable security yielding 4.0 percent and a comparable tax-exempt security yielding 1.2 percent, whereas the market yield on the tax-exempt would be 2.0 percent.

---

48. *General Tax Reform,* Panel Discussions, pt. 1, p. 34.

There is reason to believe, moreover, that the yield differential is smaller than that which would be necessary to bring about an exact equivalence for the weighted average of all holders. The yield differential is almost certainly less than that required to compensate for the tax advantages enjoyed by individual holders as a group and probably less than the tax advantages of corporate and individual holders taken together. This is true because yields must be high enough to attract marginal investors, who are subject to tax rates lower than the weighted average for all holders, and to induce high-income buyers to acquire more of the securities than they would if the differential exactly equaled the tax advantage. Prudent investors will insist on a margin as insurance against a future reduction of tax rates. In 1970 the market yield of high-grade corporate bonds was 24 percent greater than the yield of high-grade tax-exempt bonds, and in 1971 the yield differential was 30 percent.[49] Treasury Department estimates imply weighted marginal rates of federal income tax for all (individual and corporate) holders of tax-exempt securities of some 45 percent in these years.[50] These figures suggest that the interest saving realized by state and local governments was only half to two-thirds the cost to the federal government of the exclusion. This can be regarded as only a rough approximation; a refined estimate would require much more elaborate calculations taking account of lower grade securities and the repercussions of the changes in investment patterns and market yields that would occur if the tax exemption were ended.[51]

The exclusion of interest on state-local securities is economically objectionable because it diverts high-income investors from stocks and other risky private investments to government securities, and thus reduces risk-taking and innovation. This objection, however, seems to have been overrated in many past discussions. At the end of 1970, the state-local security holdings of households, personal trusts, and nonprofit institutions accounted for only 2.4 percent of the total financial assets of this sector.[52] Another objection to the exclusion is

---

49. The comparison is between Moody's Aaa corporate bonds and Standard & Poor's high-grade municipals, as reported in *Economic Report of the President, January 1973*, p. 260.

50. Derived from Treasury Department estimates published in *General Tax Reform*, Panel Discussions, pt. 1, p. 29, and total interest payments of state and local governments as shown in table 6-7.

51. See Ott and Meltzer, *Tax Treatment of State and Local Securities;* Harvey Galper and John Petersen, "An Analysis of Subsidy Plans to Support State and Local Borrowing," *National Tax Journal*, vol. 24 (June 1971), pp. 205–34; Peter Fortune, "The Impact of Taxable Municipal Bonds: Policy Simulations with a Large Econometric Model," *National Tax Journal*, vol. 26 (March 1973), pp. 29–42.

52. Federal Reserve System, "Flow of Funds Accounts, 1945–1972," pp. 83–84.

that choices between investment in the public sector and investment in the private sector are biased. This criticism is hard to evaluate because it is uncertain whether the interest rate significantly affects the amount of borrowing and spending by state and local governments.

The exclusion of interest on state-local securities has been defended as a necessary or desirable feature of federalism, regardless of constitutional requirements. The historic doctrine that each level of government should be completely immune from taxation by the other level, however, seemingly is being superseded by the opinion that a successful federal system requires only that each level be protected from discriminatory, and hence possibly destructive, impositions. Federal and state salaries have been taxable by both levels of government for the past thirty-five years with no apparent harm to the federal system. If the federal government were to tax interest on state-local securities, it is generally agreed that Congress should make clear that there would be no objection to nondiscriminatory state taxes on the interest on federal securities.

Although the tax immunity of interest on state and local government securities has resulted in inequities, it would be unfair simply to withdraw the exemption from outstanding issues. Investors have bought the securities at prices and yields reflecting the expectation of continued tax exemption and would suffer capital losses if the interest were made taxable. Withdrawal of the exemption only for interest on future issues would not immediately end the problem—indeed, it would result in windfall gains for holders of outstanding issues which would acquire a scarcity value—but it would stop the growth of tax-exempt interest.

The failure to win acceptance for proposals to tax interest on future issues, together with increased sensitivity to the financial problems of state and local governments, has stimulated interest in proposals that the federal government pay a direct subsidy to state and local governments which elect to issue taxable securities. Since the revenue loss to the federal government due to tax exemption appears to exceed the interest saving to state and local governments, it should be possible to select a subsidy rate (applicable to interest payments) that would be advantageous to both levels of government and would encourage the voluntary relinquishment of the tax-exempt status of state-local issues.[53] It would be necessary to revise the subsidy from time to time to take account of changing conditions in financial

---

53. See Galper and Petersen, "Analysis of Subsidy Plans"; Fortune, "Impact of Taxable Municipal Bonds"; Robert P. Huefner, "Municipal Bonds: The Costs and Benefits of an Alternative," *National Tax Journal*, vol. 23 (December 1970), pp. 407–16.

markets. This approach could greatly reduce existing inequities, but it seems unlikely that it would entirely eliminate tax-exempt issues. As state and local borrowing was diverted to taxable issues, the supply of tax-exempt issues would shrink relative to demand, and yields on both outstanding issues and new issues would decline. Unless the federal subsidy were repeatedly raised and finally brought to a very high level, it would always be possible for some governments to borrow more cheaply by issuing tax-exempt securities than by issuing subsidized taxable securities. As a means of assisting state and local governments, the explicit subsidy would be more efficient than the tax exemption, but the allocation of benefits among state and local governments would not conform closely to need as measured by the standards usually adopted or proposed for grants-in-aid.

The ending of the tax immunity of future issues of state-local securities would be desirable from the standpoint of equity and economic efficiency and, in my judgment, would not pose a threat to a healthy federal system. Short of this, the adoption of an explicit subsidy plan that would induce state and local governments to reduce their reliance on tax-exempt securities voluntarily would be a step forward.

ROBERT S. McINTYRE & DEAN C. TIPPS, INEQUITY & DECLINE: HOW THE REAGAN TAX POLICIES ARE AFFECTING THE AMERICAN TAXPAYER AND THE ECONOMY

Center on Budget and Policy Priorities (1983), pp. 75-8, 81-2.

Industrial Development Bonds. One of the stranger quirks of the tax code allows states and localities to "lend" their tax exemptions to private companies, which then can issue tax-exempt bonds to finance new investments. Use of such "Industrial Development Bonds" has grown rapidly in recent years, and by 1982 tax-free bonds issued for private purposes accounted for more than half of the tax-exempt bond market—up from 25 percent in 1976.

IDBs are tremendously popular with both their public sponsors and their private beneficiaries. For the latter, generally corporations, they provide a government handout that can cut interest expenses on major capital projects by 30 percent or more—the equivalent of a 20 percent to 25 percent up-front government subsidy or tax credit. Sponsoring states, cities, towns, and public agencies see IDBs as an apparently cost-free tool to attract businesses and spur development.

But, of course, the situation is not really so rosy. Left holding the bag are the federal Treasury and the majority of American taxpayers. Not only is the national government funding (but not administering) an open-ended business subsidy program, but it typically costs the Treasury between three and four dollars for every two dollars in subsidy received by its business "welfare clients."[7] The rest of the Treasury's losses end up as windfall gains to the banks and high-bracket individuals who purchase the bonds, further undercutting the fairness of the tax system.

State and local authorities like to brag about how they have used IDBs to lure businesses and "create jobs" (by taking them from somewhere else). But IDBs are ubiquitous: businesses can get virtually any state or community to authorize them. Thus, it is hard to see how IDBs can have much effect on business location decisions.

States and localities cannot really be blamed, of course, for their lack of restraint in lending their favored tax status. The fact that areas of the nation are competing with one another for jobs makes it seem foolhardy for any one jurisdiction to try to draw the line on its own. Where states and

---

7. Tax-exempt bond rates historically have averaged 65 percent to 75 percent of taxable bond rates. The average tax bracket of bond-holders, however, has been 43 percent. Thus, every 30 cents saved by a company issuing tax-free bonds costs the Treasury 43 cents, meaning a $2.87 Treasury loss for every $2.00 in interest reduction. Recently, as tax-exempt rates have climbed to more than 80 percent of taxable rates, Treasury's cost has become more than double the private business gain.

localities can be faulted is for not coming to Washington and seeking an end to this damaging tax-subsidy competition.

State and local governments actually have an important self-interest in promoting federal action to curb IDB financing. Pumping all these handouts to businesses through the tax-exempt bond market inevitably raises the cost of state and local borrowing for traditional governmental purposes, such as schools, roads, and sewers. As the quantity of tax-free bonds (and other tax-free shelters) goes up, competition to attract buyers increases. As a result, states and cities must increase the interest rates they pay on bonds to make them more attractive to potential purchasers.[8] By 1982, tax-exempt bond rates had climbed from their traditional 65 percent to 75 percent of taxable rates up to 80 percent to 85 percent, adding nearly 20 percent to state and local borrowing costs.

In 1968, when the IDB market first began to take off, Congress tried to restrict the use of the bonds through enactment of a general prohibition on their issuance. But Congress then riddled this prohibition with exceptions for quasi-governmental activities and projects it deemed of particular social utility. As of 1981, IDBs were allowed without restriction for low-income housing; sports facilities; convention centers; airports; docks; mass-transit facilities and vehicles; parking lots and garages; sewage and solid-waste disposal facilities; certain gas, electricity, and water facilities; student loans; and nonprofit hospitals and schools; and, with some restrictions, for subsidized mortgages. In addition, a so-called small-issue exception made virtually any business project costing less than $10 million eligible for IDB financing.

In recent years, the "small-issue" exception has threatened to engulf the whole system. By 1981, the volume of new issues qualifying under the provision had reached $10.5 billion, a sevenfold increase just since 1976. This represented more than 40 percent of total IDBs and more than 20 percent of the entire tax-exempt bond market. A 1981 Congressional Budget Office report estimated that "small issues" could multiply nearly fivefold again just between 1981 and 1986 and could amount to as much as $49 billion a year by 1986.

The publication of these rather startling CBO estimates came at about the same time that IDBs began to arouse growing criticism from other quarters. "Horror stories" surfaced about IDBs being used to finance massage parlors, golf courses, and fast-food restaurants. Local businesses began complaining that chain operations like K-Mart and McDonald's were using IDBs to gain an unfair competitive advantage.

In 1982, the Treasury Department responded to these complaints and to the specter of huge potential federal revenue losses by proposing a number of sensible restrictions on IDB financing. Under the Treasury plan:

8. Cities and states appreciated this market-glut problem when it came to "All-Savers Certificates"—the 1981 law allowing financial institutions to issue what are, in effect, small tax-exempt bonds—and lobbied against All-Savers, citing its potential harmful impact on the tax-exempt market.

(1) Businesses using IDB financing would have been denied most of the benefits of ACRS accelerated depreciation, thereby cutting in half the advantage from using tax-free bond financing.

(2) States and localities lending tax exemptions would have been required to make a token financial commitment of $10,000 for every $1 million in private bonds authorized (or, alternatively, would have had to assume liability for paying off bond-holders in the case of default by the business issuing the bonds), thereby creating at least a little incentive for more critical evaluation of proposed bond issues.

(3) Large businesses, such as K-Mart, no longer would have been able to use tax-exempt "small issues." The plan would have denied eligibility to companies with more than $20 million in total capital expenditures over the previous six years and would have limited total small-issue IDBs outstanding nationally to $10 million per firm.

(4) States and cities could only issue bonds after a public hearing, allowing businesses that did not relish tax-subsidized competition and taxpayers who did not want to pay for the required state/local contribution to at least register their opposition.

The administration's proposals were greeted with a groundswell of opposition from state and local "industrial development officers" around the nation, who feared that the new restrictions would be effective. Responding to heavy lobbying by these officials, Congress junked most of the administration's plan. Both the state/local contribution requirement and the rule denying IDBs to large companies were dropped, and the limitation on accelerated depreciation was basically gutted. The public-hearing requirement survived, but without the government-contribution rule, such hearings are not likely to attract many irate taxpayers.

Still needing to raise some money in the next few years in the IDB area, Congress decided to focus its actions on IDB "horror stories" rather than on the structural changes the Treasury Department had proposed. The result, which produces only one-third the revenues of the Treasury approach, is a statutory compendium of specific activities that *cannot* be financed with IDBs, a list whose *ad hoc* nature is comical.

Totally prohibited from IDB financing, as a result of the 1982 act, are: hot-tub and sun-tan facilities (but not saunas and Jacuzzis); skating rinks (but not bowling alleys); massage parlors (but not gambling casinos); tennis clubs and golf courses (but not video-game arcades); and "racquet-sports facilities (including handball . . . courts) [sic]."

A somewhat looser restriction applies to auto-repair shops (but not to boat-repair facilities), eating and drinking establishments (McDonald's, for example), and recreation and entertainment facilities generally. K-Mart, for some reason, emerged unscathed.

Watching this list expand and contract may provide some amusement in future years, but the problem of private use of tax-exempt financing remains serious. Fortunately, Congress will not be able to avoid some further examination of IDBs. Since the 1982 act provides for expiration of the small-issue exception after 1986, Congress will again have to confront the issues in the IDB area in the relatively near future when it determines whether to extend the small-issue exception.[9] Only if state and local governments—which probably have the most to lose unless IDBs are brought under control—are willing to cooperate can we hope to reach a coherent solution.

9. There is another reason that it is important for Congress to reevaluate IDBs soon. A number of communities recently have entered into deals with private investors involving sale-leasebacks of town halls, public libraries, municipal sewer systems, and the like. These extraordinary arrangements are structured so that investors can take advantage of IDB financing, accelerated federal tax depreciation, and in many cases, the investment tax credit. In return, the investors pass on some of their interest and tax savings to the communities. One result is to shift part of the cost of local public investments to the federal Treasury. Equally important to local officials, they can avoid having to go before voters with requests for new bond issues.

These municipal abuses appear to have inspired the Defense Department to attempt similar budget and tax end-runs. The Pentagon now hopes to get around federal budget constraints by leasing, rather than purchasing, a number of new weapons systems. Already in the pipeline are billions of dollars in weapons leases, involving such things as "Aggressor" aircraft, Rapid Deployment Force ships, and cargo planes. The staff of the Joint Committee on Taxation estimates that the cost to the federal government from these rather bizarre transactions is at least 12 percent more than outright purchases. But the Pentagon is not troubled by these increased expenses. Its purpose is to shift the cost of new planes and boats away from the current defense budget and onto the Treasury in the form of tax losses (and also onto future generations of Americans in the form of increased defense liabilities in later years).

C. QUASI–BUSINESS AND INVESTMENT RELATED ADJUSTMENTS: THE DEDUCTION FOR INTEREST PAYMENTS

MICHAEL J. McINTYRE, "AN INQUIRY INTO THE SPECIAL STATUS OF INTEREST PAYMENTS"

1981 Duke Law Review 765 (1981), pp. 766–810.

I. INTRODUCTION

Interest is a type of rental payment—an amount paid for the use of borrowed money.[1] Yet the tax code's treatment of interest payments differs markedly from the treatment afforded other types of rental payments. Interest payments, with a few exceptions,[2] are currently deductible regardless of the use made of the borrowed money.[3] In contrast, the deductibility of other rental payments depends primarily on the taxpayer's use of the rented property. For example, the tax code prohibits the deduction of rental payments when the taxpayer's use of the rented property is personal.[4] Similarly, rental payments used to create or improve a capital asset must be capitalized.[5]

Many commentators have criticized some features of the special status of interest payments.[6] They have frequently objected, for exam-

---

1. For a discussion of this capsule definition, see Asimow, *The Interest Deduction*, 24 U.C.L.A. L. REV. 749, 751 (1977).

2. See note 8 *infra*.

3. I.R.C. § 163(a) provides: "General Rule—There shall be allowed as a deduction all interest paid or accrued within the taxable year on indebtedness." This general allowance was found in the personal income tax act adopted in 1913. Tariff Act of 1913, ch. 16, § IIB, 38 Stat. 167. It was also contained in the personal income tax enacted during the Civil War. Act of Mar. 3, 1865, ch. 78, § 117, 13 Stat. 479.

For a summary of the scant legislative history concerning the interest deduction in the personal income tax system, see Asimow, *Principal and Prepaid Interest*, 16 U.C.L.A. L. REV. 36, 62-63 (1968); Berger, *Simple Interest and Complex Taxes*, 81 COLUM L. REV. 217 (1981). For the history of the interest deduction under the corporate income tax, see Warren, *The Corporate Interest Deduction: A Policy Evaluation*, 83 YALE L.J. 1585, 1585-86 (1974).

4. Compare I.R.C. § 162(a)(3) (permitting deduction for "rentals . . . required to be made as a condition to the continued use or possession, for purposes of the trade or business . . . .") with I.R.C. § 262 ("no deduction shall be allowed for personal, living, or family expenses"). This rule is so well established that cases arise only at the fringes. *See, e.g.*, Summers v. Commissioner, 33 T.C.M. (CCH) 695 (1974) (rental payment to church for wedding party nondeductible personal expense); Rev. Rul. 68-12, 1968-1 C.B. 96 (Congressman's rental of apartment in his district nondeductible personal living expense).

5. I.R.C. § 263(a) prohibits deductions for amounts paid to acquire a capital asset, including construction costs. *See* Commissioner v. Idaho Power Co., 418 U.S. 1, 16-17 (1974). Treas. Reg. 1.471-11(c)(2)(i)(d) (1973) requires taxpayers to treat rental payments as an inventory cost when the rented property is used to produce inventory items.

6. *See, e.g.*, R. GOODE, THE INDIVIDUAL INCOME TAX 150-52 (rev. ed. 1976); J. PECHMAN, FEDERAL TAX POLICY 86 (rev. ed. 1977) (recognizing as important the problem of mismatching of

ple, to the deductibility of interest on loans that finance the purchase of consumer durables, such as home mortgages.[7] Congress has responded periodically to perceived abuses resulting from the special status of interest payments by enacting narrowly drawn exceptions to that special status.[8] No one, however, has proposed a theoretically defensible, yet practicable, system for tracing interest payments to the use made of the "rented" money—a requirement for a tax system that would treat interest like other rental payments. Indeed, although no one has challenged the propriety of determining the tax significance of rental payments other than interest by referring to the use made of the rented property,[9] several distinguished commentators have argued forcefully that tracing interest to the use made of the borrowed funds is administratively infeasible, theoretically objectionable, or both.[10]

---

income caused by a current interest deduction on loans used to acquire assets producing deferred gains); Bittker, *Income Tax Deductions, Credits, and Subsidies for Personal Expenditures*, 16 J. LAW & ECON. 193 (1973). For a concise analysis of the traditional arguments for and against a deduction for home mortgage interest and an extensive list of references to the literature, see Pomp, *Mortgage Interest and Property Tax Deduction: A Tax Expenditure Analysis*, 1 CANADIAN TAX. 23 (1979). See also W. Hellmuth, *Homeowner Preferences* in COMPREHENSIVE INCOME TAXATION 163, 172-79 (J. Pechman ed. 1980). The multitude of problems one encounters in attempting to identify interest payments are analyzed in Asimow, *supra* note 1, at 751-72.

7. *See* Pomp, *supra* note 6, at 23-24.

8. Remedial rules are found in I.R.C. §§ 163(d) (placing $10,000 ceiling on deduction for investment interest in excess of investment income), 170(f)(5) (preventing both an interest deduction and a deduction for charitable gift for same payment), 189 (requiring construction period interest to be capitalized by individuals, but permitting ten-year writeoff), 263(g) (requiring interest payments relating to certain straddle transactions to be capitalized), 264 (preventing deduction for interest paid to carry certain life insurance and annuity contracts), 265 (prohibiting deduction for interest paid to carry tax-exempt bonds), 267(a)(2) (prohibiting deduction for interest incurred by accrual basis debtor but not paid to cash basis creditor where debtor and creditor are related parties), 279 (limiting deduction for interest paid as part of cost of a large corporate acquisition), 385 (authorizing regulations distinguishing corporate debt from corporate equity), 461(g) (limiting deduction for prepaid interest), 465 (limiting deduction for interest paid on certain nonrecourse debts and other debts in which taxpayer bears no risk of personal liability for repayment).

9. The chief arguments for a special status for interest payments apply with equal force to other types of rental payments, as the following example illustrates. Consider *C* and his tax clone *D*, each of whom owns a lake front cottage, which each rents out every summer for $1,000. Assume also that one summer *C* and *D* want to vacation at the lake themselves. *C* rents a cottage identical to his own from a neighbor for $1,000, and continues to rent out his own cottage for $1,000. *D* decides, instead, not to rent his cottage, but to use it himself. If *C* could deduct his $1,000 rental payment he could use it to offset his $1,000 rental income and end up in exactly the same tax position as *D*. Assuming it is desirable to equalize the tax treatment of those who rent and otherwise similarly situated taxpayers who enjoy imputed income from their own assets, *D* should be taxed on his imputed income or *C* should be given his deduction, even though *C*'s rental payments for a summer vacation constitute personal consumption.

The author is indebted to May Ping Soo Hoo for suggesting this example.

10. *See* Gunn, *Is an Interest Deduction for Personal Debt a Tax Expenditure?* 1 CANADIAN TAX. 46 (1979); White & White, *Tax Deductibility of Interest on Consumer Debt*, 5 PUB. FINANCE Q. 3 (1977).

These commentators attempt to defend the universal interest deduction of current law by demonstrating that a tracing requirement would be administratively unworkable and would give taxpayers who could finance purchases by drawing down their savings an unfair advantage over taxpayers who borrow to make the same purchases.[11] Section II of this article refutes these arguments by articulating the principles that should govern the deductibility of interest in an ideal income tax system based on Haig/Simons principles[12] and by demonstrating that a tax system that consistently applies those principles would preserve the essential features of the tracing requirement generally applicable to other types of rental payments.[13]

The current tax system, of course, is not a pure Haig/Simons system. Perhaps its most significant departure from Haig/Simons principles is that it includes only realized income in the tax base. Section III develops and defends tracing rules that would operate fairly, at modest administrative cost, in an "ideal" realization system. Finally, Section IV illustrates the critical importance of good tracing rules in a tax system that departs even further from a Haig/Simons system by treating income from some sources more favorably than income from others.

II. A Defense of Tracing in an Ideal Income Tax System Based on Haig/Simons Principles

Taxpayers are as individualistic as snowflakes. They may differ in wealth and income, in their consumption and saving patterns, in their

---

11. White and White, for example, argue that the disallowance of an interest deduction on consumer debt would favor "asset finance over debt finance," a result they condemn. White & White, *supra* note 10, at 5. This contention is essentially a restatement of the widely cited arguments made earlier by M. White. White, *Proper Income Tax Treatment of Deductions for Personal Expense*, *in* 1 HOUSE COMM. ON WAYS AND MEANS, 86TH CONG., 1ST SESS., TAX REVISION COMPENDIUM 365 (Comm. Print 1959).

12. Simons defined income as follows:
Personal income may be defined as the algebraic sum of (1) the market value of rights exercised in consumption and (2) the change in the value of the store of property rights between the beginning and end of the period in question. In other words, it is merely the result obtained by adding consumption during the period to "wealth" at the end of the period and then subtracting "wealth" at the beginning. The *sine qua non* of income is gain, as our courts have recognized in their more lucid moments—and gain *to* someone during a specified time interval. Moreover, this gain may be measured and defined most easily by positing a dual objective or purpose, consumption and accumulation, each of which may be estimated in a common unit by appeal to market prices.
H. SIMONS, PERSONAL INCOME TAXATION 50 (1938) (emphasis in original).

For Robert Haig's somewhat different formulation, see Haig, *The Concept of Income—Economic and Legal Aspects*, in READINGS IN THE ECONOMICS OF TAXATION 59 (R. Musgrave & C. Shoup eds. 1959).

13. In contrast to the treatment of other rental payments, commentators have uniformly treated interest as a current cost. For example, Musgrave and Musgrave assert that interest paid in a business setting "is properly deductible in computing taxable income. It is a cost of doing business, just as are wage payments." R. MUSGRAVE & P. MUSGRAVE, PUBLIC FINANCE IN THEORY AND PRACTICE 307 (2d ed. 1976). The tax code, however, requires taxpayers to capitalize their wage payments if those payments are made to construct or acquire a capital asset.

degree of enterprise, in their natural endowments, in their general appearance, and in countless other ways that affect their ability to obtain and enjoy economic benefits. A tax system that accounted for all the considerations that affect an individual's taxable capacity would not be a system at all—it would be complete chaos. All practical tax systems select a small number of quantifiable considerations that are used as either complete or partial proxies for the taxable capacity of individual taxpayers. An ideal income tax ignores differences in the taxable capacity of individuals, including arguably relevant differences in wealth and consumption, unless those differences effect a change in the income of those individuals.[14] Stated most simply, similarly situated taxpayers under an ideal income tax are taxpayers with equal incomes.

Among tax specialists, the Haig/Simons definition of income is most commonly used in specifying the features of an ideal income tax. According to this income concept, the tax code should require taxpayers to include in income the benefits obtained from interest payments whenever those benefits constitute personal consumption or produce a net increase in accumulated savings.[15] This deceptively simply rule leaves unresolved the problem of determining when these benefits constitute consumption or accumulation, as the following example illustrates.

The Airline Ticket Example. Assume that both *A* and *B* have a net salary income of $12,000 in years one and two, and that both own a $1,000 money market certificate paying 10% interest. Assume also that both *A* and *B* plan to vacation away from home, and for that purpose, they both purchase in year one a $1,000 airline ticket. *A* finances the ticket purchase by cashing in his money market certificate. *B* finances the purchase by borrowing $1,000 at 10% annual interest. In year two, *A* will receive no interest income on the cashed certificate and will have no interest payments to make, leaving $12,000 of salary income subject to taxation. *B* will receive $100 interest income on his certificate, giving him a total income of $12,100, but he will have to make a $100 interest payment on his loan. After *B* makes that payment, both he and *A* will have the same $12,000 for consumption and accumulation.[16]

---

14. For a discussion of the strategy of a tax based chiefly on money income, see Andrews, *Personal Deductions in an Ideal Income Tax*, 86 HARV. L. REV. 309, 327-30 (1972). *See also* McIntyre & Oldman, *Taxation of the Family in a Comprehensive and Simplified Income Tax*, 90 HARV. L. REV. 1573, 1593 (1977).

15. For the Haig/Simons definition of income, see note 12 *supra*. Because the Haig/Simons income concept includes consumption and accumulation, interest payments would, by definition, be taxable when they fall into either category. But as explained in the text accompanying notes 19-22 *infra*, payments attributable to accumulation would enter the tax base only indirectly, through their impact on the taxpayer's store of goods at the end of the taxable period.

16. The example modifies the one offered by White and White, *supra* note 10, at 4, in two respects. First, White and White posit a situation in which an individual taxpayer faces the choice of either drawing down assets or borrowing. Their example does not address the fairness of an

Thus equal tax treatment of *A* and *B*, achieved under current law by giving *B* an interest deduction, is intuitively appealing. But as will be seen,[17] achieving this result in a Haig/Simons system requires modification of the tracing rules applicable to other types of rental payments.[18]

In discussing tracing rules one must not confuse these issues with issues that arise in characterizing payments after the tracing issues have been settled. Assume, for example, that the proceeds of a loan are properly traced to the purchase of an airline ticket. If the ticket was used for business purposes, then tracing, in effect, determines the character of interest payments on the loan. Technically, however, conclusions drawn from the use of the ticket determine the character of the interest payments. When the use of the ticket is ambiguous, a combined vacation and business trip for example, then tracing is only a step in the process of characterizing the payments.

A. *The Theory of Tracing.*

Because of the difficulty of directly measuring the consumption of individual taxpayers, every tax system, including one based on Haig/Simons principles, must look to sources of income as the starting point in identifying the tax base and in computing and collecting the tax.[19] A taxpayer who asserts that he should have some portion of

---

interest deduction, because a fairness argument, in contrast to the efficiency argument addressed by White and White, must compare the tax burdens on two or more taxpayers who are similarly situated. Second, White and White do not specify what assets the taxpayer can draw down for financing his consumption, a matter of great importance in both a tax on realized income and a Haig/Simons tax applied in a world with high transaction costs for liquidating some types of investments. The example in the text assumes that the taxpayers hold easily liquidated assets.

17. See text accompanying notes 22-23 *infra*.

18. In an ex ante consumption tax, equality of burdens could be achieved by exempting the interest income B earned on his money market certificate. A tax on potential income could achieve equality of burdens by taxing A on the income he could have earned if he had not called his money market certificate. For a brief discussion of these alternatives, see McIntyre, Book Review, 26 WAYNE L. REV. 1181, 1187-89 (1980).

19. No tax administration could conceivably determine each taxpayer's actual consumption by recording the value of all consumption expenditures (C). As a practical matter, consumption would have to be computed indirectly from presumably knowable information about income sources and about the change in value of assets held by the taxpayer. The following formula would yield Haig/Simons income (HSY):

(1) Total income sources (money income plus the money equivalent of property and services received during the taxable year)(S); plus

(2) Net increase in the value of assets held both at the close and the start of the year over their value at the start of the year ($OA_1 - OA_0$); plus

(3) Value of assets acquired during the taxable year and held at the close of the year (AA); minus

(4) Acquisition costs (AC); minus

(5) Profit seeking expenses (E); minus

(6) Personal expense deductions excludable from a refined consumption concept (PD).

gross income excluded from his taxable income must show that he has made expenditures—out of income sources, loan proceeds, or accumulated wealth—that qualify as a cost of earning income or that otherwise satisfy the tests for deductibility in the tax system. To make this showing, the taxpayer must trace his expenditures to their tax-significant use. For example, the payment of money to a university might be a deductible donation or a nondeductible tuition payment. Thus, tracing is a familiar, fundamental, and necessary feature of any net income tax system.

Because interest, by definition, is money paid to acquire the use of borrowed funds, tracing an interest expenditure to its initial use poses no special problem. Borrowed funds, however, are almost invariably used as a medium of exchange. This secondary use, the use made of the goods and services received in exchange for the borrowed funds, determines whether the interest payments qualify for exclusion from the tax base.[20] Thus the obvious problem for the taxpayer is that physically tracing borrowed dollars can in some cases be impossible,[21] and

---

The above formula mixes consumption and accumulation. Consumption could be computed, however, by measuring accumulation and subtracting it from the sum of consumption and accumulation yielded by the above formula. Accumulation would equal the net value of all assets held by the taxpayer at the close of the taxable year (NW_1), minus the net value of assets held by the taxpayer at the start of the year (NW_0).

That formula may be expressed symbolically as follows, using the symbols defined above:
$HSY = S + (OA_1 - OA_0) + AA - AC - E - PD$
The elements of the traditional Haig/Simons definition may be expressed as follows:
$HSY = C + NW_1 - NW_0$
$NW_1 = AA + OA_1 - L_1$
$NW_0 = SA + OA_0 - L_0$
$C = S - AC - E - PD + (L_1 - L_0) + SA$
(where SA is the value of assets on hand that were valued at the start of the year and that were sold or exchanged during the year, and $L_1 - L_0$ is the net increase in liabilities at the close of the year over the liabilities at the start of the year).

The above formula excludes from Haig/Simons income the economic gain that accrues during the taxable year on assets held at the start of the year and sold for consumption during the year. In theory that element of gain could be taxed by valuing the assets at the time of sale, but that would be impractical. It would require recording the value of consumption expenditures, which the source formula is intended to avoid. See note 65 *infra* for an example illustrating this point.

20. Though rented property other than money is not commonly exchanged for other goods and services, on those occasions when it is, the tax code determines the tax-significant purpose of the rental payment by looking at the use made of the goods or services acquired in the exchange. For example, if an employer permitted an employee to vacation at a rented beach cottage, the employer usually could deduct the rental payment so long as he paid the rent in order to compensate the employee for services rendered. *See* Treas. Reg. §§ 1.162-7 (1958), 1.274-2(d)(iii) (1963).

21. The following example illustrates the impossibility of tracing in some instances. Consider F, a commercial farmer, who wants to spend $1,000 for his daughter's wedding reception and another $1,000 for feed for his hogs. In anticipation of these expenditures, F deposits $2,000 in his checking account—$1,000 from his savings account and $1,000 from an unsecured bank

can cause his tax liability to be determined by his tax planning ability, rather than by his material well-being.

The airline ticket example illustrates the undesirable tax consequences of a rule that would require the taxpayer to trace the loan proceeds. In that example, physical tracing would prevent B from deducting his interest payment, a result that is intuitively unappealing, but easily avoided. The tax-sophisticated B would shuffle his affairs in the following manner. First, he would call his money market certificate and use the proceeds to buy his airline ticket. Then he would take out a $1,000 loan, using the proceeds to purchase a money market certificate identical to the one he had just called. The use of the loan proceeds would then be a cost of acquiring an asset, includible in income under Haig/Simons only to the extent that the fair market value of B's accumulation at the end of the taxable year exceeded his accumulation at the beginning of the year. Because B's payment of interest on the loan would not increase the value of his money market certificate, the money he expended to pay the interest charge would not be includible in his tax base.[22]

B should not be taxed on the portion of his gross income used to pay interest because no legitimate tax policy objective is served by a tracing rule that operates merely as a trap for the unwary. A tracing rule in an ideal income tax should presume that the taxpayer had spent his loan proceeds for a purpose other than consumption when he actually did so or when he could have done so merely by restructuring the form of his transaction. The taxpayer should lose his deduction, however, whenever his interest payment could be linked with an expenditure that arguably constituted consumption regardless of the changes he could have made in the form of his transaction.[23] Such a rule would

---

loan. F later writes two $1,000 checks, one to the wedding caterer and one to the grain merchant. He also pays $100 of interest on his loan. Under these facts, F's actions in depositing his funds laundered their source.

22. Assume, for example, that T, a taxpayer, starts the taxable year without any savings and earns $10,000 in wages during that year. Assume also that he borrows $1,000 during the year, which he uses to buy a money market certificate with a face amount of $1,000, which earns $100 in interest income. Assume finally that he pays $100 in interest on his loan and spends the balance of his income on consumption. Employing the formula set forth in note 19 *supra*, T would have Haig/Simons income of $10,000 computed as follows: (1) $10,000 plus (2) $0 plus (3) $1,000 minus (4) $1,000 minus (5) $0 minus (6) $0.

23. Assume, for example, that R, a taxpayer, starts the taxable year holding land worth $1,000. He earns $10,000 during the year and borrows $2,000. Assume that he spends all his available dollars on consumption. Under these assumptions, if R uses $1,000 of the loan proceeds, he is able to consume without selling his land. The other $1,000 of the loan, however, could not be traced to anything but consumption under any conceivable tracing rule.

In the above example, tracing would determine the character of an interest payment if the character of the actual or hypothetical use of the loan proceeds was unambiguous. If the loan

remove the trap for the unwary without creating a special status for interest payments distinct from the tax treatment accorded other types of expenditures.

The proposed rule for interest payments would be simple to apply due mainly to the tax treatment of acquistion costs under a practical Haig/Simons system. Because practical Haig/Simons uses gross income as the starting point in identifying the tax base, all acquisition costs—even those made to purchase consumer durables—would be deductible. The accumulation component of income would enter the tax base only once through the valuation of assets held by the taxpayer at the close of the taxable year.[24] When this treatment of acquisition costs is combined with the proposed tracing rule, a borrower could deduct interest payments on a loan to the extent that his loan proceeds in the year of the loan did not exceed the value of his assets (net of liabilities from prior years) on hand at the close of that year. For taxpayers with a positive net worth at the end of the taxable year, the proposed tracing rule would identify their interest payments as deductible acquisition costs.[25] Only taxpayers whose borrowings exceeded the value of their assets would need to be concerned about the mechanics of tracing.

---

proceeds were traced to an ambiguous expenditure—an entertainment expenditure that arguably constituted a business expense and arguably constituted consumption, for example—then tracing would be the first, but not the final, step in characterizing the interest payments on the loan.

24. Consider, for example, Mr. T, a taxpayer with no assets at the start of the taxable year who earns gross wage income for the year of $10,000: $1,000 of which he spends for business expenses; $6,000 of which he spends on a work of art; and $3,000 of which he spends on consumption. Assume that at the close of the taxable year, the art piece was worth $11,000. Under the classical Haig/Simons income definition, Mr. T's net income for the year would be $14,000, computed by valuing his consumption during the year—$3,000—and adding to it the net change in his savings—the value of the art piece at the close of the taxable year. The cost of the art piece and the amount of his business expenses would have no direct impact on his income; indirectly they would reduce his income by reducing resources otherwise available for consumption or for the acquisition of other assets.

A Haig/Simons system that initially included all income sources in income would need to give Mr. T a deduction for his acquisition costs in order to prevent those costs from entering the tax base twice. Thus, Mr. T would compute his income under the above facts by taking his gross wage income of $10,000, subtracting his acquisition costs of $6,000 and his business expenses of $1,000, and adding the value of his art piece at the close of the year, for total income of $14,000. The chief advantage of this alternative method of measuring income is that it obviates the need to measure directly the value of the taxpayer's consumption. For a more formal discussion of the relationship between a classical Haig/Simons system and one that begins with gross income, see note 19 *supra*.

25. Like all other acquisition costs, interest payments properly traced to the acquisition of an asset would have no direct effect on taxable income under the classical formulation of the Haig/Simons income definition, but would be deductible in a Haig/Simons system that uses gross income as the starting point in specifying the tax base. Consider for example, Mr. S, a taxpayer, who started the taxable year without any savings and who earned $10,000 in wages during that year. Assume that he borrowed $1,000 during the year, which he used to buy a nonappreciating money market certificate paying $100 annual interest. Assume finally that Mr. S. paid $100 in interest on his loan and spent the balance of his income ($9,000) on consumption. Under these

Taxpayers who borrowed in excess of their assets would first trace their loans to the actual or to a deemed reacquisition of those assets. The balance of their loan proceeds would then be traced to their current expenses, first to their deductible business expenses and then to their personal consumption expenses. Only interest paid on loans traceable to consumption would not be deductible. The taxpayer would bear the burden of proving the amount of business expenses paid, though to avoid the trap for the unwary, he would not be required to trace the borrowed funds to the business expense.

B. *The Argument for Denying a Deduction for Interest Attributable to Consumption.*

Taxpayers who purchase consumption goods with borrowed money pay a cost in addition to the purchase price. The extra cost is interest—the rental fee paid for the use of the borrowed money. That a cost of consumption falls within the definition of consumption seems to be a self-evident proposition. But that proposition is hotly disputed among tax specialists.[26]

Advocates of the universal interest deduction (UID) turn the argument for classifying interest as consumption on its head. They contend that because interest makes consumption more costly for borrowers than for savers, it should be excluded from the definition of consumption.[27] The following example illustrates both the crux of their argument and the response of this article by showing the potential impact of the interest deduction on the relative burdens of borrowers and similarly situated taxpayers who draw down their savings.[28]

---

facts Mr. *S* would have Haig/Simons income of $10,000. Using the classical Haig/Simons formulation, that result would be reached by adding his consumption of $9,000 to the $1,000 net increase in his savings. Using gross income as the starting point, Mr. *S* would get that same result by subtracting from his gross income his acquisition costs of $1,100 (the cost of the money market certificate plus the interest payment) and adding to gross income the value of his money market certificate at the close of the taxable year. Using the formula set forth in note 19 *supra*, Mr. *S* would compute his Haig/Simons income as follows: (1) $10,000 plus (2) $0 plus (3) $1,000 minus (4) $1,100 minus (5) $0 minus (6) $0.

26. See Gunn, *supra* note 10, at 49. Gunn argues correctly that interest on consumer debt should not be classified as consumption merely because of the taxpayer's subjective intent in incurring the debt. But Gunn's attack is not relevant to the argument addressed here for classifying interest as consumption. The correct argument for classifying interest as consumption arises because the taxpayer exchanges borrowed dollars for consumption goods. Subjective intent has relevance in determining the character of expenditures only when the tax-significant purpose of the expenditure is ambiguous—as may occur, for example, with certain business-related entertainment and travel. No such ambiguity about the use of borrowed funds exists, however, when the taxpayer borrows money to finance a vacation.

27. *See, e.g.*, Gunn, *supra* note 10, at 48-49.

28. This example bypasses issues concerning the design of tracing rules by considering tax-

The Ant/Grasshopper Example. Consider two taxpayers, both of whom have a net salary income of $12,000. Mr. Ant, a thrifty person, holds a $1,000 money market certificate earning 10% interest; Mr. Grasshopper, who is a spendthrift, has accumulated no savings at all. Assume that Mr. Ant and Mr. Grasshopper both spend $1,000 on a personal vacation. Mr. Ant finances his vacation by cashing in his demand certificate. Mr. Grasshopper finances his by borrowing the $1,000 at 10% interest. Assume also that Mr. Grasshopper pays $100 in interest on his loan, and that he and Mr. Ant spend all of their remaining net income on food and recreation. Both have enjoyed the benefit of a vacation worth $1,000, but Mr. Ant has $100 more than Mr. Grasshopper to spend on food and recreation. Unless permitted a deduction for his interest payment, Mr. Grasshopper will pay the same amount of tax as Mr. Ant despite this difference in spending power.

Mr. Ant undoubtedly enjoys an economic advantage over Mr. Grasshopper. But all differences in the economic conditions of taxpayers do not justify differences in tax burdens. Differences in economic conditions must reflect differences in income before they merit response in an ideal income tax system.[29]

---

payers who use all their gross income (after taxes) either to pay interest or to purchase goods that indisputably constitute consumption.

29. Apparently, White and White believe that a difference in taxable capacity means that there is a difference in income. They state:

> The income definition generally accepted as ideal is that formulated by Simons (1938: 50) as the algebraic sum of consumption and net change of assets over an accounting period. By this definition, the act of asset accumulation in one period implies accretion of income in subsequent periods because of the positive rate of return that will ordinarily be earned, whereas the act of consumption does not.
>
> Suppose, for example, an individual chooses a traveling vacation in year 1, the cost of which exceeds his alternative of vacationing locally by the amount of transportation expense. In year 2 his Simons income will be lower than if he had chosen a local vacation and saved the transportation expenses, by the amount of interest on that saving. This will be true regardless of how he finances the travel: if he does it by drawing down his own assets, interest earned on assets in year 2 will be lowered; if he finances the travel by incurring debt, interest payments in year 2 will reduce the net interest component of his income. In other words, the act of consumption in the present, in and of itself, implies sacrifice of future income irrespective of the means by which the consumption is financed.
>
> Now, if tax law definition of income is to conform to the Simons concept, the effect of the traveling vacationer's consumption in period 1 on his income in period 2 must be allowed for in the computation of taxable income. If the individual finances the travel by drawing down his own assets, the tax allowance is automatic—the interest income that would otherwise be included in taxable income in period 2 is simply not there. If, on the other hand, the travel is debt-financed, then deduction of the resulting interest cost must be explicitly allowed in period 2; otherwise taxable income would be overstated relative to Simons income.

White & White, *supra* note 10, at 4.

Mr. Ant's economic advantage over Mr. Grasshopper stems from his previously accumulated wealth. Because of his savings, Mr. Ant is able to spend in excess of his income without incurring interest expense. Mr. Ant would have enjoyed the same relative economic advantage over Mr. Grasshopper whether Mr. Grasshopper had borrowed nothing, and paid no interest; or had borrowed more than $1,000, and paid over $100 interest. Society could tax Mr. Ant on the economic advantage conferred by his savings by enacting a wealth tax, but it could not tax him systematically on that advantage under an ideal income tax.[30]

The UID does not equalize the burden on a taxpayer with accumulated wealth and one without such wealth when the taxpayer without wealth fails to borrow. It undercompensates the taxpayer without wealth, according to wealth tax criteria, whenever he borrows less than the amount of the savings consumed by the taxpayer with accumulated wealth. It overcompensates the taxpayer without wealth whenever he borrows more than the amount that the taxpayer with accumulated wealth spends out of savings.[31]

There is serious question, moreover, about the need for any adjustment in tax burdens on account of the economic advantage resulting from accumulated wealth, at least when an ideal income tax has been in operation from time immemorial.[32] Consider the following variation on the Ant/Grasshopper example. Assume that Mr. Ant and Mr. Grasshopper both begin their income producing lives without accumulated wealth and that each has a fixed salary of $12,000. Assume also that in their first income-producing year, Mr. Ant saves $1,000 and Mr. Grasshopper saves nothing. Assume finally that in their second year,

---

Gunn rejects White and White's argument but defends the UID on the ground that in a Haig/Simons income tax system, tracing disadvantages taxpayers whose income is derived from labor. Gunn, *supra* note 10, at 48-49. Presumably, Gunn would not extend his argument to interest payments made in the ideal realization system described in Section III or the tax system that made the source distinctions described in Section IV.

30. For a thoughtful discussion of this point, see Andrews, *Fairness and the Personal Income Tax: A Reply to Professor Warren*, 88 HARV. L. REV. 947, 956-58 (1975).

31. Consider two taxpayers, A and G. A has savings of $1,000 earning a 10% return and G has no savings. A has earnings of $12,000 and G has earnings of $12,000. Assume A spends his savings on consumption, forgoing his potential investment income. If G borrows $500 and pays interest of 10%, he will pay a higher tax than A even if he is permitted to deduct his $50 interest payment. If G borrows $10,000 for consumption and pays interest of $1,000, an interest deduction will permit him to pay less tax than A, even though G's income was the same as A's and his consumption was greater than A's.

32. The best argument in favor of a wealth tax is that an income tax inherently tends to perpetuate the status quo. If the distribution of wealth prior to the introduction of the income tax is considered unfair, then a wealth tax or a consumption tax should be added to the tax system to help diminish that perceived unfairness. *See* Andrews, *supra* note 30, at 957.

they behave exactly as they did in the first example. Under these assumptions, the economic advantage represented by Mr. Ant's $1,000 nest egg has been reflected in the income tax burden imposed on him during the first taxable year. That economic advantage provides no basis for an extra income tax burden on Mr. Ant or a diminished burden on Mr. Grasshopper in later years.

Mr. Ant's economic advantage in the above example is a necessary by-product of the decision to make actual rather than potential income the base of the income tax. As many commentators have noted, that choice of bases does not always work to the advantage of savers.[33] In many situations, it forces savers to pay a so-called "double tax" on savings, as the following variation on the Ant/Grasshopper example illustrates.

Assume that Mr. Ant and Mr. Grasshopper both begin their tax lives without any accumulated wealth and with an annual income stream from wages of $12,000. Assume also that Mr. Ant saves $1,000 in year one and Mr. Grasshopper saves nothing. Assume finally that Mr. Ant earns $100 on his savings in years two and three and then spends the $1,000 he saved in year one on a vacation in year four. Under these facts, Mr. Ant will be taxable on $100 of investment income in years two and three and thus will pay higher income taxes than Mr. Grasshopper over the four-year period. The two taxpayers had equivalent economic opportunities during that period, however, because Mr. Grasshopper could have earned interest income in years two and three if he had elected to save in year one.

C. *Economic Implications of Tracing*.

In a world without taxes, an individual's choice between financing consumption by borrowing and financing consumption by drawing down assets would turn on the complex interplay of many considerations.[34] The two considerations emphasized by advocates of the UID are the interest rate at which the individual can borrow money and his estimated rate of return on the assets he holds. Advocates of the UID assert that an ideal income tax that requires tracing would make the choice of drawing down assets more attractive than it would be in a

---

33. *See, e.g.*, Dyer, *The Relative Fairness of the Consumption and Accretion Tax Basis*, 1978 UTAH L. REV. 457, 485-87.

34. Those considerations would include, among others: (1) the rate of return the taxpayer could earn on his retained assets; (2) the rate at which he could borrow; (3) his ability to borrow at any rate; (4) the transactional costs involved in drawing down his assets; (5) his preference for liquidity; (6) his subjective evaluation of his retained assets; (7) his expectations about changes in economic conditions; and (8) the nature of his ownership rights in his retained assets.

tax-free world by lowering the after-tax return on assets without changing the after-tax cost of borrowing.[35] This assertion is intended not only as a defense of a UID but also as a criticism of the physical tracing rule generally applicable to expenditures other than interest.[36] It is not a valid criticism, however, of the modified tracing rule proposed in this article.

This article advocates a tracing rule that denies taxpayers a deduction for interest only to the extent that their borrowings exceed their assets. Denying an interest deduction to taxpayers without any assets obviously does not affect their choice between borrowing and drawing down assets, because they have no such choice. Taxpayers with assets who do face this decision should be permitted to take an interest deduction. These taxpayers would be denied an interest deduction only when their borrowings exceed their assets. But at that point they would no longer have the choice of drawing down assets.[37]

This tracing rule would ameliorate the economic defect of the UID—its tendency to encourage taxpayers to borrow for consumption. In a world without taxes, an individual who borrows in order to consume would have to pay the market interest rate on his loan. The UID allows an individual to use the deduction given for interest on his consumer loan to reduce his taxes otherwise due.[38] Consequently, the taxpayer's effective interest rate on the consumer loan falls below the market rate.[39]

---

35. *See, e.g.*, Gunn, *supra* note 10, at 47.

36. *Id*.

37. Assume, for example, that *P*, a taxpayer, borrows $1,000 to buy a television at a time when he holds $500 in his savings account and has no other assets. The first $500 of the loan proceeds will be traced to the savings account so that interest on that portion of the loan will be deductible. *P* will get no interest deduction on the $500 balance, but he will not have a tax incentive to draw down assets, because spending his $500 will change the tracing for the loan proceeds, making them nondeductible.

38. Assume, for example, that *C*, a taxpayer who holds no assets at the start of the taxable year, has a salary income of $10,000 and no other income. Assume also that he borrows $1,000 at the start of the year and pays interest of $100. He spends the loan proceeds and his salary income on personal consumption. In a society that does not tax income, *C*'s out-of-pocket interest cost is $100. In a tax system that imposes a 40% tax on net income and gives a UID, *C* could use his $100 interest deduction to shelter $100 of consumption from tax, thereby saving $40. His out-of-pocket interest cost, therefore, is only $60. This example, of course, abstracts from possible effects of an income tax on the market rate of interest.

39. If we assume, as economists often do, that an ideal tax operates in an ideal world populated by economically rational persons, then a pure physical tracing rule without the modifications advocated here probably will not favor the choice of drawing down assets over borrowing because taxpayers will structure their borrowing to avoid the trap for the unwary which the rule creates. Curiously, economists generally assume that the only solution to a trap for the unwary is a tax system in which all forms of economically equivalent transactions receive the same tax treatment. Lawyers, in contrast, generally cease to worry about such pitfalls once taxpayers have been in-

III. THE DEDUCTIBILITY OF INTEREST PAYMENTS IN A SYSTEM THAT TAXES ONLY REALIZED INCOME

All tax systems use realized income, not Haig/Simons income, as their starting point in defining the tax base. In a realization system no gain or loss is included in the tax base until it materializes in, or is "realized" by, a transaction. The realization system recognizes that annual valuation of the assets of all taxpayers, as Haig/Simons demands, is not feasible.[40]

The tax base in a realization system differs from that of a system based on Haig/Simons in three respects. All three differences affect principally the taxation of gains or losses on assets. First, the tax base in a realization system does not include Haig/Simons gains or losses that arise but are not realized during the current tax year. Second, the tax base in a realization system includes gains and losses that arose under Haig/Simons in a prior year but are not realized until the current year. Finally, the tax base in a realization system would be reduced by an estimate of the loss in value of wasting assets by using depreciation or some other cost-recovery method.[41] Other than these three exceptions, the bases of the ideal realization system and the Haig/Simons system are identical.[42]

---

formed about the techniques for avoiding them. The difference in outlook may occur because economists often are paid to design rules that avoid such inequities, whereas lawyers often are paid to lead taxpayers around the traps that tax statutes inevitably create.

40. Commentators generally have not attempted to defend the realization rule on theoretical grounds. *See, e.g.*, Shoup, *The White Paper: Accrual Accounting for Capital Gains and Losses*, 18 CANADIAN TAX J. 96 (1970). In the recently adopted tax-straddle legislation Congress requires taxpayers to offset their realized straddle losses with their unrealized gains before claiming any losses—a significant departure from the realization doctrine. I.R.C. §§ 1092, 1256 (added by Economic Recovery Tax Act of 1981, §§ 501, 503, Pub. L. No. 97-34, 95 Stat. 323, 327).

41. *See* Brown & Bulow, *The Definition of Taxable Business Income*, in COMPREHENSIVE INCOME TAXATION 241, 244 (J. Pechman ed. 1977).

42. The following definitions express the relationship between the two bases. Realized income is equal to:

    (1) Total gross income received during the taxable year (money income plus the money equivalent of other acquired property and services), minus the sum of
    (2) Basis of assets disposed of during the year, plus
    (3) Estimated depreciation, plus
    (4) Profit seeking expenses, plus
    (5) Personal expenses excludable from the refined consumption concept.

Haig/Simons income is equal to:

    (1) Realized income, plus
    (2) Unrealized income arising in the taxable year, minus
    (3) Realized income that arose in a prior taxable year, plus
    (4) The excess of "real" depreciation (the actual change in value, during the taxable year, of assets held by the taxpayer) over estimated depreciation.

In a Haig/Simons system all interest payments, except those attributable to personal consumption, are deductible from the taxpayer's income sources in computing taxable income. Inter-

The interest deduction rules proposed in this section are patterned after the rules generally accepted as applicable to expenditures other than interest in a realization system. An ideal realization system includes in the tax base the personal consumption and accumulation components of realized income, and denies a deduction for expenditures not traceable to current profit-seeking activities or to some other deductible use.[43]

Expenditures attributable to the acquisition of an asset used for business or pleasure become part of the taxpayer's cost basis in the asset. Basis is an unnecessary concept under Haig/Simons because each year the gain or loss in the value of the asset is recognized in the tax base; under the realization system, the amount received on the disposition of an asset, less its basis, defines taxable gain or loss. If the taxpayer is entitled to a depreciation or similar deduction in the current year, he must reduce the asset's basis by the amount of the deduction.[44]

The need to determine the historical cost basis of the asset complicates the treatment given to interest payments in a realization system. Interest payments financing either current consumption or realized accumulation generally can be taxed as under Haig/Simons, but interest

---

est payments attributable to accumulation enter the tax base indirectly through their impact on the taxpayer's store of wealth on hand at the close of each taxable year. See note 19 *supra*.

43. Some commentators argue that only profit-seeking expenses should be deductible from income sources in an ideal tax on realized income. *See* S. SURREY, PATHWAYS TO TAX REFORM 12-14, 20-22 (1973). Others suggest that a deduction for some personal expenses, such as medical costs, would provide a better measure of net accretion. *See* Andrews, *Personal Deductions in an Ideal Income Tax*, 86 HARV. L. REV. 309, 331-43 (1972); Turnier, *Evaluating Personal Deductions in an Income Tax—The Ideal*, 66 CORNELL L. REV. 262 (1981). This dispute is beyond the scope of this article.

44. Most tax analysts would add interest to the basis of assets acquired with borrowed funds when the interest is paid prior to the construction of the assets, but they have not generalized this rule for all interest payments. *See* I.R.C. § 189. Tax analysts have realized the need, however, to capitalize payments other than interest when those payments are made to acquire a capital asset. The following example illustrates the contrast between the proper treatment of rental payments in a Haig/Simons tax and a realization system. Consider the *XYZ* Power Company, a taxpayer that has undertaken to build an electric generating plant for use in its business. Assume that the construction costs for the plant total one million dollars, which includes a $100,000 rental fee paid during the taxable year for use of cranes and other heavy equipment. Under Haig/Simons the rental fee would not enter directly into the tax base, even if it were paid out of current income sources. Instead, *XYZ* would compute its taxable income by adding together its consumption for the year, presumably zero, and the net change in its worth for the year. Because the power plant will constitute a portion of *XYZ*'s wealth at the close of the taxable year, the costs of acquiring the plant, including the $100,000 rental fee, indirectly enter into the tax base.

Under a realization system, the $100,000 rental fee would constitute part of *XYZ*'s basis in the power plant, recoverable in later years through deductions for depreciation. The rental fee would not reduce *XYZ*'s taxable income for the year, even if the fee were paid out of current income sources. In effect, a tax on realized income would trace the $100,000 rental fee to the construction of the generating plant and would treat it as the cost of an undivided one-tenth share of the plant.

payments financing unrealized accumulation must be traced to the benefit financed and are deductible only if the benefit financed is introduced into the tax base. The following variations on the airline ticket example illustrate this problem.

Assume, as in the original airline ticket example,[45] that A and B each has an annual salary income of $12,000 and each holds an asset worth $1,000. Assume, however, that instead of money market certificates paying 10% annual interest income, each holds vacant land that has not appreciated in value since the time of purchase. Assume finally that A buys the ticket for his vacation from the proceeds of the sale of his land and that B finances his ticket by borrowing $1,000 at 10% interest. Under a strict physical tracing rule, B would not receive a deduction for his interest payments, since he used his loan proceeds for personal consumption. In contrast with a Haig/Simons system, no deduction would be allowed even if B could trace the loan proceeds to a deemed repurchase of his land, because land is a nondepreciable capital asset and no acquisition costs are deductible until gain or loss is realized. This result is intuitively appealing because it causes both A and B to have taxable income of $12,000 and thus to pay equal taxes. To achieve this result the tax system requires a practicable and theoretically justifiable method for tracing the proceeds of the loan to their tax-significant use.[46]

Although a proper tracing rule would have to tie loan proceeds to their tax-significant use to justify denying B his current deduction, the rule would also have to be constructed to minimize traps for the unwary taxpayer. Consider the following variation. The tax-sophisticated B, faced with a physical tracing rule, sells his land, uses the proceeds to purchase his airline ticket, and then repurchases his land with the proceeds of his loan. The shuffle would not make his interest payments deductible, but it would cause them to be added to his basis in the land, instead of being attributed to personal consumption. This type of trap for the unwary has no analogue in a Haig/Simons income tax system because taxpayers in that system receive the same tax benefit from capital expenditures as they receive from current profit-seeking expenditures.[47]

Eliminating such traps is not always desirable. Assume that A and B are both holding bonds worth $1,000 paying 10% annual taxable in-

---

45. See text accompanying notes 16-18 *supra*.
46. Without a workable tracing rule, the tax treatment of all interest payments must be identical because the system is unable to attribute such payments to the financing of accumulation as opposed to consumption.
47. Both would be deductible. See note 19 *supra*.

terest. Also assume that *B* purchased his bond for $800, while *A* paid the face amount of $1,000. Assume finally that *A* sells his bond to finance his trip and *B* borrows $1,000 to purchase his airline ticket. Under a Haig/Simons system *B* would be permitted to trace his interest payments to the deemed repurchase of his bond and therefore would get his interest deduction. Under a realization system, however, this result is intuitively unappealing, because an actual sale and repurchase of the bond would force *B* to realize a $200 taxable gain. Thus the deemed repurchase rule would not only eliminate a trap for the unwary, but it would also give *B* a tax advantage that he could not otherwise obtain.

As a final example, assume that *A* and *B* are both holding XYZ stock worth $1,000, which is appreciating at the rate of 5% annually and pays 5% annual dividends. Assume also that *A* sells his stock and that *B* gets his $1,000 by borrowing at 10% annual interest. Under these assumptions, *A* and *B* would pay equal taxes only if *B* were allowed a deduction for half of his interest payments—an impossible result under any tracing rule. Yet equal treatment of *A* and *B* has the same intuitive appeal in this case as it had under the facts of the first variation of the airline ticket example.[48]

Equal treatment of *A* and *B* can be achieved by treating the interest payments as part of the cost of the current income stream from the XYZ stock, and by permitting *B* to recover that portion of the cost currently. But the theoretical justification for such a departure from the generally accepted cost-recovery mechanisms of a realization system requires a special tracing rule capable of matching interest payments to the income stream they finance.

A. *Proposed Tracing Rules*.

To solve the problems discussed and to give all taxpayers the benefits of expert tax planning, the ideal realization system should employ the following two tracing rules. Rule One directs taxpayers to trace the proceeds of purchase-money loans—for example, home mortgages and consumer credit loans—to the purchases the loan proceeds finance. Rule Two has three components and governs the tax consequences of interest paid on untied loans.[49] The first component presumes that tax-

---

48. See text accompanying notes 16-18 *supra*.
49. This article does not attempt a comprehensive definition of a "tied" or an "untied" loan, but simply classifies as "untied" all loans not of the purchase money type. An untied loan does not depend on the existence of security for the loan, but rather on the limitation on the use of the loan proceeds. Thus "fungible" and "nonfungible" might be more descriptive terminology. Most initial home mortgages are tied loans but most second mortgages are untied loans.

payers spend the proceeds of untied loans on purchases made during the taxable year in which the loan proceeds were received. The burden should be on the taxpayer to rebut this presumption. The second component establishes a conclusive presumption that taxpayers contracting more than one loan during the taxable year spend the proceeds of their loans in the order the proceeds were received. The third component directs taxpayers to match their actual purchases made during the tax year with the proceeds of untied loans according to the following accounting conventions:

> First, to current business expenses for the year;
> Second, to purchases of depreciable properties or other income producing properties that generate an annual deduction under the tax system's cost recovery mechanisms;[50]
> Third, to purchases of other income producing property;
> Fourth, to purchases of consumer durables; and
> Fifth, to current consumption expenses.

Allocation according to the above plan would attribute untied borrowed dollars and their associated interest payments to the use that would give the taxpayer the tax benefits he could have achieved through optimal tax planning under a physical tracing rule that operates without conventions.[51] The following example illustrates how the plan would operate for taxpayers making untied loans.

Q, an investment consultant who has a gross business income of $26,000, takes out an unsecured loan of $14,000 during the taxable year. Assume that his only asset at the start of the year is a personal residence, purchased for $60,000, on which he has an outstanding purchase-money mortgage of $40,000. Assume also that he has made the following expenditures during the year: $4,000 for interest on his home mortgage; $1,000 for job-related travel; $5,000 for the purchase of a money market certificate; and $3,000 for remodeling his home. Assume finally a balance of $27,000 for personal consumption, with a reserve for taxes. Under these assumptions Rule One would not directly come into play because Q made no purchase-money loans during the year. Unless Q produced evidence to the contrary, the proceeds of

---

50. These purchases would usually be of depreciable property, but could also be of certain income-producing intangibles that would provide a current deduction under the cost-recovery mechanisms suggested in the text accompanying notes 66-67 *infra*. The ordering among types of income-producing property could easily be provided by an operating system in a way that minimized traps for the unwary.

51. Taxpayers would be entitled to a deduction greater than the maximum allowable under a physical tracing rule whenever an asset acquired before the loan had appreciated in value by the time the loan proceeds had been spent. Under a physical tracing rule, the taxpayer would be forced to realize his gain to be able to trace his loan proceeds to the appreciated asset. See note 65 *infra*.

the $14,000 loan would be attributed under Rule Two to expenditures made during the taxable year. The first $1,000 of the loan proceeds would be allocated to the job-related travel. Interest for that portion of the loan would be deductible when paid. The next $5,000 of the loan would be allocated to the money market certificate and capitalized.[52] Three thousand dollars would then be allocated to the renovation of the house and $4,000 to the payment of interest on the purchase-money mortgage. Interest paid for these portions of the loan would become part of Q's basis in his home.[53] The balance of $1,000 would be allocated to personal consumption. Only interest tied to the personal consumption portion of the loan would provide no present or future tax benefit to Q.

B. *The Practicability of Physical Tracing.*

1. *Rule One: Physical Tracing for Purchase-Money Loans.* Physically tracing borrowed funds to a particular use is sometimes difficult and occasionally impossible. For example, a taxpayer who deposits his borrowed funds in a checking or savings account destroys the possibility of physical tracing because his bank balance makes no distinction between deposits on the basis of source.[54] In a substantial number of situations, however, physical tracing is easy. For home mortgages and most other loans made to acquire real property, the lender requires the borrower to spend the loan proceeds for a previously agreed upon use. Often the lender will send the loan check directly to a seller in order to protect his security interest in the purchased asset. Most consumer credit given by department stores and other retail outlets can be linked easily to particular purchases, though revolving credit plans complicate the tracing problem.[55] Similarly, wholesalers and distributors usually receive trade credit from their suppliers for identified goods. Virtually all installment sales contracts tie the installment loan to an identified purchase. The above types of purchase-money loans represent the bulk

---

52. The interest paid for that portion of the loan would be recoverable under the tax system's cost recovery mechanisms for income-producing intangibles. See text accompanying notes 66-67 *infra*.

53. The $4,000 mortgage interest would be added to Q's basis in his home under Rule One.

54. See note 21 *supra*.

55. Customers charging more than one item usually pay interest on their total unpaid balance without any specific tracing of interest payments to particular purchases. After some payments of interest and principal have been made, it becomes impossible, absent some accounting convention, to know the amount of the unpaid principal on any one of the charged purchases. This tracing problem has significance, however, only if some of the charged purchases had a business purpose and some had a personal purpose.

of commercial loans made in the United States.[56]

The result of tying purchase-money loans to specific purposes is that instead of fungible dollars,[57] purchase-money borrowers receive goods and services in exchange for their promises to pay interest and principal on their loans. As shown by the variations of the airline ticket example, physical tracing of purchase-money loans does not create traps for the unsophisticated unless three conditions exist. First, the borrower must have available a source of funds, other than his loan, which he can use to finance his consumption. Second, he must be able to use those funds without incurring tax on an unrealized gain. Finally, the borrower must be free to divert his loan proceeds from the consumption purchase to the one that will generate a tax benefit, *i.e.*, he must have the choice between a purchase-money loan and an untied

---

56. The table below shows amounts borrowed by individuals through United States Credit Markets in 1979:

By Sector and Instrument	Amount	Percent
Households:	$165	80%
Mortgages	109	53
Consumer Loans	44	21
Other	12	6
Farms:	26	13
Mortgages	16	8
Other	10	5
Nonfarm Noncorporate	16	8

Billions of dollars, figures are rounded.
Source: Financial and Business Statistics, 66 Fed. Res. Bull. A44 (Sept. 1980).

Mortgages and installment credit loans represented about seven-eighths of all commercial loans made to individuals in 1979. Of the $382 billion in consumer credit outstanding (other than mortgages) during 1979, 30% was for installment automobile loans, 14% was for revolving installment loans, 4% was for installment mobile home loans, and 32% was for other installment loans. Only 19% was for noninstallment loans. 66 Fed. Res. Bull. A42, A44 (Sept. 1980).

57. Many commentators assume that the proceeds of a loan can be spent for anything the taxpayer desires. They then conclude that fungibility makes a farce of tracing. *See* Note, *The Deductibility of Interest Costs by a Taxpayer Holding Tax-Exempt Obligations: A Neutral Principle of Allocation*, 61 VA. L. REV. 211, 221 (1975).

Gunn restates the classical fungibility argument against tracing as follows:

> But even if taxpayer purpose could somehow be established, denying interest deductions to those who borrow for personal as opposed to business reasons would make no sense. Compare a taxpayer who borrows $100,000 to buy business assets, and who later uses his own cash to buy a $100,000 house with another who borrows the same amount to buy a house and later uses money not borrowed to buy business assets. The first might be said to have had a business motive for borrowing, and the second a personal motive. Yet each, after buying the business assets and the house, is in the same economic position as the other; each has the same gross income, the same interest payments, and the same annual consumption. A taxpayer's motive for borrowing is not only hard to find, it is not even worth looking for.

Gunn, *supra* note 10, at 47. In Gunn's example, the apparent unfairness to the person using borrowed funds to purchase his house is illusory because the taxpayer could have easily avoided the less favorable tax consequences by using the borrowed dollars for business. He has identified a trap for the unwary, not a fundamental fairness problem.

loan. Those borrowers who can meet all three conditions, however, will be confronted by the previously discussed traps for the unwary taxpayer.[58] Those traps are tolerable in a tax system based on realized income because they arise infrequently.[59]

The most important purchase-money loan is the home mortgage. Although few home purchasers have the option of making an untied loan, a significant number probably have some discretion concerning the size of their down payment.[60] Because lending institutions usually favor large down payments,[61] perhaps they could be relied on to eliminate the trap for the unwary by informing borrowers of the possible tax advantage of untied loans.[62]

Borrowers who could obtain nonrecourse loans would probably never get caught by a trap for the unwary for two reasons. First, nonrecourse borrowers typically are knowledgeable about the tax consequences of tied and untied loans.[63] Second, the nonrecourse feature of such loans would probably be so important to the borrower that he would never choose to make an untied loan. A lending institution would never give a borrower a nonrecourse loan without getting a security interest in previously specified property acquired with the loan proceeds, because a nonrecourse loan without such a security interest would be practically uncollectible.

Similarly, taxpayers obtaining trade credit would usually be sophisticated enough to know about the traps for the unwary created by a physical tracing rule for purchase money loans. Also, they would often have business constraints that would make it impossible for them to finance their trade purchases with an untied loan. In any case, trade debtors would rarely receive a major tax advantage from an untied loan because interest on trade credit would usually be a current busi-

---

58. See text accompanying note 22 *supra*.

59. The vast majority of borrowers appear unable to meet even the least stringent of these conditions, *i.e.*, negotiate an untied loan. Most loans made in the United States are tied to specific purchases. See note 56 *supra*.

60. Some taxpayers have the resources to carry a larger mortgage while keeping some assets in reserve, but, given the high cost of borrowing in recent years, this breed of taxpayer is rapidly disappearing.

61. The larger the down payment, the smaller the risk of loss in the event of default on the loan.

62. No trap for the unwary will arise for those taxpayers who do not make purchases that generate a tax benefit during the taxable year.

63. For example, many nonrecourse loans are obtained in tax shelter transactions, in which the participants almost by definition would know the tax implications of their actions. For a discussion of the problem of nonrecourse debt in tax shelter transactions, see Popkin, *The Taxation of Borrowing*, 56 IND. L.J. 43, 53-65 (1980).

ness expense, hence immediately deductible, or an inventory cost deductible soon after purchase as part of the cost of goods sold.

The only group of taxpayers likely to suffer any hardship from a physical tracing rule for purchase money loans would be those making consumer purchases on an installment plan. For the following reasons, however, the pitfalls awaiting this group would be negligible. First, many consumer debtors do not have the borrowing power to obtain an untied loan. Second, because the interest rate on consumer credit is often higher than that on untied loans, those who can obtain an untied loan will have a financial incentive independent of taxes to do so. Third, many borrowers do not make deductible expenditures out of savings or current income sources during the taxable year in which the consumer purchases are made. Finally, many taxpayers could be taught to avoid the pitfalls of tracing, just as many have been taught the advantages of the UID.

2. Rule Two: Modified Physical Tracing for Untied Loans. A Haig/Simons system would avoid traps for the unsophisticated by permitting taxpayers to trace the proceeds of their loans not only to assets acquired during the current taxable year but also to the deemed reacquisition of assets on hand at the start of that year. As illustrated by the variations on the airline ticket example, such a tracing rule in an ideal realization system would do more than merely eliminate these pitfalls. It would also permit taxpayers holding appreciated property a tax advantage that they could otherwise obtain only by recognizing their accrued gain on the appreciated property.[64] For this reason the tracing rules for untied loans should require taxpayers to trace the proceeds from untied loans to the acquisition of assets purchased during the taxable year in which the loan proceeds were spent.

The only theoretical shortcoming of the above rule is that it would produce a trap for certain taxpayers holding unappreciated property at the start of the taxable year.[65] Those taxpayers would occasionally be

---

64. See text following note 47 *supra*.
65. Another apparent shortcoming of the proposed tracing rule is that it would permit a taxpayer to trace his loan proceeds to a deemed acquisition of property that had appreciated during the current taxable year but prior to the time the taxpayer had actually obtained his loan proceeds. A contrary rule, however, would be nearly impossible to administer and would cause taxpayers in some instances to manipulate the timing of the receipt of their loan proceeds.

The tax advantage here is analogous to the one that arises in a Haig/Simons income tax system when taxpayers use property for consumption that has appreciated in value during the year in which it was consumed. Arguably that gain would be taxable in a tax system that taxed "the market value of rights exercised in consumption." See note 12 *supra*. But as a practical matter, a Haig/Simons system that uses sources of income as the starting point in assessing tax burdens would have difficulty reaching such gains. See note 19 *supra*.

in a position to minimize their taxes by actually selling and then reacquiring their unappreciated property. This shortcoming could not be easily eliminated because the presence or absence of unrealized gains is unknowable in a realization system. The significance of this shortcoming is undoubtedly modest.

Rule Two also eliminates potential tax losses for taxpayers who either cannot prove that they have spent their loan proceeds during the current year or cannot trace the proceeds of two or more loans to the year's expenditures. It does so by establishing a rebuttable presumption that taxpayers spend the proceeds of their loans during the taxable year in which they actually receive those proceeds, and by establishing a conclusive presumption that taxpayers spend the proceeds of their loans in the order in which those proceeds are received.

The proposed tracing rules serve three separate functions. First, they keep tracing simple by requiring the taxpayer to do little more than is now required of him. In order to receive a deduction for any interest used to finance a purchase he need only prove that he made an expenditure—as he is required to do under the present tax system. Second, the rules eliminate most traps for the unsophisticated, thereby assuring fairness. Third, by giving the taxpayer the benefit of several presumptions, the rules minimize both the enforcement burden on the tax collector and the record-keeping responsibilities of the taxpayer.

C. *Cost Recovery Mechanisms for Nondepreciable Assets Acquired with Borrowed Money.*

Two special problems arise in an ideal realization system when interest payments are made on a loan that financed the acquisition of an income producing asset. One problem concerns the timing of the deduction for interest payments when those payments are made in years following the year in which the taxpayer used the borrowed money to acquire a depreciable asset. This problem is beyond the scope of this article. The second problem involves the proper cost recovery mechanisms for interest paid to acquire income-producing intangibles and other nonwasting assets—the problem illustrated by the second variant on the airline ticket example.[66] This section proposes and defends some practical solutions to this second problem.

Consider, for example *J*, the owner/manager of a drygoods store, who purchases a gallon of green paint on day one for $10. On day six, she purchases an identical can of green paint for $12. On day ten, she hires two painters, one to paint the basement of her house and the other to paint the storeroom of her drygoods store. By using the $10 paint for pleasure, *J* would never pay tax on the $2 appreciation—under Haig/Simons or a realization system—unless her consumption was measured by the fair market value of goods devoted to consumption at the time of their use rather than by the purchase price of those goods.

66. See text following note 47 *supra*.

A tax system built strictly on Haig/Simons principles would automatically link the timing of a deduction for interest paid to acquire an asset with the taxation of the gain on that asset. For example, assume that a taxpayer borrows $1,000 to buy a parcel of land, paying $100 per year in interest on the loan. The land increases in value by $200 each year and the taxpayer sells the land after five years for $2,000. Under a Haig/Simons tax system, the taxpayer would compute his annual accumulation by subtracting the fair market value of his assets on hand at the start of the taxable year from the fair market value of his assets on hand at the close of the year. The taxpayer would therefore include in each year's income $200 of unrealized gain on the land, but he would exclude from income the $100 expended to pay his interest cost.

A tax system that deviated from Haig/Simons by taxing only realized gains would match the gain from the sale of the land against the costs of producing that gain by capitalizing the annual interest payments. At the time of sale, the taxpayer would have a basis in the land of $1,500—the sum of the $1,000 purchase price and the five $100 interest payments—and hence a gain of $500. Capitalizing interest payments achieves the correct theoretical result whenever the taxpayer's gain from the asset purchased with borrowed funds comes solely from capital appreciation. In those situations, delaying the deduction for interest until the asset is sold vindicates the fundamental tax-accounting principle of a realization system that deductions should be matched with the income they generate.[67] Merely capitalizing all interest payments that are traced to the acquisition of an asset, however, produces incorrect results for assets that are generating a current income stream.

For traditional wasting assets, such as machinery, a realization system permits the taxpayer to take a current deduction for a portion of each interest payment through the tax code's depreciation mechanism.[68] But commentators have argued that a realization system should not permit taxpayers to deduct any portion of the cost of acquiring so-called nonwasting assets—stocks and bonds are classic exam-

---

67. *See, e.g.*, ACCOUNTING PRINCIPLES BD., APB STATEMENT NO. 4, BASIC CONCEPTS AND ACCOUNTING PRINCIPLES UNDERLYING FINANCIAL STATEMENTS OF BUSINESS ENTERPRISES, Oct. 1970, *reprinted in* FINANCIAL ACCOUNTING STANDARDS BOARD, FINANCIAL ACCOUNTING STANDARDS, ORIGINAL PRONOUNCEMENTS AS OF JULY 1, 1978, 437, 466:
   Expenses are the costs that are associated with the revenue of the period, often directly but frequently indirectly through association with the period to which the revenue has been assigned. Costs to be associated with future revenue or otherwise to be associated with future accounting periods are deferred to future periods as assets.
68. For a summary of the simplifying assumptions inherent in common systems of depreciation, see Kahn, *Accelerated Depreciation—Tax Expenditures or Proper Allowance for Measuring Net Income?*, 78 MICH. L. REV. 1 (1979).

ples—until taxpayers have sold or otherwise disposed of those assets.[69] That treatment may be defensible whenever the acquisition costs closely approximate the anticipated proceeds from disposition. When nonwasting assets are purchased with borrowed money, however, the total acquisition costs—including interest payments—usually exceed the proceeds from disposition. Under such circumstances at least some portion of the acquisition cost should be matched with the current income generated by those assets, as the following example illustrates.

Consider M, who has $1,000 of savings which he uses to purchase a four-year bond with a face amount of $1,000 and a 12% annual return. Ownership of the bond confers on M two intertwined though distinct rights: the right to receive the face amount of the bond after four years, and the right to four annual interest payments of $120. If M were to allocate his cost basis between those two rights according to their respective fair market values, his annual net interest income would be reduced, but the increase in the annual unrealized gain from his right to collect the face amount of the bond would offset the reduction in his net interest income. Consequently, his realized and unrealized annual net gains would equal the $120 interest payment made by the issuer of the bond, regardless of how his basis was allocated. A realization system would impose no great hardship on M by prohibiting him from dividing his cost basis between his current income right and his right to collect the face amount of the bond.

The equities would change if M financed his purchase of the four-year bond by borrowing $1,000 at 10% annual interest. Assuming that the loan remained outstanding for four years and was then paid off, M would pay a total of $1,400 to acquire the bond—the $1,000 purchase price plus $400 in interest. Under these facts, a realization system would seriously mismatch the timing of M's deduction for acquisition

---

69. For a discussion of alternative treatments of intangibles, see M. CHIRELSTEIN, FEDERAL INCOME TAXATION: A LAW STUDENT'S GUIDE TO THE LEADING CASES AND CONCEPTS 24-32 (2d ed. 1979).

Bittker and Stone pose a famous question based on a variation of the facts of Helvering v. Horst, 311 U.S. 112 (1940). In *Horst* a father held a negotiable bond with negotiable interest coupons attached. He clipped one of the coupons before its due date and gave it to his son, who subsequently cashed the coupon. The Court held that the father was taxable on the interest coupon, relying on the horticultural metaphor that the owner of a tree is taxable on the fruit of that tree. *Id.* at 120. Bittker and Stone ask who would have been taxed on the interest income if the father had given the bond to his daughter and the interest coupon to his son. *See* B. BITTKER & L. STONE, FEDERAL INCOME, ESTATE, AND GIFT TAXATION 445-46 (5th ed. 1980). One answer, described in the text, is to allocate the father's cost basis in the bond between his right to interest income and his right to repayment of principal in acordance with the fair market value of those rights at the time of the gifts. The result is that the bare bond and the interest coupons are treated as discount bonds, taxable to the holder under the normal rules for bonds issued at a discount.

costs and the income generated by those costs if it were to prohibit any cost recovery until the bond matured. The maximum amount reasonably attributable to *M*'s right to collect the face amount of the bond would be $1,000 because that is the total he will receive when the bond matures.[70] The balance of his acquisition costs—the $400 in interest payments—should be allocated to his current income right. The current income right should be viewed as a wasting asset, because its value decreases annually as the income generated by that right is collected. Straight line amortization of the $400 cost of that right produces an annual deduction of $100, the exact amount of *M*'s annual interest payment. The cost of acquiring the income right is thus properly matched with the benefit obtained from that right.

The above example illustrates an acceptable tax treatment for assets, such as bonds, that produce current taxable income without any likelihood of capital appreciation.[71] For assets such as common stock, which taxpayers usually hold both for current dividend income and for capital appreciation, a full current deduction for interest payments would be too generous. In theory, the taxpayer should allocate his total acquisition costs, including interest payments, between his current income right and his anticipated proceeds from disposition, presumably

---

70. This discussion assumes that the current income generated by the intangible is subject to tax. Obviously if the income were exempt, then the expenses allocated to the current income would not be deductible.

The exemption for interest on state and local bonds provided in I.R.C. § 103 has caused Congress to deny a deduction under I.R.C. § 265 for interest paid to carry those bonds. Tracing loans used to purchase such bonds has been problematic for two reasons. First, because interest is otherwise deductible, the taxpayer, to preserve his deduction, merely must show that an alternative source of funds was used to purchase the tax-exempt bonds. Second, many tax analysts consider it unfair that taxpayers with savings should be permitted to purchase their taxable assets with borrowed funds and their exempt assets with savings. As illustrated by the Ant/Grasshopper example, no such unfairness exists so long as the taxpayer has been previously taxed on his savings. Of course the exemption of the interest income is itself unfair under traditional income tax principles.

Canada presently prohibits a deduction for personal debt but permits an unlimited deduction for reasonable business debt. It has encountered serious tracing problems with its system. *See* Bale, *The Interest Deduction Dilemma*, 21 CANADIAN TAX J. 317 (1973). The Canadian experience illustrates the intractible problems presented by partial tracing. These problems would not arise in a tax system that conditions all interest deductions on the ability of the taxpayer to prove a deductible use of his loan proceeds.

The Canadian government has recently announced its intention to limit the annual tax deduction for interest on investments to the amount of investment income (excluding capital gains) earned in the year. Excess interest payments will be characterized as capital losses or carried forward as a deduction against future investment income and capital gains. *See* DEPT. OF FINANCE, CANADA, *Budget Paper* 25 (1981).

71. Bonds can, of course, generate capital gains and losses through changes in the prevailing interest rate. But the anticipated income from bonds is usually from interest income, not capital appreciation.

on the basis of their respective fair market values. But as a practical matter such an approach is unattractive, because the values of those intertwined rights are virtually unknowable before disposition. Also, taxpayers frequently do not know their total acquisition costs in the year of purchase because the total depends on the amount of interest paid during the term of the loan, a period that is often unfixed or changed.

The realization system could achieve an administratively feasible and theoretically defensible result if the current deduction for interest paid to acquire a nondepreciable asset were limited to the amount of current income generated by that asset, the excess interest being added to the taxpayer's basis in the asset. In the two polar cases—all income generated by capital appreciation and no income generated by capital appreciation—that rule would approximate the correct theoretical result. The rule would also produce an essentially correct result in intermediate cases, but only when the taxpayer's annual rate of return on his investment equals the rate of interest he is paying on his loan.[72] Because economic forces in a perfectly rational economy would equal-

---

72. Assume, for example, that A purchases an intangible asset with a 10 year life for $100. Assume also that it produces an annual yield of $10, half in current royalty income and half in capital appreciation. Assume finally that A is paying $10 per year interest on a 10-year loan, the proceeds of which were used to buy the intangible asset. In a theoretically correct system, A's annual interest payments would be allocated between the right to annual royalties and the right to capital appreciation on the basis of the fair market value of each of those rights. Those rights presumably would be valued by discounting the income streams that each was expected to produce. Since the two expected income streams are the same for all years, they have equal value. Thus, half of each interest payment would be allocated to the royalty income and be currently deductible and half would be allocated to capital accumulation and be capitalized. The identical result is obtained by limiting the interest deduction to current realized income.

Under less stylized facts, a theoretically correct result would not be reached by limiting the interest deduction to current realized income. Assume, for example, that A paid only $8 annual interest on his loan, with the result that A would have net income each year of $2. Since the net royalty income would be taxable currently and the net capital appreciation income would not be taxed until realized, the capital appreciation income would have a higher fair market value than the royalty income. Thus more than half of the $8 interest payments should be allocated to capital appreciation.

As a further variation, assume that A was paying $10 annual interest but that A's loan was for only five years. Under the normal rules for acquisition costs other than interest, each of the five interest payments made on the loan should be allocated over the 10 year life of the asset. Assuming for simplicity a straight line method of allocation, then only one-tenth of the $10 interest payment made in the first year should be allocated to income earned in that year. Arguably one-tenth of the interest payments made in later years should also be allocated to the first year, although tax accounting rules generally prohibit taking a deduction for interest until the interest has been paid. Even if interest paid in later years can be allocated to the first year, the total interest allocated to that year would not exceed five-tenths, or one-half, of the annual interest payment. Since half or more of that portion of the payment is attributable to the capital appreciation income stream, no more than one-quarter of the $10 interest payment ($250) made in the first year should be deductible as a cost of the royalty income.

ize average rates of return on investment and average interest rates, it is likely that the circumstances of the real world will tend somewhat in that direction.[73] Even if the result in intermediate cases is a crude approximation of the theoretically correct result, it is far more accurate than the result of the UID.[74]

D. *Fairness of Tracing in a Realization System.*

1. *Fairness in Theory.* A Haig/Simons income tax would permit taxpayers with accumulated wealth to minimize their taxes by financing their nondeductible purchases with saved rather than borrowed dollars. As illustrated by the Ant/Grasshopper example, this result is fair so long as taxpayers with accumulated wealth have paid tax in a prior period on the income out of which that wealth was saved.[75] The tracing rules proposed here provide a similar advantage to taxpayers with accumulated wealth, but only if the wealth is held in the form of unappreciated assets. Taxpayers with unrealized gains would be precluded from obtaining a tax advantage that should be enjoyed only by those whose accumulated wealth arose from income already taxed in a prior period.

2. *Fairness in Practice.* Because of the restrictive view of taxable capacity inherent in an ideal tax on realized income, fairness issues under that tax can never be resolved incontrovertibly on a theoretical basis. The practical consequences of tracing, therefore, are an important part of the fairness argument on its behalf. The tracing rules proposed above[76] would automatically solve three practical problems that cannot be solved under the UID, the only practical alternative to tracing, except through ad hoc remedial legislation. Such legislation is inconsistent with the UID ideal.

(a) *Sham transactions.* Most law students learn of the tax policy problems created by the special status of interest payments by studying *Knetsch v. United States*.[77] The taxpayer in *Knetsch* sought to create a tax shelter for himself by purchasing a deferred annuity bond from the

---

73. Economists routinely make this dubious assumption about the real world.
74. The assumption that economic forces at work in the real world tend to equalize rates of return and interest rates is similar to the one made in most of the methods of depreciation that are not intended as an investment subsidy. For example, straight line depreciation assumes that the income generated by an asset will be earned in equal annual amounts over the useful life of the depreciable asset. For accelerated depreciation that intentionally mismatches income and costs, the timing problem for interest payments is beyond the scope of this article.
75. See text accompanying notes 29-33 *supra*.
76. See text accompanying notes 49-51 *supra*.
77. 364 U.S. 361 (1960).

Sam Houston Life Insurance Co. and by paying for the bond by borrowing from the company. He then satisfied his obligation to pay interest on his loan by borrowing further from the insurance company, using his expectancy under the annuity bond as security for the loans. Because interest payments were currently deductible and the expectancy on the deferred annuity bond was not taxable until realized, the taxpayer showed a substantial paper loss on the transaction, which he sought to use to offset his income realized from other sources. The Supreme Court held that the taxpayer was not entitled to deduct the interest paid to the insurance company, despite unambiguous language in the tax code to the contrary.[78] The Court based its decision on the controversial ground that the transaction was a sham.[79]

The sham transaction doctrine has proved useful to the Internal Revenue Service in controlling outrageous abuses of the interest deduction. But this ad hoc doctrine creates its own set of problems, because tax theory does not specify when it should be applied.[80] The tax shelter problem illustrated by *Knetsch* would not arise in a realization system that adopted the proper tracing rules. Because the loan in *Knetsch* was a purchase-money loan, interest on the loan would become part of the cost of acquiring the deferred annuity bond and would not be deductible currently. The taxpayer would exclude those costs from his tax base in later years under the tax code's cost-recovery rules for annuity contracts—that is, the cost could be used to offset annuity income when he begins to receive annuity payments under his deferred annuity bond.[81]

By requiring the taxpayer to capitalize his interest payments, the tracing rules would accurately match the deduction for the interest payments with the income they helped generate. Thus, the tracing rules would destroy the *Knetsch* tax shelter on a principled basis and would, incidentally, destroy analogous tax shelter schemes built on the timing differential between deferred unrealized gains and interest deductions under the UID.[82]

---

78. *Id.* at 367-69. I.R.C. § 163(a) then, and now, permitted a deduction for "all interest paid or accrued within the taxable year on indebtedness." See note 3 *supra*.

79. 364 U.S. at 365-66. Of course the transaction had no economic substance, and the court reached the correct result. But it reached that result only through a forced interpretation of the statute. *See* Blum, *Motive, Intent, and Purpose in Federal Income Taxation*, 34 U. CHI. L. REV. 485, 517-18 (1967).

80. For a collection of cases raising the sham issue, see S. SURREY, W. WARREN, P. McDANIEL & H. AULT, FEDERAL INCOME TAXTION: CASES AND MATERIALS 561-64 (1972).

81. *See* I.R.C. § 72 (permitting a portion of each annuity payment to be treated as a return of capital).

82. In an attempt to destroy the tax benefits of tax motivated straddle transactions, Congress recently required taxpayers engaging in most commodity transactions to capitalize their interest

(b) *Construction period interest payments*. Many commentators have attacked the indefensible tax shelter opportunities created by a current deduction for interest paid on a construction loan prior to the completion of the construction.[83] They have argued correctly that in a realization system the UID mismatches construction period interest payments with the income those payments help generate.[84] Commen-

---

payments and other carrying charges incurred in order to purchase or hold the commodities. I.R.C. § 263(g) (added by Economic Recovery Tax Act of 1981, § 502, 95 Stat. 327). This provision is consistent with the theory of the interest deduction advanced in this article. The tracing problems that will arise in enforcing this section would be substantially eliminated by the adoption of a tracing requirement for all interest payments.

83. *See, e.g.*, W. ANDREWS, BASIC FEDERAL INCOME TAXATION 468-69, 669 (2d ed. 1979).

84. I.R.C. section 189 requires individual taxpayers to capitalize their construction-period interest payments over a 10 year period. (Section 189(c) applies the 10 year period to nonresidential property after 1981 and to residential property, except low-income housing, after 1983). In theory, the payments should be capitalized over the useful life of the constructed asset, but the 10 year rule is arguably fairer and easier to administer in a tax system that permits a current deduction for most interest payments. For an explanation of the congressional reasons for adopting I.R.C. § 189, see STAFF OF THE JOINT COMMITTEE ON TAXATION, 94TH CONG., 2D SESS., GENERAL EXPLANATION OF THE TAX REFORM ACT OF 1976 25-26 (Comm. Print 1976), *reprinted in* S. SURREY, W. WARREN, P. MCDANIEL & H. AULT, FEDERAL INCOME TAXATION, 192-94 (2d ed. Supp. 1979).

The table below illustrates the significance of the construction period interest issue for many taxpayers. It shows the pattern of deductions under a UID and under the tracing rules proposed in section IIIA for interest paid on a loan that finances the construction of an asset placed in service three years after interest payments begin on the construction loan. For simplicity, the table assumes that the taxpayer computes his depreciation deductions using the straight line method of depreciation.

ANNUAL INTEREST DEDUCTIONS ON FIVE YEAR LOAN USED TO ACQUIRE FOUR YEAR MACHINE WHEN DEPRECIATION BEGINS THREE YEARS AFTER YEAR OF FIRST INTEREST PAYMENT

Year	Depreciation Deduction for $80 Purchase Price	Year 1 A B C	Year 2 A B C	Year 3 A B C	Year 4 A B C	Year 5 A B C	Total Deductions A B C
1	0	0 0 8	0 0 0	0 0 0	0 0 0	0 0 0	0 0 8
2	0	0 0 0	0 0 8	0 0 0	0 0 0	0 0 0	0 0 8
3	0	0 0 0	0 0 0	0 0 8	0 0 0	0 0 0	0 0 8
4	20	2 2 0	2 2 0	2 2 0	2 2 8	2 0 0	30 28 28
5	20	2 2 0	2 2 0	2 2 0	2 2 0	2 4 8	30 32 28
6	20	2 2 0	2 2 0	2 2 0	2 2 0	2 2 0	30 30 20
7	20	2 2 0	2 2 0	2 2 0	2 2 0	2 2 0	30 30 20

This table assumes a business machine costing $80 with four-year-useful life, being depreciated under the straight line method, with depreciation beginning three years after the first interest payment. Column (A) under each year and under total deductions represents the allowable interest deductions on the assumption that the allowable deduction with respect to an interest payment may not exceed total interest already paid on the loan. Column (B) represents allowable interest deductions on the assumption that no depreciation deduction is allowable with respect to an inter-

tators have failed to notice, however, that mismatching occurs whenever interest payments constitute either a capital cost or an inventory cost. Construction period interest is merely a prominent example of that mismatching.

The tracing rules proposed above would eliminate the tax shelter opportunities created by the mismatching of construction period interest payments with the income they help generate. The tracing rules do not distinguish between construction period and postconstruction interest payments because the tax-significant purposes of construction period and postconstruction interest payments on the same loan are necessarily identical. Interest payments on any loan financing the acquisition of an asset become part of the taxpayer's basis in that asset, recoverable under the tax system's cost-recovery mechanisms. Taxpayers would usually recover their construction period interest payments through depreciation deductions over the useful life of the constructed asset.

(c) *Inflation*. Under inflationary conditions, much of what lenders and borrowers usually characterize as interest might be better characterized as prepayment of principal. Consider, for example, a borrower who takes out a three-year loan of $10,000, paying 14% annual interest, when the annual rate of inflation is 10%.[85] In this situation, a substantial portion of the borrower's nominal interest payments are compensation to the lender for his loss caused by the borrower repaying the $10,000 principal in dollars of reduced value. Only a small fraction of each periodic payment constitutes a rental fee for the use of borrowed money.[86]

In a realization system that systematically adjusts tax obligations for inflation, the borrower would match the prepayment-of-principal component of his nominal interest payments with the cancellation of indebtedness income he realized when he paid off his loan obligation in devalued dollars.[87] In theory, the prepaid principal would exactly off-

---

est payment until that interest has been paid. Column (C) represents the allowable interest deductions resulting from a UID.

85. The definition of inflation is partly a function of the index used to measure it. Indices of inflation inherently measure average changes in the purchasing power of currency.

86. *See* R. MUSGRAVE & P. MUSGRAVE, *supra* note 13. The difficulties that economists have struggled with in specifying the "real" interest role are recounted in McIntyre, *supra* note 18, at 1186-87. Economists estimate that despite high nominal interests rates in recent years the real rates have been very low, even negative. *See How Inflation Erodes the Income of Fixed-Rate Lenders*, 11 REAL ESTATE REV. 43, 50, *reprinted in* BROOKINGS GENERAL SERIES REPRINT 372 (1981).

87. Assume for example that a taxpayer with a three year loan of $10,000 pays annual interest of $1,400 and the annual inflation rate during the three year term is 10%. Under an indexing

set the cancellation-of-indebtedness income whenever market forces, in establishing the interest rate, had accurately predicted the true rate of inflation. An unforeseen inflation rate would produce a windfall gain either for the borrower or for the lender.

In the real world the tax system determines tax obligations in nominal dollars unadjusted for inflation. This computational method gives the borrower two advantages he would not enjoy in an inflation-proof tax system. First, he is not taxed on the cancellation-of-indebtedness income arising from the repayment of his loans in devalued dollars. Second, he is not forced to characterize any of the nominal interest payments as prepaid principal, which would reduce his current deduction. Neither of these advantages can be eliminated easily, for in real world situations the rental fee and the prepayment-of-principal components of nominal interest payments are difficult to distinguish.[88]

The proposed tracing rules would play an important role in limiting the second of the tax advantages just described. Under a tracing system, if a loan had financed personal consumption, the prepayment-of-principal component would provide the borrower with no tax benefit because there would be no interest deduction.[89] Similarly, the prepayment-of-principal component of interest paid on a loan used to acquire an asset would become part of the borrower's cost basis in the acquired asset, and would be deductible only through the tax system's cost-recovery mechanisms.[90] This capitalization requirement, by delaying the deduction for interest payments, would have the salutary effect of reducing the improper tax benefit obtainable under the UID for the prepaid principal component of interest. The following example illustrates this effect.

A, a taxpayer, purchases a business asset for $1,000, financing the purchase completely with a ten-year commercial loan. Assume that A pays annual interest on his loan of 14% and that the expected and actual inflation rate is 10% for all relevant periods. If the asset purchased is land, a nondepreciable asset, then A would capitalize his interest

---

mechanism only $400 per year of the nominally interest payment is characterized as interest and $1,000 is characterized as nondeductible payment of principal. Finally, under the hypothesized indexing mechanism the taxpayer's payment of what is nominally principal is also indexed so that in year three he is treated as having paid only $7,000 in satisfaction of his loan. Under these facts the taxpayer has cancellation of indebtedness income of $3,000 in year three which exactly offsets the $3,000 of nominal interest that was nondeductible.

88. McIntyre, *supra* note 18, at 1186-87.

89. This conclusion would be subject to the proposed tracing rules giving the taxpayer the benefit of the doubt in appropriate cases.

90. This article does not discuss the timing of the deduction for interest payments made in years following the year in which the taxpayer used the borrowed money to acquire a depreciable asset.

payments and receive no tax benefit for them until he disposed of the land. When he ultimately sold the land, the improper benefit he would then obtain from a deduction for the prepaid principal component of interest would offset the improper detriment he would suffer from the use of historical cost, unadjusted for inflation, as his basis in the land. Under the UID, he would get the improper benefit when the interest was paid and would not suffer the offsetting improper detriment until the land was sold.

If *A* in the above example purchased a depreciable asset with his $1,000 loan proceeds, he could recover his nominal interest payments over the useful life of the asset. To the extent that he recovered the prepaid principal component of his interest payments through depreciation, he would be getting an improper benefit, though generally a smaller benefit than he would get under the UID.[91] He would also be suffering an improper detriment from the use of historical cost, unadjusted for inflation, as his basis for depreciation. Under the straight-line method of depreciation, the timing of the improper benefit from the deduction for the prepaid component of interest would be coordinated with the improper detriment from the use of unadjusted cost as the basis for depreciation. The UID would not coordinate the improper benefit with the improper detriment.

E. *Some Economic Effects of Trading in a Realization System.*

An unwanted but unavoidable consequence of an ideal realization system is a tax bias in favor of investments that produce economic income in the form of unrealized appreciation. The UID substantially increases this bias, for it allows taxpayers who use borrowed funds to purchase appreciating assets to deduct their interest payments when made, rather than when they realize the income those payments helped generate. This mismatch of the timing of deductions and income makes it economically attractive for taxpayers to invest in appreciating assets even when the expected return on those assets is less than the projected interest payments.[92] The *Knetsch* case illustrates the tax shel-

---

91. For nondepreciable assets, the deductibility of the interest payments would be postponed until the time that the gain on the borrower's "cancellation of indebtedness" income is realized, thereby eliminating the timing advantage otherwise resulting from inflation.

92. Assume, for example, that *T*, a taxpayer in the 50% tax bracket, purchases vacant land with $1,000 of borrowed funds. Assume also that the land yields an annual deferred gain of $90 and that *T* takes annual interest deductions of $100. After six years, *T* would have a real loss of $60 on the transaction. Under a UID, however, *T* would have received annual tax reductions of $50 with a discounted value of $240 (assuming a 10% discount rate). That benefit would be offset in part by the tax on the nominal income in year five of $400, which would have a discounted value of $137. The net tax benefit of $103 would more than offset the real loss of $60.

ter opportunities created by such a mismatch.[93] The proposed tracing rules would eliminate the mismatch, and thereby prevent the economic waste that the UID stimulates.

Tracing also tends to reduce the bias in favor of borrowing over drawing down assets which results from the combination of a UID and a realization rule. A realization system, regardless of its treatment of interest, encourages taxpayers holding appreciated assets to finance their purchases by borrowing rather than by disposing of their appreciated assets, because disposing of such assets triggers the realization of gain and borrowing historically does not.[94] By reducing the effective cost of borrowing below the market rate of interest, a UID increases the bias against disposing of appreciated assets and introduces a new bias against disposing of unappreciated assets.[95]

The bias against drawing down assets resulting from a UID has undesirable economic consequences for two reasons. First, by inducing taxpayers to continue to hold assets they would sell in a world without taxes, the bias arguably reduces the efficiency of the market as an allocation device in some instances. The effect is especially critical when investment in productive resources is distorted.[96] In addition, by in effect subsidizing taxpayers who borrow for consumption purposes, the bias tends to favor consumption over investment, an undesirable outcome whenever total societal investment is inadequate.

During inflationary periods the economic gains to society from tracing will increase substantially. By permitting taxpayers a current deduction on the portion of their interest payments that represents prepayment of principal, the UID gives taxpayers a tax incentive to spend money, especially on consumption goods, consumer durables, and assets whose yield comes in the form of capital appreciation. The tax

---

93. See notes 77-79 *supra* and accompanying text.

94. See Popkin, *supra* note 63, for a challenge to that traditional treatment of borrowing.

95. Ironically, commentators favoring a UID would make neutrality between borrowing and drawing down assets the decisive issue in the choice between a UID and a tracing system. See note 11 *supra*.

96. The tax bias against drawing down appreciated assets created by a realization rule probably is benign in some instances, although economists typically argue to the contrary. For example, society has little or nothing at stake when the potential tax on unrealized gains discourages taxpayers from shuffling their stock portfolios, because the identity of the owner of the stock of a publicly traded corporation has no obvious effect on the net income produced by that corporation.

To the extent that the tax cost of realizing gains mitigates the tendency of a realization system to stimulate overinvestment in assets producing unrealized income, it adds to the efficiency of the economy. *See* McIntyre, "*How Serious a Problem is Capital Gains Lock-in?*," 12 TAX NOTES 1492 (1981). The tax bias produced by a UID, however, is neither benign nor helpful, because it stimulates consumption, not investment, and increases the attractiveness of investing in assets producing unrealized gains without reducing the tax disincentive against disposing of profitable investment assets.

incentive for such purchases tends to exacerbate inflation, both by stimulating an already overstimulated demand and by reducing the effectiveness of higher interest rates as an inflation control mechanism. In contrast, tracing would prevent taxpayers from getting a current deduction for interest on loans that financed such purchases. It would thereby eliminate the undesirable effects of the UID.

IV. THE IMPORTANCE OF TRACING IN TAX SYSTEMS THAT TAX ACCORDING TO INCOME SOURCE

Source distinctions are endemic in all real world tax systems, despite the Haig/Simons admonition against them. Although the types of source distinctions vary considerably among national tax systems, all governments provide for special treatment of capital gains,[97] imputed income from home ownership,[98] and the foreign income of their nationals.[99] The United States, for example, provides preferential treatment for capital gains,[100] an exemption for imputed income from home ownership,[101] and a tax credit for taxes paid to foreign governments on foreign source income.[102] The merits of these source distinctions are beyond the scope of this article.[103] Whatever their merits, they should be limited to net income from the favored sources, rather than gross income. The tracing rules set forth in Section III would play an indispensable role in confining source preferences to net income.

A. *Capital Gains*.

All existing tax systems, except those that exempt capital gains entirely, defer the taxation of capital appreciation income until that in-

---

97. For a general discussion of alternative treatments of capital gains, see R. GOODE, *supra* note 6, at 176-86.
98. For a survey of national attempts to tax imputed income from home ownership, see Merz. *Foreign Income Tax Treatment of the Imputed Rental Value of Owner-Occupied Housing: Synopsis and Commentary*, 30 NAT'L TAX J. 435 (1977) (reporting that 42 countries make some attempt at taxing the imputed rental value of personal residences).
99. For a general discussion of alternative methods of taxing foreign income, see UNITED NATIONS, DEPARTMENT OF ECONOMIC AND SOCIAL AFFAIRS, TAX TREATIES BETWEEN DEVELOPED AND DEVELOPING COUNTRIES 39-44, U.N. Doc. 57/ECA/110 (1969) [hereinafter cited as TAX TREATIES].
100. I.R.C. § 1202 (excluding 60% of net gains from income).
101. No tax code provision established this exemption. Rather, the imputed income has been excluded from the tax base through custom and administrative inaction. At one time the exclusion was justified on the constitutional ground that imputed income was not realized for purposes of the sixteenth amendment. *See, e.g.*, Helvering v. Independent Life Ins. Co., 292 U.S. 371, 379 (1934) (dicta).
102. I.R.C. §§ 901-908.
103. A tax system must necessarily administer its tax on foreign income and imputed income differently, even if it decides to impose uniform burdens on such income.

come has been realized.[104] Most systems then tax the realized capital gains at either a reduced rate or, equivalently, exempt a portion of the gains from the income base.[105] In combination with the UID, these preferences create dramatic tax shelter opportunities for borrowers, as the following example illustrates.

Consider T, a taxpayer in the 50% tax bracket, who purchases an appreciating asset with $1,000 of borrowed money. Assume that over a three-year period the asset appreciates at a 10% annual rate to $1,331, and that T then sells the asset for that amount. Assume also that T pays annual interest of $100 on his loan. T therefore realizes gross income of $331 on the purchase and sale of the asset, and has paid total interest of $300. Under the proposed tracing rules he realizes net income of $31 in the third year from the whole transaction. Assuming a preferential capital gains rate of 20%, he will pay $6.20 in tax on his gain in that year.

In contrast, under a UID system, T's capital gain would have been $331, resulting in a tax of $66.20. He also would have taken annual interest deductions of $100 against his ordinary income, for a total tax savings of $150.[106] The net tax on the whole transaction would have been negative $83.80. In addition, because his interest payments were deductible before his capital gains were realized, he will enjoy a cash flow advantage as well.[107]

The above example may understate the tax benefits of the UID. Higher interest rates, higher tax rates on ordinary income, longer holding periods, and lower capital gains rates all magnify those benefits. In effect, a UID creates a negative income tax for high bracket taxpayers who borrow to finance the purchase of appreciating assets.[108] No tax system should intend such a result.

---

104. At one time Canada considered accrual taxation of gains on publicly traded securities. *See* Shoup, *The White Paper: Accrual Accounting for Capital Gains and Losses*, 18 CANADIAN TAX J. 96 (1970).

105. The United States once did both. With progressive rates, the relationship between a preferential rate and a partial exemption will not be the same for all taxpayers. *See* Wetzler, *Capital Gains and Losses*, in COMPREHENSIVE INCOME TAXATION 115 (J. Pechman ed. 1977).

106. The $150 total is the sum of the deductions for three years of $100 multiplied by the 50% tax rate.

107. For an example of this deferral benefit, see note 92 *supra*.

108. *See* Halperin, *Capital Gains and Ordinary Deductions: Negative Income Tax for the Wealthy*, 12 B.C. INDUS. & COM. L. REV. 387 (1971). *See also* S. SURREY, W. WARREN, P. MCDANIEL & H. AULT, FEDERAL INCOME TAXATION: CASES AND MATERIALS 450 (Supp. 1979).

B. *Imputed Income From Home Ownership.*

Many tax analysts believe that an income tax based on Haig/Simons principles would tax as consumption the economic benefit obtained by homeowners from living rent free in their homes.[109] This economic benefit would also be taxable in the realization system described in section III, because that system determines taxable consumption according to Haig/Simons principles. Some governments have actually made half-hearted attempts to tax imputed income from home ownership.[110] The United States has never seriously considered taking that step, probably because of the obvious political and administrative obstacles.[111]

The question arises how a tax system that omits imputed income from the tax base for administrative reasons should treat interest payments on home mortgages. In the pure Haig/Simons system described in Section II, interest payments are excluded from the tax base because the payments do not enter into the valuation of the homeowner/taxpayer's assets at the end of the year and, because the payments finance the acquisition of an asset, they do not constitute a consumption expense.[112] Similarly, in the ideal realization system the taxation vel non of imputed income has no effect on the deductibility of mortgage interest. As with all interest paid on a loan financing the purchase of an asset (including a personal residence), the payments constitute an acquisition cost to be added to basis.[113]

The question therefore becomes whether it is more consistent with Haig/Simons principles simply to exclude imputed income from home ownership from the tax base or to tax the imputed income through some theoretically imperfect method. For an imperfect realization system based on Haig/Simons principles, such as that found in the United States, the answer to this "second best" question is clearly the latter.

At a minimum, such a tax system should classify personal residences as nondepreciable property, thereby denying homeowners the deductions for depreciation that arguably should have been permitted if the in-kind benefits from home ownership had been taxable under an

---

109. *See, e.g.*, R. GOODE, *supra* note 6, at 117; W. Hellmuth, *supra* note 6. For a suggestion to the contrary, see McIntyre & Oldman, *Taxation of the Family in a Comprehensive and Simplified Income Tax*, 90 HARV. L. REV. 1573 n.120 (1977).

110. See note 98 *supra*.

111. Congress considered taxing imputed income early in the history of the income tax. *See* E. SELIGMAN, THE INCOME TAX, 439, 448-49 (1911).

112. See text accompanying note 22 *supra*. These reasons for excluding home mortgage interest payments from the tax base are independent from the question of the tax treatment of imputed income.

113. See text accompanying notes 43-44 *supra*.

ideal realization system.[114] The effect of this classification would be to deny taxpayers a current deduction for home-mortgage interest.[115] As a further refinement, homeowners, regardless of whether they are mortgagors, should be required annually to reduce the basis in their homes by the amount of depreciation that would have been allowed if these in-kind benefits had been taxable, without receiving a compensating reduction of income.[116] This refinement would substantially reduce the tax advantage homeowners enjoy over renters.[117]

For an otherwise pure Haig/Simons system that omits the in-kind benefits of home ownership from the tax base, the "second best" question is more complex. As a practical matter, only two treatments of mortgage interest are worth considering. One is to continue the policy of a pure Haig/Simons system of permitting a deduction for home mortgage interest. The effect would be to exclude both the in-kind benefits of home ownership and the income sources traced to home mortgage interest from the tax base. The alternative, which this article recommends, is to tax the imputed income indirectly, at least in some situations, by denying all taxpayers the right to deduct home mortgage interest.

The choice between the two approaches turns on the ability of each to treat fairly three groups of taxpayers—homeowners with large mortgages, homeowners without a mortgage or with a relatively small mortgage, and renters—because the relative tax burden on these groups is principally affected by the choice.

Some commentators argue that the "second best" case for denying a deduction for interest traceable to home mortgages is a weak one because such a rule, in their view, is fair to renters in comparison to homeowners with large mortgages, but unfair to homeowners with large mortgages in comparison to other homeowners. Whether the fairness in the former situation outweighs the unfairness in the latter depends, they contend, on a complex "second best" calculation[118] that

---

114. I.R.C. § 167(a) now achieves this result by limiting depreciation deductions to "property used in the trade or business" or "property held for production of income."

115. See Section III.C. *supra*.

116. For a discussion of the use of basis adjustments for taxing imputed income indirectly, see Epstein, *The Consumption and Loss of Personal Property Under the Internal Revenue Code*, 23 STAN. L. REV. 454, 457-59 (1971).

117. Homeowners would still receive a timing advantage over renters because homeowners would not be taxed on their imputed income until they sold their home. Indirect taxation through basis adjustments would be inconsistent with the rollover of gains permitted under I.R.C. § 1234, and, a fortiori, the exclusion of those gains for certain taxpayers under I.R.C. § 105.

118. *See* R. MUSGRAVE & P. MUSGRAVE, *supra* note 13, at 256-58; Shoup, *Deduction of Homeowner's Mortgage Interest, Interest on Other Consumer Debt, and Property Taxes, Under the Indi-*

economists are unable to make.[119] Their position is intuitively appealing; if home mortgage interest is included in the tax base, all homeowners would enjoy an in-kind benefit from home ownership, but only those homeowners with mortgages would suffer a compensating penalty from a denial of the mortgage interest deduction. This argument is flawed, however, in much the same way the argument against treating interest like other rental payments is flawed.[120]

Consider two taxpayers, *W* and *M*, each earning an annual salary of $30,000 and each holding a $50,000 money market certificate paying interest at an annual rate of 10%. Assume that each buys a $50,000 personal residence, *W* financing his purchase by drawing down his money market certificate and *M* financing his by taking out a $50,000 home mortgage at an annual interest rate of 10%. Assume also that the houses produce in-kind annual net income of $5,000. In a pure Haig/Simons system, *W* and *M* each have a taxable income of $35,000 and would both bear the same tax burden. In a Haig/Simons system that excluded imputed income from the tax base but otherwise conformed with the proposed rules, the burdens of *W* and *M* would still be the same. *W*'s only taxable income would be his $30,000 salary. Although *M* would have a $30,000 salary plus the $5,000 income on his money market certificate, *M* would get a deduction of $5,000 for his mortgage interest payment because that interest, under the proposed tracing rules, constitutes a cost of holding the money market certificate.[121]

As an alternative example, consider two taxpayers, *A* and *G*. *A* has a salary income of $30,000 and an interest income of $5,000 from a $50,000 money market certificate. *G* has a salary income of $35,000. A pure Haig/Simons system would impose the same tax burden on *A* and *G*. Now assume that *A* and *G* each purchases a home for $50,000, *A* financing the purchase by cashing in his money market certificate and *G* taking out a $50,000 home mortgage. A Haig/Simons system that excluded imputed income from the tax base and denied homeowners a

---

vidual Income Tax: The Horizontal Equity Issue, 27 CANADIAN TAX J. 529 (1979); White & White, *supra* note 10, at 5-6.

119. For a suggested approach to this computation, see C. SHOUP, PUBLIC FINANCE 45-47 (1969).

120. White and White, for example, discuss the economic consequences of physical tracing on the one hand and a UID on the other. They do not address the consequences of the tracing system discussed in Section II. *See* White & White, *supra* note 10, at 5.

121. This tracing rule simply removes a trap for the unwary because in a Haig/Simons system that adopts a strict physical tracing rule, a tax-sophisticated *M* would finance his house purchase by drawing down his money market certificate and would then use his borrowed funds to purchase an identical certificate.

deduction for home mortgage interest would impose a greater burden on *G* than *A*, because *G* has a taxable income of $35,000 and *A* has a taxable income of only $30,000, even though both would have $30,000 to spend after the home purchase. This difference in burdens, however, does not justify the fear that denial of a deduction for home mortgage interest would favor homeowners with no mortgage or with a relatively small mortgage over other homeowners.

The above example is virtually identical to the Ant/Grasshopper example.[122] The only difference is that the consumption expense in the Ant/Grasshopper example is a vacation; in the above example it is a house. A vacation and a house are analogous because when the tax system excludes the in-kind benefits of home ownership from the tax base, the effect of the exclusion is to treat home ownership as a consumption expense—not as a cost of acquiring an income producing asset.[123] Thus the lesser burden on A is the normal consequence of an income tax that allows taxpayers to liquidate their savings without incurring tax liability on their potential income from those savings lost by the liquidation.

C. *Foreign Income and the Interest Deduction Source Rules.*

Many countries tax their nationals—corporations and individuals—on their worldwide income, but a nation's claim to exclusive tax jurisdiction stops at its borders. To avoid multiple taxation of income arising from transnational business operations, most countries acknowledge that primary tax jurisdiction over foreign source income belongs to the country in which the income was generated. This doctrine is often implemented through the mechanism of the foreign tax credit.[124] Although the rules vary, generally countries using the foreign tax credit permit their nationals to credit some or all of the income taxes paid to foreign governments.[125]

The United States tax code permits nationals to use the foreign tax credit to offset taxes otherwise due on their foreign source income. But it imposes a limitation on the credit in order to prevent taxpayers from

---

122. See text preceding note 29 *supra*.
123. Because of the problems of measuring the dollar value of the annual benefits to owners from consumer durables, consumption tax advocates have concluded that the purchase of such assets should be treated as a current consumption expense and the yields should be excluded from the base of the consumption tax. *See, e.g.*, TREASURY DEPARTMENT, BLUEPRINTS FOR BASIS TAX REFORM 121-22 (1977). The same logic applies for an income tax that generally includes consumption as a component of the tax base but does not tax the in-kind benefits from ownership of consumer durables.
124. E. OWENS, THE FOREIGN TAX CREDIT 2-3 (1961).
125. *See* TAX TREATIES, *supra* note 99, at 40-41.

using the credit to reduce their taxes on income arising in the United States.[126] To compute the limitation on the credit, nationals must multiply their tentative United States tax liability by a fraction: the numerator is their total net income from foreign sources and the denominator is their total net worldwide income.[127] In applying this formula, taxpayers obviously must distinguish between domestic source and foreign source net income.[128]

Taxpayers must know the source of their interest payments in order to reduce their gross foreign source income—defined in some detail in the United States tax code[129]—to net foreign source income. Neither the tax code nor general tax-accounting rules provides guidance to taxpayers in determining the source of their interest payments.[130] In tax accounting the question does not arise, because taxpayers are permitted to deduct their interest payments currently without establishing a link between those payments and the income they helped generate.

To fill the statutory void, the Treasury Department issued detailed source rules in early 1977[131] which link interest payments made during the taxable year with the book value of the taxpayer's assets held during that year.[132] Under the Treasury's linking formula, a taxpayer computes his interest payments allocable to foreign sources by multiplying his total interest payments for the taxable year by a fraction: the numerator is the book value of assets held by the taxpayer outside the

---

126. For an explanation of the limitation on the credit, see UNITED NATIONS, DEPARTMENT OF ECONOMIC AND SOCIAL AFFAIRS, UNITED STATES OF AMERICA: INCOME TAXATION OF PRIVATE INVESTMENTS IN DEVELOPING COUNTRIES 21-26, U.N. Doc. ST/ESA/39 (1976).

127. I.R.C. § 904. This limitation is called the "overall limitation," in that it applies to the overall income from foreign sources and is not applied on a country to country basis—the rule employed by most other countries.

128. Taxpayers must determine the source of their income in dozens of situations. Besides the limitation on the credit, the most important purpose of the source rules is in determining income of nonresident individuals and corporations subject to tax in the United States. *See, e.g.*, I.R.C. §§ 871, 881.

129. I.R.C. §§ 861-864.

130. I.R.C. § 861(b) states, in relevant part, that from the gross income items specified in § 861(a) "there shall be deducted the expenses, losses and other deductions properly apportioned or allocated thereto and a ratable part of any expenses, losses, or other deductions which cannot definitely be allocated to some item or class of gross income."

131. The regulations were issued on Jan. 6, 1977. 42 Fed. Reg. 1195 (1977). For a practitioner-oriented review of the regulations, see Fuller & Granwell, *The Allocation and Apportionment of Deductions*, 31 TAX LAW. 125 (1977). For a general introduction to the conflict over the regulations, see Kresge, *Allocation, Apportionment of Deductions to U.S. Income: Analyzing the Prop. Regs*, 40 J. TAX. 42 (1974).

132. The Treasury's source rule also contained many special rules that can only be explained as concessions to political exigencies. *See* R. McIntyre, Comments of Tax Reform Research Group on Proposed Regulations Dealing with Allocation and Apportionment of Deductions Between Domestic and Foreign Source Gross Income, Dec. 16, 1976 (unpublished comment submitted to Treasury Department).

United States and the denominator is the book value of all his assets worldwide.[133]

The following example illustrates, in a simplified setting, the consequences of the Treasury's assets formula source rule. It dramatizes the rule's deficiency by positing a situation in which none of the taxpayer's gross income arises in the country in which his assets are located. In more typical situations—when taxpayers have at least some assets in the country in which they are earning income—the results under the Treasury's rule accidentally overlap with the results from a rule that matches interest deductions with the income they helped generate.

Assume that the Transnational Bank Company, a New York corporation, borrows one million dollars at 10% interest in the United States credit market, and relends the money at 12% interest to a customer residing in Brazil. Assume further that the bank's headquarters are in New York and it has no fixed assets outside the United States. Assume finally that the bank's net income from United States operations is $400,000.[134] Under the Treasury's interest deduction source rule, the $100,000 in interest payments made by Transnational on the one million dollars reloaned in Brazil are considered a United States source deduction because all of Transnational's assets are located within the United States. Under the source rules for gross income, the $120,000 received from the Brazilian customer would be foreign source gross income.[135] Thus, Transnational would report net foreign income of $120,000 and net United States source income of $300,000.

This mismatching of deductions with gross income improperly limits the tax jurisdiction of the United States by permitting the bank to offset taxes due on its United States source income with a credit for taxes paid to a foreign government. As a further illustration, assume that Transnational pays a Brazilian withholding tax of 25% on its $120,000 Brazilian income. The United States tax code would permit Transnational to take a foreign tax credit for the taxes paid to Brazil subject to the limitation formula described above. Applying a proper interest deduction source rule, Transnational would have net income from Brazil of only $20,000—$120,000 of gross income minus the $100,000 cost of earning the income. Assuming a United States tax rate

---

133. Treas. Reg. § 1.861-8(e)(2) (1977).

134. For simplicity, the example assumes that no problems arise in reducing gross income from United States sources to net income.

135. Generally, the source of gross interest income is the place of residence of the borrower. *See* I.R.C. §§ 861(a)(1), 862.

of 50%, the limitation on the foreign tax credit would be $10,000.[136] Using the Treasury's assets formula, however, the limitation is $60,000.[137] This limitation allows the entire Brazilian withholding tax of $30,000 to be credited. The foreign tax credit, therefore, cancels out the United States tax liability on all of the Brazilian source net income and on $40,000 of the United States source income.[138]

Although the Treasury thought that its assets formula would properly link interest payments with the income they helped generate, its reasoning was faulty. The Treasury accepted the theory of some UID advocates that because loan proceeds are fungible, interest on a loan cannot be traced to purchases made with the loan proceeds. Burdened with this theory the Treasury reasoned that a cost unrelated to any particular item of income must be a cost of all past and present income, as well as all future income that has been and may be generated by expenditures made by the taxpayer.[139] This conclusion left the Treasury in a quandary, because no one can possibly know either the amount of potential gross income from a taxpayer's expenditures or the source of

---

136. [Under a proper source rule for interest deductions the limitation would be computed as follows:

Tentative U.S. Tax (50% of 420,000) = 210,000

Net World-wide Income = 420,000
Limitation (210,000 × 20,000 + 420,000) = 10,000

137. Under the Treasury's assets formula the limitation would be computed as follows:

Tentative U.S. Tax (50% of 420,000) = 210,000

Net World-wide Income = 420,000
Limitation (210,000 × 120,000 + 420,000) = 60,000[

138. Assuming U.S. net income of $400,000, the normal U.S. tax, computed at a 50% rate, would be $200,000. With the improper limitation on the credit, however, the Treasury would collect only $180,000, or $20,000 less than its due. That $20,000 tax reduction is equivalent to an exemption of $40,000 for a taxpayer in the 50% bracket.

139. Treas. Reg. § 1.861-8(e)(2)(i)-(ii) (1977) contains the collection of buzz words which passes for the theoretical foundation of the Treasury's interest deduction source rule:

> Interest—(i) *In general*. The method of allocation and apportionment for interest set forth in this paragraph (e)(2) is based on the approach that money is fungible and that interest expense is attributable to all activities and property regardless of any specific purpose for incurring an obligation on which interest is paid. This approach recognizes that all activities and property require funds and that management has a great deal of flexibility as to the source and use of funds. Normally, creditors of a taxpayer subject the money advanced to the taxpayer to the risk of the taxpayer's entire activities and look to the general credit of the taxpayer for payment of the debt. When money is borrowed for a specific purpose, such borrowing will generally free other funds for other purposes and it is reasonable under this approach to attribute part of the cost of borrowing to such other purposes. . . .
>
> (ii) *Allocation of interest*. Except as provided in subdivisions (iii) and (iv) of this subparagraph, the aggregate of deductions for interest shall be considered related to all income producing activities and properties of the taxpayer and, thus, allocable to all the gross income which the income producing activities and properties of the taxpayer generate, have generated, or could reasonably have been expected to generate.

that gross income. The Treasury was forced, therefore, to seek some measurable quantity that could serve as a proxy for both total potential gross income and the source of that potential income. It believed that the fair market value of the taxpayer's current assets would be the best available proxy.[140] But to simplify the administration of its source rule, it decided that interest payments should be allocated ratably to the book value of the taxpayer's assets.[141]

A tax code that adopts the tracing rules advocated in this article would eliminate the source of deduction problem that the Treasury Department has wrestled with unsuccessfully. These tracing rules match interest payments with the income they helped generate—the fundamental requirement for a theoretically defensible source rule. Because taxpayers would not be permitted during the current taxable year to deduct interest payments allocated to future income, the tax authorities would not have to make fanciful guesses about the source of that future income. Instead, the payments would be capitalized and would be linked in later years with the income they helped generate. The tax system's cost-recovery mechanisms would then take over to allocate the appropriate offsets. More generally, the tracing rules determine the character of interest payments, and the source rule applicable to payments of that character controls the deduction of the interest payments.[142]

V. Conclusion

This article makes three departures from prior inquiries into the nature of interest payments. First, the assumption that interest usually constitutes a current expense—what some economists call "negative income"—must be rejected.[143] Rather, one should recognize that many and probably most borrowers contract to pay interest in order to acquire income producing assets or consumer durables. Thus interest usually constitutes a capital expenditure, and its deductibility should be governed generally by the tax rules designed for such expenditures. Second, one must repudiate the fungibility fallacy: the persistent idea that the fungibility of money precludes the tracing of loan proceeds to their tax-significant use. Indeed, most loans are of the purchase-money

---

140. *See* Treas. Reg. § 1.861-8(e)(2), T.D. 7456, 1977-1 C.B. 200, *as amended by* T.D. 7749, 1981-10 I.R.B. 27.
141. Treas. Reg. § 1.861-8(e)(2), T.D. 7456, 1977-1 C.B. 200, *as amended by* T.D. 7749, 1981-10 I.R.B. 27.
142. For example, interest payments attributable to the production of inventory goods would be linked with the gross receipts earned on the sale of the inventory.
143. R. Musgrave & P. Musgrave, *supra* note 13, at 256-57.

type and are not truly fungible. More importantly, the tracing of fungible loan proceeds presents a formidable administrative problem because the tax code makes tracing a condition for deductibility in only a few, selected cases. When all loan proceeds must be traced, and tracing produces broad tax benefits, the borrower becomes anxious to demonstrate the tax-significant purpose of an interest payment. He becomes the willing ally of the tax administration in enforcing the tracing rules.

Finally, this article defends the tax advantage that savers would enjoy over those without savings in an income tax system that rejects the UID. Inherent in an income tax is an economic bias in favor of current consumption over deferred consumption, a bias exemplified by the so-called "double tax" on savings. Those who complain of the double tax generally recognize that they are arguing to replace the income tax with an entirely different type of tax such as an expenditure tax.[144] The less known corollary of the famous double tax on savings, however, is the bias in favor of financing consumption by drawing down savings rather than by borrowing, because those who draw down savings avoid the second leg of the potential double tax on those savings. Commentators who argue for eliminating that feature of an income tax by adopting the UID should realize that they are not arguing merely for a special status for interest payments; they are challenging the income tax itself.

---

144. McIntyre, *supra* note 18, at 1187.

D. PERSONAL EXPENSE DEDUCTIONS

1. CHARITABLE CONTRIBUTIONS

WILLIAM D. ANDREWS, "PERSONAL DEDUCTIONS IN AN IDEAL INCOME TAX"

86 Harvard Law Review 309 (1972), pp. 344–56.

III. THE CHARITABLE CONTRIBUTION DEDUCTION

Since 1917 a deduction has been allowed for contributions to religious, educational, and charitable organizations.[58] The deduction is subject to some rather complicated but relatively generous percentage limitations;[59] it also contains some quite complicated provisions and restrictions dealing with contributions of appreciated property and of limited interests in property.[60] Currently, the deduction is claimed on 95% of returns with itemized deductions, or 46% of all returns.[61] The aggregate amount deducted in 1970 was $12.9 billion or about 2% of total adjusted gross income.[62] The revenue cost of the deduction has been estimated at $3.475 billion per year or about 4.0% of total personal income taxes.[63]

The charitable contribution deduction is generally described as a subsidy to charitable giving and thus to the activities of qualified charitable organizations.[64] The effect of the deduction

---

[58] Act of October 3, 1917, ch. 63, tit. XII, § 1201(2), 40 Stat. 330 (now CODE § 170). For consideration of some of the problems associated with the provision of a deduction for charitable contributions, see C.H. KAHN, *supra* note 42, at 46–91; SYMPOSIUM: TAXATION AND EDUCATION (Proceedings of Special Conf. of American Alumni Council, 1966, R. Finehout ed.); TAX INSTITUTE OF AMERICA, *supra* note 3; Rabin, *Charitable Trusts and Charitable Deductions*, 41 N.Y.U.L. REV. 912 (1966); Stone, *Federal Tax Support of Charities and Other Exempt Organizations: The Need for a National Policy*, 20 U. So. CAL. 1968 TAX INST. 27; Taggart, *The Charitable Deduction*, 26 TAX L. REV. 63 (1970); Taussig, *Economic Aspects of the Personal Income Tax Treatment of Charitable Contributions*, 20 NAT'L TAX J. 1 (1967).

[59] CODE § 170(b).

[60] CODE §§ 170(a)(3), (b)(1)(D), (e), (f).

[61] 1970 STATISTICS, *supra* note 44, at 22, 40.

[62] *Id.* Charitable contributions were 2.9% of total adjusted gross income on returns with itemized deductions.

[63] TAX EXPENDITURE BUDGET — 1971, at 5; see 1973 BUDGET, *supra* note 47, at 507.

[64] *E.g.*, R. GOODE, *supra* note 3, at 169–70; TAX EXPENDITURE BUDGET — 1971, at 5; Surrey, *Federal Income Tax Reform*, *supra* note 1, at 384–85. See generally TAX INSTITUTE OF AMERICA, *supra* note 3.

has been likened to a matching gift program under which an employer makes matching gifts to charities supported by its employees. There is something peculiar, of course, about the Government spending funds with so little control over their allocation or use. Furthermore, this is an unusual matching gift program because the rate at which gifts are matched varies directly with the taxpayer's marginal tax rate bracket: wealthy taxpayers find their gifts much more generously matched than do lower bracket taxpayers. A 70% bracket taxpayer can make a $100 contribution at an after-tax cost of only $30; by way of tax reduction, therefore, the Government can be seen as contributing $70 to match the taxpayer's $30, for a matching rate of 233%. By similar computation, a 40% bracket taxpayer will find that the Government provides a matching grant of only $40 for his charitable contributions of $60, or a 66 2/3% matching rate; a 20% bracket taxpayer will find the Government's rate for matching his contributions to be only $1 for every $4 he contributes, or 25%; and one too poor to pay any income tax in any event will find the Government unwilling to make any matching grant at all. In the case of a contribution of appreciated property by a 70% bracket taxpayer, the analysis can be extended to indicate that the Government will take over the whole cost of the contribution, and even pay the taxpayer a 5% tax-free bonus to boot.[65]

Professor Bittker, however, has made several arguments for viewing the charitable contribution deduction as a legitimate refinement of the notion of taxable income. *See* SYMPOSIUM: TAXATION AND EDUCATION, *supra* note 58, at 29–31; TAX INSTITUTE OF AMERICA, *supra* note 3. *See also* C.H. KAHN, *supra* note 42, at 88–89.

Characterization of the deduction for contributions to religious organizations as a tax expenditure or subsidy has constitutional as well as policy implications. Professors Surrey and McDaniel have asserted that the deduction raises the same constitutional objections as would a program of direct government assistance in the form of matching grants, since in their view the deduction is only another way of making such grants. McDaniel, *Federal Matching Grants for Charitable Contributions: A Substitute for the Income Tax Deduction*, 27 TAX L. REV. 377, 409–11 (1972); Surrey, *Federal Income Tax Reform, supra* note 1, at 393 n.68; Surrey, *Tax Incentives, supra* note 1, at 714 & n.9; *see* Stone, *Federal Tax Support of Charities and Other Exempt Organizations, supra* note 58, at 55. If the deduction can be seen as a rational refinement in the definition of what it is we seek to tax, as is argued in this paper, then it will be easier to defend constitutionally. *Cf.* Walz v. Tax Comm'n, 397 U.S. 664 (1970) (exemption of churches from general property tax does not violate first amendment since tax exemption does not cause same involvement as direct subsidy); Bittker, *Churches, Taxes and the Constitution*, 78 YALE L.J. 1285 (1969) (discussing exemption of churches from various taxes). *But cf.* McGlotten v. Connally, 338 F. Supp. 448 (D.D.C. 1972) (concerning tax exemption for racially discriminatory fraternal order).

[65] *See* note 111 *infra*; Surrey, *Federal Income Tax Reform, supra* note 1, at 388; *cf.* Rudick & Gray, *Bounty Twice Blessed: Tax Consequences of Gifts of Property to or in Trust for Charity*, 16 TAX L. REV. 273 (1961).

But I do not believe, nor do I think most serious practical students of the subject believe, that the charitable contribution deduction is as irrational as this explanation makes it sound. To be sure, there are anomalies arising out of the allowance of a deduction for the fair market value of appreciated property without any offsetting recognition of gain.[66] But as to simple cash contributions, the charitable deduction makes more sense than tax expenditure analysis would indicate. If we want our theories to express our judgments, therefore, we should seek to give the deduction a better explanation.

As in the case of the medical expense deduction, there are substantial grounds for excluding from our definition of taxable personal consumption whatever satisfactions a taxpayer may get from making a charitable contribution. The charitable contribution deduction is quite different from the medical expense deduction since there is no reason to view the charitable contribution as offsetting some particular personal hardship like disease or injury. But there are other good reasons why a charitable contribution may rationally be excluded from the concept of taxable personal consumption. In the case of alms for the poor, for instance, the charitable contribution results in the distribution of real goods and services to persons presumably poorer and in lower marginal tax brackets than the donor. These goods and services, therefore, should not be taxed at the higher rates intended to apply to personal consumption by the donor. In the case of philanthropy more broadly defined — the support of religion, education, and the arts — benefits often do not flow exclusively or even principally to very low bracket taxpayers. But the goods and services produced do have something of the character of common goods whose enjoyment is not confined to contributors nor apportioned among contributors according to the amounts of their contributions. There are a number of reasons for defining taxable personal consumption not to include the benefit of such common goods and services. The personal consumption at which progressive personal taxation with high graduated rates should aim may well be thought to encompass only the private consumption of divisible goods and services whose consumption by one household precludes their direct enjoyment by others.

Various objections can be made to this analysis. It can be argued that the exercise of power over the distribution of goods and services is what constitutes taxable personal consumption even if that power is exercised in favor of somebody else. Or it can be argued that the pleasure or satisfaction one presumably gets from supporting philanthropic enterprises is a component of consumption. But at least this analysis and the objections to it focus on the problem of how to treat philanthropy as an intrinsic

---

[66] *See* pp. 371-72 *infra*.

issue of personal tax policy, instead of just assuming that the purpose underlying the deduction must be something outside the realm of tax policy.

It is convenient to take up first the case of alms for the poor, then philanthropy more broadly defined, and finally the special problems that arise when charitable contributions are made out of accumulated wealth rather than current earnings.

A. Alms for the Poor

Consider a taxpayer who simply contributes some of his earnings to an organization which redistributes them to or for the needy. In such a case the consumption or accumulation of real goods and services represented by the funds in question has been shifted to the recipients rather than the donor and should not be subjected to taxation at rates designed to apply to the donor's standard of living and saving. If the redistributed funds are used for ordinary consumption by the recipients, then in principle the funds should be taxed to the recipients at their rates — although in practice the recipients' total income may often fall below a taxable level. The matter is essentially one of rates. Under a graduated rate schedule the personal consumption and accumulation of well-to-do taxpayers is intended to be curtailed much more than that of the poor. Yet if a wealthy taxpayer were to be taxed at his high rate even on the income that he donated to the poor, the probable effect would be a reduction in the amount received by the donees. For all practical purposes, such a scheme would tax the consumption of the poor at the rate intended for the wealthy taxpayer. The effect of the charitable contribution is to avoid this result.

Moreover, the charitable contribution deduction operates to treat a taxpayer who redistributes his income by giving alms like other taxpayers who effect a redistribution of income directly. A businessman, for example, may pay generous wages, higher than he would have to pay in order to secure the services he needs. If he does so, within reason, we would not tax him on the additional income he could have earned by paying less. He has arranged his business in a way that diverts more income to employees and less to himself; the tax law generally will deal with the income as so redistributed.

More to the point, perhaps, a doctor might choose to spend one day a week in a clinic without charging for his services. More generally he might simply treat impecunious patients for less than the going rate. In either case he has foregone in favor of the patients whom he treats some of the personal consumption and accumulation he could have had. We do not tax the doctor on the value of his services or the excess of the value of his services over the fee he charges. We tax the doctor only on the personal consumption and accumulation he achieves by the exercise of his profession, not on what he could have achieved if he chose to maximize his personal financial gain.

Another professional man, a tax lawyer for example, may have skills that are not so directly useful to the poor as those of the doctor. If he wishes to devote part of his professional energies to the welfare of the poor, the efficient way to do it may well be to continue practicing his profession for paying clients but to turn over part of his fees for distribution among the poor or for the purchase of other services to meet their needs. The charitable contribution deduction operates to treat the tax lawyer like the doctor, by taxing him only on the amount of personal consumption and accumulation he realizes from the practice of his profession, not on what he could have realized if he had not given part of his fees away.

But this analogy between the tax lawyer who makes charitable contributions and the doctor who performs services directly for the poor suggests another that will serve to raise a number of difficulties with this analysis. If the doctor provides services free for some of his friends and relations, remote or immediate, in practice, at least, we would not seek to tax him on the value of such services. But if the tax lawyer turns over part of his fees to his friends and relations we would not allow him a deduction. Why is there any more reason to be persuaded by the analogy in the case of poor recipients than related recipients?

1. The Problem of Ordinary Gifts. — In the case of an ordinary gift between friends or relations, the donor is allowed no deduction even though he has in one sense given up the personal consumption or accumulation that the donated funds might have purchased. On the other hand, we do not tax the recipient of the gift, even though clearly his personal consumption or accumulation will be enhanced. The result is that income earned by one taxpayer and then given to another who devotes it to personal consumption or accumulation is taxed once and only once, albeit to the donor rather than the donee whose consumption and accumulation it ultimately supports. Ideally, perhaps, the tax should be on the donee rather than the donor. But it is much simpler for everyone concerned to leave ordinary interpersonal gifts out of the computation of income on both sides. And if the income tax rates of the donor are appropriate for consumption or accumulation by the donee, the result is perfectly acceptable.

What warrant is there, however, for thinking that the donor's rates are fit for the donee's consumption or accumulation? Perhaps it is assumed that interpersonal gifts occur mostly between members of the same family or between people of similar social and economic status whose income tax rates are likely to be similar. But that is not a very realistic assumption, particularly in the case of intrafamily gifts which often go from a high bracket adult to a child in a lower bracket.

A sounder explanation for our treatment of at least intrafamily gifts may rest upon the fact that consumption is largely a household rather than an individual function. In the most usual case one member of a household earns the income which supports the whole household, and the convenient way to collect a tax is to impose it on the earner individually. But the rate and exemption schedules [67] applicable to the breadwinner are designed to cover consumption and accumulation by the whole household without regard to the precise way in which consumption is distributed among household or family members and without distinctions between intrafamily transfers by way of support and transfers by way of gift. In other words, income is ultimately to be taxed at rates appropriate to the househould whose consumption it supports although those rates are expressed in terms of an individual rate schedule applied to the breadwinner.

I do not suppose the tax has been consciously designed on this premise. The more common view is that income is to be taxed to him who earns it, regardless of whose consumption it goes to support. But, again, much of what we do with the income tax can be better understood if we reinterpret it as an indirectly measured tax on personal consumption and accumulation.[68] And while people participate in the production sector on an individual basis, consumption and accumulation are largely household functions. Therefore, it is sensible to view the individual income tax on the breadwinner as an indirectly measured tax on the consumption and accumulation of the household.

On the face of it the taxation of spouses' incomes on a joint return would seem to be consistent with this interpretation, while the failure to include children's income on their parents' return would not. In fact, the case may be viewed the other way around. To be sure, if the tax is on household consumption plus accumulation, then it should be measured by total household income. But differences in sources of income may indirectly reflect differences in consumption and accumulation that should be taken into account. In particular, when a spouse or a child has his or her own earnings, there has been a sacrifice of leisure time (which in the case of a child may involve substantial educational opportunities) or services performed in kind within the household, as compared with a household in which only one person has any earnings. Reporting children's earnings on separate returns may serve to reduce aggregate tax liability in a way that takes rough indirect

---

[67] CODE §§ 1, 151.
[68] See pp. 327–30 supra.

account of this sacrifice,[69] while the joint return and split income provisions applicable to a working spouse operate inappropriately to obliterate any difference in rates between households where both husband and wife work and households where one spouse remains at home.[70]

This is not the place even to begin to explore all the implications or problems of viewing the individual income tax as an indirectly measured tax on household consumption and accumulation. The purpose of sketching that view here is only to suggest a pattern that would make it rational to treat ordinary gifts differently from charitable contributions, letting the recipient's consumption of the gift be reflected in the donor's return and taxed at his rates in the former case but not in the latter. If we interpret the difference in treatment this way, it implies that the household whose consumption is indirectly reflected on an individual's income tax return is not defined rigidly in terms of prescribed re-

---

[69] This explanation will not account for the separate taxation of children's property income. Perhaps in general children's property income is accumulated rather than consumed, and accumulation is more of an individual function and less of a household function than consumption. Or perhaps the opportunity to divert some property income to children is just an indirect step in the direction of letting aggregate household tax rates be determined by something nearer per capita rates of income and consumption and accumulation. Perhaps there simply is no adequate explanation for our treatment of children's property income. Indeed, Congress has recently concluded that such income ought to be ineligible for the low income allowance, which is a household consumption concept. *See* CODE § 141(e)(2) (added by Revenue Act of 1971, Pub. L. No. 92-178, § 301(c), 1971 U.S. CODE CONG. & AD. NEWS 577).

[70] In 1969 a lower rate schedule was adopted for unmarried taxpayers than for married taxpayers filing separately. CODE §§ 1(c), (d) (amended by Tax Reform Act of 1969, Pub. L. No. 91-172, § 803, 83 Stat. 678). The consequence is that two unmarried persons with approximately equal individual incomes will have a lower total tax burden than a married couple with the same total income. The discussion in the text suggests that what justifies the reduced rate is the fact that both work, not that they are unmarried. It may be the case that unmarried persons are more likely all to hold jobs, while one member of a married couple frequently provides services at home in kind. But that pattern is not universal, and there is no reason for the tax law to be written to try to make it so. In particular, the tax on two married persons who both have earnings should be no higher than on two unmarried persons with the same income.

Similarly, the low income allowance, as enacted in 1969, and the maximum percentage standard deduction are available only once per couple among the married, but once per person among the unmarried. CODE §§ 141(b), (c), (d) (amended by Tax Reform Act of 1969, Pub. L. No. 91-172, § 802, 83 Stat. 676). It would be better if they were made available once for each employed individual whether married or not.

The child care allowance, made much more generous in 1971, does reflect the loss of child care services performed in kind at home when the last available adult goes to work. CODE § 214 (amended by Revenue Act of 1971, Pub. L. No. 92-178, § 210, 1971 U.S. CODE CONG. & AD. NEWS 574). But care for children under 15, and for other dependents incapable of caring for themselves, is not the only kind of valuable service a housewife quits when she takes a job outside her home.

lationships. Instead, it is more flexibly conceived as embracing all his friends and relations to whatever extent he may in fact choose to support or entertain them at his expense.[71] Within the extended household, so conceived, it is likely that tax rates may be more or less comparable, except as lower marginal rate brackets reflect leisure time that justifies at least a somewhat higher aggregate rate. In any event, the complexity and variety of the transfers of consumption benefits among persons so related is such that any attempt to get all benefits on the individual returns of those who enjoy them would be hopeless. Consumption is in large part a shared activity among friends and relations.

Against this background the charitable contribution deduction may be seen as eliminating from a taxpayer's return only that consumption which he shifts beyond the confines of his own household, even as rather broadly and flexibly conceived. It thus provides an escape from the convenient rule, which taxes the donor on the consumption represented by his gifts, in those cases where the rate differential, and consequently the relative hardship arising from application of the convenient rule, is likely to be most significant and where an organization exists for the collection and disbursement of funds which makes it practical to establish and audit the amount of redistribution from donor to recipients. This interpretation not only suggests what some of the definitional problems surrounding charitable contributions may be,[72] but also suggests, perhaps serendipitously, why the deduction is defined in terms of identity of a qualified donee organization, instead of directly in terms of the use to which funds are put.[73]

---

[71] Compare in this respect the Carter Commission Proposals in Canada under which household would have been defined, for the purpose of exempting donative transfers, rather narrowly and precisely in terms of prescribed ages and relationships. Upon reaching majority a child would have been considered to be leaving his parents' household and would have been taxable on whatever property he took with him at that point in time. *See* 1 REPORT OF THE ROYAL COMMISSION ON TAXATION 19 (1967); 3 *id.* at 130–39. In 1969 the Government rejected the Commission's proposals for taxing the family as a single unit. *See* E.J. BENSON, PROPOSALS FOR TAX REFORM 14–15 (1969) (Ministry of Finance White Paper).

[72] *See, e.g.*, Havemeyer v. Commissioner, 98 F.2d 706, 707 (2d Cir. 1938) (deduction allowed for contributions to an association which made distributions to persons of whom the court said: "They were mainly, though not entirely, old family retainers and all were needy and worthy.").

[73] Having cited Henry Simons in connection with so much of this argument, I must concede the differences between us at this point. He argued that gifts and inheritances ideally should be included in income of the recipient since they support consumption or accumulation, though he sometimes acknowledged that practical considerations would prevent inclusion of every small gift in kind and might require a separate rate schedule and system of cumulation for such items. Furthermore, he recognized but rejected the possible corollary argument that the

2. *The Problem of Imputed Income.* — Comparing the doctor with the tax lawyer, however, raises another set of objections. We do not tax the doctor on services performed free, it may be said, because no income is considered to be realized unless something is received in exchange for the performance of services. That reason has no application to the tax lawyer who is paid for his services, whatever he may subsequently do with the fees. It can be argued, accordingly, that our failure to tax the doctor on the performance of uncompensated services, whether for the poor or for his friends and relations, is only an example of favored treatment which we extend to imputed income generally.

But that line of argument admits the criterion of realization into our concept of an ideal personal tax where it does not belong. It is true that we do not generally tax imputed income from services performed within the household, but that fact represents a concession to practical considerations rather than any underlying principle of fair distribution of tax burdens. There is no way to prove it logically, but I think the exemption of imputed income from services performed outside the home in a charitable enterprise is something we feel to be right in principle, not merely for reasons of convenience. If that judgment is correct, then there is a policy basis for extending the same treatment to the tax lawyer who contributes a portion of his income to the poor.

There frequently are limitations that make the nontaxation of imputed income from services performed within the household acceptable in practice even if wrong in principle, but which do not apply to the performance of services outside the household. The goods or services one can produce for use within his own household are limited in value because the processes employed cannot

---

donor should get a deduction since his consumption and accumulation are reduced by the amount of his gift. PERSONAL INCOME TAXATION 56–58, 125–47, 211–12. Simons' proposal to include gifts in income, without any deduction for the donor, has always seemed to me the weakest part of his program. In his later work Simons himself appears to have backed off from his proposal that gifts be included in income as such, advocating instead "attention to the possibility of replacing the existing Estates and Gift Taxes by a more sensible form of tax *on beneficiaries* of donative transfers." FEDERAL TAX REFORM, *supra* note 25, at 37 (emphasis in original).

Simons seems, moreover, to have disapproved of the charitable contribution deduction. He offered arguments against selective deductibility of worthy donations on the grounds that they all represent personal consumption since they are not for the sake of making money, and that power is the object of the tax. PERSONAL INCOME TAXATION 139–41. But, strangely, he included no explicit denunciation of the existing provision for deducting charitable contributions, and abolition of the deduction did not appear as part of his program. *Id.* at 205–20. His central argument, again, was against distinctions in treatment on account of differences in sources of gains available for consumption or accumulation.

be brought to bear upon a large enough volume of production to generate the kind of high pay that the performance of specialized services will command in an exchange economy. A doctor performing services within his own household, for example, will not usually find enough sickness to be able to produce a large volume of medical services, relatively speaking, beyond the reach of the tax law.[74] Similarly, while an entertainer may earn large fees for performing before large audiences, the imputed income that escapes tax when he performs at home for his family is very limited if measured by the relative size of his audience. There is thus imposed on the enjoyment of imputed income from services within the home a kind of built-in limit that makes it practically acceptable to omit such services from the computation of taxable income, even if in principle they should be included.

But there is no such built-in limitation with respect to the performance of services in kind for a charity. A doctor may indeed perform a significant percentage of his professional services for less than a full fee on a charitable basis. Or an entertainer may perform for charity before a large audience. If we think it is right not to tax the doctor or entertainer on these services,[75] which do not have the built-in value limitation, a more basic principle must underlie that exemption than the concession to practicality which operates in the case of imputed income from the performance of services within the household. And in that event the principle should be extended to the tax lawyer as well.

In effect, with respect to the performance of services for the ultimate objective of enhancing one's private standard of living, the test of taxability is participation in the exchange economy. The doctor or the tax lawyer can perform services within the

---

[74] A person who devotes full time to domestic chores in his own home may, of course, produce just as much free of tax as he could have earned and been taxed on by doing the same work in someone else's household. But domestic service is a relatively low paying form of work, partly because it does not seem to be as amenable to the economies of specialization as other occupations. Moreover, the performance of domestic services in kind within the household by one adult member of a family is so widespread that the practical thing may be to take it as the norm, and then to try to make some compensating allowance for families without an unemployed adult to keep the house in order. The deduction for child care represents a step in that direction. We might well go further. See note 70 *supra*.

[75] A problem may arise in the case of a benefit performance when an entertainer performs for paying patrons under arrangements that provide for the payments to go to charity. If the entertainer has not used up his available charitable contribution limit, it will not generally matter whether income is imputed to him because if it is there will be an offsetting charitable contribution deduction. When the deduction limit is reached, however, it will make a difference. *But cf.* CODE § 114.

household free of tax; but as soon as either performs services outside the household in exchange for something to be consumed within the household, he will be taxed. However, when the ultimate objective is not to support consumption within the household, either directly or through exchange, then the rationale for limiting the performance of taxfree services to those occurring within the household disappears. The amount of medical services the doctor can perform on a charitable basis will not be practically limited by the amount of sickness within his own household, but the exclusion of the value of these services from taxable income can be justifed since they do not support the doctor's aggregate personal consumption or accumulation. There is no reason why the tax lawyer should not be equally free to bestow the benefit of his professional skills upon the poor, free of income tax at his rates, by selling his services and turning over the proceeds.

3. *Consumption as Power.* — A more general argument against a deduction for almsgiving is that the tax should be apportioned on taxpayers' power to consume, however that power may be exercised. The income tax is supposed to be a tax based on ability to pay, not on what one does with that ability. To say that the ultimate object of the tax is consumption plus accumulation does not foreclose that argument, because consumption can be construed to embrace any exercise of power over the disposition of consumer goods and services even if that exercise does operate to benefit others.[76]

The difficulty with defining taxable consumption as the exercise of power over the disposition of goods and services is that we cannot, and probably would not want to, carry such an approach very far. Only a part of the power that people exercise over the allocation and distribution of economic resources is represented by the expenditure of money. The direct influence of people participating in political and economic affairs cannot practically be subjected to income taxation.[77] Moreover, we probably would not want to tax the exercise of power as such because the effect would be to channel some of the energies of the people involved away from these activities toward earning the funds with which to pay the taxes.

We do not tax people who exercise power through direct par-

---

[76] "Personal income connotes, broadly, the exercise of control over the use of society's scarce resources." PERSONAL INCOME TAXATION 49. *But compare id.* at 49–50 ("[c]onsumption as a quantity denotes the value of rights exercised in a certain way (in destruction of economic goods)") *with id.* at 57 ("If it is not more pleasant to give than to receive, one may still hesitate to assert that giving is not a form of consumption for the giver.").

[77] This argument is more fully developed at pp. 363–64 *infra.*

ticipation on what they could have earned if they had devoted their full energies to earning money. By analogy, it is reasonable not to tax others on what they have earned and could have kept for their own use if they choose not to keep it. If we take a broad view of how the tax falls on people who lead different kinds of lives, of how we intend it to fall, and of how it is practical to make it fall, it is not according to their powers that we should tax people but according to their standards of living and personal saving. And that is very much a matter of what they have chosen to do with their powers.

It will be answered that the tax is not on power generally, but on a power that could have been exercised for the taxpayer's private benefit, whether it was so exercised or not. But even that power cannot be measured with any accuracy by realized income. The doctor who works for a clinic is similarly exercising a power which he could have used to secure a higher level of personal consumption and accumulation for himself. So too is the businessman who pays generous wages, or the clergyman or teacher who could have earned more money at another calling. It would be impractical and undesirable to try to tax all such people on what they might have earned if they had set their minds to the business of earning money.

4. *The Pleasure of Giving.* — Finally, there is a kind of argument against the allowance of a deduction for alms to the poor which is based not on power but on pleasure. The argument is that one who makes a charitable contribution must get some pleasure or satisfaction from his act which he considers equal to what he could have gotten from some other use of his funds.[78]

---

[78] For some rudimentary speculation about the character of this pleasure or satisfaction see SYMPOSIUM: TAXATION AND EDUCATION, *supra* note 58, at 45–46 (Brazer: "If we assume that the contributor to education realizes a continuing flow of satisfaction from having made his contribution, it is not stretching matters too far to regard his gifts as investments which produce a non-pecuniary, non-taxable yield. They are, in this sense, similar to investments in art objects."); *id.* at 51 (Harriss: "I am more inclined to think that the benefits from contributions, at least the kinds many of us make, are satisfactions which are less lasting, more fleeting, than one gets from the purchase of an art object. A gift of this type is not really an investment for many of us so much as consumption."); *id.* at 60 (White: "Rather, Brazer's assumption that the contributor derives a glow of satisfaction from his contribution seems to me more appropriate."); *id.* at 61 (White, in a slightly different context: "I would like to dwell a little bit further on this relationship between the before and after tax giving, since it seems to me important and some source of confusion at least to me in all of the discussion that we have had so far . . . . The gratification of the pure desire to give seems to me to be fulfilled by an allocation of funds that otherwise would be available to provide utility through consumption or wealth accumulation, which would be after tax income, not before tax.").

Some wealthy people dress for dinner; some ride to hounds; others make substantial charitable contributions. *Chacun à son goût.* Whatever a man chooses to do with his money should be classed as personal consumption for him.

But there is a difference between dinner clothes and charitable contributions. Wearing dinner dress represents some diversion of economic resources, real goods and services, *away from* the satisfaction of other people's needs. The effect of almsgiving, on the other hand, is to cause real economic resources to be directed *toward* the satisfaction of the needs of the poor. Thus, the imposition of a tax on this latter kind of expenditure will ultimately fall on the poor in a sense that it will not in the case of dinner dress. The satisfaction one gets from making a charitable contribution is in this respect like a great many of the rest of life's best satisfactions which people can enjoy without diverting economic resources away from other people and which we do not try to take into account in assessing income taxes.

Taxable consumption in the end does not and cannot provide an accurate reflection of either power or pleasure. It is, rather, simply the accumulation or utilization of economic resources, measured at market value, for private consumption within the taxpayer's household. That definition is consistent with the practical purpose of the tax — to divert some economic resources to public uses in a manner that will reduce disparities in standards of living and saving. One might wish also to reduce inequalities in power or pleasure more generally, but those wishes are beyond what it is practical to expect an income tax to accomplish.

These speculations seem to me to confirm the desirability of trying to define taxable income in terms of material benefits to the recipient rather than nonmaterial satisfactions to the donor.

2. MEDICAL EXPENSES

ALAN L. FELD, "ABORTION TO AGING: PROBLEMS OF DEFINITION IN THE MEDICAL EXPENSE TAX DEDUCTION"

58 Boston University Law Review 165 (1978), pp. 166-7, 177-81, 193-6.

The medical expense deduction entered the income tax scheme in 1942, in the course of the transition of the federal income tax from essentially a levy on the wealthy to a popular-based tax. The limited comment in the committee report states that the deduction was designed to mitigate the heavy burden of wartime taxation when income was used for health care and to maintain a "high level of public health and morale."[4] In other words, Congress found it inappropriate to tax at high rates income applied by the taxpayer to medical expenses.

Some commentators see the medical expense deduction as an appropriate adjustment in determining the taxpayer's ability to pay income tax.[5] In this view, medical expenditures differ radically from a taxpayer's other personal consumption choices and should not be taxed similarly:

> What distinguishes medical expenses from other personal expenses at bottom is a sense that large differences in their magnitude between people in otherwise similar circumstances are apt to reflect differences in need rather than choices among gratifications.[6]

Others, however, criticize the medical expense deduction as a poorly framed tax subsidy which, like any deduction or other tax expenditure, is far more valuable to high-bracket than low-bracket taxpayers and carries no benefit for those too poor to fall within the tax system.[7] The revenue cost of the deduction was estimated to be in excess of $2 billion in 1977.[8]

Under both views, questions of line drawing arise. We might suppose that so fundamental a question as whether the deduction is regarded as an adjustment to income reflecting actual ability to pay or as a subsidy

---

[4] S. Rep. No. 1631, 77th Cong., 2d Sess. 6 (1942). *See also* Sierk, The Medical-Expense Deduction—Past, Present and Future, 17 Mercer L. Rev. 381, 382 (1966).

[5] *See* Andrews, Personal Deductions in an Ideal Income Tax, 86 Harv. L. Rev. 309 (1972).

[6] *Id.* at 336.

[7] *See* Surrey, Tax Incentives as a Device for Implementing Government Policy: A Comparison with Direct Government Expenditures, 83 Harv. L. Rev. 705, 720 (1970). In noting the inequities inherent in a deduction as opposed to a direct subsidy, Professor Surrey remarked:

> What HEW Secretary would propose a medical assistance program for the aged that cost $200 million, and under which $90 million would go to persons with incomes over $50,000, and only $8 million to persons with incomes under $5,000? The tax proposal to remove the 3% floor under the medical expense deductions of persons over 65 [Tax Reform Bill of 1969, H.R. 13,270, 91st Cong., 1st Sess. § 914] would have had just that effect.

Id. at 722.

[8] Staff of Joint Comm. on Internal Revenue Taxation, 95th Cong., 1st Sess., Estimates of Federal Tax Expenditures 9 (Comm. Print 1977).

should affect resolution of definitional problems. But these divergences in view are directed to the wisdom of including the deduction in the statute. Once the legislative decision has been made, it becomes necessary under both views to reconcile the deduction with the general prohibition against the deduction of personal expenditures.[9] All agree that it would be wrong to extend the medical deduction to expenditures that enhance the taxpayer's well-being rather than restore it after a mishap. If the deduction serves as a subsidy, the statute should be construed to address medical emergencies, not personal frolics. If, on the other hand, the deduction is viewed as an adjustment necessary to assess an individual's true income— that amount available for consumption and accumulation—then the statute should be narrowly construed to cover only those expenditures dictated by medical need.

* * *

IV. Food, Drink and Travel

A taxpayer on a special diet may not deduct its cost to the extent that it merely equals usual food expenses.[73] But if a physician prescribes the

---

[9] *See* I.R.C. § 262.

[73] *See, e.g.,* Newman v. United States, 68-1 U.S. Tax Cas. ¶ 9411 (W.D. Ark. 1968); J. Willard Harris, 46 T.C. 672 (1966); Doris V. Clark, 29 T.C. 196, 200 (1957); George H. Collins, 24 T.C.M. (CCH) 1190 (1965).

special diet and the taxpayer can establish the excess cost of the special diet over a normal diet, he may deduct the excess; indeed, the taxpayer may deduct the expense of a nip of brandy prescribed by a physician to relieve angina pains.[74] Although neither the statute nor the regulations condition deduction of these expenses on a physician's supervision, this requirement, supplied by cases and rulings, serves the salutary function of distinguishing special diets dictated by medical needs from those that proceed from more idiosyncratic motives. When taxpayers who were allergists established that they suffered severe adverse physical reactions from artificial chemical additives in foods, the Tax Court allowed them to deduct the added cost of natural foods.[75] Absent medical evidence of physical reaction, however, organic foods and vitamins are nondeductible expenses even if the taxpayer believes them to be good for health.[76] If the excess cost of the special diet constitutes medical care, costs of transportation to obtain such care have been held to be deductible as well. Thus, in holding deductible the additional cost of preparing salt-free meals in restaurants, the Tax Court also allowed a deduction for the amount paid by the taxpayer for taxicabs to those restaurants.[77]

The cases apply a two-pronged test, referred to earlier as a "but for" test. Under this standard, in order for a taxpayer to justify deduction of an expense that serves both medical and other personal functions, he must establish that the expenditure was necessary to treatment and would not otherwise have been incurred.[78] Rather than requiring the trier of fact to engage in the difficult and sometimes impossible task of determining which of two motives predominated, this test identifies the marginal cost occasioned by the medical need and grants a deduction for it. In addition to providing a more administrable rule than a primary motive test, the but-for test conforms to the apparent rationale of section 213, to permit deduction for expenses that are extraordinary in nature.

---

[74] Rev. Rul. 55-261, 1955-1 C.B. 307, 312 (cautioning that the alcohol cannot be "a substitute for . . . beverage normally consumed by [taxpayer]").

[75] Theron G. Randolph, 67 T.C. 481 (1976). The taxpayers had carefully documented the additional cost, so that the court did not have to contend with questions of proving the amounts expended to treat the allergy. *Id.* at 486-87.

[76] Princess E. L. Lingham, 36 T.C.M. (CCH) 649, 654 (1977) (self-imposed organic diet did not have direct or proximate relationship to the diagnosis, treatment, or prevention of disease).

[77] Leo R. Cohn, 38 T.C. 387, 391 (1962), *nonacq.* 1963-1 C.B. 5, *acq. on other issues*, 1963-1 C.B. 4. *But cf.* Cohn v. United States, 240 F. Supp. 786 (N.D. Ind. 1965) (deduction not allowed for the same taxpayer in a later year for the extra cost of an accommodation with kitchen facilities, in which his wife could prepare salt-free meals, over usual lodging). The earlier *Cohn* case exemplifies the difficulty in limiting the scope of the deduction without requiring the taxpayer to mitigate his expenses. *See* text accompanying notes 139-40 *infra.* The taxpayer may deduct the cost of taxicabs to a restaurant because he cannot obtain salt-free meals at his hotel, without any showing that this was the least expensive way to do so. This approach makes administration of the deduction easier at the expense of some claims that arguably should be denied.

[78] Joel H. Jacobs, 62 T.C. 813, 819 (1974).

One important set of distinctions between medical care and personal recreation involves expenditures for food and lodging incidental to travel for medical purposes. The 1939 Code included as medical care the cost of travel to obtain medical care.[79] As used elsewhere in the Code, travel expenses include food and lodging,[80] and such expenses were deductible as medical care. Wealthy taxpayers who traveled long distances to resort areas to recuperate from operations, or for other medically related reasons, could therefore deduct the full cost of wintering in Florida and the like. To prevent this practice, the 1954 Code substituted the narrower word "transportation" for "travel." Responding to the legislative history,[81] the regulations ruled out deduction of the cost of food and lodging incident to the travel.[82] In *Commissioner v. Bilder*,[83] the Supreme Court upheld this reading of the statute. A heart specialist had advised the taxpayer, a forty-three-year-old attorney with a history of heart ailments, to spend his winters in a warm climate. He rented an apartment in Florida, which he occupied with his family. The taxpayer deducted both the cost of transportation to Florida and the rent for the apartment. Finding that the trip was taken for treatment of a specific illness, and not to enjoy a vacation, the Tax Court allowed deduction of the plane fare and a portion of the rent attributable to the taxpayer's own living expense.[84] The Third Circuit extended deductibility to the full amount of the rent.[85] But the Supreme Court reversed and disallowed all of the claimed rent deduction, relying heavily on the legislative history to support its reading of the statute.[86]

The same legislative history was relied upon to *allow* deduction of food and lodging expenses in *Montgomery v. Commissioner*.[87] The taxpayers in *Montgomery* sought to deduct expenses for motel rooms and restaurant meals incurred in traveling between their home and the Mayo Clinic. The Sixth Circuit affirmed the Tax Court in allowing the deduction, reading the 1954 amendment as eliminating only deductions for expenses incidental to "resort area" medication but retaining deductions for food and lodging en route to medical care.[88] The Seventh Circuit went one step further, extending deductibility to a special post-operative care situation.

---

[79] Int. Rev. Code of 1939, § 23(x), 56 Stat. 825-26 (1942).
[80] *See* I.R.C. § 162(a)(2).
[81] *See* H.R. Rep. No. 1337, 83d Cong., 2d Sess. app. 60 (1954), *reprinted in* [1954] U.S. Code Cong. & Ad. News 4017, 4197; S. Rep. No. 1622, 83d Cong., 2d Sess. 219-20 (1954), *reprinted in* [1954] U.S. Code Cong. & Ad. News 4021, 4856.
[82] Treas. Reg. § 1.213-1(e)(1)(iv) (1957).
[83] 369 U.S. 499 (1962).
[84] 33 T.C. 155 (1959).
[85] 289 F.2d 291 (3d Cir. 1961).
[86] 369 U.S. at 502-03 (citing S. Rep. No. 1622, 83d Cong., 2d Sess. 219-20 (1954); H.R. Rep. No. 1337, 83d Cong., 2d Sess. app. 60 (1954)). Both committee reports discuss the hypothetical case of a patient traveling to Florida to alleviate chronic ailments; they concluded that transportation expenses should be deductible, but not living expenses while in Florida.
[87] 51 T.C. 410, 413-14 (1968), *aff'd*, 428 F.2d 243 (6th Cir. 1970).
[88] 428 F.2d 243, 245-46 (6th Cir. 1970).

In *Kelly v. Commissioner*,[89] the taxpayer had undergone surgery in New York after suffering an appendicitis attack while there on a business trip. His hospital discharged him shortly after the operation because of a room shortage, but his physician advised him not to return home immediately. The taxpayer rented a hotel room until his doctor decided he was strong enough to leave New York. The taxpayer deducted the cost of lodging and food at the hotel. The Commissioner disallowed the deduction under section 1.213-1(e)(1)(v) of the regulations, which allows the deduction of food and lodging only for inpatient hospital care and for care in an institution other than a hospital.[90] In effect, the Seventh Circuit treated the hotel room as an "institution" within the regulations because it was necessary to the taxpayer's recovery.[91]

The 1954 amendment, the regulation and *Bilder* reflect a general concern to prevent deduction of expenses for personal enjoyment in the guise of medical expenses—here, vacations in generally attractive surroundings. In both *Montgomery* and *Kelly*, the element of personal enjoyment as an admixture to the medical care was minimal, and in that respect the result is sound. Applying the "but for" test, it is clear the expenses both were related to treatment and would not have been incurred without medical reasons. The difficulty is in limiting deductibility to such cases, while disallowing expenses motivated both by medical care and personal consumption elements. The distinction is frequently easy to make. Thus, in Revenue Ruling 76-79,[92] the taxpayer, on his doctor's advice, took a cruise with a group of physicians. While on the cruise ship, the physicians reviewed the patient's medical records, performed certain tests on him and reported the progress of his condition to his home physician. In addition, they provided seminars on the taxpayer's physical condition and supervised his dietary program. The taxpayer could have obtained similar medical services in his home town. The ruling disallowed all the expenses except those directly related to examination of the medical records, performance of tests and transmission of the results to the patient's personal physician.[93] A case for deductibility would have been made if the services had been unique and not otherwise obtainable. But sometimes the distinc-

---

[89] 440 F.2d 307 (7th Cir. 1971).

[90] The other requirement for complete deductibility under Treas. Reg. § 1.213-1(e)(1)(v)(a) (1957)—that medical care be a principal reason for the institutionalization—clearly was met.

[91] *But see* Loren Wilks, 27 T.C.M. (CCH) 1086 (1968) (denying deduction for lodging during outpatient treatment for terminal cancer). The decision in *Kelly* makes sense to the extent that the services received from the hotel merely served as a substitute for the services the taxpayer would have received in the hospital had there been room. The Seventh Circuit made no effort to account for the difference, if any, between hospital and hotel costs.

[92] 1976-1 C.B. 70.

[93] The ruling stated that the seminars promoted only the taxpayer's general well-being and thus were nondeductible. *Id.* Compare the disallowance under section 162 of professional education expenses in a vacation setting. Reuben B. Hoover, 35 T.C. 566 (1961) (allowing deduction of only that portion of the expense of a lecture cruise that the court estimated to equal the cost of attending lectures at a university).

tion between medical and personal expense is not so clear. In Revenue Ruling 75-187,[94] the taxpayers underwent treatment for a sexual problem, concededly a medical expense. Their physician advised them that the probability of successful treatment would be enhanced if they resided at a hotel rather than at the hospital during the treatment period. Without citing *Kelly*, the ruling found the lodging cost nondeductible because, in the Service's view, it was indistinguishable from a stay in any other personal residence.[95] Applying the but-for test, the opposite result should obtain. The taxpayers presumably continued to maintain their normal residence; the hotel expense was in excess of their normal living expense and was incurred only to obtain the best medical treatment.[96]

Other long distance travel may involve an admixture of personal or recreational motive. A taxpayer who travels to another location for alleviation of a particular ailment and not for general health improvement may deduct his transportation.[97] The cost of transporting his nurse—or spouse acting as his nurse—is also deductible.[98] And a taxpayer may deduct the transportation cost of visiting a physician in another city if he has more confidence in him—notwithstanding that he spends some time in social or recreational activities on the trip—provided that the trip's primary purpose is medical.[99] As in the business expense area, the cost of transportation need not be allocated so long as the primary motive is not personal or recreational.[100] When the taxpayer uses his own automobile to provide medical transportation, he may deduct either the out-of-pocket costs paid by him or the standard mileage allowance of seven cents per mile.[101] Neither method is intended to allow for depreciation on the automobile. This is consistent both with the statutory limitation of the deduction to a "payment" for medical expenses and with the regulations' general rule allowing medical capital expenses to be deducted in the year of payment. For these purposes, depreciation is not a payment.[102]

---

[94] 1975-1 C.B. 92.

[95] The ruling did cite Wade Volwiler, 57 T.C. 367 (1971), in which the taxpayer's daughter resided separately in a rooming house as part of her psychiatric care. The Tax Court disallowed the deduction of the rooming house cost on the grounds that it was not a medical institution or otherwise specially equipped for treatment. It should be noted that there was no duplication of the daughter's residence expense in that she resided only in the rooming house, although she could have avoided even that expense by living at home.

[96] *See also* Sidney J. Ungar, 22 T.C.M. (CCH) 766 (1963) (allowing deduction of rent of an apartment used in lieu of a hospital room).

[97] Rev. Rul. 58-110, 1958-1 C.B. 155.

[98] Carasso v. Commissioner, 292 F.2d 367 (2d Cir. 1961), *cert. denied*, 369 U.S. 874 (1962); Leo R. Cohn, 38 T.C. 387, 390 (1962), *acq.* 1963-1 C.B. 4; I.T. 3786, 1946-1 C.B. 75, *declared obsolete*, Rev. Rul. 69-43, 1969-1 C.B. 310, 312. *See also* Robert M. Rose, 52 T.C. 521 (1969), *aff'd per curiam*, 435 F.2d 149 (5th Cir. 1970), *cert. denied*, 402 U.S. 907 (1971) (transportation expenses of one parent accompanying child for medical care deductible, but not those of a second parent who followed later).

[99] Stanley D. Winderman, 32 T.C. 1197 (1959), *acq.* 1960-2 C.B. 7.

[100] *Compare id. with* Treas. Reg. § 1.162-2(b)(1) (1958).

[101] Rev. Proc. 74-24, 1974-2 C.B. 477.

[102] *See* Maurice S. Gordon, 37 T.C. 986 (1962) (depreciation on automobile used to transport son to doctor not deductible under section 213). *But cf.* Sanford H. Weinzimer, 17

VII. OLD AGE

Aging frequently brings its own special wrinkles to the medical expense problem. One often litigated question concerns whether a taxpayer may claim deductions for health care expenses of an elderly parent or other relation. The taxpayer may do so if the patient is a dependent of the taxpayer—a person bearing a stated relationship to the taxpayer and having more than half of his support provided by the taxpayer during the taxable year.[166] Litigation usually focuses upon the support test. The tax concept of "support" is not well defined,[167] and the Code itself provides little elucidation. Moreover, when there are competing sources of funding to provide support—as when the elderly person has some of his own income, or other siblings of the taxpayer provide funds—the determination whether one particular taxpayer provided more than half the support may be difficult. The statute now provides some guidance on the latter question by permitting two or more taxpayers who together contribute over half the support to determine by agreement which of them will claim the deduction.[168] In this manner, taxpayers obtain certainty in planning, and the Commissioner does not risk two taxpayers claiming the same individual as a dependent.

If a taxpayer incurs significant expenses for an elderly parent's medical care, deductibility of the expense may be a considerable benefit, far exceeding in importance the additional personal exemption. But the expansion of public programs of support for the needy, as well as private and public medical insurance programs, may push the taxpayer's percentage of support of his parent to less than half if these other sources are

---

T.C.M. (CCH) 712 (1958) (allowing deduction for depreciation of specially equipped automobile necessary to transport handicapped person to work). The result in *Gordon* was carefully preserved in Commissioner v. Idaho Power Co., 418 U.S. 1, 16 & n.11 (1974), which construed the words "paid out" in section 263 to include depreciation of certain equipment. The Court noted that payment for purposes of the medical expense or charitable deduction excluded depreciation, but found that line of authority irrelevant to the application of section 263.

[166] I.R.C. § 152(a). The taxpayer may claim an additional personal exemption for a dependent parent only if the latter earned less than $750 of gross income in the year. I.R.C. § 151(e). The gross income requirement does not carry over to the medical expense deduction.

[167] *See* Comment, *Turecamo v. Commissioner:* Treatment of Benefits Received Under the Medicare Program for Purposes of the Dependency Exemption Support Test, 126 U. Pa. L. Rev. 673 (1978). *See also* I.R.C. § 677(b); Rev. Rul. 59-357, 1959-2 C.B. 212; Rev. Rul. 56-484, 1956-2 C.B. 23.

[168] I.R.C. § 152(c). Similar rules permit divorced or separated parents to allocate dependent status. *See* I.R.C. § 152(e).

taken into account. In *Turecamo v. Commissioner*,[169] the taxpayers provided food, lodging, clothing and entertainment for Mrs. Turecamo's mother, Mrs. Kavanaugh. During the year in question, Mrs. Kavanaugh was hospitalized for two months. Her total bill amounted to $11,096, $10,435 of which was paid by basic Medicare benefits (part A benefits).[170] The taxpayers paid the balance and other medical expenses, which amounted to $3531. They deducted this amount and also claimed a personal exemption for Mrs. Kavanaugh as a dependent. The Commissioner disallowed these deductions, arguing that the part A benefits constituted part of Mrs. Kavanaugh's support for that year and that the taxpayers had therefore provided less than half her support. The Tax Court and the Second Circuit held for the taxpayers.

Both courts were faced with two lines of decision that converged in *Turecamo*. The Tax Court had held that welfare payments and other benefits of a social welfare nature, although excluded from the recipient's gross income, counted as support provided by the recipient for himself.[171] The Service had ruled that part A basic Medicare benefits were of this character and must be included in the support computation as having been provided by the recipient.[172] On the other hand, health insurance had been consistently counted toward support when premium payments were made but not when the insurance company paid out proceeds.[173] Given this background, the Service ruled that supplementary Medicare benefits (part B benefits) counted toward support when the premiums were paid, but the part B benefits themselves should be excluded from support.[174] Both the Tax Court and the Second Circuit rejected the public welfare benefits argument and instead analogized part A payments to insurance. In reaching this conclusion, the Second Circuit found it persuasive that the program spread risks among the class of beneficiaries. Moreover, the court concluded that large, random payments should not be allowed to distort the relationship between the Turecamos and Mrs. Kavanaugh; the *Turecamo* result also facilitates planning with a view to tax consequences.[175]

Once the taxpayer establishes the dependency relationship, he still must show that the expense is for medical care. Sometimes the care is provided at home. The expense of a companion or housemaid is deemed purely

---

[169] 554 F.2d 564 (2d Cir. 1977), *aff'g* 64 T.C. 720 (1975).

[170] *See* Social Security Act, subch. XVIII, 42 U.S.C. §§ 1395-1395pp (Supp. V 1975).

[171] Helen M. Lutter, 61 T.C. 685 (1974), *aff'd per curiam*, 514 F.2d 1095 (7th Cir.), *cert. denied*, 423 U.S. 931 (1975); Eddie L. Carter, 55 T.C. 109 (1970), *acq.* 1971-2 C.B. 2; Rev. Rul. 71-468, 1971-2 C.B. 115.

[172] Rev. Rul. 70-341, 1970-2 C.B. 31, 32.

[173] Mawhinney v. Commissioner, 355 F.2d 462 (3d Cir. 1966) (per curiam), *aff'g* 43 T.C. 443 (1965); Rev. Rul. 64-223, 1964-2 C.B. 50. *But see* Samples v. United States, 226 F. Supp. 115 (N.D. Ga. 1963) (medical bills covered by insurance are still includable in computation to determine whether taxpayer supports brother).

[174] Rev. Rul. 70-341, 1970-2 C.B. 31, 32.

[175] There is no risk under the *Turecamo* result that the Treasury might be whipsawed by duplicative dependency claims, because only one taxpayer will be able to claim that he provided more than half the support under the court's computation.

personal,[176] while expenses for nursing care, including board, are treated as medical expenses.[177] In a few instances, the Tax Court has allowed a deduction even when the person who provides the care is a relative of the taxpayer.[178]

Nursing home care presents further definitional problems. Nursing homes often provide food, lodging and other benefits normally treated as nondeductible personal expenses. The regulations call for a factual determination of whether and to what extent care in such an institution should be treated as a medical expense.[179] If the availability of medical care in the institution is a principal reason for the individual's presence there, all costs incidental to providing such care, including meals and lodging, are deductible; if the individual's condition is such that the availability of medical care is not a principal reason for his presence in the institution, only that portion of the cost directly attributable to nursing or other conventional medical treatment qualifies for a deduction. Medical care need only be one of the "principal" reasons. In *W.B. Counts*,[180] the Commissioner sought to disallow the cost of placing the taxpayer's father in a nursing home after the mother had been admitted to recover from a stroke, on the ground that the father's presence was motivated by a desire to be near his wife. The taxpayer successfully defended the deduction by showing that the father's condition confined him to bed and required nurse supervision. But in *John Robinson*,[181] the taxpayer was unable to live alone and care for himself. The principal reason for residing at the nursing home was to preserve his general dignity in his remaining years. The Tax Court held this insufficient to warrant a medical deduction.

Even if the cost of the nursing home is not fully deductible as a medical expense, the specific portion allocable to medical care may be claimed. The taxpayer, however, has the burden of showing what part of the general fee is attributable to this expense.[182] The same rule applies to payment of a lump sum fee to the retirement home: the expenditure is deductible if the home provides a separate statement which, based on prior experience, allocates a portion of the fee to provision of medical care.[183]

In some instances, taxpayers have successfully claimed charitable con-

---

[176] *See* Rev. Rul. 58-339, 1958-2 C.B. 106 (portion of housemaid's salary attributable to nursing care may be deducted). Note that, if the expenses are necessary to enable the taxpayer to be gainfully employed, they may be taken as a credit under section 44A if the parent is incapable of caring for himself.

[177] Treas. Reg. § 1.213-1(e)(1)(ii) (1957).

[178] Walter D. Bye, 31 T.C.M. (CCH) 238 (1972) (niece); Estate of Myrtle P. Dodge, 20 T.C.M. (CCH) 1811 (1961) (daughter).

[179] Treas. Reg. § 1.213-1(e)(1)(v) (1957). Compare the treatment of special schools, discussed at text accompanying note 51 *supra*.

[180] 42 T.C. 755 (1964).

[181] 51 T.C. 520 (1968).

[182] *See* James J. Matles, 23 T.C.M. (CCH) 1489 (1964); Rev. Rul. 67-185, 1967-1 C.B. 70.

[183] Rev. Rul. 75-302, 1975-2 C.B. 87. *But see* Rev. Rul. 68-525, 1968-2 C.B. 112 (portion of fee allocable to construction of an infirmary is not deductible, because such construction is not medical expense of taxpayer).

tribution deductions for lump sum payments to nursing homes in which the taxpayers or their relatives will live. In such situations the home is an exempt charity, and the relevant question becomes whether the payment was made in exchange for the home's promise to support the elderly person, barring a deduction, or was a gift, proceeding out of "disinterested generosity."[184] The Eighth Circuit allowed such a deduction when the payment was an unconditional endowment gift without any promise of lifetime care; it reversed as clearly erroneous a finding by the Tax Court that the motive for the gift was admission to the home and receipt of other benefits.[185] But, more recently, the Seventh Circuit held nondeductible the payments made by a son under a founder's gift plan, on the ground that the payment was to gain admittance for the taxpayer's mother.[186] Similarly, when a charity requests a gift from an applicant based on the nature of the accommodations applied for, the Service will consider the payment nondeductible as a charitable contribution.[187]

---

[184] Duberstein v. Commissioner, 363 U.S. 278, 285 (1960) (defining gift for purposes of I.R.C. § 102) (quoting Commissioner v. LoBue, 351 U.S. 243, 246 (1956)).

[185] Wardwell's Estate v. Commissioner, 301 F.2d 632 (8th Cir. 1962); *cf.* Dowell v. United States, 553 F.2d 1233 (10th Cir. 1977) (connection between taxpayer's "sponsorship gift" to retirement home and later receipt of residential benefits from home was not so strong as to bar deductibility of gift under I.R.C. § 170).

[186] Sedam v. United States, 518 F.2d 242 (7th Cir. 1975), *rev'g* 74-1 U.S. Tax. Cas. ¶ 9442 (S.D. Ind. 1974). *See* Rev. Rul. 58-303, 1958-1 C.B. 61.

[187] Rev. Rul. 72-506, 1972-2 C.B. 106.

E. DEDUCTIONS FOR PERSONAL SAVINGS

NOTE, "COSTS AND CONSEQUENCES OF TAX INCENTIVES: THE INDIVIDUAL RETIREMENT ACCOUNT"

94 Harvard Law Review 864–886 (1981).

The Individual Retirement Account (IRA)[1] is a tax incentive designed to encourage retirement savings for those outside traditional pension plan coverage. In the seven years since its introduction, however, the IRA has failed to generate substantial retirement savings, and its only significant effect has been to provide a tax haven for upper income taxpayers. Like many other incentive programs that have been incorporated into the Internal Revenue Code, the IRA inefficiently reduces federal revenues while undermining the progressivity of the graduated income tax. To overcome these defects, Congress should replace the IRA tax incentive with a direct subsidy for retirement savings.

I. HISTORY OF THE IRA TAX INCENTIVE

In 1974, Congress passed the Employee Retirement Income Security Act (ERISA),[2] a bill designed to "encourag[e] the growth and development of voluntary private pension plans."[3] The Act sets uniform minimum standards for all employee benefit plans and limited tax incentives to plans that provide additional retirement benefits.[4] Because one of the goals of

---

[1] Throughout this Note, IRA refers to four tax deductible savings mechanisms — trust, annuities, bonds, and custodial accounts — offered taxpayers not covered by other pension plans. *See* note 13 *infra*.

[2] Employee Retirement Income Security Act of 1974, Pub. L. No. 93-406, 88 Stat. 829 (codified in I.R.C. and scattered sections of 5, 6, 18, 29, 31, 42 U.S.C.).

[3] 120 CONG. REC. 8702 (1974) (statement of Rep. Ullman), *reprinted in* [1974] U.S. CODE CONG. & AD. NEWS 5166, 5166.

[4] ERISA is a complex, comprehensive piece of legislation administered through the Departments of Labor and the Treasury. Under Title I, Labor regulates most employee benefit plans established by employers or employee organizations engaged in or affecting interstate commerce. ERISA § 4, 29 U.S.C. § 1003 (1976). Then, under Title II, Treasury offers favorable tax treatment to employers with pension plans meeting further qualifications. Only by satisfying these conditions can an employer deduct portions of its annual plan contribution from gross income. ERISA § 1013(c)(1), I.R.C. § 404(a)(1) (amended 1978). Generally, the qualification requirements under the tax code are more strict than the Title I regulations, demanding between a 56% and a 70% minimum employee participation in the plan, ERISA § 1011, I.R.C. § 410(b), and setting a more rapid vesting schedule for benefits, ERISA § 1012, I.R.C. § 411 (amended 1976). Title II restricts annual deductible contributions to an individual's pension to 25% of the individual's compensation, with an upper limit of $25,000. ERISA § 2004(a)(2), I.R.C. § 415(c) (amended 1976, 1978, 1980).

the legislation was "to make the tax laws relating to [pension] plans fairer by providing greater equality of treatment under such plans for the different taxpaying groups involved,"[5] ERISA offered the self-employed increased deductions for contributions to Keogh plans,[6] and it established the IRA[7] for employees not covered by qualified pension plans. The IRA remedied earlier legislation under which the retirement savings of employees in qualified plans were tax exempt, yet the savings of workers whose employers did not establish qualified plans were not.[8] Because the IRA promised to correct this inequity[9] at a relatively small cost,[10] it won overwhelming

---

Another set of guidelines governs contributions to a "defined benefit plan" that guarantees a definite pension payment, normally a percentage of final salary. ERISA § 2004(a)(2), I.R.C. § 415(b) (amended 1976, 1978, 1980). Under qualified plans, employees recognize income when they receive the benefits from the plan, either after retirement or upon terminating plan participation. I.R.C. § 61(11).

For more detailed descriptions of ERISA, see generally Chadwick & Foster, *Federal Regulation of Retirement Plans: The Quest for Parity*, 28 VAND. L. REV. 641 (1975); Preminger, Jennings & Alexander, *What Do You Get with the Gold Watch? An Analysis of the Employee Retirement Income Security Act of 1974*, 17 ARIZ. L. REV. 426 (1975); Snyder, *Employee Retirement Income Security Act of 1974*, 11 WAKE FOREST L. REV. 219 (1975); Note, *The Pension Reform Act of 1974: Brave New World of Retirement Security*, 27 U. FLA. L. REV. 1044 (1975).

[5] S. REP. No. 383, 93d Cong., 1st Sess. 1, *reprinted in* [1974] U.S. CODE CONG. & AD. NEWS 4890, 4890 [hereinafter cited as SENATE REPORT].

[6] "Keogh" plans, named for the Congressman who introduced the Self-Employed Individuals Tax Retirement Act of 1962, Pub. L. No. 87-792, 76 Stat. 809, *reprinted in* [1962] U.S. CODE CONG. & AD. NEWS 945, originally provided self-employed taxpayers an annual tax deduction for retirement savings up to 10% of earned income, with an upper limit of $2,500. ERISA increased this deduction to 15% of earned income, with an upper limit of $7,500. ERISA § 2001(a)(1)–(2), I.R.C. § 404(e)(1)–(2) (amended 1976); *see* Schmitt, *The Pension Reform Act of 1974 and the Self-Employed Person*, 63 ILL. B.J. 512 (1975).

[7] ERISA § 2002, I.R.C. §§ 219, 408, 409, 4973–4974, 6693 (amended 1976, 1978, 1980).

[8] *See* H.R. REP. No. 807, 93d Cong., 2d Sess. 126, *reprinted in* [1974] U.S. CODE CONG. & AD. NEWS 4670, 4791 [hereinafter cited as HOUSE REPORT]; *Private Pension Plan Reform: Hearings Before the Subcomm. on Private Pension Plans of the Senate Finance Comm.*, 93d Cong., 1st Sess. 359 (1973) (statement of Treasury Secretary Shultz). *See also* Hickman, *Pension and Profit-Sharing Plans: The Quintessential Tax Shelter?*, in PROCEEDINGS OF TAX FOUNDATION'S 25TH NATIONAL CONFERENCE 22 (1974) (describing inequities of pre-ERISA system and endorsing administration's pension reform, one of several proposals that shaped ERISA).

[9] *See 7 General Tax Reform: Panel Discussion on Pensions, Profit Sharing, and Deferred Compensation Before the House Ways and Means Comm.*, 93d Cong., 1st Sess. 918–19 (1973) (statement of Frank Cummings) ("[Y]ou can do an enormous favor to 50% of the workforce who are not covered by any private pension plans. . . . [T]he average American worker detests loopholes because they are always for some other guy. This is one loophole that would be for everybody . . . .").

[10] Congressional analysts estimated the IRA deduction would cost the federal government in lost tax revenue between $270 million and $355 million per year in

endorsement during congressional hearings.[11]

The IRA,[12] essentially unaltered since the passage of ERISA, allows an employee not participating in a qualified pension plan to deduct from gross income limited contributions made into retirement accounts, approved annuities, or certified bonds.[13] The employee can contribute up to fifteen percent of her compensation, but not more than $1,500 per year.[14] More-

---

1973 dollars ($503 to $661 million in 1980 dollars). SENATE REPORT, *supra* note 5, at 36 ($270 million estimate based on maximum annual contribution of $1,000), *reprinted in* [1974] U.S. CODE CONG. & AD. NEWS 4890, 4921; HOUSE REPORT, *supra* note 8, at 41 ($355 million estimate based on maximum contribution of $1,500 or 20% of compensation), *reprinted in* [1974] U.S. CODE CONG. & AD. NEWS 4670, 4707.

[11] *See* STAFF OF JOINT COMM. ON INTERNAL REVENUE TAXATION, 93D CONG., 1ST SESS., DIGEST OF STATEMENTS ON PROPOSALS FOR PRIVATE PENSION PLAN REFORM pt. 1, at 75–77 (Comm. Print 1973); *id*. pt. 2, at 59–60 (30 of 31 written statements submitted to the Ways and Means Committee discussing IRA's supported the tax incentive); STAFF OF JOINT COMM. ON INTERNAL REVENUE TAXATION, 93D CONG., 1ST SESS., DIGEST OF TESTIMONY ON PENSION PLAN REFORM 45–47 (Comm. Print 1973) (15 of 18 testifying on private pension plans before the Senate Finance Subcommittee on Private Pension Plans supported IRA tax incentives); STAFF OF JOINT COMM. ON INTERNAL REVENUE TAXATION, 93D CONG., 1ST SESS., SUMMARY OF TESTIMONY ON PROPOSALS FOR PRIVATE PENSION PLAN REFORM 29–31 (Comm. Print 1973) (all 21 of those testifying before the Ways and Means Committee supported tax incentives).

[12] For a thorough and up-to-date explanation of the IRA provisions, see Stanger & Mills, *Individual Retirement Accounts, Individual Retirement Annuities, and Retirement Bonds*, 38 N.Y.U. INST. FED. TAX. 32.1 (1980). *See generally* Craine, *Individual Retirement Accounts*, 11 TULSA L.J. 215 (1975); Stevenson, *The New Individual Retirement Accounts: What They Are and How They Operate*, 42 J. TAX. 91 (1975).

[13] The deduction, ERISA § 2002(a), I.R.C. §§ 62(10), 219(a) (amended 1976), is for savings put into nonforfeitable trusts exclusively benefiting the individual or signified beneficiary, ERISA § 2002(b), I.R.C. § 408(a) (amended 1976, 1978, 1980), for premiums on qualified annuity or endowment contracts, ERISA § 2002(b), I.R.C. § 408(b) (amended 1976, 1978), for purchases of qualified nontransferable bonds, ERISA § 2002(b), I.R.C. § 409 (amended 1976, 1978, 1980), or for funds placed in custodial accounts. ERISA § 2002(b), I.R.C. § 408(h) (amended 1976). The IRA deduction is not available to taxpayers participating in other qualified pension plans. ERISA § 2002(a), I.R.C. § 219(b)(2) (amended 1976).

[14] ERISA § 2002(a)(2), I.R.C. § 219(b)(1). IRA rollovers are an exception to the $1,500 annual contribution limit. ERISA § 2002(b), I.R.C. § 408(d)(3) (amended 1978, 1980). If an employee participating in a qualified ERISA plan were to leave her company, she would be allowed to place her vested portion of the ERISA plan into an IRA and postpone tax on the disbursement. ERISA § 2005(g)(5), I.R.C. § 402(a)(5) (amended 1976, 1978). Rollovers into IRA's create special tax problems for taxpayers because those who use the rollover forgo the opportunity to income average or claim capital gains treatment. *See* Note, *Qualified Plan Distributions: Tax Deferral, ERISA and the IRA*, 45 FORDHAM L. REV. 389 (1976). *See generally* Zelinsky, *The Taxation of Qualified Employee Plan Benefits: A Brief Stroll Through the "Statutory Thicket*," 53 CONN. B.J. 475 (1979). This Note does not examine IRA rollovers.

over, interest earned on the retirement account and any gains on its investments are not taxed as income in the year they are earned.[15] Typically, the IRA participant only pays taxes on the retirement account when the assets are distributed,[16] but then all the disbursements are taxed as ordinary income without the benefit of a capital gains allowance.[17] To ensure that IRA's are used only for retirement savings, Congress restricts the use and withdrawal of funds in IRA's before retirement.[18]

The response to the IRA provision was largely positive. One optimistic commentator concluded the "IRA provision [would] potentially affect more Americans than any other provision of ERISA."[19] Investment advisors urged executives to take advantage of the IRA deductions,[20] and analysts speculated future legislation would extend federal tax support of individual retirement savings just as ERISA had increased deductions for Keogh plans.[21]

A. The Attraction of IRA's

The IRA unquestionably increases the return on retirement savings.[22] By deferring the tax liability on contributed income until distribution, the IRA offers participating taxpayers an interest-free loan in the amount of the deferred taxes on both the contributions to the account and the interest earned on those contributions.[23] Consequently, without an IRA, a tax-

---

[15] ERISA § 2002(b), I.R.C. § 408(e)(1).

[16] Except for transfers associated with IRA rollovers, see note 14 supra, and the withdrawal of funds in excess of annual contribution limits, ERISA § 2002(b), I.R.C. § 408(d)(4) (amended 1976), distributions out of IRA's are included in gross income, ERISA § 2002(b), I.R.C. § 408(d)(1) (amended 1978).

[17] IRA distributions could include funds raised from long-term capital gains, such as the profit from the sale of stocks held more than one year, which would ordinarily receive favorable tax treatment under I.R.C. §§ 62(3), 1202, 1223.

[18] See pp. 868–69 infra.

[19] Craine, supra note 12, at 216. See also Anreder, Up the IRA!, BARRON'S, Mar. 17, 1975, at 5 (claiming 40 million Americans would be eligible for IRA's).

[20] E.g., IRAs: A Hot Deal for Some, BUS. WEEK, Dec. 29, 1975, at 112 (citing the IRA rollover as a particularly attractive feature). See also Willie Loman Would Be Pleased, SALES MANAGEMENT, Sept. 8, 1975, at 60–63; IRA — A Legit Tax Loophole, AM. DRUGGIST, Jan. 1, 1975, at 8.

[21] See Anreder, supra note 19; Stevenson, supra note 12, at 95. See generally note 6 supra (describing Keogh plans).

[22] The IRA deduction raises the participant's return on savings to the tax-free rate of return. See Graetz, Implementing a Progressive Consumption Tax, 92 HARV. L. REV. 1575, 1598–611 (1979).

[23] For every dollar of pretax income, a taxpayer in the 20% bracket would ordinarily pay 20 cents in taxes, but if that dollar is placed in an IRA, the government,

payer in the twenty percent tax bracket who allots $1,000 of pretax income each year to a ten percent savings account would accumulate $90,627 after taxes by the end of thirty years. But the same taxpayer, with an IRA, would have $131,595 after taxes at the end of thirty years, or an additional forty-five percent.[24] Beyond its attraction as a tax deferral, the IRA also benefits taxpayers who anticipate their marginal tax rate will decline because their income will be lower in retirement.[25]

But statutorily imposed safeguards substantially reduce the IRA's attractiveness for some taxpayers. A participant can be penalized for withdrawing funds before she reaches the age of 59.5,[26] or failing to begin distribution by the age of 70.5.[27] In

---

in effect, lends the taxpayer the 20 cents until the dollar is withdrawn and the tax must be paid. Furthermore, with a 10% return on IRA funds, for example, the taxpayer earns 10 cents of income a year on which taxes are deferred.

[24] In a normal 10% savings account of a 20% bracket taxpayer, $1,000 of pretax income would generate an $800 after-tax deposit, and since the taxpayer would have to pay taxes on the interest earned on that deposit, the taxpayer's after-tax rate of return would be 8%. So, $1,000 of pretax income deposited in a savings account in the first year will create $7,450 of after-tax income at the end of 30 years ($1,000 × (80%) × $(1.08)^{29}$. However, that same $1,000 of pretax income, if committed to an IRA, would produce $12,690 of after-tax income at the end of 30 years, ($1,000) × $(1.10)^{29}$ × (80%). The longer the funds are compounded at the pretax interest rate (10% in this example), the greater the benefit to the taxpayer. The equations describing the tax savings generated by annual contributions over a given number of years are

(1) After-Tax Balance of Normal Savings After "n" Years = $\sum_{i=1}^{n}$ (annual contribution) × (1 − tax rate) × (1 + (interest rate) × (1 − tax rate))$^{(n-i)}$; and

(2) After-Tax Distribution from IRA After "n" Years = (1 − tax rate) × $\sum_{i=1}^{n}$ (annual contribution) × (1 + interest rate)$^{(n-i)}$.

[25] During income-producing years, a taxpayer may be in a 50% bracket, but then during retirement be in only a 40% bracket. If so, the taxpayer would have an increased incentive to defer taxes until her retirement years. See note 33 infra. The tax code also favors the elderly. E.g., I.R.C. § 37 (tax credit for the elderly); id. § 151(c) (additional exemption allowed for those over 65). These preferences lower the effective tax rate for the elderly, making it advantageous to declare income after reaching 65 years old.

[26] A 10% excise tax is imposed on distributions made before the beneficiary reaches 59.5 years old, ERISA § 2002(b), I.R.C. §§ 408(f), 409(c), unless a disability, as defined by I.R.C. § 72(m)(7), forces the distribution.

[27] Because the IRA is meant to encourage savings for retirement and not simply the building of wealth, once the taxpayer reaches 70.5 years old, no further IRA deduction is permitted, ERISA § 2002(a), I.R.C. § 219(b)(3), and distribution of the account must begin, ERISA § 2002(b), I.R.C. §§ 408(a)(6)–(7), (b)(3)–(4), 409(a)(3). Failure to distribute can entail a 50% excise tax on the difference between the minimum required distribution and the amount distributed. ERISA § 2002(e), I.R.C. § 4974 (amended 1976, 1978).

addition, by placing funds in an IRA, a participant surrenders some control over her assets[28] and may not use the account as collateral for borrowing.[29]

Given their unique advantages and disadvantages, IRA's do not present a realistic retirement savings option for all taxpayers. First, the taxpayer must be aware that the IRA deduction is available.[30] Second, a participant must have both enough income beyond what is needed for minimal consumption to be able to save, and sufficient additional capital accumulation to be able to supply unexpected cash needs without being forced to violate the IRA premature distribution limitations.[31] Third, if the taxpayer plans to borrow funds, she must have assets outside the IRA to serve as collateral. Fourth, if the taxpayer wants to retain control over IRA assets, she must have a sufficiently large account to negotiate a flex-

---

[28] Since an approved trustee, usually a bank, must administer the IRA, the participant has no direct control over the assets, ERISA § 2002(b), I.R.C. § 408(a) (amended 1976, 1978, 1980). A participant's control over an IRA account depends on the size of the account and its location. Participants with large IRA's, typically started with qualified rollovers, *see* note 14 *supra*, can negotiate an individualized trust agreement with a commercial bank through which the participant retains effective control over the assets. Participants with smaller accounts can maintain flexibility by keeping the account at a brokerage house and moving the assets among the house's investment pools, such as bonds or stocks, depending on the financial climate. *See Brokerage Firms Cash In on IRAs*, BUS. WEEK, Sept. 15, 1975, at 81; *Swinging with the New IRA Plans*, BUS. WEEK, June 30, 1975, at 92. Those holding IRA's in savings accounts have less control because they must move to a new account to change their investment medium.

[29] Pledging an Individual Retirement Account as collateral or borrowing on an Individual Retirement Annuity causes immediate distribution, ERISA § 2002(b), I.R.C. § 408(e)(3)–(4).

There are two further statutory restrictions on the use of IRA's. First, if a taxpayer deposits more than the allowable annual contribution and if that excess is not part of a qualified rollover, then the taxpayer must pay a 6% annual excise tax on the excess contribution until it is withdrawn. ERISA § 2002(d), I.R.C. § 4973 (amended 1976, 1978, 1980). Second, ERISA prohibits a variety of transactions, notably the exchange of IRA assets between the owner and other interested parties. ERISA § 2003(a), I.R.C. § 4975(c) (amended 1976). If IRA funds are used in violation of these prohibited transaction guidelines, the account loses its tax-exempt status and the assets are distributed immediately, ERISA §§ 2002(b), 2003(a), I.R.C. § 408(e)(2), or a 5% excise tax is levied on the amount transacted, ERISA § 2003(a)–(b), I.R.C. § 4975(a)–(c) (amended 1976).

[30] A study in 1976 showed newspaper advertisements the most common source of IRA information. INSTITUTE OF FINANCIAL EDUCATION, IRA BASICS FOR SAVINGS ASSOCIATIONS 87 (1980).

[31] In addition, involuntary distribution may create a more serious penalty for lower bracket taxpayers because a lump sum distribution could force them into a higher bracket, while a high income user may always be taxed at the same 50% maximum rate regardless of when the funds are distributed.

ible trust agreement or be sufficiently sophisticated to seek an appropriate investment medium.[32] Finally, the tax deferral — the heart of the IRA — offers a more attractive shelter the higher the taxpayer's bracket. While the twenty percent bracket taxpayer would enjoy a forty-five percent increase in retirement savings by participating in an IRA, a fifty percent tax bracket taxpayer would reap a 148% increase by using the account.[33] Thus, the structure of the IRA suggests it would attract chiefly higher income taxpayers, who save for retirement even without tax incentives.[34]

B. The Spread of IRA's

Soon after Congress enacted ERISA, financial intermediaries began marketing the IRA's. Commercial banks,[35] savings and loan associations,[36] insurance companies,[37] and even brokerage houses[38] qualified as IRA trustees[39] and saw the IRA as a profitable new product. By 1979, savings and loan associations along with commercial banks emerged as the dominant repositories for IRA's,[40] positioning the IRA as a substitute for traditional savings accounts.[41]

Either because of its attractiveness as a tax shelter or because of the financial intermediaries' promotional efforts, the IRA became an increasingly popular savings instrument: in 1978, more than 2.7 million taxpayers contributed $3.0 billion

---

[32] See note 28 supra.

[33] Using the methodology outlined in note 24 supra, a taxpayer in the 50% bracket who commits $1,000 of pretax income annually for 30 years in a 10% account would have an after-tax accumulation in a savings account of $33,219 (equation 1) and an after-tax distribution from an IRA of $82,247 (equation 2). Using an IRA would be even more advantageous if the taxpayer's tax rate fell during retirement. For instance, for a taxpayer whose tax rate drops from 50% to 40%, the IRA would yield a 197% increase in after-tax savings. See p. 868 supra.

[34] Benefiting the upper brackets increases the tax burden on other brackets since additional revenues must be raised to compensate for the revenue loss. See Halperin, An Evaluation of ERISA, 17 B.C. INDUS. & COM. L. REV. 739, 795 (1975).

[35] See, e.g., More Banks Are Promoting IRAs To Build Savings And Profits, BANKING, Aug. 1975, at 62.

[36] See, e.g., 'Hot Line' Delivers Fast, Full Answers to IRA Questions, SAVINGS & LOAN NEWS, Feb. 1978, at 80.

[37] See, e.g., Individual Retirement Account: The Problem and the Opportunity, NAT'L UNDERWRITER, Feb. 8, 1975, at 1, 6.

[38] See, e.g., Brokerage Firms Cash In on IRAs, supra note 28.

[39] In the case of thrift institutions, Congress had to amend § 5(c) of the Home Owners' Loan Act of 1933 to allow the institutions to serve as IRA trustees. See Act of July 25, 1975, Pub. L. No. 94-60, 89 Stat. 301 (amended paragraph codified at 12 U.S.C.A. § 1464(l) (West 1980).

[40] The relative market share for IRA's developed as follows:

[41] See n. 41 on page 377.

to IRA's.[42] As a result of these contributions, the funds in

ESTIMATED FUNDS IN INDIVIDUAL RETIREMENT ACCOUNTS
(percentages at year end)

Institution	1976	1977	1978	1979
Savings & Loans	34.7	39.3	41.1	41.2
Commercial Banks†	24.7	23.4	24.2	25.1
Life Insurance Companies	26.1	19.9	17.8	16.6
Mutual Savings	11.7	14.3	13.8	13.7
Mutual Funds	2.4	2.6	2.8	3.1
Treasury Bonds	0.4	0.5	0.4	0.3
Total	100.0%	100.0%	100.0%	100.0%
Total (millions)	$4,315	$6,751	$10,528	$14,806

† Because commercial banks report only aggregate IRA and Keogh deposits, this row has been computed under the assumption that the ratio of IRA deposits to total IRA and Keogh deposits in commercial banks has remained the same — 0.758 — since March 1976, when commercial banks last provided a breakdown. *See* Board of Governors of the Federal Reserve System, Individual Retirement Accounts and Keogh Accounts at Selected Financial Institutions as of March 31, 1976, at 1–2 (June 1976) (on file at Harvard Business School Library).

Adapted from American Council of Life Insurance, Pension Facts, 1980, at 16 (forthcoming); AMERICAN COUNCIL OF LIFE INSURANCE, PENSION FACTS, 1978–1979, at 16 (1979); AMERICAN COUNCIL OF LIFE INSURANCE, PENSION FACTS, 1977, at 19 (1977). For the 1976–1978 data, this table includes revisions obtained from the American Council of Life Insurance, Washington, D.C. These estimates understate the volume of funds in IRA's because assets held by brokerage houses and trusts are not included.

[41] *See A Boomlet in Liberalized IRAs*, BUS. WEEK, Dec. 25, 1978, at 142; *Bank IRA Activity: A Good Start, With More Action To Come*, BANKING, Mar. 1976, at 96. These financial intermediaries, led by the savings and loan trade associations, have tried to promote IRA accounts because retirement savings provide long-term deposits that improve the intermediaries' financial stability. *See, e.g.*, Skowbo, *Who Needs IRA and Keogh Accounts? You Do.*, MARKETING SCOPE, Winter 1977, at 20, 21. Because savings and loans traditionally invest in long-term mortgages, they are eager to match these assets with long-term liabilities like IRA's. *See* INSTITUTE OF FINANCIAL EDUCATION, *supra* note 30, at 16; FEDERAL HOME LOAN BANK BOARD J., Oct. 1980, at 46 (statistical series). However, even for savings and loan associations, IRA's constitute 1.4% of deposits. *See* Zabrenski, *Changes in S&L Account Structure: October 1979–March 1980*, FEDERAL HOME LOAN BANK BOARD J., Aug. 1980, at 21, 27.

[42] Internal Revenue Service, News Release No. IR-80-55 (Apr. 21, 1980). Between 1975 and 1978, IRA contributions grew as follows:

Year	Contributions (millions)	Percent Increase Over Previous Year
1975	$1,436	—
1976	1,968	+37%
1977	2,458	+25%
1978	2,984	+21%

INTERNAL REVENUE SERVICE, PRELIMINARY REPORT, STATISTICS OF INCOME — 1978, INDIVIDUAL INCOME TAX RETURNS 25 (1980); INTERNAL REVENUE SERVICE,

IRA's grew from $4.3 billion in late 1976 to $14.8 billion by the end of 1979.[43]

Despite their growing popularity, IRA's did not generate the widespread participation congressional sponsors envisioned. The benefits of IRA's reached not even ten percent of the forty million eligible participants.[44] Even more significant was the emerging inequity in the IRA deduction's usage.[45]

STATISTICS OF INCOME — 1977, INDIVIDUAL INCOME TAX RETURNS 24 (1980); INTERNAL REVENUE SERVICE, STATISTICS OF INCOME — 1976, INDIVIDUAL INCOME TAX RETURNS 32 (1979); INTERNAL REVENUE SERVICE, STATISTICS OF INCOME — 1975, INDIVIDUAL INCOME TAX RETURNS 28 (1978). But IRA's contribute a small fraction of total capital formation. For instance, in the fourth quarter of 1977, the gross private investment was $307 billion, on seasonally adjusted annual basis. ECONOMIC REPORT OF THE PRESIDENT 257 (1978).

[43] See note 40 supra. Nevertheless, IRA's constitute a trivial portion of the $8 trillion of assets held by individuals. See Tax Incentives for Savings: Hearings Before the House Ways and Means Comm., 96th Cong., 2d Sess. 8-9 (1980) (statement of Ass't Secretary of the Treasury Donald C. Lubick) ($4.5 trillion in tangible assets and $3.5 trillion in financial assets).

The funds in IRA accounts exceed the total amount of deducted contributions because some funds arrive through qualified rollovers — presumably in excess of the amount of funds distributed from IRA's. Early on, because ERISA regulations forced many companies to discontinue their private pension plans, up to 36% of IRA funds may have arrived through rollovers. See Skowbo, supra note 41, at 23. Since then, corporations have adapted to the ERISA regulations, and the majority of new IRA funds, probably close to 80%, come from deductible contributions. For instance, in 1978, the IRS reported $3.0 billion of IRA contributions and the financial intermediaries announced a $3.8 billion increase in funds in IRA accounts. See notes 40, 42 supra.

[44] See pp. 870-71 supra; note 19 supra; Employee Contributions to IRA's and Other Pension Plans: Hearings Before the Subcomm. on Private Pension Plans and Employee Fringe Benefits of the Senate Finance Comm., 96th Cong., 1st Sess. 113, 136 (1979) (statement of Deputy Ass't Secretary of the Treasury Daniel Halperin) [hereinafter cited as Employee Contributions to IRA's].

[45] The inequitable distribution of IRA benefits had been predicted. During congressional testimony on ERISA, experts had warned that allowing the IRA deduction would "be helping the high-bracket people." General Tax Reform: Panel Discussions Before the House Comm. on Ways and Means, 93d Cong., 1st Sess. 1124 (1973) (statement of Daniel Halperin). See also HOUSE REPORT, supra note 8, at 166 (Supplemental Views of Representatives James C. Corman and Sam Gibbons), reprinted in [1974] U.S. CODE CONG. & AD. NEWS 4670, 4835; Halperin, supra note 34, at 790. But see [Ass't Secretary of the Treasury for Tax Policy] Hickman, supra note 8, at 26 (IRA's "will provide meaningful benefits for the tens of millions of lower income persons who are thrifty and wish to use it").

Moreover, experience in Canada, which adopted a tax incentive similar to the IRA in 1957, suggested that only the affluent participated in such programs. See Private Pension Plan Reform: Hearings Before the Subcomm. on Private Pension Plans of the Senate Finance Comm., 93d Cong., 1st Sess. 883-85 (1973) (statement of Merton Bernstein) (top percentile of taxpayers made a disproportionate 29% of Canadian IRA contributions) [hereinafter cited as Private Pension Plan Reform]. But see id. at 1192-95 (statement of Norman Tarver) (when employee contributions to qualified plans, allowable under Canadian law, are added to independent retirement savings, statistics reveal more comparable participation across tax brackets although a greater

While over fifty percent of taxpayers making more than $50,000 and eligible for IRA's in 1977 had opened accounts,[46] less than two percent of those eligible and earning less than $20,000 took advantage of the IRA tax deduction.[47] Consequently, an overwhelming share of IRA deductions benefited higher income taxpayers,[48] in sharp contrast to early predic-

---

percentage of higher bracket taxpayers still participated). (Of course, aggregate figures on employee contributions to retirement savings were not directly relevant since the American deduction, unlike the Canadian, was not available to qualified plan participants.) *See generally Retirement Income Security for Employees Act, 1972: Hearings Before the Subcomm. on Labor of the Senate Comm. on Labor and Public Welfare*, 92d Cong., 2d Sess. 603–04 (1972) (statement of Norman Tarver).

[46] In 1977, the estimated utilization rate by tax bracket was

Adjusted Gross Income (dollars)	Estimated Eligible Taxpayers (millions)	Estimated Number of IRA's (millions)	Utilization Rate
0–5,000	17.6	0.04	0.2%
5–10,000	13.3	0.18	1.4%
10–15,000	10.5	0.35	3.3%
15–20,000	7.4	0.40	5.4%
20–50,000	6.2	1.35	21.8%
50,000+	0.4	0.21	52.5%
Total	55.4	2.53	4.6%

Employee Contributions to IRA's, supra note 44, at 136. As IRA's become better known, an even greater percentage of eligible upper bracket taxpayers should open accounts. *See Private Pension Plan Reform, supra* note 45, at 1195 (statement of Norman Tarver) (close to 70% of Canadian taxpayers earning more than $25,000 in 1969 contributed to IRA-like accounts).

[47] *See* note 46 *supra*. Less than one million of the 48.8 million eligible taxpayers earning less than $20,000 in 1977 contributed to IRA's. While many of these taxpayers are interested in opening IRA's, the most frequently given reason for not opening an account is a reluctance to tie up funds until retirement. *See* INSTITUTE OF FINANCIAL EDUCATION, *supra* note 30, at 84–85. Potential participants may be discouraged by IRA introductory brochures that include warnings of early withdrawal penalties. *Id.* at 94. *See Getting the Ire Out of IRAs*, MONEY, Nov. 1978, at 119.

[48] The distribution of deductions between 1975 and 1978 was

Adjusted Gross Income (dollars)	Thousands of Dollars			
	1975	1976	1977	1978
0–5,000	12,310	25,998	31,670	26,944
5–10,000	100,579	132,333	145,366	167,907
10–15,000	217,764	254,118	298,557	305,434
15–20,000	234,862	325,594	338,624	374,844
20,000+	870,930	1,230,399	1,643,491	2,109,295

See sources cited note 42 *supra*. Those making less than $20,000 a year made smaller contributions to their IRA's on average than did those making more than $20,000:

tions that most IRA benefits would go to taxpayers with incomes under $15,000.[49]

C. Proposals to Amend the IRA

The IRA's failure to stimulate savings among lower income taxpayers weakened arguments that the incentive could provide equality between employees covered by qualified pension plans and those not covered.[50] Nevertheless, support for the savings incentive has persisted.

In 1979, several bills proposed to expand tax incentives for retirement savings by allowing deductible employee contributions to qualified ERISA pension plans.[51] Advocates of these proposals, again arguing for tax equality between qualified

---

$834 per participant compared with $1,054. See note 46 supra. Comparing contributions made by different brackets substantially understates the imbalance in the distribution of IRA benefits because the deductions are much more valuable to those in higher brackets.

[49] See Private Pension Plan Reform, supra note 45, at 360 (statement of Treasury Secretary Shultz) ("It is estimated that 56% of the tax benefits will go to persons with income below $10,000 and 88% will go to persons with income below $15,000.").

[50] See pp. 865–66 supra. Some IRA advocates argue that wealthier taxpayers monopolize the IRA deduction only because lower income taxpayers cannot save at all. See, e.g., Tax Incentives for Savings: Hearings before the House Ways & Means Comm., 96th Cong., 2d Sess. 337 (1980) (statement of Matthew F. Newman) [hereinafter cited as Tax Incentives for Savings]. Of course, if lower income taxpayers do not save under any circumstances, then the IRA's basic function of providing horizontal equity between those covered by qualified plans and those uncovered can never be realized. But studies show that lower income taxpayers do save; they just do not save in IRA's. See Skowbo, supra note 41, at 23 (those earning less than $10,000 a year made 40% of all savings and loan association deposits, but only 9% of IRA deposits in savings and loan associations).

[51] E.g., S. 209, 96th Cong., 1st Sess. § 203, 125 CONG. REC. S560 (1979) (allowing limited deductions for employee contributions to qualified plans); S. 557, 96th Cong., 1st Sess. (1979) (introduced Mar. 7, 1979) (extending IRA deduction to all taxpayers regardless of participation in qualified plans); H.R. 5665, 96th Cong., 1st Sess. § 203 (1979) (introduced Oct. 22, 1979) (increasing IRA deductions and offering deductions to qualified plan participants). See also Miscellaneous Pension Bills: Hearings Before the Subcomm. on Private Pension Plans and Employee Fringe Benefits of the Senate Finance Comm., 96th Cong., 1st Sess. pt. 1 (1979).

Permitting deductible employee contributions to employer plans would not be unprecedented. In 1978, Congress created the Simplified Employee Pension (SEP), an employer-established program into which employees can make deductible contributions. Revenue Act of 1978, Pub. L. No. 95-600, § 152(c), 92 Stat. 2763, I.R.C. § 219(b)(7) (amended 1980). If the employer's contribution does not equal the lesser of $1,500 or 15% of the employee's compensation, the employee can contribute the difference to the SEP and deduct her contribution. The Senate Report that introduced the SEP concept also recommended that participants in qualified plans be permitted to supplement employer contributions under $1,500, S. REP. No. 1263, 95th Cong., 2d Sess. 88–91, reprinted in [1978] U.S. CODE CONG. & AD. NEWS 6851-54, but the conference report rejected the recommendation, H. CONF. REP. No. 1800, 95th Cong., 2d Sess. 211-12, reprinted in [1978] U.S. CODE CONG. & AD. NEWS 7198, 7215-16.

plan employees and IRA savers, claimed that many employees, covered by employer plans and therefore denied access to IRA's, never receive benefits from their ERISA plans because they changed jobs before their benefits vest.[52] Notwithstanding opposition from Treasury Department officials and union representatives,[53] support for permitting individual contributions grew during the Ninety-Sixth Congress, and, when the Senate Finance Committee reported on the Tax Reduction Act of 1980,[54] it recommended that employees covered by qualified plans be allowed to contribute fifteen percent of their compensation, up to $1,000, into qualified plans or IRA's. The Committee also proposed the contribution limit for normal IRA's be raised to $1,750.[55]

Although not incorporated into the Tax Reduction Act of 1980, several other proposals during the Ninety-Sixth Congress sought to encourage a more even pattern of IRA usage across income brackets. One recommended the IRA deduction be replaced by a less regressive tax credit,[56] while another suggested making high-income employees' contributions to qualified plans deductible contingent upon minimum participation by all employees.[57] But few members of Congress endorsed these limitations on the IRA deductions.

Throughout 1980, pressure to increase the IRA incentive mounted, perhaps in part due to the upcoming congressional elections. One Member of Congress endorsed expanding the IRA deduction to include savings for first home purchases and college tuitions;[58] a witness recommended that taxpayers be allowed $100,000 of nondeductible contributions to IRA's that would earn tax-free interest.[59] Although legislators still hoped to expand the coverage of private retirement savings with the

---

[52] See Employee Contributions to IRA's, supra note 44, at 180–84 (statement of the Institute of Electrical & Electronics Eng'rs and the Eng'rs & Scientists Joint Comm. on Pensions).

[53] See id. at 112–37 (statement of Deputy Ass't Secretary of the Treasury Daniel Halperin) (arguing employee contributions would still be more attractive to upper income brackets); Tax Incentives for Savings, supra note 50, at 447–59 (statement of AFL–CIO Urban Affairs Dep't Director Henry B. Schechter) (deduction for employee contributions weakens employer-sponsored plans).

[54] H.R. 5829, 96th Cong., 2d Sess., reported in S. REP. NO. 940, 96th Cong., 2d Sess. (1980).

[55] S. REP. No. 940, 96th Cong., 2d Sess. 8 (1980).

[56] H.R. 5693, 96th Cong., 1st Sess. (1979) (introduced Oct. 24, 1979).

[57] S. 75, 96th Cong., 1st Sess., 125 CONG. REC. S264 (1979) (proposal would only guarantee the deduction to those making less than the step one of GS-14 U.S. Civil Service salary grade, which is indexed to inflation — $32,442 in 1979).

[58] [1980] 312 PEN. REP. (BNA) A-11.

[59] [1980] 302 PEN. REP. (BNA) A-23 (statement of David Silver, President, Investment Co. Institute).

IRA,[60] the deduction was increasingly seen as part of a broader program to stimulate capital formation,[61] and support for the IRA rested on the assumption that such a tax incentive would increase the level of national savings.[62]

II. Structural Defects in the IRA

Though reincarnated as a capital formation program, the IRA still suffers from two flaws characteristic of tax expenditures designed to influence private decisions. First, tax incentives like the IRA tend to be inefficient: every benefit placed in the Internal Revenue Code to induce behavior is extended to those who already practice the desired behavior as well as those who actually modify their behavior.[63] Second, tax incentives like the IRA can reduce the progressivity of the tax structure, forcing the lower bracket taxpayers to shoulder a larger proportion of the tax burden.[64]

A. Capital Formation and IRA's: A Costly Inducement

While there is no consensus as to the precise relationship between savings rates and tax incentives to promote savings,[65] a recent congressional study isolated two effects of such a tax incentive on savings.[66] Initially, because the tax incentive will raise the effective interest rate on savings, taxpayers might

---

[60] *See, e.g.*, S. REP. NO. 44, 96th Cong., 1st Sess. 26 (1979); *Employee Contributions to IRA's, supra* note 44, at 117 (remarks of Senator Bentsen) ("we have to encourage savings to be able to get the capital formation that we need in this country"). Corporate spokesmen also endorsed the IRA as an appropriate means of increasing the supply of capital. *See* President's Comm'n on Pension Policy, Public Hearing: Pensions and Tax Policy 1-2 (Sept. 12, 1980) (statement of John M. Baitsell, ERISA Industry Committee).

[61] *See generally Tax Incentives for Savings, supra* note 50.

[62] IRA proponents generate support for the deduction by pointing to countries that have similar programs. *See, e.g., Employee Contributions to IRA's, supra* note 44, at 118 (remarks of Senator Bentsen) (reported success of French savings plan).

[63] For instance, the IRA deduction is available to those who saved for retirement without the incentive and to those who save for retirement only because of the incentive.

[64] *See* pp. 878–80 *infra*.

[65] *Compare* Boskin, *Taxation, Saving, and the Rate of Interest*, 86 J. POL. ECON. S3 (1978) (taxes that lower the effective interest rate reduce welfare by restricting savings), *with* David & Scadding, *Private Savings: Ultrarationality, Aggregation, and "Denison's Law,"* 82 J. POL. ECON. 225 (1974) (savings rate is insensitive to interest rate). *See generally* Howrey & Hymans, *The Measurement and Determination of Loanable-Funds Saving*, in WHAT SHOULD BE TAXED: INCOME OR EXPENDITURE? 1 (J. Pechman ed. 1980).

[66] Congressional Budget Office, Withholding on Interest and Dividend Income 25–26 (Aug. 1980) (Staff Working Paper).

shift part of their income from consumption to savings.[67] But only a limited amount of savings qualifies for the tax incentives, so taxpayers who already save more than this limited amount cannot respond to the "incentive effect."[68] The evidence indicates the IRA deduction has a slight "incentive effect": the small number of lower income taxpayers who have taken the IRA deduction[69] suggests very little of the tax incentives goes to enticing new retirement savings.[70] Besides the "incentive effect," any tax incentive generates an "income effect."[71] The tax incentive increases the income of all taxpayers who take advantage of the tax incentive — even those who would have saved without the incentive.[72] Theoretically, these taxpayers will save part of that new income.[73]

Balanced against the benefits from an increase in savings generated by the tax incentive is the program's revenue cost. For every new saver who reduces her consumption in response to the incentive, the federal budget forgoes revenue up to the limit of the tax incentive. But unless the tax incentive is limited to those who would not have saved without the IRA deduction,[74] the Treasury must also offer the tax benefit to all other taxpaying savers even though the program has no posi-

---

[67] For instance, a 20% bracket taxpayer who saves in a 10% savings account enjoys an effective after-tax rate of return of 8%, but placing the deposits in an IRA would increase her after-tax rate of return to 10%. However, whether higher interest rates create more savings is debatable. *See* note 65 *supra*.

[68] For the taxpayer who already saves $1,500 a year, the IRA provides no incentive to increase savings beyond that amount, except inasmuch as the deduction provides her additional income, some of which might be saved, *i.e.*, the income effect.

[69] In 1977, 1.6 million taxpayers earning more than $20,000 a year contributed $1.6 billion to IRA accounts. An additional one million taxpayers earning less than $20,000 a year contributed $0.8 billion. *See* notes 46, 48 *supra*.

[70] To determine the IRA's incentive effect requires an estimate of how many of the participating taxpayers are actually contributing new savings, *i.e.*, savings that would not have been made without the IRA incentive. Wealthy taxpayers contributing to IRA's in many cases would have saved at least $1,500 a year without the tax incentive. *See* HOUSE REPORT, *supra* note 8, at 166 (Supplemental Views of Representatives James C. Corman and Sam Gibbons), *reprinted in* [1974] U.S. CODE CONG. & AD. NEWS 4670, 4835. Also, intuitively, since a relatively small number of people are using IRA's, *see* note 46 *supra*, the participants must be largely traditional savers who open IRA's to take advantage of their higher yields.

[71] The "income effect" is common to all tax reductions.

[72] If the IRA increases the yield on the first $1,500 of savings from 8% to 10%, *see* note 67 *supra*, a taxpayer who saves $1,500 a year with or without an IRA could increase her income $30 simply by participating in the IRA program.

[73] *But see* note 75 *infra* (explaining how an increase in the rate of interest might reduce savings); P. SAMUELSON, ECONOMICS 237 (9th ed. 1973) (paradox of thrift suggests increased savings could reduce national income).

[74] It is, however, difficult to imagine how such a limitation would be designed.

tive effect on their saving habits.[75] The revenue cost for a savings program might dwarf the amount of savings generated.[76]

Although there have been no empirical studies on IRA's, the available data suggest the IRA deduction is, in fact, an expensive way to stimulate savings. The Congressional Budget Office estimated the tax expenditure for IRA's to be $911 million in fiscal 1979.[77] In the overlapping calendar year, 1978, the Internal Revenue Service reported $3.0 billion of deposits made into IRA accounts.[78] So, at the very least, the Federal Treasury paid close to thirty-three cents for every dollar of IRA savings. But since over seventy percent of IRA contributions were made by those in tax brackets over $20,000,[79] many of whom were probably already saving at least $1,500 a year, the government's cost per dollar of new savings contributed must have been much higher, quite possibly in excess of one dollar for every dollar of new IRA savings.[80]

B. The IRA and the Federal Tax System: Decreasing Progressivity

The IRA generates new savings inefficiently because most participants are upper income taxpayers who transfer old savings into IRA accounts. But, even if this inefficiency did not exist, the IRA incentive, like many other tax deductions, would have a regressive impact on the federal tax structure, providing a greater benefit to higher bracket taxpayers than to lower bracket taxpayers.[81]

---

[75] In fact, if a taxpayer has a fixed savings target for the end of 20 years, the IRA's higher yield would actually reduce her annual savings. See Feldstein, *The Rate of Return, Taxation and Personal Savings*, 88 ECON. J. 482 (1978). Similarly, if the taxpayer simply wished to share the benefit of the increased rate of return between present and future consumption, she would also reduce her savings.

[76] For instance, the new exemption for interest and dividend income will create less new savings than it will cost in lost revenues. Congressional Budget Office, *supra* note 66, at 27.

[77] President's Comm'n on Pension Policy, Tax Treatment of Pension Contributions and Benefits 3 (Nov. 29, 1979) (statement of J. Douglas Sorensen, Treasury Dep't).

[78] See note 42 *supra*.

[79] See note 48 *supra*.

[80] If 60% of funds deposited by those earning less than $20,000 a year and 75% of deposits by those earning over $20,000 would have been saved anyway, then the program cost the government $1.04 for every new dollar of savings. Most bankers working with IRA's on a day-to-day basis agree that a large fraction of IRA contributions would be saved even without the tax incentive.

[81] This regressive effect is exacerbated by the high usage of IRA's among upper income bracket taxpayers, see note 46 *supra*, but even if there were equal usage across tax brackets, the deduction would still be regressive, see p. 870 *supra*.

The IRA tax incentive is one of several Internal Revenue Code sections enacted to favor income from capital.[82] Other examples include the expanded deduction for interest and dividends[83] and the increasingly favorable treatment of capital gains.[84] Like a partial deduction for income saved, these partial exclusions for returns on capital blend elements of a consumption tax into the income tax system.[85] But in contrast to most proposals for a pure consumption tax, which include a more progressive tax on expenditures,[86] grafting these deductions and exclusions onto a progressive income tax often simply redistributes wealth to higher income brackets. For instance, even if all taxpayers took advantage of a $100 savings deduction, the deduction would return fifty dollars to those in the fifty percent bracket and only twenty dollars to those in the twenty percent bracket.[87] As several commentators have

---

[82] The Treasury Department estimates that tax expenditures to encourage individual savings and investment will cost the government about $70 billion in fiscal 1981. See *Tax Incentives for Savings*, supra note 50, at 8 (statement of Ass't Secretary of the Treasury Donald C. Lubick).

[83] I.R.C. § 116; see Thuronyi, *The Dividends and Interest Exclusion — A Negative Vote*, TAX NOTES, Jan. 7, 1980, at 3.

[84] In 1978, Congress increased the preferential treatment for long-term capital gains by raising the deductible portion of capital gains from 50% to 60%. I.R.C. § 1202. The Senate Finance Committee's proposed Tax Reduction Act of 1980 would have further enlarged the deduction to 70%. See S. REP. No. 940, supra note 55, at 9.

[85] An income tax system taxes consumption plus increases to wealth (net savings) while a consumption tax system taxes only consumption. See Andrews, *A Consumption-Type or Cash Flow Personal Income Tax*, 87 HARV. L. REV. 1113, 1117 (1974) (seminal work on consumption tax). See also WHAT SHOULD BE TAXED: INCOME OR EXPENDITURE?, supra note 65. Theoretically, when tax rates are constant, a tax on consumption (and not savings) is identical to a tax on wages (and not income from investments). In both cases, savings grow at a pretax rate of return: a consumption tax is simply levied when funds are withdrawn from savings while a tax on wages is levied when the income is earned and before it is transferred to savings. See Warren, *Fairness and a Consumption-Type or Cash Flow Personal Income Tax*, 88 HARV. L. REV. 931, 938–41 (1975). But see Warren, *Would A Consumption Tax Be Fairer Than an Income Tax?*, 89 YALE L.J. 1081, 1094–95 (1980) (this equality may break down if the accumulation of wealth has value beyond the consumption) [hereinafter cited as Warren — 1980].

[86] See Andrews, supra note 85, at 1174–75. If accompanied by the appropriate alteration of tax rates, the change to a consumption tax system need not shift the tax burden across tax brackets, but the new tax schedule would have to be even more progressive than the current income tax schedule. See Graetz, *Implementing a Progressive Consumption Tax*, 92 HARV. L. REV. 1575, 1581–82 (1979). Equivalence between income and consumption taxes is possible so long as the accumulation of wealth has no independent value and all distributions, such as gifts, are considered consumption. See Graetz, supra, at 1624–26; Warren — 1980, supra note 85, at 1121–22.

[87] Of course, the deduction provides no benefit to those who do not save and those who do not pay taxes.

noted,[88] the attraction of taxing consumption as opposed to savings encourages the incorporation of consumption tax elements into the tax system, but because there is no concomitant restructuring of the basic tax rates, the most important impact of these provisions is to redistribute wealth to the higher income brackets. If the previously existing income tax structure represents a consensus as to how the burden of financing government should be distributed among tax brackets, then the enactment of provisions like the IRA not only distorts that distribution to the advantage of higher brackets, but does so in a less than straightforward way.

C. Additional Flaws in the IRA

Yet dissatisfaction with sub rosa income redistribution is not the only reason for objecting to piecemeal enactment of a consumption tax. By favoring certain classes of savings, Congress encourages taxpayers to channel assets to these investments, precipitating an inefficient allocation of resources.[89] Furthermore, the enactment of these individual incentives, which produce little new savings, is undesirable if, relying on these programs to boost savings, Congress ignores more promising solutions to the capital formation problem.[90]

III. THE FUTURE OF THE IRA

Although Congress created the IRA to equalize the tax treatment of employees covered and uncovered by private pension plans, the program has not provided that horizontal equity,[91] and has in fact exacerbated vertical inequities in the tax system. Proposed amendments of the IRA deduction should therefore be evaluated by their capacity to correct the basic shortcomings of the current incentive. First, as a practical matter, a proposal should address the IRA's inequitable distribution among tax brackets. Then, on a structural level, the

---

[88] *See, e.g.*, WHAT SHOULD BE TAXED: INCOME OR EXPENDITURE?, *supra* note 65, at 305 (conference discussion).

[89] *Cf.* Thuronyi, *supra* note 83, at 5 (tax incentives for certain savings favors sources of consumption). Indeed, proponents of tax incentives for savings argue that incentives would bring more funds to sectors like housing than the sectors would receive absent government intrusion into the market. *See, e.g.*, *Tax Incentives for Savings*, *supra* note 50, at 114 (statement of William S. Mortensen on behalf of the National Savings & Loan League).

[90] One often mentioned proposal to increase capital formation is the repeal of regulations on interest rates offered by thrift institutions. *See, e.g.*, Congressional Budget Office, *supra* note 66, at 30.

[91] *See* pp. 864–66 *supra*.

proposal should eliminate the IRA's inefficient expenditure of federal revenues and its regressive impact on the federal tax system. If none of the proposals can ameliorate the IRA's practical and structural defects, the appropriate response might be the repeal of the entire IRA program.

A. Prospects and Perils of Amending the IRA

The proposed amendments to the IRA fall into two classes: those expanding the IRA's benefits and availability, and those designed to rectify the inequitable distribution of IRA benefits. None of these proposals would overcome the current legislation's deficiencies.

Proposals to expand the IRA deduction, either by raising the contribution limit,[92] permitting new types of savings to be deducted,[93] or extending the program to new groups of taxpayers,[94] would only magnify the original legislation's inadequacies. High bracket taxpayers would still monopolize usage, gaining an even greater tax benefit,[95] and the progressivity of the tax system would be further eroded.[96] Moreover, even if such an increase were to stimulate some new savings, the national fisc would pay dearly in lost revenue.[97]

Legislative proposals to equalize the usage of IRA's across tax brackets are also inadequate. Replacing the IRA deduction with a tax credit would do much to equalize the attractiveness

---

[92] *See* p. 875 *supra*.

[93] *See id.*

[94] *See id.*

[95] *See* pp. 872–74 *supra*. The factors that led to unequal utilization of the IRA deduction would presumably accompany any extension of the program. *But see Private Pension Plan Reform, supra* note 45, at 1193–95 (statement of Norman H. Tarver) (Canadian experience shows lower income employees more likely to contribute to employer plans than to set up private savings accounts; however, Canadian plans often require employee participation). Of course, in the past, inequitable distribution of a tax incentive's benefits has not stopped Congress from enacting the incentive. *See* S. REP. NO. 1263, 95th Cong., 2d Sess. 270–74 (1978), *reprinted in* [1978] U.S. CODE CONG. & AD. NEWS 6761, 7030–35 (Additional Views of Senator Gaylord Nelson).

[96] *See* pp. 878–80 *supra*. Extensions would share the current IRA's regressive impact.

[97] *See* p. 878 & note 80 *supra*. Another hidden cost of increasing the IRA contribution limit would arise if the deduction were sufficiently high to encourage a large number of employees to desert qualified plans. Because IRA contributions are fully vested, young workers, who are more likely to leave their jobs before plan benefits vest, might well prefer IRA's to plan participation. An exodus of workers from qualified plans could diminish plan coverage and cost employers their tax deduction, *see* note 4 *supra*, ultimately decreasing total private pension plan coverage. Fearing such a result, union leaders have consistently testified against increasing the IRA deduction limit. *See Tax Incentives for Savings, supra* note 50, at 447–59 (statement of AFL-CIO Urban Affairs Dep't Director Henry B. Schechter).

of IRA's to taxpayers with different incomes.[98] But because the current proposal for IRA tax credits would exempt interest earned on IRA assets, the credit program would also be somewhat regressive, and like the current IRA deduction, the program would be more attractive to upper income tax brackets than to lower income brackets.[99] A credit program would also create serious administrative problems in deterring early distribution.[100]

The other proposals to equalize usage of IRA's across tax brackets entail statutorily imposed restrictions on IRA participation based on income.[101] Although legislation to promote equal participation is theoretically possible, these programs

---

[98] *See* President's Comm'n on Pension Policy, *supra* note 60, at 10 (statement of Ass't Secretary of the Treasury Daniel I. Halperin). A tax credit is deducted from a taxpayer's tax liability, not from her gross income, and is therefore equally beneficial to all taxpayers as long as their tax liability is at least as large as the tax credit. The congressional proposal for IRA credits has recommended a 25% credit be granted on IRA contributions, subject to the same annual limits as those under the current law. *See* H.R. 5693, 96th Cong., 1st Sess. (1979) (introduced Oct. 24, 1979). Interest earned on IRA funds would be tax free, and distributed funds would not be included in gross income.

[99] For example, investing in a 10% savings account, a taxpayer in the 20% bracket would get an after-tax rate of return of 8% while a taxpayer in the 50% bracket would only get 5%. If both of those taxpayers switched into an IRA for 30 years and received the proposed 25% tax credit for their deposits, they would both be enjoying an 11.1% annual return, but the 20% taxpayer's rate of return would have increased by more than 35% while the 50% taxpayer's return would have increased by more than 120%.

A pure credit without any interest exemption would have no regressive impact, but it would cause serious administrative problems. Putting the entire tax incentive at the time of deposit would make the IRA extremely attractive to those close to retirement but less attractive to those further away. This feature would diminish the pure credit's usefulness as a stimulus of long-term savings, and it also would create a possibility for misuse — deposits could be made immediately before retirement only to be withdrawn soon afterwards.

[100] So long as the penalty for early withdrawal is less than the tax credit, some taxpayers may be willing to make temporary deposits into the IRA and then withdraw the funds to take advantage of the difference between the credit and the penalty. Even if the penalty, currently 10%, were increased to equal the credit, taxpayers would still be motivated to make deposits into IRA's to enjoy the tax-free interest. However, the possibility for such misuse exists with the current IRA deduction even though early withdrawals are infrequent. *See* Internal Revenue Service, News Release, *supra* note 42 (IRS reported less than 1% of IRA participants prematurely withdrew funds in 1978). But premature withdrawals may someday become a problem because the IRA's are so attractive to upper income bracket taxpayers. A 40% bracket taxpayer with a 10% savings account is better off opening an IRA and paying the early withdrawal penalty so long as the funds are deposited for at least three years. *See* Collins, *Estimating the Benefits of Individual Retirement Accounts: A Simulation Approach*, 14 J. CONSUMER AFF. 124, 130–35 (1980) (describing when IRA's should be used for intermediate-term savings).

[101] *See* p. 875 & note 57 *supra*.

may present an untenable burden on the institutions administering IRA's.[102] Even if the deduction could become more efficient by evenly distributing IRA usage across tax brackets,[103] it would still have a regressive impact on the tax system.[104]

B. An Alternative Approach

All of the recommendations to amend the IRA deduction fail because they accept the federal tax code as the appropriate mechanism for encouraging retirement savings. Although the IRA has always been conceived of as a tax incentive, it need not be. As far as the taxpayer is concerned, the IRA tax deferral is no more than a means of increasing her effective return on retirement savings.[105] A direct subsidy from the federal government for funds held in a retirement savings account could provide a similar incentive.[106]

The subsidy could be in the form of extra interest paid by the government on all funds held in qualified IRA's.[107] Under such a program, contributions to IRA's would no longer be deductible, nor would distributions be taxed. Interest earned in the account and the federal subsidy would, however, be included in the taxpayer's gross income.[108] The penalty for premature withdrawal from the IRA would simply be the

---

[102] Even though some tax benefits are only available to low income taxpayers, e.g., tax credits for the elderly, see I.R.C. § 37, lobbyists have strongly opposed proposals to vary the availability of the IRA deduction based on the participant's tax bracket. See, e.g., Employee Contributions to IRA's, supra note 44, at 138 (statement of Michael Klein, Jr., Price Waterhouse & Co.).

[103] This is based on the assumption that a higher percentage of lower income participants would not have saved without the IRA. See note 70 supra.

[104] See p. 870 & note 33 supra; p. 878 supra.

[105] See note 67 supra.

[106] A senior Treasury Department official has endorsed combining an interest subsidy with a tax incentive to encourage retirement savings. See President's Comm'n on Pension Policy, supra note 60, at 9-11 (statement of Ass't Deputy Secretary of the Treasury Daniel I. Halperin).

[107] An IRA subsidy program would be analogous to student loan subsidies for which banks lend money to students at below-market rates and the government reimburses the banks for the difference between those rates and the prevailing market rates. See 20 U.S.C.A. § 1078 (West 1978 & Supp. 1980), as amended by Education Amendments of 1980, Pub. L. No. 96-374, 94 Stat. 1367.

[108] The trustee would administer the subsidy program, applying to the government for the subsidy and depositing it into the participant's account. Income taxes on the interest and subsidy would then be withdrawn from the account annually, through either trustee withholding or mandatory participant withdrawals. Forced distribution of taxes is essential to ensure equivalent contribution limits for all tax brackets. Furthermore, if these taxes could not paid be out of the IRA, then participants would in effect be forced to make annual IRA contributions in the amount of the account tax liability.

forfeiture of the annual subsidies and whatever interest had accumulated on those subsidies.[109]

C. Conclusion

The IRA subsidy surpasses both the current deduction and the proposed tax credit in progressivity, equity, and efficiency. The subsidy's advantage lies in the equal benefit it offers all tax brackets.[110] The IRA deduction and, to a lesser extent, the proposed credit both provide a greater financial reward to the fifty percent bracket taxpayer than to the twenty percent bracket taxpayer; the subsidy, however, offers the same reward to both.[111] This equality of benefit prevents the regressive impact common to the deduction and the credit.[112] It

---

[109] To handle premature withdrawals, the trustee would have to record deposits in two separate accounts, one for participant contributions and their interest, and another for government subsidies and their interest. If a participant were to make a premature withdrawal, the trustee would simply deduct the withdrawal from the contribution account and rebate a corresponding amount out of the subsidy account to the government. Since the participant would have already paid tax on the funds in the subsidy account, any amount rebated to the government would be deductible from the participant's gross income in the year of the premature withdrawal.

[110] The effective rate of return on normal savings depends on the available interest rate and the saver's tax bracket. In a 10% account, savings of a 20% bracket taxpayer will grow at 8% after taxes while savings of a 50% bracket taxpayer will grow at 5%. Because an interest subsidy would simply increase the available interest rate, the effect of the subsidy would be the same for all tax brackets. For instance, if the subsidy added 3% to the market's 10%, then the taxpayer in the 20% bracket would earn 10.4% after taxes (up 30%) and the taxpayer in the 50% bracket would be earning 6.5% (also up 30%).

The deduction, credit, and subsidy have the following effects on taxpayers in the 20% and 50% tax brackets:

RATE OF RETURN
(after-tax yield on 30-year deposit in 10% account)

	20% Taxpayer Rate of Return	20% Taxpayer Increase over Savings	50% Taxpayer Rate of Return	50% Taxpayer Increase over Savings
Savings	8.0%	—	5.0%	—
IRA Deduction	10.0%	25%	10.0%	100%
IRA Credit (25%)	11.1%	38%	11.1%	121%
IRA Subsidy (3%)	10.4%	30%	6.5%	30%

See notes 67, 99 supra.

[111] The IRA deduction helps the 50% bracket taxpayer 4.0 times more than it helps the 20% bracket taxpayer. The proposed IRA credit, with 30-year deposits, helps the 50% taxpayer 3.2 times more. The IRA subsidy offers the same benefit. See note 110 supra.

[112] See p. 878 supra; p. 882 supra.

also removes one of the major reasons for the disproportionate high-income taxpayer response to the IRA deduction.[113] Furthermore, because the uniform benefit of the IRA subsidy would presumably bring a higher percentage of lower income taxpayers with their new savings to IRA's, the subsidy would be a more efficient stimulus of new savings for capital formation.[114] Finally, because the IRA subsidy would be an annual outlay in the federal budget, the expense of the incentive would be far more visible than that of the current IRA deduction or the proposed credit. Congress could therefore more critically evaluate the value of such an annual outlay in comparison to competing federal programs.[115]

Although an IRA subsidy would provide a better incentive for retirement savings than either the current deduction or the proposed alternatives, it would share some of their inadequacies.[116] Therefore, Congress might prefer to repeal the entire IRA program,[117] either immediately or gradually by maintaining the current contribution limit and letting inflation wither

---

[113] *See* p. 870 *supra*.

[114] This conclusion rests on the assumption that lower income taxpayers are more likely to respond to the "incentive effect" and contribute new savings. *See* note 70 *supra*.

[115] Incentive programs imbedded in the tax code have traditionally been better protected from budget ceilings and sunset laws than direct outlays. *See* Surrey & McDaniel, *The Tax Expenditure Concept: Current Developments and Emerging Issues*, 20 B.C.L. REV. 225, 300–36 (1979).

[116] Like a deduction or credit, the IRA subsidy would still be given to those who save anyway, making the subsidy somewhat inefficient. In addition, because the structure if not the tax savings of the IRA subsidy is unattractive to lower income taxpayers, *see* pp. 869–70 *supra*, the benefits of the IRA might be somewhat inequitably distributed across tax brackets. Furthermore, the subsidy could still precipitate an inefficient allocation of investment or lull Congress into believing it had addressed the problem of inadequate capital formation. *See* p. 880 *supra*.

The IRA subsidy could also create administrative problems, but the procedures for offering IRA's under a subsidy program, though different from the current regulations, need not be more burdensome. Currently, IRA trustees and custodians have to make regular reports to the Internal Revenue Service. Under a subsidy, the financial institutions would have to apply to a government agency, presumably the Department of Labor, to receive their subsidy allowances, and would in all likelihood assume responsibility for promoting the subsidy and explaining its operation to potential participants. The cost of these services would be shared by those who benefit from the subsidy: the institutions that use the IRA funds and IRA participants who enjoy the basic benefit of the subsidy.

[117] But even though the IRA subsidy may never be a truly efficient program — in terms of either stimulating capital formation or expanding retirement savings — Congress may wish to retain the program in some form because it provides the semblance if not the fact of horizontal equity between employees covered and uncovered by qualified plans.

the tax incentive.[118] However, if political support for retirement savings incentives forces Congress to continue an IRA program,[119] it should do so with the IRA subsidy.

---

[118] By maintaining the $1,500 contribution limit since 1974, Congress has been slowly repealing the IRA deduction.

[119] The 97th Congress may enact IRA-expanding legislation similar to provisions in the Tax Reduction Act of 1980. *See* p. 875 *supra*.

POINTS AND COUNTERPOINTS

1. During periods of inflation, taxpayers who purchase depreciable assets with their own funds have their real income overstated if they are required to take normal depreciation deductions based on historical costs without any kind of inflation adjustment. This is not necessarily true, however, for those who purchase depreciable assets with borrowed funds, since the "loss" of real depreciation deductions may be offset by a "gain" from the repayment of the loan in inflated dollars. Thus some form of accelerated depreciation arguably could be a useful counter to inflation for equity investors but not for debt investors. But even for equity investors, the use of accelerated depreciation as a counter to inflation is problematic, since accelerated depreciation may favor some types of assets over others. For example, the credits and accelerated deductions available under the 1981 accelerated cost recovery system created a sharp bias in favor of short-lived assets. Avoiding such biases is not easy, since the relative impact of accelerated depreciation on particular classes of assets is very sensitive to the rate of inflation.

2. During the debates over the 1981 Tax Act, Alan Auerbach and Dale Jorgenson, both economists at Harvard University, proposed what they called a "first-year capital recovery system." Under their plan, taxpayers would be permitted to deduct the discounted value of their expenditures for depreciable assets in the year of purchase, using the "real" interest rate prevailing at the time of purchase as the discount rate. For example, assuming a real interest rate of four percent, a taxpayer properly entitled to three annual depreciation deductions of $1,000 would be permitted to deduct $2,888 in the first year and nothing in the subsequent years under the Auerbach-Jorgenson plan. How does the Auerbach-Jorgenson plan adjust for inflation? Must the inflation be anticipated? How can Congress discover the "real" interest rate? How would leasing transactions be treated under the plan? How are taxpayers likely to respond to a system that never permits them to deduct their total acquisition costs? Auerbach & Jorgenson, "Inflation-Proof Depreciation of Assets," *Harvard Business Review*, September-October 1980, pp. 113–118.

3. When, if ever, would accelerated depreciation constitute a tax expenditure? Assuming a stable currency and an asset subject to normal wear, would an ideal tax on realized income—

which appears to be the model underlying the tax code of most tax jurisdictions—ever permit depreciation deductions in excess of the rate necessary to reflect the real loss in value of the depreciating assets? For a defense of some form of accelerated depreciation and for the ensuing debate, *see* Kahn, "Accelerated Depreciation—Tax Expenditure or Proper Allowance for Measuring Net Income?" 78 *Michigan Law Review* 1 (1979); Blum, "Accelerated Depreciation: A Proper Allowance for Measuring Net Income?!!" 78 *Michigan Law Review* 1172 (1980); Kahn, "Accelerated Depreciation Revisited—A Reply to Professor Blum," 78 *Michigan Law Review* 1185 (1980).

4. Who is the proper taxpayer on income sources used to finance entertainment—the one enjoying the entertainment, the one providing it, or no one? See Halperin, "That's Entertainment," *Tax Notes*, Sept. 11, 1978. *See also* McIntyre, "A Solution to the Problem of Defining a Tax Expenditure," supra Chapter III.

5. Consider the following comments on the problems of tax-exempt revenue bonds:

> "The use of tax-exempt revenue bonds issued—nominally—by state and local government was to a large extent brought under control in 1968. But today it is again out of control. The extensive use of these bonds for industrial pollution control, single family housing, private hospitals, and student loan programs are all developments not expected in 1968 when these uses were not covered by the legislation restricting industrial revenue bonds. Further, the use of the dollar exemption by large corporations for new buildings or as a method of financing acquisitions of existing enterprises is a distortion of that exemption—a distortion that indicates it was ill advised, though in 1968 it seemed necessary to enactment of the 1968 legislation. Revenue bonds are now a major aspect of industrial and commercial financing and are the largest component—around 70 percent—of all tax-exempt bonds. Clearly, these revenue bonds must once again be brought under control—and if done correctly this means their elimination.

* * *

> "If revenue bonds can be eliminated, so that tax-exempt bonds are confined to direct governmental functions, then attention should again be given to the alternative route of elective taxable bonds with a direct federal subsidy to the issuing government for a portion of the interest. This approach would reduce the inequitable benefits now obtained

by high bracket buyers and would also increase the federal assistance provided to state and local governments through their bonds. A provision along this line might be the so-called Danforth elective credit, under which a bondholder in lieu of claiming tax exemption could elect to make the bond taxable and then receive a tax credit. The net fiscal effect is the same as elective taxable bonds plus direct federal subsidy to the issuing government but the approach may be found more suitable by some state and local finance officers." (Footnotes omitted.)

Surrey, "Our Troubled Tax Policy: False Routes and Proper Paths to Change," *Tax Notes*, February 2, 1981, pp. 179–97, 192.

6. Should banks be permitted a deduction for interest payments made to their depositors when the proceeds of those deposits are traceable to the purchase of tax-exempt bonds? Should a taxpayer who uses tax-exempt securities as collateral for a loan ever be able to deduct interest payments made on that loan?

7. Taxpayers can always arrange their affairs to make it impossible to trace physically the proceeds of their loans by, for example, commingling their loan proceeds with their savings. How should the tax system respond to this possibility? Should it treat the borrower more generously than it would a taxpayer who cannot remember what he spent his money on but who would like to claim a tax deduction in any case?

8. Who would win and who would lose from a substantial curtailment of the interest deduction? In answering this question, keep in mind that many taxpayers now take a standard deduction. Also consider the kinds of taxpayers, if any, who can borrow money in excess of their net worth.

9. In a lengthy attack on William Andrews' defense of the deductions for charitable gifts and medical expenses, Mark Kelman argues, *inter alia*, that most charitable giving provides donors with real benefits that ought to be considered in fixing their taxable capacity. Consider the following brief excerpt:

"The real world of charitable deductions has several significant characteristics: First, the charitable deduction is a serious tax issue only to the rich. In 1968, those with incomes over $1 million a year gave gifts averaging 25.9 percent of income. Those with income from $500,000 to $1,000,000 gave 18.8 percent of their income in gifts; and those with incomes from $100,000 to $500,000 gave 10 percent of their income in gifts. No discernible subgroup of the class of taxpayers with annual incomes between $10,000 and $50,000 gave more than 3.3 percent of their income in gifts. Second, the character of gifts from high-income givers is inevitably reciprocal in a way not necessarily true for the low-income donor. The average annual contribution of those earning over $1 million a year is $287,651, compared with between $90 and $478 for those with incomes below $50,000. Gifts of that size presumably draw some individual attention from recipients, charitable conduits, or the donor's community.

* * *

"In 1962, 61 percent of all charitable donations went to churches. Those who do not make 'significant donations' give almost entirely to churches: Those earning less than $15,000 a year give average donations to hospitals and educational institutions of $6 or less. While only 1.1 percent of religious contributions came from those earning more than $50,000 a year, 33.1 percent of donations to educational institutions came from those taxpayers.

"The charitable world, then seems to be made up largely of two types of gifts. First, there are small gifts by lower income donors to churches. These may be relatively insignificant for tax policy purposes, but they certainly involve a rather direct quid pro quo. Second, there are large gifts by the rich to educational institutions and hospitals, which divert resources to institutions that the rich choose, which often (particularly in the case of educational donations) benefit the class the rich want to be benefiting, and which involve a great deal of reciprocity, at least in the form of attention and deference. This second class of donations seriously undermines vertical tax equity because large amounts (and percentages) are at stake. Thus, real world complexity undercuts even further an already questionable defense of the charitable deduction." (Footnotes omitted.)

Kelman, "Personal Deductions Revisited: Why They Fit Poorly in an 'Ideal' Income Tax and Why They Fit Worse in a Far from Ideal World," 31 *Stanford Law Review* 831 (1979), pp. 856–58.

10. The figures quoted above by Mark Kelman might lead one to believe that capitalism gives its greatest rewards to those with the biggest heart. Would that it were true! In fact, much of what passes for charitable giving on the Form 1040 is charity in form only. For many years, some of the most profitable—and notorious—tax shelters have been those designed to abuse the deduction for charitable contributions. These shelters take

many forms, but they typically have two operative features: the gift of hard-to-value commodities, which the tax-shelter promoters claim have a value out of all proportion to their costs, and a receiving charity which is willing to assert that the property will be used to advance its tax-exempt function. This latter feature allows the shelter to avoid the impact of a 1969 tax reform, which limited the deduction for gifts of tangible personal property—the kind most susceptible to overvaluation abuses—to the taxpayer's basis in the donated property plus 60 percent of the unrealized capital gain.

The following excerpts from a series of stories on the former gem and mineral curator of the Smithsonian Institution illustrate how taxpayers sometimes convert the charitable deduction into a tax shelter:

> "In December 1977, three Florida attorneys and a former judge donated thousands of carats of aquamarines, tourmalines, amethysts and topaz to the gem and mineral collection of the Smithsonian Institution.
>
> "In recognition of their gifts they were presented gold, silver, and bronze medals and inducted into the Smithsonian honorary society * * *.
>
> "Each of the four donors had deducted his part of the gifts from his income taxes as charitable contributions appraised at five times the amount they paid for the stones less than one year earlier. The gifts cost about $70,000 and the donors took $350,000 in tax deductions over the next two years—a savings of nearly $100,000 in taxes (over and beyond their $70,000 investment in the gems) * * *.
>
> " 'I'm not so naive as to think most gifts given to museums aren't tax shelters,' says [the former gem and mineral curator]. 'They certainly are * * *. You can tell why the gifts [are] given by the fact they come in in November and December of the year—the end of the tax year. They don't come in July. I can put two and two together.' "

Washington Post, March 29, 1983, pp. A1, A8.

Tax shelters like the one described by the *Washington Post* have been attacked, sometimes with success, by the Internal Revenue Service. The Service should have even greater success in the future, due to the several anti-fraud provisions enacted in the 1982 Tax Act. But the abuse of the charitable deduction goes far beyond tax fraud transactions. Taxpayers typically get a bigger tax deduction than the loss in taxable capacity represented by their gifts whenever they make gifts of appreciated property.

How can Congress eliminate the abuses of the charitable contribution deduction? Should Congress limit the charitable deduction to contributions made in cash or a cash equivalent? In light of the performance of such reputable charities as the Smithsonian Institution, can the charities themselves be relied upon to police abuses? What would the impact be of a requirement that taxpayers realize as a taxable gain the difference between the amount they claimed as a charitable deduction and their basis in the donated property?

Many reputable charities have vigorously opposed sensible reforms of the charitable deduction because of a well-founded fear that a charitable contribution provision which met minimum fairness standards would substantially curtail "charitable" giving by the rich. But in the absence of far-reaching reforms, what remains of the case for the charitable deduction on tax policy grounds? What reforms would be needed to make the deduction a cost-effective subsidy?

11. Did Congress make a mistake in permitting taxpayers who take the standard deduction also to take the deduction for charitable contributions? What arguments, if any, can be made on fairness grounds in favor of that policy? What arguments, if any, on tax incentive grounds? Is it likely that the tax administration can effectively audit small contributors on their claimed deductions? Is it not likely that the tax administration will create, in effect, an administrative "standard charitable deduction" and only challenge claimed deductions in excess of that amount? How much additional giving would you anticipate from those now able to deduct their charitable gifts and retain the standard deduction? Assuming some additional giving, who are the likely recipients?

12. Is the tax code definition of medical expenses, as interpreted by the courts and the tax administration, consistent with Haig/Simons principles? Under William Andrews' view of Haig/Simons, would a taxpayer with a heart condition be permitted a medical expense deduction for an elevator in her home? Or should the tax system assume that those who cannot climb stairs will live in ranch houses or first floor apartments? Does Alan Feld's description of the medical deductions permitted for nursing care suggest that Congress intends to aid those in need? What, if anything, of the Congressional purpose emerges from the definition?

13. The *Harvard Note* quite properly objects to the IRA deduction on the ground that it favors the well-to-do. But the IRA deduction is probably less regressive than many other sav-

ings incentives found in the tax code. For example, it is certainly less regressive than the capital gains deduction and ACRS, and is probably less regressive than the exclusion for interest earned on state and local bonds and the All-Savers exclusion. What changes, if any, might make the IRA deduction progressive? Assuming such measures could be devised, should tax reformers then support the IRA deduction? That is, assuming they do not believe they have the votes to eliminate all savings preferences, should they attempt to fashion tax measures that offset the regressivity of the "unavoidable" preferences? Who would be the losers from such a strategy, assuming it were successful?

14. Why should consumption tax advocates oppose the IRA deduction? Some consumption tax advocates contend, incorrectly, that the IRA deduction could function as a reasonable transitional mechanism in moving from an income tax to a consumption tax. They suggest that by broadening the IRA preference to permit withdrawals for uses other than retirement, such as, for example, housing purchases, the income tax would gradually evolve into a consumption tax. What is wrong with this strategy? Consider, for example, the tax shelter problems it poses. How would an income tax with a general IRA-type deduction differ from the consumption tax recommended in *Blueprints*?

VI. CAPITAL GAINS

The capital gains preference has many defenders, but no one can offer a justification for that preference commensurate with the tax code's definition of a capital gain. Consider, for example, the oft-repeated claim that the preference stimulates productive investment by entrepreneurs, That rationale for the preference arguably explains its application to the gains of venture capitalists, but it is antagonistic to the preference given to hoarders of gold coins and other collectibles. Nor does that rationale explain why real estate developers who actively pursue their business are denied the preference, but those who merely sit on their holdings of real property are awarded it. In fact, almost none of the fine distinctions that have plagued courts and enriched lawyers since the capital gains preference became law have anything at all to do with the role of the preference as an investment incentive.

Other rationales for the capital gains preference fit equally poorly to the tax code's capital gains definition. If the preference is supposed to adjust for illusory inflation gains, as some of its proponents allege, why are inventory assets explicitly excluded from capital gains treatment and why the distinction mentioned above between types of real estate profits? The once fashionable lock-in argument for the preference fits the code definition no better. A light tax on capital gains may indeed reduce the lock-in effect of the deferral privilege, but why should policy makers care whether taxpayers are locked into their stamp collections, their tax shelter investments, or even their publicly traded stocks and bonds, since the efficiency of the economy is neither helped nor hindered in any documented way by changes in the ownership of such assets? In sum, the broad capital gains preference, when tested against its alleged functions, is incoherent and will remain incoherent until Congress defines the scope of the preference to match some specified public policy.

While tax experts await the millennium, they still must struggle to understand the impact of the capital gains preference on the fairness and efficiency of the federal income tax. The three selections below each contribute in different ways to that goal. The first selection, after summarizing the historical arguments for the capital gains preference and explaining their weaknesses, sets forth a complex proposal for restructuring the tax treatment of capital gains to exclude illusory inflation gains from the tax base. The Brinner-Munnell proposal has no natural constituency and is unlikely ever to become part of the tax code, but in explaining why their proposal would work in theory, the authors make a contribution to our understanding of the complex interplay of the inflation "penalty" and the deferral "bonus" that transcends the political context in which their proposal was offered.

The second selection, written by the chief economist for the Joint Committee on Taxation, summarizes the political confrontations over the past decade between those who are antagonistic to the broad capital gains preference and those who favor an expansion of that preference.

The final selection sets forth a proposal for accrual taxation of one major category of capital gains—gains accruing on marketable securities. Proposals of this type have been entertained in academic quarters for more than a decade and have been considered actively by the Canadian government on at least two occasions. The proposal offered here is inspired by recent Congressional action to destroy the tax shelter possibilities of commodity straddles.

Supplemental Readings. S. Surrey, "Definitional Problems in Capital Gains Taxation," House Committee on Ways and Means, 2 *Tax Revision Compendium* 1203, 1204–25 (1959), reproduced in F. Sander & D. Westfall, *Readings in Federal Taxation* (1970), pp. 552–72; *Report of the Ministerial Advisory Committee on Inflation and the Taxation of Personal Investment Income* (Canada, Sept. 30, 1982); J. Wetzler, "Capital Gains and Losses," in *Comprehensive Income Taxation* 115 (J. Pechman, Ed. 1977); Bossons, "Economic Effects of the Capital Gains Tax," 29 *Canadian Tax Journal* 809 (1981); A. Quale, "The Capital Gains Tax," in R. Musgrave & M. Gillis, *Fiscal Reform for Colombia* 352 (1971); Waggoner, "Eliminating the Capital Gains Preference. Part I: The Problems of Inflation, Bunching and Lock-in," 48 *University of Colorado Law Review* 313 (1977); Slawson, "Taxing as Ordinary Income the Appreciation of Publicly Held Stock," 76 *Yale Law Journal* 623 (1967).

no natural constituency and is unlucky to become part of the tax code.

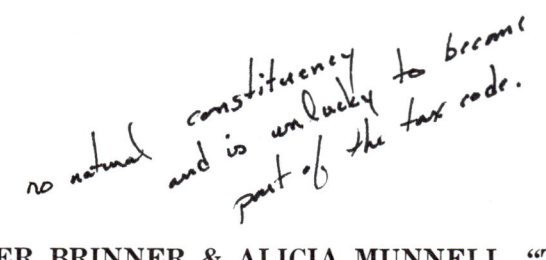

ROGER BRINNER & ALICIA MUNNELL, "TAXATION OF CAPITAL GAINS: INFLATION AND OTHER PROBLEMS"

New England Economic Review, September-October 1974, pp. 3–21.*

IN this period of high inflation and a depressed stock market, attention has once again focused on the appropriate taxation of capital gains. Much of the discussion has centered on two issues—first, the inequity of taxing illusory gains caused by inflation and second, the relationship of capital gains taxation to the declining stock market activity. In response to these concerns, there has been considerable support for reduction in capital gains taxation.[1] We agree that the current inflation justifies a reappraisal of capital gains taxation, but we find the proposals currently being considered in the Congress to be inappropriate solutions.

The essence of the Congressional proposals is that the proportion of a capital gain included in taxable income would decrease with the length of the period the investor holds the asset. Under the present law 50 percent of a gain is typically included in income subject to taxation; the proposed legislation would provide for this percentage (the "inclusion ratio") to decline to a minimal level of 25 percent for assets held for more than 25 years.[2] A Senate Finance Subcommittee has already held hearings on this type of proposal,[3] and the House Ways and Means Committee has recently approved such a formula.

A declining inclusion ratio is not the appropriate adjustment either to offset the effects of inflation or to stimulate investor activity. Due to the erratic behavior of both prices and the stock market, no arbitrary inclusion proportion can adequately correct for the inflationary component in gains derived under widely diverse circumstances. Furthermore, survey data indicate that a declining inclusion ratio would actually provide additional incentive for investors to postpone the sale of highly appreciated assets and this tendency would exacerbate the liquidity problems currently

---

* Roger Brinner is an Assistant Professor of Economics at Harvard University. Alicia Munnell is an Economist at this Bank.

[1] The advocates of tax reduction constantly emphasize a causal relationship between the stock market malaise and capital gains taxation. There is little evidence to support this contention. The poor performance of the stock market is due to much more fundamental economic and political problems than capital gains taxation.

[2] The reasoning behind this proposal is that 1) the longer an asset has been held the larger the portion of the gain which can be attributed to inflation, and 2) the declining inclusion will reduce the lock-in effect by encouraging individuals to sell appreciated assets at lower tax rates and thereby stimulate stock market activity.

[3] *Stockholders Investment Act of 1974*, Hearings before the Subcommittee on Financial Markets of the Senate Committee on Finance, *93rd Congress 2nd Session* (February 5 and 6, 1974).

plaguing the stock market. This reluctance to sell appreciated assets and thereby postpone tax payments is usually referred to as the "lock-in" effect.

The purpose of this article is to develop an alternative set of reforms to deal with inflation and the lock-in effect while, at the same time, making the taxation of capital gains more consistent with the principles of tax equity. The reform proposed for eliminating inflationary gains from the tax base is simply to express the purchase price of each asset in terms of current dollars by inflating with the consumer price index.[4] The full gain, calculated as the difference between the actual sale price and the inflated purchase price, can then be included in taxable income.

The proposed reform to reduce the "lock-in" effect consists of eliminating the two aspects of the current law which provide incentives for investors to hold onto appreciated assets. First, an interest charge should be introduced to offset the advantages of postponing the payment of tax liabilities until the asset is sold and the capital gain is realized. The interest charge can be expressed as a percentage of the gain after adjustment for inflation, so that for an asset held five years 105 percent of the adjusted gain would be included in income and this percentage would increase to 128 percent for an asset held 25 years.[5] This scheme, of course, contrasts sharply with the proposals for a schedule of declining proportions although the resultant tax burden will be lower under our proposal whenever inflation has produced substantial illusory gains.

An interest charge will eliminate the advantages of deferral and reduce somewhat the incentive to postpone the sale of appreciated assets. However, the second and most important deterrent to selling appreciated assets, especially among older persons, is the possibility of escaping taxation altogether by transferring the assets to one's heir. Therefore, closing this avenue of tax avoidance is the second element of the reform aimed at reducing the lock-in effect.

For a better understanding of the inequity of taxing inflationary gains and the sources of the lock-in effect, this article will first describe the appropriate treatment of gains within a comprehensive income framework. The second part of the article will summarize the current income tax treatment of gains, the inherent problems in the present approach, and the need for reform. Part III will develop the reform proposals mentioned above. The final section deals with the administrative changes required to implement the inflation adjustment and interest charge reforms.

I. Tax Equity and Capital Gains

Whether or not capital gains should be taxed as ordinary income, taxed at lower rates, or excluded from taxable income has been the subject of continuous controversy in the United States since the introduction of the individual income tax in 1913. Most tax experts, however, would probably agree that if taxes are to be levied in accordance with ability to pay and income is selected as the tax base, then all capital gains, both realized and unrealized, should be included in taxable income. As an index of taxpaying capacity, income should be defined broadly to include all accretion to wealth regardless of its source and irrespective of whether it is regular or fluctuating, expected or unexpected, realized or unrealized.[6] Capital

---

[4] A similar inflation adjustment has also been suggested by Milton Friedman, "Using Escalators to Help Fight Inflation," *Fortune*, July 1974, pp. 94-97, 174, 176.

[5] The derivation of these percentages is explained in Part IV. See pp. 18-20.

[6] Henry Simons, *Personal Income Taxation* (Chicago: University of Chicago Press, 1938).

gains, just like wages, salaries and income from investments, represent an increase in economic well-being which can be spent or saved. Even gains which have not been realized through the sale of the asset constitute an increase in economic power equivalent to that obtained by accumulating and investing ordinary income. In short, from the standpoint of tax equity there are no valid grounds to accord special treatment to capital gains. All accretion, including both realized and (theoretically) unrealized gains belongs in the tax base.

While theoretical considerations would lead to the full taxation of gains as they accrue, practically it is very difficult to tax unrealized gains. Furthermore, some would contend that even realized gains should not be taxed at full rates. Several of the most popular arguments for the favorable treatment of capital gains are as follows:

"Bunching"—Gains realized in any one year have accrued over a period of years and therefore it is unfair to tax them at high marginal rates in the year they are realized. This is a valid argument but could easily be answered by broadening the income-averaging provisions currently included in Federal tax law. Once capital gains are classified as ordinary income, it is clear that the averaging provisions which are appropriate for other highly fluctuating income streams such as farm and professional earnings are equally appropriate for capital gains.[7] Therefore, while the problem is of significant concern, it could be avoided simply by averaging and is not a persuasive argument for taxing gains at preferred rates.

Double Taxation—Since a portion of capital gains comes from corporate securities, there is some argument that capital income from this source is overtaxed. Assuming that the growth in the value of the stock reflects the increase in invested capital from retained earnings,[8] then this source of income is taxed once at the corporate level at 48 percent and then taxed again when individuals realize their gain by selling appreciated securities. It is therefore legitimate to question to what extent the special treatment of capital gains serves to offset the corporation income tax.

The concept of equitable taxation applies only to individuals and therefore, corporate profits should theoretically be attributed to individual shareholders and taxed at the shareholder's margin rate. Within this framework, it is true that if realized and unrealized capital gains were taxed in full, there would be no legitimate reasons for retaining the corporate profits tax. Distributed corporate profits would be taxed as dividends in the shareholder's income, while retained corporate profits would appear as capital gains.[9]

Since there is no rationale for full taxation of all gains *and* taxation of corporate profits, how seriously should the existence of corporation tax be considered when evaluating capital gains reform? There are two fairly strong arguments for minimizing the importance of the double taxation argument. First, as shown

---

[7] An alternative possibility would be to divide the gain or loss realized by the number of years the asset has been held, compute the tax liability on that fraction and multiply by the number of years in the holding period. Averaging would thus be done separately for the volatile capital gain portion of income.

[8] This is a reasonable assumption in the long run. Data for 1871 to 1960 reveal a fairly close correspondence between retentions and stock prices. See Martin J. Bailey, "Capital Gains and Income Taxation" in Arnold C. Harberger and Martin J. Bailey (eds.), *The Taxation of Income from Capital* (Washington: The Brookings Institution, 1969).

[9] We have assumed that in the long run, corporate shares will increase dollar for dollar of retained earnings. However, if retained earnings are not reflected in stock prices then there is no basis for taxation since there has been no increase in the individual's economic well being.

in Table 1, for 1962, the latest year for which data are available, capital gains in corporate stock accounted for only 30 percent of total net long-term realized gains reported by individuals. The fact that 70 percent of gains arose from noncorporate sources indicates that the double taxation argument should not be used to prevent reform in general.

Table 1

DISTRIBUTION OF LONG-TERM CAPITAL ASSET SALES REPORTED ON INDIVIDUAL INCOME TAX RETURNS, BY TYPE OF ASSET, 1962

	Net Gain (billions)	Percent of Total Net Gain
All Assets	$11.8	100.0
Corporate Stock	3.6	30.2
Real Estate	2.5	21.0
Instalment Sale Proceeds	1.5	12.6
Partnerships & Fiduciaries	1.0	8.4
Assets Used in Trade or Business	.9	7.6
Livestock	.7	5.9
Liquidation Distributions	.6	5.0
All Other	1.1	9.2

SOURCE: U.S. Treasury Department, Internal Revenue Service, *Statistics of Income, 1962, Sales of Capital Assets Reported on Individual Income Tax Returns* (Washington: U.S. Government Printing Office, 1966), p. 5.

The second consideration to keep in mind is that the double taxation argument is based on the very controversial assumption that the corporation income tax results in lower profits rather than being shifted forward into higher prices to consumers. The incidence of the corporation tax is an empirical question, but unfortunately the evidence to date is contradictory.[10] If indeed the corporation income tax is reflected in higher prices as many economists argue, then there is no double taxation.

These two factors, the uncertainty about who pays the corporation tax and the fact that only 30 percent of gains come from corporate stock, seriously undermine the double taxation argument against full taxation of real capital gains. On the other hand, if full taxation of both realized and unrealized gains were achieved, economists would generally support the reduction or elimination of the corporation income tax to the extent that the burden of the tax does indeed fall on profits.

Lock-in Effect—It has been argued that taxation of capital gains leads to a "lock-in" effect of appreciated securities which in turn reduces liquidity, impairs the mobility of capital and may magnify fluctuations in stock market prices. Whereas any tax on only realized gains would tend to lock in investments, taxing unrealized gains on a current basis would avoid the lock-in phenomenon. The strength of the lock-in effect comes, therefore, not so much from the tax itself as from the knowledge that the effective tax rate is reduced if realization of the gain is postponed.[11]

Inflation—Most of the recent concern about capital gains reform has been stimulated by the current high rates of inflation and the inequity of taxing gains that merely reflect in-

---

[10] M. Krzyzaniak and R. A. Musgrave, *The Shifting of the Corporation Income Tax* (Baltimore: Johns Hopkins, 1963); Richard A. Musgrave and Peggy B. Musgrave, *Public Finance in Theory and Practice* (New York: McGraw-Hill Book Co., 1973) pp. 407-410; A. Harberger, "The Incidence of the Corporation Income Tax," *Journal of Political Economy*, June 1962.

[11] Under current law individuals can benefit from postponing their tax payment because of the following three provisions: 1) the six-month holding rule before gains are given preferential treatment, 2) the deferral of taxes which grants an interest-free loan from the Treasury and 3) the opportunity to escape tax entirely, if the asset is transferred at death.

creases in the general price level. Actually, the case for full taxation of capital gains has been momentarily overstated in order to emphasize the basic manner in which capital gains should fit into a comprehensive income tax. In fact, capital gains that merely reflect increases in the general price level are illusory and should not be taxed. An individual who owns an asset that doubles in value at the same time that the consumer price index doubles in value is really no better off in terms of purchasing power than he was before. Only gains in excess of those reflecting movements in the general price level should be taxed.

One might ask why it is not just as necessary to adjust wages, interest and dividends for inflation. The answer is that, abstracting from certain difficulties presented by a progressive tax rate structure, the proportion of spending power derived from wage income taken as tax revenue is independent of the rate of inflation. In contrast, the proportion of spending power derived from capital gains is highly dependent on the rate of inflation—the higher the rate of inflation, the larger is the proportion of such purchasing power collected as a tax. Given that the tax authority is seeking to collect a given fraction of each taxpayer's ability to pay, it is essential that the proportion be independent of the rate of inflation.

For example, consider the case of a worker who earned $10,000 of taxable income in 1964 and still earns $10,000 in 1974. Assuming a 25 percent tax rate, the worker's tax bill remains constant at $2,500. The fact that the consumer price index rose substantially over the decade means that his purchasing power fell by approximately one-third from 1964 to 1974 but it also means that the purchasing power loss represented by his $2,500 tax bill has fallen by one-third. Therefore, the tax remains a stable 25 percent reduction of purchasing power.[12]

This situation contrasts sharply with the tax position of an individual with capital gains income in an inflationary period. First, consider an investor whose stocks rise in value from $100,000 to $110,000 in a period of stable prices. His gain in purchasing power is $10,000 and his tax payment would be 25 percent or $2,500. Compare this situation with an alternative period in which consumer prices rose 5 percent. The investor's taxable gain is still $10,000, and thus he again incurs a $2,500 tax liability. Unfortunately his purchasing power rose by only $5,000 and he is therefore forced to relinquish 50 percent of this in taxes—twice the proportion he had to pay when prices were stable.

In short, under the current laws, a comparison of the taxes levied in an inflationary period with a situation of stable prices reveals that the same proportion of purchasing power will be collected from wages, but a higher proportion will be collected from capital gains income. Therefore, to insure equitable tax treatment of all types of income, inflationary gains should be eliminated before taxes are levied.

In summary, the arguments generally put forth to justify preferential treatment of capital gains are not persuasive. Instead, most of the concerns relating to bunching gains in the year of realization, taxing inflationary gains and the problems created by the lock-in effect can be resolved by taxing *real* gains in full with extensive averaging provisions.

II. Treatment of Gains Under the Income Tax

Although the basic principles of tax equity imply that capital gains should be taxed in full

[12] This is true whether the worker's wages stay ahead, fall behind, or keep pace with the price of goods he must buy.

as they accrue like ordinary income, in the United States and most European countries they have been assigned a preferred status. As shown in Table 2, the treatment of gains in the United States has varied significantly since the introduction of the personal income tax in 1913. From the beginning, however, only realized gains have been taxed and except for the brief period from 1913 to 1917, when capital gains were treated as ordinary income, gains have consistently been taxed at preferential rates.

The period 1934-37 is particularly interesting in that the preferential treatment of gains took a form very similar to that currently under consideration by Congress. The proportion of the long-term gain included in taxable income declined from 80 percent for assets held less than two years to 30 percent for assets held 10 years or more. There is considerable evidence that the high rates in upper brackets combined with the direct incentive of lower taxes for longer holding periods did actually discourage wealthy individuals from selling assets and realizing their capital gains.[13]

While the tax treatment of realized capital gains changed frequently during the 1920s and 1930s, taxation of gains has been fairly consistent since 1942. At present, short-term gains, which are gains arising from assets held for less than six months, are treated as ordinary income and included in full in taxable income. In the case of long-term gains, only one-half of the gain is included in income. In addition, as of 1969 there is a "minimum tax" of 10 percent on the excluded half of the gains.[14] Nevertheless, capital gains are still given preferential treatment (see Table 3), and this preferred status is based on three special provisions.

1. *Exclusion:* only 50 percent of the accumulated realized gains are included in income. The excluded half of the gains are subject to only a 10 percent "minimum tax."
2. *Deferral:* gains are not taxed when they accrue and the tax is deferred until the gains are realized. This allows individuals to postpone their tax payment and thereby receive an interest-free loan from the Treasury.
3. *Escape through Bequests:* capital gains escape income tax completely if they are passed from one generation to another through bequests.[15]

The effect of these provisions, of course, is to reduce the effective rate on the taxation of capital gains below that levied on ordinary income. Because most of the capital gains occur in the upper income brackets, this preferential treatment primarily benefits wealthy in-

---

[13] In fact, in 1938 when a maximum rate of 15 percent for assets held over two years was reinstituted, individuals with incomes over $100,000 increased their realization of net long-term gains by 144 percent while net gains in all other income groups fell 28 percent. The increase among high-income individuals occurred despite adverse economic conditions (the recession that dominated the second half of 1937 deepened in 1938). Furthermore, the experience in the following year tends to confirm that, indeed, the large realizations of 1938 did reflect pent-up desire to sell assets: in 1939, net long-term gains of individuals with incomes of $100,000 fell by more than 60 percent, while gains for all other taxpayers increased slightly. Lawrence H. Seltzer, *The Nature and Treatment of Capital Gains and Losses* (New York, National Bureau of Economic Research, 1951).

[14] The minimum tax, introduced in the Tax Reform Act of 1969, is levied at a 10 percent rate on the amount of tax preference income of individuals and corporations over and above 1) a $30,000 exemption and 2) the ordinary tax for that year. Among the types of income included in preference income are the excluded half of long-term capital gains, accelerated depreciation allowances and depletion deductions in excess of cost.

[15] In the case of gifts, the gain is taxed only if the assets are later sold by the recipient.

Table 2
THE TREATMENT OF CAPITAL GAINS AND LOSSES FOR INDIVIDUALS, 1913 TO PRESENT

Date	Holding Period to Qualify for Preferential Treatment	Tax Treatment of Gains	Losses
1913-15	—	All gains taxed in full as ordinary income	Losses not deductible
1916-17	—	All gains taxed in full as ordinary income	Losses deductible up to amount of gain
1918-21	—		Losses fully deductible against all income
1920	2 years	12.5% maximum rate on net long-term gains	
1924-33	2 years	12.5% maximum rate on net long-term gains	Long-term net loss allowance limited to 12.5% maximum tax credit
1934-37	1-2 years	20% of gain excluded from taxable income	Same proportions of losses excluded, up to ceiling of $2,000
	2-5 years	40% of gain excluded	
	5-10 years	60% of gain excluded	
	over 10 years	70% of gain excluded	
1938-41	1½-2 years	1934-37 scheme with maximum rate of 20%	
	over 2 years	1934-37 scheme with maximum rate of 15%	
1942-69	6 months	Either 1) 50% of gains included and taxed as ordinary income or 2) 25% ceiling rate applied to total gains	Losses deductible from gains and ordinary income up to $1,000 with carryover provisions[a]
1970 to present	6 months	Maximum rate on gains increased to 35% and 10% minimum tax introduced on excluded gains[b]	Only 50% of long-term losses may be offset against ordinary income up to $1,000 limit

[a] Net long-term loss deductible from ordinary income up to $1,000 limit in any one year, with 5-year carryover period. Short-term losses combined with long-term losses could be used 1) to offset capital gains to the full amount of the carryover balance and 2) to offset ordinary income up to $1,000 in each year. In 1964 the loss offset up to $1,000 of ordinary income was extended to an indefinite period.

[b] Maximum rates were 29½% in 1970, 32½% in 1971 and 35% thereafter.

SOURCES: Lawrence H. Seltzer, *The Nature and Treatment of* Capital Gains and Losses (National Bureau of Economic Research, 1951); Martin David, *Alternative Approaches to Capital Gains Taxation*, (The Brookings Institution, 1968); Joseph A. Pechman, *Federal Tax Policy, Revised Edition* (The Brookings Institution, 1971).

Table 3

MAXIMUM EFFECTIVE TAX RATES ON AN ADDITIONAL DOLLAR OF EARNED INCOME AND CAPITAL GAINS INCOME, 1913 TO PRESENT

Year	Earned Income	Long-term Capital Gains	Capital Gains as a % of earned
1913-15[a]	7 %	7 %	100.0%
1916	15	15	100.0
1917	67	67	100.0
1918	77	77	100.0
1919-21	73	73	100.0
1922-3[b]	56	12.5	22.3
1924	46	12.5	27.2
1925-28	25	12.5	50.0
1929	24	12.5	52.1
1930-31	25	12.5	50.0
1932-33	63	12.5	19.8
1934-35[c]	63	37.2	59.0
1936-37	79	45.6	57.7
1938-39[d]	79	15	19.0
1940	81.1	16.5	20.3
1941	81	15	18.5
1942-43[e]	88	25	28.4
1944-45	94	25	26.6
1946-47	86.45	25	28.9
1948-49	82.13	25	30.4
1950-51	91	25	27.5
1952-53	92	25	27.2
1954-63	91	25	27.5
1964	77	25	32.5
1965-67	70	25	35.7
1968	75.25	26.875	35.7
1969	77	27.5	35.7
1970	71.75	32.21375	44.9
1971	60	34.25	57.1
1972 to present	50	36.5	73.7

a From 1913 to 1921, long-term gains were not distinguished from ordinary earned income.
b From 1922 to 1933, long-term gains are those on capital assets held longer than 2 years.
c From 1934 to 1937, long-term gains were divided into several classes; the rate in this table refers to assets held over 2 years but less than 5 years.
d From 1938 to 1941, assets were of only 2 classes; this rate refers to the longer holding period, 2 years and over.
e From 1942 to the present, gains from assets held over 6 months are treated as long-term gains.

SOURCES: Joseph A. Pechman, *Federal Tax Policy,* Revised Edition (Brookings Institution, 1971); Lawrence H. Seltzer, *The Nature and Tax Treatment of Capital Gains and Losses* (National Bureau of Economic Research, 1951).

dividuals. Table 4 provides estimates of the distributional implications of including in taxable income both 1) 100 percent of nominal realized capital gains and 2) the full value of gains assumed to be realized when assets are transferred by gift or bequest.[16] The table clearly shows that the benefits of preferential treatment accrue primarily to those individuals with incomes of $50,000 and over.

[16] As mentioned earlier, taxes should be levied only on real gains. Therefore, the magnitude of the increased tax liability is definitely overstated since the estimates include taxes on illusory inflation gains.

Furthermore, it is precisely the preferential provisions of the income tax that lead to the lock-in effect. The primary deterrents to the sale of appreciated assets appear to be the six-month holding period rule, the advantage of deferral and the opportunity to escape taxation entirely if the asset is transferred at death. As indicated earlier, the preferential treatment of capital gains applies only to those assets which have been held for at least six months. This time period was introduced to differentiate between the "speculator" and the regular investor. Since the tax rate is halved for most

Table 4
DISTRIBUTIONAL EFFECTS OF PREFERENTIAL TREATMENT OF CAPITAL GAINS, 1972

Income Class[a] (thousands)	Total Income[b] (millions)	Tax Liability, Present Law Amount (millions)	Tax Liability, Present Law Percent of Income	Liability with Full Taxation of Gains[c] Amount (millions)	Liability with Full Taxation of Gains[c] Percent of Income
Under $3	$ 7,968	$ 36	0.5	$ 36	0.5
3 to 5	27,610	475	1.7	482	1.7
5 to 10	145,033	7,655	5.3	7,823	5.4
10 to 15	216,483	18,843	8.7	19,257	8.9
15 to 20	180,340	19,354	10.7	19,932	11.0
20 to 25	109,886	13,301	12.1	13,896	12.6
25 to 50	142,941	20,707	14.5	23,090	16.2
50 to 100	41,178	9,672	23.5	12,044	29.2
100 to 500	31,355	9,241	29.5	13,519	43.1
500 to 1,000	4,360	1,324	30.4	2,314	53.1
1,000 and over	7,109	2,279	32.1	4,201	59.1
	$914,262	$102,888	11.3	$116,596	12.8

[a] These income classes are defined on the basis of adjusted gross income as defined under the Internal Revenue Code as amended through 1971 and include the following: ½ of realized gains, $17.1 billion; constructive realization of gain on gifts and bequests, $10.4 billion; exempt state-local bond interest, $1.9 billion; other preference income, $1.2 billion; dividend exclusion, $2.2 billion; interest on life insurance policies, $9.9 billion; home owners' preferences, $15.5 billion; and transfer payments, $79.8 billion.

[b] Income is expanded adjusted gross income as defined in footnote (a).

[c] Full taxation of capital gains includes taxing 100% of nominal long-term gains and constructive realization of capital gains on gifts and bequests.

SOURCE: Joseph A. Pechman and Benjamin A. Okner, "Individual Income Tax Erosion by Income Classes," in Joint Economic Committee, Congress of the United States, *The Economics of Federal Subsidy Programs* (Washington: U.S. Government Printing Office, 1972) Tables 2, 3, A-2 and A-3.

investors if they hold the asset for at least six months, there is considerable incentive to postpone the sale.

The second important deterrent to the sale of appreciated assets is found in the opportunity to enjoy an interest-free loan from the Treasury by postponing sale and thereby postponing the payment of taxes on the gain.

The third and probably the most important deterrent to selling an asset is the possibility of escaping taxation altogether by transferring the asset to one's heir. The heirs are permitted to step-up the base for future tax calculations to the value of the asset at death, which makes this provision a major contributor to the lock-in effect, especially among older individuals.

Two important points emerge from this discussion of capital gain preferences. First, the current treatment of gains favors high-income individuals. The second implication is that to reduce lock-in a system is needed that eliminates the tax-free loan and makes individuals bear an interest charge for postponing tax payments. Furthermore, reform of realized capital gains taxation without dealing with the problems of unrealized gains transferred at death will only be moderately beneficial in terms of equity and may actually be harmful to capital mobility by increasing the incentive to postpone realization.

III. Capital Gains Reform

The following proposals, which are designed to tax noninflationary gains in full with an interest charge to offset the advantages of deferral and to insure constructive realization at death, will not only lead to a more equitable system, but should also decrease the lock-in effect and thereby increase the mobility of capital. The reform can be divided into three parts:

1. *Real Gains:* tax real gains in full like ordinary income (maximum rate of 50 percent) with extensive averaging provisions and full loss offset against ordinary income.
2. *Interest:* introduce an interest charge which will offset the benefit of deferring the tax until realization.[17]
3. *Constructive Realization:* treat gains as if they were realized when transferred by gifts of bequests.

These provisions are not aimed so much at merely increasing the effective rate of tax on capital gains as at developing a more equitable and simplified tax system. Several of the changes such as taxing only real rather than nominal gains, more liberal averaging and deductibility of losses may actually reduce the liability of some taxpayers. A close look at each of the proposed changes will indicate that they are administratively feasible as well as desirable.

Real Gains—The easiest way to eliminate the effect of inflation in the measurement of long-term capital gains is to express both the original cost and the sale price in comparable units of value. Since all items on the income tax return are expressed in current dollars, it is more convenient to inflate the purchase price to the current price level. For example, if an investor has an asset purchased in 1936 for $1,000 that he wants to sell in 1973 at an appreciated price of $6,942, to calculate his real gain he will express $1,000 in 1973 prices which yields a new purchase price of $3,209 and a real gain of $3,735 compared to a nominal gain of $5,942.

This example is included in Table 5, which shows the real and nominal gains resulting from an initial investment of $1,000 for each of the selected years, assuming it appreciates in line with the average Standard and Poor (S&P) index. The ratio of real to nominal gains displayed in the last column shows the percentage of the nominal gain that should be included in taxable income to eliminate inflationary gains from the tax base. The enormous variation in this ratio substantiates the earlier argument that neither the current 50 percent inclusion nor the proposed declining inclusion ratio could be a proper inflation adjustment. It is not even generally true that the longer the asset is held, the larger the share of the gain that can be attributed to inflation. As the table indicates, for the average S & P stock purchased in 1920 90 percent of the gain is real, while for the stock purchased in 1971 there is essentially no real gain.

No arbitrary inclusion ratio can adjust for the changes in the price level. However, if price level adjustments are to receive serious consideration some practical problems have to be discussed, such as what is the proper index of price level. Since we are concerned with individuals' ability to purchase goods and services, the relevant index is one of consumer purchasing power. Despite its limitations, the consumer price index (CPI) published by the Bureau of Labor Statistics would probably be

---

[17] Under this system, an interest credit will also be available to compensate for postponing the realization of capital losses.

Table 5

REAL AND NOMINAL GAINS, 1920-73 SELECTED YEARS

Purchase Date	1973 Sale Price[a] (1973 $)	Purchase Price[a]	Nominal Gain	Consumer Price Index[b] (1973=100)	Purchase Price[c] (1973 $)	Real Gain	Inclusion Ratio (Real as % of Nominal)
1920	$13,459	$1,000	$12,459	45.1	$2,218	$11,241	90.2%
1936	6,942	1,000	5,942	31.2	3,207	3,735	62.9
1941	10,937	1,000	9,937	33.1	3,018	7,919	79.7
1946	6,288	1,000	5,288	44.0	2,275	4,013	75.9
1951	4,808	1,000	3,808	58.5	1,711	3,097	81.3
1956	2,304	1,000	1,304	61.2	1,635	669	51.3
1961	1,573	1,000	573	67.3	1,485	88	15.4
1966	1,260	1,000	260	73.0	1,369	(109)	(41.9)
1970	1,291	1,000	291	87.4	1,144	147	50.5
1971	1,093	1,000	93	91.1	1,097	(4)	(4.3)

a. Assume $1,000 purchase of stock in indicated year at Standard & Poor's 500 stock price index average for year, sold at average 1973 S&P price. Converted to 1973 dollars through CPI.

b. A consistent CPI series is available 1913-present, and the BLS has constructed a similar series for the years 1800-1913.

c. $1,000 in indicated year converted through CPI to 1973 dollars.

a pretty fair indicator of economic well-being. Since it is the conventional, generally accepted and best known measure of price changes, it appears to be an appropriate choice.[18]

The price-level adjustment is a much simpler and more equitable method to adjust for inflation than any arbitrary inclusion ratio. However, taxing 100 percent of the deflated real capital gains will require several modifications in current practices to insure that gains are not overtaxed. First, real losses should be deductible in full not just against capital gains, but also against ordinary income. This will insure a symmetrical treatment of gains and losses. A full loss offset will also encourage risk-taking since the government shares fully in the losses as well as the gains.

A second modification is required to insure that gains which have accrued over a period of years are not taxed at the high marginal rates applicable in the year the gain is realized. A simple averaging plan can avoid this difficulty. As mentioned earlier, the administratively most feasible plan is to divide the gain or loss by the number of years the asset has

---

[18] Swedish law provides for re-evaluation of the base and apparently uses the equivalent of our CPI. However, when French tax law provided for a similar re-evaluation, the economic series used related first to wholesale industrial prices and then, in 1959, to two new separate series related respectively to fixed assets and securities. This approach must be based on the assumption that investors characteristically use receipts from sales of capital assets to purchase other assets. However, deflation by means of an index of the price of capital assets would eliminate genuine gains associated with increases in earnings and relative prices of capital goods rather than simply illusory gains due to inflation. See Report of the Committee on Sales, Exchanges and Basis of the Section of Taxation of the American Bar Association, "Price-Level Basis Adjustment—a Modest Proposal," *The Tax Lawyer,* Winter 1973.

been held, compute the tax liability on that portion and then multiply by the number of years in the holding period. This is a very reasonable and practical way to avoid the "bunching problem" which will become more acute as capital gains are taxed in full.

A third change in the existing structure is to reduce the maximum marginal rate to 50 percent, the same maximum rate applicable to wage income. The whole argument for taxing real capital gains in full is based on the proposition that all income should be included in the tax base regardless of source. In this framework, there is no legitimate argument for taxing real gains at a higher rate than wage income. In fact, it seems reasonable that the 70 percent rate on unearned income was designed primarily to compensate for the preferential treatment accorded capital gains. Once the full value of real capital gains is included in the tax base there is no need to maintain the 70 percent rate for unearned income and the tax laws can thereby be simplified.

The importance of these changes to a typical investor can be verified by the comparison of the investor's tax liability under the current law and under the proposed inflation reform. (See Table 6.) In 6 of the last 13 years, an investor who turned over his portfolio annually would pay less tax or have a larger loss-offset under the inflation reform than under the present legislation. In fact, the total value of the reduction in tax liability for these six years exceeds the increased liability in the other seven. This net reduction primarily reflects the fact that the reform proposal fully recognizes the real bur-

Table 6

A COMPARISON OF TAX LIABILITIES ON $10,000 PORTFOLIO (TURNED OVER ANNUALLY): CURRENT LAW VS. INFLATION REFORM ADJUSTMENT

Year	Annual Growth in Standard & Poor's Common Stock Index	Annual Growth in Consumer Prices	Tax due Under Current Law (25% of net gain or loss)	Tax due Under Inflation Reform Adjustment (50% of inflation-adjusted gain)	Change in Tax Liability
1961	18.66%	1.07%	$466	$880	$414
1962	−5.87	1.15	−147	−351	−204
1963	12.01	1.23	300	539	239
1964	16.46	1.31	411	758	347
1965	8.36	1.67	209	334	125
1966	−3.30	2.91	−83	−310	−227
1967	7.82	2.83	196	250	54
1968	7.36	4.21	184	158	−26
1969	−0.87	5.36	−22	−312	−290
1970	−14.94	5.92	−374	−1,043	−669
1971	18.11	4.30	453	691	238
1972	11.10	3.30	277	390	113
1973	−1.62	6.23	−41	−392	−351

den of capital losses as well as eliminating the illusory inflation component of gains.

Interest—While the first part of our tax reform proposal consists of taxing real gains in full at the same rate applicable to ordinary income, the second part deals with introducing an "interest" charge to reflect the advantage of postponing tax payments from the time a gain has accrued, i.e., an asset price has changed, to the time an asset is sold. The postponement obviously gives preferential treatment to capital gains which are taxed only when realized, compared to the treatment of wages which are taxed annually as they are received.

If an asset appreciates $1,000 in real terms in the first year and simply maintains its real value thereafter, but is taxed only after 10 years at a rate of 35 percent, the government is, in effect, granting a $350 loan for a period of 10 years. If the interest rate is 5 percent, then the investor can earn $220 in compound interest on the $350 loan and the effective tax liability is reduced from $350 to $130, because he has been able to defer the tax for 10 years. If the investor can postpone paying his tax for 20 years, the interest earned of $579 will exceed the tax liability by $229. This taxpayer's gain is a loss to other taxpayers who must finance the $350 loan in the interim: the government must wait for 10 years for this sum, hence other taxes or borrowing must rise by an equal amount. Equal treatment of real gains and wage income would call for the addition of an interest charge.

Because the goal of this charge is to neutralize the advantages of tax postponement, the exact amount to be charged in a pure system would depend, of course, on the interest rate, the individual's tax bracket, and the length of time the asset has been held. For simplicity, the charge can be expressed in terms of the

Table 7

REQUIRED INCLUSION PERCENTAGE TO REFLECT INTEREST CHARGE FOR BENEFITS OF DEFERRAL

Interest Rate = 5% per year

Marginal Tax Rate	Holding Period of the Asset (years)			
	5	10	15	25
20	107.9%	118.2%	128.8%	151.0%
30	106.9	115.7	124.7	142.9
40	105.9	113.3	120.7	135.4
50	104.9	110.9	116.9	128.4

SOURCE: Authors' estimates. For details of the underlying model consult: Roger Brinner, "Inflation, Deferral and the Neutral Taxation of Capital Gains," *National Tax Journal*, December 1973.

percentage of the inflation-adjusted capital gain to be included in taxable income. The matrix of inclusion ratios for various values of holding periods and tax rates for an interest rate of 5 percent is presented in Table 7. The table indicates that a taxpayer with a 50 percent marginal rate would include 105 percent of his real gain in taxable income if he had held the asset for five years. Under the same conditions the inclusion ratio climbs to 128 percent for an asset held 27 years.[19]

The interpretation of this inclusion ratio can

---

[19] The interest charges which were the basis for the inclusion ratios in Table 7 were calculated on the assumption that the gain accrued evenly over the period in question. This means that investors who made all their gains in the beginning of the period would be charged too little interest, while those who made their gains at the end would be overcharged, but this problem is not as serious as it might seem. First, in most cases the gain is made early in the holding period so that most investors will escape paying the full interest charge. Second, investors who are actually overcharged on one asset will probably be undercharged on others, so that over an investor's lifetime the interest charged will more than average out.

be clarified by example. Consider an asset purchased for $1,000, appreciating in purchasing power at a compound rate of 5 percent per year so that at the end of each of the following five years its value is, respectively, $1,050.00, $1,102.50, $1,157.63, $1,215.51, and $1,276.28. The real capital gains or income accruing in the successive years are thus $50.00, $52.50, $55.13, $57.88, $60.77 for a total of $276.28. If the asset is sold after five years and the tax is paid on these accumulated gains, the investor has postponed his tax payment on the $50.00 gain for four years, the $52.50 gain for three years, the $55.13 gain for two years and the $57.88 gain for one year and interest should be charged. If the interest rate is 5 percent, the total charge should be:

$$\$25.00(1.05)^4 - \$25.00 = \$5.39$$
$$\$26.25(1.05)^3 - \$26.25 = \$4.14$$
$$\$27.56(1.05)^2 - \$27.56 = \$2.82$$
$$\overline{\$28.94(1.05) - \$28.94} = \overline{\$1.45}$$
$$\text{Total Interest Charge } \$13.80$$

Before calculating the tax due on the gain, as always one should be allowed to subtract any costs including interest which are incurred obtaining income.[20] Thus, his net gain subject to taxes is $276.28 − $13.80 = $262.48, his tax bill is 50 percent of this or $131.24 and the total due the government is the tax plus the interest charge or $145.04. Rather than require each taxpayer to duplicate these calculations the Internal Revenue Service could supply standard inclusion proportions of factors such as those in Table 7. In this case we need to know what multiple of the investor's capital gain, when taxed at his standard 50 percent tax rate, would produce $145.04. The simple algebra is presented below:

$$\$145.04 = (\text{Inclusion Proportion}) \times (\text{Capital Gain}) \times (\text{Tax Rate})$$

Therefore Inclusion Proportion =

$$\frac{\$145.04}{(\text{Capital Gain}) \times (\text{Tax Rate})}$$
$$= \frac{\$145.04}{\$276.28 \times .05}$$
$$= 1.05$$

In other words, by requiring an investor to include 105 percent of the inflation-adjusted gain which has accrued over a five-year interval in taxable income, the Internal Revenue Service can collect the appropriate interest charges for the tax postponement over the preceding five years.[21] This 105 percent of course corresponds to the entry in the last row of the first column of figures in Table 7. If we duplicated this algebra using other intervals and other tax rates, we would derive the other entries in the Table.

The inclusion proportion necessary to collect the appropriate interest charge varies with the tax rate and the length of time an asset has been held: the higher the tax rate, the lower is the proportion; the longer the holding period, the higher is the proportion. However, from a practical standpoint, it is probably advisable to use the schedule corresponding to the 50 percent tax rate for all investors. The slight resultant tax break given to lower-income investors would stimulate their return to the market and partially compensate for other tax shelters whose value rise with one's tax bracket, such as the municipal bond interest exclusion.

---

[20] These are approximate calculations designed to illustrate the principles involved. The exact procedures recognize the interest costs offsets to income as they accrue and thereby somewhat reduce the amount borrowed from the government.

[21] In the case of capital losses, the investor will be able to deduct more than 100 percent of the deflated loss to compensate for postponing realization.

Table 8 indicates the sensitivity of the inclusion proportion to the interest rate the government charges for tax postponement. The rows of this table present the proportions for four different interest rates, all under the assumption of a 50 percent tax bracket. As one would expect, the 5 percent interest rate (analyzed in the last row of Table 7 and reproduced as the second row in Table 8) requires that the inclusion proportion exceed 100 percent by approximately twice as much as a 2.5 percent interest charge and by approximately half as much as a 10 percent interest charge. Although market interest rates fluctuate widely, the long-run averages are fairly stable. Since the interest charges are most significant for assets which have been held for a long period of time, use of a long-run average is both practical and reasonable.

Table 8

SENSITIVITY OF INCLUSION RATIO TO THE INTEREST RATE

Marginal Tax Rate = 50%

Interest Rate	Holding Period of the Asset (Years)			
	5	10	15	25
2.5%	102.5%	105.5%	108.6%	114.7%
5.0%	104.9	110.9	116.9	128.4
7.5%	107.2	116.1	124.7	140.8
10.0%	109.5	121.1	132.1	151.5

SOURCE: Authors' estimates. For details of the underlying model consult: Roger Brinner, "Inflation, Deferral and the Neutral Taxation of Capital Gains," *National Tax Journal*, December 1973.

Introduction of an interest charge would increase both the equity and efficiency of the system. The charge would insure that individuals no longer benefit from postponing their tax until realization. This approach seems simpler than other suggestions such as periodic taxation of unrealized gains. Furthermore, the charge for deferral should reduce the "lock-in" effect since investors no longer gain by postponing taxes and also have the psychological impact of recognizing that they will have to include a larger share of the gain in income and consequently pay higher taxes the longer they hold the asset.

Constructive realization—Whereas full taxation of real capital gains combined with an interest charge for deferral are desirable changes both to deal with inflation and to increase the mobility of capital, no significant reform is possible without eliminating the loophole that allows gains to escape income tax completely when transferred by bequest. As long as this provision exists, individuals will have an enormous incentive to postpone realization of their gains.

It has been proposed that the accrued gains be taxed at death as if they were realized and this procedure is referred to as "constructive realization." Averaging and allowing the recipients to spread payments over an extended period of time would minimize inequities and forced liquidations. Actually, a constructive realization provision was enacted in Canada in 1971 and has been proposed repeatedly in the United States.

If constructive realization is too dramatic a change then perhaps a more modest scheme requiring the heir to use the original cost as his base when computing gains on future realization might be acceptable.[22] In any case, this avenue of tax avoidance should be closed. This provision is an important part of any thorough capital gains tax reform program.

---

[22] This type of reform was proposed both in 1964 and 1969.

IV. Administrative Procedures

Figure 1 displays the materials which might be substituted for the current capital gains tax forms in order to make the inflation and interest adjustments.

At present, the taxpayer subtracts his cost (current column e) from his gross sales price (current column d) and writes the difference in the final column (current column f). The revised form requires that the taxpayer make two additional calculations when computing his capital gain. These simple calculations are reflected in the substitution of columns f, g, and h for column F on the current form.

Under the proposed revision, the taxpayer would first adjust the cost by using the appropriate number from column (1) of the tables

Figure 1
SUGGESTED REVISION OF SCHEDULE D
FOR LONG-TERM CAPITAL GAIN TAXATION

CURRENT FORM:
Part II Long-term Capital Gains and Losses—Assets Held More Than 6 Months

a. Kind of property and description (Example, 100 shares of "Z" Co.)	b. How acquired. Enter letter symbol (see instructions)	c. Mo., day, yr. (Put date sold above dotted line and date acquired below dotted line)	d. Gross sales price	e. Cost or other basis, as adjusted, cost of subsequent improvements (if not purchased, attach explanation) and expense of sale	f. Gain or (loss) (d less e)
6					

REVISED FORM:
Part II Long-term Capital Gains and Losses—Assets Held More Than 6 Months

a. Kind of property and description (Example, 100 shares of "Z" Co.)	b. How acquired. Enter letter symbol (see instructions)	c. Mo., day, yr. (Put date sold above dotted line and date acquired below dotted line)	d. Gross sales price	e. Cost or other basis, as adjusted, cost of subsequent improvements (if not purchased, attach explanation) and expense of sale	f. Cost Multiplied by Inflation Adjustment	g. Inflation-Adjusted Gain (d less f)	h. Gain Multiplied by Interest Adjustment
6							
100 shares, XYZ Corp.		8/23/73 6/19/63	$2000	$1000	$1395	$605	$671

Figure 1 (Cont.)

TABLE TO ACCOMPANY SCHEDULE D

Date of Purchase	(1) Inflation Adjustment	(2) Interest Adjustment	Date of Purchase	(1) Inflation Adjustment	(2) Interest Adjustment
1929	2.492	1.480	Jan. 1970	1.127	
1930	2.557	1.471	Feb.	1.122	
1931	2.808	1.461	Mar.	1.117	
1932	3.126	1.452	Apr.	1.111	
1933	3.299	1.442	May	1.106	
1934	3.193	1.432	June	1.101	1.024
1935	3.113	1.422	July	1.098	
1936	3.081	1.412	Aug.	1.095	
1937	2.976	1.402	Sept.	1.089	
1938	3.031	1.392	Oct.	1.083	
1939	3.074	1.382	Nov.	1.079	
1940	3.049	1.371	Dec.	1.074	
1941	2.901	1.360	Jan. 1971	1.072	
1942	2.620	1.350	Feb.	1.070	
1943	2.468	1.339	Mar.	1.068	
1944	2.427	1.328	Apr.	1.065	
1945	2.373	1.318	May	1.059	
1946	2.188	1.307	June	1.054	1.012
1947	1.913	1.295	July	1.052	
1948	1.776	1.284	Aug.	1.049	
1949	1.793	1.273	Sept.	1.047	
1950	1.776	1.262	Oct.	1.045	
1951	1.644	1.250	Nov.	1.043	
1952	1.609	1.239	Dec.	1.039	
1953	1.597	1.227	Jan. 1972	1.037	
1954	1.590	1.216	Feb.	1.032	
1955	1.595	1.204	Mar.	1.031	
1956	1.571	1.193	Apr.	1.030	
1957	1.518	1.181	May	1.026	
1958	1.478	1.169	June	1.025	1.000
1959	1.466	1.157	July	1.021	
1960	1.443	1.145	Aug.	1.019	
1961	1.428	1.133	Sept.	1.014	
1962	1.412	1.121	Oct.	1.011	
1963	1.395	1.109	Nov.	1.008	
1964	1.376	1.097	Dec.	1.005	
1965	1.354	1.085	1973	1.000	1.000
1966	1.316	1.073			
1967	1.279	1.061			
1968	1.228	1.049			
1969	1.165	1.037			

in the second half of Figure 1. For example, assume that he had purchased 100 shares of XYZ Corporation in 1963 for $1,000 and sold the shares in 1973 for $2,000. He notes that the entry in column (1) opposite 1963 is 1.395, multiplies this by his $1,000 cost and enters the result, the *inflation-adjusted cost* of $1,395, in column F of the revised form. He subtracts this new cost from his sale price (column d) and enters the result, the *inflation-adjusted gain* of $605, in column g.

The final step recognizes the interest charge he implicitly owes the government because he has not paid taxes on the income from his investment throughout the 10 years he has owned his shares. The individual now refers to column (2) of the tables and multiplies his inflation-adjusted gain by the proper figure. The hypothetical investor of the previous paragraph would find the entry to be 1.109 which, when multiplied by the $605 gain, produces the taxable gain of $671. This amount would then be fully included in taxable income.

The inflation adjustments are calculated by dividing the consumer price index for January of the income year, 1973 in the example, by the consumer price index for the time of purchase. The table of Figure 1 allows for *monthly* differ-

Table 9

RESPONSE OF INVESTOR ACTIVITY TO CAPITAL GAINS TAX RATES THAT DECLINE WITH THE LENGTH OF HOLDING PERIOD

Respondents were asked to state their investment behavior if the maximum capital gains rate was geared to a sliding scale, i.e., would decrease as the holding period increased, would be applicable not only to future transactions but to present holdings. The hypothetical scale presented to respondents follows:

Holding period:	Maximum rate (Percent)
6 months	25
5 years	22.5
10 years	20
15 years	17.5
20 years	15
25 years	12.5
30 years or longer	10

Change in Investment Activity	Total	Income Under $100,000	Income Over $100,000	Under 35	35-54	55-64	65 and over
			(Percent of Total Responses)				
No change	78	76	58	81	74	80	76
Less Active	16	7	30	16	22	12	15
More Active	6	17	12	3	4	8	9

SOURCE: U.S. Senate, Ninety-Third Congress, *Hearings Before the Subcommittee on Financial Markets of the Committee on Finance* on S.2787 and S.2842, February 5 & 6, 1974, Impact of Possible Capital Gains Tax Changes on Investor Behavior, Study No. 1571. Prepared by Oliver Quayle & Co., Table P, p. 234.

entials for the preceding three years and annual differentials for longer-held assets.[23] The three-year criterion for monthly rather than average differentials is obviously arbitrary and could be expanded or shortened.

Conclusion

Congress is currently considering a proposal to reform capital gains by including in taxable income a proportion of the gain which would decline with the length of the holding period.

Although capital gains taxation is definitely in need of reform, this proposal is an extremely inappropriate solution. It would not effectively deal with inflation and would only exacerbate the lock-in problem. Indeed, the results of a recent study commissioned by the New York Stock Exchange indicate that a tax rate which declines with the holding period would actually decrease stock market activity. (See Table 9.)

As an alternative reform, we have made three proposals: 1) tax real gains in full and allow full offsets of real losses against ordinary income, 2) introduce an interest charge for tax payment postponement and 3) eliminate the loophole permitting gains to escape taxation altogether when transferred by bequest. These changes would insure both an equitable tax system and increased mobility of capital.

---

[23] Monthly adjustments are required to avoid distorting investor decisions such that investors would tend to purchase securities toward the end of the year and sell in the beginning of succeeding year in order to receive an unjustified 12-month inflation adjustment. The interest adjustments do not increase as rapidly with the holding period, hence monthly differentials do not appear necessary under any circumstances.

JAMES W. WETZLER, "RECENT DEVELOPMENTS IN U. S. CAPITAL GAINS TAXATION"

1978 Conference Report, Canadian Tax Foundation (1980), pp. 368–75.

No tax issue has generated more sustained controversy in the United States than the taxation of capital gains. Those commentators who want to move in the direction of an income tax with a broader base and lower rates recommend reducing the tax preference for capital gains because it causes a significantly larger erosion of the upper-income tax base and more complexity than any other tax preference. On the other side, many analysts consider the entrepreneur, the person who organizes and builds up a new business, to be the driving force in a capitalist economy and believe that failure to give preferential tax treatment to capital gains, the successful entrepreneur's principal source of income, would undermine our economy and society in some fundamental way. They argue that capital gains taxes discourage sales of appreciated assets, reducing economic efficiency. Moreover, in a period of inflation and negative after-tax real rates of return to savers, the traditional supporters of capital gains tax preferences are joined by those homeowners who believe that appreciation in the value of their homes is their best protection against inflation.

In the United States the interplay of these forces has led to frequent changes in the method of taxing capital gains. Since 1969 we have gone through a rather violent cycle — first raising capital gains taxes by about 20% between 1969 and 1976, and then recently lowering them just below the pre-1969 rates. My intention now is first briefly to survey the history of U.S. capital gains taxation up to 1969, then to discuss the nature and causes of the sizable increase in capital gains taxes enacted in 1969 and 1976, and finally to analyse in some detail the changes made earlier this year. I hope such a history of our trials and tribulations will be useful to you in deciding what to do in Canada.

U.S. CAPITAL GAINS TAXES BETWEEN 1913 AND 1969

The original U.S. income tax, enacted in 1913, taxed capital gains as ordinary income, but in 1921 Congress enacted a special 12½% alternative capital gains rate. That rate can be compared to a 58% top rate on ordinary income enacted in the 1921 Act and a 25% top rate prevailing through the latter part of the 1920s. The 1921 capital gains tax cut was part of a general conservative trend which swept the United States after the first world war, personified in fiscal matters by the Secretary of the Treasury, Andrew Mellon. Indeed, some editorial writers have recently used the Mellon tax cuts of the 1920s as their model for the appropriate U.S. policy for the 1970s and 1980s.

By 1934, however, several things had changed. The conservative ideology of Presidents Harding, Coolidge, and Hoover had been replaced by Franklin D. Roosevelt's New Deal. Also, the top tax rate on ordinary income had risen back up to 56%, making the 12½% capital gains rate a much larger tax preference than in the late 1920s. In response, Congress raised capital gains taxes by enacting a "sliding scale" inclusion ratio, under which the percentage of capital gains included in taxable income declined from 100% for short-term gains to 30% for gains on assets held more than ten years.

The sliding scale, however, was short-lived. Dissatisfaction focused on its tendency to encourage investors to postpone sales of assets which had appreciated in value (a characteristic which does not prevent people from recommending the sliding scale forty years later). In 1938, the sliding scale was replaced by a two-pronged capital gains preference — a 50% exclusion for long-term capital gains or, alternatively, a 15% alternative rate on the whole gain. Then, in 1942, the alternative rate was raised to 25% as part of the general wartime tax increase. This system stayed in place for twenty-seven years.

THE TAX REFORM ACTS OF 1969 AND 1976

In both 1969 and 1976 Congress passed significant tax reform bills, which together raised capital gains tax rates by about one-fifth. While the major tax bills of the 1920s, 1930s, and 1940s were presidential initiatives, the tax reform Acts of 1969 and 1976 were explicitly congressional initiatives, the Nixon and Ford administrations actively opposing the capital gains tax increases contained in them.

The 1969 and 1976 Acts increased capital gains tax rates in six ways.

— The 1969 Act put a $50,000 ceiling on the amount of capital gains eligible for the 25% alternative rate (this represented a $400 million tax increase at 1978 income levels).

— They imposed a 15% minimum tax on certain tax preferences, including the excluded half of capital gains. The minimum tax was to be paid in addition to the regular income tax (a tax increase of $1.3 billion at 1978 levels).

— The 1976 Act repealed the rule allowing an heir to compute the gain on inherited property based on its fair market value at the time of inheritance, and instead required recipients of bequests to use the cost or other basis of the decedent in computing the taxable gain (initially a small tax increase, but eventually building up to over $1 billion at 1978 levels).

— The 1969 Act raised the capital gains tax rate for corporations from 25% to 30% (a tax increase of $300 million at 1978 levels).

— The 1976 Act increased the holding period defining long-term capital gains from six months to one full year (a tax increase of $400 million at 1978 levels).

— The 1969 Act put a 50% maximum tax rate on earned income (compared to a 70% top rate on ordinary income) but reduced the amount of earned income eligible for the rate by the individual's tax preferences, including the excluded half of capital gains. This "poison" of earned income was equivalent to an additional 10% tax on certain capital gains and, together with the minimum tax, raised the marginal tax rate on capital gains to $49\frac{1}{8}\%$ in certain instances.

The estimated revenue gain of $2.4 to $3.4 billion from these capital gains tax increases (depending on whether one counts the initial or the long-run impact of carry-over of basis) might be compared to the expected 1978 revenue yield from capital gains taxes of $9 billion from individuals and $1.7 billion from corporations. Thus, in 1969 and 1976 the United States enacted a 20% increase in its capital gains tax, an increase which would eventually have grown to 30%.

The most striking point about the capital gains tax increases enacted in 1969 and 1976 is that they were not accompanied by a debate about the intrinsic merits of capital gains tax preferences. Rather, they occurred as responses to other problems faced by the tax-writing committees of Congress.

The saga of how the United States came to raise its capital gains tax by about one-fifth during the tenure of two conservative Republican presidents is a fascinating one, and I only have time to mention the highlights. It begins with the appointment by President Kennedy of Stanley Surrey as the chief tax policy officer of the Treasury Department. By 1968 Surrey's office had completed a major set of tax reform proposals, and while the Johnson administration showed little interest in them, pressure from congressional liberals caused them to be made public at the beginning of the Nixon administration. The Surrey proposals were based on the proposition that, at least as far as high-income taxpayers were concerned, the main objective of tax reform was to provide greater uniformity in effective tax rates. Other traditional objectives of tax reform, such as tax simplification and a more neutral impact of the tax system on economic decisions, were given relatively short shrift.

On the last day of business of the Johnson administration, the Secretary of the Treasury, Joseph Barr, testified at a congressional hearing and made a widely publicized statement that the United States faced a taxpayers' revolt because too many high-income people were paying little or no federal income tax. As it happened, Congress had just enacted a 10% income tax surcharge to finance the Indochina War, and the combination of the publicity surrounding the Surrey proposals, Secretary Barr's inflammatory statement, and the pain of each taxpayer's having to add 10% to a tax liability that he no doubt already considered much too large led to a flood of mail demanding tax reforms. The result was the *Tax Reform Act* of 1969.

The capital gains tax increases in that Act were carefully limited to high-income people. The minimum tax and the preference "poison" under the maximum tax each had $30,000 exemptions, so that they only applied to someone with more than $60,000 of capital gains, and the $50,000 ceiling on the 25% alternative tax applied only to individuals with gains exceeding $50,000.

A similar story underlies the 1976 increase in capital gains taxes, which was also not accompanied by much debate on the merits of capital gains tax preferences. The prime impetus for the 1976 tax reform bill was the rapid growth in the mass marketing of leveraged tax shelters in the early 1970s. These shelters were typically partnerships which promised first-year deductions of several dollars for each dollar invested. It was widely agreed that legislation was needed to stop what was rapidly becoming a national scandal.

How did this concern with tax shelters turn into a second major increase in capital gains taxes? The answer lies hidden in congressional procedures. In 1974 Congress had enacted a new mandatory congressional budget process under which, for the first time, Congress set for itself a binding revenue floor and a spending ceiling so that the budget could be considered as a whole rather than as a series of disconnected revenue and spending measures.

For fiscal year 1977, beginning on 1 October 1976, the revenue floor had to be low enough to accommodate $17.3 billion to extend several expiring temporary anti-recession tax cuts enacted in 1975. To create pressure for tax reform, liberal congressmen amended the initial budget resolution to allow for only $15.3 billion of tax cuts, thereby putting the tax-writing committees of Congress in the distinctly unpleasant position of having either to enact $2 billion of tax increases, to fail to extend the full $17.3 billion of tax cuts, or to undercut the new budget process. The $2 billion figure was concocted without any consideration of precisely what politically feasible tax reforms could raise that much revenue.

Now, while the U.S. tax system contains quite a large number of tax preferences, there is only one place to raise large amounts of revenue from high-income people by reducing tax preferences, and that is the capital gains tax preference. Furthermore, this could be done indirectly by beefing up the minimum tax enacted in 1969. Thus, the 1976 Act increased the revenue raised from individuals by the minimum tax, almost entirely from the capital gains tax preference, from about $200 million to about $1.4 billion, and it increased the number of minimum taxpayers from 20,000 to 240,000. As in 1969, a major increase in the capital gains tax occurred for reasons entirely unrelated to the arguments for or against capital gains tax preferences.

THE REVENUE ACT OF 1978

With one exception, there was no immediate adverse reaction to the capital gains tax increase enacted in 1976. The exception was carry-over of basis, which tax lawyers and other estate planners almost immediately criticized on the grounds of extraordinary complexity. (Carry-over of basis requires the heir to learn what is the decedent's basis, sometimes a difficult task; and, as drafted, it also encouraged people to bequeath appreciated assets to low-bracket heirs or charities and other assets to high-bracket heirs. Also, the specific law passed in 1976, drafted in considerable haste, contained some more easily avoidable complexities.) In response, the 1978 Act has deferred the application of carry-over of basis until 1979, giving Congress time to attempt to resolve the issue of how to treat capital gains at death. (As a non-lawyer, I cannot help but wonder how the tax bar would have reacted to a provision with equal complexity which provided a $1 billion carry-over basis credit instead of a tax increase.)

Through 1977, President Carter proceeded with his program of tax reform. The early drafts of the program included an ambitious plan to tax capital gains as ordinary income, to cut the maximum tax rate to 50% for all income, and to reduce the double taxation of dividends. The recommendations which President Carter sent up to Congress in January 1978, however, contained only a modest increase in the capital gains tax through further tightening of the minimum tax and repeal of the 25% alternative rate.

As it turned out, not only was there very little congressional support for higher capital gains taxes, but there was a strong undercurrent of doubt about what had been done in 1969 and 1976. As I have argued, in the 1969 and 1976 Acts Congress did not really make a conscious decision to raise capital gains taxes significantly, and support for those tax increases was woefully thin.

What underlay the decision to cut the capital gains tax this year was dissatisfaction over the performance of the U.S. economy. Our inflation rate has remained high, at least by American standards. Business investment, as a percentage of gross national product, is lower in the United States than in any major industrial country, and a larger proportion of our investment goes to replace our large stock of existing capital. The recent rapid growth in labour force participation, especially by women, means that the amount of capital per worker in the United States, a major determinant of productivity growth, has been growing only very slowly, in comparison not only with other countries but also with our own history. Corporate stock prices are only slightly higher today than they were in 1968, indicating a major erosion of real values, and equity capital for new businesses is very hard to come by.

Our low rate of investment has persisted despite the application of the old remedies of easy money, individual tax cuts to stimulate demand, and such targeted business tax cuts as the Investment Tax Credit. The desire for some new, more effective, investment stimulus created an environment conducive to a capital gains tax cut.

The second cause of widespread support for a capital gains tax cut was the effect of inflation on the real wealth of middle-class households. The after-tax rate of return, adjusted for inflation, is now negative for most assets owned by middle-class Americans, with the exception of their homes, and people are increasingly seeing the appreciation of their homes as their best protection against inflation.

This preoccupation with capital gains on homes presents an interesting political economic problem. To the extent that households put ever larger portions of their wealth into their homes, business investment in productive assets is reduced, and the economic difficulties flowing from inadequate investment are aggravated. However, the political forces pushing us towards ever more lenient tax treatment of owner-occupied housing are well-nigh irresistible.

Indeed, in its version of the 1978 Act, the House of Representatives passed a once-in-a-lifetime exclusion from taxable income for up to $100,000 of capital gain on the sale of a home. (The United States now taxes such gains when they are not reinvested in a new home.) In the Senate, concern over the economic impact of this change, and possible inequity towards people whose wealth was in assets other than their home, caused the exclusion to be cut back significantly; and the final version of the bill excludes the first $100,000 of gain on a home only for taxpayers aged fifty-five or over.

There was also concern over the interaction between inflation and the tax on capital gains. It is now becoming fairly well known that inflation raises the real burden of an income tax, not only by narrowing the real value of rate brackets and eroding the real value of such fixed dollar amounts as the personal exemption, but also by systematically overstating taxable income from capital. The recent acceleration of U.S. inflation, after a decline from 12% in 1974 to 5% in 1976, has generated a good deal of pessimism about our ability to control inflation (evidently shared by the traders in foreign exchange markets) and has greatly increased the support for eliminating many of the distorting effects of inflation on the tax system.

The effect of inflation in distorting the definition of capital income is most easily seen by the layman in the case of capital gains, although because of the large tax preferences for capital gains the problem is really more serious elsewhere. Recognizing the inequity of taxing capital gains which only parallel inflation and clearly in the mood to cut capital gains taxes, the House of Representatives, in a surprise move, voted decisively to index for inflation the basis of assets for the purpose of determining capital gain or loss. The indexing was to apply to inflation occurring after 1979.

The vote, first in the Ways and Means Committee and then in the full House, put the staff in the position of having to draft a capital gains indexing proposal. Our effort, along with some very useful comments on the draft by tax lawyers, has enabled us to learn quite a lot about the difficulties of indexing capital gains, a proposal which appears in almost everybody's comprehensive capital gains tax reform packages.

One problem is that indexing inherently involves a good deal of complexity for individual taxpayers. Consider, for example, someone who buys stock on a monthly investment plan and reinvests his dividends four times a year. When he sells the stock, such a taxpayer would have to make sixteen separate basis adjustments for each year in which he holds the stock.

A second problem results from the political difficulty of applying indexing to debt, where the indexing adjustment involves additional taxable income for the borrower. Failure to index debt requires denying indexing to lenders as well, which involves a complex set of rules to prevent taxpayers from converting ineligible assets to eligible assets such as, for example, by setting up a corporation which owns debt securities. Denying the benefits or costs of indexing to both lenders and borrowers is revenue-neutral if both have the same marginal tax rate; however, this policy will encourage borrowing by high-bracket taxpayers to finance purchases of assets eligible for indexing and could lead to serious tax-shelter possibilities.

These technical issues were not prominent in the debate on indexing, although they will probably arise if indexing for capital gains is reconsidered in the future. The Carter administration vehemently opposed indexing and secured its defeat, making the straightforward argument that the House provision would cause sizable revenue losses in future years and the somewhat speculative argument that indexing, by cushioning people from the ill effects of inflation, would deplete the ranks of dedicated inflation fighters.

Let me return to the main line of my story. As late as the end of 1977 virtually no one in Congress was thinking seriously about cutting capital gains taxes; the only question was whether they were to be raised further in connection with the Carter tax reform program.

During the year some presidents of California electronics companies had come around to see Congressmen and their staffs and had argued that the 1969 and 1976 capital gains tax increases had caused our economic problems by drying up sources of venture capital for new businesses. Their argument impressed Rep. William Steiger, a young, politically moderate Congressman from Wisconsin, and he introduced a little-noticed bill to roll capital gains taxes back to their pre-1969 levels, hoping to generate some discussion of the problem. Specifically the amendment deleted capital gains from the minimum tax and from the preference "poison" under the maximum tax and set a 25% top rate on both individual and corporate capital gains.

In Congress and in the editorial pages of many newspapers around the country the Steiger amendment picked up support at an astonishing rate. The *Wall Street Journal* announced its support for the Steiger amendment in a widely read editorial entitled "Stupendous Steiger".

The underlying reasons for the widespread congressional support for lower capital gains taxes were the things I outlined earlier — dissatisfaction with the nation's economic performance, the desire to accommodate homeowners, and concern about the inequity of taxing nominal capital gains in periods of inflation. As a vehicle for responding to these concerns, the Steiger amendment had one obvious deficiency: it would have cut taxes for only 380,000 of the 4.7 million tax returns with taxable capital gains (out of 67 million returns with some tax liability). This fact was downplayed or ignored in most press accounts of the amendment, which typically described the amendment as cutting *the* capital gains tax rate from 49⅛% to 25%. In fact, as Treasury data were later to show, the average marginal capital gains tax rate is only 16%, up from 14% before 1969. Only a very unusual taxpayer could be subject to the theoretical maximum rate of 49⅛%. Thus, the complexity of the law, originally a factor which enabled tax reformers to "sneak through" a major increase in capital gains taxes, began to work in favour of those who wanted to lower capital gains tax rates by facilitating misinformation about the law.

Also contributing to the intellectual confusion, and to support for the amendment, were a series of studies on its economic effects conducted or sponsored by supporters of the amendment. Typically these studies assumed (or derived) an increase in stock prices resulting from the amendment (40% in one case, 10% in another, and 5% in a third) and programmed that assumption into one of the major econometric models, generating increased business investment, lower unemployment, and greater tax revenues. As is confirmed by our stock market's 10% drop in the two weeks after enactment of the bill, these predictions were laughable, but they were widely quoted in the press and had some impact on Congress.

In addition to the indexing provision and the exclusion for gains on residences, the House of Representatives passed a compromise proposal embodying about one-half as large a tax cut as the Steiger amendment. The House bill would have deleted capital gains from the minimum and maximum taxes (à la Steiger) and repealed the 25% alternative rate on the first $50,000 of capital gains (as President Carter had proposed). Thus, the basic rule for capital gains would simply have been the exclusion of one-half the gain from taxable income.

The Carter administration, of course, opposed the Steiger amendment and the House compromise, thereby continuing what is becoming a tradition of executive opposition to congressional policy on capital gains. Initially the administration's arguments emphasized their belief that a capital gains tax cut would be a less equitable and less efficient stimulus to investment than the corporate tax rate reduction and expanded investment tax credit which had been proposed by the administration. These theoretical arguments against cutting capital gains taxes were not very successful; therefore the administration began emphasizing statistics showing that the Steiger amendment would remove from the income tax rolls about three hundred people with incomes exceeding $100,000. From this point on, the issue became not whether to cut capital gains taxes but rather how to do so in a way that kept those three hundred people on the tax rolls.

The Senate responded to the concern about high-income non-taxpayers by fashioning their capital gains tax package to include a reasonably tough minimum tax. The price for this, from the administration's standpoint, however, was an over-all capital gains tax cut much larger than the one in the House bill. The Senate, while accommodating the administration by deleting the House indexing proposal and cutting back the generous House exclusion for gains on residences, increased the general capital gains exclusion from 50% to 70%. The Senate repealed the existing add-on minimum tax and replaced it with an alternative minimum tax which worked as follows: taxpayers would add to their taxable income their tax preferences (including the excluded part of capital gains), subtract a $20,000 exemption, compute a minimum tax at rates between 10% and 25%, and pay this minimum tax only if it exceeded their regular tax liability. The Senate also lowered the corporate capital gains rate from 30% to 28%.

The final version of the *Revenue Act* of 1978, completed in a wild all-night session of Congress just before adjournment, basically follows the Senate approach, but with a 60% exclusion. In addition, the present add-on minimum tax is retained for most preferences other than capital gains. The over-all capital gains tax reduction is slightly larger than the increase which occurred in 1969 and 1976. Owing to the new minimum tax, which will raise about $700 million at 1978 levels, capital gains taxes will be higher than before 1969 for those people who pay little regular income tax. For most recipients of capital gains, however, the tax will be about 20% lower because of the 60% exclusion.

CONCLUSION

I do not want to draw any conclusions about what Canada should do about its capital gains tax, because I am not very familiar with the Canadian situation. Let me just note that you now have an opportunity to observe the effects of a major capital gains tax reduction in the United States, and I urge you to study our experience when deciding what to do yourselves about what will probably always be a vexing problem in personal income taxation.

NOTE, "REALIZING APPRECIATION WITHOUT SALE: ACCRUAL TAXATION OF CAPITAL GAINS ON MARKETABLE SECURITIES"

34 Stanford Law Review 857–876 (1982).

Since the Supreme Court's landmark decision in *Eisner v. Macomber*, capital gains income has not been subject to taxation until the taxpayer sells the underlying capital asset.[1] Although *Macomber*'s treatment of capital gains income does not reflect economic reality,[2] the courts and the Internal Revenue Code[3] generally require realization—i.e., sale of the appreciated asset—before income will be recognized and taxed. This "realization" requirement enables high-income taxpayers to defer the payment of taxes on large amounts of unrealized capital gains income.[4]

---

1. 252 U.S. 189 (1920). A broad reading of *Macomber* might imply a constitutional requirement that a capital gain be realized before it can be taxed. The Supreme Court has never explicitly overruled *Macomber*, but commentators believe that such an interpretation has been discarded and that Congress can tax all increases in wealth, realized or not. *See, e.g.*, Stone, *Back to Fundamentals: Another Version of the Stock Dividend Saga*, 79 COLUM. L. REV. 898, 916–17 (1979). The realization requirement has never been rigorously applied. *See, e.g.*, Helvering v. Horst, 311 U.S. 112 (1940); Helvering v. Brunn, 309 U.S. 461 (1940). Since the *Macomber* decision in 1920, the Supreme Court has found an absence of realization to be significant in only one 1924 case. *See* Weiss v. Stearn, 265 U.S. 242 (1924). In general, the Treasury and the Internal Revenue Service have been given wide discretion to determine when realization has occurred. Cohen, *Taxing Stock Dividends and Economic Theory*, 1974 WIS. L. REV. 142, 148 n.19. Professor Chirelstein reflects the modern consensus when he argues that today the realization requirement is "an administrative rule and not a constitutional . . . requirement of 'income.'" M. CHIRELSTEIN, FEDERAL INCOME TAXATION ¶ 5.01, at 69 (2d ed. 1979). It is likely, then, that the Court will allow Congress to tax unrealized capital gains if Congress so desires.

2. When the value of a taxpayer's assets increases, he has economic income whether or not he sells the appreciated assets. H. SIMONS, PERSONAL INCOME TAXATION 50 (1938).

3. I.R.C. § 1001 (1976). But note that Congress has not required realization when the opportunity for abuse exists. *See, e.g., id.* § 551 (taxation of shareholder on undistributed income of personal holding company); *id.* § 951 (taxation of shareholder on undistributed income of "controlled" corporation).

4. Deferral is one of the principal elements of a capital gain and, indeed, of any tax shelter. By deferring recognition of income for tax purposes, a taxpayer is able to delay paying taxes and effectively obtains an interest-free loan from the government. *See generally* Dep't of the Treasury, The President's 1978 Tax Program 64–70 (Jan. 30, 1978), *reprinted in* W. ANDREWS, BASIC FEDERAL INCOME TAXATION 654-58 (2d ed. 1979).

The realization requirement, which allows deferral, combined with other portions of the tax law—I.R.C. § 1014 (1976 & Supp. III 1979) (tax-free, stepped-up basis at death) and *id.* § 1202 (Supp. III 1979) (60% of long term capital gains excluded from ordinary income taxa-

CAPITAL GAINS

In the Economic Recovery Tax Act of 1981,[5] Congress, for the first time since *Macomber*, eliminated the realization requirement for a major category of capital assets—commodities futures contracts.[6] The Act's "mark-to-market" system treats commodities gains and losses as if the contracts were sold on the last day of the tax year. Congress eliminated the realization requirement on commodities futures because taxpayers were abusing it to avoid paying taxes. This note explores the advantages and disadvantages of taxing the appreciation on all capital assets, and argues that unrealized capital gains income from certain other marketable securities should be taxed even though the appreciated assets have not been sold.[7]

Part I of this note discusses the realization requirement and its abuse in the area of commodity straddles. Part II explores the arguments for and against a realization requirement. Part III argues that the advantages of taxing the appreciation of capital assets outweigh the disadvantages for one category of capital assets—the marketable securities of publicly held corporations—and proposes a scheme for taxing them.

I. THE REALIZATION REQUIREMENT

In *Eisner v. Macomber*,[8] the Supreme Court held that a shareholder could not be taxed on stock dividends received from a distributing

---

tion)—has made it beneficial for taxpayers to favor capital gains over other forms of income. Capital gains can be deferred until the taxpayer sells the asset. When appreciated assets are transferred at death, the bases increase to current fair market value. *Id.* § 1014 (1976 & Supp. III 1979). Finally, when the appreciated asset is ultimately sold, 60% of the realized income is exempt from ordinary income taxation. *Id.* § 1202(a) (Supp. III 1979).

5. Pub. L. No. 97-34, 95 Stat. 172 (to be codified in scattered sections of 26 U.S.C.).

6. Under the 1981 Tax Act, regulated futures contracts must be treated as if they were sold on the last day of the tax year, and any gain or loss determined by the fair market value of the contract at that time. Any capital gain or loss is treated as if (1) 40% of the gain or loss is a short term capital gain or loss, and (2) 60% of the gain or loss is a long term capital gain or loss. *Id.* §§ 501-504, 95 Stat. 172, 323-31 (to be codified in scattered sections of 26 U.S.C.); *see* H.R. CONF. REP. NO. 215, 97th Cong., 1st Sess. 258, *reprinted in* U.S. CODE CONG. & AD. NEWS 371, 432-33 (Supp. Aug. 1981). *See generally* FED. TAXES (P-H) REPORT BULLETIN: HANDBOOK ON THE ECONOMIC RECOVERY TAX ACT OF 1981 ¶¶ 186-189 (1981); STAND. FED. TAX REP. (CCH) ECONOMIC RECOVERY TAX ACT OF 1981: LAW AND EXPLANATION ¶¶ 321-323 (1981).

7. In the late 1960s and 1970s, some commentators suggested that stock appreciation should be taxed annually as ordinary income. *See Hearings on the Subject of Tax Reform Before the House Comm. on Ways and Means*, 91st Cong., 1st Sess. 4275 (1969) (statement of Martin David & Roger Miller) [hereinafter cited as David & Miller]; COMPREHENSIVE INCOME TAXATION (J. Pechman ed. 1977); Slawson, *Taxing as Ordinary Income the Appreciation of Publicly Held Stock*, 76 YALE L.J. 623 (1967).

8. 252 U.S. 189 (1920).

corporation. The Court assumed that mere appreciation in the value of an asset is not income, and that in order to be taxed, a taxpayer's gains must be realized.[9] Since the new shares received represented nothing more than the shareholders' prior interest redefined in smaller units, the Court concluded that no income had been realized.[10]

Macomber generated extensive criticism and commentary,[11] but neither Congress nor the courts have, until recently, been willing to tax gains accruing to capital assets without their realization. The realization requirement allows some taxpayers to avoid substantial amounts of taxes; for example, it enabled taxpayers to use tax-oriented commodity straddles to defer payment of taxes.

In a commodity straddle,[12] the taxpayer simultaneously holds two commodities futures contracts: one requiring him to buy a commodity in a future month, and the other requiring him to sell an identical amount of the same commodity in another month. Because of the offsetting nature of the two legs of the transaction (one "long" and the other "short"), a change in the price of the underlying commodity will usually cause the value of one contract to increase and the value of the other contract to decrease. When that occurs, the taxpayer can close out the losing leg of the straddle before the end of the tax year, realizing the loss for tax purposes, but not realizing the gain. Furthermore, the taxpayer can then secure the gain by immediately purchasing a position identical to the one just liquidated, but with a different delivery date. The straddle was an effective tax avoidance mechanism because it gave taxpayers absolute control

---

9. *Id.* at 207.

10. *Id.* at 208-09.

11. *See* R. MONTGOMERY, INCOME TAX PRACTICE 1921, at 598-612 (1921); E. SELIGMAN, STUDIES IN PUBLIC FINANCE 99-123 (1925); Clark, *Can Shares of Stock be Exempted from Taxation in the Hands of Shareholders*, 54 AM. L. REV. 689 (1920); Clark, Eisner v. Macomber *and Some Income Tax Problems*, 29 YALE L.J. 735 (1920); Powell, *Stock Dividends, Direct Taxes, and the Sixteenth Amendment*, 20 COLUM. L. REV. 536 (1920); Seligman, *Implications and Effects of the Stock Dividend Decision*, 21 COLUM. L. REV. 313 (1921); Seligman, *Are Stock Dividends Income?*, 9 AM. ECON. REV. 517 (1919); Warren, *Taxability of Stock Dividends as Income*, 33 HARV. L. REV. 885 (1920).

12. Commodity straddles have also been called butterfly straddles. *See* Lowenstein, *Practioners of Exotic Tax-Shelter Tactic Watch Nervously as U.S. Court Test Begins*, Wall St. J., Apr. 6, 1981, at 25, col. 4. The straddle mechanism will work with traditional commodities futures contracts or with any other futures contracts that allow the taxpayer to enter into a straddle position. *See generally* Dailey, *Commodity Straddles in Retrospect: Federal Income Tax Considerations*, 47 BROOKLYN L. REV. 313 (1981). The transaction, for example, will work with Treasury bill futures.

over the timing of their gains and losses for tax purposes.[13]

To curb this tax-avoidance device, Congress, in the Economic Recovery Tax Act of 1981, required that all regulated futures contracts be "marked-to-market" at year end.[14] Taxpayers must pay taxes on their commodity gains (or deduct their losses) even though they may not have closed out their positions before the end of the tax year and thereby realized income in the traditional sense.[15] The mark-to-market approach effectively eliminates the abuse of commodity straddles by removing the taxpayer's control over when gains and losses are realized for tax purposes.[16]

Congress's reaction to the use of commodity straddles to defer

---

13. Because of the exceptionally small margin requirements for a commodity straddle, *see* Dailey, *supra* note 12, at 321; Rev. Rul. 185, 1977-1 C.B. 48, 49 (margin required to finance taxpayer's straddle transaction was "¼th of 1 percent of the total futures contracts purchased"), a taxpayer could take out a large number of contracts and generate an arbitrarily large tax loss. By engaging in a series of straddles, the taxpayer could defer income for an indefinite period of time or spread realization of the income over a period of years. *See generally* Lowenstein, *supra* note 12.

Commodity straddles could be used not only to defer taxes, but also to convert short term capital gains into long term capital gains. To recharacterize a short term capital gain in this manner, the leg of the straddle containing the unrealized gain had to be the long leg. (A short position would always generate a short term capital gain.) If an appreciated long position was held for more than 6 months (the statutory holding period) and thereafter sold at a gain, the resulting gain would be long term. But if a taxpayer had a long term capital gain and engaged in a commodity straddle to defer recognition of the gain until the following year, he could inadvertently convert the long term capital gain into a short term capital gain. *The Treasury Proposal to Revise the Tax Treatment of Commodities Transactions*, 12 TAX NOTES 83, 85 (1981).

14. *See* note 6 *supra*.

15. Because of the unique accounting practices of the United States Commodity Futures Exchanges, a trader has essentially realized his gain or loss even though he may not have closed out his position. A trader in commodity futures maintains an account with his broker and the account is credited or debited with his gains or losses on a daily basis. If the trader has gained, he may withdraw those funds from his account at any time; if he has lost, the trader must cover his losses before the next business day. *See* STAND. FED. TAX REP., *supra* note 6, ¶¶ 321-325.

16. Prior to the 1981 Act, taxpayers could use exchange-traded stock option straddles to defer income. A stock option is a right (but not an obligation) to buy or sell 100 shares of a given stock at a certain price (the "strike" price) on an agreed-upon date. A "put" is an option to sell 100 shares at a guaranteed price, while a "call" is an option to buy 100 shares at a guaranteed price. Like commodities futures contracts, stock options have been standardized so that they can be freely traded on the exchanges. Stock options provide a good vehicle for a tax straddle because, like commodities futures contracts, they allow the taxpayer to leverage himself heavily so that small price movements can lead to large gains and/or losses. *See generally* L. ENGEL & P. WYCKOFF, HOW TO BUY STOCKS 200-11 (6th ed. 1977). The 1981 Tax Act omits any reference to stock options, and some observers believe that stock option straddles are still available to taxpayers who wish to defer the realization of short term capital gains for tax purposes. *See Better off having profits taxed in '82*, Chicago Tribune, Nov. 10, 1981, § 3, at 17, col. 4.

and avoid payment of taxes calls the realization requirement into question for the first time since *Macomber*. Since the realization requirement is simply an administrative rule,[17] it is possible that Congress will extend the mark-to-market approach to other capital assets. The next Part explores the advantages and disadvantages of a tax on the appreciation of other capital assets.

II. THE ADVANTAGES AND DISADVANTAGES OF TAXING APPRECIATION WITHOUT REALIZATION

The realization requirement is a significant administrative rule in any income tax system;[18] it determines what increments of wealth will be presently taxed and what increments will be taxed in the future. The realization requirement enables taxpayers to strategically target gains and losses for particular tax years. This Part discusses the advantages and disadvantages of requiring the taxpayer to recognize all income in the year it accrues.

---

17. M. CHIRELSTEIN, *supra* note 1, ¶ 5.01, at 69.

18. In recent years, commentators have debated whether an individual's tax liability should be based on his ability to pay (measured by his income or wealth) or on how much he removes from society (measured by his consumption). *See* WHAT SHOULD BE TAXED: INCOME OR EXPENDITURE? (J. Pechman ed. 1980). The argument favoring ability to pay has largely won out in the United States, where income taxes and property taxes generate the vast majority of governmental revenues. R. MUSGRAVE & P. MUSGRAVE, PUBLIC FINANCE IN THEORY AND PRACTICE 207-08 (2d ed. 1976). In European countries, by contrast, consumption-oriented value added taxes are prominent. *Id.* at 330.

The underlying theory of a consumption tax is that individuals should pay taxes not on what they put into society, but on what they remove from the pool of goods and services produced by society. *Id.* at 220-21. Although the federal government derives most of its income from income taxes, recent changes in the tax laws have moved the federal tax structure closer and closer to a consumption-based tax. Liberalized depreciation allowances, investment tax credits, and research and development tax credits are likely to eliminate the corporate income tax as a major source of federal revenues by 1990. *See* Thurow, *The Next Merger Wave*, NEWSWEEK, Sept. 14, 1981, at 73.

Another factor pushing the federal tax system towards a consumption-based tax is the recent decline in long term capital gains tax rates from a maximum of 35% only a few years ago, to 28%, and now to 20%. The liberalized treatment of pension plans, including Individual Retirement Accounts and Keogh Plans, also helps to move the federal tax structure towards a consumption-based tax.

In recent years the consumption tax has received substantial academic support. *See* Bradford, *The Case for a Personal Consumption Tax*, in WHAT SHOULD BE TAXED: INCOME OR EXPENDITURE?, *supra*, at 75, and sources cited therein. The implications for the realization requirement are significantly different under a consumption tax than under an income tax. Because a consumption tax is concerned with the timing of consumption and not with the timing of income receipts, the appreciation of a capital asset is not a "taxable event." Consumption taxation occurs when individuals purchase goods and services. The source of funds (be it borrowing against appreciated assets, sale of assets, or earnings) is irrelevant. The realization issue is thus unimportant from the consumption tax perspective.

A. The Advantages of Annually Taxing Appreciation

The federal tax system relies primarily on the personal income tax to generate governmental revenues, and generally favors taxing the appreciation of capital assets in the year the appreciation occurs.[19] Taxing without regard to realization has three principal advantages: It broadens the tax base, it improves the equity of the tax system, and it encourages efficient asset sales.

1. Broadening the income tax base.

Under an income tax, income is taxed unless substantial policy reasons justify excluding it from the tax base.[20] The annual appreciation in the value of capital assets is part of the tax base and should be taxed unless doing so can be shown to be substantially disadvantageous. Eliminating the realization requirement for capital assets would result in unrealized capital gains being included in the tax base; exclusion reduces the size of the tax base and forces the remaining items to bear a higher tax rate.[21]

2. Improving the equity of the income tax.

A second advantage of eliminating the realization requirement is that it would improve the equity of the tax system. Wealth in the United States is generally more concentrated than income.[22] Because of the realization requirement, the wealthiest members of soci-

---

19. R. MUSGRAVE & P. MUSGRAVE, *supra* note 18, at 231.
20. In 1938, economist Henry Simons proposed that personal income should be defined to be "the algebraic sum of (1) the market value of rights exercised in consumption and (2) the change in the value of the store of property rights between the beginning and the end of the period in question." H. SIMONS, *supra* note 2, at 50. Since then, the Haig-Simons definition of income has become the starting point for income determination for most public finance economists and tax commentators. *See, e.g.*, Galvin, *More on Boris Bittker and the Comprehensive Tax Base: The Practicalities of Tax Reform and the ABA's CSTR*, 81 HARV. L. REV. 1016 (1968); Musgrave, *In Defense of an Income Concept*, 81 HARV. L. REV. 44 (1967); Pechman, *Comprehensive Income Taxation: A Comment*, 81 HARV. L. REV. 63 (1967); Pechman & Okner, *Simulation of the Carter Commission Tax Proposals for the United States*, 22 NAT'L TAX J. 2 (1969). *But see* Bittker, *Comprehensive Income Taxation: A Response*, 81 HARV. L. REV. 1032 (1968); Bittker, *Income Tax Reform in Canada: Report of the Royal Commission on Taxation*, 35 U. CHI. L. REV. 627 (1968); Bittker, *A "Comprehensive Tax Base" as a Goal of Income Tax Reform*, 80 HARV. L. REV. 925 (1967).
21. In 1966, the deferral feature alone cost the Treasury about $4 billion, and the tax-free stepped-up basis at death cost another $4 billion. David & Miller, *supra* note 7, at 4298. Had these revenues been collected, the top marginal income tax rate (then 70%) could have been reduced to 50% and the estate and gift taxes completely abolished with no loss in revenue. *Id.* at 4278-79.
22. The wealthiest 20% of American households hold roughly 76% of all net wealth, and the wealthiest 1% hold 20% of all net wealth. By contrast, the 20% of the population with the

ety can defer the payment of taxes on substantial amounts of unrealized capital gains income. This ability to defer taxes amounts to an interest-free loan from the government to the taxpayer; consequently, the realization requirement allows the wealthy to keep more funds invested, increases the return on their initial investment, and allows them to defer even more taxes. Furthermore, when they eventually sell their capital assets, the deferral means that fewer real dollars are paid in taxes.[23] The result is that the effective rate of tax on the appreciation of capital assets is much lower than the nominal rate.

The principle of vertical equity requires that individuals be taxed according to their ability to pay.[24] Well-to-do taxpayers have a greater ability to pay than low-income taxpayers, and therefore should bear relatively larger tax burdens.[25] The realization requirement allows well-to-do taxpayers to defer payment of taxes on unrealized capital gains income and, in some cases, to escape payment of taxes entirely through section 1014's stepped-up basis at death. Section 1014 increases the basis of a capital asset to its fair market value at the date of the owner's death; appreciation that has accrued on the asset is never taxed.[26] High-income taxpayers with substantial

---

highest money incomes received only 41% of all money income. R. MUSGRAVE & P. MUSGRAVE, *supra* note 18, at 348.

23. Especially in times of rapid inflation, it is important to distinguish between nominal and real values. Prices and values are usually stated in nominal amounts that incorporate changes in the purchasing power of the dollar. Thus, if an item costs $1.00 today and in the next year inflation is 15%, the item will cost $1.15 next year. The nominal price has increased by 15 cents, but the real price (measured in constant or real dollars) has remained the same. *See generally* M. CHIRELSTEIN, *supra* note 1, at 331-36 app.; P. SAMUELSON, ECONOMICS 255-58 (11th ed. 1980).

24. *See generally* Sneed, *The Criteria of Federal Income Tax Policy*, 17 STAN. L. REV. 567, 576-77, 581 (1965).

25. Most proponents of an income tax argue that income taxation should either be proportional (all taxpayers pay taxes that are equal to roughly the same percentage of their income) or progressive (taxpayers pay taxes that are an increasing percentage of their incomes as their incomes rise). R. MUSGRAVE & P. MUSGRAVE, *supra* note 18, at 215-19. Income taxes should not be regressive (taxpayers pay taxes which are a decreasing percentage of their incomes as their incomes rise) because such a tax structure would be in conflict with one major goal of an income tax: that tax burdens should be distributed in relation to the ability to pay.

26. I.R.C. § 1014 (1976 & Supp. III 1979) has been criticized because it allows the asset's appreciation to escape taxation entirely. *See, e.g.*, David & Miller, *supra* note 7, at 4278. In 1976, Congress passed legislation which would have phased out § 1014 and provided that the original basis of an asset transferred at death would be "carried over" to the new owner. Tax Reform Act of 1976, Pub. L. No. 94-455, § 2005, 90 Stat. 1525, 1872-77 (codified in part at I.R.C. § 1023 (1976)). Congress has recently backtracked from that position, however, and indefinitely postponed the elimination of § 1014, which means that the basis of an asset transferred at death will continue to be stepped up to current market value. Crude Oil Windfall

amounts of capital gains income are thereby able to pay taxes on a smaller percentage of their income than lower-income taxpayers.[27] Eliminating the realization requirement would improve the general equity of the income tax by increasing its progressivity.[28]

3. *The "lock-in" phenomenon.*

The realization requirement and the stepped-up basis at death combine to lock investors into their investment portfolios. Because taxpayers do not have to pay taxes on the increase in value of an asset until they sell or exchange it, taxpayers will resist selling appreciated property even though they may have better available investments, or are in need of cash.[29] The investors are said to be "locked in" because of the tax penalty that they would incur if they were to sell their property and realize the gains.[30] If the investor is well-to-do and elderly, the lock-in problem becomes even more acute: The incentives to hold an asset until death so that the basis can be increased to market value—allowing the unrealized gain to escape taxation entirely—become even greater.

The lock-in problem not only inconveniences investors who would prefer to sell their appreciated assets, but also impedes the flow of capital from one investment to another. Older investments that are no longer as profitable as newer ones tend to be kept longer, and new investments have more difficulty attracting capital than would be optimal. Eliminating the realization requirement would mean that capital gains income would be taxed regardless of whether the asset had been sold. Taxpayers would therefore have no incentive to retain less profitable investments to avoid paying taxes, and the lock-in phenomenon would be eliminated.

Profits Tax Act of 1980, Pub. L. No. 96-223, § 401, 94 Stat. 229, 299–300. *See generally* [1980] 6 STAND. FED. TAX REP. (CCH) ¶ 4524.01.

27. *See* M. DAVID, ALTERNATIVE APPROACHES TO CAPITAL GAINS TAXATION 88 (1968).

28. The current treatment of capital gains income also reduces the horizontal equity of the tax system. Taxpayers with identical amounts of earned income and unrealized capital gains income are taxed very differently. *See* R. MUSGRAVE & P. MUSGRAVE, *supra* note 18, at 244–45.

29. The 1981 Tax Act has reduced the significance of the lock-in problem by decreasing the maximum tax rate on long term capital gains. Pub. L. No. 97-34, § 102, 95 Stat. 172, 186 (amending I.R.C. § 1 (Supp. III 1979)). Investors are locked in because of the tax penalty that they incur when selling their assets. A lower long term capital gains tax rate decreases the penalty for selling and reduces the significance of the lock-in problem.

30. R. MUSGRAVE & P. MUSGRAVE, *supra* note 18, at 247. Of course, if capital assets have lost value, the tax system creates an incentive to sell the asset so that the loss can be recognized for tax purposes, thus reducing the individual's tax liability.

B. *Problems With Taxing Appreciation*

Although eliminating the realization requirement will increase the theoretical accuracy of the tax system, in application it could encounter significant problems. These problems relate to the valuation of capital assets, the "paper" nature of unrealized capital gains, the effect on the capital markets, and the economic responses of private parties to the change in the tax rules.

1. *Valuation and liquidity.*

One argument against taxing unrealized capital appreciation is that capital assets cannot be accurately valued until they are sold.[31] Some assets are easier to value than others. Closing stock prices appear in the financial sections of major newspapers and are accurate indicators of value. Valuing real estate or partnership interests, on the other hand, requires an appraisal and involves significant administrative costs.[32] Silver and art collections are still harder to value, the results even more uncertain, and the attempt to value even more expensive.

The difficulty of valuation is linked to the liquidity of the asset: The less liquid an asset, the harder it is to value and the less reliable is the result. There is a continuum of capital assets ranging from those that are very liquid and very easy to value—such as short term U.S. Treasury bills—through those that are somewhat harder to value and that are somewhat less liquid—such as real estate and interests in partnerships—down to those that are illiquid and impossible to value—for example, collections and specialized machinery. The difficulty of valuing assets is a substantial problem in taxing the appreciation of assets on the illiquid end of the continuum. On the other hand, stocks, bonds, and other marketable securities are very easy to value and can readily be converted into cash; therefore, valuation and liquidity problems do not pose a barrier to including their appreciation in the tax base.[33]

---

31. *Id.* at 246.
32. *See generally id.* at 350-53.
33. There are cases, however, where valuation and liquidity pose significant questions even though the underlying assets are marketable securities. One such situation occurs when a few shareholders own a majority of a corporation's equity, and thousands of investors in the investing public own only a fraction of the corporation's equity.

An example of this phenomenon is the Apple Computer Company, which went public in 1980. In its first public offering, Apple sold approximately 10% of its equity. At the time,

2. Paper gains and cash flow problems.

Even if valuation could be performed accurately, the gain is only a "paper gain"—one that accrues even though the taxpayer receives no cash. This paper gain can be lost at any time until the taxpayer sells the underlying asset.[34] Shareholders with substantial paper gains in one year are at risk until they liquidate their investment; they can easily lose the profit if the market falls in subsequent years. If the asset is illiquid and the investor is unable easily to convert the asset to cash, or if he can do so only at a substantial cost, taxing the unrealized capital gains income may create inequity.

Because a paper gain does not generate cash, taxing such a gain can create cash squeezes. Taxpayers may have tax liabilities, but not the cash necessary to pay them. To pay their taxes, they will be forced to sell some of their assets. If the taxpayers cannot borrow against their unrealized gains,[35] they will have to sell assets they

---

some of its major officers held as much as 15% of the firm's equity. APPLE COMPUTER, INC., PROSPECTUS (Dec. 12, 1980).

The trades of the investing public generally determine the market price for the stock, but if the large shareholders were to attempt to sell any significant portion of their holdings, the market price would be substantially depressed. Because the market is "thin," it does not provide large shareholders with the high degree of liquidity normally associated with publicly held stocks. *See generally* J. COHEN, E. ZINBARG & A. ZEIKEL, INVESTMENT ANALYSIS AND PORTFOLIO MANAGEMENT 98-110 (rev. ed. 1973). The lack of liquidity implies that the market valuation may not accurately reflect stock value because the shareholder could not sell his holding at the market price. Under these circumstances, it would seem unfair to tax the holdings of large shareholders as if they could be sold at the market price. In this case, the accuracy of the market-based valuation becomes the issue.

If the large shareholder is part of a group of shareholders who own a controlling interest in the corporation's stock, however, the value of his shares is probably understated by the market. *See* W. CARY & M. EISENBERG, CASES AND MATERIALS ON CORPORATIONS 684 (5th unabr. ed. 1980). Controlling interests typically sell at a premium because they provide their owners with control of the corporation. *Id.* Valuing the holdings of controlling shareholders at the market price therefore understates the value of their holdings. If the holdings are valued at the market price, controlling shareholders receive a built-in tax break because they are not taxed on the premium associated with their holdings. This suggests that large shareholders are not disadvantaged by having their holdings taxed at the market value, because their stock may actually be worth more than the market price.

34. *See* L. ENGEL & P. WYCKOFF, *supra* note 16, at 188; *see also* R. MUSGRAVE & P. MUSGRAVE, *supra* note 18, at 245-47.

35. As long as the maximum tax rate is below the margin requirement, a shareholder can easily borrow from his broker to pay his taxes by taking out a margin loan. When making a margin loan, the broker retains the shareholder's securities as collateral. Under current Federal Reserve Board Regulations, shareholders can borrow up to 50% of the total value of their stock in a margin account. *See* L. ENGEL & P. WYCKOFF, *supra* note 16, at 181-89.

Taxing appreciation at long term capital gains rates therefore does not create a cash flow problem, but if the tax rates were greater than the margin requirement, the investor could be forced to liquidate some of his assets to pay his tax bill.

otherwise would have retained.

3. *Effect on equity markets.*

Annually taxing stock appreciation would drive down stock prices, or at least cause them to increase less rapidly, because it would reduce a stockholder's after-tax return.[36] Corporations that raise capital in the equity markets would therefore find equity capital to be relatively more expensive; they would have to sell more shares at a lower price to raise the same amount of capital.[37]

For most large corporations, increasing the cost of equity capital would not be troublesome because capital requirements can be met by borrowing funds and using retained earnings.[38] But some sectors of the economy must frequently go to the equity markets and would be particularly hurt by an appreciations tax. Public utilities, for example, have an enormous need for capital and frequently go to the equity and debt markets.[39] Similarly, high-growth companies[40] must frequently raise additional equity capital and could be adversely affected by an appreciations tax. Because of their rapid expansion, high-growth companies may not be able to generate enough capital through retained earnings and debt to finance optimal or efficient rates of growth. These firms are forced to go to the equity markets. And in the case of smaller high-technology firms and start-up companies, debt capacity is limited and equity capital may be the only viable alternative.[41]

The higher cost of equity capital can be expected to cause some corporations to decide not to issue equity and to delay or curtail expansion plans and purchases of capital equipment. Investors who were willing to take a certain amount of risk for a given return may be unwilling to take as much risk when an appreciations tax reduces the after-tax rate of return. As a result, less growth will occur in some

---

36. *See generally* J. VAN HORNE, FINANCIAL MANAGEMENT AND POLICY 19-23 (2d ed. 1977).

37. *Id.*

38. W. CARY & M. EISENBERG, *supra* note 33, at 1172; *see also* Slawson, *supra* note 7, at 638.

39. The American Telephone and Telegraph Company is probably the nation's largest utility. The number of outstanding shares of AT&T increased from 582,024,000 in 1975 to 754,825,000 in 1980. Over the same period, long term indebtedness increased from $31,793,326 to $41,225,000. AM. TELEPHONE & TELEGRAPH CO., ANNUAL REPORTS (1975-1980). *See generally* M. FARRIS & R. SAMPSON, PUBLIC UTILITIES: REGULATION, MANAGEMENT, AND OWNERSHIP 202-04 (1973).

40. High-growth companies are typically semi-conductor or high-technology firms.

41. *See generally* J. VAN HORNE, *supra* note 36, at 229-96.

of the most dynamic and productive sectors of the economy.[42]

Corporations currently in need of capital have a number of incentives to borrow rather than to sell equity: Interest is deductible,[43] investment bankers charge substantially smaller underwriting fees,[44] and debt does not dilute equity ownership interests. Taxing the appreciation of corporate stock would give corporations yet another reason to prefer debt. Although dividends are now taxed twice— once at the corporate level and once at the individual level—retained earnings are exempt from the individual tax.[45] Stock appreciation reflects, in part, the increased value of a company due to retention and investment of earnings.[46] Taxing the annual appreciation of corporate stock would eliminate a portion of the present favorable tax treatment of retained earnings, but interest payments would still be deductible. A corporation would prefer a higher debt/equity ratio.[47]

A primary reason that corporations are interested in obtaining debt financing is that the leverage provided by borrowed funds increases return on equity so long as the firm's before-tax rate of return is greater than the interest rate it must pay on the funds that it borrows.[48] But lenders require borrowers to make interest payments regardless of the borrower's financial condition. Interest payments are fixed costs, whereas dividend payments are not.[49] When a leveraged

---

42. This problem would be more acute if the appreciations tax were levied at the relatively high rates for ordinary income rather than at the relatively low rates for long term capital gains.

43. I.R.C. § 163(a) (1976).

44. L. ENGEL & P. WYCKOFF, *supra* note 16, at 30. A corporation therefore nets a much larger percentage of the issue value of a debt offering than it nets of an equivalent equity offering.

45. I.R.C. § 1001 (1976 & Supp. III 1979).

46. There is a substantial amount of debate over what factors influence the price of a corporation's stock, and the findings are far from definitive. *See, e.g.*, W. SHARPE, PORTFOLIO THEORY AND CAPITAL MARKETS (1970); Gordon & Shapiro, *Capital Equipment Analysis: The Required Rate of Profit*, 3 MGMT. SCI. 102 (1956); Markowitz, *Portfolio Selection*, 7 J. FIN. 77 (1952); Miller & Modigliani, *Dividend Policy, Growth and the Valuation of Shares*, 34 J. BUS. 411 (1961); Sharpe, *Capital Asset Prices: A Theory of Market Equilibrium Under Conditions of Risk*, 19 J. FIN. 425 (1964). *See generally* J. COHEN, E. ZINBARG & A. ZEIKEL, *supra* note 33, at 737-91; J. FRANCIS, INVESTMENTS: ANALYSIS AND MANAGEMENT 231-87 (2d ed. 1976), and sources cited therein.

47. What constitutes an acceptable level for a firm's debt/equity ratio varies from industry to industry and is also a function of management's preferences for financial risk. *See generally* J. VAN HORNE, *supra* note 36, at 229-96.

48. *But see* Modigliani & Miller, *The Cost of Capital, Corporation Finance and the Theory of Investment*, AM. ECON. REV., June 1958, at 261. The Modigliani-Miller thesis, however, is not generally accepted because it is based on unrealistic assumptions. *See* J. VAN HORNE, *supra* note 36, at 239-53.

49. *See* L. ENGEL & P. WYCKOFF, *supra* note 16, at 18. A corporation that borrows

firm is profitable, it has a higher return on equity than it would if it had obtained all of its funding through the sale of equity. After covering its fixed interest costs, its remaining profit is spread over a smaller equity base. On the other hand, the presence of fixed interest costs and the smaller equity base cause a leveraged firm's return on equity to fluctuate much more than its earnings before interest and taxes.[50] Increasing a firm's debt levels thus leads to a more volatile after-tax earnings record, which means the investment is riskier.[51]

A firm can acquire large fixed interest commitments by borrowing heavily at relatively low interest rates, or by borrowing less heavily at relatively high interest rates.[52] This suggests that corporations will not be willing to raise large amounts of capital by borrowing. But an appreciations tax will make raising equity capital seem relatively expensive, and the corporations may be reluctant to pay the returns that the equity markets demand. With less new capital raised through debt and less new capital raised through equity, there could be less investment and slower economic growth, particularly in the sectors most dependent on equity.

An appreciations tax also seems likely to increase the pressures for higher dividend payments, further reducing a corporation's available cash. Under current tax law, dividends are taxed twice, while retained earnings are taxed only at the corporate level.[53] With an appreciations tax, both retained earnings and dividends would be taxed twice, and the bias against paying dividends would be reduced.[54] In

---

funds is obligated to make interest payments to its lenders regardless of how well it is doing. Interest payments are therefore fixed costs, whereas dividend payments in theory are fully discretionary. On the other hand, dividends will usually be paid even if the corporation is losing money because corporate boards are reluctant to decrease or skip an established dividend. So, although dividends are theoretically discretionary, they are not painlessly varied. *Id.*

50. *See id.* at 37–38.

51. *See generally* Friedman & Savage, *The Utility Analysis of Choices Involving Risk*, 56 J. POL. ECON. 279 (1948); Sharpe, *supra* note 46. Because investors tend to be risk averse, riskier investments tend to be discounted in value.

52. Since the late 1960s when Slawson and David & Miller were writing, interest rates have risen substantially. *See* W. SHARPE, INVESTMENTS 227 (1978). A corporation that borrows today will acquire a large fixed-interest obligation at a lower debt/equity ratio than a corporation that borrowed in the late 1960s. Target debt-equity ratios should therefore be lower, suggesting that prudent corporations will not want to borrow to the same extent that they would have a few years ago. Furthermore, some firms are simply averse to borrowing because they believe that there are enough inherent business risks in their businesses and that it would be unwise to add financial risks. *See generally* J. VAN HORNE, *supra* note 36, at 166–223.

53. I.R.C. §§ 61, 1001 (1976 & Supp. III 1979).

54. To the extent that retained earnings are reflected in higher stock prices, the bias

addition, shareholders, especially those with substantial holdings, could be expected to demand higher dividends to provide cash to pay the appreciations tax. If the corporation did not pay higher dividends, some shareholders could be expected to choose to sell some of their holdings so that they could pay their taxes, thereby depressing the stock's price.[55] And this, in turn, would make the cost of equity capital even greater to the corporation.

4. *Private responses to changed rule.*

Since some assets are more liquid and more easily valued than others, most proposals to eliminate the realization requirement target specific groups of assets.[56] To avoid thorny valuation and liquidity problems, these proposals would tax only the appreciation of those capital assets that are easily valued and relatively liquid. Other capital assets would continue to be taxed as they are under the current tax law. Unfortunately, the decision to tax only some assets' capital appreciation probably would cause private investors to shift their funds from assets subject to the appreciations tax into assets not subject to the tax, thereby distorting optimal investment behavior.[57]

In tax law, the problem of drawing lines between taxed and untaxed behavior is troublesome because there are powerful financial incentives to be on the untaxed side of the line, and large amounts of capital tend to flow from more heavily taxed investments into those less heavily taxed. If only stocks traded on major exchanges were taxed, there would be a tremendous incentive not to be listed on the exchanges. If shares of all publicly held corporations were taxed, there would be a drive to "go private" or stay private.[58] If commer-

---

against paying dividends would be completely eliminated if the tax on appreciations used the same rates that are applied to dividends (ordinary income rates). If appreciations were taxed at long term capital gains rates while dividends remained taxed at ordinary income rates, the bias against paying dividends would be reduced but not eliminated.

55. Corporate decisionmakers, who are often large shareholders or who receive options as part of their compensation packages, may be willing to increase dividends (keeping less income as retained earnings) to provide shareholders with cash so that they can pay the appreciations tax without selling shares of stock. Some modern securities valuation theorists argue that stock prices react favorably to increased dividend payments. *See* M. GORDON, THE INVESTMENT, FINANCING AND VALUATION OF THE CORPORATION (1962). *But see* Miller & Modigliani, *supra* note 46. *See generally* note 46 *supra* and sources cited therein.

56. Slawson, for example, would impose an appreciations tax only on the stock of publicly held companies (500 or more shareholders). Slawson, *supra* note 7, at 651. David and Miller's proposal is more general and would reach all capital assets. David & Miller, *supra* note 7, at 4281.

57. *See generally* Sneed, *supra* note 24, at 586–87.

58. *See Master Inc. Increases Offer to Buy Its Stock*, Wall St. J., July 11, 1979, at 41, col. 6;

cial real estate is taxed and residential real estate is not, capital will flee the commercial real estate market into the residential market. Arbitrary line-drawing in the tax area creates substantial economic distortion; any division between those assets made subject to the appreciations tax and those assets not made so should seek to minimize this distortion.

III. An Approach to Taxing Appreciation

Though the disadvantages of taxing appreciation of capital assets are substantial, Congress has chosen to do so in the commodity futures area, and may act again. This Part briefly assesses a previous proposal for taxing capital appreciation and then proposes an alternative approach that would more effectively mitigate the disadvantages of taxing appreciation.

A. *Slawson's Proposal*

In 1967, David Slawson suggested that stock appreciation of publicly held corporations be taxed as ordinary income.[59] At the time he proposed this ordinary income treatment of unrealized gains, ordinary tax rates peaked at 70%.[60] Slawson's proposal could have made it quite difficult for some investors to pay their taxes and thus could have forced them to sell their stock. It also would have driven up the cost of capital for corporations dramatically, thereby making it more difficult for them to raise capital.[61] Since interest rates have risen substantially since 1967,[62] prudent corporations would not want to borrow to the same extent that they would have a few years ago.[63]

When Firm Goes Private via Assets Sale, SEC Staff Warns, Holders Must Get Data, id., Feb. 16, 1979, at 10, col. 1.

59. *See* Slawson, *supra* note 7.
60. J. Pechman, Federal Tax Policy 255 (rev. ed. 1971).
61. Slawson argued that such a tax would not harm corporations that have to go to the equity markets if new stock issues were made exempt from the appreciations tax for 15 to 20 years after they entered the category of publicly traded stocks. Slawson, *supra* note 7, at 652. But such an exemption would cause corporations to issue series of common stocks (common stock tax free until 1995, common stock tax free until 1997, etc.) rather than having a single class of common stock. Each series of stock would presumably trade at a slightly different price, depending on the value of the tax deferral characteristic. Equity markets would resemble the bond markets. Because trading in a corporation's stock would be split up among the various classes of stock, none of the individual classes would have the liquidity that a single class of stock has today. Equity markets would therefore be less efficient in matching buyers and sellers, and transactions costs would increase (the bid/ask spread would be larger).
62. *Compare* W. Sharpe, *supra* note 52, at 227, *with Money Rates*, Wall St. J., Dec. 28, 1981, at 13, col. 3.
63. *See* note 52 *supra*.

The effect of taxing stock appreciation at ordinary income rates would be to reduce the total amount of capital that corporations would seek. In short, Slawson's proposal would not have reduced the disadvantages of taxing stock appreciation.

B. *An Alternative Proposal*

To tax the appreciation of capital assets, the rate of taxation must reflect the nature of the income; in other words, a tax on capital gains income needs to be limited to a capital gains rate. Taxing appreciation at capital gains rates would, like Slawson's proposal, achieve the advantages of eliminating the realization requirement while concomitantly reducing the disadvantages. Therefore, the Congress should amend the Internal Revenue Code along the following lines:

(1) Marketable securities of publicly held corporations should be marked to market at the end of the tax year.[64] The appreciation of these capital assets will be taxed in the year of accrual at long term capital gains rates.[65] By taxing only marketable securities—stock, bonds, and options—of publicly held corporations, the problems of valuation and liquidity that exist with other classes of capital assets are avoided. And the use of relatively low rates should ease the cash flow problems that result from taxing appreciation.[66]

(2) Publicly held corporations should be defined to include those corporations that have 500 or more shareholders and gross as-

---

64. As a consequence, the distinction between short term and long term capital gains for the marketable securities of publicly held corporations will be eliminated. Because of the differential treatment of short term and long term capital gains, an investor who holds stock that has increased in value from $50 per share to $100 per share in 10 months currently may hold onto the stock for another 2 months to qualify for the long term capital gains tax rate even if he knows that it will fall $10 per share during the 2 months. The holding period requirement creates a problem similar to the lock-in problem. By eliminating the distinction between short and long term capital gains for the stock of publicly held corporations, an appreciations tax cures this perversity and makes it easier for capital to flow among marketable securities.

65. Alternatively, a tax liability for past unrealized gains could be accrued. The liability would increase or decrease each year as the asset's value increased or decreased. The liability would incur interest, but it would not be due until the asset was sold or transferred at death or by gift. This approach eliminates the liquidity problem, removes the need for liberalized capital loss carryback and carryforward provisions and withholding provisions, and limits the value of deferral and the significance of lock-in. The requirement that the tax liability be paid when the asset is sold or transferred is necessary to prevent unlimited deferral of the tax payment.

66. The need to obtain cash to pay taxes will never force a shareholder with a controlling interest to sell shares and lose his controlling interest. Because the appreciations tax applies long term capital gains rates, a shareholder should always be able to borrow on margin to pay his taxes. *See* note 35 *supra*.

sets greater than or equal to $1 million. Since some marketable securities are more liquid than others,[67] the amendment should limit appreciations taxation to the marketable securities of publicly held corporations as defined by the Security Act Amendments of 1964.[68] The Act requires that all corporations with 500 or more shareholders and $1 million or more in gross assets comply with certain proxy and filing requirements.[69] Because these corporations have to fulfill the Act's proxy and reporting requirements, it will be relatively easy for them to integrate the withholding process into their information processing systems and to issue end-of-year reports for securities holders. This division will, naturally, create some adverse incentives: Corporations will strive to have fewer than 500 shareholders. Choosing this point as the dividing line, however, subjects the vast majority of corporate securities in the United States to the appreciations tax.[70] Most of these securities are traded on public exchanges or through National Association of Securities Dealers brokers, and can easily be valued.

(3) Averaging provisions, including liberal capital loss carryforwards and carrybacks, should be adopted. If a shareholder pays tax on appreciation in one year and suffers a loss in a subsequent year, the carryback provision should provide a credit or refund on the previously paid taxes. Likewise, if current losses exceed previous gains, they should be carried forward to be applied against subsequent years' capital gains.

(4) To ease the transition in the first year of the tax, stock prices on January 1st of the year of adoption should be taken as the base for calculating the first year's appreciation.[71] In any year, shareholders should only be taxed on the appreciation that has occurred in the previous 12-month period. The difference between the stock price on January 1st of the year of adoption and the adjusted basis should not be taxed until sale or exchange of the asset.[72]

---

67. *See generally* T. SIMPSON, MONEY, BANKING, AND ECONOMIC ANALYSIS 7 (1976).

68. Act of Aug. 20, 1964, Pub. L. No. 88-467, § 3, 78 Stat. 565, 565-69 (codified in scattered sections of 15 U.S.C.). This is the same definition of a publicly held corporation that Slawson used. Slawson, *supra* note 7, at 651.

69. The rationale for choosing 500 shareholders as the cutoff point is that with so many shareholders, the stock is certain to be traded. The purpose of the $1 million gross asset screen is to exclude corporations for whom the costs of compliance are high in relation to the gain to be obtained with compliance.

70. Slawson, *supra* note 7, at 628 & n.22.

71. After the first year, the last year's valuation will provide the base upon which to calculate appreciation.

72. The purpose of this provision is to ease the transition into the appreciations tax.

(5) The basis for marketable securities affected by this proposal should be stepped up to current market value when transferred at death or by gift, but the recipient of these securities should have to recognize the unrealized accumulated appreciation as capital gains income in the year in which the assets are received.[73] This provision is needed because unrealized capital gains income that has accrued before this proposal is adopted could otherwise entirely escape taxation.

(6) When an investor purchases or sells stocks or bonds, the broker executing the order should be required to notify the corporation whose securities have been transferred of the amount of securities involved and the price at which the transaction occurred. Publicly held corporations should be required to provide holders of securities and the Internal Revenue Service with annual income statements showing the gain or loss in the value of their securities. These statements could resemble the form 1099's that savings institutions cur-

---

There is an inherent conflict between easing the transition and eliminating the lock-in problem; easing the transition means delaying the elimination of lock-in.

If a stock had appreciated substantially before adoption of the appreciations tax, there would still be some incentive not to sell the stock, because the pre-appreciations tax portion of the gain would not be taxed until the asset was sold or transferred. On the other hand, eliminating the tax-free stepped-up basis at death removes the possibility that the gain will escape taxation forever and limits the ability of the taxpayers to defer even previously accrued capital gains. Younger investors will want to reinvest their funds if they know of a better investment, and older investors will no longer be able to hope that their unrealized stock gains will fully escape taxation. As time goes on, the pre-appreciations tax on unrealized gains will become a smaller and smaller percentage of all stock gains, and the significance of the lock-in problem will therefore decrease.

An alternative approach which might make the transition more difficult, but which would eliminate lock-in more quickly, would be to give taxpayers the option to realize a portion of their previously unrealized capital gains over a few years in exchange for marking the basis up to the current market value. For example, taxpayers could be given the option of realizing 10% of the appreciation that had been unrealized at the time that the appreciations tax was adopted in each of the first 5 years following adoption. Each year, their bases would be increased by 200% (10/5) of the amount they realize. In 5 years, their bases would equal market value even though they paid tax only on 50% of the previously accrued gain.

The precise percentages are not important; it *is* important that the option be structured to make declaring the gain now and paying the tax now appear favorable when compared to deferring realization of the gain. This type of preference would be needed to induce taxpayers to write up their assets immediately. To the extent that taxpayers elected this option, the lock-in problem would be more quickly eliminated. For another alternative approach, see note 65 *supra*.

73. Alternatively, no gain could be recognized at death, but the stepped-up basis provisions of I.R.C. § 1014 (1976 & Supp. III 1979) could be eliminated. The original basis and holding period could then be carried over for property transferred at death or by gift. This alternative would be more favorable to those who inherit capital assets, but would delay elimination of the lock-in problem. The availability of funds through margin loans insures that cash would be available to cover the tax liability from the provision proposed in the text.

rently provide.[74] Where substantial appreciation has occurred, a portion of the dividends should be withheld and paid to the Treasury, and the end-of-year statements should show these payments.

Of course, any proposal to tax the annual appreciation of corporate equity will reduce the ability of firms to raise new equity capital, because it will reduce investors' after-tax rates of return. Taxing appreciation at a top rate of 20%,[75] however, can be expected to have fewer detrimental effects than taxing at a maximum rate of 70% or 50%.[76]

Imposing an appreciations tax on corporate equity may encourage some investors to leave the stock market and invest in real estate or other forms of investment[77] that are not subject to the appreciations tax. It seems unlikely, however, that the capital shift would be very large. The capital gains appreciations tax simply is at too low a rate—presently 20%.[78] In addition, the stock and bond

---

74. For one possible design for the withholding form, see David & Miller, *supra* note 7, at 4285.

75. *See* I.R.C. § 1 (West Supp. Nov. 1981); *id.* § 1202 (Supp. III 1979).

76. Corporate cash flows should increase dramatically in the next decade as the corporate income tax disappears. *See* Thurow, *supra* note 18, at 73. This change will increase retained earnings and provide corporations with more cash.

77. The major category of capital assets that is excluded from the appreciations tax is real estate. There are a number of reasons for not taxing the annual appreciation of real estate. Parcels of land are difficult to value accurately and, depending upon the economic climate, can be difficult to sell. *See generally* J. DUE & A. FRIEDLAENDER, GOVERNMENT FINANCE: ECONOMICS OF THE PUBLIC SECTOR 469-72 (5th ed. 1973). Borrowing is available through the second mortgage market, but at a relatively high interest rate and only for short periods of time. In addition, real estate is already subject to an ad valorem property tax.

It may be that commercial and income-producing properties should be subject to the appreciations tax and residential (owner-occupied) housing exempted from it. Although the valuation and liquidity problems are significant factors for both commercial and residential properties, commercial property owners probably have better access to the funds that would be needed to make the annual tax payments. *See generally* W. SHARPE, *supra* note 52, at 212-16. The most compelling reason for the distinction, however, is that society places quite a premium on the idea of home ownership, and it is probably simply not feasible to require retired individuals to pay an income tax annually on the appreciation of their homes. The value attached to home ownership is reflected in I.R.C. § 1034 (West 1967, Supp. 1981 & Supp. Nov. 1981) (tax-free rollover of gain on sale of principal residence). *See generally* R. SOMMERFELD, FEDERAL TAXES AND MANAGEMENT DECISIONS 267-69 (3d ed. 1981). Even if the funds needed were available through the second mortgage market, people may feel a great difference between asking a homeowner to borrow to pay a tax on the unrealized gain on his home and asking an investor to borrow to pay taxes on the unrealized capital gains income from his marketable securities.

78. By comparison, in 1980 single individuals with taxable incomes of $8500 faced a 21% marginal tax rate on their federal income taxes. I.R.C. § 1 (West Supp. Nov. 1981). Because a worker with $8500 of wages must also pay payroll taxes on that income, his marginal tax rate is actually even higher.

exchanges are probably better equipped to handle large amounts of capital and to provide investors with a high degree of liquidity than are any other investment institutions. Furthermore, many of the large institutional holders of marketable securities—pension funds and trusts, for example—are either exempt from income tax, and will therefore not be affected, or are obligated to invest in marketable securities.[79] The flow of capital out of stocks should, therefore, be small, and the distortive effects of the tax should not be significant.

IV. Conclusion

In the Economic Recovery Tax Act of 1981, Congress for the first time explicitly repealed the realization requirement for a major category of capital assets. This note discussed the advantages and disadvantages of taxing unrealized capital gains income, and proposed that Congress extend the capital gains tax to the appreciation on all marketable securities of corporations with 500 or more shareholders and gross assets of greater than or equal to $1 million. Eliminating the realization requirement for this group of assets will achieve the advantages of annual taxation, while taxing at a capital gains rate will reduce the correlative disadvantages. Adopting this approach will achieve true tax reform at a reasonable cost.

Mark L. Louie

---

79. *See* M. BERNSTEIN, THE FUTURE OF PRIVATE PENSIONS 42 (1964).

POINTS AND COUNTERPOINTS

1. What policy goals, if any, justify the following distinctions in the tax treatment of capital gains:

   (a) Ordinary income for authors on the sale of a copyright but capital gains for inventors on the sale of their patents?

   (b) Ordinary income for farmers raising cattle for meat but capital gains for farmers holding cattle for breeding, dairy, or sporting purposes (bullfights?)?

   (c) Ordinary income for coal miners scrabbling coal out of a mine for wages but capital gains (sometimes) for owners of coal mines on their sale of coal?

2. During the 1978 debates over capital gains policy summarized above by James Wetzler, the proponents of reduced capital gains taxes argued that a cut in rates would "pay for itself" through a substantial net increase in realizations. One well publicized study claimed that a cut in capital gains rates to the 1973 level would produce a threefold increase in realizations. Feldstein, Slemrod, & Yitzhaki, "The Effects of Taxation on the Selling of Corporate Stock and Realization of Capital Gains," 94 *Quarterly Journal of Economics* 777 (1980). A later study claimed that "[m]uch of this large measured effect was caused by an incorrect statistical procedure" and "much of the remainder was the response of taxpayers to fluctuations in their own effective tax rates, as opposed to the level of statutory capital gains rates." J. Minarik, "Capital Gains," in *How Taxes Affect Economic Behavior* (H. Aaron & J. Pechman, Eds. 1981). In the comments following the Minarik paper, James Wetzler offers an excellent criticism of both the Minarik study and the Feldstein-Slemrod-Yitzhaki study. He shows that neither study provides a theory of investor behavior that would permit anyone to interpret their empirical findings. He notes, however, that the amount of revenue actually raised from gains realized in 1979 is closer to the outcome predicted by Minarik's equation than to the outcome predicted by Feldstein, Slemrod, and Yitzhaki.

3. When does lock-in impose efficiency costs on society? Economists traditionally argue that lock-in always causes a misallocation of resources, since an investor holding asset A who wants to sell and purchase asset B is induced by taxes to continue holding asset A. Why would resources be misallocated simply because investors are inhibited from changing their portfolios? Assume, for example, that assets A and B are publicly

traded bonds. Since any sale of those bonds implies a purchase, the disinvestment by one person requires an investment by another. Since one investor in a publicly traded bond cannot make better use of it than another, what change in resource allocation arises from the trade? Arguably only lock-in of tangible business property and analogous assets would impose efficiency costs. Under some conditions, lock-in might even be desirable. For example, during a period of capital shortage, society could benefit if lock-in induced some holders of investment property to defer consumption.

4. How should Congress define a capital asset? Is there any way to answer that question without first identifying the purpose of the capital gains preference? Can the purposes of the capital gains preference be discussed realistically without noting the political influence of those benefiting from it?

5. Would it be possible to design an investment incentive that was at least as effective as the capital gains preference in stimulating investment and that avoided the dramatic negative impact of the capital gains preference on fairness? How? Would an effective incentive give its rewards only after the investment gains had been realized? Is the delay a reasonable way of avoiding a subsidy to unsuccessful investments?

6. Is it fair to tax gains on marketable securities on an accrual basis without also extending accrual taxation to other types of gains? That is, which is fairer—to equate taxpayers holding marketable securities with wage earners and bank depositors or to equate them with equal-income cattle breeders, real estate investors, etc., who would continue to enjoy deferral?

7. The Canadian government has proposed legislation that would permit taxpayers to elect accrual taxation of "real" capital gains on marketable securities, with nominal inflation gains exempt from tax. Taxpayers would invest through approved accounts that would be valued at the end of each taxable year. The amount taxed would be the difference between the market value and the taxpayer's adjusted basis in the account. That basis would equal the cost basis, increased by accrued gains previously taxed and indexed for inflation. Accrued losses would be deductible without the normal limitations. Is the proposed Canadian legislation desirable for the United States? At a minimum, would it serve as an effective riposte to those who complain about the taxation of illusory gains? Could that technique be expanded to include other assets, such as interest-bearing certificates? If interest accounts were included in the package, should those paying nominal interest be denied an interest deduction? How? Should persons holding assets in qualified ac-

counts be denied an interest deduction on loans that finance the purchase of such assets? How?

8. Is the capital gains preference a tax expenditure? Is it possible to argue, for example, that the preference for coal mine owners and inventors is a tax expenditure, but the preference for stockholders is not? Assuming that at least some part of the preference is a tax expenditure, could that part withstand a tax expenditure analysis?

9. An important issue in capital gains taxation is the proper tax treatment of appreciated property at death. Many commentators argue that death should be treated as a realization event. Others would require the recipients of inherited property to take a carry-over basis in the inherited property. In 1976, Congress enacted legislation which adopted the carry-over approach, although it permitted a number of exemptions from that treatment, principally for low- and middle-income taxpayers. This reform would have significantly increased the progressivity of the income tax and reduced the lock-in effect created by the stepped-up basis rule. According to Treasury Department estimates, about $20 billion of untaxed appreciation passed at death in 1979. About 60 percent of this unrealized appreciation is earned by persons leaving gross estates in excess of $175,000. *See* Gutman, "Federal Wealth Transfer Taxes After the Economic Recovery Tax Act of 1981," 35 *National Tax Journal* 253 (1982).

Congress repealed the carry-over rule prior to its implementation, largely in response to the claim that it would impose difficult administrative burdens on high-income taxpayers. The Tax Section of the American Bar Association, for example, lobbied against the carry-over rule on this ground. Many commentators, however, dismiss the complexity argument as a makeweight. Consider the following response to the Senate Finance Committee Report's "attempt to rationalize repeal" of the carry-over-at-death rule:

> "The literature is devoid of complaints by those who receive the benefit of similarly complex carryover basis provisions in the Code. If it is so hard to cope with carryover basis at death, why has section 1015 worked without much comment for gifts? Congress could have greatly reduced the complexity of section 1023 by eliminating the 'fresh start' adjustment and other softening adjustments. Alternatively, it might have levied capital gains taxes on the net unrealized appreciation at death as a part of the final in-

come tax return of the decedent or the decedent's estate. Significantly, Congress did not address the problem it identified, but instead simply repealed the provision." (Footnotes omitted.)

Osgood, "Carryover Basis Repeal and Reform of the Transfer Tax System," 66 *Cornell Law Review* 297, 305 (1981)

VII. THE PROPER TAX CONSEQUENCES OF FAMILY SHARING PRACTICES

The economic well-being of individuals living with members of their family differs from that of unattached individuals in two important respects. First, the standard of living of a family breadwinner is usually lower than that of an unattached individual who has the same wage or property income but who does not have any support obligations. Second, family members on the receiving end of family sharing typically enjoy a substantially higher standard of living than their independent income sources would suggest. Tax specialists often disagree on the proper tax consequences of these common economic features of family living. Some commentators argue that because family living is ultimately a matter of individual choice, the economic benefits of sharing should be ignored in establishing tax burdens. Other commentators would look at the outcome of family sharing in determining taxable capacity. Most tax jurisdictions have adopted at least some measures intended to reflect the real changes in economic circumstances that typically result from family sharing patterns. All of these measures, however, have required some practical compromises with theory, since sharing is neither universal among family members nor unique to family members.

In Section A, below, Boris Bittker traces the history of family taxation in the United States and sets forth the conflicts in values and interests which have made that history so tempestuous. Section B provides a forum for that ancient debate between the advocates of a joint filing system for married couples and the advocates of an individual filing system. As presented here, that debate has two new twists. The first selection shows how a joint filing rule follows almost axiomatically from the recently articulated principle that income should be taxed to the person whose economic well-being that income augments (the "benefit principle"). The second selection attacks the benefit principle by drawing upon the expanding economics literature on the exchange theory of marriage.

Sections C and D explore techniques for limiting the ability of taxpayers to avoid the bite of the federal progressive rate structure through income shifting mechanisms—all of which depend, for their success, on the solidarity of the family unit. In Section C, Martin McMahon attempts to revitalize the case for aggregating the income of children and their parents that was made by the Canadian Royal Commission on Taxation (1966) and which is summarized in the Bittker selection. Section D takes an alternative tack—a reform of the family trust rules. Dan Throop Smith would completely eliminate the trust as a taxable entity by taxing trust income in all cases either to the grantor (or his estate, if he is dead) or to the beneficiaries. This approach would give increased importance to the question of when the grantor should remain taxable, which is the subject of the selection by David Westfall.

The 1981 Tax Act substantially reduced part of the infamous marriage penalty discussed in Sections A and B by granting a special deduction to two-earner married couples. The penalty remains, however, for some two-earner couples, especially those with high and relatively equal individual incomes. One-earner couples obtained no relief from the marriage penalty they suffer from their failure to get a divorce and to split income through the alimony deduction.

Supplemental Readings. Coven, "The Decline and Fall of Taxable Income," 79 *Michigan Law Review* 1525, especially 1536–1564 (1981); Gann, "Abandoning Marital Status as a Factor in Allocating Income Tax Burdens," 59 *Texas Law Review* 1 (1980); H. Brazier, "Income Tax Treatment of the Family," in *The Economics of Taxation* (H. Aaron & M. Boskin, Eds.) 223–246; C. Newton, "Marital Status and the Federal Personal Income Tax," in 6 *Studies in Taxation, Public Finance and Related Subjects—A Compendium* (1982), pp. 32–41.

A. HISTORICAL CONTEXT

BORIS I. BITTKER, "FEDERAL INCOME TAXATION AND THE FAMILY"

27 Stanford Law Review 1389 (1975), pp. 1391–1414.

A persistent problem in the theory of income taxation is whether natural persons should be taxed as isolated individuals, or as social beings whose family ties to other taxpayers affect their taxpaying capacity.[1] From its inception, the federal income tax law has permitted every taxpayer to file a personal return, embracing his or her own income but excluding the income of the taxpayer's spouse, children, and other relatives. On the other hand, married couples may elect to consolidate their income on a joint return, many exemptions and deductions take account of family links and responsibilities, and the income or property of one member of a family is sometimes attributed to another member for a variety of tax purposes. The Internal Revenue Code, in brief, is a patchwork, its history being a myriad of compromises fashioned to meet particular problems.

While this tension between rugged individualism and family solidarity permeates the entire Code, four broad questions capture the major themes:

— Should family members—husbands, wives, children, or others—be required, allowed, or forbidden to amalgamate their separate incomes in order to compute a joint tax liability?

— If amalgamation is either permitted or required, what should be the relationship between the tax liability of a family on its amalgamated income and that of a person living outside any family unit on his or her individual income?

— Should the taxpayer—whether an individual or a family entity—receive a tax allowance for supporting children, parents, or other relatives?

— How should the tax law treat transfers, sales, and other financial and property arrangements between family members, and for what tax pur-

---

1. *See* Treasury Department, *The Tax Treatment of Family Income*, reprinted in Hearings on Revenue Revisions Before the House Comm. on Ways & Means, 80th Cong., 1st Sess., pt. 2, at 846 (1947) [hereinafter cited as Treasury Department]; COLWYN COMM'N, REPORT OF THE ROYAL COMMISSION ON INCOME TAX, CMD. NO. 615 (1920); ROYAL COMMISSION ON THE TAXATION OF PROFITS AND INCOME, SECOND REPORT, CMD. NO. 9105, at 37 (1954); H. GROVES, FEDERAL TAX TREATMENT OF THE FAMILY (1963); W. VICKREY, AGENDA FOR PROGRESSIVE TAXATION 274–301 (1947); Thorson, The Selection of a Tax Unit Under the Income Tax—The Individual Versus the Family Unit, April 20, 1962 (unpublished dissertation, University of Wisconsin) [hereinafter cited as Thorson Dissertation]; Klein, *Familial Relationships and Economic Well-Being: The Family Unit Rules for a Negative Income Tax*, 9 HARV. J. LEGIS. 361 (1971); Oldman & Temple, *Comparative Analysis of the Taxation of Married Persons*, 12 STAN. L. REV. 585 (1960); Pechman, *Income Splitting*, in 1 HOUSE COMM. ON WAYS & MEANS, 86th Cong., 1st Sess., TAX REVISION COMPENDIUM 473 (Comm. Print 1959); Shoup, *Married Couples Compared with Single Persons Under the Income Tax*, 25 NAT'L TAX ASS'N BULL. 130 (Supp. 1940); Surrey, *Family Income and Federal Taxation*, 24 TAXES 980 (1946); Thorson, *An Analysis of the Sources of Continued Controversy Over the Tax Treatment of Family Income*, 18 NAT'L TAX J. 113 (1965). *See also* note 4 *infra*.

poses (if any) should the law attribute the income or property of one family member to another?

The responses of today's law to these questions are, of course, influenced by the need for revenue, by the Internal Revenue Service's capacity to audit returns and enforce the rules, by legislative and administrative efforts to minimize inconsistencies within the statute and regulations, and by other objectives, constraints, and values that are "internal" to the tax system. But the impact of these factors on Congress, the Treasury, and the public has always depended on a much more influential context—society's assumptions about the role of marriage and the family.

We are living in a period of unprecedented debate about the status of marriage and the family. Citizens, moral philosophers, political groups, legislators, and judges are questioning many traditional legal distinctions between men and women, between informal alliances and ceremonial marriage, between legitimate and illegitimate children, between the role of the family and the role of the state, and between the power of parents and the rights of children. In such an era, it is fatuous to expect the premises underlying the Internal Revenue Code to escape inquiry or to suppose that income taxation has a "logic" of its own capable of supplying certitudes to a society wracked by doubts.

For these reasons, the Internal Revenue Code's current answers to the questions set out above are ripe for reexamination. The goal of this Essay is to examine the theories and pressures that shaped today's Internal Revenue Code and to suggest how its provisions may fare in the maelstrom of changing social attitudes toward marriage, women's rights, the two-job couple, communal living patterns, birth control, population growth, and intrafamily rights and liabilities. I hope this will be a useful inquiry, despite the paucity of confident answers and the certainty that any tax reforms spawned by today's social trends will be as particularistic and transitory as the laws they supplant.

I. Consolidation of Family Income

A. *Theoretical Considerations*

1. *The case for consolidation.*

By and large, tax theorists have espoused the doctrine "that taxpaying ability is determined by total family income regardless of the distribution of such income among the members of the family," rather than the contrary theory "that the family as a unit has no combined taxpaying ability per se; that its taxpaying ability is composed of the separate taxpaying abilities of its individual members; and that the taxpaying ability of each of these is determined by the amount of income of which he or she is the owner without reference to the income of the other members of the family."[2] The philosophy of consolidation was recently championed in an influential report by the Canadian Royal Commission on Taxation.[3] Its legislative proposals in this area were not enacted, but the Commission's statement in favor of consolidating family income is an excellent exposition of the social premises that underlie this position:

> We conclude that the present [Canadian tax] system is lacking in essential fairness between families in similar circumstances and that attempts to prevent abuses of the system have produced serious anomalies and rigidities. Most of these results are inherent in the concept that each individual is a separate taxable entity. Taxation of the individual in almost total disregard for his inevitably close financial and economic ties with the other members of the basic social unit of which he is ordinarily a member, the family, is in our view [a] striking instance of the lack of a comprehensive and rational pattern in the present tax system. In keeping with our general theme that the scope of our tax concepts should be broadened and made more consistent in order to achieve equity, we recommend that the family be treated as a tax unit and taxed on a rate schedule applicable to family units. Individuals who are not members of a family unit would continue to be treated as separate tax units and would be taxed on a schedule applicable to individuals. . . .
>
> We believe firmly that the family is today, as it has been for many centuries, the basic economic unit in society. Although few marriages are entered into for purely financial reasons, as soon as a marriage is contracted it is the continued income and financial position of the family which is ordinarily of primary concern, not the income and financial position of the individual members. Thus, the married couple itself adopts the economic concept of the family as the income unit from the outset. In western society the wife's direct financial contribution to the family income through employment is frequently substantial. It is probably even more true that the newly formed family acts as a financial unit in making its expenditures. Family income is normally budgeted between current and capital outlays, and major decisions involving the latter are usually made jointly by the spouses. . . .
>
> Where the family grows by the addition of children, further important financial and economic decisions are made in the family as a unit. Questions of the extent of education, time of entrance into the labour force and, frequently, choices of a career are decided on a family basis, although of course there are many exceptions to this statement. In some circumstances the income of the child is added to the family income, and, even where this is not done directly, the fact that a child has income of his own will have some bearing on the main family expenditure decisions. Certainly when the child becomes self-supporting he is nor-

---

2. Treasury Department, *supra* note 1, at 851. For citations to the comments of tax theorists, of whom very few have favored basing tax liability on individual income, *see* Thorson Dissertation, *supra* note 1.

3. REPORT OF THE ROYAL COMMISSION ON TAXATION (Carter Commission) (1966). *See* Bittker, *Income Tax Reform in Canada: The Report of the Royal Commission on Taxation*, 35 U. CHI. L. REV. 637 (1968); Groves, *Taxing the Family Unit: The Carter Commission's Proposals and U.S. Practice*, 22 NAT'L TAX J. 109 (1969); Note, *Tax Treatment of the Family: The Canadian Royal Commission and the Internal Revenue Code*, 117 U. PA. L. REV. 98 (1968).

mally expected to relieve the family of further expenditure on his behalf. Thus, the income position of children has an important bearing on the family income, although frequently in an indirect way.[4]

This rationale implies that the tax on a family with a given amount of consolidated income should be the same regardless of the proportion of each spouse's contribution to their total income,[5] and it also suggests, though less clearly, that the ratio of parent-child contributions should also be irrelevant. A corollary of this emphasis on the family's consolidated income is that legal ownership of property and income within the family should be disregarded in judging its taxpaying capacity. For at least 50 years, a major theme in the taxation of income from property transferred within the family has been that bedchamber transactions are suspect because the allocation of legal rights within the family is a trivial matter.[6]

But the persons concerned may have a less cavalier attitude toward their legal rights. Taxpayers pass up many opportunities to reduce their taxes by intrafamily gifts,[7] possibly from ignorance or inertia, but perhaps because they attach more significance to their legal rights than academicians assert. The contemporary women's rights movement is a reminder of the long struggle for married women's property laws, whose underlying premise was that the division of legal rights between husband and wife is a significant matter, not a trivial one. Of course, the legal recognition of the property rights of married women may have brought with it, or resulted from, a fundamental change in matrimonial psychology, causing the legal rights acquired by the wife to be as irrelevant as those retained by the husband, at least while the marriage lasts. But it is far from self-evident that the property rights won by married women are inconsequential. Moreover, at least among upper-income taxpayers, it is not uncommon for separate accounts to be maintained for property owned by each spouse at the time of the marriage, inherited thereafter, or accumulated from earnings or household allowances, especially if the household includes children of a prior marriage. It may be, therefore, that tax theorists have excessively downgraded the importance of legal rights within the family, and that a swing of the pendulum is in the offing.

---

4. 3 REPORT OF THE ROYAL COMMISSION ON TAXATION, *supra* note 3, at 122-24.
5. For the special case of the two-job married couple, *see* notes 117-45 *infra* and accompanying text.
6. A representative illustration of this theme, which was accepted by judges with the same enthusiasm as by tax theorists and administrators, is Helvering v. Clifford, 309 U.S. 331, 335 (1940): "We have here at best a temporary reallocation of income within an intimate family group. . . . It is hard to imagine that respondent [the transferor] felt himself the poorer after this trust had been executed or, if he did, that it had any rational foundation in fact." Of course, this conclusion may well have been justified, but despite its tough realism, transfers with no strings attached have been customarily accepted at face value, even though the transferor might feel no poorer after making a gift "within an intimate family group."
7. *See* C. SHOUP, FEDERAL ESTATE AND GIFT TAXES 21-25, 32-49 (1965).

Since 1948, however, the Internal Revenue Code has imposed the same liability on all equal-income married couples, whether the combined income is generated by the earnings or investments of one spouse or both and without regard to the division of ownership between them. So long as family harmony prevails, equal-income married couples can purchase equal quantities of goods and services and probably make their economic decisions in a substantially identical fashion. These common characteristics have been regarded by most theorists as more important in fixing the tax liability of equal-income married couples than differences in their ownership of property, even though technical ownership may become crucial if the marriage is dissolved. For this reason, the 1948 statutory principle of equal taxes for equal-income married couples has been "almost universally accepted" by tax theorists,[8] except for suggestions that a two-job married couple should not pay as much as a one-job married couple with the same joint income.[9]

2. Tax-equality or marriage neutrality?

There is, however, a cloud on the horizon. It is increasingly argued that the income tax on two persons who get married should be neither more nor less than they paid on the same income before marriage. This call for a marriage-neutral tax system stems sometimes from the conviction that the state should neither encourage nor discourage marriage by a tax incentive or penalty, and sometimes from a belief that ceremonial marriages in today's society are not sufficiently different from informal alliances to warrant a difference in tax liability. A legislative bill to achieve a marriage-neutral federal income tax has gained a large and diverse Congressional following in both the House of Representatives and the Senate.[10] Proponents of this reform, however, often overlook the fact that, given a progressive rate schedule, a marriage-neutral tax system cannot be reconciled with a regime of equal taxes for equal-income married couples.

This collision of objectives is easily illustrated. If we assume a rate schedule taxing single persons at the rate of 10 percent on the first $10,000 of income and 25 percent on amounts above $10,000, the taxes paid by four unmarried persons on the amounts of taxable income set out in Table 1 would be as shown therein.

If Alpha marries Beta and Theta marries Zeta, and all four continue to earn the same amount of income as before marriage, the consolidated

---

8. J. PECHMAN, FEDERAL TAX POLICY 87–88 (rev. ed. 1971).
9. See notes 117–45 *infra* and accompanying text.
10. H.R. 715, 93d Cong., 1st Sess. (1973). For hearings on this bill and its predecessors see *Hearings on Tax Treatment of Single Persons and Married Persons Where Both Spouses are Working, Before the House Comm. on Ways & Means*, 92d Cong., 2d Sess. (1972) [hereinafter cited as *1972 House Hearings*]. For discussion of H.R. 715 see note 136 *infra*.

TABLE 1

Hypothetical Income and Taxes Before Marriage

	Taxable Income	Tax
Alpha	$10,000	$1,000
Beta	10,000	1,000
Theta	4,000	400
Zeta	16,000	2,500

income of each married couple will be $20,000. If their marriage is to have no effect on their tax liabilities, Alpha-Beta should continue to pay a total of $2,000 and Theta-Zeta a total of $2,900 in taxes. But if this difference in their tax burdens is deemed to be unwarranted, and a new rate schedule is prescribed for married couples that will cause Alpha-Beta and Theta-Zeta to pay the same tax since they have the same joint income ($20,000), marriage will either (1) decrease the tax burden for both couples, (2) decrease it for one and leave the other's unchanged, (3) decrease it for one and increase it for the other, (4) increase it for one and leave the other's unchanged, or (5) increase it for both—depending on the rate schedule applicable to married couples. In tabular form, using the couples described in Table 1, these possibilities are as shown in Table 2.

In short, we cannot simultaneously have (a) progression, (b) equal taxes on equal-income married couples, and (c) a marriage-neutral tax burden.[11] A corollary of this conclusion is that a tax system with a progressive rate schedule can be marriage-neutral if individual legal rights over income and property are controlling even after marriage and each spouse reports his or her own income, but not if the tax is based on the couple's consolidated income.

For these reasons, advocacy of a marriage-neutral tax system collides directly and irretrievably with a dominant theme of tax theory for at least 50 years—the irrelevance of ownership within intimate family groups. This principle, together with its implication that taxpaying capacity is best measured by consolidated marital or family income, not only has been regularly expounded in the scholarly literature and preached in the classroom, but also has been a major influence on Congress and the judiciary. As will be seen, however, these ideas at one time had powerful challengers, who may belatedly come to be honored as unsung heroes if today's advocates of a marriage-neutral tax system carry the day.

---

11. It should be noted that this dilemma, as demonstrated by Table 2, arises even when two-job married couples are compared with each other; it is not restricted to the effect of marriage when only one spouse is gainfully employed outside the home.

TABLE 2

Effect of Marriage on Taxes

If the Tax on Married Couples with $20,000 of Taxable Income Is:	Marriage Will Have the Following Effect on the Tax Burden Shown in Table 1:	
	Alpha-Beta	Theta-Zeta
1. Less than $2,000	Decrease	Decrease
2. $2,000	No change	Decrease
3. More than $2,000 but less than $2,900	Increase	Decrease
4. $2,900	Increase	No change
5. More than $2,900	Increase	Increase

3. The income of children.

Returning to the Canadian Royal Commission's rationale for taxing families on their consolidated income, it will be recalled that the Commission advocated consolidation of the income of children as well as the income of spouses.[12] In a society whose children are expected to work and to contribute their earnings to the family pool without voicing any opinions on the way funds are used, the case for consolidation is strongest. But even in a society that accords more financial independence to children, their earnings affect the economic behavior of the parents; as the children's income grows, the parents are relieved of pressure to support the children currently and to pass on an inheritance to them. The larger the *aggregate* pool of resources, it is argued, the greater the group's capacity to pay taxes.

The theory is not without appeal. But the justification for consolidating family income is not "tax logic," or any other factors peculiar to the tax system, but rather a social phenomenon—more precisely, the observer's perception of social realities. The Canadian Royal Commission itself implicitly acknowledged this by proposing a series of limits to the inclusion of children's income in the family's consolidated tax base.[13] First, consolidation was to be compulsory only if the children were minors or disabled. Other children, whether living with their parents or not, were excluded, except that students between 21 and 25 years of age could elect to have their income included in the family tax base. Moreover, minors over the school-leaving age could elect to be excluded if employed and living apart from their parents. Finally, regardless of a child's age, gifts and bequests received by him (which were to be included in taxable income under another Commission proposal) could be deposited in an "Income Adjustment Account," a quasi-trust device for holding the property intact until the child's de-

---

12. 3 Report of the Royal Commission on Taxation, *supra* note 3, at 123–24.
13. *Id.* at 132–34.

parture from the family unit (usually at 21) and taxing the accumulated income to him at that time. This exception to consolidation was evidently confined by the Commission to property acquired by gift or bequest in the belief that such property is more likely to be treated as sacrosanct by the parents than would be the child's personal earnings. If so, we have one more illustration of the pervasive influence of social customs—actual or perceived—on the tax system.

These exceptions to the principle of consolidation acknowledge that children should eventually be regarded as autonomous persons whose taxpaying capacity is independent of their parents. Other draftsmen might draw the line elsewhere, but presumably even the most committed proponent of consolidation would abandon it at some point—whether it be when children reach 18 or 21, become self-supporting, leave the parents' home, get married, or have children of their own.

4. *Defining the group whose income is to be consolidated.*

If income is to be consolidated, the entity subject to this treatment must be defined, *e.g.*, "married couple," "family," "household," etc. Sociologists may find it useful to study groups that engage in joint decisionmaking or that manifest a common interest in the economic well-being of their members, but it would be difficult if not impossible to administer a law that employed such squishy phrases.[14] Any more precise definition, however, will inevitably exclude groups that are only marginally different, so far as relevant economic or social relationships are concerned, from those within the magic circle. If married couples are taxed on their consolidated income, for example, should the same principle extend to a child who supports an aged parent, two sisters who share an apartment, or a divorced parent who lives with an adolescent child? Should a relationship established by blood or marriage be demanded, to the exclusion, for example, of un-

---

14. In recent years draftsmen and administrators of social welfare programs have wrestled continually with the problem of defining family and household units. *See, e.g.*, United States Dep't of Agriculture v. Moreno, 413 U.S. 528 (1973), where a statute that defined a household eligible for federal food stamps as "a group of related individuals, who . . . are living as one economic unit sharing common cooking facilities and for whom food is customarily purchased in common" was held to be unconstitutional as a discrimination against households containing unrelated individuals. *See also* Hurley v. Van Lare, 380 F. Supp. 167 (S. & E.D.N.Y. 1974) (reduction of welfare allowance based on presence of a "lodger" in household is unconstitutional); Klein, *supra* note 1, at 388 (discussing constitutionality of statutory rules based on the permanence of a sexual liaison between two unmarried persons, describing the California concept of a "man assuming the role of spouse" ("MARS"), and referring to "spouselike persons"); Lerman, *The Family, Poverty and Welfare Programs: An Introductory Essay on Problems of Analysis and Policy*, in Subcomm. on Fiscal Policy of the Joint Economic Comm., 93d Cong., 2d Sess., Studies in Public Welfare, paper 12, part *I*, The Family, Poverty, and Welfare Programs: Factors Influencing Family Instability (Comm. Print 1974).

For discussions of the relationship of family and household patterns to public welfare programs, see *id.*, pt. II, at 181.

married persons who live together, homosexual companions, and communes?

The most objective boundary lines are those based on legal characteristics such as marital status, obligation to support, or right to inherit. Under existing law, the principal determinant of the tax burden is marriage, a status that is usually unambiguous.[15] In a society that increasingly questions the legitimacy of traditional legal distinctions, however, one is tempted to substitute social "realities" in defining the boundaries of the group whose income is to be consolidated. But every departure from readily established definitional lines increases the problem of enforcement. If the tax on two unmarried persons depends on whether they live together, for example, how is their status to be verified by the Internal Revenue Service without an intolerable intrusion into their private lives?[16] The attempt of social workers to apply the "man in the house" rule to deny welfare payments suggests the difficulties that would be encountered by the Internal Revenue Service in auditing claims that taxpayers are, or are not, living together.[17] If the assertions of status on tax returns were taken at face value in order to minimize or eliminate costly and abrasive investigations, the revenue loss resulting from improper claims might be very large; perhaps more important, conscientious taxpayers would be offended by the government's refusal to enforce its own rules against others. For these reasons, it does not seem feasible to consolidate the income of a group unless its boundaries can be crisply defined and readily verified.

B. *The Realm of Practice—1913 to 1948*

Turning from theory to practice, we find that the tension between the "individual" and "family unit" approaches to federal taxation has had a tortuous history since 1913, when the sixteenth amendment was ratified. The twists and turns in legislative, judicial, and administrative practices provide abundant evidence of the inevitable conflict of values that attend any statutory decision in this area. So much light is cast on current issues by this history that an examination in moderate depth of the principal lines of development is warranted, if not unavoidable.

---

15. The principal source of ambiguity in ascertaining marital status is an out-of-state divorce of debatable validity. *See, e.g.,* Estate of Borax v. Commissioner, 349 F.2d 666 (2d Cir. 1965), *cert. denied,* 383 U.S. 935 (1966).

16. In Sweden, we are told, the social and legal lines between marriage and informal cohabitation have become quite hazy, but unmarried persons who live together are treated as a tax unit only if they were previously married (in which event the dissolution of their marriage is a suspect "tax divorce") or have borne children. *See* Sundberg, *Marriage or No Marriage: The Directives for the Revision of Swedish Family Law,* 20 INT'L & COMP. L.J. 223 (1971). To aid the enforcement of these provisions, Swedish taxpayers must state annually in their tax returns whether they are living with another person. *See id.* at 223.

17. *See* note 14 *supra.*

1. *The early statutes and the courts:* Lucas v. Earl.

Despite the all but universal preference of theoreticians for the consolidation of family income, the tax legislation enacted by Congress was dominated by an individualistic approach at the outset. This focus on individuals rather than married couples, families, or households was implicit as early as 1913, when the introductory words of the first taxing statute based on the sixteenth amendment imposed a tax "upon the entire net income arising or accruing from all sources . . . to every citizen of the United States . . . and to every person residing in the United States, though not a citizen thereof."[18] The Revenue Act of 1916 made the point explicit by taxing "the entire net income received . . . by every individual."[19] The right of married couples to file a joint return (first recognized by statute in 1918) was not an exception to this individualistic bias, since the same rate schedule applied to both separate and joint returns, with the result that joint filings were disadvantageous except in unusual circumstances.[20]

This early Congressional decision to tax individuals rather than families[21] was buttressed by a series of judicial decisions—whose importance in the development of the federal tax system can hardly be exaggerated—holding that a taxpayer who earns or is otherwise entitled to receive income cannot assign it, for tax purposes, to another taxpayer, even if the transfer is effective under state law. The leading case, *Lucas v. Earl,*[22] involved an agreement between husband and wife for an equal division between them of all earnings, investment income, gifts, and other receipts during their marriage. The agreement was executed in 1901 and hence was innocent of a tax avoidance objective. Despite this, the Supreme Court held in a much-quoted opinion by Mr. Justice Holmes that the husband was taxable on the full amount of his personal service income:

> [T]his case is not to be decided by attenuated subtleties. It turns on the import and reasonable construction of the taxing act. There is no doubt that the statute

---

18. Act of Oct. 3, 1913, ch. 16, § II(A)(1), 38 Stat. 166.
19. Ch. 463, § 1(a), 39 Stat. 756. The 1894 Income Tax Law placed a similar emphasis on individuals: "[A tax] shall be assessed . . . upon the gains, profits, and income received . . . by every citizen . . . and every person residing . . . ." Act of Aug. 27, 1894, ch. 349, § 27, 28 Stat. 553. So did the income tax law of the Civil War era: ". . . there shall be levied . . . upon the annual . . . income of every person residing . . . ." Act of July 1, 1862, ch. 119, § 90, 12 Stat. 473.
20. A joint return could increase a generous couple's deductions for charitable contributions by increasing their adjusted gross income and hence raising the deduction ceiling which is determined by a percentage of adjusted gross income. *See also* Helvering v. Janney, 311 U.S. 189 (1940) (capital losses of one spouse deductible from capital gains of other spouse in computing "aggregate income" on pre-1948 joint return).
21. At one time, the legislative decision against consolidation may have stemmed from doubts about its constitutionality. *See* H.R. REP. No. 1040, 77th Cong., 1st Sess. 17–22 (1941), *reprinted in* 1941–2 CUM. BULL. 413, 427–31; Hoeper v. Tax Commission, 284 U.S. 206 (1931); Paul & Havens, *Husband and Wife Under the Income Tax,* 5 B'KLYN L. REV. 241, 266–71 (1936).
22. 281 U.S. 111 (1930). The taxpayers were domiciled in California; however, during the taxable years involved, the California community property system did not confer a sufficient interest on the wife to permit her to report half the husband's earnings on her separate return. *See* note 44 *infra* and accompanying text.

could tax salaries to those who earned them and provide that the tax could not be escaped by anticipatory arrangements and contracts however skillfully devised to prevent the salary when paid from vesting even for a second in the man who earned it. That seems to us the import of the statute before us and we think that no distinction can be taken according to the motives leading to the arrangement by which the fruits are attributed to a different tree from that on which they grew.[23]

Under *Lucas v. Earl*, it became virtually impossible for a taxpayer with income from wages, salaries, or professional fees to shift these items to other taxpayers such as a spouse or child.

But dividends, interest, rents, and other forms of investment income were affected very differently by *Lucas v. Earl* than income from personal services. The "tree" (to use Justice Holmes' metaphor) that produces investment income, according to the courts, was the underlying property itself, so that the income is taxable to the person owning the property when the income arises. Thus, taxpayers wanting to shift the tax liability for investment income to their spouses or children found it possible to do so with impunity, if they were prepared to give up ownership of the underlying securities, bank account, rental real estate, or other property.[24] In essence, legal ownership of the property came to be controlling, no matter how strong the emotional ties between the donor and donee.

2. *What might have been: a tax world without* Lucas v. Earl?

The opinion in *Lucas v. Earl* is late-vintage Holmes, magisterial in tone, studded with quotable phrases,[25] and devoid of analysis. It is by now so entrenched in the thought of tax experts that an income tax system without *Lucas v. Earl* is hard to imagine, rather like envisioning the English language without Shakespeare or the King James translation of the Bible. But the effort is worth making, since it will help to expose some half-hidden premises in the tax treatment of family income.

What if the Supreme Court had thought that the language of the statute and the "intent" of Congress, both murky at best, required the husband-wife agreement (whose validity in determining their property rights under state law was acknowledged) to be honored for tax purposes as well? Assuming Congressional acquiescence in this result, married couples would then have been able to split their income for both private and tax purposes,

---

23. 281 U.S. at 114–15.
24. If a taxpayer balked at a complete divestiture of ownership, a partial transfer would sometimes suffice. The tortuous and often hazy statutory, judicial, and administrative boundaries between effective and ineffective transfers are, of course, a major subject of inquiry in law school courses in federal income taxation.
25. The credit for "giving rise to a truly lamentable host of horticultural metaphors," assigned by Molloy to Helvering v. Horst, 311 U.S. 112 (1940), actually belongs to *Lucas v. Earl. See* Molloy, *Some Tax Aspects of Corporate Distributions in Kind*, 6 TAX L. REV. 57, 61 (1950).

and all equal-income married couples making this election would have paid the same amount of federal income taxes. As an objective of federal tax policy, this result of equal taxes on equal-income married couples has been widely approved by tax theorists,[26] yet the effort of Mr. and Mrs. Earl to achieve a tax burden that was independent of their proportionate contributions to their joint income was repulsed by *Lucas v. Earl*, and generations of law students have been led to applaud the decision.

Mr. and Mrs. Earl were prophets without honor in another respect. By establishing for themselves a marital regime of equal ownership and equal control of their joint income in 1901, they foreshadowed an idea that contemporary women's rights advocates often present as novel, and that many regard as worthy of being imposed by law on all married couples. Moreover, it was only by equalizing their financial positions that they put themselves in a position to claim the tax advantage of equal-income separate returns. Though their tax claim was rejected, the income-splitting joint return authorized by Congress in 1948, which with only minor changes is still in effect, achieves the tax result that Mr. and Mrs. Earl were seeking. It does so, however, without requiring husband and wife to equalize their ownership *inter se*; in this respect, the Earl agreement might be regarded as an improvement over the 1948 statutory reform.[27] In retrospect, therefore, it is not fanciful to suggest that the taxpayers in *Lucas v. Earl* might well have been praised for an agreement embodying a sound principle of marital partnership that, had it been upheld, would have furthered an equally sound principle of tax law, instead of being castigated for seeking refuge in what Mr. Justice Holmes called "attenuated subtleties."

The Supreme Court is nothing if not supreme, however, and the Holmsian epigrams in *Lucas v. Earl* carried the day. The propriety of the decision became an article of faith with tax theorists,[28] and it soon was regarded as a guardian of the progressive rate structure. In fact, however, the judgment of the court of appeals, which was reversed by the Supreme Court, was equally compatible with any desired degree of progression. To illustrate this point, assume a rate schedule that exempts the first $100,000 of income and taxes all income above that level at 100 percent. Under *Lucas v. Earl* as decided, a married breadwinner would become subject to the 100 percent rate as soon as his or her salary exceeded $100,000, which is the same point at which a single person would become subject to the 100 percent rate. Had

---

26. See note 8 *supra* and accompanying text.

27. For proposals to accord federal tax effect to "marital partnerships" established by married couples in common law states to create property rights similar to those arising in community property states, *see* H.R. 3842, 80th Cong., 1st Sess. (1947), *reprinted in Hearings on Revenue Revisions Before the House Comm. on Ways & Means*, 80th Cong., 1st Sess., 762 (1947); Altman, *Community Property: Avoiding Avoidance by Adoption in the Revenue Act*, 16 TAXES 138 (1938).

28. I do not exculpate myself for worshiping false gods.

Lucas v. Earl gone the other way, a married couple would become subject to the 100 percent rate only if their aggregate income exceeded $200,000; the first $200,000 would be exempt, but this is the same amount that two single persons could enjoy tax-free if each had a salary of $100,000.

Which approach serves the cause of progression better depends on one's views about the relationship between a married couple's tax burden and the tax burden of single persons with the same amount of income. If the best reference point is the tax paid by two single persons of whom one has the same income as the husband and the other the same income as the wife— the *Lucas v. Earl* result—then that case "protects" the progressive rate schedule. But if the married couple's taxpaying capacity is more nearly comparable to that of two single persons each with one-half their income, *Lucas v. Earl* makes no contribution to—indeed, interferes with—the achievement of progression. There is nothing in the principle of progression that requires taxpaying capacity to be determined by looking to the source of income, in disregard of the fact that it is shared by a married couple or family. For this reason, the common notion that the principle of *Lucas v. Earl*, as applied to married couples,[29] was an essential buttress to the progressive rate schedule is fallacious.

A final aspect of *Lucas v. Earl*'s exaggerated reputation as a guardian of progression has served to obscure its responsibility for an objectionable distinction between earned and investment income. When *Lucas v. Earl* was decided, it was already established law that taxpayers with investment income could make intrafamily gifts that would be effective in computing their federal tax liability, if they were willing to relinquish control over the underlying income-producing property.[30] Against this background, *Lucas v. Earl* imposed a disability on wage earners and salaried taxpayers[31] that cannot be easily reconciled with a concern for progression. To the contrary, if income splitting had been made as freely available to them as to taxpayers with investment income, the result would have been a tax structure whose progressive rates—at whatever level Congress chose to fix them—would have applied more equitably as between married couples with earned income and married couples with an equal amount of investment income. This disparity between earned and investment income persisted until the enactment in 1948 of the income-splitting joint return.

---

29. As applied outside the family context (*e.g.*, to prevent the shifting of income from a taxpayer to trusts, corporations, or other entities in which he has a beneficial interest), however, *Lucas v. Earl* clearly serves to protect progressivity.

30. *See* note 24 *supra* and accompanying text.

31. Sole proprietors and partners in business firms, whose personal service income is mingled with income from invested capital, are less restricted by *Lucas v. Earl*. Despite its rejection of "attenuated subtleties," the decision did not automatically negate the effectiveness of partnership and close corporation arrangements between taxpayers active in the business and their spouses or children, and these devices are often honored by the Internal Revenue Service and the courts.

Finally, in retrospect one can discern still another irony in *Lucas v. Earl*. In holding that the marital partnership established by Mr. and Mrs. Earl was an "anticipatory arrangement" that for tax purposes could not be allowed to override the fact that under private law the husband's salary vested in him as soon as the services were performed, it simply gave precedence to one "anticipatory arrangement" (the employer-employee contract) over another (the husband-wife contract), on the ground that the first had taken hold an instant before the second.[32] This may have been a reasonable reading of a murky statute, but in making policy, there is no valid reason to allow the time when their legal rights vested to determine whether the husband or the wife should be taxed on the income in question. Moreover, although *Lucas v. Earl* did not explicitly denigrate the husband-wife contract as a "bedchamber" reshuffling of legal rights, it was taken to imply that such arrangements should be viewed with suspicion because legal rights within the family unit are inconsequential.[33] But if their reshuffling of legal rights is to be disregarded, why attach any greater importance to the *original* division of ownership between husband and wife? Should not equal-income couples pay the same tax, regardless of how their legal rights are originally allocated or subsequently rearranged between them? Congress answered this question in the affirmative in 1948, and the seeds of this legislative decision were buried in *Lucas v. Earl*, even though it held that the statute before it required a negative answer to the same question.

3. *The community property system:* Poe v. Seaborn.

Individualism thus came to reign supreme in the formative years of federal income taxation in the sense that every individual was taxed on his or her "own" income. In states with a common law property system, the result was that the taxes paid by married couples with equal amounts of aggregate income varied greatly, depending on whether their investment income was divided between them or not and, in the case of personal service income, on whether there was one breadwinner or two. In the community property states of the Southwest and Pacific Coast, however, where marriage is treated as a partnership that vests in each spouse a present interest in one-half of the couple's joint income, whether derived from personal services or from their community property, tax equality of equal-income married

---

32. This reading of *Lucas v. Earl* is confirmed by the same Court's unanimous decision in Poe v. Seaborn, 282 U.S. 101 (1930), that the husband's earnings in a community property state are, in effect, already subjected to the wife's one-half interest when the salary is paid to him. In a community property state, in other words, the marriage agreement causes the wife's rights to vest before the salary is paid and any contrary employer-employee agreement comes too late; in a common law state, the husband-wife and employer-employee contracts are given just the opposite order of precedence.

33. *See* note 6 *supra*.

couples came to be the prevailing principle.[34] But this result was reached only after the Treasury and the courts fumbled uncertainly for many years with the proper treatment of community income. Were wages, for example, to be reported by the wage earner, or one-half by each spouse? If personal service income was invested, who should report the subsequently received dividends, interest, and rents? These questions first arose in 1913,[35] but they were not definitively answered until 1930, when the Supreme Court held in *Poe v. Seaborn*[36] that each spouse was taxable on one-half of the community income.

Until then, the Treasury had to fend for itself in administering a taxing statute that referred vaguely to "the net income of each individual" but that had to be applied in states whose community property systems give the wife a "present interest" in one-half of the community income, but vest the husband with the exclusive right to manage the property free from any duty to account for his stewardship while the marriage lasts.[37] His managerial powers amount to something less than full ownership of the community income, of course, but even in common law states the husband's "own" income is burdened by legal restrictions, including a duty to support his wife during marriage, make proper provision for her on divorce, and transfer a specified part of his estate to her if she survives him.[38]

When debating the tax significance of these legal differences between the community property and common law systems, the commentators were usually overwhelmed by their own rhetoric. Thus, the community property system was extolled as "a heritage of the great free peoples," to be contrasted with a common law system that treated women as "inferior beings, entitled only to a subordinate place in the social order" and that owed its origin "to the fact that Scandinavian pirates, descending on the coasts of France, adapted to their use a code of marital property laws deemed appropriate to the daughters of the vanquished" and then imposed it on the English after the Norman Conquest.[39] Denying that this contrast between civilization and barbarism is helpful in creating a tax structure for the twentieth

---

34. Local law left room for "separate" income, which was taxable to one spouse or the other in the same way that he or she would be taxed in a common law state, but these items (*e.g.*, income excluded from the community by agreement between the spouses, and some receipts during marriage that under state law did not become community income) were ordinarily of minor importance.

35. The question could also have arisen under the Civil War and 1894 Income Tax Acts which were based on individual income, *see* note 19 *supra*, but the modest rates made the issue rather unimportant.

36. 282 U.S. 101 (1930).

37. *See, e.g.*, ch. 1608, §8, [1969] Cal. Laws 3342 (amended 1973). Prior to the 1973 amendment, which did not take effect until 1975, the husband was vested with the right to manage and control the community property. The amendment gave both spouses equal powers of control. *See* CAL. CIV. CODE § 5125 (West Supp. 1974).

38. These gender-based obligations may now or in the future be matched by correlative obligations on the wife but they were unique to the husband during the period under examination here.

39. Brief for Atty's General of Calif., Ariz., Idaho, La., Nev., N.M., Tex., & Wash. as Amici Curiae at 62, 67–69, 71–72, Fernandez v. Wiener, 326 U.S. 340 (1945).

century, other commentators argued that the "marital partnership" recognized by the community property states is without significance while the marriage lasts, because of the husband's broad managerial powers, and that "the wife's role is essentially that of a back-seat driver who may carp and criticize, but may not take the wheel."[40] The Supreme Court, for its part, has described the husband's authority as an "expansive and sometimes profitable control over the wife's share" terminating only on his death, so that it is only then that she gains "full and exclusive possession, control and enjoyment" of her share of the community property.[41]

The husband's broad power to manage all community property led the Treasury, in its first ruling on the subject, to require him to report all community income.[42] In 1919, however, the Treasury beat a partial retreat from this theory by acknowledging the couple's right to split investment income from community property on separate tax returns, while continuing to require the husband to report all community income generated by the personal services of either spouse. This position was, in turn, abandoned when the Attorney General ruled in 1920 and 1921 that the community property systems of Arizona, Idaho, Louisiana, Nevada, New Mexico, Texas, and Washington gave the wife a "vested interest" in one-half of all community income, and that each spouse was therefore taxable on his or her share. As to California, however, the Attorney General ruled that the wife had only "a mere expectancy" under local law, rather than a vested interest."[43]

The exclusion of California from the Attorney General's protaxpayer opinion was upheld in 1926 by the Supreme Court in *United States v. Robbins*.[44] The Court accepted the government's theory that the wife had no more than "a mere expectancy" in California community property, but also went on to intimate that there was a broader ground for taxing the husband, viz., the fact that "he may spend [community income] substantially as he chooses," even "if he wastes it in debauchery."[45] This language was interpreted by the Treasury as an invitation to reexamine the status of community income in even the most orthodox community property states, and the Attorney General cleared the road for a series of test cases by reconsidering and withdrawing his 1920 and 1921 opinions. While not con-

---
40. 1 R. PAUL, FEDERAL ESTATE AND GIFT TAXATION 55 (1942).
41. Fernandez v. Wiener, 326 U.S. 340, 355 (1945).
42. *See* Maggs, *Community Property and the Federal Income Tax*, 14 CALIF. L. REV. 351, 354-57 (1926).
43. *See id.* at 356-57.
44. 269 U.S. 315 (1926). The Court reserved judgment on the effect of a 1917 revision of California law intended to insure favorable federal tax treatment. Further changes in 1927 (providing that husband and wife have "present, existing, and equal interests [in community property] under the management and control of the husband") finally succeeded in bringing California into the circle of "true" community property states. *See* United States v. Malcolm, 282 U.S. 792 (1931).
45. 269 U.S. at 327.

ceding that these opinions were erroneous, the Attorney General expressed the view that the community property systems in some of these states bore a close resemblance to the California system that had just been held ineffective in the *Robbins* case, while others differed considerably from it; therefore, he withdrew the earlier opinions, so that the issue could be submitted by the Treasury to the courts.[46]

Three years later, *Poe v. Seaborn* and three companion cases[47] reached the Supreme Court, and—17 years after the issue first arose—finally elicited an authoritative judicial resolution of the community property imbroglio. The government summarized its argument for taxing all community income to the husband in these words:

> The wife's vested interest in the community property is no more than a right to devise by will or to receive upon the dissolution of the community one-half of the then existing community property with the right in the interim to have the property devoted to such purposes as are in the honest judgment of the husband appropriate for the advancement of community interests. She has no positive powers of control and cannot, to any substantial degree, interfere with the broad powers of control given to her husband.
>
> The husband accordingly is the spouse having the right to control and manage the community property in Washington [the state of residence in *Poe v. Seaborn*] and should be made liable for Federal income tax on the entire community income. This requirement is the more reasonable in view of the fact that under the philosophy of the community property system in that State the community is a legal unit and in view of the further fact that the husband as well as the community is liable on all contracts which he makes for the community.[48]

Whether by design or accident, none of the four test cases involved community income attributable to the wife's personal services, but the government's theory would have taxed even this type of income to the husband, along with his own earnings and any income from the investment of community property.

The government's argument, however, did not carry the day. After reviewing the legal incidents of community property in Washington, where the taxpayers in *Poe v. Seaborn* were domiciled, the Court held that, despite the husband's managerial control, "the entire property and income of the community can no more be said to be that of the husband, than it could rightly be termed that of the wife."[49] The *Robbins* case was distinguished, as based on peculiarities of California law.[50] Buttressing its conclusion with references to the legislative history of the taxing statutes, the Court con-

---

46. 35 Op. Att'y Gen. 265 (1927). *See also* I. T. 2457, VIII–1 Cum. Bull. 89 (1929)
47. Goodell v. Koch, 282 U.S. 118 (1930) (Arizona); Hopkins v. Bacon, 282 U.S. 122 (1930) (Texas); Bender v. Pfaff, 282 U.S. 127 (1930) (Louisiana).
48. Brief for Appellee at 8, Poe v. Seaborn, 282 U.S. 101 (1930).
49. 282 U.S. at 113.
50. *See id.* at 116.

cluded that one-half of the community income was taxable to each spouse. On the same day the Court reached the same result for Arizona, Texas, and Louisiana (the states involved in the three other test cases),[51] and the Internal Revenue Service promptly added Idaho, Nevada, and New Mexico to the list of recognized community property states.[52]

Following *Poe v. Seaborn*, the tax status of a married couple in a community property state differed from that of a married couple in a common law state in two fundamental ways. First, each community property spouse paid the same tax as an unmarried person with one-half the aggregate community income. This result obtained in common law states only in the unusual case of a married couple whose income was earned or received in equal amounts by each spouse. A corollary of this geographical disparity was that marriage usually reduced (and divorce increased) a couple's income taxes if they resided in a community property state[53] but were neutral tax events for couples in common law states. Second, the federal tax burden for equal-income married couples was identical in community property states, whether the income was attributable to one spouse or to both. In common law states, by contrast, the tax liability of equal-income married couples could vary widely, since it depended on the amount attributable to each spouse.

4. *The 1941 defeat of mandatory joint returns.*

Its assault in the courts on the tax advantages of community property having been conclusively repulsed in *Poe v. Seaborn*, the Treasury turned to the legislative arena. Indecisive preliminary skirmishes in 1933, 1934, and 1937[54] were followed by a full-scale battle in 1941, when the Treasury persuaded the House Committee on Ways and Means to recommend enactment of a provision for mandatory joint returns, designed to eliminate the geographical disparity between the community property and common law states by equalizing the tax on married couples with the same aggregate income.[55]

---

51. *See* note 47 *supra*.
52. *See* Mim. 3853, X-1 CUM. BULL. 139 (1930).
53. In an echo of *Poe v. Seaborn*, the Supreme Court held in 1971 that a community property spouse was taxable on her half of the community income, even if she was "not really aware of the community tax situation, and not really in a position to ascertain the details of the community income." United States v. Mitchell, 403 U.S. 190, 205 (1971). The traditional forensic roles of taxpayer and government were reversed in this case, where the taxpayer sought to minimize and the government to magnify the importance of her community property rights. A legislative remedy for the tax-avoider's innocent spouse was provided by the enactment in 1971 of §§ 6013(e) and 6653(b) (last sentence) to the INT. REV. CODE OF 1954 [hereinafter cited by section]. *See also* § 981 (citizen married to nonresident alien may "elect out" of foreign community property laws); for background of this election, *see* 3 J. MERTENS, LAW OF FEDERAL INCOME TAXATION § 19.32a (1942).
54. *See* Thorson Dissertation, *supra* note 1, at 57-58.
55. *See* H.R. REP. No. 1040, *supra* note 21.
    Mandatory joint returns would also have had an important impact within the common law states, where they would have equalized the tax paid by couples with investment income, who were

The most explosive feature of the House Committee's 1941 recommendation was the imposition of the same tax on a married couple's consolidated income as on a single person with the same amount of income. This aspect of the 1941 proposal would have meant an increase in the tax burden for almost all married couples in community property states, as well as for couples in common law states if both spouses had income from personal services or investments. Conversely, two unmarried taxpayers with separate sources of income would have to pay a heavier tax if they got married than if they lived together without benefit of clergy, and many married couples would be able to reduce their tax burden by getting divorced. Quite naturally, therefore, opponents of the proposal assailed it as "a tax on morality."[56]

The House Committee on Ways and Means sought to disarm this criticism in advance by solemnly announcing:

> It is not believed that the joint return will result in any increase in the divorce rate in the United States or adversely affect the morals of American families. A compulsory joint return in Great Britain has been required since 1914, and their divorce rate is not as high as in the United States.
>
> The rate of divorces by each 1,000 of population in 1935 was, in the United States, 1.71 percent as against 0.10 percent in England and Wales. The number of divorces for each thousand marriages was, in 1935, in the United States, 164 divorces for each 1,000 marriages, in England and Wales, 12 divorces for each 1,000 marriages.[57]

---

able to split their income by intraspousal gifts of income-producing property, with the tax on couples with earned income, who had been barred by *Lucas v. Earl* from splitting their income for tax purposes. *Cf.* notes 22–24 *supra* and accompanying text.

The term "mandatory joint return" is ambiguous; as envisioned in 1941, the plan required husbands and wives to apply to their joint income the same rate schedule that was used by single taxpayers. The sting, therefore, resulted less from the proposed compulsory aggregation of marital income than from the rate schedule, and it could have been increased, reduced, or eliminated by a different rate schedule. The split-income plan enacted in 1948 included a favorable rate schedule for joint returns; joint returns were optional in theory, but the new rate schedule was an offer "that could not be refused" (except in special circumstances, *see* notes 78–79 *infra* and accompanying text), and this meant that joint returns became mandatory in fact for almost all married couples. *See* notes 67–77 *infra* and accompanying text. The same carrot-and-stick approach is employed by the reform proposed by Pechman; married couples would not be compelled to file joint returns, but an unfavorable rate schedule for married couples filing separate returns would make the filing of such returns costly unless their income was equally divided. *See* Pechman, *supra* note 1. Because the usage is so widespread, I have used the term "mandatory joint return" to refer to marital aggregation combined with an unfavorable rate schedule.

56. Any structural provision that increases the taxes paid by two single persons if they get married can be described as a "marriage penalty," unless the same burden will be imposed on them if they cohabit without benefit of clergy. Since the latter measure is not politically likely, constitutional, or enforceable, *but see* Sweden's example *supra* note 16, a "marriage penalty" can also be termed "a tax on morality" or "a subsidy to sin." Publicists have not refrained from using these colorful terms. *See 1972 House Hearings, supra* note 10, at 153 (testimony of Oscar Gray). Opposition to mandatory joint returns that impose a heavier burden on married couples than is borne by two single taxpayers with the same aggregate income is not confined to American taxpayers. British tax law consolidating marital income was vigorously attacked from a socialist perspective in Webb, *A Revolution in the Income Tax,* in How to Pay for the War 233 (1916), with the same rhetoric: "Legal matrimony would become prohibitive. A substantial premium would even be put on desertion."

57. H.R. Rep. No. 1040, 77th Cong., 1st Sess. 14 (1941), 1941–2 Cum. Bull. 413, 424.

Although the Committee did not explicitly say so, there was a more effective way to defuse the "immorality" allegation than these fragmentary statistics (which were not even limited to the taxpaying segments of each country's population)—a separate rate schedule for joint returns under which a married couple would pay twice the tax paid by a single person with one-half the couple's income. But this was a costly way to protect the institution of marriage, since it would have drastically cut the income taxes paid by married couples in common law states. Though accepted in 1948, a tax reduction of this magnitude, given the government's insatiable need for revenue on the eve of World War II, was not in the cards.

But neither, as quickly became apparent, was the mandatory joint return. The political response to the House Committee's proposal was tempestuous:

> Of course, the provision was "un-American." The contention was that by making the marital relation a taxable privilege the "sly and tricky" provision was arbitrary and against public policy in that it struck at the institution of marriage, was an attack upon the family, and promoted celibacy. The charge was that it penalized fidelity and awarded perfidy. The argument continued into many other aspects of this same general theme. It was asserted that the provision discouraged marriage by young couples.
>
> The [opponents of mandatory joint returns] became champions of emancipated womanhood. The provision was an encroachment on the independent status and social, economic, and political individuality of women which had been won only after a long, hard struggle. It revived the old common law fiction which made the wife a chattel. Thus it was a step backward and contrary to the trend of American policy, which more and more treated women on an absolute equality with men. A famous phrase in a dissenting opinion of Justice Holmes came into this argument. The provision brought back the horse and buggy days of 1880 when the legal pattern made the husband and wife one "and that one the husband." It was also erroneously alleged that the provision took the money of one person to pay the taxes of another, and that the provision upset the established property laws of the sovereign community property states. In addition, many congressmen argued that the provision was unconstitutional though there was little doubt among fair-minded people that it would be upheld by the Supreme Court.[58]

Bowing to the storm, the House voted to eliminate the mandatory joint return provision from the bill that became the Revenue Act of 1941. The Senate Finance Committee then recommended a milder remedy, limited to community income, taxing personal service income to the spouse who earned it and investment income to the spouse entitled to manage and

---

58. R. PAUL, TAXATION IN THE UNITED STATES 275 (1954). The tone of these references to the status of married women has become more than a little jarring with the passage of time. A bit of historical irony in Paul's final sentence is that he himself had expressed doubts about the constitutionality of mandatory joint returns only 5 years earlier. *See* Paul & Havens, *supra* note 21, at 266–71.

control it under local law.[59] This proposal, in turn, was rejected by the Senate.

5. *The spread of community property.*

The income tax advantages of community property having come unscathed through these judicial and legislative battles,[60] there was a stampede at the state level to share in its benefits. Oklahoma—true to its sobriquet, the "Sooner State"—had already started in 1939 by authorizing its married citizens to elect to be governed by a newly enacted community property system, and Oregon followed its lead by enacting a similar statute in 1943. In 1944, however, the Supreme Court decided in *Commissioner v. Harmon*[61] that the Oklahoma and Oregon do-it-yourself laws were substantially the same as the income-splitting contract between husband and wife that was held to be ineffective for federal tax purposes in *Lucas v. Earl*. The Court went on to announce that only a non-elective system of community property, "made an incident of marriage by the inveterate policy of the State," could qualify for income splitting under *Poe v. Seaborn*.[62] As the dissenting Justices (Douglas and Black) cogently argued, however, community property is an optional arrangement even in the original community property states, since it is dependent on the marital decision to live in a community property state and to refrain from exercising the option, available in most community property states, to hold all acquisitions during marriage as separate rather than community property.[63] Thus, the result of the *Harmon* case was that the community property system was effective for federal income tax purposes if under local law the couple could "opt out" of it, but not if they had to "opt in."

While it was easy for the scholar to ridicule *Harmon*'s distinction between a condition precedent and a condition subsequent, it was almost as easy for the legislator to sidestep its result with a new statute. Oklahoma and Oregon promptly replaced their optional community property systems with

---

59. *See* S. REP. No. 673, 77th Cong., 1st Sess. 9–12, 36 (1941), *reprinted in* 1941-2 CUM. BULL. 466, 474–76, 494–95.

60. The estate tax advantages of community property, however, were drastically cut back by the Revenue Act of 1942, which required community property to be included in its entirety in the estate of the first spouse to die, unless attributable to the surviving spouse's personal services or separate property and in any event taxed the first estate on the one-half subject to that spouse's testamentary control. *See* Revenue Act of 1942 ch. 619, § 402, 56 Stat. 941, *amending* Int. Rev. Code of 1939, ch. 2, § 811(e) 53 Stat. 122. The Supreme Court held the amendments constitutional in Fernandez v. Wiener, 326 U.S. 340 (1945). Similar changes were made in the gift tax. *See* Revenue Act of 1942, ch. 619, § 453, 56 Stat. 953. These rules might have become the prototype of changes in the income tax area, but they were repealed in 1948, when Congress authorized income splitting for all married couples and concurrently enacted the estate and gift tax marital deductions. *See* S. REP. No. 1013, 80th Cong., 2d Sess. 26–29, *reprinted in* 1948-1 CUM. BULL. 285, 303–06. *See also* note 73 *infra* and accompanying text.

61. 323 U.S. 44 (1944).
62. *Id.* at 46.
63. *Id.* at 53–56. *See* Shoenhair v. Commissioner, 45 B.T.A. 576 (1941), and cases there cited.

mandatory ones, but neither tempted fate by going on to permit their married citizens to elect out of the new law, despite the fact that the ostensibly mandatory systems of some original community property states contained this escape hatch. Their new statutes were later accepted as effective by the Internal Revenue Service.[64] Hawaii, Nebraska, Michigan, and Pennsylvania soon joined the community property parade, and by 1948 a similar step was under discussion in states as far removed from the civilizing mission of Spanish law as Massachusetts and New York.[65] An influential New York study warned that adoption of a community property system was fraught with difficulties and urged that every effort be made to get a federal solution, but it also recommended state self-help if Congress did not act promptly.[66]

C. *1948: The Optional Joint Return*

The community property epidemic—which some enthusiasts praised as a married women's liberation movement—forced Congress to confront, once again, the problem of geographical disparity in the tax burdens borne by married couples. But the range of legislative choice, viewed realistically, was quite narrow. A revival of the remedy proposed by the House Ways and Means Committee in 1941—a mandatory joint return, with the couple's consolidated income taxed at the rate applicable to single persons—would have invited a renewal of the old attack ("a tax on morality").[67] Moreover, those who succeeded in defeating the proposal in 1941 would now have the "new" community property states as allies in the legislative battle. The 1941 Senate Finance Committee's proposal[68] to tax community income to the person who earned it was no more appealing; it too would invite opposition from both old and new community property states, and it had the additional defect of focusing on personal service income, while leaving married couples free to split their investment income by intraspousal gifts. A third possibility for Congress was to do nothing, a strategy that would probably have been followed by universal adoption of the community property system at the state level, regardless of any local misgivings about its nontax merits.

Instead of standing pat, Congress decided in 1948 to authorize all married couples to aggregate their income and deductions on a joint return and to pay a tax equal to twice what a single person would pay on one-half

---

64. *See* I.T. 3782, 1946–1 Cum. Bull. 84 (Oklahoma); I.T. 3743, 1945–1 Cum. Bull. 142–43 (Oregon).
65. *See* Note, *Epilogue to the Community Property Scramble: Problems of Repeal*, 50 Colum. L. Rev. 332 n.4 (1950) and statutes cited therein. Pennsylvania's statute was held unconstitutional in Willcox v. Penn Mut. Life Ins. Co., 357 Pa. 581, 55 A.2d 521 (1947).
66. Annual Report of the State Tax Commission, 27–43 (New York 1947).
67. *See* note 56 *supra* and accompanying text.
68. *See* note 59 *supra* and accompanying text.

their consolidated taxable income.[69] In its impact on the federal revenue, this device was virtually the same as standing idly by while the whole country adopted the community property system, but enactment of the income-splitting joint return meant that the political credit for reducing taxes was concentrated on Congress rather than dispersed among the state legislatures.

Though the economic case for a massive tax reduction was not overwhelmingly persuasive, the idea had great political support in 1948, and for many the income-splitting joint return was an attractive device to effectuate a reduction. Unlike an across-the-board cut in tax rates, the joint return could be supported as a way of terminating both the historic disparity between community property and common law states and the special opportunities for intraspousal income splitting that were available to married couples with income-producing property. The Senate Finance Committee offered this summary of the merits of the income-splitting joint return:

> Adoption of these income-splitting provisions will produce substantial geographical equalization in the impact of the tax on individual incomes. The impetuous enactment of community-property legislation by States that have long used the common law will be forestalled. The incentive for married couples in common-law States to attempt the reduction of their taxes by the division of their income through such devices as trusts, joint tenancies, and family partnerships will be reduced materially. Administrative difficulties stemming from the use of such devices will be diminished, and there will be less need for meticulous legislation on the income tax treatment of trusts and family partnerships. In effect, these amendments represent the adoption of a new national system for ascertaining Federal income tax liability. The adoption of these amendments will extend substantial benefits to residents of both community-property and common-law States.[70]

Placing the legislative decision in a broader context, Surrey added this endorsement:

> If tax reduction of [great] magnitude was to be afforded [to middle and upper bracket taxpayers], it was wise tax policy to use the dollars of tax reduction to accomplish needed reform and build an improved tax structure. The best chance for a more equitable and economically effective tax system lies in the intelligent allocation of any tax reduction. The adoption of a presently acceptable solution to the family income problem represents the one bright spot in the Revenue Act of 1948.[71]

---

69. A 1947 Treasury study paved the way for this legislative action and also canvassed the major alternatives to the split-income plan. *See* Treasury Department, *supra* note 1. The Treasury study, in turn, was foreshadowed by a 1946 article by Surrey, *supra* note 1, who was then Tax Legislative Counsel to the Treasury, and the income-splitting proposal was frequently called the "Surrey Plan." *See* Surrey, *supra* note 1. As enacted, however, it did not embrace the income of minor children, although this was recommended in Surrey's 1946 article. *Id.* at 986.

For a fuller discussion of the 1948 legislation, *see* Surrey, *Federal Taxation of the Family—The Revenue Act of 1948*, 61 HARV. L. REV. 1097, 1103-16 (1948).

70. S. REP. No. 1013, *supra* note 60 at 26.
71. Surrey, *Federal Taxation of the Family supra* note 69, at 1106.

As anticipated, once the privilege of income splitting was extended to married couples in common law states, the "new" community property states lost their taste for Spanish law and repealed their statutes.[72] The joint return became virtually universal for married couples, except for those too hostile to cooperate in signing the return and for a few unusual situations in which separate returns had minor residual advantages.[73]

At the time, the Revenue Act of 1948 seemed to have added a chapter "[t]o the long history of the treatment of family income [that] is likely to be the last for many years."[74] In fact, new chapters were added by Congress in 1951, 1954, and 1969.[75] Moreover, the basic 1948 decision to equalize the tax burden on married couples with equal aggregate income has itself come under attack recently,[76] though it was once widely thought to be settled "for all time."[77]

---

72. See Note, note 65 *supra*, at 337-47.
73. If income is divided about equally and one spouse incurs substantial medical expenses, separate returns may increase the medical expense deduction by reducing the 3% floor of § 213(a)(1). *See also* § 152(e)(2), which may make separate returns preferable for some low-income taxpayers because one (or even both) can then qualify as a dependent of a third person. Until the enactment of § 1211(a)(2) in 1969, separate returns could be advantageous if both spouses had capital losses, since $2,000 of ordinary income could then be offset by their capital losses, while only $1,000 could be offset on a joint return.
74. Surrey, *Federal Taxation of the Family, supra* note 69, at 1104.
75. *See* notes 82-90 *infra* and accompanying text.
76. *See* notes 92-107 *infra* and accompanying text.
The 1947 Treasury study discusses at length the problem of aggregating the income of children with that of their parents. *See* Treasury Department, *supra* note 1, at 861-63.
77. Pechman, *supra* note 1, at 475.

B. TAXATION OF MARITAL PARTNERS

MICHAEL J. McINTYRE, "INDIVIDUAL FILING IN THE PERSONAL INCOME TAX: PROLEGOMENA TO FUTURE DISCUSSION"

58 North Carolina Law Review 469–489 (1980).*

Many married persons, probably most, pool some or all of their individual income sources with their spouses.[1] The exact sharing patterns of couples are unknown and probably unknowable, because sharing is often an unconscious act unaccompanied by careful record keeping.[2] If we consider the major items in a family budget, nevertheless, we can plausibly argue that extensive sharing is virtually unavoidable. In most marital partnerships, the distribution of benefits from

---

* Professor of Law, Wayne State University Law School. A.B. 1964, Providence; J.D. 1969, Harvard.

For a popular summary of many of the arguments made in this paper, see McIntyre, *Prolegomena to Future Arguments for Individual Filing in the Personal Income Tax*, TAX NOTES, June 18, 1979, at 763-67.

1. For a summary of the empirical basis for the widespread belief that married persons pool income, see Thorson, *An Analysis of the Sources of Continued Controversy over the Tax Treatment of Family Income*, 18 NAT'L TAX J. 113 (1965).

2. Suppose we observe two lovers in a soda parlor drinking through straws from a single ice cream soda. We understand easily enough that sharing is taking place, but we cannot determine how much soda each party is getting. Any attempt to measure the flows through the straws scientifically would require an intrusion into the scene that would undoubtedly bias the results. Questioning the lovers, moreover, is unlikely to yield reliable data, because the nature of the sharing virtually precludes detailed awareness of the amount of soda each party is consuming. Marital

expenditures for housing, utilities, furnishings, insurance, food, transportation, vacations, taxes, support of children and clothing are unlikely to favor one spouse over the other to a substantial degree. Even in marital partnerships in which the spouses make a determined effort to maintain spending authority over their individual income sources,[3] the benefits of marital expenditures will tend to be shared; any other pattern would undermine communal living and ultimately destroy most marital bonds. Full sharing is especially likely in two-job marital partnerships, because financially independent spouses are unlikely to tolerate any other pattern.[4]

The reality, or perceived reality, of marital pooling is the economic underpinning for the joint filing rule that has been a feature of the personal income tax in the United States since 1948.[5] Under the joint filing rule, husbands and wives are required (or induced by the promise of lower taxes) to aggregate their individual income sources as a step in the computation of their tax burden. Given the assumption of marital pooling, aggregation of marital income is essential if the tax system is to reflect systematically the real changes in an individual's personal consumption and net change in savings that are thought to accompany communal living. Because the sum of personal consumption and the net change in savings is a traditional index of material well-being under the income tax,[6] the assumption of marital pooling supports a formidable prima facie case for joint filing.[7]

---

income sharing may be less romantic, but the problem of monitoring the sharing patterns of married couples parallels the problem of measuring the soda consumed by each lover in my example.

3. For equal income couples, whether each partner obtains half the community income by spending out of one pot or by keeping control over his or her income sources is irrelevant for tax policy purposes; the benefits enjoyed by each spouse are the same under both systems.

4. Some supporters of individual filing assert that an assumption of [equality] between spouses is less realistic with the changing status of women in society and with the increase in the number of two-job couples. *See, e.g.*, Munnell, *The Couple Versus the Individual Under the Federal Personal Income Tax*, in ECONOMICS OF TAXATION (M. Boskin & H. Aaron eds.) (to be published by the Brookings Institution); H. Brazer, Income Tax Treatment of the Family (March 15, 1979) (copy on file in office of the *North Carolina Law Review*). The basis for that assertion is unstated. Munnell feels that the increase in divorce also undermines the case for joint filing, apparently on the ground that income pooling requires stable marriages. *See* Munnell, *supra*, at 4. Assessing tax on an annual basis seems to take care of the marriage stability concern. In fact, the availability of divorce suggests that the number of women trapped in an unequal relationship probably has diminished in recent years.

5. For a thorough discussion of the history of family taxation in the United States, see Bittker, *Federal Income Taxation and the Family*, 27 STAN. L. REV. 1389 (1975).

6. For the classic statement of the income concept, see H. SIMONS, PERSONAL INCOME TAXATION 59-102 (1938).

7. For the presentation and a detailed analysis of this argument, see McIntyre & Oldman, *Taxation of the Family in a Comprehensive and Simplified Income Tax*, 90 HARV. L. REV. 1573

Promoters of the individual filing rule—the chief alternative to joint filing—generally have failed to confront this prima facie case for the joint filing rule.[8] No serious effort has been made to challenge the assumption of widespread marital pooling or to dispute its relevancy in determining an individual's taxable capacity. Nor have the individual filing advocates developed an affirmative theoretical justification for their position. Instead, they have focused their attention on two asserted side effects of the joint filing rule. The first, analyzed in part I below, is the allegedly bizarre set of rewards and penalties produced by changes in marital status under a joint filing regime. The second, taken up in part II, is the alleged discrimination produced by the joint filing rule against secondary workers, the overwhelming majority of whom are presumed to be wives working in paid employment outside the home. These side effects, the argument goes, hopelessly discredit the joint filing rule, leaving individual filing as the only viable choice.

My objective in this Article is to demonstrate the weakness of the current case for the individual filing rule and to establish the essential elements of any future arguments for individual filing worthy of serious attention. I do not attempt to build a viable case for individual filing. In the context of current economic and social conditions in the United States, I doubt that a tenable case for individual filing is possible. What I hope to do is to convince the proponents of an individual filing rule that they must address seriously the tax policy implications of marital pooling if they are to join issue with their critics.

(1977). *See also Hearings on the Tax Treatment of Married Couples and Single Persons Before the House Comm. on Ways and Means*, 96th Cong., 2d Sess. (1980) (statement of Robert S. McIntyre, Public Citizen's Tax Reform Research Group, on "The 'Tax on Marriage' and Related Matters").

8. For recent articles championing an individual filing rule, see H. Brazer, *supra* note 4; Gerzog, *The Marriage Penalty: The Working Couples' Dilemma*, 47 FORDHAM L. REV. 27 (1978) (advocating voluntary individual filing for two-job couples); Munnell, *supra* note 4; Quester, *Women's Behavior and the Tax Code*, 59 SOC. SCI. Q. 665 (1979); Rosen, *Is It Time to Abandon Joint Filing*, 30 NAT'L TAX J. 423 (1977); Wenig, *Marital Status and Taxes*, in UNMARRIED COUPLES AND THE LAW 190-273 (G. Douthwaite ed. 1979).

In Canada, which has an individual filing rule, defenders of the *status quo* have challenged the reality and significance of family sharing patterns. For a lively debate, see *Taxation of the Family*, 1 CANADIAN TAXATION 4 (1979) (including London, *The Family as the Basic Tax Unit*, *id.* at 4; Dulude, *Joint Taxation of Spouses—A Feminist View*, *id.* at 8; McIntyre, *Economic Mutuality and the Need for Joint Filing*, *id.* at 13; Dulude, McIntyre, London, Woodman, Lakey & Wolfson, *A Panel Discussion*, *id.* at 16).

Some advocates of the community property system for marital property acknowledge, at least implicitly, the fairness arguments for the joint filing rule. They would deny income splitting in common law jurisdictions, however, in order to induce those jurisdictions to change their marital property laws. Issues relating to the reform of marital property regimes are tax issues only incidentally and are beyond the scope of this Article. For a discussion of these issues, see Bartke, *Marital Sharing—Why Not Do It By Contract*, 67 GEO. L.J. 1131, 1178 n. 323 (1979).

I. Marriage Neutrality and Individual Filing

An income tax that employs a joint filing rule cannot be marriage neutral. The case for joint filing rests, first of all, on the premise that married couples typically pool income and, second, on the premise that the real changes in an individual's economic circumstances that are produced by marital pooling should be reflected in determining a married person's taxable capacity. A lack of marriage neutrality, therefore, is not an embarrassment to the supporters of a joint filing rule. To join issue with the advocates of joint filing, the supporters of an individual filing rule cannot assume without argument that a marriage neutral tax system is per se good. They must be prepared to challenge the proposition that married couples typically pool income, or show why that fact should be ignored in a tax system that attempts to distribute burdens in accordance with each individual's real income.

Joint filing advocates, of course, do not suggest that all types of marriage nonneutrality, or even all the nonneutralities of current United States law, are desirable. Few if any supporters of joint filing, for example, favor the "tax on marriage" produced by the system of multiple rate schedules under United States law. The "tax on marriage" found in the tax regimes of many European countries, which results from the combination of spousal income aggregation and only one rate schedule, also is not favored.[9] The only nonneutralities that can be defended on principle are those that result from real or assumed changes in a person's taxable capacity as a result of marriage or, of course, divorce.

Two marriage nonneutralities of the income tax are commonly espoused by the advocates of a joint filing rule. The first is produced by implementing a policy that requires married couples with equal income to pay equal tax.[10] For example, this policy would mandate that Terry and Lee, a married couple, each with individual income sources of $10,000, pay the same total tax as Pat and Jean, another married couple who have respective net incomes of $5,000 and $15,000. This result, which flows directly from a joint filing rule, is impossible under an individual filing system. The rationale for the result is that, for couples pooling income sources, the taxable capacity of each partner is his or her share of the total marital income, independent of the source of the

---

9. For a summary of the tax regimes of many European countries, see ORGANISATION FOR ECONOMIC CO-OPERATION AND DEVELOPMENT, THE TREATMENT OF FAMILY UNITS IN OECD MEMBER COUNTRIES UNDER TAX AND TRANSFER SYSTEMS (1977).

10. *See* McIntyre & Oldman, *supra* note 7, at 1589-92.

income. Even tax theorists favoring individual filing are comfortable with this result.[11] Moreover, the result has broad public support.

The second marriage nonneutrality favored by joint filing advocates is the treatment under current United States law of alimony payments. Under Internal Revenue Code sections 71 and 215, alimony is deductible by the payor and taxable to the recipient. This permits a form of income splitting between formerly married persons, paralleling the implicit income splitting afforded to married persons under the rate schedule for married couples.[12] The justification for this treatment is that the personal consumption and savings of the payor is reduced by the alimony payment, while the consumption and savings of the payee is concomitantly increased. This result also is a popular feature of the United States tax laws among tax specialists and the public. In fact, all the advocates of individual filing who have addressed this issue favor a continuation of the alimony deduction.[13]

Given the apparent acceptability of at least some marriage nonneutrality, the per se argument for a marriage neutral tax system is hopelessly undercut. No tax regime can be advanced on the basis of a principle that necessarily and systematically produces results that are acknowledged to be unfair. Therefore, a plausible argument for individual filing based on marriage neutrality considerations must be far less sweeping and more refined than the per se argument discredited above.

Two lines of argument are still open to those who would defend individual filing on marriage neutrality grounds. First of all, the two nonneutralities discussed above are not the only ones produced under the joint filing rule of current law. In addition, we have the infamous "tax on marriage" imposed on many two-income married couples and the frequently misunderstood "tax on remaining unmarried" imposed on cohabiting persons with substantially unequal incomes who are

---

11. *See, e.g.*, Rosen, *supra* note 8, at 423. Some commentators, however, would favor unequal treatment of equal income spouses to offset the alleged benefits from household services of one-job couples. *See* note 29 *infra*.

12. *See* I.R.C. §§ 71, 215. Under current law, the rate schedule for married couples implicitly assumes an income split between the spouses of approximately 85/15 for middle income taxpayers. The rate schedule was constructed in accordance with a congressional mandate that the tax burden on a single person not exceed 120% of the tax burden on two married persons with the same aggregate income. For a fuller explanation of the implicit income splitting of current United States law, see McIntyre & Oldman, *supra* note 7, at 1584-85. For a detailed description of the implicit income splits at various income levels after the 1978 tax act, see Statement of Tax Reform Research Group, *supra* note 7.

13. For example, none of the advocates of individual filing referred to in note 8 *supra* argue against the alimony deduction.

sharing income but are not married. These nonneutralities, one might contend, are sufficiently important and unfair that they overcome the acknowledged virtues of the joint filing rule. The merits of this contention and its common variations are discussed in subsection B below.

The second line of argument is based on the contention that an individual's taxable capacity should be measured by the income he earns or, in the case of property income, the income he controls by ownership of an income-producing asset. Under this approach, marriage neutrality would be mandated unless marriage resulted in a change in ownership rights. Advocates of individual filing have asserted that this income attribution rule, which I call the property interest rule, is correct as a matter of principle but have never revealed the theoretical underpinning of the rule. In section A below, I articulate both the foundation and the inadequacies of this asserted principle.

A. The Unsound Case for Attributing Income to the Earner

An unstated principle underlying the prima facie case for joint filing set forth above is that the proper taxpayer on an item of income is the person who uses or benefits from that income. If income is defined as the sum of personal consumption and the net change in savings, this principle would tax consumption to the consumer and savings to the saver. More generally, the principle asserts that if income is used to measure an individual's material well-being for tax purposes, the proper taxpayer on an income item is the one whose material well-being is increased by that income item.[14] This benefit rule is compatible with the property interest rule outside the family context because for unattached individuals the "owner" of income and the "beneficiary" of income are typically the same person. For married couples, however, the tax rules seem to be in conflict.[15] A refutation of the benefit rule, therefore, appears to be a necessary precondition for developing a principled defense of the property interest rule. Supporters of the property interest rule have not attempted this refutation, nor are they likely to seriously challenge this fundamental and commonsensical principle of taxation.

The property interest rule formulated above, nevertheless, need not conflict with the benefit rule if we use a broad enough definition of

---

14. See McIntyre & Oldman, *supra* note 7, at 1592-99.
15. See *id.* at 1593.

income. If we assume, as some economists suggest, that an individual's income includes the value of all his or her human choices, measured by market criteria, the apparent conflict between the benefit rule and the property interest rule, at least within the family context, vanishes. Anyone who earns income or owns an asset that produces income obviously has exercised an economic choice when he or she shares that income with a spouse. That choice may be required under a marriage contract or, *a la* Mr. Earl in *Lucas v. Earl*,[16] by a private contract. However we identify the choice, a market analysis of marital behavior suggests that a husband, for example, who shares his earnings with his wife reaps an economic benefit from that sharing.[17] Under market criteria, the value of that choice is presumed to be the value of the money or other property relinquished. It is the value of this choice, not the actual market consumption or savings enjoyed by the donee spouse, that would be taxed to the donor spouse under the property interest rule. Because the donee spouse who actually spends or saves the income also exercises an economic choice, pooled income or gifts would end up being taxed to both the donor and the donee.[18]

What the above analysis suggests is that a principled defense of the property interest rule is possible, but only if a defense is also provided for taxing individuals on the value of their economic choices instead of

---

16. 281 U.S. 111 (1930).

17. A market analysis of family dealings has become commonplace. For a discussion of the theory and references to the literature, see Sawhill, *Economic Perspectives on the Family*, DAEDALUS, Spring 1977, at 115. The following statement by a prominent economist suggests an awakening of the economics profession to the dangers of inappropriately imposing an exchange model on family transactions:

> Economic analysis is very useful and does provide a number of insights even about the behavior of marriage partners. I would only suggest that we may be beginning to push market analysis beyond its functional limits in trying to find price surrogates for all the activities of our waking hours, and in trying to explain everything in terms of economic values. This is not a new idea, for both Karl Marx and Adam Smith would have been horrified by the notion that the exchange process is the origin of all values. Moreover, this kind of reductionism is at variance with another tendency in economics—the effort to broaden its concepts of accounting to include such concerns as the quality of life and social responsibility of corporations. Besides, it may be a matter of great satisfaction not to engage in cost accounting and *quid pro quo* exchanges in our leisure time and in our close and informal relationships with other people.

Johnson, *The Limits of Economic Analysis: Should We Try to Price Everything?*, 4 J. INST. SOCIOECON. STUD. 30, 40 (1979).

18. The "double taxation" of gifts has been viewed by many tax specialists as an inescapable consequence of a comprehensive tax base. For an interesting discussion of recent developments, see Head, *The Simons-Carter Approach to Tax Policy: A Reappraisal*, in WIRTSCHAFTSWISSENSCHAFT ALS GRUNDLAGE STAATLICHEN HANDELNS 191, 200-01 (P. Bohley & G. Tolkemitt eds. 1979). In my view, the double tax problem is avoided by treating the beneficiary as the proper taxpayer and market consumption and savings as the proper object of taxation. *See* Dodge, *Beyond Estate and Gift Tax Reform: Including Gifts and Bequests in Income*, 91 HARV. L. REV. 1177, 1182-88 (1978); McIntyre & Oldman, *supra* note 7, at 1598 n.90.

on the income they actually receive. In effect, the defense of the property interest rule depends on first developing a justification for taxing individuals on potential income. A tax on potential income is a popular plaything of the economics profession. It appeals to those economists who purport to place primary emphasis on the achievement of efficiency in the design of an income tax.[19] They find some merit, for example, in taxing people on the value of their leisure time on the theory that a failure to tax leisure provides a tax incentive to those who choose to do nothing in lieu of working in paid employment in the taxable sector of the community. Our existing income tax, however, in no way resembles a tax on potential income. Nor has any serious effort been made to specify the tax base of a potential income tax, to overcome the obvious obstacles to administering such a tax or to develop any arguments concerning the fairness of such a tax. In sum, a case for the property interest rule linked to the case for a tax on potential income is no case at all, at least for the present.

B. Tax on Marriage and Other Nonneutralities as the Basis for Individual Filing

Much of the criticism of the current program of family taxation in the United States is directed at the so-called "tax on marriage" that arises because two married persons, each with substantial individual income sources, generally would pay less tax if they got a divorce and filed as single persons. Although a variety of features of the tax code can produce this phenomenon, most have nothing to do, by everyone's admission, with the choice between joint and individual filing.[20] Of

---

19. The champions of the so-called optimal tax theory generally treat efficiency as the principal goal of the income tax. Their search for efficiency requires a quantification of all nonmarket choices, including leisure. For a statement of the efficiency goal and references to this expanding literature, see Rosen, *Application of Optimal Tax Theory to Problems in Taxing Families and Individuals*, in 1 COMPILATION OF OTA PAPERS (Office of Tax Analysis, U.S. Dep't of the Treasury, Paper 21, 1976).

The case for a tax on potential income has some similarities to the case made by some economists for a consumption tax. For a discussion of the common roots of the tax on consumption and the tax on potential income and a criticism of both, see McIntyre, Book Review, 26 WAYNE L. R. 1181 (1980).

20. The various marriage penalties of current United States law are summarized in H. Brazer, *supra* note 4.

The House Ways and Means Committee held hearings on the tax treatment of married and single persons on April 2-3, 1980. In anticipation of those hearings, the Staff of the Joint Committee on Taxation published a 68 page report, JOINT COMM. ON TAXATION, 96th CONG. 2D SESS., THE INCOME TAX TREATMENT OF MARRIED COUPLES AND SINGLE PERSONS (Comm. Print 1980) [hereinafter cited as JOINT COMMITTEE REPORT], that summarized some of the proposals for solving the "tax on marriage" problem. Curiously, the Report virtually omitted any reference to income splitting as a solution to that problem.

those relevant to the subject matter of this Article, the most talked about cause of the tax on marriage derives from the introduction of special rate schedules for single persons by the 1969 tax act. Proponents of individual filing claim that the fairest way to eliminate this tax on marriage would be for the United States to return to the pre-1948 system of individual filing with one rate schedule. In subsection 1 below, I analyze that claim and demonstrate its serious weaknesses. I then discuss, in subsection 2, the related claim that the joint filing rule is unfair to certain single persons by imposing on them a penalty for failing to marry.

1. Marriage Neutrality and the Married Person

Most tax theorists would agree that the tax on marriage is an unhappy feature of the United States system of family taxation. No convincing tax policy argument has been advanced for placing a higher tax burden on cohabiting couples who marry than on those who live together in a less formal relationship.[21] Nor do social policy concerns support the tax on marriage. The joint filing rule need not be abandoned, however, in order to deal with the tax on marriage problem. A system of joint filing with full income splitting, as was adopted in the United States in 1948, completely eliminates the tax on marriage. Within the context of the current United States system of multiple rate schedules, the tax on marriage could be substantially eliminated for most two-income couples through the granting of a special marital allowance for the second earner.[22] Therefore, the case for individual filing based on the tax on marriage problem requires a showing that the solution under an individual filing rule is superior to those available under the joint filing rule.

As its advocates assert, an individual filing rule could end the tax on marriage caused by the multiple rate schedules of current United States law. It would not produce, however, a marriage neutral rate

---

21. For a summary and criticism of the defenses of the tax on marriage, see Bittker, *supra* note 5, at 1419-28. *See also* Gerzog, *supra* note 8, at 31-36.

22. Several proposals for a special deduction are explained in McIntyre, *Taking Account of Marriage*, PEOPLE & TAXES, October 1977, at 3-6. A special credit is advocated in Z. Giraldo, Tax Policy and the Dual-Income Family: The "Marriage Tax" and Other Inequities, at 3-9 to 3-13 (Center for the Study of the Family and the State, Institute of Policy Sciences and Public Affairs, Duke University 1978). Giraldo concludes that income splitting and the problem of geographical nonneutrality make an individual filing election undesirable. She refutes the argument that these problems are less intractable now than they proved to be prior to 1948. *Id*. at 3-5 to 3-8. Rosen has suggested that the problems have been solved in Canada. *See* Rosen, *supra* note 8, at 428 n.10. For a pointed rebuttal, see Bird, *On the Importance of Tax Details: Joint vs. Individual Filing*, 31 NAT'L TAX J. 203 (1977).

structure unless the deduction permitted for alimony payments were eliminated as well. Under current United States law, and under any system of individual filing with an alimony deduction, two unmarried persons with substantially unequal individual income sources could reduce their total tax bill by marrying, getting a divorce and then equalizing their taxable incomes through alimony payments.[23] For example, if Pat, with income of $15,000, married and then divorced Lee, with income of $5,000, an alimony payment of $5,000 paid by Pat to Lee would leave the couple with equal taxable incomes, the optimum position for unmarried couples who are being taxed individually under a progressive rate schedule.

The tax on marriage produced by the alimony deduction is the mirror image of the more famous tax on marriage produced by the multiple rate schedules of current United States law. The chief victims of the alimony tax on marriage are one-income couples and other couples with substantially unequal incomes. Equal income couples, who pay the maximum tax on marriage produced by the multiple rate schedules, suffer no tax on marriage from the alimony deduction.

As discussed above, the alimony deduction is a popular feature of our tax laws, which even the champions of a marriage neutral tax system seem unwilling to abandon. Assuming the permanence of the alimony deduction, those advocates of individual filing who have been most uncompromising in their call for an end to the tax on marriage have actually been touting a system they condemn—joint filing with full income splitting. Every other tax regime has to tolerate a tax on marriage, at least to some extent.

The analysis above debunks much of the tax on marriage rhetoric that has been marshalled for an individual filing rule. Two lines of argument, both unpromising, remain open to those who would pursue an individual filing solution to the marriage penalty. First, one might develop a principled basis for abandoning the alimony deduction. Without the alimony deduction to contend with, the supporters of individual filing at least could claim that their favored tax regime would end the tax on marriage problem. Because the alimony deduction is a necessary corollary of the benefit rule, a principled attack on the alimony deduction most likely would require a defense of the property interest rule for attributing income to individual taxpayers. The

---

23. For a full explanation of this alimony tax on marriage, including a table showing the amount of the penalty, see Wenig, *supra* note 8, at 257-59, 261.

argument for the property interest rule is discussed and rejected in section I *A* above.

The other line of argument involves a direct appeal to social policy goals independent of traditional tax policy concerns. In effect, the proponents of individual filing would concede, *arguendo*, that joint filing is the correct tax policy choice, but would contend, nevertheless, that the assumed cost in tax equity from the individual filing rule is more than offset by some social policy gains produced by individual filing. This argument is similar to those often made for tax incentives in that the special deduction, credit or other allowance that constitutes the incentive is said to produce economic or social benefits that outweigh the departure from accepted notions of tax fairness.[24] The crux of this social policy argument would be a comparison of the social consequences of an individual filing rule, including the cost in fairness and the social cost of the alimony tax on marriage, with the social consequences of the various alternative tax regimes that employ a joint filing rule.[25] The beginning of the argument would be a comparison of the social consequences of the alimony tax on marriage under individual filing with the consequences of the more famous tax on marriage under the various joint filing regimes. Because the consequences of both marriage penalties probably are modest, a quick victory for either approach on marriage neutrality grounds is unlikely. The argument, therefore, would have to be expanded to consider the panoply of social consequences of each of the many tax regimes possible under an individual filing rule and under a joint filing rule. Supporters of individual filing thus far have not even attempted to pursue this complex and exceedingly difficult undertaking.

2. Marriage Neutrality and the Single Person

An apparent defect of the joint filing rule is that it applies only to married persons, although the reason for the rule—the economic consequences of income pooling—would justify joint filing for some unmarried couples as well. As a result, one-income unmarried couples (and other unmarried couples with substantially unequal individual income sources) pay higher taxes under a tax regime employing a joint filing

---

24. For a discussion of the use of tax expenditure concepts to analyze social policy arguments made on behalf of tax rules, see McIntyre, *A Solution to the Problem of Defining a Tax Expenditure*, 14 U.C.D.L. REV. 427 (1980).

25. The calculus should include the administrative costs of policing income-splitting arrangements and the social cost of a loss of geographical neutrality. For a discussion of these problems, see Z. Giraldo, *supra* note 22, at 3-5 to 3-7.

rule than the fairness criteria implicit in the joint filing rule would support. The reason for this result is obviously one of administration. Because the tax administration cannot be put in the position of verifying the actual sharing patterns of couples, marriage is used as the bright line test for pooling arrangements.[26]

A compromise with a normative tax rule for administrative reasons need not discredit a tax rule; otherwise, no administratively feasible tax system could be justified. The case for abandoning joint filing because of the plight of certain unmarried couples requires a showing that an alternative tax regime employing an individual filing rule would be a better approximation of the assumed ideal than a joint filing regime that used marriage (or some alternative) as a prerequisite for income pooling. Because all sharing patterns are ignored systematically under an individual filing rule, however, it would be mere happenstance if an individual filing regime were a second best solution to the problem of accounting for the economic consequences of income pooling.

As a practical matter, individual filing would be a plausible second best response to the economic consequences of income pooling only if pooling were a way of life for most married and unmarried persons. To take the extreme, if everyone were pooling with someone, then ignoring all pooling arrangements would give a fairer result than using marriage as the prerequisite for pooling. Income pooling outside of marriage, however, is unlikely to become a way of life for significant numbers of individuals, requiring as it does the subordination of individual economic welfare to that of the household.

In estimating the extent of income pooling outside of marriage, we must not equate cost-sharing arrangements with income pooling. Cost sharing is indeed common; friends, lovers, relatives, even virtual strangers often agree to join a household and share common expenses. The crux of income pooling, however, is the equalization of benefits for

---

26. Bittker argues that the group whose income is to be consolidated should be delineated by boundary lines that can be "crisply defined and readily verified." Bittker, *supra* note 5, at 1399. Marriage, of course, satisfies these criteria.

According to recent census data, 1.3 million households in 1979 were shared by unrelated adults of the opposite sex; these households contained 2.7 million unmarried partners. For the same year, 96.5 million men and women were married and living with their spouses. Thus, the unmarried partners represented only about 3% of all persons living together as couples in 1979. The census data do not contain information on the number of unrelated adults of the same sex living together. Nor do they show the extent of pooling among unmarried couples. *See* BUREAU OF THE CENSUS, CURRENT POPULATION REPORTS, NO. 349, at 20 (1980), *quoted in* JOINT COMMITTEE REPORT, *supra* note 20, at 27-28.

each member of the pool. Whether or not unmarried housemates typically agree to equalize unequal incomes has little to do with the phenomenon of cost sharing.

In addition to its alleged failure to account properly for the pooling of income by unmarried persons, some critics complain that the joint filing rule provides an irrational incentive to single persons who do not have a housemate to go find one and get married.[27] In their view, marriage gives a tax bonanza to unattached individuals who find and marry someone with little or no income. For example, if Adrian, an individual with wages of $20,000, seeks out and marries Fran, who has no income sources, Adrian's taxes would go down under most tax regimes employing a joint filing rule. This tax savings is said to make the lower income spouse, typically the wife, a tax shelter for the husband.

This tax reduction by marriage is not a necessary consequence of joint filing. The mandatory joint return with only one rate schedule, a system once common in Europe and still operating in the Philippines, provides no rate advantage for persons who marry.[28] Any joint filing system that provides for full or partial income splitting, however,

---

27. *See, e.g.*, Mess, *For Richer, For Poorer: Federal Taxation and Marriage*, 28 CATH. U.L. REV. 87, 90-91 (1978).

The alleged incentive may be viewed from two perspectives. Some commentators do not view a spouse who has no independent income sources as a legitimate taxpayer. P. STERN, THE RAPE OF THE TAXPAYER (1973), for example, speaks of "the little woman" as a valuable "asset" of the husband. A tax wise single person, according to this perspective, can "purchase" this asset and reap a tax bonanza. From another perspective, the unattached single person always has a phantom partner on the hook, ready to materialize whenever the single person wants to make the tax wise decision to marry. The single person always has a tax incentive to marry the phantom, since a hypothetical mate does not in fact reduce the single persons's real consumption and savings (i.e. income). Michael Moss, for example, illustrates the "discrimination" against single persons by showing how much less tax a single person, X, would pay if X married another single person, Z. Moss, *supra* note 27, at 92 n.20. If Z were a real person sharing income with X prior to the marriage, we have the "tax on remaining unmarried" discussed above. As long as Z remains a figment of the imagination, however, Z does not represent any drain on X's resources. For a similar perspective, see *Hearings on the Tax Treatment of Married Couples and Single Persons Before the House Comm. on Ways and Means*, 96th Cong., 2d Sess. (1980) (statement of Emil Sunley, Deputy Assistant Secretary of the Treasury, on the tax treatment of married and single taxpayers), *reprinted in* Treasury Dep't News, April 2, 1980, at 8.

28. The mandatory joint return with only one rate schedule is, in my view, the least fair system of family taxation commonly discussed. In a society that strives for equality between the sexes, it is particularly inappropriate because it forces two married people to pay tax as if they were one individual. Full or partial income splitting, of course, recognizes the separate tax status of each spouse. Historically, the mandatory joint return with one rate schedule was a response to property rules giving management of marital income to the husband. In effect, that system is a form of individual filing, with all marital income attributed to the husband in accord with local property law.

always produces a tax savings when a high income person marries a lower income person.

The wife as tax shelter argument, nevertheless, is faulty because it misapprehends the relationship between the joint filing rule and a progressive rate structure. Under joint filing with income splitting, married persons are assumed to be sharing their incomes. In the example above, once Adrian and Fran married, their individual circumstances presumably would change. With full income splitting, half of Adrian's income of $20,000 would go for the benefit of Fran. Under a progressive rate structure, the tax on two individuals, each with $10,000 of income, is lower, by definition, than the tax on one individual with an income of $20,000. If the tax regime assumed that splitting were less even than a 50/50 split, as is assumed implicitly by the United States system of multiple rate schedules, the tax savings from marriage would be reduced, but the rationale would be the same. Individuals whose income goes down, whether by marriage or otherwise, ought to pay less tax than they did at their higher income level.

II. The Alleged Discrimination of the Joint Filing Rule Against Working Wives

Much of the support for individual filing comes from those who see the joint filing rule as discouraging married women from working outside the home. In section *A* below, I examine that disincentive claim from the perspective of an individual contemplating entry into the labor market. In section *B*, I analyze that claim in light of the economic literature on the labor supply response of married women to taxes.[29]

A. *Some Commonsense Objections to the Discrimination Charge*

At first blush, the claim that joint filing discriminates against wives working outside the home appears frivolous, even mischievous.[30] As discussed in part I above, the intent of joint filing is to tax married

---

29. I do not discuss in the text the economic literature that purports to show that the failure to tax imputed income from self-performed household services biases the tax system against women who want to work in paid employment outside the home. The issue of what nonmarket items to include in the tax base arises under both individual filing and joint filing regimes. For the case against taxing self-performed services, see McIntyre & Oldman, *supra* note 7, at 1607-24. The defects of individual filing as a second best response to the imputed income issue are addressed in *id.* at 1623-24.

30. In light of the sensitivity of men and women in the United States to real and perceived gender-based discrimination, a false claim of gender bias is indeed mischievous.

persons, male and female, on their material well-being, as measured by the income they actually enjoy, without regard for the source of the income or, incidentally, the sex of the beneficiary. In operation, joint filing necessarily applies in exactly the same way to husbands and wives; by definition, for every husband who files a joint tax return, there is a wife doing likewise. In operation and intent, therefore, the joint filing rule is gender neutral.

Fair-minded critics of joint filing concede, as they must, that the rule itself is gender neutral. They contend, nevertheless, that, under current social and economic conditions, joint filing acts as a disincentive for married women to work outside the home. Married persons, they assert, typically view the husband as the person primarily responsible for support of the household. Therefore, whatever work decision the wife may make, the husband will work anyway. Because of this perspective, many married women allegedly see any income they may earn as the marginal marital income. Consequently, under joint filing, they perceive themselves as taxed on the first dollar of income they earn at the rate applicable to the last dollar of their husband's earnings.[31]

This disincentive argument against joint filing must be refined substantially before it can provide any support for an individual filing rule. A fundamental weakness of the argument is illustrated by the following example. Assume we have a farmer, Mr. F, who grows wheat that he can sell for a profit of $1,000 per bag. Assume that he has the capacity to produce 100 bags of wheat a year. Assume further that profits from

---

31. For alternative versions of this argument, see Boskin, *The Effects of Government Expenditures and Taxes on Female Labor*, AM. ECON. REV., May 1974, at 251, 254; Quester, *supra* note 8, at 670; Rosen, *Tax Illusion and the Labor Supply of Married Women*, 58 REV. ECON. & STAT. 167 (1976); P. Musgrave, Women and Taxation (paper presented to Congress of International Institute of Public Finance, September 1979). No evidence is offered to show that the wife is the marginal taxpayer. Rosen, for example, simply states that "in this paper we follow the reasoning of Bowen and Finegan: 'It seems *reasonable to suppose* that in most families the (potential) earnings of the wife are more "marginal" than the earnings of the husband and that the marginal tax rate to which the family is subject is therefore viewed as being particularly applicable to the wife's earnings.'" Rosen, *supra*, at 167 n.2 (quoting W. BOWEN & T. FINEGAN, THE ECONOMICS OF LABOR FORCE PARTICIPATION 136 (1969)) (emphasis added). For a more lengthy discussion, see Quester, *supra* note 8, at 670-71. Quester contends that "sex discrimination in earnings implies that the average couple will be better off if it is the husband, rather than the wife, who works full-time in the market . . . ." *Id.* at 671. From this observation, she concludes that the husband is the primary earner and the wife pays the marginal tax. *Id.* Under Quester's thesis, the high marginal rate facing the wife could be avoided if the wife refused to file a joint return, and elected instead to use the individual schedule of I.R.C. § 1(d). This action, of course, is unlikely because it would reduce the net income of the couple and, therefore, the wife's net income. That wives almost universally elect to file the joint return rather than use the pre-1969 singles' rate schedule is solid evidence that the wife is not forced to pay the marginal tax.

the sale of the wheat are taxed for the first $50,000 of income at 20% and at 50% for the remainder. Assume finally that Mr. F, for purposes of his own, puts his wheat in blue bags until he has 50 bags full and then puts the wheat in pink bags.

From the point of view of Mr. F, the progressive rate structure discourages the production of pink bags of wheat, for his after tax return on a pink bag is $500, while his net return on a blue bag is $800. That perspective, of course, is nonsensical. The tax system treats all wheat profits alike. It is Mr. F who, for idiosyncratic reasons, identifies pink bags as the bags at the margin.

The tax system, similarly, treats all marital income alike. If a married woman, because of a stereotyped view of marriage, views herself as the marginal worker, we might bemoan the social conventions that have encouraged that perspective, but we have no cause for complaint against the tax system. The assumption of joint filing is that married couples pool income. For marital partners who are pooling income, taxes reduce the resources of the marital community available for sharing. If splitting is on a 50/50 basis, the real burden of any tax on the couple is shared equally by the spouses. For married couples who are not pooling, the burden of the tax on the community will be a matter of negotiation. Given the option of divorce, few wives are likely to bargain so poorly as to end up paying tax at the top marginal rates applicable to the couple.

Another weakness in the disincentive argument against joint filing is the lack of data showing that most married women working outside the home perceive themselves, albeit incorrectly, as paying tax as the marginal worker. The plausibility of alternative perceptions is illustrated by the following example. Assume that H, the husband, and W, the wife, are married, that H has wage income of $20,000, that W has wage income of $10,000 and that H and W have income from a joint savings account of $500. During the year, H and W are both subject to withholding at the source on their wages; because of his higher income level, H has substantially more withheld than W. Nothing is withheld, of course, on the interest income. When the joint return is filed in April, H and W get a tax refund of $100. Under these conditions, is W likely to perceive herself as paying a substantial part of the taxes withheld from H's salary? Would the perception be likely to change if H and W had to make a tax payment in April of $500?

The weaknesses in the disincentive argument against joint filing illustrated above appear to be fatal ones. If married couples pool income, the real burden of the tax on either spouse necessarily is borne in fact by the community. Even if pooling is incomplete, the withholding of taxes at the source on wage income makes it improbable that the working wife will be forced to pay the taxes already withheld from the husband.

Whether wives *perceive* the joint filing rule as imposing a disincentive to work is difficult to resolve conclusively.[32] Even if a substantial number of married women do suffer from this false perception, however, a repeal of the joint filing rule, unless justified on other grounds, is hardly an appropriate response. To call for a repeal of joint filing on that ground is in effect to call for a tax subsidy for husbands and wives with a stereotyped view of marriage.

B. *Labor Supply Response of Married Women to Taxes as an Argument Against Joint Filing*

Over the past decade, economists have attempted to estimate the work response of husbands and wives to changes in income and social security tax rates. Measuring the work response of married persons has turned out to be a complex endeavor. Economic theory would predict the following labor supply responses of married persons to increases in taxes: (1) hours worked would decrease because the reduction in the net return from paid labor would make other uses of time relatively more attractive (the "substitution" effect); (2) hours worked would increase because a married couple with fixed budget needs would have to work more hours to satisfy those needs (the "income" effect); and (3) hours worked by the husband would increase and hours worked by the wife would decrease, or vice versa (the "cross-substitution" and "cross-

---

32. Rosen has attempted to determine the labor response of married women and concludes, with some qualifications, that "[m]arried women do in fact seem to react to tax rates in the 'rational' manner of standard economic theory." Rosen, *supra* note 31, at 170. This study, however, does not test the working woman's perception of the effect of joint filing. Rosen "assumed for simplicity that the husband's work effort is fixed institutionally and there are no cross-substitution effects." *Id.* at 169. The tax rules used in his calculations are based on the assumption that "the wife is in effect taxed at the same marginal rate as the last dollar earned by the husband." *Id.* at 167. *See also* Rosen, *Taxes in a Labor Supply Model with Joint Wage-Hours Determination*, 44 ECONOMETRICA 485 (1976).

In the United Kingdom, the Inland Revenue Department recently announced a change in the treatment of married women under the tax department's withholding mechanism. Under the current practice, the full marital allowance is allocated to the husband, with the result that the entire wages of the wife are subject to withholding. Under the new procedure, the marital allowance will be allocated to the wife, unless it appears that the wife's earnings will exceed the husband's or the couple requests that the wife be treated as the marginal worker. This change does not affect the total tax burden imposed on the couple; it may, however, change perceptions about the distribution of the burden between spouses. INLAND REVENUE PRESS RELEASE, Dec. 4, 1979.

income" effects). Economic theory says nothing about the overall impact of these responses.[33]

Empirical studies are likewise inconclusive. A number of studies indicate that wives respond to higher taxes by reducing their hours of work. Husbands tend to have an opposite but less pronounced reaction.[34] These reactions, however, may be cancelled out by the cross responses. One recent study found, for example, that the cross effects produce an overall increase in the labor supply as a result of an increase in taxes.[35] Earlier studies found the cross effects to be less substantial.[36] These earlier studies, however, assumed that the wife was the marginal taxpayer in the marital partnership, a perspective that was discredited in section *A* above.[37]

Some supporters of individual filing contend, nevertheless, that the labor supply literature provides a basis for favoring an individual filing rule. Some commentators read the literature as showing that joint filing is inefficient in that it allegedly reduces the supply of economic goods and services that otherwise would be produced.[38] Others claim it shows that joint filing perpetuates traditional husband/wife role patterns because it encourages women who otherwise would choose to work outside the home to stay at home.[39] Neither of these readings of the literature is accurate.

First, the supporters of individual filing rely on studies of the labor supply response to family taxation that measure only the economic responses at the margin of women already in the labor force. None of these studies claims to measure the effect of taxes on the decision to

---

33. For a more technical description of these effects, see Rosen, *supra* note 19.

34. *See, e.g.*, Hall, *Wages, Income, and Hours of Work in the U.S. Labor Force*, in INCOME MAINTENANCE AND LABOR SUPPLY 102 (G. Cain & H. Watts eds. 1973).

35. *See* Leuthold, *Taxes and the Two-Earner Family: Impact on the Work Decision*, 7 PUB. FINANCE Q. 147, 154-56 (1979).

36. *See, e.g.*, Boskin, *The Economics of Labor Supply*, in INCOME MAINTENANCE AND LABOR SUPPLY 163 (G. Cain & H. Watts eds. 1973).

37. *See* text accompanying notes 30-32 *supra*.

38. *See, e.g.*, Rosen, *supra* note 19, at 11. Rosen notes that individual filing also would be inefficient. The optimal result, from an efficiency perspective, would give a large tax benefit to high income working wives, a modest tax benefit to upper middle class working wives and no benefit to lower income persons.

39. *See, e.g.*, Quester, *supra* note 8, at 673. *See also* P. Musgrave, *supra* note 31, at 2, 4. Musgrave suggests that the tax code produces a "doll house" effect by reflecting and reinforcing a dependent status for women. *Id.* at 1-2. In Henrik Ibsen's *A Doll's House*, we may recall that Nora ultimately was liberated through increased self-awareness, not through an amendment to the Norwegian tax code. Musgrave does not suggest that joint filing necessarily collides with the interests of women; her conclusion is that joint filing should be retained, with some special allowances for working wives. *Id.* at 10.

enter the labor market.[40] Since 1940, the percentage of married women in the labor force has increased from under seventeen percent to nearly fifty percent. Participation of unmarried women has also increased substantially during this period, but at a less rapid rate.[41] These data provide some basis for believing that taxes are not a significant barrier to married women who desire to enter the labor market.[42] These figures show nothing, however, about the effect of taxes at the margin on hours worked by married women.[43]

Second, the consistent finding of the studies that women are more tax sensitive than men does not show that the joint filing rule is inefficient. Whether a tax provision is inefficient depends on the overall effects of the provision on the production of economic goods and services. The cross effects of the joint filing rule must be considered, therefore, in determining its efficiency. As stated above, one recent study found the overall job response of married couples to a marginal change in taxes to be positive—a marginal increase in taxes would increase the total hours worked, and a decrease in taxes would decrease hours worked.[44] Earlier studies have reached the opposite conclusion,

---

40. Measurement of the labor response of women is based on data collected by the Bureau of Labor Statustics from two sources: a sample survey of households using interview techniques and questionnaires submitted by employers. *See* BUREAU OF LABOR STATISTICS, U.S. DEP'T OF LABOR, EMPLOYMENT AND EARNINGS: JANUARY 1979, at 203 (1979). No data, obviously, is available on the value of self-performed services. For a description of the problem of defining self-performed services, see McIntyre & Oldman, *supra* note 7, at 1609-13. Attempts have been made to quantify the value of self-performed services, but the estimates necessarily are crude and reveal nothing about marginal values. *See* Rosen, *supra* note 31, at 169. Even if data were available, the decision to enter the labor force cannot be comprehended by comparing the marginal return from a job in the labor market to the marginal return from housework. The decision to enter the labor force is different in kind from the decision of someone in the labor market to work an additional hour.

41. *See* U.S. BUREAU OF THE CENSUS, STATISTICAL ABSTRACT OF THE UNITED STATES 404 (table 655) (99th ed. 1978).

42. Needless to say, these figures do not demonstrate that taxes have had *no effect* on the decision of married women to enter the labor market; perhaps the growth in the participation rate would have been higher or lower under an alternative regime.

43. A finding that the United States tax system poses a significant barrier to women entering the labor market would have important political implications; a finding that taxes merely affect the number of hours worked by part-time female workers probably would have no political impact. An entrance barrier suggests the tax law is locking women in the home; an effect on hours worked means at most that the tax law is inducing women employees to go home a little early.

44. *See* Leuthold, *supra* note 35, at 158-59. The author states:

> The results of this study are interesting in light of recent Administration proposals to amend federal income tax treatment of two-earner families to reduce the so-called marriage penalty in the tax code. As a result of the marriage penalty, two-earner families often find their tax liabilities higher than if they were to divorce and be taxed as two single taxpayers. To the extent that reforms to reduce the marriage penalty also lower the marginal rate of tax on two-earner families, the results of this study suggest that hours of work and the division of work between the husband and wife will be affected. According to the results of this study, a reduction in the marginal rate of income tax on

but those studies were tainted by the false assumption that the tax-sensitive wife pays at the highest marginal rates imposed on the marital partnership.[45]

This discussion of the efficiency of joint filing has proceeded under the implicit assumption that efficiency is an appropriate standard for measuring the worth of a tax rule. That assumption, however, is unwarranted. Throughout the income tax history of the United States, fairness has been the primary value to be maximized.[46] In many contexts, fairness and efficiency are complementary, but when efficiency is a function of the tax sensitivity of groups of taxpayers, the two criteria are at war. A system that permits women to pay less tax than men, single persons less than married ones, blacks less than whites or old less than young[47] because of differences in their feelings about taxes seems monstrously unfair and, incidentally, an invitation to chaos in the tax laws. Such madness, however, is a logical consequence of building a personal income tax on efficiency principles.[48]

III. Conclusion

The case for joint filing would be overwhelming if marriage were always a true partnership, with each spouse sharing equally in the

---

two-earner families can be expected to cause a realignment of work responsibilities within two-earner families with wives working a larger share and husbands a smaller share of total family labor time. At the same time, total family labor time can be expected to decrease for white families and remain unchanged for black families.

45. *See* text accompanying notes 33-39 *supra*.

46. The political support for the 16th amendment to the United States Constitution, for example, is explainable on fairness, rather than efficiency grounds. Historically, efficiency criteria have been important when fairness criteria provided no guidance or the efficiency effects were very substantial. For discussion of the historical preeminence of fairness criteria among followers of Henry Simons, see Head, *supra* note 18, at 193-95.

47. Leuthold found, for example, that "an increase in the marginal tax rate leads white families to work longer hours and black families to work shorter hours in total." Leuthold, *supra* note 35, at 156.

48. The statement in the text puts me at odds with those who would restructure the United States income tax according to so-called optimal tax theory criteria. The optimal tax theory literature has attempted to ascertain how the tax rules could be rewritten to minimize changes in behavior in response to the tax. If data were sufficient to carry out the enterprise and if a cost-free tax administration could be obtained, the optimal tax theorists would be able to construct a tax that was paid exclusively by those without the economic power to shift any portion of the tax. The tax so constructed would be an "optimal" tax system!

For a friendly lampoon of the optimal tax theory, see McIntyre (a.k.a. Walter T. McDuck), *Optimal Tax Act Passes: Income Tax Replaced by Lump Sum Levy*, Tax Notes, April 2, 1980. That piece points out that an optimal tax payable in coin is nonneutral when applied to nonmarket income, since a person working in the nonmarket sector cannot pay the tax without shifting to the market sector, whatever his preference for nonmarket income. For example, the British once imposed a lump sum levy on blacks in the nonmarket agricultural sector in order to force them to take paying jobs in the South African diamond mines.

marital income by voluntary agreement, reinforced by community property law. In contrast, individual filing would be the obvious rule if married persons typically had no common economic interests and sharing was rare. In the United States and many other countries, marital relationships are characterized by widespread but not universal sharing, with limited reinforcement by local property law. This untidy situation is the root cause of the legitimate debate over the proper tax effect of family circumstances.

Most of those arguing in favor of individual filing, nevertheless, fail to address the issue of marital sharing or address it only tangentially. This Article demonstrates the inadequacy of that approach.

NOTE, "THE CASE FOR MANDATORY SEPARATE FILING BY MARRIED PERSONS"

91 Yale Law Journal 363 (1981), pp. 367-78.

C. The Defects of Joint Filing

The adoption of the new joint return in 1948 permitted a tax reduction for individuals who married, unless their incomes were already earned so equally that income splitting provided no benefit. Congress came to regard this marriage "bonus" as excessive,[12] particularly because married couples were perceived as enjoying economies of scale in the purchase of food, housing, and other goods and services.[13] Congress' desire to reduce the marriage bonus led in 1969 to the adoption of a new schedule of tax rates that limited a single person's tax liability to no more than 120% that of a married couple with the same income.[14]

The adoption of the new singles' schedule has created its own problems. For the couple whose income is earned primarily by one partner, tax liability is still reduced upon marriage. But a married couple whose income is earned equally by each spouse now suffers an increase in tax burden under joint filing. To prevent such couples from filing separately to take advantage of the 1969 singles' schedule, Congress provided that married couples filing separate returns must be taxed under the old singles' schedule, now the most disadvantageous of all.[15] The changes in 1969 thus reduced the marriage bonus at the cost of creating a new marriage penalty. The present joint filing system is consequently characterized by an arbitrary system of incentives and disincentives for marriage that are determined by a couple's income and the proportions in which that income is

---

12. By 1969, a single individual might pay as much as 42% more tax than a married couple with the same income. JOINT COMMITTEE ON TAXATION, *supra* note 2, at 23. Congress regarded this disparity as too great. *Id.*

13. While two may not live as cheaply as one, it was argued, a married couple could still live more cheaply than two single individuals; for example, apartments could be shared and one newspaper or automobile would do instead of two. Bittker, *supra* note 1, at 1422-25. Some commentators suggest, however, that the argument that married couples enjoy economies of scale that single persons do not is problematic, because single persons also have the option of living in a household with family members or other individuals. H. GROVES, *supra* note 11, at 94 n.2; Pechman, *Income Splitting*, in H. STEIN & J. PECHMAN, ESSAYS IN FEDERAL TAXATION 49, 55-56 (1959); Surrey, *Family Income and Federal Taxation*, 24 TAXES 980, 985 (1946). In fact, most singles do share households. *See* Gerzog, *supra* note 4, at 35 (62.5% of single persons share their homes with another).

14. Tax Reform Act of 1969, Pub. L. No. 91-172, 83 Stat. 487 (1969).

15. Rosen, *supra* note 1, at 427. Separate filing by married persons still may be advantageous under limited circumstances. *See* note 2 *supra*.

earned by each spouse.[16] While there is no evidence as to the number of taxpayers who have actually refrained from entering marriage or who have sought divorce solely for tax reasons, the amounts of tax liability involved can be considerable. For a couple whose total income in 1979 was $50,000, marriage could result in an annual tax bonus of $3,344 or an annual tax penalty of $2,674, depending on the percentage of joint income earned by each spouse.[17] That marriage penalty has resulted in some well-publicized cases of happily married couples who obtained annual "tax divorces."[18] Even if the effects of joint filing do not extensively influence most taxpayers' behavior, the existence of penalties and bonuses for marriage has been widely criticized as an arbitrary and undesirable government intrusion into private activity.[19]

A second major disadvantage of joint filing is the creation of a second earner's disincentive. Joint filing discourages a non-working person with a working spouse from employment, because his first dollar earned will be taxed at the same high marginal rate as the last dollar earned by the couple's primary earner.[20] A second earner within a couple must also sac-

---

16. As a general rule, marriage will increase a couple's tax burden whenever the lesser-earning spouse earns 20% or more of the couple's total income, and decrease a couple's tax burden whenever the lesser-earning spouse earns less than 20%. Gerzog, *supra* note 4, at 28. *See also* JOINT COMMITTEE ON TAXATION, *supra* note 2, at 29 (table of effect of marriage on individual's tax liability according to family income and percentage of family income earned by lesser-earning spouse). The magnitude of the marriage penalty or bonus may also be affected by the number of dependents in the household; in 1951, Congress enacted the Head of Household (HOH) rate schedule, which gives unmarried or divorced taxpayers supporting dependents half the income-splitting benefits of joint filing. That is, it taxes their returns at a rate midway between that applied to a married couple's joint return, and that applied to a single person's return. The HOH schedule thus increases the divorce "bonus" for spouses earning equal incomes who support dependents. JOINT COMMITTEE ON TAXATION, *supra* note 2, at 23, 37.

17. JOINT COMMITTEE ON TAXATION, *supra* note 2, at 29 (table showing effect of marriage on tax liabilities at selected income levels and earning splits between husband and wife).

18. Feld, *Divorce Tax Style*, 54 TAXES 608, 609 (1976); Haitch, *Tax Split*, N.Y. Times, Feb. 15, 1981, § A, at 49, col. 5. In 1976, the Internal Revenue Service ruled that it will not recognize such divorces for tax purposes because they are "sham" transactions. Rev. Rul. 76-255, 1976-2 C.B. 40. Two taxpayers challenged the Service's position in the United States Tax Court. *Boyter v. Commissioner*, 74 T.C. 989 (1980). The Tax Court, however, never reached the Commissioner's argument that taxpayers' annual divorces were a sham, holding against taxpayers on the theory that the divorces were legally invalid, having been obtained in foreign courts that had no jurisdiction to grant them.

19. *See, e.g.*, note 4 *supra* (original concern for marriage neutrality primarily concern to avoid marriage disincentives; recent commentators also criticize creation of incentives for only legal, heterosexual unions); Munnell, *supra* note 3, at 247-49 (tax burden should not vary with marital status); Richards, *Discrimination Against Married Couples Under Present Income Tax Laws*, 49 TAXES 526, 536-38 (1971) (same). *But see* McIntyre, *supra* note 1, at 472 (marriage penalty undesirable, but marriage bonus justifiable recognition of real changes in individual's economic circumstances that occur upon marriage).

20. In the absence of any income tax, individuals would choose to work only as long as the extra income from an additional hour of paid employment exceeds the value of an additional hour of leisure time. Income taxes reduce an individual's net wage, creating incentives to work longer hours to maintain previous levels of consumption (the "income effect"). They also create incentives to work shorter hours, by increasing the value of leisure time relative to the individual's declining net wage (the "substitution effect"). Because the income and substitution effects conflict, the overall impact of taxes

rifice time that otherwise might be spent providing household and childcare services, which are not taxed as imputed income.[21] Further, second earners entering employment face additional nondeductible work-related expenses.

With the growing acceptance of two-earner couples,[22] the possible economic inefficiency[23] associated with the second earner's disincentive has become a source of increasing concern.[24] Further, because most second earners are married women,[25] the disincentive is also criticized for rein-

on the number of hours spent in paid employment depends on the relative strengths of these effects. Studies of the labor force participation of males indicate that income taxes have little effect on participation, perhaps because factors other than money play an important part in motivation. See Munnell, *supra* note 3, at 264 (labor force participation of adult males largely unaffected by tax rates); *cf.* Rosen, *supra* note 1, at 426 n.15 (increase in family income through wife's employment has little effect on husband's labor force participation). Empirical studies of the labor force participation of married women, who are generally the second earners within a married couple, see note 25 *infra*, suggest that their labor force participation is very sensitive to changes in their tax rate. JOINT COMMITTEE ON TAXATION, *supra* note 2, at 36. Several researchers have found married women's response to a tax increase to be greater than unity; that is, a 10% decrease in net real wage due to a tax increase will result in a more than 10% decrease in the number of hours spent in paid employment. Munnell, *supra* note 3, at 265; Rosen, *supra* note 1, at 426. One commentator has criticized these studies on the ground that they measured only the marginal responses of women already in the workforce, and not the behavior of married women making the initial decision to enter employment. McIntyre, *supra* note 1, at 486-87. Intuition suggests, however, that married women deciding to undertake paid employment would be even more sensitive to tax rates, because they must also face the threshold loss of their household and childcare services, and incur threshold employment-related expenses.

21. It can be argued that the disincentive associated with the loss of imputed income derives not from joint filing but from the failure of the tax system to tax imputed income from such self-performed services. Due to the difficulties that would have to be overcome to tax such imputed income fairly, however, taxation of imputed income has generally been dismissed as unfeasible. See p. 377 *infra*.

22. D. RICE, DUAL CAREER MARRIAGE 1-4 (1979). During the early 1940's, only about 15% to 20% of married couples contained two earners. By 1980, this figure had risen to nearly 50%. Munnell, *supra* note 3, at 261.

23. Economic efficiency is achieved when individuals allocate scarce resources so as to obtain the highest possible level of satisfaction. G. BREAK & J. PECHMAN, *supra* note 3, at 7. For example, a person will allocate his time between work and leisure in the most efficient manner by working until the income from an additional hour of employment equals his subjective value for an hour of leisure. An economically efficient tax raises revenue while minimizing the incentives for taxpayers to alter their original, efficient behavior. U.S. DEP'T OF THE TREASURY, BLUEPRINTS FOR BASIC TAX REFORM 49 (1977) [hereinafter cited as BLUEPRINTS].

24. Any income tax is inherently inefficient, because it alters the wage rewards associated with the allocation of time to paid employment. Brazer, *supra* note 1, at 227. The current use of the married couple as a single taxable unit, however, exacerbates this inefficiency. Married women are much more sensitive than men to changes in their tax rates, see note 20 *supra*, and much more likely to alter their employment behavior inefficiently to avoid tax. Yet married women, generally the second earners in a couple, face the greatest marginal tax rates under the joint filing system. Separate filing is consequently superior to joint filing on efficiency grounds. Brazer, *supra* note 1, at 227-28; Munnell, *supra* note 3, at 263-65; Rosen, *supra* note 1, at 426-27.

25. The description of married women as "second" earners is not intended to imply that their employment is somehow less important or significant than that of men. Married women are "second" earners in the sense that their employment appears to be much more discretionary; they enter or leave the market place frequently while the employment of married men remains constant. See JOINT COMMITTEE ON TAXATION, *supra* note 2, at 36; Munnell, *supra* note 3, at 264; Rosen, *supra* note 1, at 426.

forcing sexual stereotypes by encouraging married women to remain at home producing more traditional household and childcare services.[26]

D. The Second Earner's Deduction

Concern over both the second earner's disincentive and the marriage penalty has induced Congress to write still another chapter in the history of the federal tax treatment of married couples. The Economic Recovery Tax Act of 1981 permits married couples with two earners a new tax deduction based on the earnings of the lesser-earning spouse.[27] In 1982, married couples filing joint returns will be allowed to deduct from their taxable income five percent of the lesser of $30,000 or the earned income of the lesser-earning spouse. For 1983 and subsequent years, the deduction will be ten percent.[28]

While the deduction provides some relief from the undesirable effects of joint filing, it stops far short of achieving marriage neutrality or eliminating the second earner's disincentive. First, the deduction does not reduce the tax bonus enjoyed by married persons whose incomes are relatively unequal.[29] Second, while the deduction reduces the marriage penalty paid by married individuals with relatively equal incomes, significant penalties still remain. For a couple whose total income in 1984[30] is $50,000, marriage could result in an annual tax penalty of $1,142.[31] Third, the deduction does not eliminate the second earner's disincentive. For example, an unmarried person undertaking employment at $15,000 a year can expect to pay twelve percent or $1,801 in tax in 1984. An individual whose spouse earns $30,000 would pay thirty percent or $4,533 in additional tax on the same income. The new ten percent deduction would decrease that

---

26. *See* Bittker, *supra* note 1, at 1433 (reasonable to describe joint filing system as biased against married women); Gerzog, *supra* note 4, at 36-37 (joint filing reinforces stereotypical notions of married women's appropriate roles).

27. Economic Recovery Tax Act of 1981, Pub. L. No. 97-34, § 103, 95 Stat. 172 (August 13, 1981).

28. SENATE REPORT, *supra* note 4, at 30. The 1981 Act also contains provisions that "flatten" the rate schedules by reducing the marginal tax rates faced by high-income taxpayers. Because of the relationship between progressivity and marriage neutrality, these rate reductions, which will be phased in fully by 1984, also reduce slightly the second earner's disincentive and the tax penalties or bonuses associated with marriage. *See* note 6 *supra*.

29. In fact, where a couple has two earners (and therefore qualifies to take the deduction) but more than 80% of joint income is earned by one spouse (so that the couple already enjoys a marriage bonus, *see* note 16 *supra*), the deduction will increase the amount of that bonus.

30. 1984 figures are used to incorporate fully the effects of the rate reductions provided by the Economic Recovery Tax Act of 1981, Pub. L. No. 97-34, § 101, 95 Stat. 172 (August 13, 1981).

31. These calculations are derived from the 1984 rate schedules provided in the Economic Recovery Tax Act of 1981, Pub. L. No. 97-34, § 101, 95 Stat. 172 (August 13, 1981), and assume that the taxpayers do not itemize and have no dependents. Under the same assumptions, a couple with a joint income of $15,000 could face a tax bonus of $338 or a tax penalty of $71 upon marriage; a couple with a $30,000 income could face a $1,458 bonus or a $731 penalty; and a couple with a $100,000 income could face a $5,935 bonus or a $3,280 penalty.

tax bill only to $4,038, or twenty-seven percent of the second earner's income.[32]

II. The Problem of Horizontal Equity

Despite the widely recognized drawbacks of joint filing,[33] no commentator has advocated its abandonment until very recently.[34] The continuing popularity of joint filing arises from the belief that it is more important to

---

32. Again, these calculations are from the 1984 rate schedules provided in the Economic Recovery Tax Act of 1981, Pub. L. No. 97-34, § 101, 95 Stat. 172 (August 13, 1981), and assume taxpayers do not itemize and have no dependents. Under those assumptions, a taxpayer whose spouse earns $15,000 would pay a tax of 20% on an additional $15,000 in earnings, and use of the new deduction would reduce this rate only to 17%. A taxpayer undertaking employment at $25,000 a year, who would pay 17% tax on that income if unmarried, would pay 30% tax if his spouse also earned $25,000 (a rate reduced to 26% by the new deduction) and would pay 40% tax if his spouse earned $50,000 (a rate reduced only to 36% by the deduction).

33. *See, e.g.*, JOINT COMMITTEE ON TAXATION, *supra* note 2, at 26-37; G. BREAK & J. PECHMAN, *supra* note 3, at 32-36. In the past, numerous proposals have been suggested to remedy, at least partially, the defects of joint filing. The 1976 childcare credit, I.R.C. § 44A, is designed to compensate for the loss of childcare and household services that occurs when both spouses are employed, and is available only to two-earner couples and single persons who incur expenses for care of a dependent in order to undertake paid employment. Other suggested proposals included a limited deduction or credit of some percentage of the earnings of the lesser-earning spouse. *See* JOINT COMMITTEE ON TAXATION, *supra* note 2, at 6-7. Somewhat similar is the "Pechman plan," under which married couples would file joint returns taxed at the same rate as unmarried individuals' returns, but would receive in addition a special deduction or credit based on the earnings of the lesser-earning spouse. J. PECHMAN, FEDERAL TAX POLICY 95-97 (3d ed. 1977). Another proposal would permit married couples to file separate returns under the 1969 singles' schedule, if they perceive such filing to be advantageous. JOINT COMMITTEE ON TAXATION, *supra* note 2, at 6; Gerzog, *supra* note 4, at 47-48. A nonprogressive, flat-rate income tax with a per-taxpayer refundable credit also has been proposed. Such a system would provide for equal taxation of couples with equal incomes, marriage neutrality, and some limited progressivity. JOINT COMMITTEE ON TAXATION, *supra* note 2, at 7; Rankin, *Plans to Ease the Marriage Levy*, N.Y. Times, Sept. 9, 1980, § D, at 2, col. 3.

In fact, none of these proposals completely remedies the defects of joint filing. A deduction or credit based on the earnings of the lesser-earning spouse fails to acheive complete marriage neutrality or elimination of the second earner's disincentive. *See* p. 369 *supra* (failure of deduction provided by the Economic Recovery Tax Act of 1981, Pub. L. No. 97-34, § 103, 95 Stat. 172 (August 13, 1981), to acheive these goals). Permitting married couples the option of filing separately under the 1969 singles' schedule would eliminate the marriage penalty, but a marriage bonus would persist for those couples whose income was earned disproportionately enough that joint filing was still advantageous, and the second earner's disincentive would persist for these couples as well. Given the importance of progressivity to the personal income tax, *see* p. 364 *supra*, elimination of this fundamental principle seems a visionary approach to the problems of marriage neutrality and the second earner's disincentive. Gerzog, *supra* note 4, at 44.

34. Rosen, *supra* note 1, who recommended mandatory separate filing in 1977 on grounds of economic efficiency, appears to be the first commentator to suggest seriously a return to the individual tax unit. More recent champions of mandatory separate filing include Brazer, *supra* note 1, and Munnell, *supra* note 3, both of whom suggest that increases in cohabitation, employment of married women, and divorce incidence have made the individual tax unit more attractive.

ensure that married couples with equal incomes pay equal tax[35] than to avoid variations in individual tax liability based on marital status.[36]

That belief is premised, however, upon an assumption that married persons pool incomes.[37] The concept of income pooling, while widely accepted,[38] remains without empirical support.[39] In fact, modern studies of

---

35. See JOINT COMMITTEE ON TAXATION, supra note 2, at 26-28 (joint filing premised on desirability of equal taxation of couples); McIntyre, supra note 1, at 470-71 (equity demands that couples with equal incomes bear equal tax burdens). Even Munnell, who supports mandatory separate filing, believes that the need for equal taxation of couples presents the "most serious" objection to separate filing. Munnell, supra note 3, at 278. Nevertheless, many of the recent proposals to remedy the defects of joint filing would also compromise the principle of equal taxation of couples. For example, the second earner's deduction recently adopted by Congress, see p. 370 supra, will ensure that two-earner couples pay less tax than one-earner couples with the same joint income. Because the benefit of that proposal increases in direct proportion to the second earner's income, couples whose incomes are earned equally by each spouse will also pay less tax than other two-earner couples with the same aggregate income, earned less evenly by each spouse. This would also be true for couples who file separately under an optional separate filing scheme. Interestingly, these equity effects have not provoked much comment. One commentator, however, has noted the detrimental effect of optional separate filing on the equal taxation of couples. See Gerzog, supra note 4, at 44-45.

36. Secondarily, joint filing provides an easy solution to the administrative problem of policing tax avoidance through interspousal transfers of income-producing assets and credits, deductions, and exemptions. Because income and deductions are attributed to the couple as a unit, allocation between spouses is irrelevant. Joint filing also solves the pre-1948 problem of geographical disparities in the tax treatment of married couples in community property and common law states, by extending the benefits of Poe v. Seaborn, note 10 supra, to all married couples. These geographical disparities, however, can also be easily eliminated under mandatory separate filing by a statutory override of community property laws for purposes of federal income taxation. See note 60 infra.

37. SENATE REPORT, supra note 4, at 29 (equal taxation of couples appropriate because married couples frequently pool incomes and consume as unit); JOINT COMMITTEE ON TAXATION, supra note 2, at 27 (attractiveness of principle of equal taxation of couples depends on extent to which spouses pool incomes and single individuals do not); McIntyre, supra note 1, at 470 (reality or perceived reality of marital pooling is underpinning for joint filing); Thorson, supra note 4, at 116 (income pooling implies married couple is appropriate taxable unit).

It should be noted that the tax system's recognition of pooling behavior through joint filing has itself been criticized as a source of horizontal inequity between similar households because children, dependent parents, cohabitating couples and homosexual companions may also pool incomes. Income could be split on a joint return not only between husband and wife, but among other household members as well. While even the supporters of joint filing have recognized that marriage is not a necessary condition for pooling, see Bittker, supra note 1, at 1398-1400; McIntyre, supra note 1, at 480, the restriction of the income-splitting benefits of the joint return to married couples has been justified as an easily administered "bright line" test for pooling arrangements. Nevertheless, a proposal to permit income splitting among family members in addition to spouses was suggested in 1946 by Surrey, then Tax Legislative Counsel to the Secretary of the Treasury. See Surrey, supra note 13, at 986.

Joint filing has also been criticized as a source of horizontal inequity between similar couples because it does not account for the real benefits that one-earner couples enjoy over two-earner couples with the same income, due to the household and childcare services a nonworking spouse can provide and the absence of an additional set of nondeductible employment-related expenses. See, e.g., Bittker, supra note 1, at 1425-26; Brazer, supra note 1, at 242; Gerzog, supra note 4, at 33. Those differences between one- and two-earner couples may persist beyond the initial entrance of the second earner into employment. Thorson, supra note 4, at 116-17. As the income of the lesser-earning spouse rises, it is likely that his employment expenses will rise as well. Similarly, less time is available for the provision of untaxed household services; at lower income levels, second earners are often employed in part-time positions. With the recent rise in the representation of two-earner couples, see note 22 supra, this inequity between one- and two-earner couples has become a greater source of concern.

38. See McIntyre, supra note 1, at 471 (no serious challenges have been made to assumption of widespread marital pooling). Even the supporters of mandatory separate filing have not challenged the income pooling assumption. See, e.g., Brazer, supra note 1, at 226; Munnell, supra note 3, at 247-48;

39. See n. 39 on page 505.

the family suggest that married persons retain the control and benefits of their personal incomes. Concern for horizontal equity in personal income taxation is therefore better served by taxing individual rather than joint income.

A. *Marital Income Sharing Patterns: Pooling or Exchange?*

Under the joint filing system, income splitting is usually justified by the assumption that, while a greater-earning spouse may have legal possession of his income, the actual control and benefits of the income will be shared equally by both spouses.[40] Because family consumption decisions are presumed to be joint decisions, both spouses are perceived to gain an equal benefit from an increase in family income regardless of which spouse earns it.

But exchange theory, one of the dominant modern perspectives on social behavior,[41] suggests that married individuals do not enjoy access to their

---

Rosen, *supra* note 1, at 425. Rather than questioning the pooling presumption, these authors have argued that the need for horizontal equity between couples is outweighed by other considerations. *See* note 34 *supra*. Pechman also accepts the premise of income pooling, but objects to the income-splitting benefits of joint filing on the ground that the decision to marry and pool income is voluntary, and should be ignored for tax purposes just like any other consumption decision. Pechman, *supra* note 13, at 55.

39. H. GROVES, *supra* note 11, at 70; McIntyre, *supra* note 1, at 469. Thorson claims to have discovered a "consensus" that married couples pool income, but he gives no empirical support for this finding. Thorson, *supra* note 4, at 116. Even commentators who accept the pooling presumption note that pooling may not occur between high-income spouses. H. GROVES, *supra* note 11, at 70; Bittker, *supra* note 1, at 1394; Thorson, *supra* note 4, at 116. Yet the benefits of income splitting are greatest for high-income couples, because low-income taxpayers are already taxed at such low rates that income splitting makes little difference; for example, a one-earner couple filing a joint return with an income of $5,000 enjoys a marriage bonus of $250, or 5% of after-tax income, while a one-earner couple with an income of $50,000 enjoys a marriage bonus of $3,344, or 9.2% of after-tax income. JOINT COMMITTEE ON TAXATION, *supra* note 2, at 29 (table showing effect of marriage on tax liability in dollar amounts at selected income levels and earnings splits between husband and wife), *id.* at 30 (table showing effect of marriage on tax liability as percentage of family income, at selected income levels and earnings splits between husband and wife).

40. *See* Bittker, *supra* note 1, at 1420-21 (married person has less legal, emotional, and social control over his income); McIntyre, *supra* note 1, at 475-76 (to tax primary earner in couple on his full income is to tax "potential" rather than actual income, and is inconsistent with principle of taxing income to individual with control or enjoyment of income); Thorson, *supra* note 4, at 116 (technical title over income does not indicate actual control or benefits that accrue to married taxpayer).

41. Although "some variant of the rational choice [exchange theory] approach has long been with us," A. HEATH, RATIONAL CHOICE AND SOCIAL EXCHANGE 184 (1976), modern American exchange theory has its roots in two seminal works: P. BLAU, EXCHANGE AND POWER IN SOCIAL LIFE (1964), and G. HOMANS, SOCIAL BEHAVIOR: ITS ELEMENTARY FORMS (1961). While exchange analysis is a relatively recent development in sociological theory, it has gained widespread appeal. It was regarded as an emerging perspective as recently as the early 1970's. W. GOODE, EXPLORATIONS IN SOCIAL THEORY 98-99 (1973) (noting "the many 'exchange theories' that have been developed of late"); Spengler, *Contemporary Approaches to Societal Analysis*, in THEORETICAL SOCIOLOGY 486 (J. McKinney & E. Tiryakian eds. 1970) (exchange analysis emerging field). By the late 1970's, however, exchange theory had become "one of the most prominent theoretical perspectives in sociology," J. TURNER, THE STRUCTURE OF SOCIOLOGICAL THEORY 215 (rev. ed. 1978). *See* P. EKEH, SOCIAL EXCHANGE THEORY 81 (1974) (exchange theory major sociological perspective); A. HEATH, *supra*, at 184 (exchange analysis "a standard tool of the mainstream sociologist"); J. TURNER, *supra*, at 278 n.1

spouse's income in a manner that would suppport the assumption of unilateral, uncompensated income transfers.[42] According to exchange theory, people will not normally incur costs without expecting compensation in one form or another, so that goal-seeking individuals must exchange resources and services.[43] Social relationships thus result from individuals' dependence upon the expenditures of other persons to accomplish their own goals,[44] and individuals enter relationships primarily to engage in a beneficial exchange of both economic and noneconomic resources.

The resources that will be exchanged within any social relationship, including marriage, need not be economic or even similar in kind.[45] When

---

(exchange theory has gained wide appeal in sociological theorizing). The basic theoretical principles are presented in P. BLAU, *supra*, and G. HOMANS, *supra*. For more modern syntheses of Homan's and Blau's works, see P. EKEH, *supra*; A. HEATH, *supra*; and J. TURNER, *supra*, at 201-309.

42. While exchange theorists do not claim that exchange is the root of all behavior, they do argue that most, if not all, social relationships can be usefully viewed as exchanges between goal-seeking individuals expecting to profit from such transactions. P. BLAU, *supra* note 41, at 88 ("Social exchange can be observed everywhere . . . not only in market relations but also in friendship and even in love."); A. HEATH, *supra* note 41, at 1-2 (social exchange the basis of a wide range of human relationships); G. HOMANS, *supra* note 41, at 13-14 (same). Exchange theory has been widely accepted as an especially useful vehicle for analysis of the marital relationship. *See* C. HARRIS, THE FAMILY 160 (1969) (marriage relationships maintained by exchange between partners); L. SCANZONI & J. SCANZONI, MEN WOMEN AND CHANGE: A SOCIOLOGY OF MARRIAGE AND THE FAMILY 11 (1976) ("Sociologists may look at many areas related to the family in terms of exchange theory."); E. WALSTER & G. WALSTER, A NEW LOOK AT LOVE 135 (1978) (considerable evidence supports application of exchange theory to dating and courtship, marital choice, and marital satisfaction); R. WINCH, FAMILIAL ORGANIZATION: A QUEST FOR DETERMINANTS 7, 98-100 (1977) (noting particular relevance of exchange analysis to familial behavior, and suggesting that exchange of male's hunting ability for female's childbearing and foodgathering abilities may have formed basis for first family units); Edwards, *Familial Behavior as Social Exchange*, 31 J. MARR. & FAM. 521-23 (1969) (social exchange evident in dating and mate selection research and in allocation of authority in the family decisionmaking process); Nye, *Choice, Exchange, and the Family* in 2 CONTEMPORARY THEORIES ABOUT THE FAMILY 1, 11-39 (W. Burr, R. Hill, F. Nye, & I. Reiss eds. 1979) (exchange theory successfully applied to several areas of familial behavior, including labor force participation of married women, sexual behavior, marital choice and dissolution).

43. The presumption of goal-seeking rationality is central to exchange theory. People are assumed to be motivated to enter social relationships by the prospect of some return, be it psychic or economic. *See* P. BLAU, *supra* note 41, at 91-92, 98; G. HOMANS, *supra* note 41, at 61-62. The benefit is not always obvious; it may spring from the satisfaction of internalized norms or the approval of third parties. Nevertheless, altruism is ultimately reduced to egoism. P. BLAU, *supra* note 41, at 17. Social relationships arise when both parties stand to benefit from an exchange; that is, when each has something the other wants. *See id.* at 92; G. HOMANS, *supra* note 41, at 61; Edwards, *supra* note 42, at 518-19.

44. *See* P. BLAU, *supra* note 41, at 14-15; Edwards, *supra* note 42, at 518-19.

45. *See* P. BLAU, *supra* note 41, at 99-100. *Cf.* R. BLOOD & D. WOLFE, HUSBANDS AND WIVES 12, 32 (1960) (income important resource in marital exchange); B. MURSTEIN, WHO WILL MARRY WHOM? 110-11 (1976) (physical attractiveness an exchangeable resource); L. SCANZONI & J. SCANZONI, *supra* note 42, at 86, 96 (sexual intimacy exchangeable resource). Individuals who rank high on one resource scale may use their advantage to obtain a spouse who ranks high on another; an individual who is very attractive physically may use his status as a desirable companion to woo a spouse who is less attractive but has more prestige and power. B. MURSTEIN, *supra*, at 110-11; E. WALSTER & G. WALSTER, *supra* note 42, at 139-41. The bargaining power associated with a resource depends not only on its absolute value but also on the available alternatives. *See* L. SCANZONI & J. SCANZONI, *supra* note 42, at 312-13. The importance of a spouse's income as a resource will be determined not only by the amount of this income but also by what the other partner might earn if he were himself to enter employment.

both spouses earn substantial incomes, there may be no exchanges of income or property between them at all, but only exchanges of noneconomic resources such as emotional support, sexual intimacy, enhanced socioeconomic status, or the satisfaction of having fulfilled a desired social role.[46] If one spouse earns more than the other, though, the greater-earning partner may transfer some of the benefits of his income to the lesser-earning spouse in return for an additional share of nonmonetary resources and services. So, for example, one spouse may exchange cash acquired through employment for household and childcare services and emotional support provided by the other spouse.[47]

Married individuals do not necessarily expect immediate compensation for every service provided to a spouse. According to exchange theory, however, there is a long-run expectation of reciprocity in marriage as in any other relationship.[48] When selecting spouses, individuals tend to choose partners with whom they believe a marital "contract" can be arranged under which the total exchange of services will leave them better off during marriage than before.[49] If an individual's exchange expectations are not fulfilled, the exchange "contract" may be renegotiated so that the relationship remains superior to other possibilities.[50] One of the best documented examples of such renegotiation is the redistribution of family decisionmaking power that accompanies a change in the distribution of income or economic resources between spouses: an increase in the eco-

---

46. Such marriages have been described as "equal partner" arrangements, in which spouses are less concerned with providing instrumental services, such as income or household services, than with exchanging expressive resources such as companionship, emotional support, and sexual intimacy. L. SCANZONI & J. SCANZONI, *supra* note 42, at 235, 287.

47. H. ROSS & I. SAWHILL, TIME OF TRANSITION: THE GROWTH OF FAMILIES HEADED BY WOMEN 45 (1975) (spouse who earns disproportionate amount of income "may use his position to redistribute family income in his favor, to establish greater authority within the family, or to obtain other nonmonetary perquisites"); L. SCANZONI & J. SCANZONI, *supra* note 42, at 124, 260, 287, 476 (describing exchange pattern as "traditional" marriage arrangement, in which husbands seek wives to perform housekeeping services and "expressive functions" of providing comfort, support, encouragement, and respect, while wives seek husbands "who appear able to provide them with the kinds of economic security, status, and material comfort they define as acceptable").

48. *Cf.* P. BLAU, *supra* note 41, at 16-17 (expectation of reciprocity in social relationships); P. EKEH, *supra* note 41, at 47 (same); Edwards, *supra* note 42, at 519 (same).

49. *See* C. HARRIS, *supra* note 42, at 160 (marriage is contractual relationship entered after bargaining on terms); B. MURSTEIN, *supra* note 45, at 272-73 (exchange theory has empirical success in predicting marital choice); L. SCANZONI & J. SCANZONI, *supra* note 42, at 110 (marriage decision reached only after mutually favorable implicit exchange "bargain" emerges); Edwards, *supra* note 42, at 521-23 (social exchange and bargaining for resources clearly evident in dating and mate selection).

50. C. HARRIS, *supra* note 42, at 160-63 (exchange continues after marriage so that marital roles are further defined through bargaining process affected by relative power of spouses); L. SCANZONI & J. SCANZONI, *supra* note 42, at 258, 321-23, 480 (marriage continual process of exchange and renegotiation under changing circumstances); E. WALSTER & G. WALSTER, *supra* note 42, at 142-45 (retaining reciprocal equity of exchange important for stable relationship); *cf.* D. RICE, *supra* note 22, at 12 (wife's decision, after marriage, to pursue career produces strain between spouses that must be resolved through renegotiation or divorce).

nomic resources that a marital partner can offer leads to a corresponding increase in that partner's control over the uses of joint income.[51]

Married persons generally attempt to resolve inequities in their relationship through renegotiation, because the process of divorce entails substantial economic and noneconomic costs.[52] Nevertheless, when extreme disparities in exchange cannot be reconciled, alternatives to the marriage become more attractive, and divorce more likely.[53]

B. *The Implications of Exchange Theory for Joint Filing: The Problem of Income Attribution*

Under exchange theory, the income-splitting benefits of the joint return can only be justified as a means of recognizing that, after interspousal exchanges of resources take place, the lesser-earning spouse will have the control and benefit of approximately one-half of joint income. Yet there are two reasons to suggest that the recognition of such marital exchanges of income through joint filing is an inappropriate and undesirable means of meeting horizontal equity concerns.

First, although attribution of one-half of joint income to each spouse is consistent with the income-pooling presumption that a lesser-earning spouse has direct access to a greater-earning spouse's income, under exchange theory the greater-earning spouse retains the benefit of his income and uses it to strike a more favorable marriage "contract." Joint filing thus gives an implicit deduction to a primary earner for that part of his income that is exchanged for nonmonetary resources and services provided by his spouse. Although taxpayers are permitted to deduct expenses incurred in the production of income or the pursuit of a trade or business,[54] they generally are not permitted to deduct the costs of goods and services purchased for personal consumption.[55] If taxpayer expenditures for enhanced status, companionship, or household and childcare services ordina-

---

51. R. BLOOD & D. WOLFE, *supra* note 45, at 12-13, 32 (decisionmaking power within married couples fluctuates between partners in accordance with spouses' changes in workforce participation and income); A. HEATH, *supra* note 41, at 105-12 (same); H. ROSS & I. SAWHILL, *supra* note 47, at 42-45 (same).

52. Individuals contemplating divorce face intangible costs such as third party disapproval and the violation of internalized norms, as well as the more obvious costs of obtaining a legal agreement and facing disruption in career and living patterns. E. WALSTER & G. WALSTER, *supra* note 42, at 146; Nye, *supra* note 42, at 26.

53. *See* L. SCANZONI & J. SCANZONI, *supra* note 42, at 11, 463-64 (divorce result of breakdown in renegotiation of marital exchange); E. WALSTER & G. WALSTER, *supra* note 42, at 146 (inequitable exchange likely to lead to dissolution of relationship); *cf.* H. ROSS & I. SAWHILL, *supra* note 47, at 41-42, 47 (wife's direct access to income through employment reduces dependency and increases attractiveness of alternatives to marriage, thereby reducing cost and increasing likelihood of divorce).

54. I.R.C. §§ 162, 165, 212.

55. I.R.C. § 262.

rily are not deductible,[56] a primary earner who exchanges income for such consumption goods within the marital bond should not be given a deduction for those "purchases."

Second, the services that may be provided by a lesser-earning spouse in exchange for cash income generally are not recognized as sources of income under the Internal Revenue Code. Even services that produce income when performed for a formal employer, such as childcare and household services, are not recognized as sources of income when they are performed by the taxpayer for himself or a household member. Other resources exchanged by spouses, such as emotional support, sexual intimacy, and enhanced socioeconomic status, are not freely exchanged in the marketplace, and hence are even more difficult to quantify. Because the exchange of such resources with a spouse adds to the taxpayer's well-being, they should in theory be taxed as imputed income.[57] Proposals to do so have been consistently rejected, however, because of the difficulties of deciding which services to tax, the problem of measuring their value without unbearable invasions of privacy, and the fact that imputed income does not produce the actual cash needed to pay tax bills.[58] Since these types of

---

56. The childcare credit might be viewed as an exception to this rule; however, it was not intended as a deduction for consumption expenses, but rather as a deduction for expenses incurred in the production of income (that is, paid employment). R. GOODE, *supra* note 3, at 156. The credit is available "only if such expenses are incurred to enable the taxpayer to be gainfully employed." I.R.C. § 44A (c)(2)(A).

57. Imputed services might be recognized as a source of income under a "comprehensive income tax," a proposed reform that has received much support in recent years. BLUEPRINTS, *supra* note 23, at 1-3; COMPREHENSIVE INCOME TAXATION vii-viii (J. Pechman ed. 1977). Comprehensive income taxation involves broadening the definition of income and taxing all income alike. The Haig-Simons definition is the one most favored by specialists; it defines personal income as the market value of consumption enjoyed during the year plus the net change in savings. Goode, *The Economic Definition of Income*, in COMPREHENSIVE INCOME TAXATION, *supra*, at 7-8; McIntyre & Oldman, *Taxation of the Family in a Comprehensive and Simplified Income Tax*, 90 HARV. L. REV. 1575 (1977). Under an ideal comprehensive tax system, the imputed income from leisure and services the taxpayer performs for himself would be included in the definition of "market value of consumption" and included in taxable income. One-earner couples would therefore pay more tax than two-earner couples with the same income because a nonworking spouse enjoys more free time for leisure and self-performed services. *Id.* at 1608. Supporters of comprehensive taxation usually reject the taxation of imputed income, however, because of the administrative difficulties. *See* note 58 *infra*. Use of a comprehensive tax base might also justify the "double taxation" of cash income transferred from a greater-earning to a lesser-earning spouse. Some have suggested this treatment for gifts and inheritances, BLUEPRINTS, *supra* note 23, at 48; Goode, *supra*, at 19-20. They argue that the beneficiary must be taxed because he clearly receives income in the form of greater consumption power, but that the donor should not be allowed a deduction because making the gift or transfer has presumably provided him satisfaction or some other element of quid pro quo, and hence is a form of consumption. *Id. But see* Goode, *supra*, at 19 (arguing under income pooling theory that family "sharing" should not be regarded as consumption); McIntyre, *supra* note 1, at 475 n.18 (rejecting double taxation of either shared income or gifts and inheritances, and recommending that such transfers be taxable to the beneficiary and deductible by the donor).

58. For a discussion of the difficulties of taxing imputed income, *see* McIntyre & Oldman, *supra* note 57, at 1607-24. Most commentators reject taxation of imputed income as infeasible. *See, e.g.*, BLUEPRINTS, *supra* note 23, at 7; B. BITTKER & L. STONE, *supra* note 3, at 84; R. GOODE, *supra* note 3, at 150-51; H. SIMON, PERSONAL INCOME TAXATION 53 (1938); Gerzog, *supra* note 4, at 34.

services are not usually recognized as sources of income, they should not be recognized as sources of income when a lesser-earning spouse provides them in exchange for cash income earned by the greater-earning spouse.

The implications of exchange theory consequently leave little justification for joint filing on grounds of horizontal equity, since the well-being of a married taxpayer depends more upon his personal income and the pattern of exchange he has established with his spouse than on the couple's joint income. Use of joint filing to deduct consumption expenditures and tax imputed income only when they result from exchanges between married taxpayers is inequitable and arbitrary; horizontal equity is served not by imposing such treatment on a few taxpayers, but by exempting all from it.[59] Mandatory separate filing is therefore preferable to joint filing on equity grounds.

---

59. Treatment of alimony payments under exchange theory may depend on how such payments are viewed. If alimony is regarded as an obligation between individuals that is created and enforced by a third party—the court—alimony payments should be taxable income to the recipient (who clearly recieves control and benefit of the income) and a deductible expense of the payor (whose loss can hardly be regarded as a voluntary consumption decision). This is the current approach. I.R.C. §§ 71, 215. Alternatively, if alimony is regarded as a means of redressing the spousal exchange inequities that lead to divorce, see p. 375 *supra*, it should be trated neither as income to the recipient nor as a deductible expense of the payor; the transfer would not have received such treatment had it taken place, as originally intended, within the marriage. The same reasoning applies if the expectation of alimony in the event of divorce was part of the marital "contract" the spouses implicitly agreed to before marriage, see p. 374 *supra*.

It seems more sensible, however, to regard alimony as an obligation created by a third party. Since alimony is awarded in less than 10% of all divorce cases, *see* Weitzman, *Legal Regulation of Marriage: Tradition and Change*, 62 CALIF. L. REV. 1186 (1974), it is hardly likely to be an implicit part of the maritial contract. Moreover, since alimony is usually awarded for the lifetime of either spouse or until remarriage of the recipient, Foster, *Alimony Awards, in* THE ECONOMICS OF DIVORCE 7 (American Bar Assoc. 1978), it is difficult to see how it might be characterized as a judicial "balancing" of existing inequities in interspousal exchange. In jurisdictions that have adopted "no-fault" divorce laws, however, alimony is sometimes made as an interim and limited award during a transition period, and the economic worth of the homemaker's contributions may be considered in determining the size of the award. *Id*. at 10-12. In such jurisdictions, judicial balancing of inequitable interspousal exchange may be an accurate characterization of alimony.

C. TAXATION OF DEPENDENT CHILDREN

MARTIN J. McMAHON, JR., "EXPANDING THE TAXABLE UNIT: THE AGGREGATION OF THE INCOME OF CHILDREN AND PARENTS"

56 New York University Law Review 60 (1981), pp. 64-8, 71, 77-9, 80-93.

II

INCOME SHIFTING AND THE PROGRESSIVE TAX

Many reasons and justifications for progressive taxation have been advanced: that progression aids in maintaining economic stability; that taxes should be levied in proportion to the benefits received, which rise more rapidly than income; that progressive taxation equalizes the sacrifice made by each taxpayer; that taxes should be levied in relation to ability to pay, which rises faster than income; and that progression reduces socioeconomic inequality.[21] Blum and Kalven

---

[21] See generally W. Blum & H. Kalven, supra note 2. Professor Sneed has identified as the seven principal purposes which have shaped the progressive structure of our income tax,

  (1) to supply *adequate* revenue, (2) to achieve a *practical* and workable income tax system, (3) to impose *equal* taxes on those who enjoy equal incomes, (4) to assist in achieving economic *stability*, (5) *to reduce economic inequality*, (6) to avoid impairment of the operation of the *market-oriented economy*, and (7) to accomplish a high degree of harmony between the income tax and the sought-for *political order*.

Sneed, The Criteria of Federal Income Tax Policy, 17 Stan. L. Rev. 567, 568 (1965) (emphasis in original). For other compilations of the purposes to be served by the income tax, see H. Groves, Postwar Taxation and Economic Progress 373-74 (1946); Heller, Some Observations on the Role and Reform of Federal Income Tax, in 1 Tax Revision Compendium, supra note 2, at 181, 182-83.

5)ze thoroughly the logical basis for each of these theories, and ʒed on their analysis, one can conclude that the strongest justification for a progressively graduated income tax is the reduction of socioeconomic inequality.[22]

The present pattern of taxation, however, discriminates in favor of families that derive some portion of their income from property. The parents in such a family can, through numerous devices, transfer income to their children prior to its inclusion in the tax base. In many, if not most, instances the primary purpose of the income shifting arrangement is the reduction of taxes. Even if they had been unable to shift the incidence of the tax, the parents would have conferred on the children all or a substantial part of the benefit of the after tax income. The ability to shift the tax burden to the children, taking advantage of their lower marginal tax rates, allows the parents to confer a greater benefit on the children for the same after tax cost than they could have in the absence of income shifting. If one assumes that at least the majority of income producing property is owned by those in upper socioeconomic classes, then the ability to reduce taxes by transferring ownership of property is inimical to the purpose of the progressive tax system—the reduction of socioeconomic inequality. Moreover, the case for the elimination of income shifting is not solely dependent on this justification for progressive taxation. Other bases on which progressively graduated taxation has been justified—that sacrifice should be equalized and that those with greater income have greater ability to pay—lead to the same conclusion.[23]

These principles are encompassed in the concept of equity, described in this context as horizontal equity—"those who are equal in

---

[22] W. Blum & H. Kalven, supra note 2; see Sneed, supra note 21, at 581-84, 582 n.58. But see R. Goode, The Individual Income Tax 17-21 (rev. ed. 1976). It may even have come to pass that justification for progressive taxation is no longer necessary and is merely academic:

> The justifications for progressive taxation do not lie in the esoteric theories often used to support it. The relative marginal value of a dollar to the poor man and to the rich man is not the basis for progressive taxation. Its real merits lie in its suitability for maintaining and extending the necessary conditions for democracy—the broad sharing of all a society's values, the stimulation of the most equitable and so, ultimately, the most healthy economic pattern and the avoidance of great extremes of wealth and poverty, or an undemocratic degree of concentration of wealth and power.

Lanning, Some Realities of Tax Reform, in 1 Tax Revision Compendium, supra note 2, at 19, 23. This comes close to saying that progressive taxation simply strikes our society, collectively, as fairer than nonprogressive taxation. As such it appears more as an end than a means to an end. However, progressive taxation as an end is merely an alternative statement of a desire to redistribute wealth.

[23] The discussion in this section, when based upon an ability-to-pay or equal-sacrifice rationale, requires the assumption of pooling. The consequences of relaxing this assumption are explored in the text accompanying notes 90-113 infra.

the relevant aspects should bear equal [tax] burdens,"[24] — and vertical equity—those who are not equal should not be treated equally,[25] *viz.*, at a minimum those with greater incomes should pay a greater amount of tax.[26] Identification of the persons whose positions are to be compared is essential to determining whether these principles of equity have been satisfied. Should comparisons be made solely between individuals, regardless of their family status, or should comparisons be made between family units?

To argue that the relevant comparison is between individuals is not necessarily inconsistent with the theory of progressive taxation in some contexts. An argument can be made that each individual should be taxed on his own personal material consumption plus savings.[27] Under such a system any unit broader than an individual would be inconsistent with the underlying theory. But the definition of income on which such a system is based differs from the definition of income under our present income tax system. Under such a structure emphasis is placed on the identity of the person expending money for satisfactions rather than on the identity of the person causing the flow of money with which these satisfactions are obtained.[28]

For many years the income tax looked solely to the individual as the taxable unit. The crucial issue was choice of the proper individual unit. Income shifting transactions were struck down, not on the basis that they distorted the unit, but because they lacked economic reality[29] or a business purpose,[30] or that they were merely assignments of

---

[24] Sneed, supra note 21, at 574. The "relevant aspects" here are ability to pay and sacrifice.

[25] Id. at 577.

[26] The principles of vertical and horizontal equity do not necessarily require a graduated progressive income tax. These standards can and will be met by a proportional income tax. Under a proportional income tax, all other things being equal, if two taxpayers have equal incomes they will pay equal taxes. If two taxpayers have different incomes the taxpayer with the greater income will pay a greater amount of taxes, although he will pay the same proportion of his income in taxes. If, however, one's view of different treatment for those in different positions requires, either dogmatically or logically, that those with greater income pay proportionately greater taxes, then vertical equity is not achieved in a proportionate tax system.

[27] This view and alternative administrative methods of implementing the theory are advanced in McIntyre & Oldman, Taxation of the Family in a Comprehensive and Simplified Income Tax, 90 Harv. L. Rev. 1573 *passim* (1977). Also see Bittker, A "Comprehensive Tax" Base as a Goal of Tax Reform, 80 Harv. L. Rev. 925, 932 (1967).

[28] For a summary of the competing theories of income: the consumption and net accretion approaches, see Sneed, supra note 21, at 577-78. Income has been selected as the tax base out of a conviction that "it accords best with ability to pay." R. Goode, supra note 22, at 11. The selection of income as the tax base and the choice of a progressive structure are separate issues. W. Blum & H. Kalven, supra note 2, at xvii.

[29] E.g., Mathews v. Commissioner, 520 F.2d 323, 325 (5th Cir. 1975), cert. denied, 424 U.S. 967 (1976).

[30] Perry v. United States, 520 F.2d 235, 238 (4th Cir. 1975), cert. denied, 423 U.S. 1052 (1976); Van Zandt v. Commissioner, 341 F.2d 440, 443-44 (5th Cir.), cert. denied, 382 U.S. 814 (1965).

income.[31] Since 1969, however, spouses have effectively been treated as a single unit for the purpose of computing taxable income.[32] Thus our system is not in fact based solely upon the individual economic unit, but considers familial relationships as an element of determining the taxable unit. With the exception of a special exception for limited amounts of earned income, the tax burden of different married couples should be, and is under current law, equal if the couples have equal income and unequal if the couples have differing incomes notwithstanding any difference in the distribution of income between the respective spouses.[33] The joint return provisions negate the effect of a

---

[31] E.g., White v. Fitzpatrick, 193 F.2d 398, 402 (2d Cir. 1951), cert. denied, 343 U.S. 928 (1952).

[32] Tax Reform Act of 1969, Pub. L. No. 91-172, § 803, 83 Stat. 487 (now I.R.C. § 1); see R. Goode, supra note 22, at 228-31; McIntyre & Oldman, supra note 27, at 1573-84. See also Commission to Revise the Tax Structure, Reforming the Federal Tax Structure 12 (1973) [hereinafter Reforming the Federal Tax Structure]. The income splitting provisions originally enacted in the Revenue Act of 1948, ch. 168, § 301, 62 Stat. 110 (amending Int. Rev. Code of 1939), have since been replaced by the separate rate schedules for married taxpayers and single taxpayers provided by I.R.C. § 1(a), (c), (d). The original reason for the joint return income splitting provisions was keyed more to the desire to equalize the treatment of married taxpayers in community property states and common law states than to equalize the treatment of different married taxpayers in either type of state having the same combined income but a different distribution between the spouses. Since income in a common law state was, under Lucas v. Earl, 281 U.S. 111 (1930), taxed to the wage earner, the tax liability for married taxpayers having identical total incomes but different intrafamilial distributions would differ. See Bittker, Federal Income Taxation and the Family, 27 Stan. L. Rev. 1389, 1404 (1975)[hereinafter Bittker, Taxation]. However, in community property states, the earnings of the couple were taxed as though earned half by each spouse. Id. at 1404-05. Thus the tax liability of two similarly situated couples, one in a common law state and one in a community property state, differed. See H.R. Rep. No. 1274, 80th Cong., 2d Sess. (1948), reprinted in 1948-1 C.B. 241, 257-60, 279-83; S. Rep. No. 1013, 80th Cong., 2d Sess. (1948), reprinted in 1948-1 C.B. 285, 301-03, 326-30. See generally Bittker, Taxation, supra, at 1412-14.

[33] From 1948 through 1980, Congress rejected any variance in the tax burden on the basis of differing proportions which the spouses contribute to aggregate family income. See note 32 supra.

Equal taxation of married couples regardless of the relative proportions in which they actually receive earned income has not been universally accepted as appropriate. The literature abounds with discussions of the possible or asserted inequity of taxing two-earner couples on the same basis as one-earner couples. Among the proposals for varied treatment are permissible separate returns at single's rates, a deduction equal to some percentage of the earned income of one of the spouses, and an earned income credit. See, e.g., H. Groves, Federal Tax Treatment of the Family 80-81 (1963); Bittker, Taxation, supra note 32, at 1431-43; Nussbaum, The Tax Structure and Discrimination Against Working Wives, 25 Nat'l Tax J. 183, 191 (1972); Richards, Discrimination Against Married Couples Under Present Income Tax Laws, 49 Taxes 526, 530-34 (1971); White, The Tax Structure and Discrimination Against Working Wives, 26 Nat'l Tax J. 119, 121 (1973). As a result in 1981, Congress enacted § 221, allowing a deduction on joint returns equal to 10% of the first $30,000 of earned income of the spouse with the lesser amount of earned income. Economic Recovery Tax Act of 1981, Pub. L. No. 97-34, § 103, —Stat.— (now I.R.C. § 221). See also Hearings on Tax Treatment of Single and Married Persons Where Both Spouses are Working Before the House Comm. on Ways and Means, 92d Cong., 2d Sess. (1972).

successful device to shift income from one spouse to the other. However, successful income shifting techniques will reduce the family's total tax burden if the income is shifted to a child, even if he is a dependent minor. Although currently permitted, this result is unjustifiable from a policy viewpoint because it gives rise to both vertical and horizontal inequities.

* * *

B. Closing the Loopholes

Intrafamilial income shifting arguably could be ended if Congress were to enact specific provisions to eliminate each tax avoidance scheme. Unfortunately, this method of dealing with tax avoidance often creates as many tax avoidance possibilities as it eliminates. One commentator described this phenomenon in the following manner: "Taxes and tax avoidance were probably born twins and are likely to continue their joint existence until the millenium of a taxless world. Avoidance is hydra-headed and, as the tax gatherers, aided by the Supreme Court, discover and cut off one escape contrivance, the taxpayer rears up another."

* * *

C. Statutory Anti-Tax Avoidance Provisions

Another possible method of eliminating the inequities created by intrafamilial income shifting is to enact a general anti-tax avoidance provision in the Internal Revenue Code. Such a provision would invalidate, for tax purposes, intrafamilial transactions the purpose of which is to avoid taxes by shifting income.[60] Both Australia and New Zealand have catchall tax avoidance provisions in their income tax statutes that render void, for tax purposes, any contract, agreement, plan, or arrangement having a tax avoidance purpose.[61] Both provi-

---

[60] The provision might be akin to I.R.C. § 269:
    a) If

        (1) any person or persons acquire, or acquired on or after October 8, 1940, directly or indirectly, control of a corporation, or

        (2) any corporation acquires, or acquired on or after October 8, 1940, directly or indirectly, property of another corporation, not controlled, directly or indirectly, immediately before such acquisition, by such acquiring corporation or its stockholders, the basis of which property, in the hands of the acquiring corporation, is determined by reference to the basis in the hands of the transferor corporation,

and the principal purpose for which such acquisition was made is evasion or avoidance of Federal income tax by securing the benefit of a deduction, credit, or other allowance which such person or corporation would not otherwise enjoy, then the Secretary may disallow such deduction, credit, or other allowance. For purposes of paragraphs (1) and (2), control means the ownership of stock possessing at least 50 percent of the total combined voting power of all classes of stock entitled to vote or at least 50 percent of the total value of shares of all classes of stock of the corporation.

[61] The Australian statute provides:

Every contract, agreement, or arrangement made or entered into, orally or in writing, whether before or after the commencement of this Act, shall so far as it has or purports to have the purpose or effect of in any way, directly or indirectly—

    (a) altering the incidence of any income tax;
    (b) relieving any person from liability to pay any income tax or make any return;
    (c) defeating, evading or avoiding any duty or liability imposed on any person by this Act; or
    (d) preventing the operation of this Act in any respect,

be absolutely void, as against the Commissioner, or in regard to any proceeding under this Act, but without prejudice to such validity as it may have in any other respect or for any other purpose.

Income Tax Assessment Act, § 260, 6 Acts of Australian Parliament 1901-1973, at 669 (1975).

In Newton v. Commissioner of Taxation, [1958] 2 All E.R. 759, 764, the court stated that § 260 was not applicable absent a purpose to avoid taxes. Such a purpose is to be found in objective facts, rather than in the taxpayer's motives. See generally Trebilcock, Section 260: A Critical Examination, 38 Austl. L.J. 237, 241-43 (1964).

New Zealand has a statute of similar import. Income Tax Act 1976, § 99, [1976] 2 New Zealand Statutes 1026-28, as amended by 2 New Zealand Statutes, Act No. 81 (1977).

sions, but more particularly the Australian statute, appear to have been only moderately successful as devices to stem income splitting arrangements, permitting certain tax avoidance schemes in which the transaction has some non-tax avoidance purpose.[62] The difficulties inherent in using the taxpayer's purpose in entering into the transaction as a basis for recognizing or voiding a transaction for tax purposes has been a major factor in that limitation.[63] Catchall provisions have also been criticized on the grounds that by their very nature they provide for the taxation of transactions that are not taxable according to the letter of the tax law, thus attributing to the legislature a purpose not found in the words of the statute.[64]

The use of motive or purpose as a test to determine the tax treatment of a particular transaction is inappropriate when dealing with the issue of income splitting among family members. The principle of proscribing the splitting of income among family members is

---

[62] For example, the Australian provision has been expressly held inapplicable where the Commissioner attempted to disallow the payor's deductions for items purchased from a related taxpayer at an inflated price. Cecil Bros. Pty. v. Commissioner of Taxation, 111 C.L.R. 430, 438-42 (Austl. 1964). Where income producing property was transferred by a taxpayer to himself in trust for the benefit of members of his immediate family, the predecessor of § 260 was held inapplicable, Purcell's Case 29 C.L.R. 464, 473-74 (Austl. 1921). Commentators have split on the applicability of § 260 to the service company or service trust, the Australian equivalent of the gift and leaseback income shifting scheme currently in vogue in the United States. Compare Pose, The Deductability by Professionals to Their Service Trusts and the Impact of Europa Oil (N.Z.) Ltd. (No. 2) v. The Comm'r of Inland Revenue (N.Z.), 51 Austl. L.J. 15, 22-27 (1977) with Cullinan, Latest Developments in Tax Planning, 49 Austl. L.J. 353, 355-56 (1975). Where, however, there is a clear attempt to assign income, the scheme will be defeated. Peate v. Commissioner of Taxation, 111 C.L.R. 443, 461 (Austl. 1964) (physician's transfer of share in medical partnership to a family company is void as against the Commissioner).

Section 99 of the New Zealand Income Tax Act has apparently been more useful in striking down "service companies." See Cullinan, supra, at 355-56 (citing Wisheart v. Commissioner of Inland Revenue, 71 A.T.C. 6001 (N.Z. 1971), as disallowing in part deductions by partnership of solicitors for amounts paid for rental of equipment and staff services to a service company of which family trusts of the partners were beneficiaries). However, where tax avoidance is not the sole purpose, such deductions have been allowed. See id. at 356 & n.16 (citing Loader v. Commissioner of Inland Revenue, 74 A.T.C. 6014 (N.Z. 1974), as allowing a deduction on similar facts based on a finding of the existence of non-tax-avoidance purposes that the sole purpose was not tax avoidance).

[63] Such a test has been criticized as a judicial standard, see Gunn, Tax Avoidance, 76 Mich. L. Rev. 733, 756-58 (1978), and as a statutory standard, see Cohen, Tax Avoidance Purpose as a Statutory Test in Tax Legislation, 9 Tul. Tax Inst. 229 passim (1960), for various reasons. For a general discussion of motive and purpose in the taxation context, see Blum, Motive, Intent and Purpose in Federal Income Taxation, 34 U. Chi. L. Rev. 485 (1967).

[64] See Trebilcock, supra note 61, at 240-41. For example, the Income Tax Assessment Act provides for the imposition of tax on those who "derive" income from property. Id. at 240. Yet in some cases courts have held taxpayers who transferred income-producing assets to be liable for taxes thereon even though they no longer derive the income, id., a result outside the letter of the law. Thus the legislature is assumed to have intended what it did not say.

not grounded on any notion that income splitting is morally or legally wrong, but rather on the ground that considerations of both horizontal and vertical equity require that the income of a family unit should be viewed as a whole for purposes of taxation, without regard to the reason, purpose, or intent behind the arrangement of the affairs of the family members which resulted in the particular distribution of income among them.[65] Thus, even those intrafamilial income splitting transactions that do not have a tax avoidance purpose would violate the fundamental principles of fairness necessary in a progressive tax structure. Since a motive test would permit such transactions, it is inadequate.

* * *

III

AGGREGATION OF FAMILY INCOME

Even if these obstacles to successful anti-tax avoidance statutes could be overcome, and income shifting substantially eliminated, inequities would remain. Families with equal incomes, but with initially unequal intrafamilial income distribution between parents and children, would be taxed unequally, thus violating the principle of horizontal equity. For example, assume that Families A and B earn $20,000 per annum, and that while all of Family A's income is earned by the parents, $5000 of Family B's income is earned by a child. Because the child's income in Family B would be taxed at lower rates than the final $5000 of Family A's income, Family B will pay less tax than Family A. Assuming that Family B pools its income, and that the justification for the progressive tax is either ability to pay or equal sacrifice, a horizontal inequity is present that would not be eliminated by the elimination of income shifting.[74] Furthermore, if Family *B's* children's income increases to $7000, a vertical inequity will occur, since the incremental $2000 will not be taxed at a higher rate than Family *A's* marginal rate.[75] Total aggregation of income at the family level would, however, eliminate the inequities created both by income shifting and by initially unequal intrafamilial income distributions, since income shifting or initially unequal distributions would not affect the family's tax burden.[76] In addition, a redefinition of the

---

[74] This, of course, requires the assumption, which is made for purposes of this Article, that the progressive income tax is a desirable system of taxation and that this country is committed to the implementation of such a tax. The argument may be made that although we have a statutory progressive rate, taxes are in fact only nominally progressive due to the numerous exclusions of income items from the tax base and to the multitudinous methods that taxpayers with high incomes use to escape the high rates. See generally W. Blum & H. Kalven, supra note 2, regarding the arguments for and against progressive taxation.

[75] Compare I.R.C. § 1(a) with I.R.C. § 1(c).

[76] As a single proposition, the proposal that the income of children be aggregated with that of their parents for computing income tax liability is not new. The idea was raised as early as 1932 and has been discussed on several occasions since then. For example, Bruton, Surrey, Thorson, and Groves all mention the issue briefly. See H. Groves, Federal Tax Treatment of the Family 70 (1963); Bruton, supra note 4, at 1192; Surrey, Family Income and Federal Taxation, 24 Taxes 980, 986 (1946) [hereinafter Surrey, Family Income]; Thorson, supra note 39, at 117-18. R. Goode, supra note 22, at 231-34, provides a more extensive comment on the rationale for aggregating minor children's income and on occasion the income of "older children and other family members," but concludes:

> It does not seem feasible, however, to work out an acceptable set of rules for aggregation of all family income. Property arrangements and family practices differ so greatly that attempts to carry out aggregation would be likely to be meddlesome and arbitrary. This would be true even if aggregation were limited to parents and minor children.

Id. at 233-34.

The Commission to Revise the Federal Tax Structure, sponsored by the Fund for Public Policy Research, recommended that minor children be included with their parents as a single tax unit. Reforming the Federal Tax Structure, supra note 32, at 19. That proposal would exclude from income $500 of a child's earned income. Id.

The most thorough discussion of the issue, including alternatives for implementation, appears in Tax Treatment of Family Income, supra note 38, at 861-63. A mandatory filing unit consisting of both the husband and wife (or survivor) and minor and certain other dependent children was also proposed in U.S. Dep't of the Treasury, Blueprints for Basic Tax Reform 103-04 (1977). Also see 1 S. Surrey, W. Warren, P. McDaniel & H. Ault, Federal Income Taxation 1283-84 (1972); Bittker, Taxation, supra note 32, at 1392-95.

The Canadian Royal Commission on Taxation suggested aggregation within the family unit for Canada. 3 Report of the Royal Commission on Taxation 117-51 (1966) (Canada) (this Commission is known as both the Royal Commission and the Carter Commission). That suggestion would have totally restructured income, estate, and gift taxation of the family and would have resulted in total nonrecognition for tax purposes of transfers from parents to children as well as total integration of income subject to detailed technical exceptions. See generally Bittker, Income Tax Reform in Canada: The Report of the Royal Commission on Taxation, 35 U. Chi. L. Rev. 637, 645-50 (1968) [hereinafter Bittker, Income Tax Reform in Canada]; Comment, Tax Treatment of the Family: The Canadian Royal Commission on Taxation and the Internal Revenue Code, 117 U. Pa. L. Rev. 98, 100-05 (1968). Nearly all of the suggestions that children's income be aggregated with that of their parents, however, are in the context of proposals for

taxable unit could bring about an end to tax avoidance through intrafamilial income shifting devices without the need for technical and complex legislation designed to attack income shifting on a transaction-by-transaction basis.[77] The broader unit would also reduce the complexities, so often decried by taxpayers, that arise from families' abilities to split income and the diligent efforts of taxpayers to do so.[78]

The problem of aggregation of children's income with their parents' income is not totally unknown to Congress. In 1944 Congress amended section 22(m), the predecessor of I.R.C. § 73, to affirmatively reject aggregation of children's earned income with their parents' income.[79] Prior to this amendment, parents were taxable on

---

mandatory joint returns for spouses. See, e.g., Bruton, supra, at 1192; U.S. Dep't of the Treasury, Blueprints for Basic Tax Reform 103-04 (1977). Indeed, it has been suggested that joint returns are a prerequisite to aggregation. Davies, The Shifting of Family Income for Income Tax Purposes, 6 St. Louis U.L.J. 281, 366 (1960).

Concededly, theoretical purity may require the mandatory aggregation of married taxpayers' income as a logical corollary of aggregating the income of children with that of their parents, but aggregation does not require mandatory joint returns. Aggregation of income and mandatory joint returns are separate issues. Indeed, the mechanics of aggregation in the context of married persons filing separate returns is discussed in the text accompanying notes 281-86 infra. The current relationship of the brackets and rates of the schedule for married taxpayers filing singly and those filing jointly, under which a married taxpayer filing singly is subject to the same marginal rate as a married taxpayer filing jointly with exactly double the taxable income, achieves effective aggregation without mandatory joint returns. Compare I.R.C. § 1(a) with I.R.C. § 1(d). See also Pechman, Income Splitting, in 1 Tax Revision Compendium, supra note 2, at 473, 475-79 (explaining the relationship between income splitting, aggregation, and the width of brackets, by which effective aggregation can be maintained notwithstanding the filing of separate returns).

[77] Cf. S. Rep. No. 1013, 80th Cong., 2d Sess., reprinted in 1948-1 C.B. 285, 301-03. In discussing the effect that the implementation of joint returns between husband and wife would have on income shifting devices then in use, the Senate Committee on Finance reported:

> The incentive for married couples in common law states to attempt the reduction of their taxes by the division of their income through such devices as trust, joint tenancies, and family partnerships will be reduced materially. Administrative difficulties stemming from the use of such devices will be diminished and there will be less need for meticulous legislation on the income tax treatment of trusts and family partnerships.

The 1948 legislation authorized interspousal income splitting and thus obviated the need to resort to interspousal income shifting devices. See Revenue Act of 1948, ch. 168, §§ 301-303, 62 Stat. 110, (now I.R.C. §§ 1(a), 1(d)).

[78] See, e.g., Lanning, Some Realities of Tax Reform, in 1 Tax Revision Compendium, supra note 2, at 19, 54-55; Surrey, Complexity and the Internal Revenue Code: The Problem of the Management of Tax Detail, 34 Law & Contemp. Probs. 673 (1969). In regard to this problem the Committee on Tax Policy of the New York Bar Association has suggested that the complexity of the Code is undermining the voluntary compliance system upon which the administration of the tax laws is based, and rendering the tax laws substantially unenforceable. A Report on Complexity and the Income Tax, 27 Tax L. Rev. 325, 329-30 (1972).

[79] Individual Income Tax Act of 1944, ch. 210, § 7, 58 Stat. 231 (now I.R.C. § 73). I.R.C. § 73 provides, "Amounts received in respect of the services of a child shall be included in his gross income and not in the gross income of the parent, even though such amounts are not received by the child."

their child's earned income if under state law they had the legal rights to that income.[80] Under the laws of the overwhelming majority of states, the parents were entitled to the earnings of their children.[81] Nevertheless, for the ostensible purpose of achieving nationwide uniformity, Congress amended section 22(m), granting children separate taxpayer status with respect to their earned income.[82] The amendment of section 22(m), however, does not indicate that Congress has considered and rejected the principles upon which aggregation of children's income is based. At the time of the amendment of section 22(m), spouses filed separate returns on the same basis as unmarried individuals.[83] The joint return provisions effectively aggregating spouses' income postdate the amendment of section 22(m),[84] and Congress simply failed to reconsider the taxation of children's income. The following sections of the Article illustrate that the principles upon which progressive taxation and joint returns for spouses are based require the aggregation of children's income with that of their parents.

---

[80] Treas. Reg. 103, § 19.51-3 (1941), provided that income derived from property was taxable to the minor child. But with respect to earned income the Regulations provided:
> If under the laws of a State the earnings of a minor belong to the minor, such earnings, regardless of amount are not required to be included in the return of the parent. In the absence of proof to the contrary, a parent will be assumed to have the legal right to the earnings of the minor and must include them in his return.

H. R. Rep. No. 1365, 78th Cong., 2d Sess., reprinted in 1944 C.B. 821, 837-38; see 4 C. Vernier, American Family Laws § 232 (1936).

[81] H. R. Rep. No. 1365, 78th Cong., 2d Sess., reprinted in 1944 C.B. 821, 837-38; see 4 C. Vernier, American Family Laws § 232 (1936). Prior to 1944 the Commissioner had issued a specific ruling as to the proper taxpayer for a minor's earned income only with respect to Louisiana. The Commissioner held that the parent should not include earned income of a minor child on his return since under Louisiana law earned income belonged solely to the child. S.M. 2045, III-1 C.B. 231 (1924).

[82] The stated purpose of the amendment to § 22(m) was to bring about uniformity of tax treatment of taxpayers in the several states, H.R. Rep. No. 1365, 78th Cong., 2d Sess., reprinted in 1944 C.B. 821, 837-38. Congress, however, conformed federal tax law to the property rights to the minority of states rather than to the majority. See text accompanying notes 80-82 supra. In light of the substantial uniformity of rights under state law and the generally applied rule of taxing transactions according to rights established and determined under state law, one can easily speculate that there existed an unstated intent to relieve parents from taxation of that portion of their children's incomes to which the parents had a legal right. If so, the amendment of § 22(m) may be another example of the institutionalization of permissible income splitting.

[83] Section 73 was enacted in 1944. See text accompanying note 79 supra. The joint return provisions were not enacted until four years later. See Revenue Act of 1948, ch. 168, §§ 301-303, 62 Stat. 110 (now I.R.C. §§ 1(a), 1(d)).

[84] Effective aggregation was implemented in 1969. See Tax Reform Act of 1969, Pub. L. No. 91-172, § 803, 83 Stat. 487 (now I.R.C. § 1); McIntyre & Oldman, supra note 27, at 1584.

A. Aggregation and Socioeconomic Inequality

Most tax theorists today agree that economic power and economic well being are generally determined on the family unit level, not on the individual level.[85] This is obviously true when income is pooled.[86] The argument in favor of total aggregation of the income of minor children with that of their parents has previously been based upon the theory that there is a joint pooling and budgeting of income. In its 1947 study, "The Tax Treatment of Family Income," the Treasury Department described the basis for aggregation as follows:

> It should be noted, however, that the case for the equal tax treatment of families (including minor children) [having equal incomes and exemptions] hinges on validity of the proposition that the income of the entire family including that of minor children, is pooled and shared by all the family: that the family is in effect a tightly knit economic entity providing a better unit for gauging taxpaying ability than its several members individually. This goes beyond technical economic considerations to the core of the sociological problems involved in the institution of the family and the home.[87]

Under the theory thus stated, the validity of aggregation depends heavily on the extent to which the income of children is pooled with that of their parents. If it is not in fact pooled, the case for aggregation is weakened. If such pooling does occur, the case for aggregation rests on the extent of pooling.

Other proponents of aggregation, including the Commission to Revise the Federal Tax Structure and the Carter Commission, have not required as extensive *actual* pooling as the Treasury study seems to

---

[85] See, e.g., H. Groves, Federal Tax Treatment of the Family 62, 70 (1963); 3 Report of the Royal Commission on Taxation 123-24 (1966) (Canada); Thorson, supra note 39, at 116. But see Glendon, Modern Marriage Law and Its Underlying Assumptions: The New Marriage and the New Property, 13 Fam. L.Q. 441, 455 (1980). The view that economic well-being is determined on the family level rather than on the individual level is also shared by social economists and social scientists. See Layard & Zabalza, Family Income Distribution: Explanation and Policy Evaluation, 87 J. Pol. Econ. S133, S133 (1979); Treas & Walter, Family Structure and Distribution of Family Income, 56 Soc. Forces 866, 866 (1978).

[86] Reforming the Federal Tax Structure, supra note 32, at 19. It is generally accepted, however, that the income of children, other than in the lower socioeconomic classes, is not actually pooled to the same extent as income between spouses and that families account for the income of children separately. See Bittker, Taxation, supra note 32, at 1394. However, children of middle and higher income families may relieve other family members of burdens by supplying their own clothes, entertainment, and other support obligations. See text accompanying notes 88-89 and note 88 infra.

[87] Tax Treatment of Family Income, supra note 38, at 862.

suggest is necessary. They have justified aggregation on the basis that the use of a child's income to meet his own consumption or savings needs and desires enhances the family's economic power or power to consume, and that, therefore, the income of the child should be taxed at the family's marginal rate.[88] Although there is not a complete pooling, the very existence of the children's income gives rise to an effective pooling by relieving the parents in whole or in part of the obligation to provide for the child.[89]

There is, however, some thought that pooling of income between parents and children is not as extensive as the pooling between spouses upon which joint returns are theoretically based.[90] Furthermore, there is little agreement on the extent of such pooling.[91] There are indeed many factual distinctions which may be drawn between different families. Some parents have less control over the use of a child's income than do other parents.[92] Some parents require that their children use their own income for necessities while others do not.[93]

---

[88] Total aggregation was advocated in 1963 by the Commission to Revise the Federal Tax Structure, sponsored by the Fund for Public Policy Research. In its Report, the Commission generally described the rationale underlying aggregation:

> Although arguments can be made for the exclusion of dependent children's income from the family unit, in most cases such income is taken into account in family decision making. In low-income families and families living on a farm, children are expected to make contributions to the general support of the family. In the middle and higher income families, children's income is often expected to meet part of the education, clothing and entertainment expenses. In all of these cases, the children's income enhances the family's power to consume and should be taxed to the family.

Reforming the Federal Tax Structure, supra note 32, at 19. A similar rationale was advanced by the Carter Commission:

> In low income families the children are often expected to make a contribution to the general support of the family; in well-to-do families the child with income is often expected to buy such things as clothing and entertainment. These expenditures would otherwise have to be made, at least in part, by the parents. In either case the income of the child increases the economic power of the family and should be taxed at the marginal rate of the family.

3 Report of the Royal Commission on Taxation 131 (1966) (Canada).

[89] Reforming the Federal Tax Structure, supra note 32, at 19; H. Groves, Federal Tax Treatment of the Family 34 (1963); Bittker, Taxation, supra note 32, at 1397. See also McIntyre & Oldman, supra note 27, at 1604.

[90] Thorson, supra note 39, at 116.

[91] Indeed, Richard Goode suggested that "it does not seem feasible, however, to work out an acceptable set of rules for aggregation of all family income. Property arrangements and family practices differ so greatly that attempts to carry out aggregation would be likely to be meddlesome and arbitrary." R. Goode, supra note 22, at 233. A similar point was made by Treas & Walter, Family Structure and the Distribution of Family Income, 56 Soc. Forces 866, 878-79 (1978), who note the inability of social scientists to construct a quantitative model of family income pooling. But see Smith, The Distribution of Family Earnings, 82 J. Pol. Econ. S163, S179-86 (1979) (analysis limited to family consisting only of spouses).

[92] See R. Goode, supra note 22, at 233.

[93] Reforming the Federal Tax Structure, supra note 32, at 19.

The ratio between the amount of parents' incomes and the amount of children's incomes used for the provision of luxuries may differ from family to family. In some families a child is expected to expend his own income for educational expenses before receiving assistance from his parents while in others he is not.[94] In some families a child's income may be so great that he takes accumulations with him upon leaving the family unit.

If one accepts the proposition that the primary justification for graduated progressive taxation is that it tends to reduce socioeconomic inequality, the case for aggregation is unaffected by the absence of complete pooling. The unit against which socioeconomic status is measured should be the unit selected for computation of the income tax, and the unit by which socioeconomic status is measured is generally accepted to be the family unit.[95] Despite these differences between particular families, there seems to be frequent agreement that a child's income "enhances the family's power to consume."[96] The basis for aggregation, which subjects a child's income to higher rates of tax, then, is that the socioeconomic advantage of the child is to be mitigated. Since his socioeconomic advantage is derived not only from his own income but also from that of his parents, their income should be considered in determining the rate of tax on his income. Conversely, since the parents' socioeconomic power is derived not only from their own income but from their child's income, their tax should reflect his income. In such an analysis, whether or not income is pooled is irrelevant; the very existence of the income enhances the socioeconomic prestige and power of the family unit and thereby justifies aggregation.

B. Aggregation and Ability to Pay

If one justifies progressive income taxation on an ability-to-pay theory,[97] rather than on the reduction of socioeconomic inequality, whether there is actual or effective pooling acquires greater significance. It has been argued that "the family as a unit has no combined taxpaying ability per se; that its taxpaying ability is composed of the separate taxpaying abilities of its individual members; and that each of these is determined by the amount of income of which he or she is the owner without reference to the income of the other members of

---

[94] See id.

[95] See note 85 and accompanying text supra.

[96] Reforming the Federal Tax Structure, supra note 32, at 19; see U.S. Dep't of Treasury, Blueprints for Basic Tax Reform 103 (1977).

[97] See W. Blum & H. Kalven, supra note 2, at 64-68.

the family."[98] This argument presumes that families do not pool income to a significant extent.

That there is either actual pooling, where the child's income helps to provide for family expenses, or effective pooling, where the child's income relieves the parents of some or all of the expenditures that they would have made on the child's behalf were it not for his income, is difficult to deny.[99] However, it may well be that the assumption that there is complete pooling in all socioeconomic strata is not the most plausible one that can be made. It seems more likely that the following broad characterizations are closer approximations of reality. At the lower socioeconomic levels, actual pooling is probably common. In the middle strata a child's earned income probably relieves parents of some expenditures on behalf of a child, and this portion of the child's income is effectively pooled. If a child's income is sufficient, however, the child's consumption or savings, as he chooses, probably exceeds that which would be possible without his own income. This is particularly true for a child's earnings from his own services, which many families view as at least partially his own

---

[98] Tax Treatment of Family Income, supra note 38, at 851. Joint returns for spouses, requiring aggregation of incomes, are justified by the factual observation that spouses do indeed pool assets and incomes jointly and function as one economic unit, with some exceptions in the upper income levels. Thorson, supra note 39, at 116. This being so, considerations of horizontal equity require equal taxes for two different married couples with identical incomes, regardless of the proportional distribution of the income between respective spouses. See McIntyre, Individual Filing in the Personal Income Tax, Prolegomena to Future Discussion, 58 N.C.L. Rev. 469, 472-73 (1980).

[99] See Becker & Tomes, Child Endowments and the Quantity and Quality of Children, 84 J. Pol. Econ. S143 (1976), which discusses varying parental contributions to children within the family based on the "endowments" of the children. In the context of a price-benefit analysis, the authors state:

> If the cost of adding to quality [of all children] were the same, even when children differed in ability or other aspects of their endowment . . . differences in parental contributions would fully compensate for differences in endowments. In other words, *within* a family, the amount invested by parents in a child would be perfectly negatively correlated with the endowment of the child.
>
> The family would contribute to equality by redistributing to less endowed children and to parents some of the increased family wealth resulting from better endowments. This conclusion is essentially a special case of a general theorem in social interactions . . . namely, if a family "head" is voluntarily transferring some of his own resources to different members, a redistribution of endowed resources among members would induce the "head" to "tax" the entire gain of those gaining and compensate fully those losing.

Id. at S153. The authors then conclude that a price effect dominates in the parents' allocation of investment in human capital, thus causing greater relative investment in developing the human resources of the better endowed children. Id. at S154. To offset the further enhanced endowment of the children who started out with greater abilities, the parents make a compensating investment in the material well-being of the children with lesser income. Id. The effect of this is to reduce the inequality in the total income of each of the children relative to any inequality in their earnings. Id. at S155.

spending money, available to satisfy a child's desires over and above those for which the parents would provide.[100] At the upper socioeconomic levels a child's income may be less likely to be used to satisfy current wants. Rather, such income may be accumulated for college or for his use after completion of his education. Such accumulation relieves pressure on parents to provide funds for a college education or to assist their offspring in his posteducational start in the world and thus effectively is pooled. Moreover, to the extent that parents at the upper end of the scale can fully afford to satisfy a child's current needs and wants, whatever portion of the income he spends on those wants effects a virtually pro tanto reduction in parental contributions to the child, and effective pooling occurs. Thus the most plausible assumption that can be made is that there is complete pooling in the lower and perhaps upper socioeconomic classes but only partial pooling in the middle class.

Can these broad characterizations of pooling justify aggregation when analyzing the progressively graduated income tax on an ability-to-pay basis? It would appear that they can indeed justify aggregation at the lower levels and perhaps at the upper levels as well. In a family unit in which income of parents and their child is actually fully pooled, a family of two parents and one child having a given amount of income should bear the same taxes regardless of how the income is distributed between the parents on the one hand and the child on the other. In the upper classes, so long as the child's income does not exceed the amount which the parents would have otherwise provided, there is effectively full pooling and aggregation therefore is warranted.

More difficult questions arise in the middle strata and at the upper end if the child has income in excess of that which the parents would have otherwise provided. Both of these situations share a common thread—the child has some income that does not reduce his parents' contributions on a dollar-for-dollar basis. This has given rise to the criticism of aggregation on the ground that, "[a]lthough a minor child's income may increase the family's 'discretionary economic power' in some instances, self-imposed or even legal restrictions on the use of such income are not uncommon."[101] The thrust of this criticism is that there is only partial economic pooling. Aggregation

---

[100] See H. Groves, Federal Tax Treatment of the Family 70 (1963); Bittker, Income Tax Reform in Canada, supra note 76, at 647.

[101] Bittker, Income Tax Reform in Canada, supra note 76, at 647. See also Groves, Taxing the Family Unit: The Carter Commission's Proposals and U.S. Practice, 22 Nat'l Tax J. 109, 112-13 (1969).

may create horizontal inequities since families with identical family income but different intrafamilial distributions would pay the same amount of taxes despite having unequal abilities to pay. Self-imposed restraints as to the actual use of a child's income, however, are difficult to justify as a rationale against aggregation if as a general rule society as a whole treats children's income as available to the family or available to reduce parental payments to a child. To the extent a child is accorded freedom to use his income as he chooses without suffering any reduction in parental support, his ability to pay taxes on his income is maximized. The argument that aggregation overstates the parents' ability to pay is specious. It is within their power to maximize their ability by reducing parental support to the child. They have simply chosen not to do so. The voluntary decisions of particular families regarding the allocation of consumption within the family have no bearing on the ability of the family unit to pay taxes. Although it is generally recognized that wealthy spouses often voluntarily impose restrictions on the commingling of assets and income,[102] this does not excuse them from the effectively mandatory joint return rates.[103] The issue is not whether aggregation would not comport with family practice in individual cases but rather whether aggregation would comport with family practices more generally than not.[104]

Nor should legal restrictions on the use of a child's income stand as a barrier to aggregation.[105] Hesitancy to accept aggregation on the grounds that a parent may lack legal control or have restricted legal

---

[102] Thorson, supra note 39, at 116.

[103] See I.R.C. §§ 1(a), 1(d).

[104] An analogy might be drawn to the issue of constructive receipt of income. If a cash basis taxpayer is entitled to an item of income which "has been set apart for him, or otherwise made available so that he may draw upon it" then he will be treated as having received the item regardless of whether or not he in fact receives the item in the year in question. Treas. Reg. § 1.451-2(a). In applying this principle to the issue in the text, the question is whether families generally treat a child's income either as an amount that the family may draw upon for its support, or as an offset against the amounts the parents must supply for the support of the child. If this is the general view, the individual practices of some families not to so treat a child's income should not justify applying a general rule in conformity with the practice of the minority.

[105] Such legal restrictions on the use of a child's income derive from the father's obligation to support his minor children. See generally Annot., 121 A.L.R. 176, 177-78 (1939). Specifically, a father who has sufficient means has an obligation to support his child regardless of the extent of the child's property. Note, Federal Tax Aspects of the Obligation to Support, 74 Harv. L. Rev. 1191, 1192 (1961). Absent special circumstances, the father cannot draw on his child's property to discharge support obligations. Annot., 121 A.L.R. at 177-78. What constitutes required support, however, is vague. Note, Federal Tax Aspects of the Obligation to Support, supra, at 1193-94. Furthermore, where a state law obligation of support is defined, it is frequently less stringent than the economic level the family desires collectively to provide to the child or that society may expect. See id. at 1194-95.

rights with respect to items of a child's income arises from being locked into the traditional concept that liability for tax on a receipt of income will lie with the person having ownership and control. When discussing the choice of the individual or family unit as a basis for taxation this concept is not relevant.[106] Certainly, a husband has no legal control over or, absent special circumstances, claim to the income of his wife, but their incomes are nevertheless aggregated to compute tax liability.[107]

In any event, the factual premise that parents lack effective control over their children's income is doubtful. First, effective control may be achieved by parents' withdrawal of discretionary contributions to their children, thus forcing the children to use their income for purposes for which the parents previously supplied funds. Additionally, even assuming that children have broad discretion with respect to income from personal services, it is highly doubtful that children have any significant income from property subject to their own control which is viewed as available for their own use. It is probable that most property of a minor child is usually acquired through gifts and bequests of his parents and other relatives, especially

---

[106] In France, for example, a minor child has no independent tax liability. His income is added to that of the head of the household who bears responsibility for him. The head of the household is liable for the full tax on the aggregate income. It generally makes no difference whether the child is in fact dependent on the parent for support. Income splitting between the head of the household and dependent children, according to statutory ratios, is then extended to the aggregated income. Harvard Law School World Tax Series, Taxation in France § 5/1.4 (1966). Under civil law, the parent has no right to income from the services of his minor child, see French Civil Code, 6k. 1, tit. IX, c.2, art. 387 (Crabb trans.) (as amended to July 1, 1976), but does enjoy usufruct of his property, id. art. 382.

[107] In a series of cases involving taxation of income of married couples in community property states, Poe v. Seaborn, 282 U.S. 101, 111-12 (1930) (Washington); Goodell v. Koch, 282 U.S. 118, 119 (1930) (Arizona); Hopkins v. Bacon, 282 U.S. 122, 123 (1930) (Texas); Bender v. Pfaff, 282 U.S. 127, 128 (1930) (Louisiana), the Government argued that all of the income of a married couple, including the investment income of the wife, domiciled in a community property state, should be taxed to the husband. The Government's theory was that the wife's vested interest was no more than a right to devise one-half of the community property by will or to claim one-half of the community property on dissolution of the marriage. E.g., Poe v. Seaborn, 282 U.S. at 111-12. The husband under state law was vested with full power of management and control. The Supreme Court rejected this argument, id. at 113, and as a result, income of married couples in community property states was taxed to the spouses in accordance with their respective vested ownership rights under state law. The Internal Revenue Service subsequently accorded such treatment to all other community property states except California. Mim. 3853, X-1 C.B. 139 (1931); cf. United States v. Robbins, 269 U.S. 315, 326 (1926) (holding that full income splitting was not available to married spouses in the community property state of California because state law gave the wife no more than "a mere expectancy" in the community property). An amendment to the California community property statutes in 1927 resulted in income of married persons subsequently being taxed one-half to each spouse. United States v. Malcolm, 282 U.S. 792, 794 (1931).

his grandparents. It seems unlikely that a child will have any control over such property or the use of the income from the property. Most often the income from property of a minor child is under the control, directly or indirectly, of the parents of the child or his grandparents, if they were the source of the property. Parents are most frequently appointed the guardians of the property of their children regardless of the source of the funds.[108]

Rarely does a child own any significant property without a guardianship.[109] Parents often are custodians of a child's property under the Uniform Gifts to Minors Act,[110] although sometimes they are counseled not to act in that capacity.[111] Finally, a child's significant property is frequently held in trust. The grantor of the trust is most commonly a parent or grandparent. Even when an independent trustee has been named, if a parent was the grantor of the trust he can and does designate the time and manner in which the trust income is to be expended for the child's benefit, although such designations are often unspecific. Grandparents, in practice, usually consult with their children—the beneficiary's parents—prior to establishing trusts for their grandchildren. Often the trust instrument requires an independent trustee to "consult" with the parents regarding the use of income for children. Thus, even if traditional notions of control as the basis for taxation are followed, the argument that aggregation is not appropriate because of the independence of the children in the use of their income is specious. Such independence generally extends only to income from a minor's services. Moreover, such independence is usually voluntary on the part of parents since in almost every state the parent has the legal right to the income of his child earned from services.[112]

---

[108] Although parents are not generally the natural guardians of the property of their children, they are generally preferred by statute. See H. Clark, Law of Domestic Relations § 814, at 247-48 (1968). Thus, absent circumstances rendering a parent unfit, the appointment of a person other than a parent as guardian of the property of a minor child is usually with the explicit or tacit acquiescence of the parents.

[109] As a practical matter, it is difficult to transfer investment property, real or intangible, outright to a child because minors are unable to contract. The exception is cash, which can be deposited in a bank account.

[110] Although any person may be named original custodian, under § 7(a) of the Uniform Gifts to Minors Act, only an adult member of the child's family, a guardian of the minor, or a trust company is eligible to become successor trustee.

[111] The drawback, if a donor parent acts as custodian of property that he has transferred to a minor, is that the property will be includable in the donor's estate if he dies during the custodianship since he is treated as having a reserved right to control the property under I.R.C. § 2038. See Rev. Rul. 70-348, 1970-2 C.B. 193. The income from custodianship property is, however, taxed to the minor child and not to his parents, unless expended in discharge of the parents' support obligation. Rev. Rul. 59-357, 1959-2 C.B. 212.

[112] See Barnett & Spradlin, Enslavement in the Twentieth Century: The Right of Parents to Retain Their Children's Earnings, 5 Pepperdine L. Rev. 673, 675-76 & n.7 (1978).

The right to exercise control over income from property not owned by the person holding control, even if unexercised, generally has been considered sufficient basis to tax the income to the person holding such control.[113] Thus, with respect to children's income, parents either have effective control or have at one time or another had the opportunity to exercise control and have voluntarily surrendered their control. Lack of parental control over the income of a child can hardly provide a solid ground from which to launch an attack on aggregation.

On balance, it would appear preferable to institute aggregation. If any horizontal inequities arise, they would be created by the voluntary decision of the family unit not to maximize the potential benefits of pooling of income. Those benefits would be available, however, and therefore the family should be taxed as if it had taken advantage of them. It has the ability to pay. Furthermore, if income is not aggregated and these horizontal inequities are avoided, vertical inequities continue. If two children each have an identical income, it is likely that the child whose parents have the greater income will receive greater satisfactions arising from the sharing of the parents' income than will the child whose parents have the lesser income. The child of the parents with a greater income will sacrifice less than the child of the parents with the lesser income if each child pays the same taxes. He therefore has a greater ability to pay. Thus, unless he pays a greater tax, there is a vertical inequity.

A similar conclusion is reached if the children have different incomes but the parents' income in each family is the same. But for their own incomes it would be expected that both children would receive the same satisfactions from their parents' income. If Child 1 has income of $2000, Child 2 has income of $3000, and each family views the child's income as his own spending money, the child with greater income has greater total satisfaction available and thus a greater ability to pay. Arguably, however, this does not support aggregation but merely individual application of a graduated progressive rate of tax to the individual income of each child. The argument in favor of aggregation is based on the fact that each child's satisfaction from his own income is not his total amount of satisfaction. Rather, since each child's parents would provide the same amount of satisfaction, measurable in terms of money, each incremental dollar of a child's own income represents marginal satisfactions beginning at

---

[113] See I.R.C. § 674(a); 2 J. Mertens, Law of Federal Income Taxation § 17.02 (1974); Rice, Judicial Trends in Gratuitous Assignments to Avoid Federal Income Taxes, 64 Yale L.J. 991, 993 (1955).

a level set by the amount received from his parents. If we accept the principle of diminishing marginal utility of money, the utility of the extra one thousand dollars of income of Child 2 diminishes more rapidly than it would if he received no money satisfactions from his parents—if the $3000 were his sole income. Thus each extra dollar to Child 2 when his total amount of satisfactions is X + $3000 (X being the amount provided by his parents) diminishes more rapidly in value against each extra dollar to Child 1 when his total amount of satisfactions is X + $2000, than it would if neither received anything from his parents.

D. TAXATION OF FAMILY TRUSTS

DAN THROOP SMITH, FEDERAL TAX REFORM
McGraw-Hill (1961), pp. 291–4.

Trusts should be ignored for income tax purposes. Trust income should continue to be taxed to the person establishing the trust unless the transfer is sufficiently permanent and complete to make it taxable to another individual or charity. This is the first major change proposed. A transfer to be sufficiently complete to shift the liability for income taxation would be subject to either the gift or estate tax on the principal amount. When one has a sufficient interest in the income from property to be taxable on it, that is, when someone else has made a sufficiently firm transfer of property to be *not* taxable on the income from it, the property would then become subject to estate or gift tax when it or the right to receive income from it was permanently transferred on to still another person. This is the second major change. To permit discretion and flexibility in handling property for a surviving spouse or minor children, an estate might be permitted to continue as a single taxable entity for some period of time, perhaps up to twenty-one years or for the life of a surviving spouse, whichever is longer, with income from any property not definitely transferred to heirs taxable to the estate.

The results of this proposal would be to wipe out completely the tax advantages of multiple trusts or even single trusts which accumulate income, as well as the multiple-generation trusts. It would not in any way destroy the usefulness of trusts for purposes other than taxation. They could continue to be used as they have been, but they would no longer receive major tax benefits which are so great as to force their creation even where trusts are not desired for other reasons.

In its simplest terms, this set of rules would provide that a person is taxable on the income from his own property and would continue to be taxable on it until he made a complete and final transfer of the property to another person. He could not get out of his tax liability by a temporary transfer to anyone else whether the other person is an individual or a trustee. To shift liability for income taxation, he would have to make a transfer of the property to another individual, with the transfer subject to the estate or gift tax if applicable. An irrevocable transfer to a trustee would qualify if a definite beneficiary were established. If the income were to go to any one of several beneficiaries at the discretion of the trustee, the transfer would not be complete and the income would still be taxable to the person establishing the trust or to his estate.

This does not seem an unduly stringent rule for tax liability. Certainly if a person left his bonds in several safe-deposit boxes with instructions to his surviving children to go to the boxes once a year to clip the coupons and divide them up in whatever way they chose for tax purposes, with the additional right to leave some of the coupons in the boxes, each of which thereby became a separate taxable entity to be taxed on any unclipped coupons, there would be a general outcry against tax avoidance. But that is exactly the result achieved by trusts, with a trustee taking the place of the safe-deposit boxes and making them legal taxable entities.

Property could still be left in trust for as many generations as the trust law permits, but when each life interest or other definite interest was terminated, the principal amount from which the income was paid would be subject to gift or estate tax. This would not curtail the usefulness of trusts for nontax purposes; they could and would still be established to prevent a squandering of capital and to assure continued income to several generations in the future, but there would be no tax advantages over normal outright bequests. We may revert again to the analogy of the safe-deposit box. If a person could leave bonds in his boxes with instructions to his children to clip the coupons but never take out the bonds except to exchange them for other bonds to be placed in the boxes, with further instructions to leave the keys to the boxes to their children who would continue the process for their lifetimes and then turn the keys over to their children who would be the great-grandchildren of the person who rented the safe-deposit boxes in the first place—if all this could be done with only an original transfer tax when the bonds were put in the safe deposit box, there would be objection to avoidance of intervening gift or estate taxes. But that is just what can be done now if one thinks of each safe-deposit box as a trustee. Trustees have all the tax advantage of the hypothetical safe-deposit box and many other advantages, because a trustee can exercise his judgment and change investments and even pay out some of the principal to maintain a customary standard of living or meet some other specified objective.

Drastic though it may seem from some standpoints, the inclusion in one's estate of the principal sum from which one receives income seems fair and reasonable if one has not been brought up to think of trusts as separate legal entities. If a person unfamiliar with them were to hear them proposed as a new device to conserve property and permit an original owner's desires to be carried out after his death, he would probably react sympathetically and regard the proposal as a good one as long as it did not create an area for tax avoidance. What is proposed here is to unravel and wipe out the entire fabric of tax maneuver that has developed around trusts and in many instances has been the sole reason for their creation.

The new rules as a matter of fairness should be applied only to trusts created in the future. As a practical means of handling property left at death for varying uses, an estate might be permitted to be continued for a considerable period as a taxable entity. A person, in a sense, would be permitted to project himself in time as a taxable entity but not to proliferate himself into a group of new nonpersonal taxable entities. Income would be taxable to the estate until the property from which it came was transferred to an heir or to a trust with sufficiently definite terms to make the income from it and the capital sum attributable to a specific individual. Estates would not be given deductions as they now are for income distributed here and there on an interim basis to various heirs, any more than a living person can shift the liability for tax on his income by distributing the income year by year to his children and prospective heirs. The law would be no more strict on an estate than on the person whose property went into the estate. It would, to repeat, permit an individual to continue himself, through his estate, as a single taxable entity but deny the possibility of creating other new nonpersonal entities.

There would doubtless be many administrative problems in working out this new concept. It is proposed here as an objective for major reform. If the concept is accepted, exceptions should be made only to avoid impossibly complicated provisions covering special situations. The approach should be to bring all aspects of the tax law into conformity with the general objective, not to make minimum changes in the tax law to give recognition to the objective while maintaining as much of the present substance as possible.

DAVID WESTFALL, "TRUST GRANTORS AND SECTION 674: ADVENTURES IN INCOME TAX AVOIDANCE"

60 Columbia Law Review 326 (1960), pp. 326–42, 345–7.

In few other areas is a lawyer's work as tax-dominated as it is in the creation of irrevocable inter vivos trusts.[1] The articles on the subject mention only in passing, if at all, the possibility that such a trust will enable a grantor to do something with his property that he could not do as readily in other ways. Emphasis is placed almost exclusively on opportunities to use the trust device to make, at a lower tax cost, the same disposition that the grantor would have made if he had created no trust.[2] The conclusion is inescapable that irrevocable inter vivos trusts usually are created primarily to save taxes and in forms dictated by tax considerations. They are part of a nationwide adventure in tax avoidance.

The consequences of this artificially induced activity in the creation of irrevocable inter vivos trusts in general, and in particular in the creation of those most favored from a tax standpoint, are matters for public concern. The time and talent of lawyers and others have been absorbed in mastering and applying some of the most complex and intricate provisions of the Internal Revenue Code. If a trust may last a long time, the draftsman of the trust instrument must seek to anticipate such a variety of hypothetical but possible eventualities that a severe strain is placed upon human ingenuity in foreseeing and dealing clearly with the problems. And the availability of trust funds for the most attractive investment at a given time often is restricted, either by legal impediments that may be imposed by the trust instrument or by trust doctrine, or by practical limitations that may result from the conservatism of

---

1. An irrevocable trust, as the term is used in this article, is a trust that is not currently subject to revocation by the grantor, either alone or in conjunction with anyone else who is not an "adverse party" within the meaning of INT. REV. CODE OF 1954, § 672(a) [hereinafter cited CODE]. Such a trust may provide for return of the trust property to the grantor at the expiration of a stated period or may be revocable by him at that time.
Trusts revocable by the grantor alone will not be discussed in this article, as such trusts are not created to save federal income taxes during the grantor's life or federal estate taxes at his death. Reasons for their creation are discussed in CASNER, ESTATE PLANNING 87-106 (2d ed. 1956). Trusts revocable by the grantor in conjunction with another person are likewise includible in the grantor's estate, CODE § 2038, although the existence of the power to revoke will not cause the income to be taxed to him if the other person is an adverse party with respect to the exercise of such power within the meaning of CODE § 672(a). The practical significance of the "adverse party" exception is, however, somewhat limited. See note 21 *infra*. A reason for the creation of a trust revocable by the grantor in conjunction with another person may be to protect the grantor from his own indiscretions. See CASNER, *op. cit. supra* at 108-09.

2. See, *e.g.*, Drew, *Paying Family Expenses and Saving Taxes*, 37 TAXES 689 (1959); Johnson, *Trusts and the Grantor*, 36 TAXES 869 (1958); Mansfield, *Short-Term Trusts and the Clifford Rules*, N.Y.U. 15TH INST. ON FED. TAX 837 (1957); Yohlin, *The Short-Term Trust—A Respectable Tax-Saving Device*, 14 TAX L. REV. 109 (1958).

the trustee or the smallness of the investing units. Of course some of these objections can be minimized, at least, by adequate drafting, common trust funds, and progressive trustees; but a basic question remains: from a public standpoint, is the game worth the candle—or would we rather play another one instead?

An equally serious objection to the contemporary stress on the use of irrevocable inter vivos trusts to save taxes is that it is a game that not all taxpayers in the same income tax bracket are equally able to play. In the first place, it is open only to players who own or can borrow property to transfer in trust. Although such borrowing may permit an individual whose income is derived from personal services to get into the game, his ability to do so is likely to be relatively limited because he may be disqualified if the trust property is security for the loan.[3] Secondly, there are wide variations in the abilities of property owners to play the game successfully, or indeed to play it at all. The least sophisticated may be psychologically hobbled by a lingering linking that persists, despite the promotional zeal of corporate fiduciaries, between trusts and combinations in restraint of trade.[4] Others on a more advanced level of sophistication may be handicapped by a lack of competent counsel and cooperative trustees. And still others may be unable to bring themselves to make commitments on the basis of predictions and projections extending for a substantial period into the future.

If the device is not truly available to all, it nevertheless achieves impressive results for a few. The size of the potential income and estate tax savings is well known, and often the gift tax cost of the transfer may be kept comparatively low. What is less widely recognized is that tax reduction may often be achieved by sophisticated taxpayers without any real loss of control over the trust property. Although this is true of the estate tax as well as the income tax, the Code sections that deal with inclusion of inter vivos transfers in the gross estate are written in sufficiently general terms to leave some scope for judicial and administrative interpretation in their application to tax-minimizing arrangements.[5] There is much less room, however, for similar

---

3. CODE § 677(a) would seem clearly to require this result, but the cases to date have based taxability of the grantor in this situation upon actual use of trust income for repayment of his debt, rather than upon the mere possibility of such use that arises from the fact that the trust property is security. See, *e.g.*, Helvering v. Blumenthal, 296 U.S. 552, *reversing per curiam* 76 F.2d 507 (2d Cir. 1935); Rev. Rul. 54-516, 1954-2 CUM. BULL. 54. *But see* Hays' Estate v. Commissioner, 181 F.2d 169 (5th Cir. 1950).

4. At least one corporate trust officer seeks to allay such suspicions by avoiding use of the term "trust" and referring to the institution's services as an "arrangement."

5. The Commissioner's contention that the "substantial ownership" concept of Helvering v. Clifford, 309 U.S. 331 (1940) is applicable to inclusion of property in the gross estate was rejected in Helvering v. Safe Deposit & Trust Co., 316 U.S. 56 (1942). But a related contention seems to have found acceptance in State Street Trust Co. v. United States, 263 F.2d 635 (1st Cir. 1959). And Lober v. United States, 346 U.S. 335 (1953) interpreted the predecessor to § 2038 in a manner that makes it extremely difficult

flexibility in the taxation of trust income to the grantor.[6] The Code provisions are detailed and specific. If the grantor has complied with the express statutory requirements for shifting taxability, the Commissioner is expressly denied use of the general definition of gross income to require inclusion of trust income in a grantor's return on the ground of his dominion and control.[7]

Congress and the Treasury have recognized the need for revision of the Code provisions dealing with taxation of trust income.[8] An Advisory Group has recommended extensive and detailed amendments, many of which have been included in a bill recently passed by the House of Representatives.[9] However, neither the bill nor the recommendations of the Advisory Group, which in this area the bill generally follows, would make any basic change in the present rules governing taxation of trust income to the grantor. The Advisory Group did not feel authorized to propose completely new approaches,[10] and the tenor of its proposals in this area suggests acceptance and endorsement of the *status quo*. The recommendations are concerned with matters of detail and seek to make the current mode of taxing grantors work more smoothly. Changes of a more fundamental nature are needed if the present tax-motivated use of irrevocable inter vivos trusts is to be checked.

This article will be chiefly concerned with only one section of the Code: section 674, which determines the effect of a power in the grantor or a nonadverse party to control beneficial enjoyment. This section appears to have

---

for a grantor to have significant discretionary powers as trustee if the trust is not to be includible in his gross estate.

It should also be noted that although §§ 2036 and 2038 refer to a right or power of the decedent, the Regulations treat powers of a trustee as powers of the decedent if the decedent had the unrestricted right to remove the trustee and appoint himself. See Treas. Reg. §§ 20.2036-1(b)(3), 20.2038-1(a)(3) (1958). And it has been intimated that an unrestricted right of removal may cause powers nominally given to the trustee to be deemed powers of the decedent even if he could not have appointed himself as trustee. See Van Beuren v. McLoughlin, 262 F.2d 315, 318 (1st Cir. 1958), cert. denied, 359 U. S. 991 (1959).

6. The Code refers to treating the grantor as the "owner" of a given portion of a trust. The result of such treatment is to require inclusion of the income therefrom in his taxable income, CODE § 671; hence, that term will be used herein. "Income" will refer to the ordinary income of the trust, exclusive of capital gains.

7. CODE § 671. Justification for thus disarming the Commissioner has been found in an assumed "need for tax certainty in the area of family property planning." See Holland, Kennedy, Surrey & Warren, *A Proposed Revision of the Federal Income Tax Treatment of Trusts and Estates—American Law Institute Draft*, 53 COLUM. L. REV. 316, 361 (1953). Such certainty is not desirable if the rules themselves fail to prevent the use of tax avoidance arrangements. See *ibid.*

8. See STAFFS OF JOINT COMM. ON INTERNAL REVENUE TAXATION AND THE TREASURY DEPARTMENT, LIST OF SUBSTANTIVE UNINTENDED BENEFITS AND HARDSHIPS AND ADDITIONAL PROBLEMS FOR THE TECHNICAL AMENDMENTS BILL OF 1957, at 8 (1956) ; *Hearings Before the House Committee on Ways and Means on General Revenue Revision*, 85th Cong., 2d Sess., pt. 3, at 2761 (1958).

9. See ADVISORY GROUP ON SUBCHAPTER J OF THE INTERNAL REVENUE CODE OF 1954, FINAL REPORT ON ESTATES, TRUSTS, BENEFICIARIES, AND DECEDENTS, in *Hearings Before the House Committee on Ways and Means on Advisory Group Recommendations on Subchapters C, J, and K of the Internal Revenue Code*, 86th Cong., 1st Sess. 257 (1959) [hereinafter cited REPORT OF ADVISORY GROUP ON SUBCHAPTER J]; H.R. 9662, 86th Cong., 2d Sess. (1960) (proposed Trust and Partnership Income Tax Revision Act of 1960).

10. See *Hearings, supra* note 8, at 2759.

played the most important role in permitting the use of irrevocable trusts to achieve tax savings without any real loss of control by the grantor. But if this abuse of an ancient and honored institution is to be fully curbed, revisions may be needed in other Code sections dealing with taxation of trust income to the grantor: section 673, which allows one type of trust to shift taxability of income from the grantor even though its duration is as short as two years; section 675, which allows a grantor to have the opportunity to borrow back that which he purportedly has given away, without loss of income tax benefits when he does so; and section 677, which allows him to retain the power to use income for the support of his legal dependents without incurring tax liability for income not thus used.

Finally, revisions may also be needed in the present rules governing taxation of trust income to persons other than the grantor. Under section 678, a non-grantor often may exercise a substantial degree of effective control over the beneficial enjoyment of trust income or principal, or both, without being taxed on income not actually distributed to him or used for the support of his legal dependents.[11] In this situation, however, the problems are quite different from those that arise with respect to taxation of the grantor. There may be a sound basis for not treating a power exercisable by someone other than the grantor as having the same tax consequences to such other person as the same power would have for the grantor if possessed by him.[12] The grantor could, if he wished, have retained complete control over the property, so that any restrictions upon his control are of his own making. A person other than the grantor, on the other hand, had no similar choice unless the grantor or testator allowed him to determine the trust provisions in this respect.[13]

Moreover, any revision of the rules governing taxation of trust income to persons other than the grantor should give due consideration to the importance of flexibility in post-death property dispositions. Creation of a discretionary inter vivos trust provides no amount of flexibility in the disposition of property during the grantor's life that he would not have enjoyed as owner if he had created no trust, so long as the property remained free from claims. Thus, an assumed need for "flexibility" in property dispositions should not

---

11. See Casner, *Responsibilities of the Corporate Trustee as to Discretionary Trusts*, 32 TRUST BULL., March 1953, p. 21, at 24-25; Pedrick, *Familial Obligations and Federal Taxation: A Modest Suggestion*, 51 Nw. U.L. REV. 53 (1956); Winton, *Taxation of Nongrantors Under Trusts for Support of Their Dependents*, 33 TAXES 804 (1955).

Minor revisions of § 678 are contained in § 109 of the proposed Trust and Partnership Income Tax Revision Act of 1960, H.R. 9662, 86th Cong., 2d Sess. (1960).

12. Of course, if a person other than the grantor partially releases a power exercisable by him alone to vest corpus or income in himself, the income tax consequences of the partial release are determined, in effect, as if he were the grantor. CODE § 678(a)(2).

13. It is not uncommon for a grantor or testator to find out before making a gift or testamentary disposition whether the prospective recipient wishes to avoid the adverse tax consequences of the possession of unrestricted rights over the property in question.

be the controlling consideration in the tax treatment of inter vivos trusts during the life of the grantor. The situation changes, however, with the grantor's death. At that time, it may be desirable, for non-tax reasons, for a grantor or testator to be able to delegate to a trustee (who may also be a beneficiary) the power that he had as owner to dispose of his property or periodically to dispose of the income from that property in the light of the changing needs of different members of his family.[14] Thus, the discussion in this article of tax-minimizing motives in the creation of discretionary trusts during the life of the grantor is not equally applicable to the use of a discretionary trust to control the post-death devolution of property of a grantor or testator. On the other hand, such post-death use may also be tax-motivated and may accordingly create problems comparable to those dealt with herein.

I. FACTORS THAT SHOULD BE RELEVANT IN DETERMINING WHETHER A POWER TO CONTROL BENEFICIAL ENJOYMENT SHOULD CAUSE TRUST INCOME TO BE TAXED TO THE GRANTOR

In *Helvering v. Clifford*,[15] the Supreme Court sustained the taxation of trust income to a grantor on the ground that "the bundle of rights which he retained was so substantial that [he] . . . cannot be heard to complain that he is the 'victim of despotic power when for the purpose of taxation he is treated as owner altogether.'" The grantor's retention of such substantial rights is generally accepted today as a sound basis for taxing trust income to him, but there are differences of opinion as to what rights are to be deemed "substantial" for this purpose.[16] In any event, substantiality should not be an exclusive test, either with respect to powers to control beneficial enjoyment or with respect to the other types of rights that presently may cause trust income to be taxable to the grantor.[17] If the definition of "substantial" remains liberal from the taxpayer's standpoint, as it appears to be today, the tax-motivated creation of trusts can be expected to continue unchecked. If, on the other hand, the definition were made so strict as to cause such arrangements to be ignored for tax purposes in all cases, a serious problem would be presented. It would be almost impossible to establish for any trust that the grantor could not exercise some amount of control over the enjoyment of the trust property, either because he reserved a power or because of his

---

14. *Cf.* CASNER, ESTATE PLANNING 566 (2d ed. 1956).
15. 309 U.S. 331, 337 (1940).
16. When the Treasury Regulations based on the *Clifford* case were promulgated, there was no unanimity as to whether they interpreted the decision correctly. *Compare* Pavenstedt, *The Treasury Legislates: The Distortion of the Clifford Rule*, 2 TAX L. REV. 7 (1946), *with* Eisenstein, *The Clifford Regulations and the Heavenly City of Legislative Intention*, 2 TAX L. REV. 327 (1947).
17. See Rice, *Judicial Trends in Gratuitous Assignments to Avoid Federal Income Taxes*, 64 YALE L.J. 991 (1955).

ability to influence the action of a trustee or beneficiary. Rather than seek to satisfy such a rigorous requirement, prospective transferors would turn to non-trust gifts if they wished to achieve the tax savings now available from the creation of trusts. And the result would be to inhibit the use of types of trusts that may serve significant non-tax purposes and that may have only a limited potential impact upon the relative burdens of different taxpayers in similar income brackets if deemed effective to shift the taxability of income from the trust property.

All three factors, it is submitted, should be considered in determining whether a power to control beneficial enjoyment should cause trust income to be taxed to the grantor: (1) whether the grantor has retained substantial rights with respect to beneficial enjoyment of the trust property; (2) whether the type of trust he created is likely to serve significant non-tax purposes; and (3) whether the potential impact upon the relative burdens of different taxpayers in similar income brackets is likely to be serious in comparison with the impact of comparable non-trust gifts.

If A gives property that he owns absolutely to B, almost all would agree that fairness requires that A not be taxed upon income that is properly deemed to be realized from the property after the gift is made. The historically and constitutionally protected rights of property generally have been assumed to include the right to rid oneself of all incidents of ownership, even though the necessary result is that the taxability of income derived from property ownership may be shifted much more easily than that of income derived from personal services.[18]

Apart from questions of fairness, there are sound reasons for believing that most donors do not make widespread use of absolute gifts solely to save taxes on income properly deemed to have been realized after the gift is made. It is true that A may have made the gift because he wanted the income taxed in B's lower bracket and because A thought that at the same time he could control, in one way or another, what B did with the property. But the potential tax savings are counterbalanced and made less significant by two factors that could even cause these savings to be nullified if A gives very much property to B: (1) The amount of taxable income that is shifted is likely to be small in relation to the value of the gift for gift tax purposes—and even if A thinks of the gift tax as a bargain-basement substitute for the estate tax (a concept accepted by only the more sophisticated donors), it is due shortly after the gift is made and can be large enough to be burdensome; (2) No new taxpayer is brought into the world by the gift; B merely has been substituted for A, and if B acquires enough income-producing property he will have tax problems of his own, if he does not already. Moreover, many donors

---

18. *Cf. id.* at 1001.

in *A*'s position have been disappointed in their expectations of keeping indirect control of property given away absolutely. Legally, *B* has the same control over property *A* gave him that he has over any of his other property: he can use it for his own purposes, or he can follow *A*'s directions. Over the years a large number of donees have found the first alternative irresistably attractive.

If *A* gives *B* not absolute ownership but rather some limited interest in property, without creating a trust, there is no similar uniformity of opinion that *A* should never be taxed upon the income that *B* derives from that limited interest. If *B*'s interest is merely income for a term of a few years, for instance, the income that *B* receives during the term is taxable to *A*.[19] And there are sound reasons, it is submitted, for making a distinction between gifts of absolute ownership and of limited interests of substantial duration, on one hand, and gifts of short-term interests, on the other. In each case, to be sure, *A* assumes the risk that *B* will prefer to use his interest for his own purposes, so that *A* will no longer be able to control that which he has given away unless *B* chooses to let him do so. Thus, there is reason to believe that in many instances the transfer, whether of absolute ownership or of a limited interest, is not made solely for tax reasons. But if *B*'s interest is limited and of short duration, *A*'s rights may be regarded as so substantial, because of his reversionary interest, that the first of the three factors referred to previously requires that *A* remain taxable on the income that *B* receives. Furthermore, a contrary rule would create a far more serious risk that the relative burdens of different taxpayers in similar income brackets would be distorted than in the case of absolute gifts or of gifts of limited interests of substantial duration. The shorter the limited interest given to *B*, the weaker is the deterrent effect of the gift tax, because the amount of annual income shifted to *B* becomes larger in relation to the value of the transfer for gift tax purposes.

II. The Present Statutory Scheme

Section 674, as it now stands, appears to reflect a congressional belief that property owners should be accorded a large measure of flexibility in choosing the kinds of interests they may create by transfers in trust, without loss of the income tax benefits otherwise obtainable by immediate, absolute gifts.[20] All should not be forced to pour their assets into receptacles fashioned from a common mold, to fit their varying dispositive desires into a Procrustean bed, even though such preferences may be shaped primarily by a desire to

---

19. *Cf.* United States v. Shafto, 246 F.2d 338 (4th Cir. 1957); Rev. Rul. 58-337, 1958-2 Cum. Bull. 13.
20. See Holland, Kennedy, Surrey & Warren, *supra* note 7, at 359.

secure a lower effective income tax rate. Accordingly a grantor is given several alternatives.

The basic choice that the grantor faces is whether he wants freedom in choosing the trustee or freedom in postponing the choice (by someone other than himself) of the beneficiaries who will actually enjoy income or principal. The Code also provides an intermediate alternative for grantors who would like a measure of each variety of freedom at the same time.

If the grantor decides he is more interested in latitude in selecting the trustee or trustees, he can name anyone, including himself, without adverse income tax consequences to him by reason of the trustee's powers to control beneficial enjoyment, so long as those powers are limited in the manner prescribed by section 674(b).[21] If, on the other hand, the grantor decides that what he wants is not so much a free hand in choosing the trustee as it is to postpone the determination of who will actually benefit from his gift, he may confer upon the trustees, if they are selected within the limitations of either section 674(c) or section 674(d), the broader discretionary powers authorized in those sections. Thus, the choice is essentially between giving the trustee the grantor really prefers limited discretionary powers and giving a trustee selected from a restricted list broader discretionary powers.

A. *Limited Discretion in the Trustee: Section 674(b)*

If the grantor is most interested in being able to select anyone, including himself, as sole trustee, without incurring adverse tax consequences for himself, the trustee's powers must be limited in the manner prescribed by section 674(b). Before considering the extent to which that section permits the trustee to be given explicit powers to affect beneficial enjoyment, it is appropriate to examine the extent to which a trustee, notwithstanding the absence of provisions in the instrument dealing explicitly with control of beneficial enjoyment, is nevertheless likely to be able to affect such enjoyment by the manner in which he exercises his usual powers as fiduciary.

1. *Usual fiduciary powers.* Although a trustee may be denied the power to change the manner in which the trust property is invested, such

---

21. In the following discussion it is assumed that the grantor does not hold the power in question with someone who is, with respect to the exercise or nonexercise thereof, an "adverse party" within the meaning of CODE § 672(a). A grantor may, as trustee, have broader powers than those described in the text if the powers are exercisable only with the consent of an adverse party. But the practical significance of the Code's recognition of adverse parties is limited by the tax consequences to such parties from the exercise of these powers. For example, if the grantor and *B*, as trustees, jointly hold powers affecting the beneficial enjoyment of the trust property, the mere existence of such a power has no adverse tax consequence to *B*; from an income tax standpoint, it is not exercisable "solely" by *B*, CODE § 678(a)(1), and from a gift and estate tax standpoint, it is exercisable only in conjunction with the creator of the power. CODE §§ 2041(b)(1)(C)(i), 2514(c)(3)(A). But its exercise in favor of someone other than *B* may constitute a transfer of *B*'s interest as a beneficiary and thus be taxable as a gift. See Treas. Reg. § 25.2514-1(b)(2) (1958). *But see* Self v. United States, 142 F. Supp. 939 (Ct. Cl. 1956).

power is customarily given, subject to whatever restrictions on its exercise may be imposed by the terms of the instrument or by local law. And the power to change investments may necessarily affect the beneficial enjoyment of the trust property. Assume that A transfers property to T as trustee to pay the ordinary income to B for ten years or until B dies, whichever event first occurs, and then to return the principal, including capital gains, to A. On its face the trust instrument gives A no right to control beneficial enjoyment, even if he himself is sole trustee; and the ordinary income of the trust is not taxable to A under either section 673[22] or section 674, although he will, of course, be taxed on capital gains realized by the trust.[23] But, as a practical matter, A may have retained, as a result of T's power to change investments, an important element of control over the ordinary income that is payable to B, and, accordingly, if such a trust is treated as shifting taxability of the ordinary income from A to B, the potential impact upon the relative burdens of different taxpayers in similar income brackets may be serious in comparison to the impact of comparable non-trust gifts.

a. *Grantor's control.* The amount of income payable to B will depend on how the trust principal is invested. The trustee may benefit B by buying securities with a high yield, or he may prefer low-yield growth stocks, which may produce an increase in the value of the principal to be returned to A on the termination of the trust. If the trustee is A himself, or someone whom A can influence, the choice of investments may be made in a manner that allows A to determine, in effect, whether income is to be paid to B or not. But in this situation the law of trusts provides substantial protection for B's interest by imposing upon the trustee a duty to dispose of unproductive property.[24] If such protection is expressly excluded by the instrument, a court should be able to find that the trust income is taxable to A on the ground that it could, in effect, be accumulated for A in the discretion of the trustee.[25] It is difficult, however, to find authority that expressly supports this conclusion.[26]

b. *Non-tax purposes.* An important non-tax motive for the creation of irrevocable inter vivos trusts may be a grantor's desire to make his depend-

---

22. See Treas. Reg. § 1.673(a)-1(b) (1958); Johnson, *Trusts and the Grantor*, 36 TAXES 869, 871 n.11 (1958).
23. CODE § 677(a).
24. See RESTATEMENT (SECOND), TRUSTS § 240 (1959); 3 SCOTT, TRUSTS § 240 (1956).
25. CODE § 677(a).
26. *Cf.* Treas. Reg. § 1.674(b)-1(b)(5)(i) (1956) (power to distribute corpus not limited by a "reasonably definite standard" if trust instrument provides that trustee's determination is conclusive). In the case of the federal estate tax marital deduction, the Code merely provides that a gift of income for life coupled with a general power of appointment would avoid the disqualification of an interest as a terminable one. See CODE § 2056(b)(5). But the Regulations have read into the statute a requirement that the property be income producing. See Treas. Reg. § 20.2056(b)-5(f)(5) (1958); Casner, *Estate Planning Under the Revenue Act of 1948—The Regulations*, 63 HARV. L. REV. 99, 101 (1949).

ents financially independent.[27] Undoubtedly there are grantors who have such desires, although it is the common experience of lawyers that many are only reluctantly induced to confer such independence in order to secure tax benefits.[28] Therefore, if the trust term is long enough to indicate that the grantor genuinely wished to confer independence upon the beneficiaries, the existence of such motives may be a factor that supports according recognition for income tax purposes to the creation of trusts with limited discretion in the trustee.

c. *Potential impact on relative tax burdens.* The most serious consideration opposed to recognition of trusts with limited discretion in the trustee as shifting taxability of the trust income from the grantor to the beneficiary is the potential discrimination between those taxpayers in a given income bracket who are able to create such trusts and those who, for one reason or another, are not. The amount of income that is shifted is no larger in relation to the value of the gift for gift tax purposes than in the case of a comparable non-trust gift of income from property for a term of similar duration, and in each case the beneficiary is legally free to ignore the grantor's desires as to the disposition of income that he receives. But the making of such non-trust gifts is deterred, it seems probable, by the difficulty in changing the form of investment once the gift has been made, as the beneficiary must concur in any such change. Therefore, if trusts with limited discretion in the trustee were deemed ineffective to shift taxability of the trust income, it appears probable that some would-be grantors would choose to make no transfer, rather than to make a non-trust gift of income that would make more difficult any subsequent changes in the form of investment that might appear to be desirable. On balance, however, the factor of potential discrimination between taxpayers does not appear to be sufficiently serious to warrant the denial of tax recognition to trusts with limited discretion in the trustee, if the trust term is long enough to be deemed "substantial" in a realistic sense.

2. *Variations permitted by section 674(b).* Section 674(b) does not stop with the basic type of trust with limited discretion in the trustee, which has just been described. It also uncritically places its seal of approval, for

---

27. See CASNER, ESTATE PLANNING 109 (2d ed. 1956).

28. Of course, to the extent that the trust income is used to discharge the grantor's legal obligation to support a dependent such a trust will not reduce his income tax liabilities. See CODE § 677(b). But the Regulations, in dealing with the taxation of trust beneficiaries, state that such an obligation exists "if, and only if, the obligation is not affected by the adequacy of the dependent's own resources." Treas. Reg. § 1.662(a)-4 (1956). Presumably, the reference in Treas. Reg. § 1.677(b)-1(b) (1956) to Code sections dealing with the taxation of trust beneficiaries incorporates as well the quoted definition of legal dependency, which is, of course, far more restrictive than that generally provided by state law. It is still more limited in comparison to the extent of the moral obligation that many parents feel to provide adult children with a professional education.

federal income tax purposes, upon types of trusts in which the discretionary power of the trustee is considerably greater.

a. *Permissible variations that reduce the need for court proceedings.* One category of permissible variations that appears to be unobjectionable consists of those that reduce the need for court proceedings as a result of the creation of the trust. In this category is the power to allocate receipts and disbursements between principal and income.[29] This necessarily increases the trustee's control over the amount the income beneficiary will actually receive,[30] but at the same time it performs an important function by reducing the need for recourse to the uncertain and unsatisfactory rules that have been developed in some states as to what falls into one category or the other.[31] Similarly, a power to apply income for or withhold it from a beneficiary under a legal disability may permit the use of income for the beneficiary and investment of that which is in excess of his current needs without the necessity for appointment of a guardian, or if a guardian has already been appointed, without subjecting such investment to the limitations imposed upon guardians.[32]

b. *Permissible variations that permit the alienation of the trust principal.* A second category of permissible variations consists of powers that are not very susceptible of being used primarily for the minimization of current income taxes but that do serve to allow principal to be alienated during the term of the trust. Thus a discretionary power in the trustee to distribute principal to or for a current income beneficiary with such distribution required to be charged against the proportionate share of principal held in trust to pay income to that beneficiary does not shift taxability of income if the beneficiary is currently entitled to all the income produced by his share.[33] Similarly, a power exercisable only by will has no effect on current income taxes prior to the

---

29. CODE § 674(b)(8).
30. This power should not, in any event, be construed to permit the trustee to diminish substantially the beneficiary's right to income. See note 24 *supra*.
31. See 3 Scott, TRUSTS § 233 (1956); Dunham, *A Trustee's Dilemma as to Principal and Income*, 26 U. CHI. L. REV. 405 (1959).
32. CODE § 674(b)(7). The Code provision goes considerably beyond what has been suggested in the text, as it does not require that the income withheld be distributed to the beneficiary if his disability terminates during his lifetime. Such a requirement would, however, introduce the complicating necessity of accounting separately for such income.
33. CODE § 674(b)(5)(B). This section does not state whether it is applicable to a discretionary power to distribute principal to a current income beneficiary if the beneficiary is not entitled, as a matter of right, to all of the income from the share held in trust for the payment of income to him. If he is not thus entitled, income may be withheld from him in one year, so that it is taxable as income of the trust. In a later year the accumulated income may be distributed to the beneficiary as "principal," and the distribution is not taxable as income to him if it falls within one of the exceptions to the five-year throwback rule contained in CODE § 665(b). Even if the throwback rule applies, the beneficiary has the benefit of a choice between different taxable years. See CODE § 668(a).

death of the holder of the power,[34] although the manner of its eventual exercise may, of course, be influenced by tax considerations.[35]

c. *Other permissible variations.* Aside from the two categories of powers just referred to and the usual power to change the form of investment of the trust property, it is submitted that the other powers that a trustee may be given under section 674(b) without adverse income tax consequences to the grantor are inconsistent with any substantial surrender of rights by the grantor if he is trustee or can dominate the trustee, are unlikely to serve significant non-tax purposes, and may have a serious impact upon relative burdens of different taxpayers in similar income brackets.[36] In the first place, the trustee (or the grantor, if he is trustee) may be given discretion to use trust income to satisfy the grantor's obligation to support his legal dependents,[37] although there is some uncertainty as to the precise effect of this provision.[38] Second, he can be authorized to withhold income from beneficiaries who are under no legal disability. Such withholding may be wholly tax motivated and not

---

34. See CODE § 674(b)(3). It has been proposed that the provision be broadened to include powers exercisable by deed if the exercise will not confer enjoyment upon anyone until after the death of the donee. See H.R. 9662, 86th Cong., 2d Sess. § 115(a) (1960) (proposed Trust and Partnership Income Tax Revision Act of 1960); REPORT OF ADVISORY GROUP ON SUBCHAPTER J 311-14.

35. If the holder of the power predeceases the grantor, his exercise of the power may create a problem that neither the Code nor the Regulations deal with explicitly. He may exercise the power to create interests that, if created by the grantor, would have resulted in taxation of the trust income to the grantor. For example, the holder of the power may direct the grantor as trustee to pay income and principal to one or more members of a group, in the grantor's uncontrolled discretion. If the grantor had created such a trust himself, the income would have been taxable to him under CODE § 674, so the critical question is whether the holder of the power is to be deemed the grantor of interests created by his exercise thereof. Under CODE § 678(a), a holder of a power is, in effect, deemed to be a grantor for other purposes if he had a power exercisable solely by himself to vest income or principal in himself. But if he did not have such a power, it would seem that the original grantor should also be deemed grantor with respect to interests created by the exercise of a testamentary power by someone else. Otherwise, a grantor could create such a power in a person who had no beneficial interest and who, therefore, might have no reason to refuse to exercise the power in the manner desired by the grantor to create the type of trust that the grantor could not himself create without continuing to be taxable on the trust income.

36. CODE § 674(b)(2) merely correlates the section with CODE § 673, relating to reversionary interests.

37. CODE § 674(b)(1).

38. The uncertainty arises from the fact that income of a trust that may be used, in the discretion of the grantor as trustee, to discharge the grantor's support obligations, could be taxable to the grantor for either of two reasons: (1) under CODE § 677, on the ground that such use of income would be, in effect, a distribution to the grantor; or (2) under CODE § 674, on the ground that the discretion to make such a distribution is a power of disposition. Taxability on the first ground is expressly limited by § 677(b) to amounts actually used for support. Taxability on the second ground is dealt with by § 674(b)(1), but that section does not indicate clearly whether the grantor may, as trustee, be authorized to divert income from any other use to the support of his legal dependents without becoming taxable on such income, whether or not such diversion in fact occurs. If the ability to use income for support obligations is the only discretionary power that the grantor possesses with respect to income, such power would appear to fall within § 674(b)(1). But if the grantor already possesses discretion to withhold income from a beneficiary under the type of power authorized by § 674(b)(6) or § 674(b)(7), may he, in addition, be given discretion to use income for support of dependents? The Regulations provide no clear answer.

justified as a means of avoiding the expense and formalities of guardianship,[39] and there need be no assurance that withheld income will ever be payable to the beneficiaries from whom it was withheld.[40] Third, the trustee may be authorized to distribute principal to one beneficiary, if his discretion to do so is limited by an appropriate standard,[41] even though the effect is to reduce the income payable to another beneficiary.[42] Finally, he may be given power to spray income among certain charitable beneficiaries,[43] thus permitting circum-

---

39. See p. 336 *supra*. It may be contended that a similar purpose is in fact served even though the beneficiary is not under a legal disability if his ability to handle his affairs is impaired because of age and it is desired to avoid the publicity that would result from proceedings for an adjudication of incompetency. However, this factor is unlikely to be present with the great majority of beneficiaries of trust income, and it is submitted that avoidance of such publicity in a minority of cases does not justify permitting the general use of a power with such great tax-minimizing possibilities.

40. CODE § 674(b)(6). * * *

41. CODE § 674(b)(5)(A). It seems to be assumed that so long as the standard is observed, the grantor lacks real power to shift enjoyment from one beneficiary to another, and that fear of suit for breach of trust will deter the grantor as trustee from straying from such observance. Both assumptions may be quite unrealistic. See p. 341 *infra*.

42. For example, assume that the current trust income is payable to beneficiary *A*, but that the principal may, in the trustee's discretion (limited by an appropriate standard), be distributed to *B*, who is not an income beneficiary. Any distribution to *B* inevitably reduces the amount of income taxable to *A*, to the extent that the principal distributed to *B* would have produced income after the date of its distribution.

If the trustee could be authorized to withhold income from *A* and at the same time to distribute principal to *B*, taxability of the withheld income could be shifted from *A* to *B*. See CODE § 662(a)(2). However, the Regulations state that CODE § 674(b)(6), which authorizes the creation of discretionary powers to withhold income from beneficiaries who are not under a disability, is inapplicable "if the power is in substance one to shift ordinary income from one beneficiary to another." See Treas. Reg. § 1.674(b)-1(b)(6)(i) (1956).

43. CODE § 674(b)(4).

vention of the percentage limit on charitable deductions[44] without the requirement of an advance decision by the grantor as to who will benefit from the circumvention.

B. *Broad Discretion in the Trustee: Sections 674(c) and 674(d)*

If the grantor decides that what he wants is not so much a free hand in choosing the trustee as it is postponement of the determination as to who will actually benefit from his gift, he can have a spray trust in the fullest sense of the word. If the trustee is properly selected, he can be given all the powers the grantor could have had and, in addition, uncontrolled discretion either to make distributions and to decide, from time to time, which of the described beneficiaries will actually receive income or principal, or, on the other hand, to accumulate income so that for the time being no one receives any.[45] It is in this situation that the Code provisions appear to reflect a remarkably naïve set of assumptions with respect to the effective exercise of control by a grantor.

1. *Grantor's control.* The statute first recognizes that a grantor may be able to dominate a trustee who is his wife, close relative, or employee.[46] This is sound, as far as it goes, but the converse is not equally true. Because a trustee does not occupy one of these relationships it does not follow that the grantor will be unable to dominate the trustee's decisions. Nor does it follow, as the Code seems to assume, that even if one or more trustees may be dominated by the grantor because of such a relationship to him, he can not dominate the trustees as a body if an equal number are not thus related.[47]

The statute then authorizes an intermediate arrangement for grantors who are unwilling to have outsiders as trustees, but who can not quite decide whom the trust should benefit. The grantor's close relatives and employees can be made the only trustees, and they can be given discretionary power to spray income among the described beneficiaries or to accumulate it, if the power is limited by a standard.[48] It apparently is assumed that the presence of the standard will stiffen the trustees' backbones so that they will not succumb to domination by the grantor in the exercise of their discretionary power. In this respect, however, the Code sounds two refreshing notes of realism: (1) If all the trustees are close relatives or employees of the grantor,

---

44. See Johnson, *Trusts and the Grantor*, 36 TAXES 869, 871 (1958).
45. CODE § 674(c).
46. See CODE § 672(c).
47. See CODE § 674(c). REPORT OF ADVISORY GROUP ON SUBCHAPTER J 317-18, and H.R. 9662, 86th Cong., 2d Sess. § 115(e) (1960) (proposed Trust and Partnership Income Tax Revision Act of 1960), would change the present requirement that one-half of the trustees be "independent" to a still milder version. Only one such trustee would be needed, if concurrence of that trustee were required for exercise of the power.
48. CODE § 674(d).

they can not be given greater powers over principal than the grantor could have been given if he himself were trustee; and (2) not even the presence of a standard will be assumed to stiffen the spine of the grantor's spouse so long as the couple is living together.

If the approach of the Code is naïve, the writers on the subject have not been. The Code would confine the assumption of trustee domination by the grantor arising out of a business relationship to the situation in which the trustee is an employee,[49] and this is commonly believed not to include professional people who perform services for the grantor.[50] But it has been pointed out that the grantor's lawyer or accountant can be named as trustee and may be expected to "exercise discretion in these matters comparable to his own."[51] Even a corporate fiduciary may be susceptible to pressure from the grantor in its exercise of discretionary powers as trustee.[52] The grantor may be a customer of the commercial department as well as the trust department, or the corporate fiduciary may anticipate serving as executor of the grantor's estate and as trustee under his will if no untoward development should mar the relationship. Quite apart from such specific pressures is the more general one that arises from the nature of a fiduciary's business. As the name implies, it is engaged in the administration of trusts. A reputation in the community for being hard to get along with is unlikely to assist the work of the new business department. Finally, the grantor may have a relative who is not on the forbidden trustee list, such as a niece or nephew or an in-law, who can be counted upon in the particular family situation to be responsive to his wishes.

Of course there are, no doubt, trustees who refuse to be influenced at all by a grantor. But the position of a trustee (if he is not also a beneficiary, and normally he can not be one without complicating his own tax position[53]) is quite different from that of the donee of an absolute gift or the beneficiary

---

49. See CODE § 672(c)(2).
50. The Regulations contain no definition of "employee" as used in CODE § 672(c)(2).
51. Yohlin, *The Short-Term Trust—A Respectable Tax-Saving Device*, 14 TAX L. REV. 109, 130 (1958).
52. See Baer, *Keeping Control of the Spray Trust in the Family: Income Tax Problems*, 34 TAXES 734, 736 (1956); *cf.* Casner, *Responsibilities of the Corporate Trustee as to Discretionary Trusts*, 32 Trust Bull., March 1953, p. 21, at 24-25.
53. A trustee who is also a beneficiary may suffer adverse tax consequences either from (1) possession of a power to vest income or principal in himself, or (2) exercise of a power to distribute income or principal to persons other than himself. Possession of a power exercisable in his own favor solely by himself makes him taxable on trust income (unless such income is taxable to the grantor) under CODE § 678; its exercise or release may be taxable as a gift under CODE § 2514(b) and may require inclusion of all or part of the trust in his taxable estate under CODE § 2041(a)(2). Exercise of a power in favor of someone other than himself may constitute such a release of a power exercisable in his own favor, with the tax consequences just mentioned. See Treas. Reg. §§ 25.2514-3(c)(4), 20.2041-3(d)(1) (1958). Similarly, exercise of a power in favor of someone other than himself may constitute a transfer of the trustee's beneficial interest, taxable as a gift. See Treas. Reg. § 25.2514-1(b)(2) (1958). *But see* Self v. United States, 142 F. Supp. 939 (Ct. Cl. 1956).

of a non-discretionary trust. A donee or beneficiary can follow the grantor's wishes, and thus permit him to continue to exercise control over that which he purportedly has given away, but the donee or beneficiary will do so only if he is able to resist the temptation to use what he has received for his own purposes. No similar temptation confronts one who is merely the trustee of a discretionary trust, unless he wishes to commit the most flagrant form of breach of trust. Thus, such a trustee may have many reasons for doing the grantor's bidding and no compelling reason for doing otherwise.

Finally, there is the matter of the assumed spine-stiffening effect of a "reasonably definite external standard" upon trustees who are in relationships that the Code recognizes as creating susceptibility to domination by the grantor.[54] The assumption is presumably based upon a belief that so long as such trustees observe the standard they lack real power to shift enjoyment from one beneficiary to another, and that fear of suit for breach of trust will deter them from being led astray as a result of pressure from the grantor. This view is more easily stated than sustained. Even a "reasonably definite" standard is far from being so precise that a given exercise or non-exercise of the discretionary power is likely to fall clearly within or without its scope.[55] And even if the trustee recognizes that following the grantor's wishes may give a beneficiary grounds for suit, he may assume that suit will not be brought, either because of the beneficiary's relationship to the grantor or his relationship to the trustee himself.[56]

2. *Non-tax purposes.* The creation of a trust in which the trustee has limited discretion, may be motivated by a desire to give a dependent of the grantor the feeling of financial independence.[57] But if the trustee has broad discretionary powers, creation of the trust will not give the beneficiaries any justified feeling of financial independence; there will be merely a substitution of dependence upon the trustee for dependence upon the grantor. Therefore, we must look elsewhere to find a non-tax reason for the creation of such discretionary trusts.

---

54. See CODE § 674(d) (power over income). Such trustees may also be given powers over principal identical to those that a grantor may himself have as trustee without causing adverse tax consequences to the grantor. CODE § 674(b)(5).

55. The Regulations state that the entire context of a provision of a trust instrument must be considered to determine whether the required standard is present, and that if the trustee's determination is conclusive, the power is not limited by a reasonably definite standard. See Treas. Reg. § 1.674(d)-1 (1956), referring to Treas. Reg. § 1.674(b)-1(b)(5) (1956).

56. The trustee may also be immunized from suit in greater or lesser degree by an exculpatory clause or by a provision in the instrument for binding approval of his accounts by the grantor or someone else. See Westfall, *Nonjudicial Settlement of Trustees' Accounts,* 71 HARV. L. REV. 40 (1957). It is uncertain whether such a clause or provision would result in a conclusion that the trustee's discretionary power is not limited by a reasonably definite standard. See note 55 *supra.* A power in the grantor to make a binding approval of the trustee's accounts, however, may itself have adverse tax consequences to the grantor. See Westfall, *supra* at 58-59.

57. See pp. 334-35 *supra.*

It has been suggested that one such reason, applicable to irrevocable inter vivos trusts generally, is to protect the grantor's family from his creditors when the grantor is about to undertake a hazardous business venture.[58] Of course a non-discretionary trust would provide the same protection from creditors, but it may be that the grantor has funds that he wants to keep available for the benefit of the persons in his family who, from time to time, will most need assistance. A trust in which the trustee has broad discretion is ideally suited to such a purpose, but it does not follow that the grantor should be freed from taxability upon the income from the trust property.

If the anticipated threat to family financial security is from business creditors, other devices, such as broad insurance protection and non-recourse loans, may provide limited liability as well as a trust.[59] Moreover, if it is deemed unduly harsh to tax a grantor upon trust income that no longer is legally his, provision could be made by the Code for placing a prorata part of the tax upon the trust.[60]

The fundamental need that is fulfilled by irrevocable inter vivos trusts with broad discretion in the trustee is that of grantors who want to make gifts but are uncertain about to whom they want to make them.[61] This paradoxical dilemma can logically be attributed to a desire to minimize taxes and at the same time to retain effective control over the disposition of the trust property by dominating the trustee. If the grantor's real desire were for flexibility in disposing of the property, he would not create a trust at all during his lifetime. He would retain ownership himself, thereby enjoying, up to the moment of his death, the maximum flexibility of disposition known to American law.

* * *

---

58. See CASNER, ESTATE PLANNING 110 (2d ed. 1956).
59. See Anthoine, *Federal Tax Legislation of 1958: The Corporate Election and Collapsible Amendment*, 58 COLUM. L. REV. 1146, 1175 (1958).
  The corporate form may also be used in conjunction with an election under subchapter S, which may eliminate federal corporate income taxes.
60. See U.S. TREASURY DEPARTMENT, FEDERAL ESTATE AND GIFT TAXES—A PROPOSAL FOR INTEGRATION AND FOR CORRELATION WITH THE INCOME TAX 50-54 (1947); cf. CODE §§ 2206-07 (recovery of portion of estate tax from beneficiaries of life insurance and recipients of appointive property included in decedent's gross estate).
61. Another possible motive is to minimize the claims of a surviving spouse. Cf. Westfall, *Estate Planning and the Widow's Election*, 71 HARV. L. REV. 1269, 1286 n.62 (1958).

If tax-motivated transfers in trust are to be discouraged, revision of section 674 is necessary. Repeal of sections 674(c) and 674(d) would bring realism to bear upon the legislative assumptions concerning the ability of grantors to influence "independent" and "related and subordinate" trustees and would greatly restrict the opportunities that now exist to secure income tax benefits by making a gift in trust without deciding who is to receive the income from the trust property. It would also encourage the selection of trustees upon the basis of ability to render fiduciary service, rather than because of a trustee's formal qualifications to exercise discretionary powers without causing adverse tax consequences to the grantor. In addition, if income tax benefits are to be denied for the creation of trusts unless the grantor has determined, at the time of creation, who shall receive the income, sections 674(b)(4), 674(b)(5)(A) and 674(b)(6) should also be repealed.

The suggested revisions of section 674 would, of course, leave many problems still unsolved. Inadequacies in the present versions of sections 673, 675, and 677 would, no doubt, continue to lead to tax-motivated transfers in trust with the retention of substantial rights by grantors. And there would remain the problem of the taxation of non-grantors who may exercise a substantial degree of effective control over the beneficial enjoyment of trust income or principal, or both.[74] Of course, any such piecemeal approach as that proposed here inevitably encounters the initial objection that it deals with but part of a still larger problem: tax-motivated property dispositions generally.[75] But if revision of the trust provisions must await a solution of the larger problem, the wait is likely to be a long one. In the meantime, a piecemeal solution, it is submitted, is better than no solution at all.

Almost every proposal for changing Code provisions to the detriment of some taxpayers encounters the fundamental objection that there has been reliance upon the old law and that such reliance has taken the form of irrevocable arrangements.[76] Congress has, in a number of situations involving

---
74. See text accompanying note 11 *supra*.
75. See, *e.g.*, Johnson & Vernon, *supra* note 71, at 1760.
76. See, *e.g.*, Novick & Petersberger, *Retroactivity in Federal Taxation*, 37 TAXES 499 (1959).

other areas of the Code,[77] and in a few involving the taxation of trust income,[78] accorded recognition to such reliance by making new provisions inapplicable to completed transfers. It would seem, however, that no exemption of existing trusts from Code changes is appropriate here.

In the first place, it is questionable whether a majority, or even a significant minority, of the living grantors of irrevocable inter vivos trusts may properly be regarded as having "relied," at the time such trusts were created, upon an indefinite continuance of the present mode of taxation of trust income. The present scheme was first enacted with the adoption of the Internal Revenue Code of 1954, and although its provisions dealing with taxation of grantors were copied in large part from the predecessor *Clifford* Regulations,[79] reliance upon such administrative regulations is not usually thought to preclude legislative change of the underlying statute. Accordingly, the allegation of reliance would appear to be limited to grantors of trusts created after August 16, 1954, the date of enactment of the Code.

Did the post-August 16, 1954 grantors indeed rely upon indefinite continuance of the Code provisions? To assume that they did so is to credit them (and their tax advisers) with a remarketable naïveté, as the Code itself made significant changes in the pre-existing mode of taxation of trust income in respects other than the taxation of grantors. Certainly no well-advised draftsman of a long term discretionary trust would neglect to include an appropriate avenue of relief in case of an adverse change in the tax law.[80]

Second, even if some of the post-August 16, 1954 grantors were indeed sufficiently naïve to rely upon an indefinite continuance of the new provisions, a revision of section 674 along the lines just described need produce no undue hardship. A grantor who is required to include trust income in his taxable income may be given the right to recover from the trust a part of his tax.[81]

---

77. See, *e.g.*, CODE §§ 269, 1551.
78. The present sections dealing with taxation of trust income to the grantor, CODE §§ 671-78, are applicable to all trusts, without regard to the date of their creation. The same may be said of the tier system and the five-year throwback rule, with two minor exceptions: § 663(b) and § 665(b)(3). In view of this statutory pattern, it is difficult to find support for the statement by one member of the Advisory Group that "Congress has always been careful to prevent a statute from operating retroactively where it is too late to change what the taxpayer has already done." *Hearings Before the House Committee on Ways and Means on General Revenue Revision*, 85th Cong., 2d Sess., pt. 3, at 2792-93 (1958).
79. See Treas. Reg. 118, § 39.22(a)-21 (1953).
80. See, *e.g.*, CASNER, ESTATE PLANNING 970-71 (2d ed. 1956) (provision for release by trustee of discretionary powers).
81. Such right of recovery should, it is submitted, be created by the Code itself, rather than by state legislation, since the problem is national in its scope. In the analogous situation of inclusion of inter vivos transfers in the gross estate for federal estate tax purposes, the scope of the federal tax apportionment provisions is quite limited. See note 60 *supra*. A large number of states have enacted state apportionment legislation. See, *e.g.*, MASS. ANN. LAWS c. 65A, § 5 (1953); N.Y. DEC. EST. LAW § 124. Variations in the state statutes have created problems, see Scoles, *Apportionment of Federal Estate Taxes and Conflict of Laws*, 55 COLUM. L. REV. 261 (1955), and

Although such a recovery would, no doubt, create problems of computation and payment, it is difficult to believe that they are insurmountable.[82] Thus, the effect would be merely to change the tax rates applicable to the income of the trust, with the increase borne, in effect, by the grantor, by means of an increase in his marginal tax bracket, or by the trust, or by both the grantor and the trust, depending upon the mode of computing the amount recoverable. It has not been seriously contended that a taxpayer is entitled to a lifetime of taxation at the rates prevailing in the year of his birth.[83] Likewise, it is submitted, fairness does not require that trust income be taxed throughout the existence of the trust under the law in effect when it was created.

---

have led to proposals for enactment of more comprehensive federal provisions, see Note, 30 IND. L.J. 217 (1955), or for uniformity in state legislation, see Scoles & Stephens, *The Proposed Uniform Estate Tax Apportionment Act*, 43 MINN. L. REV. 907 (1959).

82. At least three methods for determining the amount of tax recoverable by the grantor from the trust deserve consideration. Assume that G, an unmarried grantor, has a taxable income of $16,000 without inclusion of $2,000 of trust income taxable to him under the proposed revision of CODE § 674. For simplicity, assume further that no part of G's or the trust's income consists of capital gains. Ignoring the dividends received, retirement income, and other credits, G's tax is $5,200 without inclusion of the trust income and $6,200 if it is included. G could be given the right to recover from the trust either (a) $1,000, the amount his tax was increased as a result of inclusion of the trust income in his taxable income; (b) $688.89, representing two-eighteenths of $6,200, or the same proportion of G's total tax as his trust income bears to his total taxable income; or (c) $380, representing the tax the trust would have paid on the $2,000 if all of its income had been accumulated.

Clearly the last is the easiest method for the trustee, as the grantor's recovery is based upon the amount of trust income alone, a figure that the trustee may be expected to anticipate and to be guided by in making distributions to beneficiaries. See U.S. TREASURY DEP'T, FEDERAL ESTATE AND GIFT TAXES—A PROPOSAL FOR INTEGRATION AND FOR CORRELATION WITH THE INCOME TAX 51-52 (1947). But, in the example given, there would be a $1,000 increase in G's tax, only $380 of which would be recoverable from the trust. On the other hand, under either the first or the second method it would be more difficult for the trustee to anticipate, in making distributions to beneficiaries, the amount that should be withheld to meet the liability for a prorata or marginal part of the grantor's tax. A compromise solution would allow such prorata or marginal recovery only to the extent of income received by the trustee after a demand therefor from the grantor. *Cf. ibid.*

83. *Cf. Hearings Before the House Committee on Ways and Means on General Revenue Revision*, 85th Cong., 2d Sess., pt. 3, at 2792 (1958).

POINTS AND COUNTERPOINTS

1. Congress is almost certain to insist that any plan for reform of the present system of family taxation in the United States retain the geographical neutrality achieved through the adoption of marital income splitting in 1948. Thus a return to separate filing for husbands and wives "reintroduces income attribution questions like those raised in *Lucas v. Earl, Poe v. Seaborn,* and *Commissioner v. Harmon* * * *. Congress has two choices for determining income attribution: (1) it could override *Poe* and thereby extend *Earl* to community property states or (2) it could override *Earl* and *Harmon* and extend *Poe* to common law states." Gann, "Abandoning Marital Status as a Factor in Allocating Income Tax Burdens," 59 *Texas Law Review* 1, 52 (1980). Which of these choices should individual filing advocates recommend to Congress? Can Congress extend *Earl* and *Harmon* to community property states without adopting page upon page of detailed property rules to fill the vacuum created by the override of the community property system? Would an extension of *Poe* differ from the marital splitting system advocated in the McIntyre selection?

2. The family law of every state enforces a set of marriage bonuses and penalties, since persons who marry someone with money or good prospects get at least inchoate rights to share in some or all of their spouse's income sources, while those who marry someone with less material wealth must support their spouse and children and usually are forced to leave their spouse some share of their accumulated income on death or divorce. These laws merely reflect an even more extensive system of bonuses and penalties created by well-entrenched social customs. Are these nonneutral features of family law and custom undesirable? Are they more or less offensive than the much less substantial, but partially offsetting, marriage nonneutralities of the federal income tax? Why?

3. Does the *Yale Note* offer a principled defense of individual filing? Or does it view the individual filing rule merely as a convenient technique for taxing some married persons on the nonmonetary benefits they obtain from their marriage relationship? For an analysis of the imputed income aspects of the exchange theory of marriage, see McIntyre & Oldman, "Taxation of the Family in a Comprehensive and Simplified Income Tax," 90 *Harvard Law Review* 1573 (1977), reproduced in part in Chapter IV.

4. A traditional argument for taxing married persons more heavily than single persons with equal monetary income is that married persons allegedly enjoy economies of scale in their utilization of household assets. The proper technique for imposing a tax on such consumer surplus, however, is an addition to taxable income, not an individual filing rule. *See* Coven, "The Decline and Fall of Taxable Income," 79 *Michigan Law Review* 1525, 1536–45 (1981). In evaluating the case for a special tax on the consumer surplus of married persons, is it relevant that over 60 percent of single persons apparently enjoy comparable economic benefits? *See Yale Note*, supra, at note 13. Are the alleged economies of scale of marriage the only type of consumer surplus that policy makers should consider taxing, or should persons be taxed in other situations when the benefits they obtain from market purchases exceed their costs?

5. Would adoption of a family assessment unit, as proposed by Martin McMahon, solve the family trust problems addressed by Smith and Westfall? Conversely, how important would it be to move toward a family assessment system if the tax avoidance opportunities afforded by family trusts were substantially curtailed?

6. Commentators have often asserted that family taxation issues would have little importance in a flat-rate income tax. This cannot be correct. All flat-tax proposals provide in some fashion for a substantial standard deduction or low income allowance. In effect, they are really disguised progressive taxes. Family taxation issues, therefore, would reemerge as tax base issues. Flat-tax designers must decide whether one-job couples and two-job couples should get the same standard deduction and whether one-job couples and unattached individuals should get the same per-capita standard deduction. What would really happen in a flat-tax is that family taxation issues would become relatively less important for high-income taxpayers and relatively more important for low-income taxpayers.

7. How would a family unit tax regime account for differences in taxable capacity due to differences in family size? Is it not clear, for example, that a family of ten with a total income of $12,000 has less taxable capacity than a family of four with the same total income? Can those differences in taxable capacity be adjusted for through dependency deductions? Are dependency deductions adequate in adjusting for these differences at middle- and upper-income levels? Is the French quotient system, which allows for substantial income splitting among members of the core family, a better alternative? For discussion, *see* McIntyre & Oldman, "Taxation of the Family in a Comprehensive

and Simplified Income Tax," 90 *Harvard Law Review* 1573 (1977), pp. 1599–607. For an analysis of the substantial reduction in the value of the dependency deductions since 1947, *see* Steuerle & Hartzmark, "Individual Income Taxation, 1947–79," 34 *National Tax Journal* 145 (1981).

8. Can a joint filing system take account of the economic consequences of nonmarital cohabitation? Can an individual filing system do this any better? What types of nonmarried partners would be treated unfairly under a joint filing system with full income splitting? Under a marital unit system like that of current law? Under an individual filing system? Is marriage the only reasonable bright-line test for income pooling? Sweden once required previously married partners sharing a household and unmarried partners with an acknowledged child to file jointly under some circumstances. Would this be a good rule for the United States to adopt? What harmful social consequences, if any, flow from a tax system that encourages couples to marry (e.g. full income splitting)? That discourages couples from marrying (e.g. joint filing without full income splitting)? That encourages couples to marry and then get a divorce (e.g. individual filing with an alimony deduction)?

VIII. TAXATION OF CORPORATIONS AND THEIR SHAREHOLDERS

In a personal income tax, who is the proper taxpayer on the income sources of a corporation? The corporation itself? Its shareholders? Those who effectively exercise control over corporate policies—i.e., the managers? Those whose material well-being the corporate income augments? This latter answer is the one dictated by the benefit principle discussed in Chapter VII, but that principle has never been applied systematically to the solution of corporate income-attribution issues. Would adoption of that principle in a Haig/Simons income tax require that the shareholders be taxed on corporate income, or can corporations themselves consume and save in a Haig/Simons sense? Assuming a decision to tax the shareholders on corporate income, is there any practical way to assess and collect a tax that effectively treats the corporation as a partnership of its shareholders? Or is a separate corporate tax an equitable response to the administrative obstacles to direct shareholder taxation on corporate income?

Assuming the inevitability of a separate corporate tax, what rules should the tax system adopt to approximate the asserted ideal of an integrated corporate and personal income tax? What tax rate should apply to corporate income? Should either the shareholders or the corporation be permitted a deduction for some or all of distributed corporate income—to prevent or minimize the so-called "double tax" on corporate profits? Aside from equity concerns, are there any efficiency grounds for some form of dividend relief? What is the reasonable trade-off between equity and efficiency in this context?

Most discussions of the design features of a corporate tax assume that the corporate tax is intended to serve as a complement to the personal income tax. But can a corporate tax stand on its own merits? In fact, the present federal corporate tax was adopted in 1909, four years before Congress enacted the personal income tax. What was its legitimate function, if any, during that four-year period? Is it reasonable for a society to seek to share in business profits quite apart from its desire to redistribute marketplace rewards? Can a corporate tax be understood as a mechanism through which society rents its production and marketing networks to capitalists who wish to use those networks for private profit? Assuming that society wishes to levy a fee for use of its networks, is the corporate tax well suited for that function? How would a corporate tax built on such benefit criteria differ from one built on traditional ability-to-pay criteria?

In the first selection, below, Richard Bird examines the various arguments that have been advanced by commentators over the years to explain the function of a corporate tax. He makes the important point that the arguments for and against the corporate tax in theory may have little or no relevance to a country which in fact has a corporate tax in place and is considering its reform or repeal. Charles McLure, the author of the second selection, has been a leading advocate of some form of integration of the corporate and personal income taxes. He analyzes here the arguments typically made for and against his position and shows why the debate over proposals for integration is not easily resolved. In the third selection, Martin Norr compares two techniques for partial integration—the tax relief to shareholders and tax relief to corporations. In the final selection, William Andrews shows how a very limited dividend relief mechanism could reduce the tax bias against corporate equity capital normally produced by a tax system that imposes a dual tax on corporations and individuals.

Supplemental Readings. J. Pechman, *Federal Tax Policy* (3d Ed. 1977), pp. 123–180; Surrey, "Reflections on 'Integration' of Corporate and Individual Income Taxes," 28 *National Tax Journal* 335 (1975); Sato & Bird, "International Aspects of the Taxation of Corporations and Shareholders," 22 *International Monetary Fund Staff Papers*, 384 (1975); McLure, "Integrating the Income Taxes: How To Do It Right," *Tax Notes*, Sept. 5, 1977, pp. 3–9; G. Esenwein & J. Gravelle, "A Comparative Analysis of the Accelerated Cost Recovery System and a Repeal of the Corporate Income Tax," in 6 *Studies in Taxation, Public Finance and Related Subjects—A Compendium* (1982), pp. 64–83; Auerbach, "Whither the Corporate Tax?: Reform after ACRS," 35 *National Tax Journal* 275 (1982).

RICHARD M. BIRD, "WHY TAX CORPORATIONS?"

In Taxing Corporations, Institute for Research on Public Policy (1980), pp. 9–24.

CHAPTER 3: WHY TAX CORPORATIONS?

Perhaps the most basic question to be considered in this study is why corporations as such should be taxed at all. Although the proverbial man in the street may not be aware of it, the prevailing view among scholars of public finance at the present time is probably that there is <u>no</u> reason for taxing corporations as such (although there may <u>be</u> some administrative advantages in withholding personal taxes at the corporate level). The ideal tax system of most public finance economists thus contains no corporate tax. In this respect, if in few others, there would appear to be a striking similarity of view between economists and most businessmen!

In reality, however, almost every country <u>does</u> tax corporations, a fact which suggests either that there <u>are</u> good reasons for taxing corporations as such, or that no tax system is ideal, or - what seeems most likely to be true - both. Moreover, it is important to note that the question of whether or not a corporation tax should be introduced into a country which does not have one is really quite different from the question of whether a long-existing corporation tax should be abolished. The answer to the latter question depends not so much on the case <u>for</u> taxing corporations as on the presumption that "untaxing" them in some way would improve the efficiency with which the tax system achieved its goals, whatever they may be.

Discussions of tax reform, whether with respect to corporate taxes or anything else, are thus soon reduced to a question of goals, since taxes are in the end only <u>instruments</u> of policy, not policy ends in their own right.[1] The <u>appropriate</u> context within which possible changes in corporation taxes must be considered is therefore this broader public policy framework rather than simply as part of the design of an "ideal" tax system. Corporate taxes serve as one way to achieve particular policy goals. From such a broader perspective, it seems clear that one of the arguments usually put forth for abolishing taxes on corporations, namely, that the reasons for taxing corporations are weak or non-existent, is essentially irrelevant. Since we already <u>do</u> tax corporations, for whatever historical reason, and since all <u>policy</u> changes involve transitional costs, often considerable in magnitude, a better argument than this seems necessary to justify the abolition of an existing corporate tax.[2] Old taxes need not be good taxes, but there must be good reasons for changing them since any change is itself costly.

TWO ARGUMENTS FOR ABOLITION OF THE TAX

The arguments for the abolition of corporate taxes seem, in the end, to come down to two. The first is the view that, because in the final analysis only people can pay taxes, the best taxes are those that are levied on people openly and directly, so they can know what is going on, and make their democratic decisions accordingly. The second argument arises from the desire to remove the various distortions of business activities and horizontal inequities that are thought to arise from the present corporate income tax.

To take the second point first, it is easy to agree that a tax which induces firms to rely more heavily on debt and less on equity finance than they otherwise would, as well as to distribute less than they otherwise would to shareholders and perhaps to take fewer risks and to invest less than would be the case in a world without corporate taxes, has virtues that are, to say the least, somewhat suspect.[3] Most such distortions in corporate decisions, however, arise from such particular features of the present corporate tax as the deductibility of interest but not dividends, less than complete dividend relief, the incomplete offset of losses, and distorted tax depreciation provisions.[4] They can therefore be offset, if desired, at least in part through revising those features of the tax rather than altering its essential nature as a tax on corporations rather than people.[5] Chapter 4 outlines two such revised corporate taxes that have been proposed in recent years - a neutral tax on rents and a tax on the flow of funds. These two taxes are basically equivalent in most respects, and the flow of funds version at least is probably also administratively feasible.

To return to the first argument mentioned above, as the Report of the Royal Commission on Taxation (1966) put it, the corporation in itself has no independent reality because it is merely a conduit through which money is channeled from some persons - the buyers of corporate products - to others - the owners of the factors of production combined in the corporate form (workers, managers, shareholders). This denial of the reality of the legal fiction of the corporation not only comes easily to the lips and pens of economists, but it is also surely fundamentally correct.

WHO PAYS THE TAX?

If corporations pay tax monies over to the government some natural person's (as opposed a legal person's) income is clearly reduced by this act: either that of consumers (who as a result either of administered prices or reduced output will pay higher prices for corporate goods), or workers (who get lower wages either immediately or in the long run because they have less capital to work with), or shareholders (who get fewer dividends and capital gains), or all capitalists (to the extent the tax lowers the rate of return on capital in general) - or some mixture of the foregoing (depending on the precise nature of the tax, the state of the economy, its degree of openness to foreign trade, the nature of other accompanying policy measures, the time period considered, and so on). As the very condensed summary of several decades of theoretical and empirical literature in the last sentence is intended to convey, however, the question of precisely <u>whose</u> income is reduced by taxes on corporations is far from simple.[6]

There are, for example, three published studies of the short-run incidence of the Canadian corporate income tax.[7] All three found substantial short-run forward shifting of the tax, ranging from 70 percent (Levesque, 1966) to 100 percent (Spencer, 1969) to 55 to 88 percent (Dusansky and Tanner, 1975). The econometric evidence, such as it is, therefore, suggests that the short-run impact of an increase in corporate taxes is much like that of an increase in sales taxes, particularly since sales taxes are also levied for the most part on products produced by corporations.[8]

In contrast, the most fully worked-out proposal for corporate tax reform yet put forth in this country - that of the Royal Commission on Taxation (1966) - is generally considered to have assumed that in the long run the corporate tax is borne by shareholders.[9] A still more recent argument is that, in the truly long run, the major impact of corporate taxes is probably borne by <u>workers</u> who, as a result of lower levels of investment, receive lower real wages than they would otherwise have in the absence of the tax (Feldstein, 1974). The relevance of the results of any of these models depends critically upon how well their assumptions describe reality, an essentially empirical question to which no one as yet has a good answer.[10]

One reason why some economists dislike the corporate income tax is thus because neither they nor anyone else understands who really does pay it (in the form of reduced real income). This uncertainty as to the incidence of the tax is, as the above discussion suggests, well-founded, but it does not quite serve to explain why the corporate tax seems to be particularly disliked by economists. The fact is that we do not <u>really</u> know who pays most other general taxes either, for example the property tax (Bird and Slack, 1978), the payroll taxes used to finance social insurance schemes, or even - so some have said - sales and personal income taxes.[11] In a world in which everything depends (at least to some degree) on everything else, this uncertainty should not be surprising. What is surprising, however, is the apparent belief of some that the corporate income tax is much worse than most other major taxes in this regard.

It is true that corporation taxes, like all other taxes, are ultimately paid by the real income of some natural persons being reduced, and that, as with other taxes, no one is completely certain _which_ persons bear this burden. But it does not follow what the tax must therefore be abolished for, so to speak, reasons of intellectual tidiness. In the end, the argument that the tax distorts important business decisions probably constitutes a sounder reason for being against the present corporate tax - even though, as already mentioned, it does not necessarily support the abolition of all taxes on corporations.

RATIONALES FOR TAXING CORPORATIONS

To this point, then, it has been suggested that even if one would not introduce a tax on corporations into an ideal tax system, there is no clear reason in principle for abolishing an existing corporate tax, though there may be good reason to modify it in certain ways. Taking the instrumental view of tax policy mentioned earlier, the more immediate policy question is therefore not whether should we tax corporations, but rather how should we tax corporations in order best to achieve our objectives in doing so? _This_ question can be answered only after a more careful exploration of some of the reasons why corporations as such are taxed. The remainder of the present section outlines briefly some possible rationales for corporate taxation. For convenience, these arguments are arranged under four broad headings - ability, benefit, control, and pragmatic.

(1) Ability to Pay Arguments

Most discussions of taxation begin with some mention of equity. This important but elusive characteristic is most commonly sought in the tax field in the form of the ability-to-pay principle. The simplest application to corporate taxes of the ability approach is to assert that the income of corporations should be taxed separately simply because corporations are separate legal entities. "The underlying rationale for corporate taxation," as one author has put it, "goes back to our legal system which looks upon the corporation as an artificial person" (Anderson, 1973, p. 147).

The full logic of this position would presumably subject corporations to the personal income tax rate schedule just like any other individual - as, indeed, some less developed countries have done. Perhaps because the results of this practice would be considered undesirable, however, such extreme application of the principle is rare. Indeed, as noted earlier, it is more normal for economists to take the opposite tack and argue that "there would seem little justification for taxing persons through the fiction of the corporation" (Buchanan and Flowers, 1975, p. 285). This denies _any_ economic reality to the legal fiction of the corporation.

Other writers have, on the contrary, asserted that the large corporation _is_ a real economic entity in modern society, separate and distinct from its owners and exercising real economic power. Those who argue this way (for example, Colm, 1955; Johansen, 1965) often distinguish the small private company associated with a few owners from the large publicly-held company.[12] The latter, unlike the former, is both "... in law and in fact, distinct from its owners. The average stockholder has no direct control over its policies...." (Henderson and Cameron, 1969, p. 164). In a modern industrial society most large aggregations of income and wealth are organized in the form of such corporations, run by salaried managers.

It is of course true, as noted above, that some or all of the taxes levied on such corporations may in some sense be borne by their shareholders - their owners, whether those owners have effective control over corporate policy or not. But _all_ taxes, not simply corporate taxes, affect different individuals differently and should, in principle, be judged on the totalilty of their effects. Although a strong equity case may be made for treating closely-held corporations like partnerships - since the owners in such firms do control decisions - in this view the level and structure of the tax on public corporations is a matter to be decided in a general public policy context, not on the basis of some essentially hedonistic equity principle. Even on equity grounds broadly conceived, as Due and Friedlaender (1977, p. 329) note, "... the tax is widely accepted ... the typical corporation accumulates large sums of wealth over which individual stockholders have no direct claim and which would not be reached effectively by other levies."

This quotation, although it ignores such possible alternative approaches as the full integration discussed in Chapter 4 below, points to another important ability argument for the corporate tax - or at least for that part of it attributable to undistributed profits - as a means of reaching such proftis and thus taxing wealth accruing in the form of increased corporate share values. To put essentially the same point another way, the benefits of "untaxing" corporations would in all likelihood be regressively distributed across income classes, probably accruing primarily to existing shareholders, who would recieve windfall gains if the tax were removed.[13] As noted earlier, even if an old tax is not a very good tax, it does not follow that the result of removing it will necessarily be good. This objection has more force when, as is the case in Canada at present, such windfall gains would not be subject to personal income tax at full rates.[14]

All such problems are, however, at most short run in nature since, through the workings of markets, any initial maladjustments as a result of the change would presumbably tend to work themselves out over time. Transitional problems may appear to present formidable difficulties, but they can never really constitute insuperable obstacles to tax reform. The question is whether the costs incurred in overcoming such barriers are outweighed by the benefits achieved once the change is made.

Another ability-to-pay approach to corporate taxation rests in part on the incidence question discussed above. Depending to a considerable extent on who is reading what, it may be concluded that the corporate income tax is in equity (and perhaps other) terms, a <u>desirable</u> element in the tax structure as a whole. In a famous early study of the U.S. corporation tax, for example, Goode (1951, p. 37, emphasis added) suggested that:

> under prospective long-run conditions in the United States a large part of corporate profits and dividends had a lower order of <u>social usefulness</u> than the income that would be taken by likely alternative taxes. This hypothesis rests on the premises that: (1) the atrophy of their leadership function has weakened the moral and economic claims of stockholders in large public corporations to the whole of profits; (2) corporate profits are an important source of large incomes and fortunes and hence of economic inequality....

In other words, if many corporate profits go to those who do little to deserve them and serve to accentuate inequality, then taxes reducing those profits may themselves be socially useful more or less in proportion as the profits are not. How convincing one finds such views probably depends more on ideology than on any available empirical information.

Some, but not all, of the incidence studies mentioned above lend some credence to the view that the corporate tax is likely to be broadly progressive in its incidence, that is, its burden is distributed across income classes so that the rich pay a relatively higher proportion of their income in tax.[15] It is important to stress, however, that even if the corporation tax <u>is</u> broadly progressive in some real sense - and such studies cannot and do not demonstrate this to be the case - it is not related in any way to the <u>personal</u> characteristics of those presumed to pay it; that is, such factors as the amount of income they receive from other sources, their family status, and so on, are not taken into account. Moreover, the recent atrophying of death taxes in this country (Bird, 1978) perhaps suggests that many Canadians seem to have surprisingly little interest in how progressive taxes are anyway.

What is arguably the most telling ability case for the imposition of corporate taxes arises from the important role of foreign investment in Canada. Although few Canadian corporations possess sufficient power in international markets to shift taxes levied on them to foreign consumers, most foreign-owned corporations do make payments abroad - as dividends, interest, royalties, or management fees, for example. These payments are, as a rule, subject to corporate taxes in the foreign country in which the receiving parent firm is resident. Most such countries, however, allow the crediting of source-country taxes (as, indeed, does Canada).[16] What this means is that if Canada does not tax the profits of a foreign-owned firm operating in Canada, those profits will be taxed anyway when they are repatriated to the country in which the parent firm is located. If Canada does tax these profits, the firm generally will pay no more taxes in total as a result: instead, there is, in effect, a transfer from the foreign treasury to ours.

There is thus a <u>very</u> strong case for levying a separate corporate income tax on foreign-controlled corporations operating in Canada.[17] Moreover, in view of the strong view traditionally taken by the United States - the principal home country of foreign investors in Canada - with respect to the so-called principle of nondiscrimination (Surrey, 1964), it is most unlikely that Canada could get away with either any sort of discriminatory profits tax levied on foreign corporations alone or very high withholding taxes on distributions to foreigners.[18] In other words, so long as the United States has a corporate income tax, so should Canada, and at about the same rates. In the end, this argument alone is probably sufficient to justify the present Canadian tax.

There are thus several ability to pay arguments, of varying degrees of persuasiveness, for retaining some form of separate tax on corporations, and in particular a corporate income tax: (1) to tap foreign treasuries - and hence to secure for Canadians a fair share of the benefits of foreign investment; (2) to supplement the income tax and reach certain forms of income and wealth more effectively than is otherwise done in the present personal tax system; and (3) to avoid bestowing an unwarranted - and economically inefficient - bonus on existing corporate owners by removing the present tax. Finally, to the extent that the corporation tax falls on pure profits (that is, those not needed to call forth effort and enterprise), it is of course an ideal tax anyway (see Chapter 4). None of these arguments, except the first (and last) is perhaps very strong, but in total they suggest there is a stronger case for corporate taxation, and in particular the taxation of corporate profits, than is often admitted.[19]

(2) Benefit Arguments

Many writers seem to find the benefit case for taxing corporations stronger than the ability arguments discussed above - although far from providing a convincing rationale for a tax of the magnitude and structure of the present corporation income tax. At least three versions of the benefit argument for corporate taxes may be distinguished in the literature: (1) general benefit, (2) special benefit, and (3) social costs.

The first of these - the general benefit argument - in its broadest formulation is more or less equivalent to a partnership principle, under which government is seen as "a sort of silent non-voting partner who shares in the profits and to some extent the losses of enterprise" (Colm, 1955, p. 98). Government is justified in so sharing because enterprises enjoy many advantages as result of government activity. Government provides the basic legal and institutional framework within which market activity takes place; it finances the education of the labour force; it attempts to maintain a high and stable level of economic activity; and so on. This rather broad and vague line of argument does not, however, provide any particular support to a tax on <u>corporate</u> profits since any sort of general business tax would seem <u>equally</u> justified on these grounds.[20]

The case for taxing corporations in particular as receiving a special benefit from government in the form of the limited liability of shareholders, perpetual life, easy transfer of ownership, and improved financing possibilities which make it easier for corporations to expand was made strongly by Goode (1951). However, even though the state has a monopoly on the incorporation privilege and could charge for these benefits if it chose to do so, it would be justified in efficiency terms in doing so only if incorporation carried with it some social costs (Musgrave and Musgrave, 1976, p. 294). The special benefit argument thus appears to reduce to a variant of what is called here the social cost argument.

Goode (1951) also suggested two variants of the social cost argument for business taxes. The first is essentially similar to the case for partnership mentioned above, namely, to charge for general government services that in some way facilitate the income-producing activities of private firms. The other is to reflect in the private accounts of firms the <u>external</u> costs their activities impose on others - for example, <u>air, water</u>, or noise pollution. In both cases, when possible, it would clearly be preferable to charge directly the firms responsible for causing the problem or benefiting from the service. Although it is perhaps possible to discern a vague rationalization for some general business tax in this line of argument, the benefit case for a corporate income tax seems clearly much weaker than that for user charges, effluent charges, and the like (Bird, 1976).

On the whole, then, it is hard to see why so many current textbook authors appear to think that the present corporate income tax is supported by <u>any</u> benefit reasoning. User charges, a tax on costs or perhaps a tax on sales, none of which should be limited to corporations, seem equal or better instruments to bring together social and private costs, in the vague terms used here. Weak as they are, the ability arguments outlined in the previous section seem as strong or stronger than such benefit arguments.

(3) <u>Control Arguments</u>

Whether or not it is accepted that corporations have a capacity to pay taxes independent of that of their shareholders, no one can deny that corporations are important in the real world. As with almost any other facet of that world, then, it should occasion no surprise that arguments have been made (1) that corporate activity should be regulated and (2) that taxes have a role to play in such regulation.[21] One may be concerned, for example, with the control of monopoly, with potential political dangers posed by very large private organizations, or with controlling profits in a period of inflation or wage restraint. In these cases and others, particular taxes on corporations may have a role to play. Excess profits taxes of various sorts and taxes graduated in accordance with the size of assets, however, seem more likely candidates for such control roles than the present corporate profits tax (Musgrave and Musgrave, 1976), although one might discern some slight rationale for the present <u>graduated</u> corporate tax rate in arguments.

More convincing justification for the deviations from uniformity which characterize the present Canadian corporate tax system – see the discussion in Chapter 2 above – may, however, be found in some other control motivations. To encourage certain industrial sectors relative to others, to encourage investment in fixed assets, to encourage small businesses relative to large, to encourage the retention rather than the distribution of profits[22] – these are among the intended purposes served by the present corporate tax structure.

No doubt all or most of these goals could be achieved as well or better through such alternative means as direct grants or subsidies. Moreover, some control purposes (for example, to curb management's control over undistributed profits) may conflict with others (for example, to encourage corporate saving). Nevertheless, in total the scope for implementing public policy afforded by a tax on corporate enterprise is, presumably to the despair of believers in <u>laissez-faire</u> and the delight of would-be interventionists, very great indeeed.

Someone once said about the public debt from the point of view of monetary management: "If it did not exist, we would have invent it." Similarly, if the corporate income tax did not exist we might perhaps have to invent it, or something very like it, in order for the governments of modern industrial states to attempt to achieve the numerous policy goals they have, perhaps unwisely, set out to accomplish.[23]

Much the same comment may be made about the potential use of the corporate income tax for purposes of macroeconomic policy. Although there is considerable dispute these days about the uses and usefulness of varying tax instruments for macroeconomic purposes (Branson, 1973), those charged with managing an economy like Canada's seem unlikely to give up willingly the apparent flexibility afforded by a separate tax on corporate profits, particularly when, as noted earlier, so much of Canada's private corporate sector is dominated by foreign interests.

ll, the case for retaining some form of separate taxation of corporations for the purpose of control thus seems moderate though, although again there is little in what has been said to suggest that the present system of corporation income taxes in any sense represents the best of all possible worlds.

Pragmatic Arguments

We do not live in the best of all possible worlds; we live, for better or worse, in this one. From this realistic, or pragmatic, perspective, there are at least three possible reasons additional to those already mentioned for continuing to tax corporations at least as heavily as we now do. Put briefly, these reasons are (1) that we now have such corporation taxes; (2) that they are politically acceptable; and (3) that none of the attractive alternatives seems feasible and none of the feasible alternatives seems attractive. These points are elaborated briefly in this concluding part of Chapter 3 and to some extent developed further in Chapter 4 below (particularly the third point).

As Brown and Jackson (1978, p. 362) put the first point in the British context recently, "a very powerful argument for any existing tax is that we have it, that people are more or less used to it, and that a switch to any alternative source of revenue could have high costs associated with change." The corporate income tax is deeply entrenched not only within the Canadian tax structure but also in the complex network of relationships that constitutes the business world. Any significant change in that tax will therefore produce a chain of windfall gains and losses throughout the economy, the uncertain magnitude and distribution of which argue against sharp changes. This is, of course, really the "old tax is a good tax" argument again. As noted earlier, transitional difficulties of this sort must not be regarded as an insuperable barrier to change. When coupled with the pervasive uncertainty of the incidence and effects of the corporate tax noted above, however, this argument does suggest that at most one should make haste slowly in this area.

Major changes in important taxes should probably be made only where there is consensus that the effects of the change, once the system is adjusted to it, will be more beneficial than the cost in equity and efficiency terms of the inevitable transitional adjustments.[24] The fact that no one is really in a position to carry out this sort of elementary cost-benefit analysis on corporate tax changes, despite all the attention paid to this area in the past, is perhaps sufficient evidence of the need for caution in making major changes.

This argument from existence, as it might be labelled, for the present corporate tax system seems more convincing than the line of argument that holds that "the tax appears to be attractive all out of proportion to its actual justification on equity or other grounds because of widespread acceptance of the belief that

a tax on business is not borne by people - and corporat_
vote" (Due and Friedlaender, 1977, p. 329). To quote an do not
cent text along similar lines: "The political decisio re-
find it very easy to impose a tax on corporate income a rs
difficult to impose a tax on individual income" (Buchan s
Flowers, 1975, p. 286).[25] In response to such remarks it
be noted that there is obviously more to political life thar
curing votes since, as shown in Chapter 2 above, corporation t
have been exploited less and less intensively in recent years.

It is somewhat surprising that the currently dominant schoo
of thought that views politicians as focusing their efforts on the
marginal voter and bureaucrats as endlessly self-aggrandizing
revenue-maximizers have apparently never asked why countries such
as Canada and the United States make so <u>little</u> use of such hidden
taxes as the corporation tax. Could it be that the reasons are
unlikely to square with their theories?[26] In any case, there is
no strong evidence in support of the cynical argument that corporate taxes reflect simple political expediency, or, perhaps, the
cynicism of the political right found in the quotations above has
been met, and overcome, by the cynicism of the left in the sense
that corporate financial influence on the political system may
have outweighed the attractiveness of "buying" votes by hiding
taxes.

Although it is not exploited to the full extent naive readers
of quotations such as those reproduced above might expect, the
corporate tax nevertheless still brings in a significant amount
of revenue in Canada (see Chapter 2). Whether one considers alternatives to taxes on corporations or alternative ways of taxing
corporations, it is therefore important to consider as well the
merits and demerits of alternative potential revenue sources.[27]
Advocates of full integration, for example, have usually assumed
that the revenue would be made up by increased personal income
taxes (primarily as a result of broadening the base through measures such as the full taxation of capital gains). <u>Would</u> it be?
<u>Should</u> it be? Advocates of substituting value-added taxes for
corporate income taxes tend to assume that the overall effects of
the substitution on growth, distribution, and so on would be, on
balance, beneficial; but would they be? These are the sorts of
questions which must be considered as carefully and empirically as
possible in order to decide whether any proposed tax substitution
is worthwhile. Unfortunately, the present state of fiscal science
in this area does not allow us to improve much on Grove's (1958,
p. 181) conclusion of two decades ago that "... the economic effects of this levy may be more favorable or less unfavorable than
those of alternative levies. And ... the same may be said of its
consequences in terms of equity." Or, one might add, the opposite
may be true!

In short, at best the melange of partial (and sometimes contradictory) arguments assembled in this Chapter may justify the
continued existence of some sort of absolute corporate taxes, per-

haps even in the form of corporate income taxes, as a sort of second-best tax. Little as this is, however, it is likely all that can be said about any feasible alternative either. In particular, if any alternative system is required to yield the same revenue from the corporate sector and all other taxes remain unchanged, the task of the would-be tax reformer is difficult indeed. These conditions, when combined with the persuasive theoretical and empirical uncertainty about the incidence and effects of the present corporate income tax, make it exceedingly difficult to meet even the mild cost-benefit test for reform proposed earlier, namely, that the expected benefits of the change clearly exceed the transitional costs.

While this conclusion does not mean that some changes in the form of the existing corporate income tax are not desirable and feasible, it does suggest that, in the absence of strong evidence to the contrary, no major upheaval of the present system seems likely to be either desirable or feasible. The major problems with all the alternatives to corporation income taxes that have so far been proposed in a sense are reduced to three: (1) revenue; (2) transitional problems; and (3) the international aspect. These are all feasibility concerns and are consequently often taken to be of little importance in the world of theoretical tax designer.[28] They are, however, the major problems of any would-be tax reformer, and the question of how corporations should be taxed in Canada is pre-eminently a problem of tax reform, not tax design.

Notes to Chapter 3

1. This is true with respect to particular tax changes even if one takes the view that the attainment of a particular sort of tax structure is itself a goal (for example, because it may restrain government growth or in some way satisfy some a priori concept of efficiency, equity, or neatness).

2. For a detailed account of the costs and difficulties of changing federal tax policies in Canada, see Good (1980). This book also develops at length the politics of tax policy, a question not discussed in the present study.

3. For conventional critiques of the corporate income tax along these lines, see almost any public finance text: e.g., Musgrave and Musgrave (1976); Due and Friedlander (1977); Boadway, (1979).

4. Moreover, all these distortions may almost as readily be argued to go the other way. Nevertheless, the distortion in business decisions due to the corporate tax, regardless of its direction, is undeniable - which is not to say that it is

necessarily undesirable (a result which would hold with certainty only in a perfectly competitive static world). Some of the problems alluded to in this note are discussed more fully later in the present paper.

5. The major exception is the presumed bias in favour of retention, which can be resolved only by full integration of corporate and personal income taxes: see Chapter 4 below.

6. Indeed, this summary is not only condensed but misleading in the important sense that even in theory only the combined effects of a corporate tax change <u>and</u> the other accompanying measures needed to hold other things equal can be seen (Shoup, 1969). In this sense, then, one can not say anything about the incidence of the corporate tax as such.

7. All these studies are subject to the serious stricture in the preceding note: nevertheless, they are mentioned here as the only empirical work on this question in Canada.

8. The common criticism that forward-shifted corporate taxes are like unplanned sales taxes is really damaging only if one is against all sales taxes or if one thinks corporate sales taxes are somehow worse than planned sales taxes. Although there may indeed be some substance to this last objection, it seems somewhat overdone as a rule. To a considerable extent it is essentially the <u>same</u> firms that pay, for example, the federal corporate income tax and the federal manufacturers' excise tax. The main differences between the two are that (1) the corporate income tax covers a wider range of industry than the sales tax (see note 4 to chapter 2 above), but (2) it is limited to profitable firms, and (3) its effective rate varies with the characteristics of the industry. It is not clear that any of these points <u>necessarily</u> counts against it. (See also the discussion of value-added taxes in Chapter 4 below.)

9. A more correct statement would be that the tax is borne by capitalists in general. Actually, much of the argument of the Royal Commission does <u>not</u> depend upon any particular assumption about shifting, as Mieszkowski (1972) has pointed out. It does, however, depend on the assumption that the total stock of capital is fixed, an assumption removed in the studies referred to in the next sentence in the text.

10. For a striking example of the importance of the assumptions in such analyses, see Asimakopulos and Burbidge (1974), who employ a completely different approach to the short-run incidence of corporate taxes than the neoclassical models used in most of the empirical studies cited above.

11. Those who find this statement of the uncertainty surrounding tax incidence hard to take are referred to Bird and Slack

(1978) and Bird and DeWulf (1973) and the references cited there.

12. For an attempt to draw a similar distinction in Canadian tax policy, see Benson (1969). Although the line between public and private is not necessarily identical to that between widely-held and closely-held the idea behind this distinction is clearly similar.

13. This result may ensue even if the existing tax is largely shifted forward in higher prices to consumers: an asymmetry in shifting and unshifting of the sort suggested by Musgrave (1968) seems quite conceivable.

14. The full capital gains tax proposed by the Royal Commission on Taxation (1966) would, of course, have dealt with this problem to a considerable extent. In the absence of such measures, however, retained earnings could escape all taxation almost indefinitely in the present tax system, if they were not taxed at the corporate level.

15. Gillespie (1976), for example, shows the corporate income tax as progressive in 1969 for income levels over $6,000, on the assumption that the tax is half shifted forward to consumers and half borne by capital owners as a whole. He also notes (p. 434) that the lowering of corporate profits tax in the 1970s would benefit the rich. As argued in Bird and Slack (1978), however, the results of such studies in no sense constitute independent evidence of the validity of the assumptions on which they are based.

16. In the case of U.S.-based firms, there are certain limitations on the foreign tax credit provisions, but the result described in the text is still the most probable outcome. For further discussion, see Jenkins (1979).

17. Jenkins (1979) estimated that Canada's tax revenues from foreign investment in the 1965-74 period ranged between 1.5 and 2.5 percent of GNP. In 1974, for example, the 'net tax contribution' of foreign investment ranged between $2.2 and $3.5 billion (Jenkins, 1979, p. 421). Since total corporate taxes in that year were only $7.2 billion (Bird, 1979a, p. 118), the contribution of the foreign-owned sector was obviously very important.

18. Present witholding taxes on payments to non-residents are severly constrained by tax treaties. Transparent gambits such as nominally levying profits taxes on all corporations but in effect exempting domestic-owned firms seem unlikely to fool U.S. authorities. For an argument that non-discrimination as a guiding principle in international tax relations should be replaced by effective reciprocity, see Sato and Bird (1975).

19. It should perhaps be stressed, however, that there is <u>no</u> conceivable ability case for <u>progressive</u> taxation of corporations, such as now exists in Canada (see Chapter 2 above). To construct such a case, one must assume that richer people own own larger corporations. If anything, the opposite seems more likely to be true, with lower-income shareholders being most likely to own shares of larger corporations (e.g., Bell Canada).

20. Sullivan (1965), for example, discusses in detail the long history of similar arguments used to justify <u>value-added</u> taxes!

21. Of course, if one believes that the best of all possible worlds is one with as little government interference as possible, none of the following arguments will be very persuasive!

22. These last two objectives conflict in Canada to some extent because there is an incentive for small businesses to distribute in order to remain small (see note 3 in Chapter 2 above).

23. To repeat: the point being made is <u>not</u> that government <u>should</u> interfere with private decisions but rather that if it desires, for whatever reason, to so interfere, the corporate tax structure provides a good venue for such action. An alternative approach is to contend that most of these interferences appear to be necessary simply because of the initial distortions occasioned by the corporate tax itself (Bracewell Milnes and Huiskamp, 1977). This view, however, is more semantic than substantive, as argued in Bird (1980).

24. Musgrave (1968), for example, discussed the Royal Commission on Taxation (1966) integration proposals in these terms and found in favour of them: it soon became apparent, however, that there was no consensus along these lines (Bucovetsky and Bird, 1972). For a more formal treatment of this argument, see Feldstein (1976).

25. There is nothing new in such views. Colm (1955, p. 96) noted years ago that "there is no other tax which brings in so much money while making so few voters angry."

26. The fear of international capital flight seems unlikely to have been seen as a constraining influence in U.S. tax policy until very recently, although it has no doubt played some role in Canadian policy (Bucovetsky and Bird, 1972).

27. Reduced government expenditure or increased deficit financing might also be considered as alternatives. The same questions – what happens to income in general? to prices? to employment? to the distribution of income and wealth? etc. – may of course be posed in these cases, as with any tax substitution.

28. Kay and King (1978, p. 5), for example, assert that the international aspect is "unimportant" and "always a secondary argument." In principle, they may be right in a general equilibrium context with a functioning international adjustment mechanism. In practice, however, they are dead wrong. As noted earlier, what Canada can do with its corporate tax structure _does_ depend very much on what the United States does (or will accept), no matter how often theoreticians assert the contrary.

CHARLES E. McLURE, JR., MUST CORPORATE INCOME BE TAXED TWICE?

Brookings Institution (1979), pp. 19–38.

CHAPTER TWO: THE PROS AND CONS OF INTEGRATION

OVER THE PAST several years the presentation of the cases for and against integration and dividend relief in the United States has evolved into a more or less standard format. Yet, rather surprisingly, the arguments used to support dividend relief in the European countries where it is actually practiced are usually quite different from the arguments commonly heard in the United States. This chapter briefly reviews the U.S. debate and then shows how it differs from the European version.[1] Whether the United States should adopt integration (or dividend relief) depends upon at least two types of infor-

---

1. Rather than give both the pros and the cons on each question in sequence, I present the argument for integration (broadly defined to include dividend relief), the argument against, and the reply, to give some continuity and integrity to the arguments on each side and to facilitate comparisons with the rationale for dividend relief as it has developed in Europe. Of course many objective observers can see valid points on both sides of the integration issue; thus the division into two opposing camps is not as clear-cut as I have made it appear. At times arguments made by proponents of integration are used to buttress the case against integration, and vice versa. (Ordinarily this is noted.) Finally, though an effort has been made to present the two sides of the debate in a balanced and unbiased manner, the reader should be aware that I have been an advocate of full integration and, with less enthusiasm, of dividend relief.

mation: the economic effects of integration (or dividend relief) and whether integration (or dividend relief) is administratively feasible. Economists are far from unanimous in appraising the economic effects in such areas as equity, neutrality, and the amount, quality, and financing of capital formation. Though in this chapter I try to raise most of the economic issues that must be addressed, I do not settle them, nor do I attempt to do so in the remainder of the book.

The Case for Integration: The Conduit View

Central to the U.S. case for integration is the view that the corporation has no independent taxpaying ability and should be seen as a conduit through which earnings pass on the way to shareholders.[2] The "conduit" theory of the corporation is important because it has implications for the form integration should take, and especially for the meaning of full integration and the proper treatment of tax preferences. Once the conduit view is accepted, it is natural to calculate the aggregate (corporate and personal) tax rates paid on corporate-source equity income at various points in the personal income distribution (as indicated by marginal personal tax rates) and compare them to the rates that would be paid on ordinary income. Table 2-1 presents one such set of comparisons; it assumes that the corporation income tax is borne by corporate shareholders, that is, that it is not shifted to other owners of capital or to consumers or workers.[3] (The implications of shifting are described below.)

2. The conduit view is most often used to justify full integration, but can be used to argue for dividend relief. For recent statements of the conduit view, see Richard A. Musgrave and Peggy B. Musgrave, *Public Finance in Theory and Practice*, 2d ed. (McGraw-Hill, 1976), pp. 291–301; and Charles E. McLure, Jr., "Integration of the Personal and Corporate Income Taxes: The Missing Element in Recent Tax Reform Proposals," *Harvard Law Review*, vol. 88 (January 1975), pp. 532–82. For a particularly provocative essay on the relation between corporations and shareholders, see William A. Klein, "Income Taxation and Legal Entities," *UCLA Law Review*, vol. 20, issue 1 (1972–73), pp. 13–74.

3. For a more detailed discussion of such a table, see McLure, "Integration," pp. 537–42. Implicit in the construction of table 2-1 and in much of the discussion of equity issues that follows is the assumption that, though capital gains and losses may occur for reasons unrelated to retentions of earnings, there is a tendency for retained earnings to be reflected initially in share prices, and hence in capital gains, on a dollar-for-dollar basis. For evidence of the validity of this assumption, see George F. Break, "Integration of the Corporate and Personal Income Taxes," *National Tax Journal*, vol. 22 (March 1969), pp. 44–49, and references cited there. Of course, it can be expected that corporate financial policies will adjust to the implied difference in costs of various sources of capital.

Table 2-1. Taxation of $100 of Corporate-Source Income under U.S. Law, 1979
Rates in percent; other data in dollars

	Dividend payout rate					
	Zero			100 percent		
Item[a]						
	0	*20*	*70*	*0*	*20*	*70*
1. Shareholder's marginal tax rate[b]	0	20	70	0	20	70
2. Corporate-source income[b]	100.0	100.0	100.0	100.0	100.0	100.0
3. Corporate income tax [46% of 2]	46.0	46.0	46.0	46.0	46.0	46.0
4. Net corporate income [2 − 3]	54.0	54.0	54.0	54.0	54.0	54.0
5. Dividends [from 4]	...	...	...	54.0	54.0	54.0
6. Retained earnings (= capital gains)[c] [from 4]	54.0	54.0	54.0	...	...	...
7. Personal tax on dividends [1 × 5]	...	...	...	0	10.8	37.8
8. Tax on long-term capital gains						
a. Maximum[d] [6 × 40% of 1]	0	4.3	15.1	...	...	...
b. Minimum[e]	0	0	0	...	...	...
9. Total tax						
a. With maximum capital gains tax [3 + 7 + 8a][d]	46.0	50.3	61.1	46.0	56.8	83.8
b. With minimum capital gains tax [3 + 7 + 8b][e]	46.0	46.0	46.0	46.0	56.8	83.8
10. Overtaxation						
a. Maximum tax on capital gains [9a − (1 × 2)]	46.0	30.3	−8.9	46.0	36.8	13.8
b. Minimum tax on capital gains [9b − (1 × 2)]	46.0	26.0	−24.0	46.0	36.8	13.8
11. Percentage overtaxation[f]						
a. Maximum tax on capital gains [10a ÷ 1]	∞	151.5	−12.7	∞	184.0	19.7
b. Minimum tax on capital gains [10b ÷ 1]	∞	130.0	−34.3	∞	184.0	19.7

a. Except for percentages, the numbers in brackets refer to the lines of this table.
b. The shareholder's marginal tax rate is assumed invariant with regard to inclusion of corporate-source income and throughout the taxpayer's life. The statutory corporate rate is assumed to be the effective marginal rate.
c. Assumes that, on the average, retained earnings give rise to capital gains on a dollar-for-dollar basis.
d. Assumes that gain is realized after the passage of a one-year holding period, but within the year in which it accrues. Short-term gains are taxed like dividends.
e. Assumes that the appreciated asset is held indefinitely or transferred at death.
f. The percentage of overtaxation of the zero-bracket taxpayer is infinite.

The combination of corporate and personal income taxes produces aggregate tax rates that are grossly inequitable compared to the statutory personal rate structure.[4] The overtaxation of dividends is greater at the bottom of the income scale than at the top. This is true whether overtaxation is measured by the number of percentage points by which the aggregate tax burden exceeds the statutory marginal tax rates at various income levels or by the excess expressed as a percentage of the statutory rate. Moreover, because of the preferential tax treatment accorded long-term capital gains, retained corporate-source income may actually be taxed at lower aggregate rates at the top of the income scale than ordinary income is.[5]

Indicative of the extra burden created at various income levels by the separate corporate income tax are figures calculated by Break and Pechman and reported in table 2-2. These show that corporate-source income is overtaxed by some 1½ percentage to 3 percentage points at the bottom of the income scale, but undertaxed by some 1 percentage to 2 percentage points at the top of the scale.[6]

---

4. For an alternative analysis of these effects, see the discussion of the "ACID test statistic," in Mervyn King, *Public Policy and the Corporation* (London: Chapman and Hall, 1977), pp. 57–58.

5. This is especially the case when relatively small, closely held corporations are concerned. It has been estimated, for example, that the 91.4 percent of corporations with less than $1 million of assets showing net income for 1974 paid an aggregate effective tax rate of only 21.5 percent. Many of these corporations would probably have qualified for subchapter S treatment (taxation as partnerships), but at most only 16 percent elected it. This suggests that tax saving motivated the choice to be taxed as regular corporations. Further evidence in support of this hypothesis is the relatively low percentage of net income (before tax) distributed to shareholders by these firms (14.1 percent, compared to 42.3 percent for firms with net income and assets in excess of $250,000,000 in 1974). See Dennis J. Gaffney and James E. Wheeler, "The Double Taxation of Corporate-Source Income: Reality or Illusion?" *Tax Adviser*, vol. 8 (September 1977), pp. 523, 526. Of course, this argument is not fully persuasive, since by increasing salaries and bonuses to shareholder-employees, the closely held corporation can reduce taxable income at the corporate level and thereby avoid one layer of the double tax while achieving most of the benefits of dividends.

There has been an unfortunate tendency in some quarters to focus on the double taxation of dividends; unfortunate, because it obscures (1) the fact that at the top of the income scale retained corporate income can be taxed at effective rates well below those on ordinary income, and (2) the fact that tax-exempt organizations and individual shareholders with incomes below levels at which personal tax liability begins pay only *one* tax, the relatively high corporate tax. The real issue is not the number of times corporate source income is taxed, but that (except by accident) it is not taxed in aggregate at the marginal tax rates of shareholders.

6. See George F. Break and Joseph A. Pechman, *Federal Tax Reform: The Impossible Dream?* (Brookings Institution, 1975), p. 93, whose calculations were

Table 2-2. Extra Tax Burdens of the Corporation Income Tax, by Adjusted Gross Income Class, 1976

| | Extra burden as a percent of adjusted AGI[a] ||
Adjusted gross income class (thousands of dollars)	With no capital gains tax from retained earnings	With 7 percent capital gains tax from retained earnings
0–3	2.2	2.4
3–5	2.8	3.1
5–10	1.3	1.5
10–15	0.7	0.8
15–20	0.7	0.8
20–25	0.6	0.7
25–50	0.6	0.8
50–100	−0.6	0.1
100–200	−2.0	−1.1
200–500	−3.5	−2.2
500–1,000	−3.4	−1.7
1,000 and over	−1.2	0.6
Total[b]	0.6	0.9

Source: George F. Break and Joseph A. Pechman, *Federal Tax Reform: The Impossible Dream?* (Brookings Institution, 1975), p. 93.
a. Adjusted AGI equals AGI plus retained corporate earnings plus corporate profits tax.
b. Includes negative incomes not shown separately.

In a related exercise, Feldstein and Frisch have calculated the distributional effects that integrating the income taxes would have at different income levels. They find that the proportion of "full income" (adjusted gross income plus corporate-source income) taken by taxes on corporate-source income would drop by 2 percentage points in the lowest income class ($0–$5,000) and by 1 percentage point for families with annual incomes as high as $30,000–$50,000, while it would rise by over 5½ percentage points for households with annual incomes in excess of $500,000.[7] Their conclusion that

---

based on the 1972 Brookings tax file. In the first column any capital gains tax resulting from retained corporate income is ignored; in the second column a uniform tax rate of 7 percent is applied to such retentions. The 7 percent rate is consistent with the estimate that higher-income shareholders probably paid an average effective rate (in present value terms) of only about 7 percent on gains realized over the period from 1926 to 1961. See Martin J. Bailey, "Capital Gains and Income Taxation," in Arnold C. Harberger and Martin J. Bailey, eds., *The Taxation of Income from Capital* (Brookings Institution, 1969), p. 37.

7. See Martin Feldstein and Daniel Frisch, "Corporate Tax Integration: The Estimated Effects on Capital Accumulation and Tax Distribution of Two Integration Proposals," *National Tax Journal*, vol. 30 (March 1977), pp. 37–52. In this exercise, which does not involve recoupment of revenue lost in integration, tax

"integration would reduce taxes relatively more for low income individuals and would actually raise taxes for high income individuals" is entirely consistent with that of Break and Pechman.[8]

Some descriptions of the inequities of an unintegrated income tax system go little further than the presentation and discussion of a table such as 2-1. But to stop there is wrong, since cursory inspection of the figures in table 2-1 indicates that the situation shown there is one of disequilibrium. That is, at all levels of income, distributed corporate income is taxed more heavily than ordinary income, and retained corporate earnings are effectively taxed at rates that (in present-value terms) can be either greater or (for high-income shareholders) less than the rates applied to ordinary income. It would be strange, indeed, if the shareholder viewed the corporation as a conduit and yet did not respond to the indicated differences in the taxation of ordinary (corporate interest and noncorporate) income, corporate-source income resulting in dividends, and undistributed corporate-source income. Rather, it is generally assumed, especially by advocates of integration, that these differentials in taxation can be expected to lead to a number of adjustments, all of which are held to be socially undesirable.[9]

First, the tendency for retained earnings to be undertaxed at the top of the income scale induces the ownership of firms with low dividend payout rates to be concentrated in the hands of the wealthy and, together with the relatively heavy taxation of dividends at all income levels, produces strong incentives to reduce dividend payout rates.[10]

---

falls as a percentage of income of all households by a 0.84 percentage point. Under an alternate scheme that leaves revenue essentially unchanged, the only substantial reductions are in the bottom two income classes ($0–$10,000), and the increase in burden at the top of the income scale is 8½ percentage points.

8. See Feldstein and Frisch, "Corporate Tax Integration," p. 49, and Break and Pechman, *Federal Tax Reform,* p. 94. Both these studies ignore investors' adjustments to changes in tax policy.

9. These arguments are presented in somewhat greater detail in McLure, "Integration," pp. 537–46.

10. Feldstein has estimated that a 10 percent increase in the opportunity cost of retained earnings, in terms of forgone dividends, results in the reduction of retentions by some 9 percent. See M. S. Feldstein, "Corporate Taxation and Dividend Behaviour," *Review of Economic Studies,* vol. 37 (January 1970), pp. 57–72. These estimates have been the subject of further exchange between Feldstein and M. A. King in subsequent issues of the *Review of Economic Studies* (for example, vol. 38 [July 1971], pp. 377–86, and vol. 39 [April 1972], pp. 231–40). Even if one accepts King's somewhat lower point estimate of the relevant elasticity, Feldstein's

Artificially high retention rates have several adverse effects. For one thing, they allow profitable firms to reinvest without passing the test of the marketplace.[11] Besides resulting in investment in projects that do not yield the highest social rate of return, this may give rise to mergers, thereby worsening competitive conditions in the economy.[12] Moreover, the tax premium on retained earnings is often said to place newer, smaller firms at a disadvantage in competing with larger established firms.[13] Relief from double taxation of dividends would reduce the tax stimulus for retention of earnings and full integration would eliminate it.[14]

---

basic conclusion that tax policy has an important impact on dividend policy seems to hold up. Furthermore, after reviewing several studies that try to determine the tax effect on dividend policy, J. Wiseman and M. Davenport in an OECD report conclude that Feldstein's results should be accepted. For a review of this and other literature relevant to the integration debate, see Organisation for Economic Co-operation and Development, *Theoretical and Empirical Aspects of Corporate Taxation* (Paris: OECD, 1974), especially pp. 38–56.

11. It allows, in the words of one British critic, the "survival of the fattest"; quoted in Organisation for Economic Co-operation and Development, *Company Tax Systems in OECD Member Countries* (Paris: OECD, 1973), p. 14, and in Harry G. Gourevitch, *Integration of Corporate and Shareholder Taxes on Income: The European Experience* (Library of Congress, Congressional Research Service, 1977), p. 15. One piece of evidence consistent with this view is found in William J. Baumol and others, "Earnings Retention, New Capital and the Growth of the Firm," *Review of Economics and Statistics*, vol. 52 (November 1970), pp. 345–55. The authors concluded that

the rate of return on equity capital ranged from 14.5 per cent to 20.8 per cent. The rate of return on ploughback, however, ranged from 3.0 to 4.6 per cent; while the rate of return on debt ranges from 4.2 to 14 per cent. Thus, it appears that the rate of return on new equity is substantially higher than the rate of return on ploughback; while the rate of return on new debt is somewhere between the rates of return to ploughback and equity [p. 353].

Yet they do not attribute the differences in rates of return to tax influences, which could go far in explaining them.

12. This would occur, for example, if acquisitions of other firms appeared more attractive to firms with excess retained profits than acquisition of physical assets, as has apparently been the case recently.

13. Of course, this argument cuts both ways. Smaller firms may be more dependent on retained earnings for expansion, especially since larger established firms are likely to have better access to capital markets.

14. If dividend relief were complete and were accompanied by reduction of the top personal marginal tax rate to the level of the corporate rate, the discrimination in favor of retaining earnings could actually be reversed. Preliminary survey evidence on the effect that dividend relief would have on dividend payout rates is in Marshall E. Blume, Jean Crockett, and Irwin Friend, *Financial Effects of Capital Tax Reforms* (New York University, Salomon Brothers Center, 1978). It is often asserted that dividend relief has had little effect on either debt-equity ratios or dividend policy in Europe. But the statistical basis for such assertions is weak.

Second, despite the attraction that retained earnings hold for some investors, the return to equity capital in the corporate sector is taxed more heavily, on the average, than interest on debt and income earned in the noncorporate sector. As a result, corporate debt-equity ratios tend to be distorted in the direction of overreliance on debt finance, and too little investment occurs in the corporate sector. It has been estimated that the annual welfare loss resulting from the differentially heavy fiscal burden on the return to corporate equity may be on the order of 0.5 percent of gross national product.[15] Although the corresponding loss that results from tax-induced increases in leverage has not been estimated—indeed it is difficult even to conceive how it would be quantified—the increased vulnerability of American corporations to bankruptcy induced by the unintegrated corporate tax should not be taken lightly.[16] Consider, for example,

15. The pioneering articles on the misallocation of resources caused by the corporate income tax are Arnold C. Harberger, "The Incidence of the Corporation Income Tax," *Journal of Political Economy,* vol. 70 (June 1962), pp. 215–40, and Arnold C. Harberger, "Efficiency Effects of Taxes on Income from Capital," in Marian Krzyzaniak, ed., *Effects of Corporation Income Tax* (Wayne State University Press, 1966), pp. 107–17. Subsequent contributions to the refinement of estimates of excess burdens (welfare losses) are Leonard Gerson Rosenberg, "Taxation of Income from Capital, by Industry Group," in Harberger and Bailey, *Taxation of Income from Capital,* pp. 123–84, and John B. Shoven, "The Incidence and Efficiency Effects of Taxes on Income from Capital," *Journal of Political Economy,* vol. 84 (December 1976), pp. 1261–83. Note that in this literature there is an assumption (often implicit) that certain activities (producing steel, automobiles, and so on) require such large amounts of capital that the limited liability afforded by the corporate form is essential, whereas other activities exhibit considerable flexibility in their form of business organization. The important distortion is against inherently corporate *activities,* not against the use of the corporate *form* of business organization.

16. For preliminary attempts to model the corporate financial decision and response to the tax differentials described above, see Martin Feldstein, Jerry Green, and Eytan Sheshinski, "Corporate Financial Policy and Taxation in a Growing Economy," *Quarterly Journal of Economics* (forthcoming, 1979), and J. Gregory Ballentine and Charles E. McLure, Jr., "Corporate Tax Integration: Incidence and Effects on Financial Structure," *Quarterly Journal of Economics* (forthcoming, 1979). These papers have the disadvantage that neither includes a progressive personal income tax, and the paper by Feldstein and coauthors assumes that all economic activity occurs in the corporate sector. The comment in that paper about the difficulty of defining a measure of incidence in a world with risk premiums (a problem also encountered by Ballentine and McLure) is also relevant for the measurement of the economy-wide risk of bankruptcy: "A more complete analysis of risk and risk aversion would be required to provide a precise welfare measure." Finally, an attempt to include progressive personal taxes (but not the corporate financial decision) in the so-called Harberger model of general equilibrium incidence analysis is made in Martin Feldstein and Joel Slemrod, "Personal Taxation,

the recent orgy of takeovers by the go-go conglomerates of the 1960s (which was financed in large part by borrowing) and the experience of the real estate investment trusts.

Finally, it has been argued that the extraordinary tax burden on capital, which can be traced in large part to the two-tier levy on corporate-source income, reduces the rates of capital formation and economic growth.[17] To the extent that capital-labor ratios are adversely affected, labor may share in the burden of the corporation income tax in the long run.[18] Moreover, whether or not capital formation and economic growth are affected, the extraordinarily heavy taxation of capital income creates an undesirable distortion in choices between present and future consumption.[19] For all these reasons it has been argued that the U.S. income taxes should be integrated.[20]

Portfolio Choice, and the Effect of the Corporation Income Tax," working paper 241 (National Bureau of Economic Research, 1978). Blume and others, *Financial Effects of Capital Tax Reforms,* report survey evidence that suggests that dividend relief would have little impact on debt-equity ratios. But British experience suggests otherwise; see King, *Public Policy,* pp. 222–27.

17. Among the important academic expressions of views of this type are: Marian Krzyzaniak, "The Long-Run Burden of a General Tax on Profits in a Neoclassical World," *Public Finance,* vol. 22, no. 4 (1967), pp. 472–91; Martin Feldstein, "The Welfare Cost of Capital Income Taxation," *Journal of Political Economy,* vol. 86 (April 1978), pt. 2, pp. S29–S51; and Michael J. Boskin, "Taxation, Saving and the Rate of Interest," *Journal of Political Economy,* vol. 86 (April 1978), pt. 2, pp. S3–S27. Note, however, that Feldstein, for example, though an advocate of integration, does not argue that integration will necessarily increase saving. See Feldstein and Frisch, "Corporate Tax Integration." Less cautious statements have been made by public officials and businessmen about the positive effects integration or dividend relief would have on capital formation. See, for example, William E. Simon, Testimony in *Tax Reform (Administration and Public Witnesses),* Hearings before the House Committee on Ways and Means, 94 Cong. 1 sess. (Government Printing Office, 1975), pt. 5, pp. 3846–61. For an expression of this view by a particularly vocal business spokesman, see Reginald H. Jones, "The Need for Capital," *National Tax Journal,* vol. 28 (September 1975), pp. 265–81. Jones also decries the tax-induced tendency toward higher debt-equity ratios.

18. See especially Krzyzaniak, "Long-Run Burden of a General Tax"; Martin Feldstein, "Incidence of a Capital Income Tax in a Growing Economy with Variable Savings Rates," *Review of Economic Studies,* vol. 41 (October 1974), pp. 505–13; and Martin S. Feldstein, "Tax Incidence in a Growing Economy with Variable Factor Supply," *Quarterly Journal of Economics,* vol. 88 (November 1974), pp. 551–73.

19. Feldstein, "The Welfare Cost of Capital Income Taxation."

20. But, as is noted in greater detail in the next section, "integration" has not meant the same thing to all its advocates, and various advocates are not uniformly concerned about all the alleged ills of an unintegrated system.

The Case against Integration: The Separate Entity View

Opponents of integration argue that, though the conduit theory of the corporation may be relevant for closely held corporations, in which the interests of the shareholders and those of the firm are closely identified, it has virtually no relevance for the large widely held corporations that dominate the U.S. business scene and pay the great bulk of corporate income taxes.[21] As has been noted in the literature, because of the separation of ownership and control the interests of the corporation may be quite different from those of its shareholders, and indeed the interests of various groups of stockholders may be in conflict, especially when dividend policy is involved.[22] Thus, Surrey has said, preference for the conduit theory and integration is no more than "tax theology" and therefore a matter about which agreement is not to be expected. In his view, the choice between integration and separate treatment "should be cast in terms of the desired overall effects of the entire tax system, taking into account the distribution of the tax burden, growth, savings, investment, and other fiscal and social aspects."[23]

Once the conduit view is rejected, the conceptual case for integration is weakened considerably. Under the separate entity view the existence, nature, and level of the corporate income tax is essentially irrelevant for the appraisal of the personal income tax, and the primary structural problem that remains is the preferential treatment of long-term capital gains, interest on state and local securities, ex-

---

21. For a strong statement of the "separatist" case against integration, see Richard Goode, *The Corporation Income Tax* (Wiley, 1951), pp. 24–43.

22. See Commission of the European Communities, "Proposal for a Council Directive Concerning the Harmonization of Systems of Company Taxation and of Withholding Taxes on Dividends," *Bulletin of the European Communities,* Supplement 10/75: *Harmonization of Systems of Company Taxation* (Luxembourg: Office for Official Publications of the European Communities, 1975), p. 8. Note, however, that this point is used in the European context to justify integration for dividends, even though dividend relief can actually accentuate such conflicts.

23. Stanley S. Surrey, "Reflections on 'Integration' of Corporation and Individual Income Taxes," *National Tax Journal*, vol. 28 (September 1975), p. 335. For expression of a generally similar view by the German Ministry of Finance, see page 44 below. That there is relatively little recent literature opposing integration is probably indicative of the suddenness with which the policy debate has arisen, rather than the absence of opposition. Moreover, "integration" has so many meanings that most groups can find a version they like.

tractive industries, and so forth, under the individual income tax. The "double taxation of dividends" has no meaning in such a context, since each tier of the two-tier system of taxing corporate-source income has independent significance.

A second line of opposition to integration is based on theoretical reasoning and empirical evidence that the corporation income tax might be shifted to consumers or to workers, rather than be borne by shareholders or even by all owners of capital.[24] If the tax is shifted, this argument goes, then it cannot have the effects usually attributed to it, including especially the double taxation of dividends. Instead, the tax is more like a payroll or sales tax than an income tax, and such shifting, Musgrave has argued, implies that a deduction should be granted for the corporation tax, not that the tax should be abolished or integrated into the personal tax.[25]

A third argument against integration, and the one that probably has the most popular and political appeal, accepts the incidence of the tax as falling on shareholders, but decries the reduction in progressivity that dividend relief would entail. Because ownership of corporate equities is concentrated in upper income families, the corporate income tax adds greatly to the overall distributional progressivity of the tax system.[26] Full integration at existing rates would, it

24. This is not the place to review the theory and evidence on the incidence of the corporation income tax. For such a review, and references to other literature, see George F. Break, "The Incidence and Economic Effects of Taxation," in Alan S. Blinder and others, *The Economics of Public Finance* (Brookings Institution, 1974), pp. 119–237, especially pp. 138–54.

25. R. A. Musgrave, "The Carter Commission Report," *Canadian Journal of Economics,* supplement 1 (February 1968), pp. 163–64.

26. Indicative of this is the incidence pattern that results if the corporation tax is allocated to shareholders in proportion to their receipt of corporate dividends. Allocating one-half of the tax to dividend recipients and one-half to recipients of capital income in general (which reduces the estimated progressivity), Pechman and Okner report the following effective rates (tax as a percentage of income) at various points in the income scale:

Population decile	Effective rate
First	1.7
Second	2.1
Third	2.2
Fourth	1.9
Fifth	1.7
Sixth	1.5
Seventh	1.6
Eighth	1.8
Ninth	2.2
Tenth	8.1

is admitted, increase progressivity even further because it would reduce the tax shelter that high-income households currently find in retained earnings. But full integration might be accompanied by reduction of the top-bracket rate under the personal tax; in that case much of any increase in progressivity integration might cause would be lost.[27] Moreover, as a political matter, it is quite conceivable that dividend relief, not full integration, might be enacted. Since it lacks the compensating closure of the capital gains loophole that advocates of full integration find so attractive, dividend relief is likely to reduce rather than increase progressivity. Feldstein and Frisch have estimated, for example, that under dividend relief tax reductions as a percentage of "full income" would range from less than 1 percent at the bottom of the income scale to some 3 percent to 5 percent at the top of the scale.[28]

Stanley S. Surrey has elaborated on this theme:

economists are talking—almost in a dreamlike world—about "full integration," which means treating the corporation like a partnership or conduit. But the business groups pushing integration are talking in terms of "partial integration," which in simple terms means tax relief for dividends. Each is thus seeking a different goal, but in the world of reality I believe the economists are being used to make "integration" a respectable issue ... while ... a fast shuffle quickly makes partial integration the path to follow if "integration" is to be pursued.[29]

Given the likelihood that neither full integration nor significant tax reform will occur, the adverse distributional implications of dividend relief, and the political difficulty of obtaining full integration once dividend relief is on the books, Surrey and others oppose even considering the issue of full integration.[30]

See Joseph A. Pechman and Benjamin A. Okner, *Who Bears the Tax Burden?* (Brookings Institution, 1974), p. 61. On annual income above $500,000 the effective rate nears 25 percent; see ibid., p. 59. Note that these figures relate to the burden of the corporate tax, not to the extra burden that tax imposes over and above what would be levied under an integrated system.

27. See Break and Pechman, *Federal Tax Reform*, p. 94, for an expression of this fear.

28. From unpublished tables accompanying Feldstein and Frisch, "Corporate Tax Integration"; the exact effect depends upon the response of dividend payout policy.

29. Surrey, "Reflections," p. 335. "Partial integration," as used by Surrey, means, of course, dividend relief.

30. Taking a somewhat different tack, McLure and Surrey have suggested that the outcome of any legislative consideration of integration is so uncertain that none

Concern over the distributional implications of integration is heightened by a consideration of the role of corporate tax preferences in reducing the effective rates of tax actually paid by corporations. Whereas the statutory marginal rate for firms paying the great bulk of corporate taxes has been 48 percent, and the average rate would have been almost as high if tax were paid on book income, the effective rate actually paid has been only about 36 to 38 percent, and differs both between and within industries.[31] It would be inequitable, some have argued, to allow integration or dividend relief at the statutory rate when in fact the effective tax does not approach that figure in many cases.[32]

Yet another equity argument against integration and dividend relief takes as its basic premise the prior capitalization of the corporate tax. If indeed the tax has been capitalized in the form of lower prices for corporate shares, present owners of such shares may not, in fact, bear the burden of the tax. Moreover, integration or dividend relief would be inequitable because it would result in windfall gains (and losses) to present owners of corporate shares.

A fourth line of reasoning against integration questions the importance of the presumed losses of welfare resulting from use of a classical system. Wiseman and Davenport argue, for example, that "it is difficult to take seriously Harberger's estimates of the loss in output resulting from the double-taxation of dividends in the corporate sector. . . . Clearly tax discrimination against particular legal

---

of the interested parties in the debate—corporate executives, investors, managers of pension funds and other tax-exempt organizations, labor unions, professional tax reformers, and public interest groups—may "want to push integration into the legislative arena and risk the roll of the legislative dice." See Charles E. McLure, Jr., and Stanley S. Surrey, "Integration of Income Taxes: Issues for Debate," *Harvard Business Review*, vol. 55 (September–October 1977), p. 181.

31. See various issues of *Tax Notes*, and particularly Richard L. Kaplan, "Disparity in Corporate Rates Raises Questions About Underlying Tax Policy," Tax Analysts and Advocates, *Tax Notes*, vol. 3 (November 17, 1975), pp. 13–37; and U.S. Department of the Treasury, *Effective Income Tax Rates Paid by United States Corporations in 1972* (GPO, 1978).

32. See Gerard M. Brannon, "Dividend Relief and Tax Reform," Tax Analysts and Advocates, *Tax Notes*, vol. 3 (August 11, 1975), pp. 3–7. In the article, Brannon, an advocate of full integration, criticized the 1975 proposal of the U.S. Treasury Department, which would have used the statutory rate in calculating dividend relief, thereby providing overly generous relief. Though Canada does so, European countries do not generally allow relief for dividends paid in excess of income on which corporate tax has been paid.

forms of enterprise or particular asset classes must involve a cost in the misallocation of capital. The cost takes the form of a loss in output, but to attempt to quantify that cost, even in the crudest sense, may result in a totally misleading impression."[33] Surrey adopts a particularly strong viewpoint on this issue:

As to efficiency and allocation of resources between corporate and noncorporate capital, it is here that the economists plant their flag of integration. . . . But if this is so, the issue of integration turns on the extent of the seriousness of those allocative effects weighed against the consequences of integration. . . . While economists may plant their integration flag on the uncertain terrain of allocation of resources, the Congress should not follow in their path. . . . The uncertainties surrounding the effects on allocation of resources of the various forms of corporate taxation are hardly the base to support a major change in the United States tax system with all the known serious and adverse consequences of such a change.[34]

In addition, the claim that tax-induced tendencies to retain earnings leads to inferior investment decisions has also been questioned.[35] Kaldor, for example, argues that only firms that have retained earnings really have access to external capital markets.[36] Moreover, it can be argued that dividend relief could lead to stratification of the market for corporate equities if it were not accompanied by reduction in the top personal tax rate—a reduction that most opponents of dividend relief would probably not welcome. That is, low-income shareholders would prefer stocks of firms with high dividend payout rates, in order to take advantage of the shareholder credit (or analogous relief under a dividend-paid deduction). But shareholders with marginal rates above the corporate rate might prefer to invest in shares

33. Organisation for Economic Co-operation and Development, *Theoretical and Empirical Aspects*, pp. 43, 44.
34. Surrey, "Reflections," p. 340. Surrey is discussing integration in the broad sense.
35. See, for example, Irwin Friend and Frank Husic, "Efficiency of Corporate Investment," *Review of Economics and Statistics*, vol. 55 (February 1973), pp. 122–27, and G. Whittington, "The Profitability of Retained Earnings," *Review of Economics and Statistics*, vol. 54 (May 1972), pp. 152–60. Both papers are summarized in Organisation for Economic Co-operation and Development, *Theoretical and Empirical Aspects*, pp. 41–42.
36. Nicholas Kaldor, "The Economic Effects of Alternative Systems of Corporation Tax," in *Report from the Select Committee on Corporation Tax, Together with Minutes of Proceedings of the Committee, Minutes of Evidence, Appendices and Index, Session 1970–71* (London: Her Majesty's Stationery Office, 1971), Appendix 15, pp. 248–56.

of firms retaining substantial portions of their earnings, in order to take advantage of the exclusion and deferral benefits of the taxation of long-term capital gains. Furthermore, tax-exempt organizations might effectively be driven from the market for corporate equities if they were not allowed the benefits of integration or dividend relief. These results, it could be argued, would not appear to improve the effectiveness of the nation's capital markets as allocators of resources.

Opponents of integration also argue that claims that integration will relieve the capital shortage are grossly exaggerated, or at least incomplete. As two proponents of integration have stated, "Corporate tax integration is not an effective instrument for achieving the goal of capital accumulation,"[37] and "It seems likely that the effects on saving would be minimal if the lost revenue were made up through tax reform that left the existing pattern of tax burdens essentially unchanged. . . . Maintenance of progressivity and raising the saving rate seem to be in direct conflict."[38]

Yet another conceptual reason for opposing integration has been provided by Stiglitz, writing in the tradition of the Modigliani-Miller literature[39] on the irrelevance of corporate financial structure.[40] Stiglitz argues that in a world without taxes or the risk of bankruptcy there is no optimal debt-equity or dividend policy and that firms sub-

---

37. Martin Feldstein, "Corporate Tax Integration and Capital Accumulation," discussion paper 437 (Harvard University, Harvard Institute of Economic Research, 1975), p. 32. For a more detailed elaboration of this position, see Feldstein and Frisch, "Corporate Tax Integration." Feldstein's conclusion is based on his earlier econometric work in Britain in which he found that the transferral of one pound of corporate net income from retained earnings to dividends would reduce total private saving by from 0.15 to 0.50 pound. See Martin Feldstein and George Fane, "Taxes, Corporate Dividend Policy and Personal Savings: The British Postwar Experience," *Review of Economics and Statistics*, vol. 55 (November 1973), pp. 399–411. For a similar analysis in the United States, see Martin S. Feldstein, "Tax Incentives, Corporate Saving, and Capital Accumulation in the United States," *Journal of Public Economics*, vol. 2 (April 1973), pp. 159–71.

38. Charles E. McLure, Jr., "Integration of the Income Taxes: Why and How," *Journal of Corporate Taxation*, vol. 2 (Winter 1976), pp. 458, 463. Preliminary survey evidence that supports this conclusion is reported in Blume and others, *Financial Effects of Capital Tax Reforms*.

39. For example, Franco Modigliani and Merton H. Miller, "The Cost of Capital, Corporation Finance and the Theory of Investment," *American Economic Review*, vol. 58 (June 1958), pp. 261–97.

40. See especially Joseph E. Stiglitz, "Taxation, Corporate Financial Policy, and the Cost of Capital," *Journal of Public Economics*, vol. 2 (February 1973), pp. 1–34.

ject to a corporate income tax would never pay dividends and would finance marginal investments from debt rather than with equity. However, far from drawing the conclusions that integrationists draw from qualitatively similar results about tax effects on dividend payout rates and debt-equity ratios, Stiglitz reasons that at the margin the corporation income tax affects neither corporate financial decisions nor the cost of capital and is therefore neutral; that is, it has none of the adverse effects on the allocation of resources attributed to it by Harberger.[41]

David Bradford has recently presented a theoretical analysis of the effects of business income taxation which can be interpreted as implying that the unintegrated corporation income tax does not necessarily have all the adverse effects on corporate financial structures commonly attributed to it.[42] In Bradford's analysis there is a tax only on distributions—with no corporate tax or capital gains tax. The essence of his argument is that such a system would not favor retention over distribution, because the present value of tax liabilities is the same whether distribution occurs currently or with a lag. In fact, the taxation of retained earnings would involve distortion against retentions and in favor of current distribution.[43] Moreover, the tax on distributions is best thought of as a lump-sum levy on those who own corporate equities at the time the tax is imposed. Thus neither debt-equity ratios, dividend payout, nor sectoral allocation of capital will be distorted. In short, the tax is completely neutral.

---

41. If, by assumption, bankruptcy is impossible, an all-debt financial policy can do no harm.

42. David F. Bradford, "The Incidence and Allocation Effects of a Tax on Corporate Distributions," discussion paper 7738 (Louvain, Belgium: Université Catholique de Louvain, Center for Operations Research and Econometrics, August 1977).

43. It may be useful to consider the analogy of the expenditure tax. As is commonly recognized, if future consumption is discounted by the market rate of interest, a tax on expenditures is neutral between present and future consumption. In contrast, an income tax discriminates against future consumption, while a tax on saving—the difference between income and consumption—is clearly distorting. If one thinks of dividends as being analogous to consumption, corporate income (dividends plus retained earnings) as being analogous to income in the debate over income versus expenditure taxation, and retained earnings as being analogous to saving, then given his very limiting assumptions, Bradford's propositions follow. Of course, more than analogy is involved: retained earnings *are* saving, and so forth.

The step from Bradford's model, which is based on the assumption of a single tax on distributions levied in a world of rational expectations, to policy conclusions about the corporate income tax is not a small and simple one. Bradford does, however, suggest that "the partial integration approach may have gotten the matter just backwards . . . insofar as partial integration amounts to eliminating a tax on distributions it may result primarily in windfall wealth redistributions, reversing the by now irrelevant wealth changes that occurred when the tax was introduced, while leaving the features of the tax system giving rise to inefficiency."[44]

A final set of objections against integration is practical rather than conceptual, theoretical, or distributional. Any form of integration would involve difficult problems in tax administration and in the taxation of international flows of corporate-source income. For full integration, the complications might be so severe as to doom any proposal. Since assessment of these problems is the focus of the bulk of this book, only a brief outline of them can be given here.

The conduit theory has implications for the nature of integration that have not been generally recognized. If the corporation and its shareholders are seen to be distinct, then there is no question that the income the corporation receives from various sources should be merged and that the different components of corporate income should lose their identities when distributed to shareholders or retained in their behalf. But the conduit theory says that the corporation has no separate existence from a fiscal point of view; thus the various components of corporate income should retain their separate characteristics in the hands of shareholders. That is, interest on tax-exempt securities held by the corporation should be received free of tax when attributed to the shareholder; long-term capital gains should be taxed as such to the shareholder, rather than as ordinary income; investment tax credits should be passed through to shareholders; and so on. It takes little imagination to realize that imple-

---

44. Bradford, "Incidence and Allocation Effects," pp. 2, 6–7. Bradford uses the term "partial integration" for what I call dividend relief. That the forces for and against integration are not monolithic can again be demonstrated by noting that Bradford, as deputy assistant secretary of the treasury for tax policy, was largely responsible for the proposal for full integration in U.S. Department of the Treasury, *Blueprints for Basic Tax Reform* (GPO, 1977).

mentation of such a pure partnership approach would be administratively difficult.[45]

Of course, if the conduit theory is not taken quite so literally, it is possible to have a system of full integration in which components of income do not retain their character in the hands of shareholders; this is essentially the approach suggested by the Canadian Royal Commission and by the U.S. Department of the Treasury in *Blueprints for Basic Tax Reform*. But even under such an impure scheme for full integration, difficult problems would have to be surmounted. How, for example, would corporate earnings be allocated to shareholders who had owned stock for less than a year? Presumably it would be necessary to choose a date of record rather than attempt day-by-day allocations to shareholders.[46] Moreover, how would operating losses be treated? Would they be passed through to shareholders or would they merely be available for carry-forward to profitable years? (Carry-back of losses, like audit adjustments of shareholder incomes for prior years, is not satisfactory, because the ownership of shares may have changed; furthermore, audit adjustments and carry-back would necessitate the reopening of the returns of prior shareholders, in any case.) What if some portfolio shareholders were corporations? What should be done if corporate-source income initially taxed to holders of common stock is subsequently distributed to owners of preferred shares? As mentioned in chapter 1, these problems should not be taken lightly. (Administrative difficulties of integration and dividend relief are considered further in chapter 5.)

Finally, even if one is willing to be less ambitious and strive for relief from double taxation of dividends only, difficult problems still arise, as can be seen from European experience. Since many of these involve the tax treatment of international capital flows, I mention only a few here. (See also chapters 3 and 6.) First, there is no doubt

---

45. See also chapter 5. It is of interest to note that, though this approach underlies the taxation of partnerships, it does not form the basis of the taxation of closely held corporations under subchapter S, the clearest case of integration of personal and corporate taxes extant in the U.S. tax code. This point is made in Edwin S. Cohen, "Possible Solutions to Practical Problems in Integration of the Corporate and Shareholder Income Tax," *National Tax Journal*, vol. 28 (September 1975), p. 361. For further discussion, see also Klein, "Income Taxation and Legal Entities."

46. The U.S. Department of the Treasury, in *Blueprints for Basic Tax Reform*, p. 70, would choose the first day of the tax year to prevent trafficking in shares of firms with losses. See also chapter 5.

that the neutral taxation of international capital flows is simplest if all nations adopt the classical, or separate, system of taxing corporate-source income.[47] The principles that have traditionally governed U.S. tax relations with other nations (primacy of source-country taxation, limited foreign tax credits in capital-exporting country, nondiscrimination, and reciprocity) are most appropriate in a world of separate corporate income taxes; in a world of integrated domestic tax systems the analogous rules are far more complex and less likely to command agreement. Of more immediate relevance, the fact that many European countries have already adopted dividend relief conditions U.S. policy choices, but does not necessarily imply that achieving neutrality will be easier if the United States adopts dividend relief than if it does not.[48] Even though dividend relief may be provided most simply in the domestic sphere through the deduction of dividends at the corporate level, a combination of preexisting tax treaties and revenue and competitive effects may effectively preclude use of that method by the United States. Thus if dividend relief is to be granted, it will probably be through the imputation method.

Finally, whether integration is provided only for dividends or is extended to retained earnings, it will be necessary to decide how tax preferences should be treated. Among the options are (1) to eliminate them entirely, (2) to eliminate them only for the corporate sector, (3) to allow them, but only if preference income is retained, (4) to allow them, but only if preference income is distributed, or (5) to allow them whether preference income is retained or distrib-

---

47. Categorical statements such as this are hazardous, since capital-import neutrality (not a particularly important goal) may be more easily achieved than capital-export neutrality (an important goal), especially in the absence of foreign tax credits. Moreover, what is true for direct investment may not be true for portfolio investment. Yet the statement in the text seems reasonable. This is affirmed in Richard M. Hammer, "The Taxation of Income from Corporate Shareholders: Review of Present Systems in Canada, France, Germany, Japan and the U.K.," *National Tax Journal*, vol. 28 (September 1975), pp. 315–16, and Mitsuo Sato and Richard M. Bird, "International Aspects of the Taxation of Corporations and Shareholders," International Monetary Fund, *Staff Papers*, vol. 22 (July 1975), p. 412. Note, however, that Sato and Bird argue that "the attempt to discourage integration because it fails to achieve nondiscriminatory treatment of resident and nonresident investors does not appear to be a realistic alternative. . . . There is no case for concluding that the international tail (nondiscrimination) should wag the domestic dog (integration)" (p. 425).

48. For more on this, including a definition of neutrality, see Sato and Bird, "International Aspects of Taxation," pp. 411–17, and chapter 6 below.

uted. In cases 3 and 4 it is necessary to have arbitrary rules for the determination of the order in which distributions are assumed to come from fully taxed and preference income. No matter which of the alternatives (other than eliminating preferences) is chosen, important technical difficulties and distortions of choices are likely to result.[49]

[49] Many opponents of intergration also dislike tax preferences. If they cannot have preferences eliminated they are likely to opt for ordering rules and tax treatment that would minimize the value of preferences.

MARTIN NORR, THE TAXATION OF CORPORATIONS AND SHAREHOLDERS

Kluwer Law & Taxation Publishers (1982), pp. 71–82.

CHAPTER 4: CHOICE OF THE LEVEL (CORPORATE OR SHAREHOLDER) AT WHICH INTEGRATION IS TO BE PROVIDED

4/A. In General

If the burden of the two-tier taxation of corporate-source income is to be eased by integration, the first question to be answered is this: at what level should integration be provided? Should an adjustment be made at the corporate level—that is, should the corporation income tax on the distributed component of the corporation's profits be reduced because that component will also be taxed in the shareholders' hands? Or should there be an adjustment at the shareholder level—that is, should the individual income tax on the shareholder's dividend be reduced to take account of the fact that the dividend is paid from profits that were previously taxed to the corporation?[1]

This chapter will discuss the arguments for and against the choice of one level or the other. This choice, however, is one of tax technique rather than of substantive effect. The choice of level does not control the amount of relief given. The integration of the corporation and the individual income taxes can achieve whatever amount of tax relief for distributed profits is desired, whether it is applied at the corporate level or the shareholder level (or at both levels). As far as the total amount of tax is concerned, the same reduction can be provided at one level just as well as at the other level.

Moreover, whatever level is chosen and whatever the formal differences between techniques of integration, integration reduces the effects of the two-tier taxation of corporate-source income by diminishing the impact on distributed profits of the *corporation* income tax, not that of the individual

---

1. Some countries (Japan and Germany, for example) use a combination of methods, which provides some reduction in the taxes on distributed earnings at both the corporate level and the shareholder level (see below).

income tax. It is the additional burden imposed by the corporation income tax (see Table 1 in Chapter 3) which is reduced or eliminated by integration.

Some methods of integration reduce the burden of the corporation income tax by operating at the corporate level; they impose a rate of tax on the distributed component of a corporation's profits which is lower than the rate imposed on the retained component. Yet even those methods of integration which operate at the shareholder level (reducing, in one way or another, the individual income tax on the shareholder's dividend receipt) do so by treating the corporation income tax merely as a collection device. The payment of income tax by the corporation on the distributed component of its profits is treated, in whole or in part, as an advance payment by the corporation on account of the income tax due from the shareholder. In other words, the corporation income tax on the distributed component of the corporation's profits is treated as a tax "withheld" for the shareholder's account from his share of that component. Only because a portion of the corporation income tax is deemed to have been paid or withheld for the account of the shareholder does the latter receive correlative relief from the individual income tax.

With the warning, then, that the discussion of the relative merits of integration at the corporate level as opposed to integration at the shareholder level involves matters of form rather than of substance, the remaining sections of this chapter will examine certain considerations that enter into the choice of the level (corporate or shareholder) at which integration is to operate in a technical sense.

4/B. Ease of Administration

Integration is generally easier to administer at the corporate level than at the shareholder level. Integration at the corporate level is not, however, entirely free of administrative difficulties; it does introduce some additional complexity into the corporate tax structure. This complexity is rarely beyond the capability of most tax administrations and corporations, however. Corporations are more skilled at bookkeeping than individual shareholders; and the computation of tax by the taxpayer, as well as audit and review by the tax administration, tends to be easier at the corporate level than at the shareholder level.

At the shareholder level, the fact that integration involves some complexity may be more serious than at the corporate level. Far more taxpayers are involved. Except in cases in which integration takes the form of an outright exemption of dividends from the individual income tax (which is true only in some relatively underdeveloped countries, as indicated in

Chapter 6), integration at the shareholder level requires some adjustment of each shareholder's tax base or tax liability. The degree of complexity involved in this adjustment varies from one method to another, as will be apparent from the discussion in Chapter 6 of particular methods. As a practical matter, some of the burden of complexity at the shareholder level may be shifted to the corporation. For example, the corporation may be required to advise the shareholder of the exact amount of the adjustment to which the latter is entitled.

Moreover, integration at the shareholder level is based on the assumption that the full tax has been paid at the corporate level on the profits from which the shareholder's dividend is paid. For a variety of reasons, however, corporations often pay tax at less than the full nominal rate. Particularly complex adjustments may be required to ensure that distribution relief is not given to shareholders with respect to taxes that have *not* been paid by the corporation.[2] At best, therefore, integration at the shareholder level tends to be more complicated for the taxpayer and more difficult for the tax administration than integration at the corporate level.[3]

4/C. Effects on Tax Revenue and Compliance

Although, as pointed out in the beginning of this chapter, tax revenues may be made equal under the two systems of integration, integration at the corporate level may in practice cost the government more in lost tax revenues than integration at the shareholder level. One argument for the use of a corporation income tax is its strength as a revenue producer. Because integration at the corporate level operates by reducing the corporation income tax on a portion of a corporation's profits (the distributed portion), however, integration at that level results in an immediate decline in the yield of the corporation income tax. Although this decline can be compensated for by an increase in the rate of tax on the retained com-

---

2. See, for example, the discussion of the French *précompte mobilière* in Chapter 6.

3. Professor Prest asserts that as far as comparisons of integration at the corporate and shareholder levels are concerned, "The arguments of principle... seem to be very weak ones"; for that reason, he thought it appropriate to go along with the views of the tax administrators that, in the English case, integration at the corporate level would be preferable because easier to administer. Prest, "Minutes of Evidence Taken 6 July 1971," in United Kingdom, Parliament, House of Commons, *Report From the Select Committee on Corporation Tax* 110.

Unlike Professor Prest, who favors integration, Professor Kaldor opposes integration. If forced to choose between alternative systems of integration, though, Professor Kaldor would also prefer it at the corporate level. Kaldor, "The Economic Effects of Alternative Systems of Corporation Tax," in United Kingdom, Parliament, House of Commons, *Report From the Select Committee on Corporation Tax* 248, 255.

ponent, such an increase may reduce retained earnings below reasonable business needs.

Integration at the shareholder level has the advantage of leaving undiminished the yield of the corporation income tax. This advantage may be more apparent than real, however. At the beginning of this chapter, it was pointed out that integration at the shareholder level in effect treats a portion of the corporation income tax as a mere prepayment of the individual income tax. With integration at the shareholder level, some of the tax collected from corporations in the first instance therefore serves merely to reduce the tax collected from shareholders in the second instance. As a result, it is difficult to isolate the impact of integration on tax revenues and to attribute this impact specifically to one level of taxation rather than another.

Nevertheless, a country contemplating the adoption of distribution relief at the corporate level must consider that the tax revenue lost at that level may not be compensated for by higher tax revenues at the shareholder level. Even if dividend disbursements increase, the relatively large number of shareholders and the problems of enforcement and administration of the individual income tax (particularly to the extent that that tax bears on unearned income) mean that a considerable degree of erosion is likely. Pointing to the efficiency of the corporation income tax as a revenue producer, Professor Surrey warned that "any approach which looks more to the shareholder for the tax on corporate profits must devise a more efficient system of collecting the tax on dividends than we possess today."[4] If this is a consideration in a developed country, such as the United States, which has an experienced and presumably efficient income tax administration, it must be an even greater consideration in developing countries in which the income tax is relatively new.

Integration at the corporate level may be appropriate, therefore, only to the extent that tax compliance at the shareholder level is good. Moreover, integration at the shareholder level may actually improve taxpayer compliance. Except in those countries in which integration takes the form of an outright exemption of dividends, the tax benefits of integration at the shareholder level are available only to the individual who reports his dividend income on his tax return and then claims integration relief. The French, for example, in defending their post-1965 system of integration at the shareholder level (see Chapter 6), emphasized that its benefits "go only

---

4. Surrey, "Statement by Assistant Secretary of the Treasury Surrey, April 21, 1966, at the School of Law of the State University of New York [at Buffalo], on Federal Tax Policy in the 1960's," in United States, Treasury Department, *Annual Report of the Secretary of the Treasury on the State of Finances for the Fiscal Year Ended June 30, 1966,* 366, 377. This speech is reproduced in Hellmuth and Oldman (eds.), *Tax Policy and Tax Reform: 1961-1969—Selected Speeches and Testimony of Stanley S. Surrey* 115, 127.

to honest taxpayers." Those who fail to report their dividend income cannot use the system.

To eliminate or at least reduce the problems of shareholder compliance, a country adopting integration at the corporate level may find it expedient to adopt a withholding system that would collect from every dividend disbursement a preliminary tax for the shareholder's account. With such a withholding system in effect, compliance may be as good under integration at the corporate level as under integration at the shareholder level.[5] In the absence of actual withholding from dividends, however, integration at the corporate level may reduce tax revenues at that level by an amount greater than that of any increase in revenues at the shareholder level.

4/D. Effect on Business and Investment Behavior

Integration is generally adopted with the hope that it will influence taxpayer behavior—for example, that it will increase the portion of corporate profits paid out as dividends or encourage equity rather than debt financing. If it is assumed that corporate managers consider the total tax on corporate-source income (the corporation income tax and the individual income tax on dividends), then the two systems of integration do not differ in their effect on such behavior (see Chapter 3). But corporate managers may not give equal attention to the two taxes imposed at the two levels. They may respond more strongly to integration at the corporate level, which directly reduces the corporation income tax. At least in the case of widely held corporations, it is often argued that what matters to management is the tax payable by the corporation itself.[6] Integration at the corporate level should therefore have a greater impact on corporate dividend policy.

In contrast, integration at the shareholder level may be said to have less effect on business decisions than integration at the corporate level. If integration is provided at the shareholder level, the tax due from the corporation is the same whether earnings are retained or distributed. For

---

5. "Having a tax withheld by a payor, that is, deducted from the payment and paid instead to the government, is universally recognized as the most effective and inexpensive way of collecting income taxes..... A withholding tax is not an income tax but a means of collecting that tax, inasmuch as whatever is collected is applied toward the payment of the total income tax liability." Yudkin, *A Legal Structure for Effective Income Tax Administration* 3/B1.

6. See Musgrave, "The Carter Commission Report," 1 *Canadian Journal of Economics* 159, 166 (1968). Professor Musgrave has also put it this way: "With widely-held corporations it may well be that management simply looks at what corporation tax must be paid at the corporate level, and not at the net payments by the shareholders." Musgrave, "Taxation of Corporations," in Canadian Tax Foundation, *Report of the Proceedings of the Twenty-Second Tax Conference* 124, 135–136.

the corporation, integration at the shareholder level means there is no discrimination against the retention of earnings. If the directors of a corporation conclude that the needs of the business require the retention rather than the distribution of earnings, no tax penalty on the corporation results. Quite apart from tax factors, retained earnings may be the cheapest and the most readily available source of corporate capital. If so, it might be appropriate to arrange the tax system so that it does not work at cross-purposes with nontax considerations.

If constructive dividends or noncash dividends (dividends in shares, for example) qualify for distribution relief, however, even integration at the corporate level may operate without unduly depleting corporate cash reserves or unduly influencing the directors' decisions about the amount of earnings to be retained. On the whole, though, integration at the shareholder level may more easily avoid tax discrimination against retained earnings at the corporate level. Belgium, for example, adopted distribution relief at the shareholder level as its primary method of integration because it feared that integration at the corporate level "would have the effect of discouraging self-financing. Self-financing is of considerable importance in Belgium...."[7]

With the change from the two-tier system of taxation, integration at the shareholder level may even permit increased retentions by corporations without causing any reduction in shareholder income.[8] Because integration at the shareholder level reduces the shareholder's tax on dividend receipts, each unit of distributed profits becomes more valuable (after tax) to the shareholder. The corporation may therefore be able to meet shareholder net (or after-tax) dividend requirements despite a reduction in its gross (or before-tax) dividend outlays. In short, integration at the shareholder level may permit an increase in the shareholder's effective income without draining the corporation of the profits needed for investment in the business.

On the whole, however, integration at the shareholder level is generally assumed to leave the shareholders (generally well-to-do individuals) with more after-tax income than they would have without integration. Whether the result will be more investment by individuals and a greater flow of funds into capital markets or more consumption expenditures depends on

---

7. "European Communities: The Corporation Income Tax Split Rate Versus the Shareholders' Tax Credit As a Means of Easing the Double Taxation Burden on Corporate Distributions," 8 *European Taxation* 197, 201–202 (1968).

8. See the discussion in Chapter 6 of the French dividend practice since France's adoption of integration at the shareholder level. As noted there, the increase in retention is not the effect of the system itself but the effect of a change in the system. In other words, a reduction of the tax on corporate-source income resulted partly in increased corporate retentions and partly in increased net dividends for shareholders.

such local variables as the presence or absence of a functioning capital market, patterns of investment and spending, and so on.

All of these considerations are theoretical, however. As a practical matter, there is no conclusive evidence that integration is effective in raising dividend distributions, promoting investment in corporate shares, or accomplishing any similar results. There is still less evidence that integration at one level is more effective than integration at the other. Professors Bird and Oldman state that "no one has ever shown that what system is employed makes much difference in economic results on saving and investment."[9]

4/E. Shifting and Incidence

The proponents of integration at the corporate level perhaps depend less on unproven assumptions about the incidence of the corporation income tax than those who support integration at the shareholder level. At present, the incidence of the corporation income tax is shrouded in doubt; the burden of the tax may be on the shareholder, or on the consumer, or on the worker, or on some combination of the three. Yet integration at the shareholder level is generally defended on the grounds that the burden of the corporation income tax falls, at least in part, on the shareholder and that the shareholder is therefore entitled to an equivalent measure of tax relief when he receives a dividend. To the extent that this assumption about incidence is incorrect, such relief may be unwarranted.

Regardless of the assumptions about incidence, however, it may be easier to defend integration at the corporate level. Suppose, for example, that the burden of the corporation income tax falls not on the shareholder but on the consumer, to whom it may be passed on as a cost. Even in this case, integration at the corporate level may be defensible as a device to reduce (tax) costs. In other words, there may always be a case for integration at the corporate level. In contrast, integration at the shareholder level may be largely defensible only to the extent that the burden of the corporation income tax actually falls on the shareholder, who gets the relief.

Any argument based on the thorny problem of incidence is likely to be inconclusive, however, and will therefore throw little light on the choice of the level at which integration should be offered.

---

9. Bird and Oldman, "Tax Research and Tax Reform in Latin America," 3-3 *Latin American Research Review* 5, 13 (Summer 1968). To the same effect, see van den Tempel, *Corporation Tax and Individual Income Tax in the European Communities* 9.

4/F. Equity and Political Factors

Whether a particular method of integration is equitable is generally measured by this test: does it remove, at all income levels, the same proportion of the additional burden imposed on distributed profits by the corporation income tax?[10] All of the alternatives for integration at the *corporate* level which are discussed below meet this test, but some of the methods proposed for integration at the *shareholder* level do not (see Chapter 6). The more common methods of integration at the shareholder level do, however, operate equitably by the test. The argument of equity does not, therefore, point to the choice of one level or the other but, rather, depends on the particular technique by which integration is implemented.

Even if it is deemed equitable according to the test above, integration at the shareholder level may involve a special difficulty of "apparent" equity. Integration at this level generally means that if only the shareholder's tax burden (rather than the combined corporation-shareholder burden) is considered, dividend income appears to be taxed less heavily than other income—earned income from labor or a profession, for example. Especially since dividend income is received primarily by well-to-do individuals, this apparent preference for a particular form of unearned income may raise more political problems than a system of integration at the corporate level. France offers an example of the political problems that may follow from integration at the shareholder level: in 1972, the Prime Minister was forced out of office after it was revealed that he had paid no income tax for several years because of the tax savings he had enjoyed (as a shareholder) as a result of France's having adopted a system of integration at the shareholder level. (This episode is discussed in more detail in Chapter 6.)

4/G. International Aspects: Effect on Nonresidents

4/G.1. In General

The above arguments are inconclusive; none is strong enough to point compellingly to the choice of one level of integration over the other. In one respect, however, integration at the shareholder level is significantly different from integration at the corporate level. This difference may be important enough to determine a country's choice of the level, corporate or shareholder, at which integration is to be provided.

The difference concerns the effect of choice of level on nonresident shareholders. Integration at the corporate level reduces the tax burden on

---

10. Pechman, *Federal Tax Policy* (rev. ed.) 142.

all distributed profits, including those paid to nonresident shareholders. Integration at the shareholder level, in contrast, ordinarily benefits only resident shareholders; it offers no benefits to nonresident shareholders.[11] A study for the European Economic Community concluded that this differing impact on resident and nonresident shareholders constitutes the "*essential difference*" between integration at the shareholder level and integration at the corporate level.[12]

In a country in which foreign ownership is so extensive as to be a matter of concern, the preferential treatment of resident, as compared to nonresident, shareholders which follows from integration at the shareholder level may be the single most important factor inducing such a country to integrate at that level. Canada and France are conspicuous examples. In 1965, France adopted integration at the shareholder rather than the corporate level because integration at the shareholder level gives relief only to resident shareholders (see Chapter 7).[13] In Canada, the Carter Commission regarded integration at the corporate level (by way of a deduction to the corporation for dividends paid) as "a reasonable alternative." However, the Commission then added[14]:

> Its main drawback, however, would arise from the deduction of dividends paid to non-residents. The allowance of such deductions would result in unwarranted revenue costs and would serve to increase the amount collected by foreign treasuries.

The United Kingdom provides another example. It adopted a new integration scheme that became effective in April 1973. The British government's first preference was for integration at the corporate level; but in the end, the government chose integration at the shareholder level. The major consideration in this choice was that integration at the shareholder level would provide no relief to nonresident shareholders—particularly U.S.

---

11. The international aspects of integration are considered in detail in Chapter 7.
12. Communauté Économique Européene, Commission, *Le Développement d'un marché européen des capitaux* 225.
13. "In 1965, when the French first introduced this system, there was strong opposition from abroad because the benefit of the [system] was not extended to foreign investors. Of course, this was the intention of the French government...." Rädler, "International Aspects—II," in Canadian Tax Foundation, *Report of the Proceedings of the Twenty-Second Tax Conference* 299, 301.
14. Canada, Royal Commission on Taxation, 4 *Report of the Royal Commission on Taxation* 44. Professor Musgrave similarly indicated Canada's preference for integration at the corporate level but recognized that it might "not be quite suitable to the Canadian setting"; given the importance of foreign shareholders in Canada, integration at the shareholder level might be preferable because it "readily permits limitation to resident shareholders." Musgrave, "Taxation of Corporations," in Canadian Tax Foundation, *Report of the Proceedings of the Twenty-Second Tax Conference* 124, 136.

parent corporations of British corporate subsidiaries. (See Chapter 7, which deals with the international aspects of integration.)

Integration at the shareholder level does more than deny relief to nonresident shareholders; it also denies relief to those resident shareholders who own shares in domestic corporations but who conceal those shares abroad. It is apparently not uncommon for residents of a country (particularly a developing country) to transfer wealth secretly to a safe haven in a foreign country (Switzerland, for example). The transfer may be made because of fear of political disturbances, fear of devaluation or exchange controls, or a desire to evade income, wealth, or death taxes. Often, some of the wealth transferred will include shares of corporations resident in the transferor's country. Even though the shares are beneficially owned by a resident of that country, they will be held by a nonresident nominee in the transferee country and, for purposes of distribution relief, will be treated as shares owned by a nonresident. Integration at the corporate level will extend distribution relief to dividends paid on these pseudo-foreign shares, but integration at the shareholder level will deny relief to dividends paid on such shares.

Much of the Italian capital transferred to Switzerland is said to consist of shares in Italian corporations. Similarly, it is believed that much of the French capital concealed in Switzerland consists of shares in French corporations. The French government's desire not to provide tax relief for dividends paid on those shares was a factor in France's choice of integration at the shareholder rather than the corporate level; in the French view, integration at the former level discourages the expatriation of capital.

Any country that has reason to fear the flight of capital or to believe that a significant portion of the shares nominally held by nonresidents is actually owned by residents must take account of this argument in choosing the level at which integration is to be offered.[15]

4/G.2. Possible Effect of New French Tax Treaty Pattern

A development in France since 1969 may, however, have reduced the force of the argument that integration at the shareholder level is in a country's national interest because it gives no relief to nonresidents. As noted earlier, France chose integration at the shareholder level in 1965, primarily to favor resident over nonresident shareholders. However, pressure from France's Common Market partners and from other capital-exporting nations (as well

---

15. Musgrave, "International Aspects—II," in Canadian Tax Foundation, *Report of the Proceedings of the Twenty-Second Tax Conference* 308, 325.

as certain changes in France's attitude toward foreign investors) led France to modify its position.

France announced that it was willing, by treaty or treaty amendment, to extend the same relief it offered to its own resident shareholders to shareholders in any country with which it had a tax treaty (see Chapter 3). Because France has treaties with virtually all developed and many undeveloped countries, there is little merit (as far as France is concerned) in the argument that a country may prefer integration at the shareholder level as a means of favoring residents over nonresidents. In fact, by the end of 1977, France has extended dividend relief to nonresident shareholders in 12 countries (Australia, Austria, Belgium, Brazil, Finland, Germany, Luxembourg, the Netherlands, Sweden, Switzerland, the United Kingdom, and the United States). Moreover, the United Kingdom, after adopting an integration scheme at the shareholder level, decided to follow the French pattern and actually extended dividend relief across its borders. By treaty arrangement, it has afforded the same treatment as France to foreign shareholders in seven European countries (Denmark, Finland, France, Ireland, Spain, Sweden, and Switzerland) and a number of less-industrialized countries.[16]

Underlying the tax treaty patterns of France and the United Kingdom is the requirement of the European Community (Common Market) treaty that capital be allowed to move freely within the Community so that the goal of a unified capital market throughout the whole Community can be attained. In other words, a resident of one member country must eventually be able to invest in the other member countries without impediments (tax or other); a corporation of one member country must, similarly, be able to raise capital in the other member countries without tax or other obstacles.[17] Countries outside the European Community have no such obligation, however. Japan, for example, does not extend to nonresident shareholders the same distribution relief that it gives residents at the shareholder level. Although Belgium is a member of the European Community, it had not, as of 1977, extended its shareholder distribution relief to nonresidents.

A developing country adopting integration at the shareholder level may therefore be able in its tax treaties to follow the Japanese and Belgian pattern (of not extending relief to nonresident shareholders) rather than the French pattern.

As a general rule, then, the fact that integration at the shareholder level favors resident over nonresident shareholders, whereas integration at the

---

16. The same treatment is provided to U.S. shareholders by the U.S.-U.K. income tax treaty which was ratified in 1980.

17. See Article 4(1) of the "Proposed Directive for the Harmonisation of Systems of Company Taxation and of Withholding Taxes on Dividends," 16 *European Taxation* 52, 59 (1976).

corporate level gives as much relief to nonresidents as to residents, remains the "essential difference" between these two levels of integration. In a number of cases, this difference appears to have been the decisive factor in the choice of the shareholder level.

4/H. Conclusion

Given the importance of local variables as well as the fact that few of the arguments considered above point strongly in one direction or the other, no definitive answer can be given to the question whether a system of integration, if it is to be adopted, should be implemented at the shareholder rather than the corporate level. Administrative capabilities, revenue needs, political factors, attitudes toward progressive taxation, national economic goals, investment and spending patterns, the presence or absence of a functioning capital market, the relative importance of nonresident shareholders, and the extent to which a country seeks to limit foreign ownership, to give a tax incentive to foreign shareholders, or merely to provide "neutrality" in the tax treatment of nonresidents—in every case, these and other local variables must be considered, and the alternatives must be weighed in the light thereof. Moreover, each of these factors will vary from time to time; for example, a system beyond the capabilities of a country's tax administration at one time may be feasible 10 or 20 years later.

In the absence of arguments that point conclusively to the choice of one level of integration over the other, it is perhaps not surprising that some countries have chosen to adopt measures of integration at both levels. Japan and Germany, for example, provide some relief for distributed profits at the corporate level and rather more relief at the shareholder level. Such a system capitalizes, at least to a limited extent, on the advantages of integration at each level. Yet by requiring tax adjustments for distributions at both the corporate level and the shareholder level, such a system of relief doubles the administrative problems of integration.

AMERICAN LAW INSTITUTE, FEDERAL INCOME TAX PROJECT—SUBCHAPTER C

"REPORTER'S STUDY OF THE TAXATION OF CORPORATE DISTRIBUTIONS" (1982), pp. 341–55.

PART II. SUMMARY OF ARGUMENT

The proposals in this Study are for refinement of what is sometimes called the classical system of taxing corporate earnings. This summary begins therefore with a description of the essential elements of the classical system (A), followed by a brief identification of the principal legal and economic issues and problems raised by that system (B), and of their interrelationships (C and D). Finally, there is another summary of the proposals themselves (E).

A. The Classical System

The classical system for taxing corporate earnings builds upon the separate legal identity of the corporation and shareholders. It contains both a corporate income tax on corporations and an individual income tax on shareholders, and provides for computation of each in a manner relatively independent of the other. Corporations are taxpayers under the former tax, and taxable on their earnings as such, whether or not distributed, and without regard to who owns their shares or to economic arguments about what individuals may ultimately bear the burden of the corporate tax. For individual income tax purposes, on the other hand, corporate shares are simply investment property whose yield is taxable without much regard to the prior imposition of a corporate tax on the earnings out of which that yield is paid.

1) *The corporate income tax.* Taxable income is defined in much the same way for corporate and individual income tax purposes; indeed many of the provisions of the income tax law apply equally to corporate and individual taxpayers. There are some provisions peculiar to corporate taxpayers, however, and some that have a special function as applied to corporate taxpayers.

The interest deduction falls in the latter category. Interest is deductible by corporations under the same statutory provision as for individuals. Section 163. But in the corporate context, debt is an alternative to stock as a source of outside capital, and the interest deduction serves to make the cost of capital raised by issuing debt deductible, while that of capital raised by issuing stock is not. The interest deduction thus creates a bias in favor of debt financing as compared with new issues of stock. But it also serves, in certain cases, at least, to reduce the bias that the corporate income tax would otherwise create against new real investment by corporations. Because of the interest deduction, a corporation that borrows to finance a new investment will not bear any net income tax burden from it unless the new investment yields more than the interest expense incurred to finance it.

Several provisions peculiar to the corporate income tax are of importance for present purposes. These all concern investments by one corporation in shares of another. In the case of any such intercorporate investment, the corporate shareholder may realize income or gain from its investment just as any other investor does, but taxation of such gain would result in earnings being subject to corporate income tax more than once, in addition to individual income tax. To avoid that result, the statute contains several relief provisions for corporate shareholders. The most general of these is the 100-percent deduction for intercorporate dividends from a subsidiary (a corporation at least 80-percent owned by the dividend recipient) and an 85-percent deduction for other dividends. Section 243. Other provisions exempt gain or loss realized on liquidation of a subsidiary, and allow filing of consolidated returns and elimination of various sorts of intercompany profits and losses under certain circumstances. Sections 332, 1501-05. While the general purpose of these provisions is sensible enough, they generate a number of particular distortions in relation to freely tradable shares, since their effect is to make corporate shares largely a taxfree form of investment for corporate investors while remaining taxable for noncorporate investors.

Another issue peculiar to the corporate income tax is the treatment of previously unrealized gain on a distribution of appreciated property to shareholders. That issue is considered at length in connection with Acquisition Proposal C1, on pages 105-119, and is not involved in this Study.

2) *The individual income tax on shareholders.* The essential features of the individual tax on shareholders in the classical system are that dividend yield is fully taxable as ordinary income, while mere appreciation in share value is not currently taxable at all, even if attributable to accumulated corporate earnings that are fully realized at the corporate level. In the American version of the

classical system, shareholder gain becomes taxable on a sale of shares, though generally only at capital-gain rates. Nondividend distributions are taxed in a variety of ways: some like dividends, some like sale proceeds, and some distributions of corporate shares not at all, like mere unrealized appreciation.

Dividends are fully taxable at an individual's ordinary income rate, without any significant offset for the corporate tax already imposed on the earnings out of which the dividend is paid, and generally without any offset for the reduction in share value caused by the distribution. There is a very limited exclusion of dividends of $100 per individual, which is a remnant from a 1954 provision originally designed to grant limited relief from double taxation of dividend income. Section 116. There has recently been discussion of a considerably more general provision giving individual shareholders credit for a portion of corporate income taxes paid on distributed earnings. Even if such a provision were adopted, however, dividends (including the amount of the credit) would be fully included in computing individual taxable income. The effect of such a credit would be to turn the corporate income tax, in part, into a withholding tax on behalf of shareholders.

Dividends are defined as distributions out of corporate earnings and profits, and distributions in excess of earnings and profits are treated as return of capital — applied first against a shareholder's basis for his shares, and then taxed as capital gain. Sections 301, 316. For corporations whose capital consists in substantial part of accumulated earnings this limitation has no effect, even if a particular distribution to a particular shareholder represents essentially a return of part of his investment because it represents earnings or appreciation in value prior to his purchase of his shares.

While dividends are fully taxable as ordinary income, accumulated corporate earnings are not subject to current individual income tax at all. So far as the individual shareholder is concerned, he is considered to have only an unrealized appreciation in the value of his shares, which is not considered to be currently taxable income. The Supreme Court once even held unrealized appreciation due to accumulated corporate earnings to be beyond the scope of shareholder income as the term "income" is used in the 16th Amendment to the Constitution, and extended that holding to accumulated earnings represented by a stock dividend of common shares on common shares, since such a dividend did not effect any essential change in shareholder interests. *Eisner v. Macomber*, 252 U.S. 189 (1920).

Nontaxation of accumulated earnings under the individual income tax is a matter of deferral rather than exemption, since a shareholder is subject to tax whenever his gain is subsequently realized. But long-term deferral is of immense importance. Besides the fact that deferred gains may escape taxation due to subsequent intervening events, deferral alone is tantamount to exemption from individual tax of earnings from investment of the gains on which tax is deferred. One function of the corporate tax is, indeed, to offset that effective exemption. See pages 348-353.

On a sale of shares, gain or loss is computed by subtracting the taxpayer's basis from his sale proceeds, and any gain so computed is subject to tax, usually at long-term capital-gain rates.

Taxable gain may be realized on a sale of shares to a noncorporate purchaser without any distribution of funds or assets out of corporate solution. Taxation of sale proceeds differs from taxation of dividend distributions in two respects. First, a taxpayer is allowed to apply sale proceeds against basis, paying tax only if there is some excess of proceeds over basis. Indeed, if proceeds fall short of basis, the taxpayer may have a deductible capital loss. Second, even if there is a gain, it is generally only taxable at long-term capital-gain rates, which currently are only 40 percent of the top rate on dividends.

Corporations sometimes make distributions in liquidation or in redemption of shares, or in the form of shares of the distributing corporation or a subsidiary of the distributing corporation. Taxation of such distributions is determined, in effect, by a scheme of competing analogies to a dividend distribution, a sale of shares, or mere unrealized appreciation. A substantially pro rata distribution in redemption of shares, for example, is taxable as a dividend; a substantially disproportionate redemption distribution or a liquidating distribution is taxed as a sale of shares; and gain goes currently unrecognized on certain forms of stock dividends and spin-offs of subsidiary shares, as in the case of simple unrealized appreciation in share value. Differentiation among distributions that are to be taxed in different ways is a major problem under the existing system of shareholder taxation.

B. Problems and Issues

Even the brief foregoing exposition serves to suggest what are the major problem areas and issues under the existing general method of taxing corporations and shareholders. They are, briefly, as follows.

1) *The debt/equity problem.* The classical system treats corporate debt more favorably than stock in two primary respects. First, at the corporate level, interest is deductible while dividends are not. If a corporation raises capital by issuing debt, it will not be taxed on operating income devoted to payment of the cost of that capital, while it will be taxed on the whole of any operating income derived from investment of equity capital. Second, at the individual level, repayment of debt is a nontaxable return of investment to the full extent of the payee's basis for his obligation, while retirement of stock may be taxed as a dividend if the payees, or their family or other associates (as defined under the statutory attribution-of-ownership rules) continue to own other shares in the corporation.

These disparities in treatment of debt and equity capital generate several problems. For one, they simply create a bias in favor of debt as against newly issued equity capital. This leads to the issue of debt securities in some circumstances in which an issue of equity would be preferable but for the tax differential. While the magnitude of the resulting distortion is debatable, almost nothing can be said in its favor. Moreover, the bias has an equity aspect as well as an incentive effect, in that it simply imposes higher burdens on those who finance through new issues of equity than on those who issue debt. This differential cannot be satisfactorily justified.

The disparity between tax burdens on debt and equity lies at the root of a morass of legal problems in distinguishing one from the other for tax purposes. In corporate practice the distinction between shareholders and creditors is largely formal, shareholders being investors whose rights are defined in the corporate charter, while creditors' rights are defined in a contract to which the corporation is merely a party. Moreover, corporate law and practice are flexible with regard to the substantive rights of both shareholders and creditors, and permit ownership of both shareholder and creditor interests by the same persons. It has hardly seemed appropriate, however, that substantial differences in tax burden be allowed to turn solely on formal differences in investors' status, and so tax administrators and courts have sought to give some substantive content to the distinction between debt and equity. Accordingly, contractual instruments giving an investor rights that are too much like those ordinarily enjoyed by shareholders may be classed as equity for tax purposes. Even unconditional debt obligations, presumably fully enforceable as such, may be treated as equity if they represent advances by shareholders that would be unlikely to be made by an investor without an equity interest. While certain relevant factors can be named, it has proved exceedingly difficult to come to any settled consensus about their relative weight or about any other form of usable standard for making the debt/equity differentiation with any satisfactory degree of clarity or certainty.

2) *Distributions other than simple dividends.* A second problem area is classification and tax treatment of distributions other than simple dividends. The rules that have emerged are quite complex, and yet often still uncertain in their application. Too often decision still depends on relatively formal or procedural distinctions. Other times it turns on arbitrary distinctions imposed by statute in an effort to avoid uncertain judgments based on a complex of disparate factors.

Beyond its difficulties in application, existing law remains unsatisfactory because of bailout opportunities that remain. If a controlling shareholder gives shares to a charity, for example, which are subsequently redeemed, it has been held several times that there is no taxable dividend to anyone — indeed there is not even any capital gain — despite the fact that the shareholder is allowed a charitable-contribution deduction for the full value of the shares. For another example, if a publicly held corporation distributes funds by purchasing its own shares in the market, there is likely to be no dividend income to anyone. Again, indeed, there may not even be any significant additional capital gain, since market sellers might have sold their shares at nearly the same price even in the absence of any corporate purchase. Privately held corporations frequently plan to distribute a substantial portion of their earnings over time on a nondividend basis, by redeeming shares. It is not clear that the resulting relative tax advantage for shareholders of such corporations is justified.

At bottom, the process of classifying distributions by competing analogies is unsatisfactory because it fails to provide any reason for the distinctions it makes. The result of virtually any distribution could be readily duplicated by combining a simple dividend with purchases and sales among shareholders, and no reason is given why it should ever be taxed substantially more lightly. That analogy would suggest, of course, that the tax burden should rest partly on continuing shareholders who may not have participated directly in the distribution. The current version of section 305 already provides that under certain circumstances a redemption may be treated as a cash dividend to redeeming shareholders and a taxable imputed stock dividend to non-redeeming shareholders, but the definition of circumstances for such treatment in section 305 is highly unsatisfactory, again because virtually any redemption distribution could be restructured in this manner.

3) *Intercorporate investment problems.* Several problems arise from the statutory provisions designed to integrate taxes on corporate holders and issuers of shares. These have not had such prominent attention as other problems, and they have not emerged primarily as problems of legal interpretation. They are instead problems of potential distortion in behavior and resulting disparities in tax burdens arising from the fact that shares whose yield is fully taxable in the hands of a noncorporate holder are essentially or mostly taxfree in the hands of a corporate holder.

One interesting and ironic recent development concerns corporate holders of shares for which the issuer makes a tender offer. The game, for such holders, is to try to tender just enough so that shares redeemed will *not* be substantially disproportionate within the meaning of section 302(b)(2), since for a corporate shareholder dividend treatment will usually involve a smaller tax burden than a sale. There are other contexts, too, in which the normal preference for exchange over dividend treatment is reversed for a corporate shareholder.

4) *Unreasonable accumulation of earnings.* Existing law is said to favor accumulation of earnings over distribution. While this effect has been accepted as to accumulation for the reasonable business needs of a corporation, penalty taxes have been imposed to prevent abuse by accumulating for the purpose of avoiding individual taxes. There is an accumulated-earnings tax, which

depends directly on findings concerning business necessity and motivation for accumulation. Sections 531-537. There is also a personal holding company tax, which applies automatically to any undistributed earnings in the case of a closely held corporation whose income is passive investment income or otherwise unlike normal corporate business income. Sections 541-547. Both the notions of close holding and personal holding company income are defined with some specificity.

The accumulated-earnings tax presents substantial problems of fair administration in the finding of facts concerning motivation and business needs. The personal holding company tax raises problems of arbitrary coverage and non-coverage resulting from the attempt to avoid amorphous factual questions.

C. Relations Among Issues

These problems and issues are often conceived in relative isolation from one another. Moreover, there is a tendency to regard corporate and individual income taxes as independent of one another, and to regard each problem issue as involving only one or the other. The problem of nondividend distributions, for example, may be seen as one of individual-shareholder taxation only. There is some inclination to see even the debt/equity problem as involving essentially and functionally independent corporate and individual tax issues.

But in fact there are important offsetting relationships between individual and prospective corporate tax burdens that make net biases much less than their separate components in connection with many transactions.

1) *Distributions.* Corporate distributions to individual shareholders, for example, have important corporate income tax implications, since a distribution will leave less capital in corporate solution where its earnings are subject to corporate tax. These corporate tax implications are less obvious than individual tax implications, perhaps, because there is no apparent issue of immediate taxability or deductibility of the distribution itself under the corporate income tax. The corporate tax implications of a distribution have to do with prospective tax burdens rather than immediate tax liability.

The corporate-income-tax benefits from effecting a distribution are widely appreciated in at least some common practical contexts. Well-advised shareholders in a closely held corporation, for example, will almost always provide for liquidation of their interests by redemption of shares even if corporate funds are not plentiful. On a sale of shares of a corporation to individual purchasers, moreover, sophisticated taxpayers and counsel understand perfectly well that there are substantial tax advantages to be realized by having the transfer financed in part through a redemption distribution. These advantages, being prospective, are of primary concern to the purchaser, not the seller, but sellers presumably gain some of the benefit of such advantages through a higher price for their shares than if they were unavailable to the purchaser. In estimating the net aggregate tax burden or benefit from a transaction, therefore, the prospective corporate tax advantages of a substantial distribution should be offset against the individual tax burdens imposed directly on selling shareholders.

Moreover, the relation between corporate and individual tax benefits and burdens, even if not consciously designed as such, is not merely sporadic and accidental. For a considerable number of common financial transactions, there is a systematic compensatory relationship between corporate and individual tax implications that greatly mitigates the problems that would arise under either tax standing alone.

For example, a dividend distribution involves immediate imposition on shareholders of an individual income tax that could readily be deferred by the simple expedient of accumulating earnings instead of distributing. The existing system of taxation is therefore sometimes said to create a bias against distribution of dividends. But there are countervailing corporate income tax implications: if funds are accumulated, their earnings will be subject to a corporate income tax that can readily be avoided by the simple expedient of distributing the funds for investment by the shareholders themselves. The immediate burden of a dividend tax on distribution must therefore be weighed against the prospective burden of corporate taxes resulting from accumulation.

Corporate and individual tax aspects of a dividend distribution will indeed balance rather neatly under certain conditions. If (1) funds are to be invested the same way in or out of corporate solution, (2) the rate of individual tax on earnings from investment by shareholders outside corporate solution is the same as the rate of corporate tax on earnings from the investment if made by the corporation, and (3) the rate of tax on the eventual distribution of funds plus earnings thereon will be the same as on an immediate distribution of the funds, then the corporate tax on earnings from accumulated funds will exactly compensate for the value of deferral of tax on the distribution itself.

Example: Consider one dollar of corporate funds available for distribution or investment. One alternative would be to hold it in the corporation to invest, say at 18 percent before tax. A 50 percent corporate tax would leave 9 percent to accumulate and compound, at which rate the dollar would triple in about 13 years. If the three dollars were then distributed as a dividend taxable at 50 percent, the shareholders would have $1.50 left.

A second alternative would be immediate distribution of the original dollar. A 50 percent tax on dividends would leave only 50 cents to invest. In 13 years, at a 9 percent after-tax rate of return, this would grow to just about $1.50, which is the same as in the first alternative.

This equivalence will hold for other rates of return and periods of investment so long as corporate and individual investment opportunities and rates of tax on investment are equal and rates of tax are the same for distribution now or later.

These conditions will frequently not be met, of course. If shareholders of a close corporation, for example, look forward to the possibility of future distributions at capital-gain rates, then there will be a bias against current dividend distributions. (On the other hand a current distribution in capital-gain form will be preferable to future dividend distributions; the corporate tax will still tend to offset the burden of acceleration of shareholder tax, leaving the rate differential in favor of capital gains essentially uncompensated.) Or if shareholders are in higher brackets than the corporate rate, the benefits of deferral alone will outweigh the burden of additional corporate tax from investing within the corporation. Finally, if the funds in question are to be used for portfolio investment in corporate stock, the intercorporate dividend tax may make the effective corporate rate on such investment substantially lower than the individual shareholder rate. These are indeed the situations in which corporate accumulation is most subject to abuse.

2) *Financing.* Another important aspect of the compensatory relationship between corporate and individual tax burdens concerns modes of financing. It is common to point out the corporate income tax disparity between debt, whose cost is deductible, and equity, whose cost is not. This is indeed an uncompensated disparity in the case of newly contributed equity. But for corporations in unregulated industries, the predominant source of equity capital is accumulation of earnings, and as to this, the nondeductibility of future distributions tends to be offset by the value of deferral of the individual tax that would have been imposed if earnings had been distributed rather than accumulated. Indeed, one can make comparisons between a corporation that accumulates earnings and one that distributes earnings but borrows to finance new investment, which will show an equivalence of outcome under exactly the same conditions as stated above for accumulation as against distribution generally.

> *Example:* A corporation is about to undertake a $30,000 expansion of real investment expected to yield 10 percent or more. Its shareholders are willing to invest for a yield of 10 percent. If the corporation borrows from its shareholders (or from others) at 10 percent, it will get a deduction for interest paid; a 10 percent yield on the project would therefore just cover the cost of borrowing, without any corporate income tax.
>
> If the corporation accumulates earnings to pay for the investment, however, there would be no interest deduction and a 10 percent return on the project would only yield about $1,620, or 5.4 percent after corporate tax. But if the shareholders are in a 46 percent bracket, distributing the $30,000 to them would only have given them $16,200 after tax; and so their after-tax cost of investment is only $16,200. The after-corporate-tax yield of $1,620 is equal to a 10 percent yield on $16,200.
>
> If the shareholders are in a higher bracket than the corporate rate, their yield on investment by accumulation of earnings, calculated in this manner, will actually exceed the before-

tax return on real investment by the corporation. If the shareholders were in a 60 percent bracket, for example, the after-tax cost to them of the $30,000 corporate investment would be only $12,000; and $1,620 would represent a 13.5 percent yield on $12,000.

If the shareholders' rate were less than the corporate rate, then accumulation of earnings would be less attractive.

For corporations that choose between debt finance and equity finance by accumulation of earnings, therefore, the whole system is much more nearly neutral than is sometimes supposed. Again the real problems, sharply defined, involve situations of uncompensated benefit or burden — in this case the uncompensated burden cast by the existing system on new equity investment.

D. Economic Appraisal

The classical system of taxing corporate earnings is often asserted to create three distinct biases. One is a bias against corporate investment as compared with noncorporate investment, since only the former is subject to corporate tax; another is a bias against equity capital as compared with debt, since there is a deduction in the corporate income tax for interest but not for dividends; and the third is a bias against distribution of dividends as against retention of earnings, since distribution results in immediate imposition of an individual income tax that can be deferred by retention of earnings. Integration of one form or another is often prescribed as a cure for all of these.

But each of these biases is only one part of the elephant; together they make a more coherent system than separate description suggests, because of the general way in which they offset one another. The bias in favor of debt, for example, tends to offset the bias in favor of noncorporate investment, by offering a way to use noncorporate funds to finance corporate investment without a corporate tax on the return. The bias in favor of retention of earnings tends to offset the bias in favor of debt over equity financing, for many corporations, since retention of earnings is a major way of raising equity capital. Finally, the bias in favor of retention tends to offset the bias in favor of noncorporate investment, in the case of internally generated corporate funds, since only by distribution can such funds by made available for noncorporate investment.

These compensatory relationships are far from perfect, in part because of differences between corporate and individual rates. Moreover, they are not perfectable so long as individual rates are graduated by reference to each individual taxpayer's total personal income. Still, these relationships make the system considerably more balanced than a consideration of each bias separately would imply.

The customary identification of biases results from measuring everything against a pattern of corporate financial behavior that is plausible but not typical except in the case of regulated utilities. That pattern is one in which a corporation distributes all its earnings as dividends and raises new capital by selling shares. As against that pattern, the existing law does indeed create biases in favor of noncorporate investment, debt finance and retention of earnings. But a more realistic description might say the result is something of a rough balance among noncorporate investment, debt finance and equity finance by retention of earnings, with a net, uncompensated bias against equity finance through new issues of shares and in favor of nondividend distributions.

That net uncompensated bias is important and deserves a cure; indeed, the purpose of the proposals in this Study is precisely to provide such a cure. But the existence of the general compensatory relationships just described makes it possible to effect a considerable cure by way of refinement rather than replacement of the existing system, without the much larger revenue costs and windfall effects that would accompany more general integration.

E. Summary of Proposals

Most of the troubles with existing law arise from two main uncompensated biases: 1) the bias against new equity investment, and 2) the bias in favor of nondividend distributions. The main proposals in this Study are to alleviate those biases by providing relief for the former and imposing a compensatory excise on the latter. If these proposals were adopted, all distributions would be subjected to more nearly comparable tax burdens, and contributions to corporate equity (negative distributions) would attract a comparable benefit (negative burden). In such a system, the compensatory relationships described in C and D above would extend to most financial decisions, and the difficult definitional problems with which present law struggles would be eliminated or reduced substantially in significance.

While the proposals complement one another in important ways, an effort has been made to analyze and present them separately, as follows.

1) *Relief for new equity.* Reporter's Proposal R1 is to relieve the bias against new equity by provision of a deduction based on newly contributed equity capital. The main proposal is for a corporate dividends-paid deduction, limited to a specified rate on the amount of net newly contributed equity capital, akin to the interest deduction that would have resulted from a debt investment. Adoption of this proposal would move a long way toward eliminating problems of differentiation between debt and equity, since it would attach comparable tax consequences to any investment of outside funds.

The main problem in implementing this proposal is defining net newly contributed investment in a manner that will exclude mere refinancing of accumulated earnings or previously contributed capital. This problem would be minimized if an appropriate tax burden were imposed generally on nondividend distributions.

2) *Nondividend distributions.* Reporter's Proposal R2 would deal with the present bias in favor of nondividend distributions by imposing some increased tax on them. One possibility would be to impute redemption distributions pro rata to continuing shareholders, as if they had received a dividend and used it to buy out redeeming shareholders. The proposal offered is simply to impose a flat-rate, compensatory excise on nondividend distributions, to be withheld and paid over to the government by the distributing corporation.

Adoption of this proposal would take much of the pressure off questions of dividend equivalence, with which present law struggles, and make it possible to be much more lenient about stock dividends and spin-offs, and the bailout opportunities they generate under existing law.

3) *Intercorporate investments and distributions.* A corporation can now purchase dividend-paying stock of another corporation and enjoy 85 or 100 percent exemption from corporate income tax on

the dividends received from this investment. A purchase of shares from noncorporate shareholders represents an indirect way of distributing funds out of corporate solution, and the intercorporate dividend deduction operates to contract the corporate income tax base accordingly, but all without any distribution, as such, by either corporation. Reporter's Proposal R3 would distinguish between direct and mere portfolio investment. In the case of portfolio investment, the dividend-received deduction and cognate provisions would be made inapplicable; with respect to direct investment those provisions would continue in effect, but purchases of shares would be treated as nondividend distributions subject to the compensatory excise in Reporter's Proposal R2.

POINTS AND COUNTERPOINTS

1. Compare the proposal for "full integration" of the corporate and personal incomes taxes espoused by Charles McLure with the proposal for accrual taxation of capital gains outlined in the *Stanford Note*, Chapter VI. Which system would result in heavier taxes on shareholders? Under what circumstances? Which is fairer? More efficient? Easier to administer? Are the two proposals inconsistent? Would an ideal income tax assess gains on corporate stock on an accrual basis *and* integrate the corporate and personal income taxes?

2. Who pays the corporate tax? Why do we want to know the answer to this question? Many economists believe that the tax is shifted to some other persons, but they are not sure to whom. The most likely candidates are: (a) all holders of capital, on the theory that the tax generally depresses the return on investment in the long run; (b) consumers, on the theory that the tax is passed on to the end users of corporate goods and services through higher prices; (c) laborers, on the theory the tax is passed backward to other factors of production; (d) shareholders, on the theory that in a market economy a tax on profits cannot be passed on to anyone; (e) some mix of all of the above, on the theory that each corporation faces somewhat different competitive conditions.

Would it matter in deciding whether to lower the corporate tax rate some modest amount and run a budget deficit which of the above answers is correct? Why? Suppose the issue were the substitution of a value added tax for the corporate tax? Would the incidence question likely have a different answer, depending upon which of these options was under consideration? Does the link, if any, between the answer to the incidence question and the use made of the answer explain why economists have had so much trouble determining the incidence of the corporate tax?

3. Who would benefit from integration of the corporate and personal income taxes? Why, in answering this question, is it crucial to know what type of integration is under consideration? Given the huge tax preferences now given to corporations, would shareholders favor a form of integration that guaranteed one full tax on corporate profits at the shareholder level? Would corporate managers favor an integration scheme that granted shareholders a partial credit for taxes paid at the corporate lev-

el, as provided in the tax systems of some European countries? For an excellent discussion of these and related issues, *see* McLure & Surrey, "Integration of Income Taxes: Issues for Debate," *Harvard Business Review*, Sept.-Oct. 1977, pp. 169–181.

4. Note the importance of the form of partial integration in the taxation of nonresident shareholders, discussed in the Norr selection. What other groups of shareholders currently do not pay taxes on their dividend income?

5. Consider the following excerpts from M. McIntyre, Pensees on Integration: Where's the Reform? *Tax Notes*, Sept. 5, 1977, pp. 11–12:

1

Why do I like the double tax on corporate profits? And why do I dislike the double tax on wage income—I mean the personal income tax and the Social Security tax? Is it because I have to pay so very little of the one and so much of the other? Our own self interest is a marvelous instrument for nicely putting out our eyes. Why does the business community rail against the double tax on profits and keep silent on the double tax on wages? Let them answer.

5

Full integration makes the simplifying assumption that a corporation is the docile agent of its shareholders. For most publicly held corporations, however, a shareholder cannot get his share of the profits at his discretion. But the assumption is not without merit, for in most cases the shareholder can get his approximate share of the profits by selling his stock. To argue for full integration is to argue against the realization rule for the taxation of gains. To argue against full integration is to argue that a corporation is not the alter ego of its shareholders.

6

If we do not think the corporation is the alter ego of its shareholders, why do we consider a corporate tax and a shareholder tax to be a double tax? Is it a double tax when a person hires a maid, and both the maid and the employer pay tax on the same income? Double taxation is a slogan, not an explanation.

8

Objection—The corporate tax is not paid by the shareholders. It is passed on in higher prices to the consumers.

Reply—If so, it results in a double tax on consumers, not on shareholders. Tax relief for shareholders therefore would be doubly wrong.

9

The economic arguments that the corporate tax is paid by consumers are so remote from the reasoning of men, and so complicated, that they make little impression; and if they should sway some, it would be only during the moment that they see the demonstrations; but an hour afterwards they fear they have been mistaken.

11

Some of the people who argue for shareholder relief on the ground that the corporation is the alter ego of the shareholder oppose current taxation of the earnings of controlled foreign subsidiaries. A domestic company is an alter ego but a foreign company is not?

12

The quiet lion waiting to walk off with the kill is the tax exempt foundation. If the corporate profits tax and the personal income tax are integrated, do we give a refund of the corporate tax to shareholders who are charities? This is the multibillion dollar question. Where is the "double tax" when a tax exempt foundation receives a corporate dividend?

6. How should corporate tax preferences be treated under an integration proposal? Should shareholders get relief from "double taxation" on profits that were not taxed at the corporate level? But would not the opposite rule—denying dividend relief for untaxed corporate profits—undercut the impact, if any, of corporate tax incentives? Is this conflict the expected result of a preference for distributions and a preference for reinvestment of profits?

†